Science Teaching
and
Development of Thinking

Anton E Lawson
Arizona State University

WADSWORTH
TM
THOMSON LEARNING

Wadsworth/Thomson Learning
10 Davis Drive
Belmont, CA 94002-3098
USA

For information about our products, contact us:
Thomson Learning Academic Resource Center
1-800-423-0563
http://www.wadsworth.com

International Headquarters
Thomson Learning
International Division
290 Harbor Drive, 2nd Floor
Stamford, CT 06902-7477
USA

UK/Europe/Middle East/South Africa
Thomson Learning
Berkshire House
168-173 High Holborn
London WCIV 7AA

Asia
Thomson Learning
60 Albert Street, #15-01
Albert Complex
Singapore 189969

Canada
Nelson Thomson Learning
1120 Birchmount Road
Toronto, Ontario MIK 5G4
Canada
United Kingdom

ISBN 0-534-04851-X

The Adaptable Courseware Program consists of products and additions to existing Wadsworth Group products that are produced from camera-ready copy. Peer review, class testing, and accuracy are primarily the responsibility of the author(s).

SCIENCE TEACHING
AND THE DEVELOPMENT OF THINKING

CONTENTS

CHAPTER 6   **CHARACTERISTICS OF EFFECTIVE
              SCIENCE INSTRUCTION**   **177**

CHAPTER 7   **WHY DON'T MORE TEACHERS USE
              INQUIRY-ORIENTED METHODS?**   **209**

REFERENCES

INDEX

PREFACE

This book is intended to serve as a text for courses in the methods of science teaching for pre-service secondary school teachers (grades 7 through 12). The book also will serve as a text for graduate-level instruction in science education, and it may also be of interest to in-service science teachers, university-level science educators, school curriculum personnel, and administrators who wish to update their knowledge of the latest developments in science teaching.

What do teachers need to know to teach science effectively? In my view, the answer to this question is found in the answers to six subordinate questions:

1. What is science?
2. Why teach science?
3. What is the nature of scientific knowledge?
4. How do scientists construct conceptual knowledge?
5. How do people develop scientific thinking skills?
6. What teaching methods best facilitate scientific knowledge acquisition (both conceptual knowledge construction and thinking skills development)?

The primary purpose of this book is to provide answers to these questions so that the reader gains both a set of useful science teaching methods and a coherent philosophy of science teaching and a psychologically and pedagogically sound theory of science instruction. A secondary, but equally important, objective is to provide readers with sufficient examples of the methods advocated so that they will be able to implement those methods in the classroom with the greatest possible success.

In short, the main thesis of this book is that students, when given the opportunity, become active constructors of knowledge. Truly effective science instruction demands that this constructive process occur, because it is the best way that science instruction can be carried on so that students can construct science concepts *and* develop their creative and critical thinking skills.

We face several genuine crises in today's world. For individuals to remain competitive in that world—indeed, to ensure that humans survive in that world—we must produce both knowledgeable and thoughtful people who are capable of making sound decisions now and in the future. This book has been written to that end.

We begin with a brief look at educational purpose and then examine the way in which science works—that is, the way in which humans construct scientific knowledge and develop the thinking skills they use in that process. We also examine the nature of the knowledge so constructed and the current status of scientific thinking patterns in adolescents. From this exploration we derive a philosophy and methodology of teaching science.

Several specific science lessons are presented that exemplify the advocated teaching methods, as are specific strategies for classroom management and student assessment. The book concludes with a look at current research in neuropsychology, which reveals that the teaching methods advocated here are founded in the way in which the brain spontaneously functions to construct, test, store, and retrieve knowledge. These chapters on neuropsychology are appropriate for the advanced reader, and they can be omitted in an undergraduate course.

The book is unique in at least two ways. First, it specifically presents methods for teaching general thinking skills in the context of science instruction. Second, it presents a research-tested theory of instruction. This theory of instruction is complete with cutting-edge work in the area of neural modeling. In these ways, the book not only has useful and practical suggestions for improving science instruction, but also contains the latest research and theory in science teaching.

▼ ACKNOWLEDGMENTS

Chester Lawson, Robert Karplus, and Jack Renner are my intellectual fathers. They are missed, but their ideas are alive and well in this book. I thank them for this. Others who have contributed ideas and advice are Michael Abraham, John Alcock, James Birk, Ken Costenson, Al Gibbs, David Hestenes, David Lawson, Jane Maienschein, Floyd Nordland, Warren Wollman, and several former students who are themselves now successful science teachers. I acknowledge my debt to these people with pleasure.

Special thanks are due to Jan Nagle, Jean Chesser, Charles Kazilek, and Rachelle Dermer, who produced the original manuscript, and to Steven Summerlight for his considerable expertise in preparing the final product. Several reviewers—O. Roger Anderson, Columbia University Teachers College; Clifford Edwards, Brigham Young University; Leonard Garigliano, Salisbury State University; Joseph Stepans, University of Wyoming; Deborah Tippins, University of Georgia; and Edward Zielinski, Clarion University—saw earlier drafts of the manuscript and made this a better book. Thanks also to the editors of Wadsworth Publishing Company, especially Suzanna Brabant, Sabra Horne, Kate Peltier, and Stacy Steiner, for their encouragement and assistance in seeing the manuscript through to publication.

Anton E. Lawson
May 1994

CHAPTER 1

TEACHING AND THE NATURE OF SCIENCE

Is this a Dagger, which I see before me,
The Handle toward my hand? Come, let me clutch thee.
I have thee not, and yet I see thee still.
Art thou not fatal Vision, sensible
To feeling, as to sight? Or art thou but
A Dagger of the Mind, a false creation?

"A Dagger of the Mind, a false creation?" Macbeth's mind has created a dagger. Order imposed by the human mind is always a created thing. That creation is found to be true or false by testing through behavior. The mind creates from sensory data and then imagines the creation to be true to allow the generation of an expectation, which is then tested in the external world. If the expectation is met, the creation is retained. If not, the creation must be replaced. So in lies a statement of how the human mind functions to construct knowledge. Do methods of science teaching follow? I think they do. The primary purpose of this book is to introduce those methods and to provide you with the knowledge necessary to incorporate them into your teaching so that students will not only learn science but also *how* to learn—that is, how to create and test their own knowledge.

▼ **EDUCATIONAL PURPOSE**

A great many opinions have been expressed concerning the educational system's primary goals. Transmission of knowledge, culture, and values and the development of conceptual understanding, attitudes, thinking skills, problem-solving abilities, and creativity are all viewed as worthy objectives. But can a common thread be pulled from these diverse opinions? In 1918 the Commission on the Reorganization of Secondary Education proposed a unity around what it called the "seven cardinal objectives": health, command of the fundamental thinking processes, worthy home membership, vocational competence, effective citizenship, worthy use of leisure time, and ethical character. Certainly these objectives are difficult to quarrel with, although stating specifically how to achieve them is not easy.

In 1961 the Educational Policies Commission published *The Central Purpose of American Education* (see Appendix A), which made a significant step in clarifying a means of obtaining, or at least working toward, these objectives. In the commission's view, of primary importance was a condition it called "Freedom of Mind," "which each individual must develop for himself" (p. 3). "To be free, a man must be capable of basing his choices and actions on understandings which he himself achieves and on values which he examines for himself. *He must be aware of the basis on which he accepts propositions as true*" (p. 4; emphasis added).

In other words, freedom of mind requires rational understanding of oneself, one's surroundings, and one's actions within those surroundings. One must be aware of the basis for establishing the truth or falsity of statements (*propositions*) made about the above. But what contributes to the attainment of this awareness?

The commission's answer was contained in what it called the "ten rational powers": "the processes of recalling and imagining, classifying and generalizing, comparing and evaluating, analyzing and synthesizing, deducing and inferring. These processes enable one to apply logic and the available evidence to his ideas, attitudes, and actions, and to pursue better whatever goals he may have" (p. 5). Without a command of these processes, people are limited to accepting the ideas, beliefs, and attitudes of others. They are not free to make their own decisions, because they do not possess the rational ability to do so. The rational powers represent the essence of the ability to think. In the words of the Educational Policies Commission: "The rational powers, moreover, make intelligent choices possible. Through them a person can become aware of the basis of choice in his values and of the circumstances of choice in his environment. Thus, they are broadly applicable in life and thus provide a solid basis for competence in all areas with which the school has traditionally been concerned" (p. 5).

With respect to attaining the seven cardinal objectives, the commission argued that the objectives all depended on the development of the rational powers, that is, the ability to think:

> *Health, for example, depends upon a reasoned awareness of the value of mental and physical fitness. . . . [It] requires that the individual understand the connection among health, nutrition, activity and environment.*
>
> *Effective citizenship is impossible without the ability to think. . . . [F]irsthand experience is no longer an adequate basis for judgment. He must have in addition the intellectual means to study events, to relate his values to them, and to make wise decisions as to his own actions. (p. 6)*

In short, development of the rational powers serves as a necessary, if not sufficient, means of obtaining the stated objectives of the schools. If we accept the commission's argument that the central (but not only) purpose of American education is the development of the rational powers, then we need to understand how instruction can be designed and implemented to facilitate the development and use of the rational powers. One important point: The development of the ability to think cannot be divorced from context. One does not develop the ability to think without some object, event, or situation to think about.

In 1966 the Educational Policies Commission, recognizing the key role that could be played by science education in developing the ability to think, published a second document, *Education and the Spirit of Science*, which emphasized science not so much as a body of accumulated knowledge but as a way of thinking, a spirit of rational inquiry driven by a belief in its efficiency and by a restless curiosity to know and to understand. The commission also emphasized that this mode of thought, this spirit, relates to questions people usually ask and answer for reasons that they may think are completely nonscientific—religious, aesthetic, humanistic, literary. Thus, the spirit of science infuses many forms of scholarship besides *science* itself.

Although the commission recognized that no scientist may fully exemplify the spirit of science and that no work may be completely objective, it is clear that the following key values underlie science as an enterprise:

1. Longing to know and to understand.
2. Questioning all things.
3. Searching for data and their meaning.
4. Demanding verification.
5. Respecting logic.
6. Considering the premises.
7. Considering the consequences.

By its nature, this list insists that students are not indoctrinated to think or act a certain way. Rather, it insists that they acquire the ability to make up their own minds, that is, to develop freedom of the mind and to learn to make their own decisions based on reason and evidence. In this sense, the values of science are the most complete expression of one of the deepest human values—the belief in human dignity. As a consequence, these values are part of any science but, more basically, of rational thought, and they apply not only in science, but also in every area of one's life.

More recently, the American Association for the Advancement of Science (AAAS) (*Science for All Americans*, 1989) echoed the importance of scientific knowledge and scientific ways of thinking within its goal of scientific literacy for all Americans. In the association's words, a scientific person "uses scientific knowledge and scientific ways of thinking for individual and social purposes" (p. 11). More specifically, the report states: "Scientific habits of mind can help people in every walk of life to deal sensibly with problems that often involve evidence, quantitative considerations, logical arguments, and uncertainty; without the ability to think critically and independently, citizens are easy prey to dogmatists, flimflam artists, and purveyors of simple solutions to complex problems" (p. 13). Regrettably, a review of the current state of affairs in the United States led AAAS to conclude that most Americans are not scientifically literate.

To achieve scientific literacy, the AAAS advocates a teaching and learning approach that starts with questions about nature, engages students actively, concentrates on the collection and use of evidence, does not separate knowing from finding out, and de-emphasizes the memorization of technical vocabulary. In other words, teach science as science is done. This theme of inquiry and de-emphasis of meaningless memorization is also evident in the National Research Council's Commission of Life Science's (1990) *Fulfilling the Promise: Biology Education in the Nation's Schools*:

"We need a much leaner biology course that is constructed from a small number of general principles that can serve as scaffolding on which students will be able to build further knowledge. . . . Concepts must be mastered through inquiry not memorization of words. The number of new words introduced must be kept to an absolute minimum" (p. 21).

The Educational Policies Commission, the AAAS, and the National Research Council are advocating science teaching not only for the production of more scientists, but also for the development of people whose approach to life is that of creative and critical thought. Thus, the central question for the science teacher is, How can science be taught to help students become skilled in creative and critical thinking? The answer proposed in this book is: by using an instructional method that actually allows students to explore nature and generate and test their own mental creations. In other words, knowledge is the result of personal "constructions" of the learner. Effective instruction must allow for this *constructivist* process to take place.

As mentioned, creative and critical thinking skills neither develop nor function independently of specific contexts; therefore, we must carefully consider the relationship between context and process in thinking and in instruction. Indeed, I will argue that the use of activities in which students truly investigate and attempt to construct their own knowledge about natural phenomena best facilitates both the construction of specific concepts and conceptual systems and the development of general thinking skills.

How then do prior knowledge and new experiences interact to facilitate the construction of new knowledge? This fundamental question will be answered by looking at the work of specific scientists as they are engaged in the process of knowledge construction.

▽ THE NATURE OF SCIENTIFIC THINKING: A LOOK AT THE WORK OF AN ETHOLOGIST

What is science? Is there one scientific method? What is scientific thinking? How do scientists construct knowledge? Scientists are primarily engaged in learning about nature. Consequently, if we are able to answer these questions, we will have discovered how people learn and, more important, how you, as a teacher, can create the conditions necessary for your students to construct knowledge, to learn. We begin an examination of these questions by carefully looking at research that we all would agree is scientific. The research chosen is that being done by Tim Caro, a British ethologist who studies predator–prey relationships in Kenya's Serengeti Plain. While studying cheetahs and gazelles, Caro became curious about the tendency of gazelles that were being chased by cheetahs to leap high in the air with their legs stiffly pointing downward and their rump fur spread so as to create a large white patch (Caro, 1986a, 1986b).

Creating Hypotheses

Caro's observation of this curious behavior, called *stotting*, led him to ask, Why do gazelles stot? Is stotting of some benefit to gazelles? Caro considered that stotting was worth being curious about because it appeared strange that a gazelle being stalked by a predator would act in such a way that seemed to slow the gazelle and make it more conspicuous and vulnerable.

Previous to Caro's investigation, another ethologist had published a tentative explanation for stotting. That explanation argued that gazelles might actually gain a survival advantage by stotting, despite appearances to the contrary, because they would be better able to survey the immediate area for predators. Caro was aware of this explanation but was unconvinced. Consequently, he created several additional explanations. One explanation was that gazelles stot in order to warn other gazelles of danger. Another explanation was that adult gazelles stot to draw attention away from their more vulnerable offspring. Still another explanation was that stotting tells the predator that it has been seen, and thus the stotting gazelle will be difficult to catch. Six additional explanations were proposed, so Caro did not simply come up with a single answer to his question, but *multiple* answers. Each amounted to an alternative explanation for stotting. Of importance is the fact that these tentative explanations were not derived by observations of the stotting gazelles but from Caro's prior knowledge of similar situations. For example, Caro knew that many other animals, when pursued by a predator, send warning signals to members of their group, so it seemed reasonable to suspect that gazelles might do the same thing.

The *American College Dictionary* (Barnhart, 1953) defines the word *hypothesis* as follows: "a proposition (or set of propositions) proposed as an explanation for the occurrence of some specified group of phenomena." Further, the same dictionary defines the word *explain* as "to make clear the cause or reason of; account for." Thus, a hypothesis is a proposed explanation, a tentative cause for some specific observation or related observation. Therefore, we can say that Caro proposed several *alternative* hypotheses to answer his question about the curious behavior of stotting.

Because hypotheses play such a crucial role in science and in other disciplines, obtaining a clear understanding of that role is absolutely essential. Hypotheses seen in this light are not merely educated guesses based on collected information. Creating hypotheses does require background information and an element of guessing, but not all educated guesses are hypotheses. Suppose, for example, that you taste a green apple and discover that it is sour. After tasting a second, third, and fourth green apple you also find them sour. So from this "education" you "guess" that all green apples are sour and, on this basis, you predict that the next green apple you taste will also be sour. Does your educated guess that "all green apples are sour" constitute a hypothesis? No. It is merely a *generalization,* that is, a general statement drawn from specific experiences by way of a process known as *induction.*[1] Is the educated guess that "the next green apple will be sour" a hypothesis? Again, the answer is no. Instead it is better referred to as a *prediction* based on simple class logic that proceeds as follows: "All green apples are sour. This is a green apple, therefore, it will be sour." The prediction that the next apple will be sour is derived by a process referred to as *deduction.*

Philosophers use the term *abduction* to refer to the process of creating hypotheses (Hanson, 1958). Abduction consists of studying the available information (observations) and devising an explanation for them. Obviously, doing so requires some education and some guessing about causes, the guessing coming not from induction or deduction, but from prior knowledge and the creative process of abduction. Abduction involves sensing ways in which the current situation is somehow similar (analogous) to other known situations and using this similarity as a source of hypotheses in the present situation. Perhaps you know that sugar molecules make candy and cookies sweet, so it seems reasonable to borrow this idea and use it as a hypothesis to *explain* the lack of sweetness in the green apples. Thus, the statement that green apples are sour *because they lack sugar molecules* constitutes a hypothesis derived by abduction. The purpose of the hypothesis is to answer the question, What *causes* green apples to taste sour?

Many science textbook authors state that induction is the process involved in the formulation of hypotheses. Brum and McKane (1989), for example, state: "Most hypotheses and theories are the product of *inductive reasoning,* the assimilation of specific observations into a generalized explanation" (p. 24). As discussed by Hanson (1958), this is wrong: "[Induction] never can originate any idea whatever. . . . All the ideas of science come to it by the way of abduction" (p. 85). All that induction provides is a general statement that by itself cannot explain anything.

To understand this point, consider once again the green apple story. The tasting of individual apples (the specific) led by induction to the statement that all green apples are sour (the general). This statement is an *inductive generalization.* Such statements that arise from induction simply summarize a set of specific data and allow that summary to be tested further. For example, the observation that the sun has risen in the east every day in the past year leads inductively to the tentative generalization that it always does so. This, in turn, leads to a prediction: The sun will rise in the east tomorrow. In science it is important not merely to find patterns of regularity, which should appropriately be referred to as *laws,* but also to explain them—that is, establish causes of these patterns of regularity. For example, one explanatory hypothesis for why the sun rises in the east proposes that it is due to the earth's rotation on its axis from west to east. Thus, an explanatory hypothesis attempts to account for one set of observed phenomena in terms of another; in this case, it accounts for the sun's rising in the east in terms of the earth's rotation.

Without abduction, Caro would not have come up with several hypotheses about stotting in gazelles. Abduction, then, emphasizes that the formulation of hypotheses is a creative open-ended process based on analogies, not one that simply involves generalizations from limited observations or educated guesses about what might happen next.

Testing Hypotheses

Once competing explanations (alternative hypotheses) for an interesting causal question have been stated, Caro's next step was to find out which alternative explanation was the best answer to the question. Because Caro could not test his explanations by direct observation (gazelles will not tell us why they stot), he had to test them indirectly.

Consider Caro's hypothesis that gazelles stot in order to draw attention away from their more vulnerable offspring. To indirectly test this idea, Caro generated an argument as follows:

Hypothesis:	*If*	gazelles stot to draw attention away from their more vulnerable offspring,
Experiment:	*and*	we observe gazelles with and without offspring
Expected Outcome 1:	*then*	young, sexually immature gazelles should not stot.
Expected Outcome 2:	*then*	adults who have no young in the herd should not stot.
Expected Outcome 3:	*then*	isolated gazelles who are feeding alone or away from their offspring should not stot.

Presenting hypothesis testing in this format clearly indicates the *hypothetical-deductive* reasoning pattern that is involved as the hypothesis under consideration and the experimental conditions (observing gazelles with and without offspring) lead by way of deduction to, in this case, three distinct expected outcomes. Deduction involves making the assumption that the particular hypothesis under consideration is correct, and imagining some experimental or observational situation that, together with the hypothesis, leads by way of an *if . . . and . . . then* reasoning pattern to one or more specific expected outcome(s). Expected outcomes are often referred to as *predictions,* but these predictions should not be confused with the sorts of predictions discussed earlier that were the result of extrapolation of past events into the future—that is, the last ten green apples were sour, so I "predict" that the next one will also be sour.

With respect to the present hypothesis, Caro's experimental results did not correspond well with his expected (predicted) results. He observed that sexually immature gazelles (adults with no young), isolated gazelles, and gazelles with offspring all stotted at the same frequency when fleeing from a cheetah. Therefore, Caro rejected this hypothesis. As a result of testing all of the hypotheses in this way, Caro rejected all but the hypothesis that gazelles stot to signal that the predator has been seen, and thus the gazelle will be difficult to catch. Support for this hypothesis came from the following reasoning and evidence:

Hypothesis:	*If*	gazelles stot to signal to the predator that it has been seen, and consequently the gazelle will be difficult to catch,
Experiment:	*and*	we observe stotting gazelles by themselves and in groups
Expected Outcome 1:	*then*	gazelles should leap so that their rumps are visible to the predator and not to other gazelles.
Expected Outcome 2:	*then*	solitary gazelles should stot just as often as those traveling in groups.
Expected Outcome 3:	*then*	predators should often abandon a stalk if the gazelle stots early.

Caro observed all of these expected outcomes (predictions) and therefore concluded that this hypothesis had been supported.

The major elements of Caro's thinking, as described, are outlined in Figure 1.1. In general the figure shows that scientific research involves raising causal questions about some unexplained observation, using abduction to create several alternative explanations (hypotheses), imagining experimental or observational conditions that allow the deduction of expected outcomes (predictions), gathering actual outcomes (data) to compare with expected outcomes, drawing conclusions about the relative support or lack of support for the initial hypotheses based on the quality of the observations and their correspondence with the predictions, and finally storing supported hypotheses (conclusions) in long-term memory and, in the case of unsupported hypotheses, searching through long-term memory for additional hypotheses to test. The possibility exists that none of the alternative hypotheses will find convincing support: The "correct" hypothesis may not have been thought of as yet. Another possibility is that the most satisfactory explanation may involve some combination of the alternatives. In other words, any specific effect may have more than one cause.

The supported conclusions of one investigation—one stored in long-term memory—are then available to be used as alternative hypotheses in a future

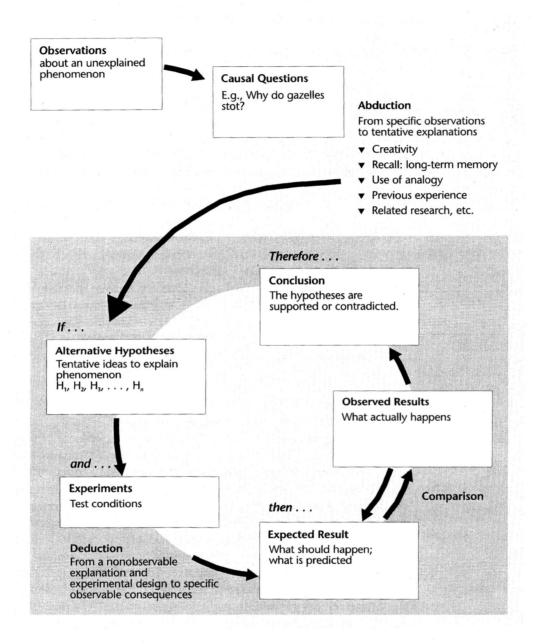

Figure 1.1 ▽ **Summary of Key Words and Scientific Processes.** These words and processes are used to investigate natural phenomena and testing.

investigation. For example, someone who believes that gazelles stot to signal predators that they will be difficult to catch may borrow this idea (using abduction) to generate the hypothesis that a particular kind of butterfly is brilliantly colored to signal a predator that it will be difficult to catch. Consequently, the research and learning process takes on a spiral pattern as shown in Figure 1.2. Presumably over time the research spiral produces more satisfactory and more generalizable explanations.

Why Hypotheses Are Neither Proven nor Disproven

The most basic test of any hypothesis (the nonobservable) is that it permits the deduction of predictions that can in turn be checked with experience (the observable). As long as experience is consistent with those predictions, the hypothesis has been supported. When experience is not consistent with predictions, the hypothesis has not been supported. It would be a mistake, however, to claim that consistency or lack of consistency of predictions with experience *proves* the truth or falsity of a hypothesis.

The reason that supportive evidence does not prove a hypothesis correct is simply because hypotheses, being the product of human imagination, are potentially unlimited in number, and any two or more may give rise to the same prediction(s) (i.e., when Hypothesis A predicts x, and Hypothesis B predicts x, the observation of x cannot tell you whether it was A or B that led to x. For example, suppose you generate the hypothesis that the sun orbits the earth. Such a hypothesis leads to the predictions that the sun will rise on one horizon, cross the sky, and set on the opposite horizon. Consequently when such a set of events is observed, the "sun-orbit" hypothesis has gained support. But it has *not* been proven, because some other hypothesis could give rise to the same set of predictions (e.g., the earth rotates on an axis).

But why are hypotheses not disproven? The logic of falsifiability reads as follows: p implies q, not q, therefore not p where p and q are two propositions. This is the logical form known as *modus tollens*. Modus tollens applies in the artificially constrained contexts of the logician but not in nature. Why not? The answer has to do with the complexity of natural phenomena and in our inability to be certain that we have accounted for *all* possible contingencies. In nature the proper logical form must read as follows: p implies q (assuming *all* other things were in fact equal), not q, therefore *probably* not p (to the extent that *all* other things were in fact equal).

Consider the following example. Suppose on a walk in a park you observe two nearly identical trees. Tree A has tall grass growing under it, while Tree B has nearly none (see Figure 1.3). Let us generate several hypotheses to account for the difference in the grass growth beneath the trees: for example, Tree B provides too much shade, Tree B drops grass-killing fruit, children trample the grass

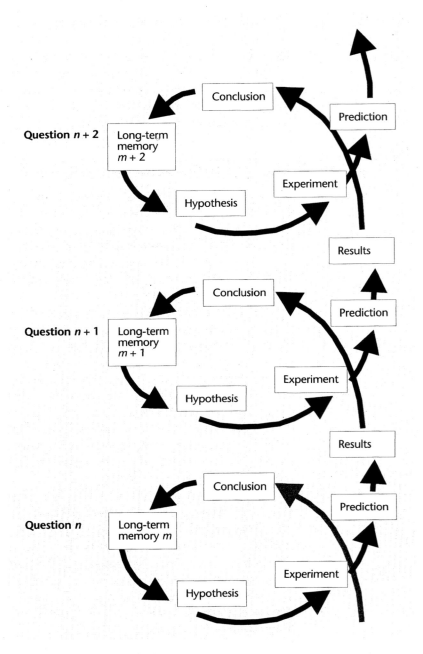

Figure 1.2 ▾ **The Hypothetical-Deductive Learning and Research Cycle.** This cycle becomes a spiral when conclusions from earlier investigations are added to the long-term memories of investigators and libraries, who thus become sources of alternative hypotheses for subsequent investigators.

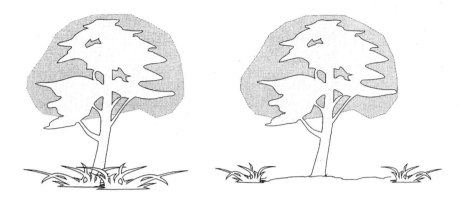

Figure 1.3 ▾ **Tree A and Tree B**

under Tree B, and the grass under Tree A is shade-tolerant. Now let us test one of these hypotheses. The first hypothesis (p) leads to the prediction (implies) that the grass should grow (q) if the branches are cut off, permitting more sunlight to reach the ground near the base of Tree B. Suppose we conduct the experiment and after several weeks we discover that the grass does not grow (not q). Have we, therefore, disproven the hypothesis? Recall that the logic of the situation reads as follows: The hypothesis (p) implies or predicts that the grass should grow after the branches are cut (q), but the grass did not grow (not q), therefore (via modus tollens) the hypothesis must be false.

Of course, it would be a shortsighted investigator who jumps to such a hasty conclusion. The correct conclusion is that the explanation has *not been supported*, but it has *not* been falsified or disproven. Too much shade may still be the reason that grass did not grow under Tree B, but it failed to grow after the branches had been cut off because (a) we did not wait long enough, (b) it was too cold for the grass to grow, (c) the soil lacked sufficient water, (d) no grass seed remained under the tree, and so on. In other words, we can never control all of the variables that might have influenced the outcome, so *some* doubt must always remain. Thus, no causal claim can be *proven* false.

▼ **THE ORIGIN AND NATURE OF THEORIES: A LOOK AT THE WORK OF CHARLES DARWIN**

Although the pattern of hypothesis creation and testing previously discussed in the work of Caro is completely general, it need not progress in precisely the way described—that is, although all the elements of the process are present, the order in which they occur may vary—nor is it all there is to doing scientific research. Some research is primarily descriptive, at least at the outset, and some deals with theory creation and test. We shall therefore take a look at the work of Charles Darwin and how his initially descriptive research led to the creation of the most important theory in the history of biology.

Gruber and Barrett (1974) analyzed Charles Darwin's thinking during the period 1831 to 1838 when he underwent a change in beliefs from a special creationist view of the world to that of an evolutionist. Darwin left a record of much of his thinking during this period in copious diaries. Figure 1.4 highlights the major changes in his worldview during this time as reflected by Gruber and Barrett's analysis of those diaries.

Darwin's view in 1831 was that the creator made an organic world (O) and a physical world (P) and that the organic world was perfectly adapted to the physical world (see Figure 1.4a). This view of the world served Darwin well, and his thoughts and behavior were consistent with this view.

Although Charles Darwin was most certainly a creationist in 1831, he was well aware of evolutionary views. In fact, Darwin's own grandfather, Erasmus Darwin, published a work titled *Zoonomia: or the Laws of Organic Life* that contained speculative ideas about evolution and its possible mechanism. Nevertheless, Charles Darwin on that day in 1831, when he boarded HMS *Beagle* as the ship's naturalist, was seeking an adventure, not a theory of evolution.

During the first two years of the voyage on the *Beagle*, Darwin read some persuasive ideas about the modification of the physical environment through time by Charles Lyell in the latter's two-volume *Principles of Geology*. At each new place Darwin visited, he discovered examples and important extensions of Lyell's ideas. Darwin was becoming increasingly convinced that the physical world was not static—it changed through time. This new conception of the physical world stood in opposition to his earlier beliefs and created a serious contradiction. If the organic world and the physical world are perfectly adapted, and the physical world changes, then the organic world must also change. This, of course, is the logical extension of the argument. Its conclusion, however, was the opposite of Darwin's original view that organisms did not evolve. Darwin also spent a considerable amount of time and energy collecting and carefully describing the various plant and animal species that he found. He was profoundly struck by their overwhelming numbers and diversity. With each new species and variety collected it became increasingly difficult to imagine that their existence was solely the work of the creator.

These perplexities put Darwin into what psychologists call a state of *mental disequilibrium* (see Chapter 3). Darwin did not immediately accept the logic of this situation and conclude that organisms must also change. In fact, not until 1837, after his return to England, was he converted to the idea of the evolution of species (Green, 1958). It seems astonishing that it would require this amount

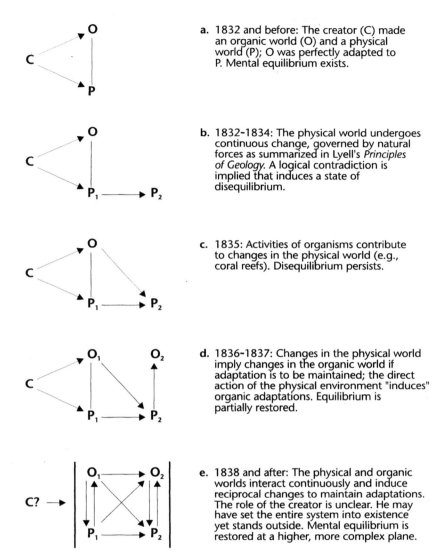

a. 1832 and before: The creator (C) made an organic world (O) and a physical world (P); O was perfectly adapted to P. Mental equilibrium exists.

b. 1832-1834: The physical world undergoes continuous change, governed by natural forces as summarized in Lyell's *Principles of Geology*. A logical contradiction is implied that induces a state of disequilibrium.

c. 1835: Activities of organisms contribute to changes in the physical world (e.g., coral reefs). Disequilibrium persists.

d. 1836-1837: Changes in the physical world imply changes in the organic world if adaptation is to be maintained; the direct action of the physical environment "induces" organic adaptations. Equilibrium is partially restored.

e. 1838 and after: The physical and organic worlds interact continuously and induce reciprocal changes to maintain adaptations. The role of the creator is unclear. He may have set the entire system into existence yet stands outside. Mental equilibrium is restored at a higher, more complex plane.

Figure 1.4 ▾ **Charles Darwin's Changing Worldview from 1831 to 1838.** This is an example of conceptual change and mental self-regulation (after Gruber & Barrett, 1974).

of time for Darwin to assimilate the logic of the situation, but even in the 2,000 pages of geological and biological notes that he made during the voyage, there is very little discussion of the evolution of organisms. What little there is opposes the idea.

Precisely how and why Darwin changed his view is not known. Figure 1.4, however, appears to be a fairly accurate summary of his changing worldview. Smith and Millman (1987) have also carefully examined Darwin's notebook (particularly the B notebook) and have characterized Darwin's mind as in a state of "exploratory thinking," meaning that, rather than accepting any particular theory, Darwin was considering various views (alternatives) to explain the situation as he saw it. If we assume that the weight of accumulating evidence forced a rejection of special creation (e.g., physical change, intermediate "forms" of organisms, an untold diversity of species larger than could reasonably be held on Noah's ark), then this exploratory thinking was aimed primarily at explaining evolution. Figure 1.4e thus represents the partial restoration of mental equilibrium as it eliminates the logical contradiction implied in Figure 1.4b.

The process of moving from equilibrium to disequilibrium and back to equilibrium is referred to as *self-regulation* (or sometimes as *equilibration*). The necessary conditions for self-regulation to take place appear to be: (a) data that are inconsistent with previous ways of thinking, (b) the presence of alternative conceptions or hypotheses (the idea of evolution), and (c) sufficient time, motivation, and thinking skills to compare the alternative ideas and their predicted consequences with the evidence.

The Use of Analogy

Once Darwin had accepted the alternative view that organisms evolve, the question of "How?" immediately arose. Of course the answer he created was through a process he called *natural selection*. But by what process did Darwin come to create the theory of natural selection?

According to the record, Darwin's search for an explanation of how evolution occurs involved several initially unsuccessful trials and a good deal of groping until September 1838. That month, Darwin read Thomas Malthus's *Essay on Population*. Darwin wrote, "I came to the conclusion that selection was the principle of change from the study of domesticated productions; and then reading Malthus, I saw at once how to apply this principle" (Green, 1958, pp. 257–258). Darwin saw in Malthus's writing a key idea that he could *borrow* and use to explain evolution. That key idea was that *artificial* selection of domesticated plants and animals was *analogous* to what presumably occurs in nature and could account for a change or evolution of species. As Gruber (1974, pp. 118–119) points out, Darwin had read Malthus before but not until this reading did he become conscious of the import of the artificial selection process.[2] But once it had been properly assimilated, Darwin turned to the task of marshalling the evidence favoring his theory of descent with modification. He turned to the facts known about plant and animal breeding, to the evidence that had first led him to doubt the fixity of species—namely, the facts concerning the geographic distribution of organic forms—and to the creatures of the Galapagos Islands. He discovered support for his ideas in the geological, anatomical, ecological, and embryological records of the period, and by the year 1842 he was ready to commit a rough draft of his entire thesis to paper (Green, 1958).

The example of Darwin's use of the analogous process of artificial selection suggests that analogy plays a central role in theory creation. The "idea" or pattern that allowed Darwin to make sense of his data was analogous to the pattern inherent in the process of artificial selection. As mentioned previously, the process of the borrowing of old ideas and applying them in new situations is known as *abduction*. Others have referred to the process as *analogical reasoning* (Karplus, 1979; Lawson & Lawson, 1979) or *analogical transfer* (Holland, Holyoak, Nisbett, & Thagard, 1986).

Examples of abduction are numerous in the history of science. Kepler borrowed the idea of the ellipse from Appolonious to describe planetary orbits. Mendel borrowed patterns of algebra to explain heredity. Kekulè borrowed the idea of snakes eating their tails (in a dream!) to create a molecular structure for benzene, and Coulomb borrowed Newton's ideas of gravitational attraction to describe the electrical forces that exist at the level of atomic particles.

Abduction, borrowing old ideas and applying them in new situations to invent new explanations, is all-pervasive. According to Pierce (in Hanson, 1958): "Abduction consists in studying the facts and devising a theory to explain them. Its only justification is that if we are ever to understand things at all, it must be that way. Abductive and inductive reasoning are utterly irreducible, either to the other or to Deduction, or Deduction to either of them" (p. 85).

Thus, theories such as natural selection are created by applying previously acquired patterns from the world of observable objects and events to explain unobservable events.

The Nature of Theories

What, then, is a theory? A *theory* is a set of basic premises or fundamental assumptions that function together to explain a class set of related phenomena. The *American College Dictionary* (Barnhart, 1953) defines theory as "a coherent group of general propositions used as principles of explanation for a class of phenomena." In this case, Darwin proposed the following six general propositions (postulates) to explain how organisms evolve (after Lewis, 1986):

1. Enormous spans of time are available for gradual geological and biological change.
2. Given favorable conditions, populations of organisms are capable of exceedingly rapid growth. This potential for rapid expansion in numbers is termed *biotic potential.*

3. Populations seldom reach their potential growth rate because of restricting environmental factors termed *limiting factors.*
4. There is *variation* among the characteristics of individuals within a species.
5. Some of the characteristics that contribute to this variation are *heritable.*
6. Individuals with certain characteristics have a better chance of surviving and reproducing than individuals with other characteristics. In other words, there is a *natural selection* of certain characteristics.

Note that natural selection is the phrase defined by the postulates. A *concept* is defined as a pattern of regularity plus a term or phrase that is used to refer to that pattern. Therefore, the phrase *natural selection* refers to the pattern Darwin hypothesized to exist in nature that was analogous to the pattern he was familiar with in animal breeding. Once a person recognizes a pattern and knows what term or phrase is used to refer to that pattern, we can say the person has acquired the concept. Because Darwin was the first person to link this pattern to the phrase *natural selection,* we can say that he introduced or "coined" the term and "created" the concept. Anyone who follows Darwin who also links the pattern to Darwin's phrase has "learned" the concept. In a very real sense, to "learn" the meaning of a new phrase or term requires that one "reinvent" or re-create the concept.

Theories such as Darwin's may or may not represent adequate explanations. Many theories of the past seemed adequate at the time but have subsequently been rejected or modified because of a lack of scientific support for the component postulates; nevertheless, they remain theories. A well-known example in biology is the theory of spontaneous generation, which consists essentially of three basic postulates: (a) Living things arise spontaneously from nonliving materials when a special "vital" force acts on the nonliving material; (b) different sorts of nonliving materials give rise to different kinds of organisms (for example, rotting meat gives rise to flies, while old rags give rise to mice); (3) spontaneous generation has occurred in the past and still occurs today. Lamarck's theory of the inheritance of acquired characteristics, and the blending theory of inheritance are other theories that have failed to find much support. Still another is the theory of special creation; although not supported by scientific evidence, it is still a theory because its postulates function together in an attempt to explain the origin of life. To determine whether a theory is a "good" one, its basic postulates must be tested in the manner previously described in the work of Caro—that is by deducing the consequences of each postulate, or group of postulates, and comparing those consequences with evidence gathered through a careful look at nature. It is by no means an understatement to say that the central purpose of modern science is to create and test comprehensive theories about nature. The issue of theory testing will be examined in more detail later.

Although research continues on evolutionary change to this day, the basic postulates of Darwin's theory of natural selection have withstood the test of time as virtually all available evidence supports their validity. Consequently, Darwin's theory of natural selection can be called an *embedded theory* (Lewis, 1987, 1988). Although the postulates of Darwin's and other embedded theories such as the cell theory, Mendel's theory of inheritance, and the theory of DNA structure and duplication (see Table 1.1 for a list of the major postulates of these theories) have become generally accepted by members of the scientific community, the possibility of coming up with a better theory or with evidence that contradicts one or more of the postulates always remains. In this sense, certainty is not attainable.

The great utility of theories, then, is that a considerable amount of information can be unified through a relatively few postulates. In science, the embedded theories—those that are well established through strong support from a wide range of studies over a considerable period of time—are the most useful. Embedded theories give structure to established knowledge (Lewis, 1987, 1988).

Some theories have been discarded or modified, but they still remain theories. Other theories, although not as well-established as embedded theories, have had and continue to have considerable influence on the development of our knowledge and understanding of nature. Still other theories attempt to explain processes but are more restricted in their application. The root pressure theory and transpiration pull theory to explain the movement of water through xylem in plants are examples. They both attempt to explain the same process, but at present no single theory satisfactorily explains all of what is involved in water movement through plants. Because these types of theories have a more limited application (in this case they are limited to one process and to higher plants), they do not play the same central role in science as do embedded theories.

Before we turn to another example of science in action, examine the following definitions of key terms.

▼ **Hypothesis:** A single proposition intended as a possible explanation for an observed phenomenon—that is, a possible cause for a specific result.

▼ **Abduction:** The mental process of creating hypotheses in which an explanation that is successful in one context is borrowed and applied as a tentative explanation in a new context.

▼ **Induction:** The mental process of deriving general propositions from a limited set of specific observations.

▼ **Law:** A general proposition that summarizes a pattern of regularity detected in nature—that is, the manner or order in which a set of natural phenomena occur under certain conditions. (Note that a satisfactory explanation for the pattern may or may not exist. For example, a force called *gravity* appears to exist that

Table 1.1 ▾ **Major Postulates of Three Embedded Theories in Biology and Kinetic-Molecular Theory**

Theory	Postulate
The Cell Theory	1. Cells are the structural and functional units of all organisms.
	2. Cells arise only from preexisting cells.
	3. Cells contain hereditary material by which specific characteristics are passed from parent cells to daughter cells.
Mendel's Theory of Inheritance	1. Inherited characteristics are determined by tiny particles called *factors*.
	2. Factors are passed from parent to offspring in the gametes.
	3. Individuals have at least one pair of factors for each characteristic in all cells except the gametes.
	4. During gamete formation, paired factors separate. Each gamete receives one factor of each pair.
	5. There is an equal chance that a gamete will receive either one of the factors of a pair.
	6. When considering two or more pairs of factors, the factors of each pair assort independently to the gametes.
	7. Factors of a pair that are separated in the gametes recombine randomly during fertilization.
	8. Sometimes one factor of a pair dominates the other factor so that it alone controls the characteristic (dominant–recessive).
Watson and Crick's Theory of DNA Structure and Duplication	1. DNA consists of a double spiral helix with the two strands of the spiral made of alternating molecules of deoxyribose and phosphoric acid.
	2. Pairs of bases form links between the two opposite deoxyribose molecules in the spiral strands. The base parts are adenine—thymine (—A—T—) and cytosine—guanine (—C—G—).
	3. The base pairs may be in any sequence along the double spiral and may be positioned —A—T—, —T—A—, —C—G—, or —G—C—.
	4. When DNA duplicates, the two bases in each pair separate, permitting the two spirals to separate.
	5. As the spirals separate, complementary nucleotides pair sequentially with the organic bases in each spiral.
	6. And as the pairing occurs, the deoxyribose attaches to the phosphoric acid of the preceding nucleotide, thus forming the strand of the new spiral.

Table 1.1 ▾ **Major Postulates of Three Embedded Theories in Biology and Kinetic-Molecular Theory (continued)**

Theory	Postulate
Kinetic-Molecular Theory	1. Matter consists of small particles (atoms and combinations of bonded atoms called *molecules*) and light, which consists of still smaller particles called *photons*. 2. Matter moves and can strike other matter and transfer some or all of its motion (kinetic energy) to the other piece of matter. 3. Photons can interact with electrons and cause them to move more rapidly. Photons may also be "released" from electrons, which causes light to be emitted and results in a reduction in the motion of the electrons. 4. Atoms differ from one another because of the different numbers of protons, neutrons, and electrons contained in each. 5. Attractive forces between atoms (i.e., molecular bonds) can be broken, causing the atoms to move apart, which in turn can cause collisions and transfers of energy. 6. Molecular bonds can be formed between atoms when they strike one another. 7. The temperature of a substance is a measure of the amount of motion of its particles (i.e., the more motion, the greater the temperature). 8. The term *pressure* refers to the force exerted on a surface by the collisions of particles (i.e., more and larger particles at higher speeds equals greater air pressure).

Source: After Lewis, 1975

causes objects to be attracted to one another, although no one has yet offered a satisfactory explanation as to how this force can act at a distance.)

▼ **Experiment:** A set of manipulations or specific observations of nature that allow the test of hypotheses or generalizations.

▼ **Deduction:** The mental process of joining a hypothesis or generalization with a proposed experiment or observation to allow the derivation of an expected outcome. The process of deduction follows the *If . . . and . . . then* linguistic form.

▼ **Prediction:** A proposition that represents a reasonable consequence (expected outcome) of an experiment or observation given that the hypothesis or generalization under consideration is assumed to be correct. A prediction is the result of the process of deduction. The term *prediction* also refers to the outcome of the process of "guessing" about future events based on an extrapolation of a pattern of regularity detected in past events. The fact that the term is used in two different ways is perhaps partially responsible for the confusion that exists in many science textbooks regarding the term's meaning.

▼ **Theory:** A collection of general propositions (postulates, assumptions) that when taken together attempt to explain a class of related phenomena.

▼ **Embedded Theory:** A theory whose general propositions have been tested and supported repeatedly so that it represents a widely accepted explanation for a class of related phenomena.

▼ **Evidence:** Actual observations of nature that can be compared with expected observations (predictions) to allow the test of alternative hypotheses or theories.

▼ **Conclusions:** Propositions that summarize the extent to which hypotheses or theories have been supported or contradicted by the evidence.

▼ **Fact:** A proposition concerning direct observation of nature that is replicated so consistently that little doubt exists as to its truth or falsity.

▼ **Scientific Method:** The collection of various activities (the most prominent of which have just been defined) that people use in their attempt to describe and explain natural phenomena accurately. The scientific method involves, but is not limited to, the following activities:

1. Raising both descriptive and causal questions about nature.
2. Inventing alternative explanations for what is observed.
3. Generating experimental or observational manipulations to allow the explanations to be tested.
4. Deducing the expected outcome(s) of experimental or observational manipulations assuming the explanation is correct.

5. Gathering and analyzing data to determine the extent to which the data agree with the expected outcome(s).

6. Generating and communicating conclusions regarding the relative support or lack of support obtained for the alternative explanations.

Keep in mind that not all that is considered scientific research involves all of these steps. Further, the order in which the steps occur may vary. Indeed, the research process is highly cyclical and may involve a considerable amount of trial and error. Therefore, use of the phrase *scientific method* in no way implies a linear and lockstep procedure for doing successful research.

▼ HOW ARE THEORIES TESTED? THE CASE OF SPONTANEOUS GENERATION

Although it is true that theory testing involves the same basic process as hypothesis testing (as described in the Caro example), the process can run into considerable difficulty if people are willing to modify a theory's initial postulates when confronted with contradictory data. A classic example of this, again from the history of biology, is the case of spontaneous generation.

In 1748 English clergyman John Needham reported experimental results that seemed to show that life can arise spontaneously from nonliving matter. In that experiment Needham put some gravy in a bottle, which he plugged with a cork. He then heated the gravy in a hot fire. He believed this would kill any living things or eggs that might be in the bottle. He put the bottle away for a few days, and when he returned to examine the gravy under a microscope, he found it teeming with tiny living creatures.

Needham concluded from his experiment that living things can arise spontaneously from the nonliving. To explain how this could happen he postulated that a special "vital," mystic force entered the bottle and acted on nonliving material to bring it to life. As stated previously, this theory of spontaneous generation consisted essentially of three postulates: (a) Living things arise spontaneously form nonliving materials when a special vital force acts on the nonliving material; (b) different sorts of nonliving materials give rise to different sorts of organisms; and (c) spontaneous generation has occurred in the past and still occurs today.

An Italian physiologist named Lazarro Spallanzani read about Needham's experiment and about his idea of the vital force. Because Spallanzani did not believe in spontaneous generation or in the vital force, he looked for flaws in Needham's experiment. To refute Needham's work, Spallanzani began with the alternative hypothesis that microbes grew in Needham's bottle because he had not sealed it tightly enough to keep new microbes out or had not heated the gravy long enough to kill the microbes or eggs that were in the gravy at the start, or both.

To test this idea, Spallanzani cleaned several bottles and put seeds in each. He then poured distilled water into the bottles, closed them by melting the necks in a flame, and boiled the contents. He boiled some for only a few minutes and some for an hour. As a control, he repeated the procedure with another set of bottles that he only plugged with corks as Needham had done.

The reasoning that guided Spallanzani's experiment can be summarized as follows:

Hypothesis:	*If*	a vital force exists that can act on nonliving matter to bring it to life,
	and	some bottles are heated and corked while others are heated and sealed by melting their necks
Prediction:	*then*	microbes should be spontaneously generated in both sets of bottles.

On the other hand,

Alternative Hypothesis:	*If*	the vital force does not exist and microbes can enter a bottle around a cork but not through a bottle neck that has been melted shut
Prediction:	*then*	microbes should be found in the corked bottles but not in the melted shut bottles.

Days later Spallanzani discovered that the bottles that had been boiled only a short time were teeming with microbes. But in those bottles that had been boiled for an hour and sealed by melting the necks, he found no microbes. He found all of the corked bottles full of microbes. Because his results did not match the result predicted by this vital force postulate, Spallanzani concluded that the vital force and spontaneous generation theory was wrong. Instead, he believed that his alternative *biogenesis* theory (life only from prior life) was correct.

To Spallanzani, his experiment seemed to be conclusive evidence that spontaneous generation and Needham's vital force did not exist. But Needham did not conclude that Spallanzani's experiment was indeed a "crucial" test and that his theory was wrong; instead, he answered Spallanzani in a way that was quite convincing to many. Needham reasoned that the fierce heat used in Spallanzani's experiment weakened and damaged the vital force so that it could no longer create the microbes.

Spallanzani was, no doubt, frustrated at Needham's claim, but again he saw a way to test this new claim. To do so, he set up a whole series of bottles with seeds that had been heated for various lengths of time. The first seeds were boiled only a few minutes, some for half an hour, some for an hour, and some for two hours, and some he baked until they were charred. After this he set up his bottles with the seeds and water, but he only sealed the tops with corks. If Needham were correct, no microbes would be found in the flasks with the charred seeds. Days later Spallanzani examined the flasks and found them all alive with microbes.

Surely Needham would not be able to refute this "crucial" evidence. But refute it he did. Although Needham had been forced to admit that fierce heat may not destroy the vital force, he countered with the ingenious claim that, while Spallanzani was heating his sealed bottles in his previous experiment, he was destroying the "elasticity" of the air. According to Needham, "elastic" air was necessary for the vital force to work. Notice what Needham is doing here. Instead of concluding that his theory is wrong, he is instead adding *ad hoc* postulates to the theory to keep its predictions consistent with the evidence— that is, he first added Postulate 4, which states that "fierce heat destroys the vital force." Then when this did not work, he added Postulate 5, which states that "elastic air is necessary for the vital force to work."

Nevertheless, once again Spallanzani set out to falsify Needham's newest idea. All of the bottles he had used previously had wide necks, so heating to seal them required a relatively long time. This, he reasoned, heated and consequently drove out a large quantity of air, which to Needham had appeared to be the result of boiling the sealed bottles, therefore his claim of less elastic air. Spallanzani instead took the same bottles and filled them partially with seeds and water. He then diminished the necks of the vessels by heating until the opening was very thin. After letting the internal and external air come to the same temperature, he put the opening to his blowpipe to seal it instantaneously so the internal air underwent no alteration. With this completed, he heated the bottles in boiling water for an hour. On opening the bottles nearly a month later, Spallanzani found, by use of a candle held near the opening, that the flame deflected away from the neck. This showed the internal air to be more "elastic," not less as Needham had argued.

Again, a "crucial" experiment had been conducted. Spallanzani had shown tremendous skill in deducing the consequences of his beliefs and putting them to the test. Consequently much of the opposition to Spallanzani quieted, although the ideas of spontaneous generation and special vital forces in living things were by no means dead. Many distinguished scientists still held fast to prior beliefs.

The question of spontaneous generation and vitalism persisted well into the nineteenth century as witnessed by the classic experiments of Louis Pasteur, who concluded: "The great interest of this method is that it proves without doubt that the origin of life, in infusions which have been boiled, arises uniquely from the solid particles which are suspended in the air" (Pasteur, 1862, p. 69). The method Pasteur refers to was simply to set up flasks with nutrient liquid as others had done before; however, instead of sealing them, he drew the necks out under a flame so that several curves were produced and some sections of the necks pointed downward. He then boiled the liquid for several minutes and allowed the flasks to cool and sit for several days. In no case did microbes develop in the liquids. This, to Pasteur and many others, seemed crucial, just as Spallanzani's experiments had seemed crucial nearly a century earlier. But even in the face of Pasteur's logic, clarity, and simplicity in his experimentation, the question was still not completely settled in some people's minds.

The Needham and Spallanzani case history reveals that testing theories is basically a matter of comparing predictions that have been derived from the theory's basic assumptions (i.e., postulates) with evidence. When a mismatch occurs between what the postulates lead one to predict and the evidence, then the basic assumptions of the theory must be modified to remain in accord with the empirical world. But when those necessary modifications become too numerous or too implausible in terms of other theories, most impartial and informed observers are willing to abandon the theory. This is especially so when a more plausible and less cumbersome alternative theory exists. The original advocates of the refuted theory are generally the last ones to give it up and may indeed never change their minds. Consider, for example, the words of Charles Darwin at the end of *On the Origin of Species*: "Although I am fully convinced of the truth of the views given in this volume, I, by no means expect to convince experienced naturalists whose minds are stocked with a multitude of facts all viewed during a long course of years, from a point of view directly opposite to mine. But I look with confidence to the future, to young and rising naturalists, who will be able to view both sides of the question with impartiality" (p. 45). The words of Max Planck (1949), writing in his autobiography, are also particularly appropriate: "A scientific truth does not triumph by convincing its opponents and making them see the light, but rather because its opponents eventually die, and a new generation grows up that is familiar with it (pp. 33–34).

How, then, are theories tested? The answer, of course, is precisely as stated previously: by generating and testing predictions derived from the theory's basic postulates. But the example of the biogenesis versus spontaneous generation controversy tells us that the process is not so simple, primarily for two reasons. First, it may be difficult to imagine ways of actually and convincingly testing the basic postulates; second, even if apparently crucial tests are generated, advocates of the theory may be able to generate additional postulates that will render these newer tests less than crucial.

SCIENCE AND RELIGION

How does science differ from religion? Do you suppose any amount of evidence could have shaken Needham from his belief in the vital force? Of course, we cannot really answer this question, but suppose that the answer is *no*. In other words, suppose that Needham has taken it as a matter of faith that the vital force exists. Consequently, his task is twofold:

1. to provide evidence consistent with this idea, and
2. if and when someone (such as Spallanzani) provides counterevidence to the idea of the vital force, propose new postulates that will keep the idea consistent with the evidence.

Compare this approach to one in which:

1. alternative explanations to a single phenomenon are generated (e.g., spontaneous generation versus biogenesis),
2. the postulates of each explanation are then generated and tested and the evidence is evaluated, and
3. the explanation that is most in accord with the evidence is tentatively accepted and the other rejected.

These two approaches represent the essential difference between religion and science. Religion asks one to believe based on faith. Science asks one to believe based on the evaluation of alternatives, evidence, and reason. This, of course, does not mean that religion is wrong and science is right, or that individual scientists cannot be deeply religious and believe some things based solely on faith. Rather, what it means is that as collective enterprises, religion and science are fundamentally different. At the extremes, a religion knows the Truth (i.e., the correct answers) before nature is consulted. And because there are many religions, there are many Truths, whereas in science the answers must be viewed as only tentative before nature is consulted. Even after nature has been consulted and support has been found for any particular explanation, scientists should still regard that explanation as only tentatively true: They should realize that the possibility always exists that someone may later create a "better" explanation or that new evidence may be found that contradicts the currently accepted explanation. The result of these differences between the world's many religious bodies of knowledge and scientific knowledge is that there are many religious perspectives, each claiming the ultimate truth and each not open to change,[3] whereas ideally there is only one collective body of scientific knowledge, which must always remain open to change with no claim, or even hope, of ever obtaining truth in any ultimate sense. Rather, scientific knowledge should be accepted as "correct" only so long as it seems reasonable in light of alternative explanations and the evidence and leads to successful behavior in nature.

▼ **THE ROLE OF OBSERVATION IN SCIENCE:
THE "CONSTRUCTION" OF OXYGEN**

How would you evaluate the following statement on a true–false quiz? "Science is a process of the discovery of the nature of things via observation." Make a mental note of your response and compare it to your view of the role of observation in scientific discovery after reading the next few pages about the discovery of oxygen.

Who discovered oxygen, and when was it discovered? If you happened to answer "true" to the previous statement about the nature of science, then the answers to these questions should be relatively easy to obtain, assuming, of course, that you do not already "know" the answers. All you need do is peruse the history of science to find out when oxygen was first "observed." But wait a minute. How can anyone observe oxygen? Have you ever seen oxygen? Are we not told that oxygen is a gas that consists of tiny moving molecules? Have you ever seen oxygen molecules? Have you ever seen any type of molecules? If you are honest, you will have to answer *no*. But do not feel bad. No one has ever seen individual molecules. Presumably, they are just too small for direct observation.[4] How then do we find out who discovered oxygen and when that discovery occurred?

The prevailing theory concerning the nature of the matter from the days well before the birth of Christ was that nature consisted of four fundamental substances: earth, fire, air, and water. Further, each of these substances, if free to move, would travel to their "natural" locations. According to this theory, nature locates earth below water, water below air, and air below fire. Therefore the reason that solid objects (earths) fall when released in the air or placed in water is because they seek their natural place below air or water. Likewise, flames (fire) rise in air because they seek their natural place above the air. The fact that the sun, the major concentration of fire, appears high in the sky (above the sky?) is consistent with this view.

The ancients not only developed comprehensive theories about nature such as these, but also made numerous observations. For example, it was well known that a candle placed under a jar burns for only a short time and then goes out. By the eighteenth century, most chemists explained this phenomenon by assuming that combustible substances, such as a candle, consist of a base material (the ancients' earth) plus something akin to the ancients' fire, which by that time had acquired the name *phlogiston*. Thus, when a candle is burned its phlogiston is released to the air in the form of the flame, and its base material is left behind. According to this "phlogiston theory" of combustion, the extinction of the flame in a closed jar occurs because the air in the jar becomes saturated with phlogiston. When the air can hold no more phlogiston, combustion stops and the flame dies. The phlogiston theory is most certainly in accord with the observations. Indeed, one can even *observe* the flame going from the candle into the air.

The phlogiston theory, however, was not entirely free of difficulties. Suppose, for example, that a metal is heated in an enclosed jar. Presumably the heating drives the phlogiston out of the metal and leaves the base substance behind in the form of ashes. When the air is saturated with phlogiston, combustion stops. If we assume that phlogiston is a substance, then it should weigh something. Consequently, a reasonable prediction is that the ashes should weigh less than the original metal because the ashes represent what is left of the metal after the phlogiston has gone into the air. Unfortunately for the phlogiston theory, the ashes actually weigh more, not less, than the original metal.

So, just as in the case of Needham's vital force, we have a theoretical postulate that leads to a prediction that is contradicted by evidence. What do you suppose the phlogistonists did? Just as Needham had done, instead of rejecting the theory, they merely postulated that phlogiston was a substance with *negative* weight! Thus, adding phlogiston to another substance decreases that substance's weight, and removing phlogiston increases its weight. In view of the ancients' four substance theory, this makes perfect sense. After all, fire seeks its natural place above air, so it should have negative weight. Lest you still think this idea of negative weight is unreasonable, consider the phenomenon of attractive *and* repulsive forces of common magnets, which was well known at the time. Clearly, it is not unreasonable merely to postulate that phlogiston has a negative weight. Once again, is this not consistent with the *observation* that flames rapidly rise in air? Small wonder that the phlogiston theory of combustion was well accepted by the scientific community of the eighteenth century even with the postulate that phlogiston has negative weight.

Several phlogistic chemists conducted experiments to explore additional aspects of combustion. They discovered, for example, that they could turn the ashes of metals back into the original metals by heating them over charcoal in a sealed jar. Charcoal was assumed to contain lots of phlogiston, so the explanation was quite straightforward. The phlogiston from the charcoal combined with the ashes (the base material of the metal) to produce the metal itself (i.e., the base plus the phlogiston). But these experiments also changed the nature of air in the jar. For example, when a mouse was placed in the jar, it died immediately, indicating that the air had been "damaged" in some way; thus, it was dubbed "damaged" air.

Phlogiston theory was not able to offer an explanation for the production of damaged air. French chemist Antoine Lavoisier considered this to be one of the most remarkable phenomena known. For Lavoisier, this unexplained phenomenon served as a source of doubt about the phlogiston theory (i.e., a source of mental disequilibrium) just as the realization in Darwin's mind that the physical world changes was a source of doubt about the theory of special creation. Consequently, when Lavoisier conducted his experiments, some of which will be discussed below, he sought a different type of explanation.

Among the numerous experiments on combustion that were reported, Pierre Bayen, a French chemist, discovered in 1774 that, when heated, the red precipitate (the ashes) of mercury could be converted to mercury (the metallic liquid), which also produced a gas. Phlogiston theory would explain the process as one in which the heat adds phlogiston to the ashes to produce the metal. However, this experiment, like the one just described, proved bothersome for the phlogistonists, not only because the released gas is unexplained, but also because Bayen was also able to convert the red precipitate into mercury without the use of charcoal, which presumably was the source of phlogiston. Bayen did note the gas released in the process, although he did not investigate its properties. In retrospect, today we can be rather certain that the gas was oxygen. Can we therefore conclude that Bayen discovered oxygen? Because Bayen had no idea what he had found, it hardly seems fair to give him the credit. By the same token, we would not conclude that someone who finds a map to buried treasure only to throw the map away has, in fact, discovered the treasure. Therefore, let us continue the story and our hunt for the discoverer of oxygen.

Joseph Priestley, an English chemist and an ardent phlogistonist, was also actively conducting experiments on combustion at the time. Priestley, unlike Bayen, had explored the properties of the gas that was released from heating the red precipitate of mercury. He discovered, for example, that when a candle was burned in the gas, it produced a "remarkably vigorous flame." He also discovered that a mouse placed in the jar with the gas lived much longer than in common air. Priestley had conducted numerous additional tests on the gas and concluded that he had obtained nitrous oxide, a species of gas already well known. Because Priestley had misidentified the gas, awarding him credit for the discovery of oxygen is also probably not fair.

In October 1774, Priestley had dinner with Lavoisier in Paris and told Lavoisier about his combustion experiments with the red precipitate of mercury. Some two years earlier Lavoisier had conducted several of his own experiments on combustion and had discovered that sulfur and phosphorus gain weight when burned (see Figure 1.5). Not only do they gain weight, but also the quantity of air in the enclosed experimental jar is reduced considerably during combustion. This led Lavoisier to suspect that something was removed from the air during combustion that may, in fact, combine with the sulfur or phosphorus. In the minds of the phlogistonists, sulfur and phosphorus gained weight because of the loss of phlogiston, which has negative weight, although they were at a loss to explain the reduced volume of air. But to Lavoisier, who had never accepted the phlogiston theory, the explanation was quite different, namely, that combustion involved the removal of something from the air that combines with the burning substance to increase its weight. Consequently, when Priestley told

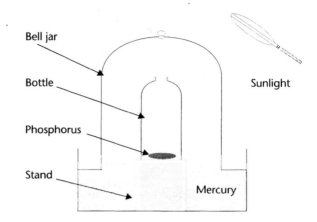

Figure 1.5 ▾ **Lavoisier's Experimental Apparatus (1).** This diagrams the apparatus that Lavoisier used to investigate changes in the weight of phosphorus when burned. A weighed piece of phosphorus is placed in a bottle of known weight, and the bottle is enclosed in a bell jar. Mercury is used to seal off the air in the bell jar from the surrounding air. When the phosphorus burns (by sunlight focused with a lens), a white substance forms within the bottle, and the mercury level rises in the bell jar. When the bottle containing the white substance was removed and weighed, Lavoisier found that the white substance weighed more than the phosphorus (after Conant, 1951). A few months after his conversation with Priestley, Lavoisier conducted his own experiments with the red precipitate of mercury. He tested the gas that was produced when the red precipitate was heated and confirmed Priestley's observation that "candles and burning objects were not extinguished in it, but the flame increased . . . and gave more light than common air." However, instead of concluding that he had indeed discovered a *new* gas, Lavoisier believed he had merely obtained common air, albeit a pure sample of common air. As he put it, "All these circumstances convinced me that this air was not only common air but that it was more respirable, more combustible, and consequently . . . more pure than even the air in which we live."

Lavoisier about his experiments with the red precipitate of mercury and the gas that was produced, Lavoisier was keenly interested, but not at all satisfied with Priestley's phlogistic interpretation.

During the early months of 1775, Priestley continued his tests on the gas that was produced when the red precipitate of mercury was heated. By a series of amazing accidents, Priestley was convinced by March 1775 that his previous interpretation was wrong. He had not obtained nitrous oxide after all. Instead,

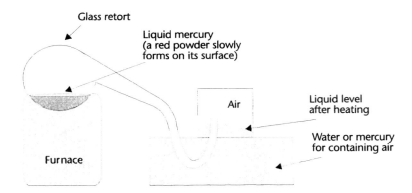

Figure 1.6 ▾ **Lavoisier's Experimental Apparatus (2).** This diagram shows that mercury heated in air absorbs a gas from the air (after Conant, 1951).

in accordance with the belief in the phlogiston theory, he concluded that the gas he had observed was air that was completely free of phlogiston, or, in the terms of the day, his experiments had produced completely "dephlogisticated" air.

Based on this work we might again be tempted to conclude that it was Priestley who discovered oxygen. After all, all one need do is change the name *dephlogisticated* to *oxygen* and we would have it. But this misses an important point. Can we really give Priestley credit for the discovery of "oxygen" when his *conception* of oxygen is so at odds with ours? We conceive of oxygen gas as a specific type of molecule that interacts with other types of molecules during combustion in a specific way. This conception is completely foreign to Priestley. To Priestley, the gas he had discovered was merely normal air devoid of a substance called phlogiston. Consequently, it hardly seems appropriate to give Priestley credit. Viewed in this way, oxygen is not a "thing" to be discovered. Rather, it is a *concept* to be invented. Did Priestley invent the appropriate concept of oxygen? No, he did not, therefore he cannot be given credit for its discovery any more than we can give Bayen credit.

Perhaps it was Lavoisier who deserves the credit. Armed with a mind well-prepared for a new conception of the combustion process, Lavoisier read about Priestley's latest experiments and was quick to "see" Priestley's "mistake" and present his own revolutionary interpretation. By 1778 Lavoisier had made his new theory of combustion clear to the scientific world. His own classic experiments, depicted in Figures 1.6 and 1.7, and, more important, his interpretation of those experiments, can be summarized as follows. Mercury heated in air produces a red precipitate and approximately one-fifth of the air disappears in the process (Figure 1.6). The red precipitate weighs more than the metal

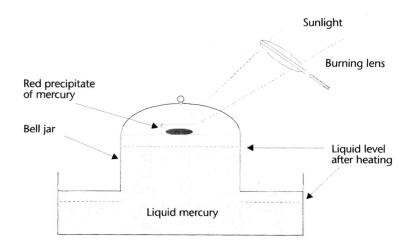

Figure 1.7 ▾ **Lavoisier's Experimental Apparatus (3).** Diagram showing Lavoisier's apparatus for heating the red precipitate of mercury and collecting the liberated gas (after Conant, 1951).

because some previously unidentified gas from the air (the one-fifth that disappeared) combined with the metal. The new gas that disappears when mercury is heated reappears when its red precipitate is heated and converted back into mercury (Figure 1.7). Lavoisier named this new gas "eminently respirable" air and later referred to it as the *principe oxygine*. With this revolutionary conception of combustion, Lavoisier had not only demonstrated no need for the notion of phlogiston, but also argued that he had discovered a *new* gas and even gave it a new name, the *principe oxygine*. Do we therefore conclude that it was Lavoisier who "discovered" oxygen? Perhaps, but this *also* may be giving him too much credit. Up to the end of his life, Lavoisier insisted that oxygen was an atomic "principle of acidity" and that oxygen gas was formed only when that "principle" united with *caloric*, the matter of heat. Thus, just as Priestley and others before him, Lavoisier really did not propose the modern view. Lavoisier's principle of acidity was not banished from chemistry until the early 1800s. The idea of caloric did not suffer the same fate until the 1860s. Of course, today we do not conceive of heat being matter; rather, heat is a measure of the amount of motion of the matter in question.

Who, then, discovered oxygen? Indeed, this question cannot be answered, except to say that no one did. In fact, no one could have discovered oxygen because, as mentioned previously, theoretical entities, such as oxygen, are not discovered. Instead, they are *invented,* and those inventions gain their meaning through their relationships with other invented entities within complex conceptual systems (theories) that themselves change and grow through time and are sometimes overthrown, as was the case of the phlogiston theory.

In conclusion, we see that the invention of the conceptual system describing oxygen's role in combustion took place in basically three phases. The first phase, which extended from the days of the ancient Greeks to well into the eighteenth century, involved exploration of a variety of phenomena, such as the burning of candles, phosphorus, and mercury, and the interpretation of those explorations in terms of concepts such as phlogiston and dephlogisticated air. The second key phase occurred when it became increasingly clear to Lavoisier during the 1770s that the old conceptual system was in error. In his view, the combustion process produced a new gas, which was given the name *oxygine*. Of course, the name itself is unimportant. Rather, the important point is that Lavoisier had conceived of something new in the combustion process. The third and final phase, which extended roughly from 1778 to the 1860s, can be considered a phase in which the modern view of oxygen's role in combustion was clarified (i.e., during combustion, oxygen gas combines with carbon to produce carbon dioxide gas) and the final vestiges of eighteenth-century chemistry such as the principle of acidity and the caloric were put to rest. Viewed in this way the process of scientific "discovery" is really a cyclic *constructive* process that consists of the *exploration* of novel phenomena, the *invention* of novel conceptions, and the *application* of the newly invented conceptions to the interpretation of old and new phenomena alike. Keep the phases of *exploration, invention,* and *application* in mind. If we intend to teach science as science is done, then science instruction should follow this exploration, invention, and application pattern. We will return to this pattern later when methods of effective science instruction are discussed.

Finally, three additional points must be made. The first point is about science. The second and third points are about science teaching. First, science is not a process of the discovery of the nature of things through observation. Rather, science is a process of the "discovery" of the nature of things via the creative invention of novel entities and theories and the test of those novel entities and theories through a comparison of their deduced consequences with observable evidence. In other words, scientific knowledge is the product of human mental construction, rather than mere observations of the "world out there." Second, because individual concepts such as oxygen derive their meaning not from observation, but from their place in imagined theoretical systems, they cannot be fully understood or learned apart from other concepts within those theoretical systems. Thus, when trying to teach complex processes such as combustion, science teachers need to think about how to teach *conceptual systems* (theories), not isolated facts or isolated concepts (Chapter 8 contains examples of teaching conceptual systems). And third, just as was the case for scientists such as Needham and Priestley, whose conceptual systems or theories were very different from those of modern-day scientists, many students enter classrooms firmly believing in ideas that we would consider scientific misconceptions. For students such as these, successfully teaching modern scientific conceptions requires much more than informing them of the modern view.

Questions for Reflection

For Questions 1 through 4 respond *true* or *false* and explain your response. Questions 5 through 13 require more in-depth answers.

1. Science is a process of discovery of the nature of things through observation.
2. Truth is attainable by way of proof through repeated observation.
3. A hypothesis is an educated guess of what *will be* observed under certain conditions.
4. A conclusion is a statement about what *was* observed under certain specific conditions.
5. In what sense is science both a process and a product?
6. Why is it more accurate to say that oxygen was invented, not discovered? Of what importance might this issue be in terms of teaching about combustion?
7. To the modern scientist, the concept of phlogiston is a "misconception." Do you think that the introduction of such misconceptions during instruction should be encouraged or discouraged? Why?
8. Which of the following do you think is the most appropriate "unit" for instruction: facts, concepts, or conceptual systems (i.e., theories)? Why?
9. During the next day or so, be on the lookout for objects, events, or situations that occur that raise questions about causes. For example, on a walk you might observe a spot of yellow grass in the middle of someone's green lawn and ask, What caused the yellow spot? Or you might be watching television only to have the picture flicker off; you might ask, Why did the picture go off? Make a list of five such causal questions.
10. For one of the five questions listed in Question 9, propose two alternative answers (hypotheses).
11. Use the *if . . . and . . . then* reasoning pattern (see Figure 1.1) to generate a prediction to the test of one or both of these alternatives.
12. For many students the process of generating and testing hypotheses seems a bit odd. Instead of simply observing the world to see if an explanation is correct, we must start by assuming that the explanation is correct so that it may be shown to be incorrect! If the explanation is *not* shown to be *in*correct, then it can be retained for the time being at least. Although this approach to learning about the world may seem backward, it nevertheless is the basic pattern of scientific thinking. Try these two puzzles to see if you can identify this "backward" thinking pattern.

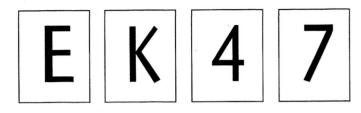

▼ **The Four Index Cards**

Observe the four index cards above. Each card has a letter on one side and a number on the other. Read the following rule:

"If a card has a vowel on one side, then it has an even number on the other side."

Suppose you want to test this idea to see if it is correct or incorrect for these four cards. Which of the four cards must be turned over to allow the rule to be tested? Explain. (*Note:* You may decide that you need to turn over more than one card.)

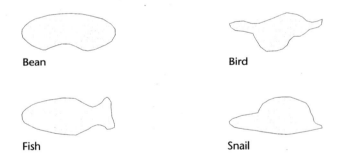

▼ **The Islands Puzzle** (after Karplus and Karplus, 1970)

This puzzle is about four islands in the ocean called Bean Island, Bird Island, Fish Island, and Snail Island. People have been traveling among these islands by boat for many years, but recently an airline started business. Carefully read the clues given below about possible plane trips. The trips may be direct, or they may include stops on one of the islands. If a trip is possible, it can be made in both directions between the islands.

First Clue: People can go by plane between Bean and Fish Islands.
Second Clue: People cannot go by plane between Bird and Snail Islands.

Use these two clues to answer Question A.

Question A: Can people go by plane between Bean and Bird Islands?

Yes   No   Cannot tell from the clues
Explain your answer.

Third Clue: People can go by plane between Bean and Bird Islands.

Use all three clues to answer Questions B and C. Do not change your answer to Question A.

Question B: Can people go by plane between Fish and Bird Islands?
Yes   No   Cannot tell from the clues
Explain your answer.

Question C: Can people go by plane between Fish and Snail Islands?
Yes   No   Cannot tell from the clues
Explain your answer.

13. By all accounts Hans was a very clever horse. According to German newspapers around the turn of the century, he could identify musical intervals, understand German, and was quite good at arithmetic. When his owner, Herr Wilhelm von Osten, asked him to add numbers, he tapped out answers with his hoof. For other questions he gestured with his head toward the appropriate pictures or objects.

Understandably, many people were skeptical about this, so a group of "experts"—two zoologists, a psychologist, a horse trainer, and a circus manager—were brought in to investigate. They watched closely as Herr von Osten asked question after question to which Clever Hans replied with near-perfect accuracy. Hans was even able to reply correctly to questions posed by perfect strangers. If the question called for the square root of 16, Hans would confidently tap four times with his hoof. The experts were unable to discover any tricks and thus were forced to conclude that Hans was a very clever horse indeed.

Do you agree with the experts? If not, how could Hans have correctly answered the questions? After reading the experts' report, a young psychologist named Oskar Pfunget proposed a different explanation. Suppose Hans was not able to think out the answers at all. Suppose instead that he was able to monitor subtle changes in the questioner's facial expressions, posture, and breathing that occurred when Hans arrived at the correct answer. Perhaps these cues could tell Hans when to stop tapping or moving his head.

How could this explanation be tested? Oskar decided he needed to use questioners who did not know the correct answers. If questioners did not know the answers, then their expressions and so on could not clue Hans, so his success rate should drop considerably. Surely enough, when the interrogator knew the answer, Hans succeeded on 9 out of 10 problems. But when the interrogator was ignorant, Hans's score dropped to just 1 out of 10. Hans had not learned arithmetic, music, or German after all. Instead, he had learned how to read people's faces and body language! In one sense Hans was not smart at all, but in another sense he was extremely perceptive.

Now see if you can identify the key elements of the scientific method from the story. Fill in the boxes in Figure 1.8 with the correct questions or statements. You can compare your answers with the correct ones in Figure 1.9.

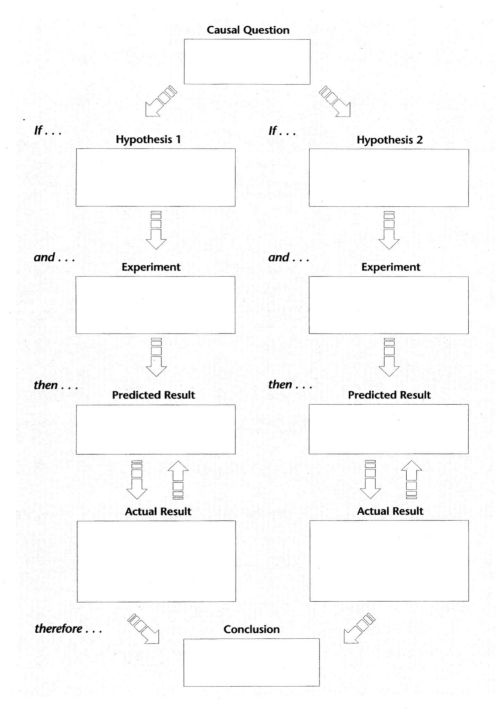

Figure 1.8 ▽ **Major Elements of Scientific Thinking (1).** Fill in the boxes with the appropriate questions or statements from the story about Clever Hans.

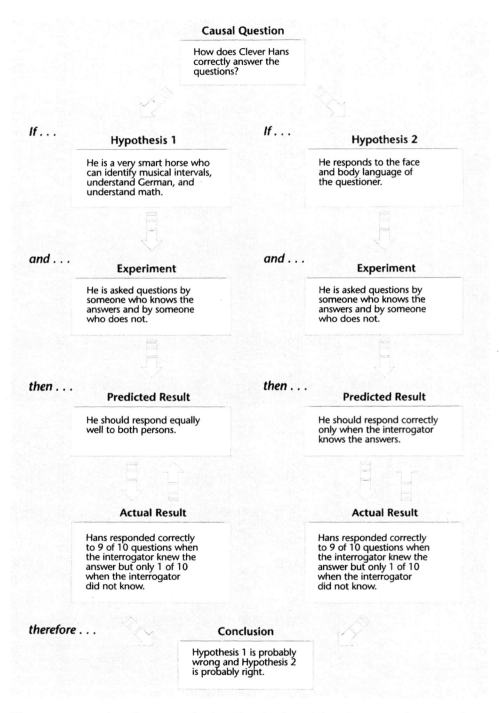

Figure 1.9 ▾ **Major Elements of Scientific Thinking (2).** The major elements of scientific thinking as identified in the story about Clever Hans.

Endnotes

1. Some authors refer to such inductively generated propositions as *generalizing hypotheses* (e.g., Baker and Allen, 1977). I prefer not to follow this convention because I think it blurs the important distinction between tentative explanations and generalizations.

2. One might well ask why Darwin did not recognize the importance of the selection process when he first read Malthus. Of course, no one knows the answer to this question for certain, but it is clear that the concept of natural selection assumes awareness of preceding concepts such as limiting factors, variation, and biotic potential. If Darwin was not aware of these ideas, or if they were not near his plane of consciousness when he read about artificial selection, it would seem unlikely that the importance of the idea in evolution would be recognized.

3. In fact, some bodies of religious knowledge are open to change, although such change does not occur in the way that scientific knowledge changes. Rather, religious change occurs by decree of the religious leaders, through the cumulative expressions of believers over long periods of time, or through the "inner light" of each participant. For example, the leader may experience a "revelation," a message from God, that directs a change in religious doctrine.

4. You might be thinking that molecules may be too small to see without a microscope but that recent photographs taken with electron microscopes have revealed individual atoms. In reality, those photographs have revealed pictures of what appear to be tiny "ball"-shaped objects. Whether these are really atoms is a matter of interpretation, not observation.

CHAPTER 2

PATTERNS OF THINKING BY SCIENTISTS AND BY ADOLESCENTS

Chapter 1 explored the work of several scientists to provide you with a better understanding of the nature of science. In a general sense science can be defined as the process by which humans attempt to understand nature. That process involves many steps, usually beginning with an encounter and an *exploration* of some puzzling, curious phenomenon that cannot be explained in terms of current knowledge. The sense of puzzlement provokes curiosity and a desire to understand, to explain. The human mind may then *invent* one or more tentative explanations based on the recollection of prior experiences that are seen to be similar in some way or ways to the current situation. This is the process of *abduction.*

If scientists are clever and energetic, they may then be able to imagine a means of putting some of these tentative explanations to the test. This is done by collecting data from nature and comparing those data with the deduced consequences of the tentative explanations. If the data and the deduced consequences are essentially the same, then the tentative explanation has been supported. If the data and the deduced consequences are not the same, then the tentative explanation has not been supported and may be rejected or perhaps modified. This is precisely how Macbeth went about testing the reality of the dagger that appeared before him. This is how all human minds function. In this sense scientists are no different than anyone else. However, in another sense, they may be vastly different, because doing science forces one to become much more conscious of this process, and consequently more likely to avoid potential pitfalls in its use and become a more effective thinker not only in one's own area of research, but also in other parts of one's life. Hence the purpose of this chapter is to look more closely at the process of science to identify some of its key elements, skills, and patterns of thinking (i.e., patterns of argumentation) and then to look at the extent to which typical adolescents have acquired those thinking patterns. Again, we will begin with an example from science, in this case, the migration of silver salmon from the Pacific Northwest.

▼ HOMING BEHAVIOR IN SILVER SALMON

Raising a Causal Question

Silver salmon are found in the cool, quiet headwaters of freshwater streams in the Pacific Northwest. Young salmon swim downstream to the Pacific Ocean, where they grow to full size and mature sexually. They then return to the freshwater and swim upstream, often jumping incredible heights up waterfalls ultimately to lay their eggs in the headwaters before they die. By tagging young salmon, biologists discovered that mature salmon actually migrate to precisely the same headwaters in which they were hatched years earlier. This discovery raised an interesting question: How do the salmon find their way to the streams of their birth?

Creating Hypotheses and Combinatorial Thinking

Several answers to this causal question can be proposed. For instance, we know that humans can navigate by sight. Perhaps the salmon do so as well. That is, they may remember certain objects, such as large rocks, that they saw when they swam downstream to the ocean. Studies of migratory animals may also suggest answers. For example, it was discovered that migratory eels, who also migrate from freshwater to saltwater and back, are enormously sensitive to dissolved minerals in water. A single eel can detect the presence of a mineral in water at concentrations as low as two to three molecules per liter. Perhaps the salmon are also sensitive to smell, and this allows them to find their way back. They may swim a short distance into various streams until they find the one that "smells" right. In other words, they are able to use their noses to detect certain chemicals specific to their home stream and then can follow a chemical path home.

Scientists also have discovered that homing pigeons are able to navigate using the earth's magnetic field. Pigeons wearing little magnets on their backs (to disrupt the magnetic field near the bird) were not as successful at finding their way home at night as a similar group of pigeons who wore small nonmagnetic metal bars on their backs. Perhaps the salmon are also sensitive to the magnetic field and this is how they find their home stream. Thus, the process of abduction—borrowing ideas from past experiences and using them as possible explanations in this new context—gives us three tentative hypotheses:

1. Salmon use sight to find their way home (i.e., they see certain landmarks recalled from their previous trip to the ocean).
2. Salmon smell certain chemicals in the water that are specific to their home stream.
3. Salmon are sensitive to the earth's magnetic field and use it to navigate.

Other possibilities remain, of course. Indeed, none of these three may be the "correct" answer. Or perhaps salmon are able to use all three or perhaps two of three. Psychologists refer to this process of generating all possible combinations of hypotheses as *combinatorial thinking*. In this case, combinatorial thinking gives us these possibilities:

1. None of the three hypotheses is correct.
2. Hypothesis 1 is correct.
3. Hypothesis 2 is correct.
4. Hypothesis 3 is correct.
5. Hypotheses 1 and 2 are correct.
6. Hypotheses 1 and 3 are correct.
7. Hypotheses 2 and 3 are correct.
8. All three hypotheses are correct.

9. One or more of the identified hypotheses in combination with one or more of the yet-to-be-identified hypotheses are correct.

Generating Predictions

Once the processes of abduction and combinatorial thinking have provided several likely possible explanations, the next task is to put one or more of them to the test. For example, biologists tested the sight hypothesis by capturing and blindfolding a group of salmon and comparing their ability to locate their home stream with the ability of a similar group of nonblindfolded salmon. The thinking pattern used to test the sight hypothesis was as follows:

Hypothesis:	*If*	silver salmon locate their home stream by sight,
Experiment:	*and*	a group of blindfolded (nonsighted) salmon is compared to a group of nonblindfolded (sighted) salmon, all other things being equal,
Prediction:	*then*	the blindfolded salmon should not be able to locate their home stream and the nonblindfolded salmon should be able to locate their home stream.

This pattern of *hypothetical-deductive* thinking is involved in all hypothesis testing.

Identifying and Controlling Variables

Notice, however, that the prediction in the previous hypothetical-deductive argument follows only to the extent that the experiment is conducted in a manner that allows only the values of one input (an independent) variable to vary. In this case the input variable is the fishes' ability to smell. All values of the other possible input variables must be held constant to the extent possible. In other words, the experiment should be controlled. Suppose, for example, that we do, in fact, find a difference in the ability of the two groups of fish to find their home stream (the outcome or dependent variable). This is the result predicted by the sight hypothesis, so we appear able to conclude that the difference results from sight and not some other variable. However, during the experiment, the blindfolded salmon may have been hindered in returning to their home stream, not by lack of sight, but by an inability to swim with blindfolds. Or perhaps simply taking the fish out of the water to fit them with blindfolds shocked the fish and disrupted their ability to swim. At any rate, the experimenter must try to avoid these potentially confounding problems as much as possible. But because one can never be certain that all such problems have been eliminated, the result of all such experiments must be interpreted with caution. Consequently, positive results can never be interpreted as "proof" of the correctness of a hypothesis. Positive results merely allow us to conclude that the hypothesis has been supported.

On the other hand, suppose both groups of salmon are equally successful at finding their home streams. Now we can be reasonably sure that the salmon use some other means of navigation—that is, the sight hypothesis is not supported. However, we cannot conclude that it has been disproved or falsified. Although logic could dictate that the hypothesis has been falsified, the real world is not that simple. Again, other unknown input variables may be operating. For example, perhaps the salmon could see under the blindfolds. This is precisely how blindfolded magicians are able to see. Or perhaps the blindfolds were not thick enough to block out all light. Or perhaps the blindfolds were indeed effective and the salmon do indeed use sight when they can, but when their sight is blocked, they use some other sense (e.g., smell) to navigate.

Drawing Conclusions

In short, the thinking involved in testing hypotheses does indeed follow a hypothetical-deductive pattern, but it also involves thinking that can be referred to as the *identification and control of variables*. The identification and control of variables is an absolutely crucial thinking pattern, but it is limited in that one can never be certain that all potentially relevant variables have been identified or controlled. Thus, all scientific conclusions, whether supportive or not supportive of a particular hypothesis, must remain tentative to some extent. Scientific arguments and evidence can most certainly be convincing *beyond a reasonable doubt*, but to the critical mind they can never be convincing beyond *any* doubt. Recall that hypotheses are neither proven nor disproven.

Probabilistic and Correlational Thinking

Let us return to the salmon example to discuss two additional patterns of scientific thinking. To test the sight idea, biologists captured and tagged salmon that had just returned to spawn in one of two streams near Seattle, Washington. The streams were the Issaquah and East Fork (see Figure 2.1). The biologists blindfolded some of the salmon and returned them approximately three-quarters of a mile below the point where the streams join. The fish were then recaptured in traps approximately a mile above the junction of the two streams as they made their way back up to the headwaters. An interesting point is that the blindfolded salmon were as successful as the nonblindfolded salmon at finding their home streams. Thus, the sight hypothesis was not supported.

The smell hypothesis was tested in a similar manner. Let us consider this test, including a look at the actual numbers of fish involved. First, 302 salmon

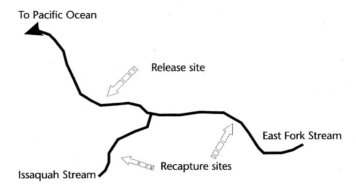

Figure 2.1 ▽ **Issaquah and East Fork Streams.** This map shows salmon release and recapture points.

were captured from the headwaters of the two streams. The biologists then tagged the fish and divided the East Fork fish into two groups. They inserted cotton plugs coated with petroleum jelly in the noses of one group of fish to block their ability to smell. These fish were referred to as the *experimental* group. The noses of the other group—the control group—were left unplugged. The scientists then divided the Issaquah fish into two groups and plugged the noses of one group just as they had done with the East Fork fish. Finally, all of the fish were taken to the release site. The fish were then recaptured in traps above the junction of the two streams (marked as recapture sites in Figure 2.1) as they returned upstream.

Not all of the 302 tagged fish were recaptured. Some fish swam either downstream or upstream but avoided the traps. Of the 153 tagged fish with unplugged noses, 45% were recaptured, while 49% of the 149 tagged fish with unplugged noses were recaptured. Additional results of the experiment are shown in Tables 2.1 and 2.2. Table 2.1 shows the results for the fish with unplugged noses. As can be seen, 46 of the Issaquah fish were recaptured in the Issaquah, and none were recaptured in the East Fork. Eight of the East Fork fish were recaptured in the Issaquah and 19 in the East Fork.

Table 2.2 shows the results for the fish with the plugged noses. Thirty-nine of the Issaquah fish were recaptured in the Issaquah and 12 in the East Fork. Sixteen of the East Fork fish were recaptured in the Issaquah, and 3 in the East Fork.

How can these data be interpreted to test the smell hypothesis? First, we must remind ourselves of the specific prediction involved. If the smell hypothesis is correct, then we can predict that the fishes that can smell (the control group) should be able to locate the correct stream, while those that cannot smell

Table 2.1 ▾ Results for Control Fish (Unplugged Noses)

	Recapture Site	
Capture Site	*Issaquah*	*East Fork*
Issaquah	46	0
East Fork	8	19

(the experimental group) should not be able to locate the correct stream. Notice in Table 2.1 that 46 of 46 of the Issaquah fish that could smell were recaptured in the Issaquah stream. Therefore, 100% of these fish were successful, as predicted by the hypothesis. But only 19 of the 27 East Fork fish (70%) that could smell found the correct stream. Eight of the 27 (30%) were not successful. Clearly the result from these 8 fish contradict the hypothesis. Why do you suppose the Issaquah fish were so much more successful than the East Fork fish?

Let us now turn to the results in Table 2.2 for the experimental fish with plugged noses. Here 39 of 51 Issaquah fish (77%) were successful in finding the correct stream. The East Fork fish were not nearly as successful: Only 3 of the 19 East Fork fish (16%) were recaptured in the East Fork stream. Thus, in both control and experimental groups the Issaquah fish, for some reason, were more successful than the East Fork fish at reaching their home stream. Perhaps the Issaquah stream is wider than the East Fork at the point where they join. Whatever the reason, the overall results reveal that 65 (46 + 19) of the 73 control group fish (89%) were successful at reaching their home stream, whereas only 42 (39 + 3) of the 70 experimental group fish (60%) were successful. The predicted percentages based on the smell hypothesis would be 100% for the control fish and 50% for the experimental fish. The prediction of

Table 2.2 ▾ Results for Experimental Fish (Plugged Noses)

	Recapture Site	
Capture Site	*Issaquah*	*East Fork*
Issaquah	39	12
East Fork	16	3

50% assumes that the fish with plugged noses will turn in to one of the two streams at random, therefore 50 of 100, or 50%, of those turns will be successful because of chance alone.

We see that the actual experimental results (89% vs. 60%) are not precisely those predicted by the smell hypothesis (100% vs. 50%). Suppose the fishes' ability to smell contributes nothing to their ability to navigate. Then the percentages for each group should be the same. Therefore, the question we need to ask is this: Is the 89% success rate of the control fish significantly better than the 60% success rate for the experimental fish? Of course, a more complex statistical analysis would be needed to determine the actual probability of a difference of this magnitude occurring because of chance, but you should have the sense that given the number of fish involved, 89% appears to be considerably higher than 60%. Therefore, the difference is probably the result of the fishes' ability to smell and not the result of chance. Therefore, we can conclude that the smell hypothesis has been supported.

The thinking pattern we have used to generate the probability statements such as 19/27, 3/19, or 65/73 is called *probabilistic thinking*. Further analysis of the data also required us to compare these probabilities to determine whether they appear to depart significantly from chance. So, for example, when we concluded that 89% was a significantly greater probability than 60%, we were using what psychologists refer to as *correlational thinking*. The use of a correlational thinking pattern allowed us to conclude that a correlation (that is, a *co relation*) most likely does exist between the fishes' ability to smell (the independent variable) and their ability to locate their home stream (the dependent variable).

Probabilistic and correlational thinking can also be used to analyze data gathered from nonexperimental situations. For example, a 25-year study of 1,969 men found a direct correlation between the amount of cholesterol in their diets and their risk of heart attack. The study reported that men who consumed more than 500 milligrams of cholesterol per day had a 22% greater probability of dying of a heart attack than men whose cholesterol intake was substantially below the 500-milligram level.

▼ ## CREATIVE AND CRITICAL THINKING SKILLS

Although this brief discussion is by no means exhaustive of the creative and critical thinking skills used by scientists, it should provide a framework for understanding important thinking patterns used by scientists in creating and testing hypotheses. Science is essentially a process of accurately describing nature and attempting to create and test theoretical systems that serve to explain natural phenomena. Thinking skills and patterns essential to the accurate description and explanation of events in nature can be divided into the following seven skills categories (after Burmester, 1952):

1. accurately describing nature
2. sensing and stating causal questions about nature
3. recognizing, creating, and stating alternative hypotheses and theories
4. generating logical predictions
5. planning and conducting controlled experiments to test hypotheses
6. collecting, organizing, and analyzing relevant experimental and correlational data
7. drawing and applying reasonable conclusions

Some of the above skills are creative, while others are critical. Still others involve both creative and critical aspects of scientific thinking. We are defining a *skill* as the ability to do something well. Skilled performance includes knowing what to do, when to do it, and how to do it. In other words, being skilled at something involves knowing a set of procedures, knowing when to apply those procedures, and being proficient at executing those procedures. Note that grade levels at which the skills should be emphasized during instruction are indicated. More will be said about this in Chapter 4 when the development of procedural knowledge is discussed. The seven general skills listed above can be further delimited into the following subskills:

1.00 Skill in accurately describing nature
  1.10 Skill in describing objects in terms of observable characteristics (K–3)[*]
  1.20 Skill in seriating objects in terms of observable characteristics (K–3)
  1.30 Skill in classifying objects in terms of observable characteristics (K–3)
  1.40 Skill in describing, seriating, classifying, and measuring objects in terms of variables such as amount, length, area, weight (K–6), volume, and density (6–9)
  1.50 Skill in identifying variable and constant characteristics of groups of objects
    1.51 Skill in identifying continuous and discontinuous variable characteristics and naming specific values of those characteristics (K–9)
    1.52 Skill in measuring, recording, and graphing the frequency of occurrence of certain values of characteristics in a sample of objects (4–6)
    1.53 Skill in determining the average, median, and modal values of the frequency distribution in 1.52 (7–9)
  1.60 Skill in recognizing the difference between a sample and a population and identifying ways of obtaining a random (unbiased) sample (7–9)

---

[*]Grade levels at which skills should be emphasized

1.61 Skill in making predictions concerning the probability of occurrence of specific population characteristics based on the frequency of occurrence of those characteristics in a random sample (7–9)

2.00 Skill in sensing and stating causal questions about nature

2.10 Skill in recognizing a causal question from observation of nature (K–3) or in the context of a paragraph or article (4–9)

2.20 Skill in distinguishing between an observation and a question (K–3)

2.30 Skill in recognizing a question even when it is stated in expository form rather than in interrogatory form (4–9)

2.40 Skill in distinguishing a question from a possible answer to a question (hypothesis) even when the hypothesis is presented in interrogatory form (7–12)

2.50 Skill in distinguishing between descriptive and causal questions (K–6)

3.00 Skill in recognizing, creating, and stating alternative hypotheses (causal explanations) and theories

3.10 Skill in distinguishing a hypothesis from a question (K–6)

3.20 Skill in differentiating between a statement that describes an observation or generalizes from the observation and a statement that is a hypothesis (causal explanation) for the observation (K–6)

3.30 Skill in recognizing the tentativeness of a hypothesis or theory (4–9)

3.40 Skill in distinguishing between a tentative explanation for a phenomenon (hypothesis) and a term used merely to label the phenomenon (4–9)

3.50 Skill in systematically creating all possible combinations of created hypotheses (7–12)

4.00 Skill in generating and stating logical predictions based on the assumed truth of hypotheses and imagined experimental conditions (K–12)

4.10 Skill in differentiating between hypotheses and predictions (4–12)

5.00 Skill in planning and conducting controlled experiments to test alternative hypotheses

5.10 Skill in selecting reasonable alternative hypotheses to test (K–12)

5.20 Skill in differentiating between an uncontrolled observation and an experiment involving controls (4–9)

5.30 Skill in recognizing that only one input factor in an experiment should be variable

5.31 Skill in recognizing the input variable factor and the outcome variable factor(s) (4–9)

5.32 Skill in recognizing the factors being held constant in the partial controls (4–9)

5.40 Skill in recognizing experimental and technical problems inherent in experimental designs (K–12)

5.50 Skill in criticizing faulty experiments when:

    5.51 The experimental design was such that it could not yield an answer to the question (4–12).

    5.52 The experiment was not designed to test the specific hypotheses stated (4–12).

    5.53 The method of collecting the data was unreliable (4–12).

    5.54 The data were not accurate (4–12).

    5.55 The data were insufficient in number (9–12).

    5.56 Proper controls were not included (4–9).

6.00 Skill in collecting, organizing, and analyzing relevant experimental and correlational data

6.10 Skill in recognizing existence of errors in measurement (4–9)

6.20 Skill in recognizing when the precision of measurement given is warranted by the nature of the question (9–12)

6.30 Skill in organizing and analyzing data

    6.31 Skill in constructing tables and frequency graphs (4–9)

    6.32 Skill in measuring, recording, and graphing the values of two variables on a single graph (7–12)

    6.33 Skill in constructing a contingency table of discontinuous variables (7–12)

6.40 Skill in seeing elements in common to several items of data (4–12)

6.50 Skill in recognizing prevailing tendencies and trends in data and in extrapolating and interpolating (7–12)

6.60 Skill in applying quantitative notions of probability, proportion, percentage, and correlation to natural phenomena and recognizing when variables are related additively or multiplicatively, setting up simple quantitative equations to describe these relationships (7–12)

    6.61 Skill in recognizing direct, inverse, or no relationship between variables (4–9)

    6.62 Skill in recognizing that when two things vary together, the relationship may be coincidental, not causal (7–12)

    6.63 Skill in recognizing additional evidence needed to establish cause and effect (see 6.62) (7–12)

7.00 Skill in drawing and applying reasonable conclusions

7.10 Skill in evaluating relevancy of data and drawing conclusions through a comparison of actual results with predicted results

    7.11 Skill in differentiating between direct and indirect evidence (4–9)

    7.12 Skill in recognizing data that are unrelated to the hypotheses (4–9)

    7.13 Skill in recognizing data that support a hypothesis (4–9)

    7.14 Skill in recognizing data that do not support a hypothesis (4–9)

7.15 Skill in combining both supportive and contradicting evidence from a variety of sources to weigh the likely truth or falsity of hypotheses (10–12)

7.16 Skill in postponing judgment if no evidence or insufficient evidence exists (4–12)

7.17 Skill in recognizing the tentativeness inherent in all scientific conclusions (10–12)

7.18 Skill in being aware of the tentativeness of conclusions about new situations even when there is a close parallel between two situations (10–12)

7.19 Skill in recognizing the assumptions that must be made in applying a conclusion to a new situation (10–12)

These skills function in concert in the mind of creative and critical thinkers as they learn about the world. When testing hypotheses, thinking follows a hypothetical-deductive pattern that is initiated not with what is observed (the real) but with what is imagined (the possible). The hypothetical-deductive thinking pattern includes key steps and the key words *if, and, then,* and *therefore.* The thinking patterns and skills of the hypothetical-deductive thinker are, in essence, learning tools essential for success and even for survival. One who possesses these skills has "learned how to learn." Indeed, if you help students improve their use of these creative and critical thinking skills, then you have helped them become more intelligent and helped them "learn how to learn."

▼ **THE NATURE OF ADOLESCENT THINKING**

How good are students at scientific thinking? The next few pages contain three scientific puzzles that have been given to students to solve. Each puzzle is followed by several typical student responses. First try to solve each puzzle and then compare your ideas with those of the students. A discussion of the student responses and what they reveal about how students think will then follow.

The Mealworm Puzzle

An experimenter wanted to test the response of mealworms to light and moisture. To do this he set up four boxes as shown in the diagram on page 54. He used neon lamps for light and constantly watered pieces of paper in the boxes for moisture. In the center of each box he placed 20 mealworms. One day later he returned to count the number of mealworms that had crawled to the different ends of the boxes.

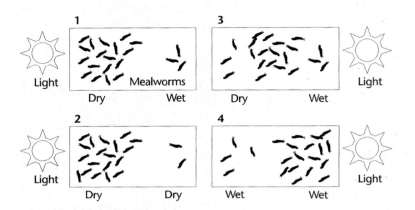

The diagrams show that mealworms *respond* to (that is, move toward or away from):

a. light but not moisture
b. moisture but not light
c. both light and moisture
d. neither light nor moisture.

Which of the above choices seems most reasonable? Please explain your choice.

The following are typical student responses to the mealworm puzzle. Read these responses and compare them with your own. Look for similarities among Type A responses and among Type B responses. Look also for differences between Type A and Type B responses.

Student A₁ (Larry, age 11):
  D *No definite pattern was followed by the mealworms.*

Student A₂ (Richard Cripe, age 18):
  D *Because even though the light was moved in different places the mealworms didn't do the same things.*

Student A₃ (Glen, age 16):
  A *They usually went to the end of the box with the light.*

Student A₄ (John Simonds, age 14):
  A *Because there are 17 worms by the light and there are only 3 by moisture.*

Student A₅ (Ron Gerard, age 16):
  A *Because in all situations, the majority go where there's light. Wetness doesn't seem to make a difference.*

Student B₁ (Cindy East, age 15):

C   *Boxes 1 and 2 show they prefer dry and light to wet and dark, Box 4 eliminates dryness as a factor, so they do respond to light only. Box 3 shows that wetness cancels the effect of the light, so it seems they prefer dry. It would be clearer if one of the boxes was wet–dry with no light.*

Student B₂ (Jamall, age 15):

C   *When the light was on the dry side they all crowded to the dry side. When it was on the wet side, an equal amount went to each side.*

Student B₃ (Ed, age 16):

C   *In Experiment 3 the mealworms are in the middle. So it's safe to assume that light was not the only factor involved.*

Student B₄ (Pam Stewart, age 17):

B   *One, two, and four show that mealworms seem to like the light, but in 3 they seem to be equally spaced. This leads one to believe that mealworms like the dryness, and the reason in pictures 2 and 4 they are by the light is because of the heat that the light produces, which gives a dryness effect.*

Student B₅ (Hong, age 17):

C   *The mealworms in all cases respond to light. However, in Box 3 mealworms are in the middle. This shows that the worms are attracted to the light but not like the situations where the dry area was next to the light. When there is no choice between wet and dry, such as in Case 4, the worms turn to the light. Note: We might also test a box like this* | **wet   dry** | *with no light to verify further the effect of moisture.*

Questions

1. What similarities did you find among the responses of Students A?
2. What similarities did you find among the responses of Students B?

The Volume Puzzle

Here are drawings of two vertical tubes (cylinders) that are filled to the same mark with water; the cylinders are identical in size and shape.

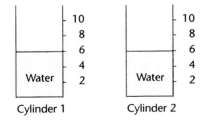

Cylinder 1   Cylinder 2

Here are two marbles, one made of steel and one of glass. Both marbles have the same volume (that is, they are the same size). The steel marble is heavier.

Glass   Steel

The steel marble is heavier than the glass one, but both marbles will sink if placed in one of the cylinders. We will put one marble in each cylinder. After we have put the glass marble into Cylinder 1, both cylinders and their contents look like this:

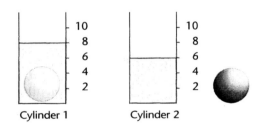

Cylinder 1   Cylinder 2

If we now put the steel marble into Cylinder 2, what will happen to the water level in that cylinder? (Tell whether it will rise, fall, or stay the same; if it rises or falls, predict the final water level in Cylinder 2.)

_____

_____

_____

_____

Explain why you predicted the result above.

_____

_____

_____

_____

The next pages present written student responses to the volume puzzle. Study the responses and compare Students A with Students B.

Student A₁ (John Simonds, age 14)

Prediction: I think Cylinder 2 would be higher to about the number 10 mark.

Explanation: Because it put more pressure onto the water. This means it would push it upward. The steel ball seems to me like it would be heavier.

Student A₂ (Richard Cripe, age 18)

Prediction: It will rise. The final water level in Cylinder 2 will be 7.

Explanation: The steel marble is heavier, therefore the water will not rise as much.

Student A₃ (Ron Gerard, age 16)

Prediction: The level of H_2O in Cylinder 2 will rise to higher than 8—probably 10.

Explanation: Because the marble in Cylinder 2 is heavier than the marble in Cylinder 1. It's just like scales: the more weight the higher it goes up.

Student A₄ (Cindy East, age 15)

Prediction: I think it will stay the same.

Explanation: I don't really know why. But it would seem the steel marble might have the weight to hold it down. The glass marble is lighter, so it pushes the water up.

Student B₁ (Rita, age 16)

Prediction: Rise to 8.

Explanation: Equal volume spheres displace the same volume of water.

Student B₂ (Pam Stewart, age 17)

Prediction: The water level in Cylinder 2 will rise to the same height as in Cylinder 1 after the glass marble is put in.

Explanation: Both marbles had the same volume, therefore the water level, after the marbles were put in, was the same in each cylinder. The weight in no way affected the degree to which the water rose.

Student B₃ (Jean, age 13)

Prediction: Cylinder 2's water level will rise to the number 8.

Explanation: Since the two marbles have the same volume they will displace the same amount of water. Eureka! (weight has nothing to do with it).

Student B₄ (Harold, age 18)

Prediction: The level in Cylinder 2 will also be 8; the same as in Cylinder 1.

Explanation: If both marbles are heavy enough to sink and are the same size, they will therefore displace the same amount of water.

Questions
1. What similarities did you find among the responses of Students A?
2. What similarities did you find among the responses of Students B?
3. What features seem to distinguish between the two types of responses?

The Frog Puzzle

Professor Thistlebush, an ecologist, conducted a field investigation to determine the number of frogs that live in a pond near the field station. Because she could not catch all of the frogs, she caught as many as she could, put a white band around their left hind legs, and then put them back in the pond. A week later she returned to the pond and again caught as many frogs as she could. Here are the professor's data.

First trip to the pond
55 frogs caught and banded
Second trip to the pond
72 frogs caught; of those 72 frogs, 12 were banded

The professor assumed that the banded frogs had mixed thoroughly with the unbanded frogs, and from her data she was able to approximate the number of frogs that live in the pond. If you can compute this number, please do so. Write it in the space below. Explain in words how you calculated your results.

_____

_____

_____

_____

The next pages present student solutions to the frog puzzle. Please read the responses and compare them with yours. Look for key differences between Student A responses and Student B responses.

Student A₁ (Terrance, age 13)
    Answer: 72
Explanation: It would be 72, because that is all she was able to catch.

Student A₂ (Ron Gerard, age 16)
    Answer: 115
Explanation: 55 were caught and banded, 55 with bands. She didn't catch every frog, so 55 and 60 would be 115.

Student A₃ (Richard Cripe, age 18)
    Answer: 115

Explanation: There were 55 frogs banded. On the second trip 72 are caught; of those, 12 are banded. So 72 plus 60 new ones makes 115.

Student A_4 (John Simonds, age 14)

Answer: 115

Explanation: I say 115 because $55 + 60 = 115$ frogs.

Student A_5 (Wendy, age 18)

Answer: About 200

Explanation: 60 frogs were caught. I'd have to try a third time (take a second sample). How big is the pond? Add 60 and 55 together. It's poor experimental data. I would come up in a third try. I'd guess 200.

Student B_1 (Cindy East, age 15)

Answer: 275

Explanation: $72 - 12 = 60$ were not banded. $55/x = 12/60$, $x = 275$, so the number of frogs is 275.

Student B_2 (Alex, age 15)

Answer: 330

Explanation: 1/6 were banded. $55 \times 6 = 330$. What this implies is that 1 out of 6 mingled with the total frogs.

Student B_3 (Carlos, age 17)

Answer: 330

Explanation: I figured that it is a proportion problem, so I set it up like this: $12/72 = 55/x$; $12x = 72 \times 55$, so using algebra I got $x = 330$.

Student B_4 (Pam Stewart, age 17)

Answer: 330

Explanation: $55{:}x$ as $12{:}72$

$12x = 3{,}960$

$x = 330$

Student B_5 (Jim, age 16)

Answer: 330

Explanation: You have to assume that in the week between the first and second sampling that none of the banded frogs died or were born. Also the assumption must be made that the frogs mingled thoroughly. This may not be the case, but anyway if you make all these assumptions the problem is simple. $12/72 = 1/6$ so 1/6th of the frogs have bands; $55 \times 6 = 330$.

Question

1. What seem to be significant differences between Student A responses and Student B responses?

▽ ## EMPIRICAL-INDUCTIVE AND HYPOTHETICAL-DEDUCTIVE THINKING PATTERNS

In reading the student responses to the three puzzles you undoubtedly recognized that Type B answers were more complete, more consistent, and more systematic—in short, they were better than Type A answers. In fact, you may have been somewhat surprised to learn that so many students gave Type A answers!

Psychologists often characterize human intellectual development in terms of four major levels or "stages" of thought processes. The first two are usually completed before a child is 7 or 8 years old. Therefore, only the last two are of particular interest to us; they are called *empirical-inductive thought* and *hypothetical-deductive thought*. Empirical-inductive thinking patterns enable the child to order accurately and describe perceptible objects, events, and situations within his or her world. Hypothetical-deductive thinking patterns allow the adolescent to go beyond descriptions and create and test hypothetical (nonobservable) explanations for what is encountered. What follows are key thinking patterns at the empirical-inductive and hypothetical-deductive levels.

Empirical-Inductive Thinking Patterns

The following patterns elaborate the empirical-inductive (EI) stage.

EI1 **Class Inclusion:** The individual understands simple classifications and generalizations (e.g., all dogs are animals; only some animals are dogs).

EI2 **Conservation:** The individual applies conservation thinking to perceptible objects and properties (e.g., if nothing is added or taken away, the amount, number, length, weight, etc. remains the same even though the appearance differs).

EI3 **Serial Ordering:** The individual arranges a set of objects or data in serial order and establishes a one-to-one correspondence (e.g., the youngest plants have the smallest leaves).

These thinking patterns enable the individual to:

1. understand concepts and simple propositions that make a direct reference to familiar actions and observable objects, and can be explained in terms of simple associations (e.g., the plants in this container are taller because they got more fertilizer);

2. follow step-by-step instructions as in a recipe, provided each step is completely specified (e.g., he or she can identify organisms with the use of a taxonomic key or determine the oxygen content of a water sample using the Winkler method);

3. relate his or her viewpoint to that of another in a simple situation (e.g., a girl is aware that she is her sister's sister).

However, individuals whose thinking has not developed beyond the empirical-inductive level demonstrate certain limitations. These limitations are evidenced as the individual:

4. searches for and identifies some variables influencing a phenomenon, but does so unsystematically (e.g., investigates the effects of one variable but does not necessarily hold the others constant);

5. makes observations and draws inferences from them, but does not initiate reasoning with the possible;

6. responds to difficult problems by applying a related but not necessarily correct algorithm;

7. processes information but is not spontaneously aware of his or her own thinking patterns (e.g., does not check his or her own conclusions against the given data or other experience).

The above characteristics typify empirical-inductive level thought previously designated as Type A responses.

Hypothetical-Deductive Thinking Patterns

The following patterns elaborate the hypothetical-deductive (HD) stage; these are used in the testing of alternative hypotheses.

HD1 **Combinatorial Thinking:** The individual systematically considers all possible relations of experimental or theoretical conditions, even though some may not be realized in nature (recall how earlier in this chapter we generated all possible combinations of the hypotheses that had been advanced to explain salmon navigation).

HD2 **Identification and the Control of Variables:** In testing hypotheses, the individual recognizes the necessity of taking into consideration all the known variables and designing a test that controls all variables except the one being investigated (e.g., recognizes the inadequacy of the Box 1 setup in the mealworm puzzle).

HD3 **Proportional Thinking:** The individual recognizes and interprets relationships between relationships in situations described by observable or theoretical variables (e.g., the rate of diffusion of a molecule through a semipermeable membrane is inversely proportional to the square root of its molecular weight; for every 12 banded frogs there are 72 total frogs, therefore, for every 55 banded frogs there must be 330 total frogs).

HD4 **Probabilistic Thinking:** The individual recognizes the fact that natural phenomena themselves are probabilistic in character and that any conclusions or explanations must involve probabilistic considerations (e.g., in the mealworm puzzle the ability to disregard the few mealworms in the "wrong" ends of Boxes 1, 2, and 4; in the frog puzzle the ability to assess the probability of certain assumptions holding true such as the frogs mingled thoroughly, no new frogs were born, and the bands did not increase the death or predation rate of the banded frogs).

HD5 **Correlational Thinking:** In spite of random fluctuations, the individual is able to recognize causes or relations in the phenomenon under study by comparing the number of confirming and disconfirming cases of hypothesized relations with the total number of cases (e.g., to establish a correlation of, say, blond hair with blue eyes and brunette hair with brown eyes, the number of blue-eyed blonds and brown-eyed brunettes minus the number of brown-eyed blonds and blue-eyed brunettes is compared to the total number of subjects).

These thinking patterns, taken in concert, enable individuals to accept hypothesized statements (assumptions) as the starting point for reasoning about a situation. They are able to reason hypothetically and deductively. In other words, they are able to imagine possible relations of factors, deduce the consequences of these relations, and then empirically verify which of those consequences actually occurs. Previously, this was referred to as Type B thinking. Table 2.3 summarizes important differences between these two levels of thought.

Science teachers who are interested in applying these ideas in their teaching should be aware that many issues relating to developmental theory are still being investigated. Researchers initially thought that all people progress through the major levels in the same invariant sequence, though not necessarily at the same rate. Recent studies suggest strongly, however, that many people do not come to use hypothetical-deductive thinking patterns effectively.

Analysis of Student Responses

Using Table 2.4 (page 64), reexamine a few of the student responses to the three puzzles. Apply some of the ideas just discussed to classify these responses into the following more descriptive categories, rather than the superficial A, B designation previously employed.

PE = pre–empirical-inductive
EI = empirical-inductive
Tr = transitional
(mixed empirical-inductive and hypothetical-deductive characteristics)

Table 2.3 ▾ **Characteristics of Empirical-Inductive and Hypothetical-Deductive Thought**

Characteristics	
Empirical-Inductive Thought	*Hypothetical-Deductive Thought*
Needs reference to familiar actions, objects, and observable properties.	Can reason with second-order relationships, hypothetical properties, postulates, and theories; uses symbols to express ideas.
Thinking is initiated with observations.	Thinking can be initiated with imagined possibilities.
Uses thinking patterns EI1 through EI3. Patterns HD1 through HD5 either are not used or are used only partially, unsystematically, and only in familiar contexts.	Uses thinking patterns HD1 through HD5 as well as EI1 through EI3.
Needs step-by-step instructions in a lengthy procedure.	Can plan a lengthy procedure given certain overall goals and resources.
Is unconscious of his or her own thinking patterns, inconsistencies among various statements that he or she makes, or contradictions with other known facts.	Is conscious and critical of his or her own thinking patterns and actively seeks checks on the validity of his or her conclusions by appealing to other known information.

HD = hypothetical-deductive

? = Not possible to classify without more information

First select one student and reread and classify his or her responses to each puzzle. Record your classification of his or her thinking patterns, thus making a "profile" of thinking for this student. Follow this procedure for at least two students (more if you have time). Then read my analysis of the thinking involved in each puzzle and my classification of each student's responses.

To further assist you in differentiating the thinking patterns involved in the three puzzles, consider the following general analysis of responses for each puzzle.

Mealworm Puzzle

Empirical-Inductive Thinking (Type A). Individuals using this type of thinking will fix on one variable to the exclusion of others. They do not detect the

Table 2.4 ⌄ **Your Classification of Student Responses**

Student (Age)	Puzzle Classification		
	Mealworm	Volume	Frog
John Simonds (14)	_____	_____	_____
Cindy East (15)	_____	_____	_____
Ron Gerard (16)	_____	_____	_____
Pam Stewart (17)	_____	_____	_____
Richard Cripe (18)	_____	_____	_____

logic of the experiment that requires variables to be identified and isolated and thus dealt with as causal agents. They see the one-to-one correspondences where one factor causes one response in one of the boxes.

Hypothetical-Deductive Thinking (Type B). Other variables are held constant, while only one is allowed to change. All possible causal factors are examined in turn to test the hypotheses that light or moisture or both are responsible for the distribution of the mealworms. The answer will be derived in a systematic manner with each possible conclusion being tested. Probabilistic thinking is also evidenced by the student's ability to ignore the few mealworms in the "wrong" ends of Boxes 1, 2, and 4.

Volume Puzzle

Empirical-Inductive Thinking (Type A). It is common sense that the weight of an immersed object is responsible for the force that lifts the displaced water. Hence the direct conclusion, given differing weights, is the greater the weight, the higher the water level. (Note that this thinking leads to the correct conclusion for equal-sized bodies that float!)

Hypothetical-Deductive Thinking (Type B). Even though the weight is dynamically responsible for lifting the water, the combined volume of water plus marble limits the height to which the water can rise in the container. Because the combined volumes are equal for the two marbles, the water will rise to equal heights if the marbles are fully submerged.

Note the intermediate concept of the combined volume or the alternate formulation that, if equal marble volumes are added to equal water volumes, the

Table 2.5 ▾ **My Classification of Student Responses**

Student (Age)	Puzzle Classification		
	Mealworm	Volume	Frog
John Simonds (14)	EI	EI	EI
Cindy East (15)	HD	Tr	Tr
Ron Gerard (16)	EI	EI	EI
Pam Stewart (17)	HD	HD	HD
Richard Cripe (18)	EI	EI	EI

final volumes will be equal. The combined or final volume is not stressed in the statement of the puzzle, but it must be introduced by the student.

Frog Puzzle

Empirical-Inductive Thinking (Type A). Differences rather than ratios are the focus. This student assumes constancy of differences and thus reasons as follows: There were 60 more unbanded than banded frogs in the recapture sample, so there are 60 more frogs in the pond as a whole; 60 plus 55 equals 115. How would a person using empirical-inductive thinking respond to the following problem? "In a new recapture sample of 50 frogs, how many do you think are banded?" These responses have been observed: (1) Impossible to do; (2) 10; and (3) −10!

Hypothetical-Deductive Thinking (Type B). Probabilistic thinking is used. Starting with the relative frequency of banded frogs in the recapture sample, this student reasons that the ratio is an estimate of the relative frequency of banded frogs in the pond. After setting 12 divided by 72 equal to 55 divided by x, the answer follows easily. This student is undisturbed by the uncertainty associated with a statistical estimate and realizes that, as an estimation, this procedure is valid.

▾ **SUMMARY**

Table 2.5 shows my classification of student responses. Notice that not all students responded consistently with EI or HD thinking patterns. Many students have been found who respond at varying levels on different tasks. This indicates that students can be at varying levels in various areas. One should not expect that a person would be operating with hypothetical-deductive thinking patterns in all contexts. The transition from empirical-inductive to hypothetical-deductive thought in biology, for example, depends not only on a general change in orientation toward problem solving, but also on specific experiences in this particular field of study.

In addition to these puzzles, Appendix G contains a classroom test of scientific reasoning that can be used to evaluate student thinking skills.

Questions for Reflection

1. Read the following excerpt from *Newsweek* ("Learning to Breathe Free," April 30, 1990, pp. 38–40. Reprinted by permission of Newsweek, Inc. All rights reserved.).

    If freedom is in large part a habit of mind, the point is made plainest in Germany, where West and East are falling together at the seams. In a West Berlin office, Daniela Nowicki had to break in a new East German secretary. "I had a lot of trouble explaining to her that the work depended on her," she says. Within two months, her co-workers were exasperated. "If the boss tells her to do that, that and that, she's OK." The unexpected paralyzes her. "She fears taking the initiative because she might do something wrong." Says Dirk Rossman, owner of a chain of drugstores actively recruiting East Germans: "Many of them can't work like West Germans. There's a pressure to produce they're not used to."

    That sort of criticism is heard everywhere. "The demoralization in our work places is famous," says Jan Petranek, a leading Czechoslovak radio commentator forced to take a factory job after 1968 and now a writer for the country's leading newspaper, Lidove Noviny. "As the French philosopher Montesquieu said, the slave only has the freedom to be lazy." President Vaclav Havel is self-deprecatingly frank about how hard it is for him to learn to run a country, and in many speeches he implores Czechoslovaks to help out by helping themselves. "The president's office is just flooded with pleas, complaints and proposals by people who are used to someone else deciding for them," says a confidant. "They are all waiting for someone else to give them a cue or an order. . . ."

    Do you think the problems discussed in this excerpt are the result of fear and pressure or might they also be the result of a lack of hypothetical-deductive reasoning skill? Explain.

2. The data in Figure 2.2 compare representative samples of Japanese and North Carolina students on several tasks that require the use of hypothetical-deductive thinking patterns. The data suggest a clear Japanese superiority. Generate several alternative hypotheses to explain this apparent

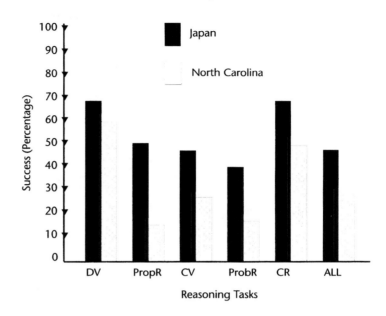

Figure 2.2 ▼ **Reasoning Abilities of Japanese and North Carolina Students.**
The bars compare the reasoning abilities of representative samples: 4,397 Japanese students and 3,291 North Carolina students (Grades 7, 8, and 9). DV = displaced volume; PropR = proportional reasoning; CV = control of variables; ProbR = probabilistic reasoning; CR = combinatorial reasoning; ALL = all tasks combined. (From Lawson, 1990.)

superiority. How might these alternatives be tested? What effect, if any, do you think this has on national competitiveness? Explain.

3. Solve each problem in the Classroom Test of Scientific Reasoning (Appendix F) and then identify the thinking patterns used on each problem.

CHAPTER 3

SCIENTIFIC KNOWLEDGE: ITS CONSTRUCTION AND DEVELOPMENT

Chapter 2 listed several creative and critical thinking patterns and skills needed for doing science—that is, for learning about nature. As mentioned, the use of these thinking patterns and skills results in the construction of new scientific knowledge. Therefore, in a sense, there are two distinct types of scientific knowledge. The first type is *knowledge of scientific processes*—how to do science. The second type is *knowledge of scientific products*—the scientific facts, concepts, and theories that the processes yield. Psychologists recognize these two general types of knowledge and refer to them as *procedural* and *declarative knowledge,* respectively. The distinction is essentially between "knowing how" (e.g., I know how to ride a bicycle, count to 100, perform a controlled experiment) and "knowing that" (e.g., I know that there are 50 states in the United States, and I know that animals inhale oxygen and exhale carbon dioxide). Anderson (1980) defines declarative knowledge and procedural knowledge in the following way: "Declarative knowledge comprises the facts that we know; procedural knowledge comprises the skills we know how to perform" (p. 222). Clearly, any discussion of teaching methods must address how to teach both declarative and procedural knowledge. Chapters 1 and 2 have already discussed the nature of scientific procedural knowledge in some detail. Therefore, the purpose of this chapter is to consider the nature of scientific declarative knowledge, to take a closer look at how it is constructed, and to explore how procedural knowledge develops during that construction process.

▼ THE NATURE OF DECLARATIVE KNOWLEDGE

From the teacher's and curriculum developer's points of view, the declarative aspects of subject matter of the disciplines are composed of a series of concepts and conceptual systems of various degrees of complexity, abstractness, and importance. These are generally seen as the primary units of instruction.

Adequately defining the term *concept* is no simple matter. Nevertheless, the following definition should prove sufficient. A concept has been formed whenever two or more distinguishable objects, events, or situations have been grouped or classified together and set apart from other objects, events, or situations on the basis of some common feature, form, or properties of both (after Bourne, 1966, p. 2). A concept can be considered a unit of thought that exists in a person's mind. Typically, terms are used to refer to these units. This does not deny the existence of nonverbalized knowledge, yet concept formation is usually seen as involving both the recognition of some common form or feature(s) from some phenomena plus some term or a combination of terms to refer to that which is common to the otherwise varied phenomena. Chairs, dogs, atoms, democracy, hunger, love, and so on all are terms to which meaning has been attributed; you know the meaning of these terms. Hence, for you these terms represent concepts. Do you know the meaning of the term *mellinark*? Probably not, therefore for you the term does not represent a concept.

Concepts do not stand alone. Rather, they are related in meaningful systems often with hierarchical structure of subordinate and superordinate concepts (Ausubel, 1963; Bruner, 1963: Gagné, 1970; Lawson, 1958; Novak, Gowin, and

Johansen, 1983; Okebukola and Jegede, 1988; Preece, 1978; Suppes, 1968). These interrelated concepts are called *conceptual systems*. An example of such a conceptual system is the ecosystem from ecological theory. This conceptual system consists of concepts such as trees, sunlight, frogs, producers, consumers, food webs, community, environmental factors, and ecosystem itself. The hierarchy of concepts—with the basic units of trees, frogs, sunlight, and so on at the bottom and ecosystem at the top—forms the conceptual system known as ecosystem. The concept of ecosystem is all-inclusive. All of the previously mentioned concepts are mentally integrated under the term "ecosystem." Figure 3.1 shows many of the subordinate concepts that must be interrelated to form the inclusive concept of ecosystem.

TYPES OF CONCEPTS

As previously defined, a concept refers to some pattern (regularity) to which a term or terms have been applied. Terms fall into different types according to the different sources of meaning. Consider, for example, the following list of terms. Decide whether a person could develop an initial understanding of these terms

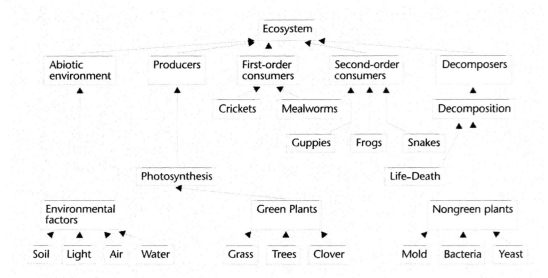

Figure 3.1 ▿ **Interrelated Concepts Subordinate to the Inclusive Concept of Ecosystem.** Interrelationships among subordinate concepts are complex but generally hierarchical. Chapter 8 will discuss curricular principles involved in teaching this conceptual system.

through (a) internal sensory impressions, (b) direct external experience and the classification and seriation of observable phenomena, or (c) inferences from experience and assumptions about imaginary, but not directly observable, objects, events, or situations:

gene	environment
hunger	light wave
density	solution
pain	electrical conductor
interaction	ideal gas

The meanings of the terms *hunger* and *pain* are derived primarily through internal sensory impressions. One can also immediately sense input such as the color green, heat and cold, sharpness and dullness, and internal states such as thirst and fatigue. The complete meaning of such inputs is derived immediately from the internal or external environment. The term *blue,* for example, derives its meaning from something that is immediately apprehended. Thus, concepts *by apprehension* are the first major type of concept (Northrop, 1947). Such concepts are well understood before children enroll in school, hence they are not objects of school instruction.

The terms *interaction, electrical conductor, solution,* and *environment* can be understood in terms of familiar actions, direct observations, and examples. In other words, the meanings of these terms are derived primarily from external experience. Such concepts serve to summarize and organize observable properties of objects, events, and situations, hence they are called *descriptive concepts*. Objects such as tables, chairs, other persons, and the room; events such as running, resting, playing, and eating; situations such as on top of, before, under, next to, and so on are not immediately apprehended in their totality. The meaning of *these objects as* terms comes through interaction with the "world out there." However, humans are not born with the ability to perceive objects in their environment as they perceive them later on (Piaget, 1952). As Northrop (1947) said, "perceptual objects are not immediately apprehended factors; they are postulates of common sense so thoroughly and frequently and unconsciously verified through their deductive consequences that only the critical realize them to be postulated rather than immediately apprehended" (p. 93). In other words, even though the properties of objects such as tables and chairs are perceptible, the objects in their totality are mentally constructed entities. We will return to this important point when we discuss the process of concept formation. Descriptive concepts also refer to perceived relations of objects and events. *Taller, heavier, wider, older, on top of, before,* and *under* are all terms that derive meaning from a comparison of properties of objects or events. To understand the meaning of such terms, the individual also must mentally construct order from environmental encounters.

The terms *gene, ideal gas,* and *light wave* must be understood as part of complex interrelationships with other concepts *(heredity, pressure, volume),* functional relationships *(ideal gas law, wave function),* or inferences from experience or idealizations. These understandings are not primarily the result of direct experiences with observable properties. Rather, the properties of such imagined entities are themselves imagined. Such concepts are called *theoretical concepts.* Said another way, theoretical concepts differ from descriptive concepts primarily because their defining properties are not perceptible. The primary use of theoretical concepts is to function as explanations for events that need causes but for which no causal agent can be directly perceived. Fairies, poltergeists, and ghosts fall into this category. Common examples from science are genes, atoms, molecules, electrons, and natural selection. The reason for the existence of theoretical concepts of imaginary objects with imaginary properties and interactions lies in a basic assumption humans make about the universe—that is, events do not occur without a cause. Thus, if we perceive certain events but cannot perceive objects or processes that cause such events, then we do not conclude that the events are spontaneous and without cause. Instead we invent unseen properties, objects, and interactions that explain the events in analogous perceptible causal terms. Because theoretical concepts are imagined and function to explain the otherwise unexplainable, they can be given whatever properties or qualities necessary in terms of the theory (that is, general explanation) of which they are a part. In other words, they derive their meaning in terms of the postulates of specific theories (Lawson, 1958; Lewis, 1980, 1988; Northrop, 1947; Suppes, 1968).

Some terms, of course, may have more than one meaning and may represent a descriptive or theoretical concept, depending on their definition. Temperature, as read on a thermometer, represents a descriptive concept. However, temperature, as a measure of the average kinetic molecular energy, is a theoretical concept. Likewise, the term *habitat,* if defined as a place where an organism lives, is a descriptive concept. Indeed, this meaning of habitat has been successfully taught to first graders. However, if *habitat* is defined as Hutchinson defines *niche*—as "an n-dimensional hypervolume every point of which corresponds to an environmental state permitting the species in question to maintain a steady state"—then the concept is clearly a theoretical one. This concept causes some graduate students difficulty. Before being classified, therefore, a term must be clearly defined.

The distinction between descriptive and theoretical concepts is not equivalent to the more familiar concrete and abstract distinction. All concepts are abstract, in a sense, abstracted from many specific instances and examples. Interaction is abstract because it is extremely general and applicable to all objects that influence one another, regardless of whether they exchange energy or momentum, modify the chemical composition, or (if living) infect with a disease. Because many direct experiences are readily available to illustrate the meaning of interaction, interaction is a descriptive concept and has been taught successfully to second and third graders.

The light wave concept is also abstract, though more restricted in applicability than interaction. Yet the meaning of *light wave* depends essentially on Maxwell's electromagnetic theory, which can be understood only through the use of functional relationships, abstract variables, idealized models, and other hypothetical-deductive thinking patterns. Hence, light wave is a theoretical concept. In biology, the concept of environment is highly abstract and general because it applies to individual cells, to entire multicellular organisms, populations of organisms, and so on. Nonetheless, once it is abstracted, many direct experiences are readily available to demonstrate its meaning. The concept of gene is also an abstraction, although of a different kind than environment. Mendel hypothesized the existence of "factors" with specific imagined properties to explain ratios of characteristics obtained through hybridized crosses of pea plants. The factors, or genes, themselves did not give rise to direct experience. The gene concept has to be understood in terms of other concepts (heredity, trait), the possible combinations of genes that produce observable effects, and a theory relating genotype to phenotype. Hence the concept of gene is theoretical.

Of significance to the teacher attempting to teach theoretical concepts such as the electron, a young child may be quite capable of imagining tiny particles and calling them electrons, if the teacher wishes, but with little or no awareness or understanding of (a) the theoretical system of which they are a part and from which they derive their actual importance, (b) the empirical situation(s) that led to the postulation of the existence of these "tiny particles" in the first place, and (c) the evidence that supports the hypothesized existence of the particles. To the young child with no understanding of the nature of theoretical systems and their relationship to empirical data, the idea of the electron and other theoretical concepts must seem to have derived meaning as if by magic or perhaps by decree of some omniscient scientist. In short, one cannot fully comprehend the meaning of any single theoretical concept without some appreciation and awareness of the theoretical system of which it is a part and of the empirical data on which that system is based (Lawson and Karplus, 1977; Shayer and Adey, 1981).

▼ TYPES OF CONCEPTUAL SYSTEMS

Concepts by apprehension, descriptive concepts, and theoretical concepts are the bricks that, when cemented together, make up the conceptual systems that represent our declarative knowledge of the world and universe, the conceptual systems that make up the laws of the land, and the philosophies and religions that guide human lives—in short, the contents of human minds.

Basically, conceptual systems are of two types, descriptive or theoretical, depending on the nature of the concepts that make up the system. A descriptive conceptual system comprises concepts by apprehension and descriptive concepts only. A theoretical system is composed of concepts by apprehension, descriptive concepts, and theoretical concepts. Examples of descriptive conceptual systems are human anatomy, early Greek cosmology, taxonomies, and games such as chess, football, and baseball. Each of these systems consists of concepts about perceivable objects and the interactions of these objects.

Theoretical conceptual systems are exemplified by atomic-molecular theory, Mendelian genetics, Darwinian evolution through natural selection, and so on. In atomic-molecular theory, the atoms and molecules were imagined to exist and to have certain properties and behaviors, none of which could be observed. However, by assigning certain properties to atoms that included combining with one another to form molecules, observable chemical changes could be explained. In the same manner, Mendel imagined genes to exist that occurred in pairs, separated at the time of gamete formation, combined when egg and sperm united, and determined the course of development of the embryo. By assuming the gene to exist and to have certain properties and behavior, Mendel could explain the observable results from crosses of plants and animals.

Each conceptual system is composed of a finite set of basic postulates that taken together define the system and certain basic concepts of that system. For example, the basic postulates of classic cell theory, Mendelian genetics, Watson and Crick's theory of DNA structure and duplication, and the kinetic-molecular theory were listed previously in Table 1.1. The postulates of these and other theories, when taken together, constitute the essence of theoretical conceptual systems used to explain how cells function, how traits are passed from parent to offspring, how the genetic material duplicates, and so on. Concepts such as cell, gene, dominance, recessive, atom, and molecule derive their meaning from the systems' postulates. As mentioned in Chapter 1, when the postulates of theories such as these become widely accepted, the theories are referred to as "embedded" theories, and then postulates take on the status of "facts."

▼ MENTAL STRUCTURES AND THE PROCESS OF SELF-REGULATION

Before turning to a discussion of how science can be taught so that students construct understanding of important concepts and conceptual systems *and* develop the ability to use important scientific thinking patterns, we must understand just how previous knowledge and thinking pattern interact to create new knowledge. Of course, the discussion of the work of the scientists discussed in Chapters 1 and 2 should have provided initial insights into this process. We will now take a closer look at the creative process by way of an activity that will involve us directly in knowledge construction.

The Pattern of Knowledge Construction

Place Figure 3.2 and then Figure 3.3 in front of a mirror and read and follow the reflected instructions. As you attempt the mirror drawing, make sure that you look only in the mirror. Do not look directly at your hand, only at its reflection. Try to become conscious of your techniques as you draw.

When finished, consider the following questions:

1. Did you improve at all during the activities?
2. What feedback, if any, from your actions was especially helpful? disruptive?
3. What strategies proved helpful?
4. Did your strategies evolve?
5. What errors persisted in spite of your best efforts?
6. Did you try right-handed versus left-handed drawing? If so, did that seem to affect the result?
7. Did you try drawing with your eyes closed? If so, did that help?

When you attempted the mirror drawing, did you discover that your initial strategies misled you? Were you forced to reflect on and modify those strategies?

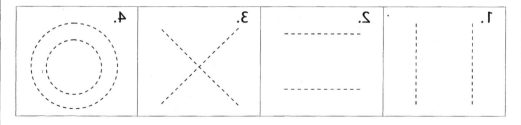

Figure 3.2 ▼ **Mirrored Drawing (1)**

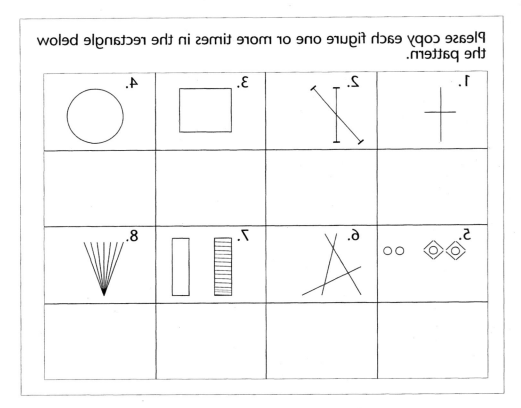

Figure 3.3 ▽ **Mirrored Drawing (2)**

This is the process of *self-regulation.* Its reflective component is the key to success. The process of self-regulation is one in which a person actively searches for relationships and patterns to resolve contradictions or to bring coherence to a new set of experiences. Self-regulation starts with the *exploration* of current thinking patterns or behaviors. It progresses to the *invention* of novel ideas or behaviors and then to their possible successful or unsuccessful *application* to current and future situations. Self-regulation results in both increased understanding of the world—that is, new declarative knowledge—and a greater awareness and refinement of one's procedure for constructing that understanding—that is, new procedural knowledge.

The Role of Mental Structures

A fundamental idea that underlies the notion of self-regulation is the concept of mental structures, or hypothesized "mental blueprints" that guide the organism's behavior. At this point in our study of human mental functioning we cannot specify the exact neurological or chemical nature of these structures. (The issue of the neurological and chemical nature of mental structures will be taken up later in Chapter 10.) As was obviously the case when we attempted to alter previous mental structures or perhaps to construct new ones while drawing in the mirror, mental structures do not come from simply making a mental record of the world, that is, by keeping eyes and ears open. Work done by Senden with congenitally blind persons provides an interesting example of this point. These persons, who gained sight after surgery, could not visually distinguish a key from a book when both lay on a table in front of them. They also were unable to report seeing any difference between a square and a circle (Hebb, 1949). Only when they were able to pick up and handle the objects did they come to recognize the visual differences that would be obvious to us. The important idea to note is this: Whether the task is to distinguish simple objects in the environment or complex processes such as photosynthesis, natural selection, or metabolism, the ability to construct the appropriate mental structures and meaningful understanding requires much more than a simple photographing of the environment. According to Jean Piaget, a person is unable to perceive a thing until his mind has constructed a structure that enables its perception (*assimilation* is his term). Without the construction of a mental structure, things that seem obvious to most adults—such as the difference between a key and a book, a square and a circle, or a plant and an animal—are simply not perceived. But this leads us to a fundamental problem. If learning is the construction and reconstruction of mental structures, and if structures are needed to perceive and to learn, and if they are not derived from simply photographing the external world, then from where do they come?

Plato's answer to this question was simple. The structures were innate and were acquired through the passage of time and development of the brain, albeit nourished by environmental encounters. Of course, at the other end of the spectrum is the belief that these structures are derived directly from the environment. This is the classical empiricist's view; but as we have already noted, this view is lacking.

Most scholars now reject the Platonic view, except to admit that certain primary structures must be present at birth. The modern view is that the construction of structures derives from a dynamic interaction of the organism and the environment. The structure derives not solely from within the organism and not solely from within the environment but from the organism's own actions within the environment. This is the process of self-regulation.

The child's self-regulatory actions lead to the construction and reconstruction of progressively more complex and powerful mental structures. Powerful mental structures are those that have broad applications. From birth, basic structures enable the child to initially experience and begin interacting with his or her surroundings. As long as that interaction is successful, the basic structures continue to guide behavior. However, because of the child's inborn drive to interact with the environment, he or she meets contradictions, that is, things that do not fit current mental structures. These contradictions produce a state of *disequilibrium*. In other words, the child's current mental structures are found inadequate and must be altered or replaced. Through continued investigation and guidance from others, the child alters or *accommodates* his or her inadequate mental structures. Once this is accomplished, he or she is then able to *assimilate* the new situation. The new structure that is constructed is then tried. If the structure guides behavior so that the child's efforts are rewarded (reinforced), then the structure is also reinforced. In this way the child builds new mental structures and adapts to new situations.

The emphasis in this process is on the *self* because the process is by its nature an internal regulation that *cannot* be circumvented using external agents. This, of course, does not suggest that a teacher cannot provide situations that can initiate self-regulation and later provide input that can help the student think through the problem to reestablish equilibrium.

In the mirror drawing context, the exploration and assimilation of new input to old mental structures quickly led to inappropriate or contradicted behavior. This resulted in disequilibrium. Hence an accommodation of these mental structures was called for. Accommodation entails (a) an analysis or breakdown of the situation to locate the source of difficulty, and (b) the invention of new plans of attack. For example, during the mirror puzzle, you may have decided to analyze a complex figure into simpler ones, then apply them before reattempting the more complex figure. Also, you have observed the effect of executing the commands "up," "down," and "right," and realized that the first two commands produce movements that go "the wrong way" in the mirror.

The result of this exploring, inventing, and applying with the mirror puzzle was new (though ephemeral) thinking patterns—that is, new actions and new ways to label and organize those actions. These self-correcting activities were constantly being tested until they had an acceptable level of positive feedback. The whole self-regulation process is directed at obtaining a stable rapport between mental structures and the environment. The basic pattern of self-regulation is shown in Figure 3.4.

Additional Examples of Self-Regulation

As a further example of the self-regulation process, consider a problem faced by my son, Matthew, when he was 14 months old. When playing with the shape-sorting toy shown in Figure 3.5, he would pick up the cylinder at the left and hunt for the correct hole into which to drop it. Because he was initially unable to find the correct hole or orient the cylinder correctly to make it fit, even if he

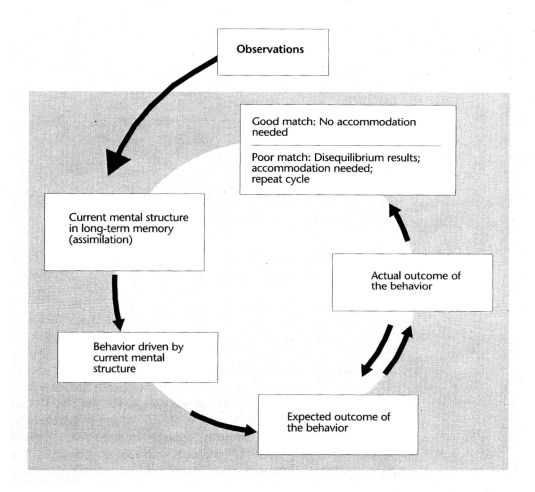

Figure 3.4 ▾ **The Cyclic Process of Self-Regulation.** Observations are assimilated by current mental structures that drive behavior that has previously been linked to specific consequences (i.e., expected outcomes). If the behavior is contradicted by feedback from the environment—that is, if there is a poor match between expected outcome and actual outcome—then disequilibrium results. Dis-equilibrium drives a search for an alternative mental structure, closer observation, or both. As a consequence, alternative mental structures are selected or constructed (mental accommodation) and tried until a good match between expected and actual outcomes occurs to restore equilibrium. Notice how the change of mental structures occurs as a consequence of contradicted behaviors (mistakes). In short, we learn from our mistakes. In reality, because no sensory input is completely identical or completely novel from past input, some assimilation and accommodation is involved in all mental processing.

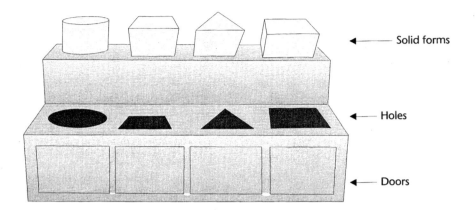

Figure 3.5 ▼ **Shape Sorter Toy.** The objective of this toy is to pick up and properly orient the solid objects on top so that they will fit into the holes below.

did choose the correct hole, he was faced with a task that could not be resolved with his current mental structures. Self-regulation was needed. Nevertheless, without too much difficulty I was able to physically assist him in fitting the cylinder into the correct hole. When he placed the cylinder above the correct hole, I was able to push the object to orient it correctly so that it fit. When he let go it would drop out of sight, and he was delighted—success! But when he then picked up the rectangular solid next to the cylinder, which hole do you think he tried to put it in? The one below the rectangular solid? Wrong. He did not even consider that hole even though it clearly is the correct choice. Instead he would try to put it into the round hole. Presumably this is because it was that behavior, the act of placing an object above the round hole and then letting go, that previously led to success. In other words, he would attempt to assimilate the new situation to the previously successful behavior. In general, successful behavior will always be repeated until contradicted. Now, of course, when the rectangular object was placed over the round hole it would not fit, so the behavior was contradicted. But only after numerous contradictions was Matthew willing to try another hole. I tried showing him into which holes the various objects would actually go, but this showing was to no avail. He had to behave himself. In other words, Matthew learned from his behaviors. Only after repeated behaviors did he find the correct holes. It was the coordination of behaviors that ultimately led to the accommodation of his mental structures and new, more complex behaviors.

At a level closer to high school teaching, consider the self-regulation needed by a bright-eyed, conscientious sophomore named Karen. When shown one wide and one narrow plastic cylinder of equal height, with equally spaced marks along their heights, she predicted that water that filled the wide one up to the fourth mark would rise higher if poured into the narrow cylinder. So far, so good. Now when the four units of water in the wide cylinder were actually poured into the narrow one, they rose to the sixth mark. Seeing this result, Karen predicted that water that rose to six in the wide cylinder would rise to eight in the narrow. As she put it, this is because it was two higher before so it would still be two higher. Now, of course, a problem is recognizable here but Karen did not see it. When Karen actually saw the water rise to nine when poured into the narrow cylinder instead of eight as she predicted, the problem surfaced. Her additive strategy simply did not work. The result was mental disequilibrium and a conscious search for a new strategy.

Trying to teach Karen to use a proportional strategy to solve the problem as well as her inability to use proportions in other appropriate situations (for example, instead of using proportional reasoning to triple a recipe, she would cook a single recipe three times!) clearly demonstrated the magnitude of the problem. Both the theory of self-regulation and experience argue that this learning is not isolated and easily remedied. Rather, it is intimately tied to a whole host of ideas (e.g., probability, correlations, control of variables) that are a part of a general way of processing information. At this level the required self-regulation takes considerable time and effort on Karen's part. As in Matthew's case this will take repeated attempts at solving problems until her inappropriate strategies are relinquished and more appropriate strategies are adopted.

Thus, whether on the sensory motor level (as was the case with the mirror puzzle or the shape sorter) or the conceptual level (as was the case for Karen struggling with proportional relationships or Charles Darwin struggling with the evolution of species—see Chapter 1, particularly Figure 1.4), the self-regulation process results in new declarative knowledge of the external world. But the process also results in increased procedural knowledge (that is, skill in constructing that knowledge through the development of explicit guides to problem solving, or thinking patterns and skills), what others have called heuristics, cognitive strategies, and the like.

Note that this "constructivist" view is quite the opposite of the traditional view that holds that intellectual development is the sum total of bit-by-bit learning experiences that the learner has acquired over the course of a variety of provoked encounters. To the constructivist, such development is the acquisition and integration of mental structures that result not from a series of externally provoked and isolated learning experiences but from a self-directed process in which the individual actively takes part in the solution of self-chosen problems that arise in the course of behaving in and trying to construct meanings in a complex environment. The individual is an explorer, a question finder, and an answer seeker. Explorations with novel phenomena raise questions. Once questions are raised, the innate need to find answers pushes the child to continue exploration and invent ideas or new strategies until answers are created that can be successfully applied to this and future situations. The learner is not a passive recipient of external information.

Disrupting Children's Spontaneous Attempts at Self-Regulation

We might usefully look at what can happen when children's self-directed attempts at self-regulation are interrupted by well-intentioned but excessive external guidance. The following example seems to capture the essence of the central educational issue raised by the constructivist view.

When my son Bobby was 2 years old, he had a set of eight small "nesting" boxes that fit one within the other in order from small to large. They could be nested or placed upside-down largest first, next largest next, and so on until each was stacked on the other to make a tower. Now, making such a tower is an extremely difficult task for a 2-year-old. Bobby could usually pick the largest box first and perhaps the next largest but most certainly, if left to himself, he would err before completing the tower. He appeared to recognize the correct solution, but he lacked the ability to arrive at it by himself.

When we played with the boxes I normally built the tower so he could see the result. Then he would knock the tower down, grab the boxes, and attempt to build it himself. Of course, it was an assumption on my part that he actually was attempting to build the entire tower. His actual motives may have been quite different. Nevertheless, his spontaneous effort went on and on.

One day, while he was playing with the boxes, I decided to find out if a concerted effort at teaching him the correct way to build the tower would be successful. When he first grabbed the largest box, I let him continue, but I intervened when he grabbed an incorrect box. "No, Bobby, that's not the correct box. This is the correct one." And so on. I continued this intervention for about ten minutes until we worked out a successful technique to unerringly build the tower. He would grab a box and then look at me for approval or disapproval. If I approved, he would add it to the first. If I disapproved, he would grab another box and so on until together we got the tower built.

Unfortunately, such a prescription had two rather serious side effects. First, it eliminated all of his spontaneous effort to build the tower. He would not add a box without looking to me for approval. His behavior had changed from spontaneous to dependent in the course of only a few minutes. And second, without me for continual guidance, he was not able to build the tower again. Seeing my own child transformed in this instance from a curious, ambitious, and energetic builder to a dependent, cautious, seeker of approval taught me not to try my heavy-handed teaching methods again.

If adults usurp the child's spontaneous and self-directed efforts by imposing nonassimilable procedures or by answering unasked questions, the child may be able to solve problems by rote or by parroting words, but the child will neither be able to solve novel problems nor be able to understand how those empty words relate to the world that he or she knows. The key educational issue raised by this discussion is clearly one of active, spontaneous, self-directed learning versus passive, outer-directed, "reception" learning. The constructivist position is that the active, spontaneous, self-directed approach is essential if the development of thinking skills and truly meaningful concept understanding are the aims.

Three Basic Mental Abilities and Self-Regulation

Three basic mental abilities are assumed to be innate: (a) pattern making and recognition, (b) drawing inferences, and (c) making comparisons. These three abilities are assumed to function in various phases of the self-regulation process, which begins with the exploration of some new, hence undifferentiated object or event. The mind draws on its current store of mental structures to assimilate the new phenomenon. The interaction of the new phenomenon plus the mental structure evokes a thought—a mental pattern. In the past this mental pattern has been linked to behavior; thus the presence of the mental pattern produces an expectation of what the subject will experience next if the previous behavior is repeated. When the previous behavior is actually carried out, the expectation can then be compared with the actual result of the behavior. If the expectation and the result are one and the same, then the new object or event will have been directly assimilated to previous mental structures and no modification of these structures will occur. However, if the expectation and the actual result are not the same, then the subject finds him- or herself with a new object or event and no structure with which to assimilate the new phenomenon. He or she has a problem and must invent a novel solution. Mental disequilibrium results. What happens now depends on available strategies. A search through other mental structures for possible solutions or a closer inspection of the phenomenon itself for an analysis of its properties may result. This latter route leads to the eventual differentiation of the phenomenon, the eventual accommodation of mental structures, and then successful application.

How Do Thinking Patterns Function in Adult Thinking?

The three basic innate mental abilities (pattern making and recognition, inference drawing, and comparison making) and empirical-inductive and hypothetical-deductive thinking patterns operate in conjunction with previous declarative knowledge in the cognitively mature individual to answer questions and create new declarative knowledge through the self-regulation process.

Empirical-inductive patterns such as classification, seriation, and correspondence operate to differentiate the parts of the new phenomenon. They are needed to order objects and observable properties and to isolate important variables. The mind's pattern-making and recognizing ability (commonly referred to as *creativity* and perhaps a function of the right hemisphere) allows the creation of patterns—hypotheses, postulates, theories, and so on—to tentatively organize the new phenomenon. This involves *abduction,* that is, the borrowing of a pattern from one's current store of concepts and conceptual systems, as was the case when Mendel borrowed algebraic patterns to organize data from the crosses of pea plants, when Darwin borrowed the idea of artificial selection to understand selection in nature, and when Coulomb borrowed Newtonian laws of planetary attraction to organize data from the interaction of electrically charged objects.

Once the new pattern has been created or invented, it must be tested. This may occur in one of three ways. Obviously, the first question that should be asked is, does the new idea actually answer the current question? Second, does the new idea fit with previously constructed concepts and conceptual systems? If the answer to this second question is no, then either the idea itself will have to be changed or some accommodation of previously constructed concepts and conceptual systems is likely to occur. A third way the new idea can be tested is through the deduction of its logical consequences and the comparing of these consequences with actual experimental results. In that this test will be conducted in the "real world"[1] and one can never be sure of having controlled all variables involved in the situation, the deductions take the form of a weak *modus ponens* and *modus tollens* (Bunge, 1967). Nevertheless, the derivation of predicted consequences requires an understanding of the need to control variables and an understanding of the probabilistic nature of phenomena. The analyses of data at this point often require what has been termed *proportional* or *correlational thinking patterns* (see Chapter 2).

If the problem solver does indeed find that the new hypothesis or theory satisfies these tests, then the result is new conceptual understanding and a new plane of mental equilibrium. If, however, any or all of these tests lead to contradictory findings, then (a) the process must be repeated with the reexamination of the phenomenon or the generation of a new hypothesis, (b) the individual must find out what went wrong with the tests, or (c) the individual may conclude that the question simply cannot be answered (at least by him or her) and will go on to something else. Such a view of mature adult thought represents the implied goal of the educational process as it encompasses creativity, effective thinking, and conceptual understanding.

Contributing Factors in Self-Regulation

The role of three main factors—*experience, social transmission,* and *maturation*—can be isolated in the general process of self-regulation. It is obvious that experience is a necessary part of learning. If there are no encounters with the environment, no contradiction of current structures arise and there is no possibility for further exploration into the situation that produced the contradiction. Obtaining a stable rapport with new mental structures needed for mirror drawing takes a lot of experience that few of us—besides dentists, who often have to work while looking in a mirror—have had.

Experience helps students to construct structures that can ultimately lead them to think hypothetical-deductively about the world around them. And experience with the materials of the discipline produces the person who can understand theoretical concepts. This says to science teachers that firsthand experiences in the laboratory or field *must* precede the introduction of new procedures and terms. The more traditional method of conducting laboratory and field activities is to introduce procedures and terms in a lecture *before* the firsthand experiences. Thus the procedures and terms are introduced on a purely verbal level. The laboratory or field is then seen by students to be a place to demonstrate that the teacher or the textbook are correct and not a place to conduct meaningful explorations and construct new knowledge. This, of course, is contrary to the spirit and pattern of scientific inquiry and is also contrary to the way in which self-regulation proceeds. Recall from Chapter 1 how we found that the pattern of scientific inquiry consists essentially of the *exploration* of phenomena, the *invention* of novel explanations and new terms, and the *discovery* of evidence to either support or refute those inventions. If we intend to teach science as science is done—that is, in the way that people spontaneously construct knowledge—then the experiences must come first.

The second factor, social transmission, also is necessary for structure building. Very young children—and some not so young—operate from an egocentric frame of reference. They do not see things objectively because they often look at them as related only to themselves. For the learners to move from this egocentric view, they need to experience others' viewpoints and thoughts. They must, in other words, interact with other people. If they do not, they have no reason to alter concepts that were initially constructed from their self-centered frame of reference. Social interaction can lead to conflict, debate, shared data, and the clear delineation and expression of ideas. All of these require that students carefully examine their current beliefs. This examination is a necessary condition for the change and construction of new concepts. For all of this to happen, however, students must be encouraged to talk with one another and their teachers. Data from an experiment must be shared, discussed, retaken, and rediscussed. Students should converse, share experience, and argue. This point is sometimes overlooked by teachers who try to incorporate "hands-on" activities into their classrooms. All of the direct experience in the world will not facilitate the construction of new conceptual knowledge unless it is accompanied by social interaction through the use of language. The factor of social interaction is invaluable; however, like physical experience, it alone is insufficient because learners can receive valuable information by language or education only if they are in a state in which they can understand this information. In other words, to receive this information, they must first have a set of direct experiences that provide a variety of sensory images to serve as reference points that ground the verbal elements.

Consider, for example, a young child riding in a car at dusk who notices that the moon, which is low on the eastern horizon, seems to be following her down the road. To her father's astonishment she exclaims, "Look Daddy, the moon is following us!" Of course, merely telling the child that the moon really is not following her will not enable her to construct the alternative view that the moon is so far away that it merely *appears* to be following her. But suppose she is asked whether the moon is also following people riding in the other direction. For example, why should the moon only follow her and not others? Might this question provoke her to begin taking another point of view?

Maturation, the third factor, must also be considered. The role of maturation is not yet well understood. Whether under maturational control or not, a child's mental capacity for processing information appears to increase more or less linearly with age. For example, when children of 5 or 6 years of age hear two digits such as 9 and 7, they can recall the digits, transpose them, and say them backward. However, if these children are asked to listen to three digits, transpose them, and say them backward, they are unable to do so. Their capacity for mentally storing and processing information seems able to simultaneously process two bits of information, but not three. By the age of 7 or 8, this capacity has increased to three numbers; and by the age of 15 or 16, it has reached a maximum of approximately seven numbers. This apparent constraint on a child's ability to store and mentally manipulate information may limit the child's ability to construct complex conceptualizations. Because the growth of this "mental capacity" may depend on the growth of the central nervous system, there is perhaps nothing teachers can do about it. They should, however, be aware of this possible constraint and whenever possible design instruction in such a way as not to overload this capacity. Perhaps the demand on mental capacity can be reduced by introducing material in such a way that it can be coordinated or "chunked" with previous material. Another possible maturational constraint will be considered in Chapter 4's discussion of the stages of intellectual development.

A personal example may help to clarify how the factors of experience and social transmission interact in the process of self-regulation to construct knowledge. In my first science course in the seventh grade, my teacher presented us with many experiments to perform. We examined the effect of various concentrations of fertilizer on the growth of plants and the effect of other environmental factors such as light, temperature, and water on the behavior of animals such as beetles, snails, and mealworms. Following each experiment we were to write a report of two or three pages explaining the problem, procedure, data, and conclusions. The reports were straightforward and, in effect, something of a bore—all except for one question that the teacher asked repeatedly: "What was the control? Did you perform a controlled experiment?" I had no ready answer to this question. In fact, the words in relation to my experiments were practically meaningless. What did the teacher mean by "control"? The insistence on something being controlled and my inability to figure what was to be controlled caused a very real state of disequilibrium. I realized that the answer to the question lay somewhere in the experiments, but just where I could not say. My teacher must have been skilled indeed, for she continued to bring in a variety of materials for us to perform experiments with, and at the conclusion of each experiment we were asked that penetrating question about controls. With each new experiment, I tried to see how I could make sense of those words in terms of the activities. During this time a great deal of thinking took place—thinking about specific activities and about specific verbal terminology. Following what must have been two or three months of such experimentation and discussion with the teacher and other students, the idea finally dawned on me. To find out if temperature made a difference in the growth of bean plants we had to make sure that all the plants were watered the same amount and had the same amount of fertilizer, and so on; otherwise I would not know for sure if the temperature made the difference. In other words, *everything* (except the temperature) had to be the same for the experiment to give us clear results. That was a controlled experiment! Immediately I could apply this idea to any experiment I performed. At last equilibrium was once again mine.

This example demonstrates that the firsthand experiences and social transmission (in this case, the teacher's introduction and continued reintroduction of the term controlled experiment) clearly have a place in promoting disequilibrium and self-regulation. The initial experimentation and the introduction of only intuitively grasped terms can produce disequilibrium. To the skilled, concerned science teacher, this disequilibrium is an opportunity to provide students with new activities involving the same concept(s). This enables students to continue their thinking and self-regulate at their own rates until they can mentally coordinate the new terms with the concrete activities to construct new knowledge and reestablish equilibrium. Subsequent research suggests that my teacher would have made my job of understanding considerably easier had she chosen intuitively understood words such as *fair test* as opposed to the more scientific term *controlled experiment:* "Did you do a fair test" rather than "Did you do a controlled experiment?" (Lawson and Wollman, 1976).

▼ HOW ARE DESCRIPTIVE CONCEPTS CONSTRUCTED?

To acquire a better sense of how self-regulation and thinking patterns operate in the construction of specific descriptive concepts, consider the drawings in Figure 3.6. The first row contains five "creatures" called *mellinarks*. None of the creatures in the second row are mellinarks. From this information, decide which creatures in the third row are mellinarks.

The problem of deciding which creatures in Row 3 is or are mellinarks is an example of descriptive concept construction. If you correctly identified the first, second, and sixth figures as mellinarks, then you have identified a pattern for the term *mellinark*. How did you do it? Outdated theories of abstraction (Locke,

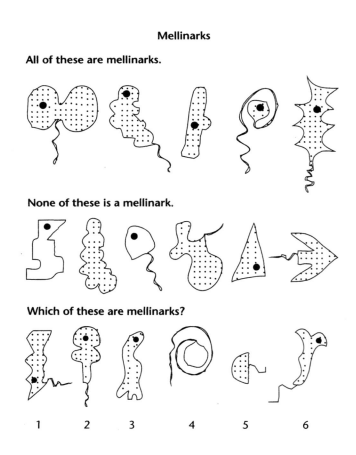

Mellinarks

All of these are mellinarks.

None of these is a mellinark.

Which of these are mellinarks?

    1   2   3   4   5   6

Figure 3.6 ▼ **Mellinarks.** These imaginary creatures are adapted from Elementary Science Study, 1974.

1690; Hume, 1739) would claim that you merely induced a set of specific characteristics and generalized it to other instances. The notion of self-regulation, on the other hand, emphasizes the importance of idea generation and test and the predictive nature of concept construction (e.g., Bolton, 1977; Holland, Holyoak, Nisbett, and Thagard, 1986; Mayer, 1983).

Let us consider a solution using the notion of self-regulation—that is, idea creation and test. In this case we will see that several features are immediately noted that allow us inductively to generate several ideas that can be tested. For example, a glance at Row 1 reveals several features of the mellinarks. They have tails. They contain one large dot and several smaller dots. They have an enclosed cell-like membrane that may have curved or straight sides. If we assume that features such as these are crucial, then which ones? The process of induction—that is, going from the observation of specific features to the generation of general statements—gives us the following ideas to be tested. Mellinarks are creatures that consist of:

1. one large dot only
2. several small dots only
3. one tail only
4. one large dot and several small dots
5. one large dot and one tail
6. several small dots and one tail
7. one large dot, several small dots, and one tail.

Idea 1 would lead one to predict that all of the Row 1 and none of the Row 2 creatures would contain one large dot. Because this is not the case, the prediction is disconfirmed, and the idea that mellinarks are creatures distinguished solely by the presence of one large dot is also disconfirmed (see Figure 3.7). The same pattern of inductive-deductive reasoning leads one to disconfirm Ideas 2 through 6 as well, leaving Idea 7, that mellinarks are defined by the presence of all three features, as "correct." Thus only the first, second, and sixth creatures in Row 3 are mellinarks.

Seen in this light, concept construction is not viewed as a purely abstractive process; it rests on the ability to generate and test alternative possibilities. In this sense one's conceptual knowledge (an aspect of declarative knowledge) depends on one's procedural knowledge. As one gains skill in using these inductive-deductive procedures, descriptive concept construction becomes easier. More will be said about this when we discuss stages in the development of procedural knowledge. In the case of the mellinarks, the concept constructed is a descriptive one, because its defining attributes are directly perceptible. We may continue to use the term induction to refer to this process of concept construction provided we do not view induction as purely abstractive. Clearly the induced features must be tested before we can be sure that we have identified the correct features.

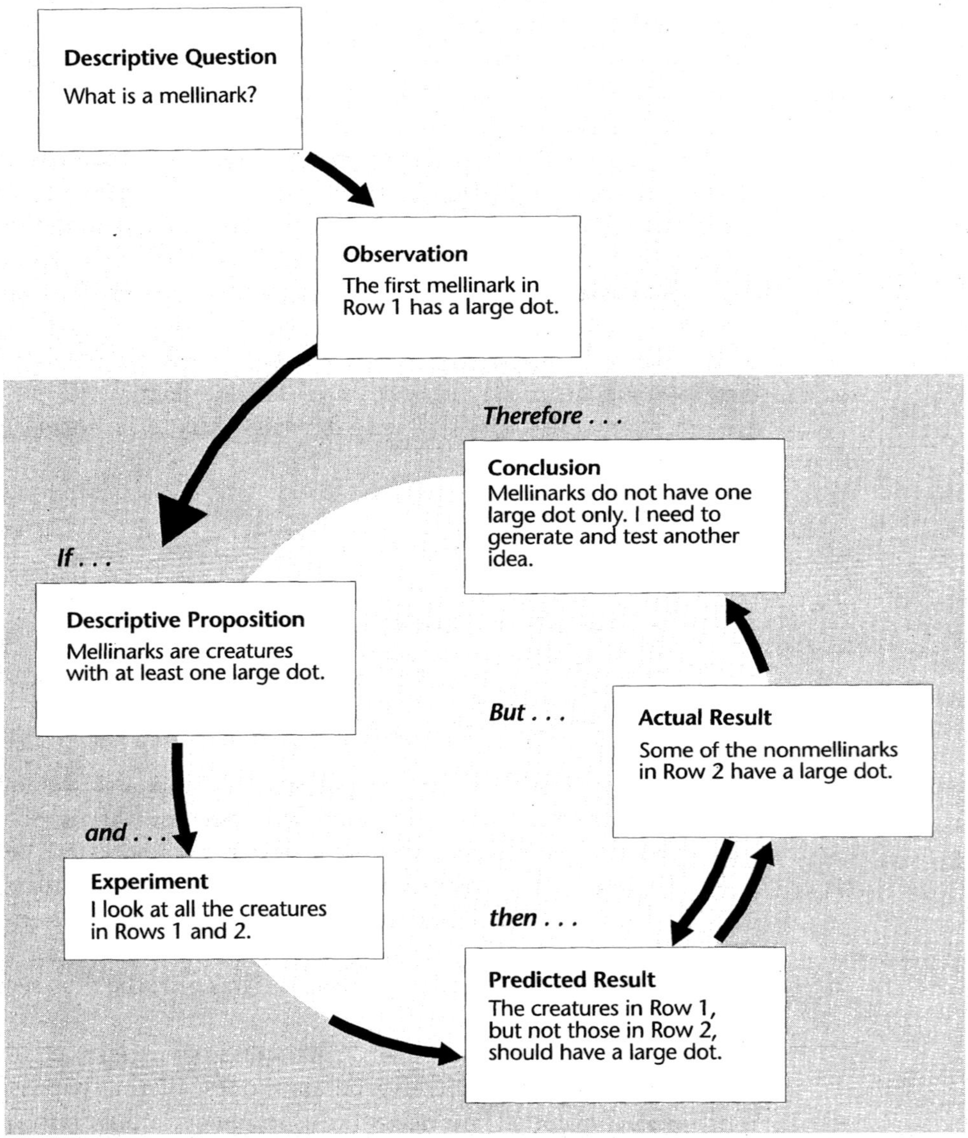

Descriptive Question

What is a mellinark?

Observation

The first mellinark in Row 1 has a large dot.

Therefore . . .

Conclusion

Mellinarks do not have one large dot only. I need to generate and test another idea.

If . . .

Descriptive Proposition

Mellinarks are creatures with at least one large dot.

But . . .

Actual Result

Some of the nonmellinarks in Row 2 have a large dot.

and . . .

Experiment

I look at all the creatures in Rows 1 and 2.

then . . .

Predicted Result

The creatures in Row 1, but not those in Row 2, should have a large dot.

Figure 3.7 ▾ **Inductive-Deductive Thinking and Mellinarks.** This thinking cycle can be used to construct the descriptive concept of mellinark. Note how ideas about what mellinarks' defining features might be are derived from direct observation of the creatures in Row 1.

▼ ## THE ROLE OF CHUNKING IN HIGHER-ORDER CONCEPT CONSTRUCTION

The human mind at any one moment is able to integrate or process only a limited amount of information. Miller (1956) introduced the term *chunk* to refer to the discrete units of information that could be consciously held in working memory and transformed or integrated. He cited considerable evidence to suggest that the maximum number of these discrete chunks was approximately seven.

Clearly, however, we all construct concepts that contain far more information than seven units. The term *ecosystem,* as mentioned, subsumes a far greater number of discrete units or chunks than seven. Further, the term *ecosystem* itself is a concept, thus it probably occupies but one chunk in conscious memory. This implies that a mental process must occur in which previously unrelated parts— that is, chunks of information (an approximate maximum of seven chunks)— are assembled by the mind into one higher-order chunk or unit of thought. This implied process is known as *chunking* (Simon, 1974).

The result of higher-order concept construction (chunking) is extremely important. It reduces the load on mental capacity and simultaneously opens up additional mental capacity that can then be occupied by additional concepts. This in turn allows one to form still more complex and inclusive concepts (i.e., concepts that subsume greater numbers of subordinate concepts). To turn back to our initial example, once we all know what a mellinark is, we no longer have to refer to them as "creatures within an enclosed membrane that may be curved or straight, one large dot and several smaller dots inside, and one tail." Use of the term *mellinark* to subsume all of this information greatly facilitates thinking and communication when both parties have constructed the concept. See Ausubel (1963) and Ausubel, Novak, and Hanesian (1968) for details of the subsumption process.

▼ ## HOW ARE THEORETICAL CONCEPTS CONSTRUCTED?

The preceding discussion of descriptive concept construction leaves two important issues unresolved. First, how does concept construction take place when the defining features are not directly perceptible, that is, when the concept in question is a theoretical one? Second, what takes place when the theoretical concept to be acquired contradicts a previously constructed concept?

Again, let us consider these issues by returning to the example of Charles Darwin as he changed his view from that of a creationist to that of an evolutionist and invented a new concept, that of natural selection. Note that the concepts of creationism, evolution, and natural selection are all theoretical, according to our previous definition.

Recall that Gruber and Barrett (1974) analyzed Darwin's thinking during the period 1831 to 1838 when he underwent a conceptual change from a creationist theory of the world (a misconception in today's scientific thinking) to that of an evolutionist (a currently valid scientific conception) and when he invented his concept of natural selection. Fortunately for Gruber and Barrett and for us, Darwin left a record of much of his thinking during this period in diaries. Figure 1.4 (page 15) highlighted the major changes in his theoretical conceptual system during this time. Evolutionary ideas were certainly in the air before Darwin's time. Recall that Darwin's own grandfather, Erasmus Darwin, published *Zoonomia: or the Laws of Organic Life* (1794–96), which contained speculative ideas about evolution. Nevertheless in 1831 when Darwin boarded the HMS *Beagle* as the ship's naturalist, he was a creationist. But during those years from 1831 to 1836 on the *Beagle*, Darwin read some persuasive ideas about the struggle for survival of organisms, collected scores of exotic specimens, and made numerous firsthand observations of strange and wonderfully diverse creatures. This reading included a two-volume work, *Principles of Geology*, by Charles Lyell, whose treatise studied not only inorganic change, but also organic change. Lyell discussed many topics, but perhaps the most influential on Darwin's thinking were his descriptions of the struggle for existence faced by all species because of changes in their physical environment. Lyell's words fired Darwin's imagination, and he became a zealous disciple of Lyell's views.

During the voyage, geology became Darwin's major concern, and he looked forward to arrival at the Galapagos Islands with great anticipation—not to study the flora and fauna, but to study the active volcanoes and tertiary rocks. But when Darwin arrived in the Galapagos in 1835 he was fascinated most by the extraordinary variety of life forms on the islands. From that time onward, geology took a second seat. By the time Darwin left the Galapagos, he felt certain that important secrets about life were hidden there; important secrets that "future comparison" might someday reveal (Green, 1958). Charles Darwin's explorations transformed him from a disbeliever in evolution to a man with a questioning and probing mind, a mind in search of explanations, a mind in disequilibrium.

Darwin apparently was converted to evolution shortly after his return to England in 1836 (Green, 1958). But his invention or construction of the conception of natural selection as its mechanism was to come still later, sometime between 1836 and 1838. You may recall from Chapter 1 that the key event in this story came in October 1838 when Darwin first read Thomas Malthus's *Essay on Population*. Darwin wrote, "I came to the conclusion that selection was the principle of change from the study of domesticated productions; and then reading Malthus, I saw at once how to apply this principle" (Green, 1958, pp.

247–248). Thus, the crucial idea had come to Darwin, the idea for which his mind had been well prepared. Again from Chapter 1 recall that this process of borrowing ideas from one area and applying them in a new area is called *abduction:* It is a key process in theoretical concept construction just as induction is a key process in descriptive concept construction. There can be no doubt that Darwin's explorations played a significant role in initiating his search for an explanation. The key idea or organizing pattern, as so often is the case throughout the history of science, came from an unexpected source. In this instance, it came from an essay on human population growth and survival. Evidently, Darwin conceived of selection as the agent of evolution, but it was not until he read Malthus that he discovered its application to the human population and then to all populations in nature—hence, *natural* selection. The panels of Figure 3.8 depict just two of the many *if . . . and . . . then . . . therefore* abductive-deductive thinking cycles that Darwin used to reject creationism and replace it with the conception of evolution through natural selection.

For the next four years Darwin turned to the enjoyable task of marshalling the evidence that favored his theory of evolution through natural selection. He turned to the facts known about plant and animal breeding, to the evidence that had first led him to doubt the fixity of species (namely, the facts about the geographic distribution of organic forms), and to the creatures of the Galapagos Islands. He discovered support for his ideas in the geological, anatomical, ecological, and embryological records of the time, and by 1842 he was ready to commit a rough draft of his entire theory to paper (Green, 1958).

The phases of equilibrium, disequilibrium, and back to equilibrium are clear in Darwin's thinking. Darwin's reading of Lyell and his voyage on the *Beagle* represents exploration that provided input that could not be assimilated into previous beliefs. This provoked disequilibrium. Darwin experienced a great deal during his explorations. He borrowed the idea of domesticated breeding, or artificial selection, and became convinced that it must also somehow apply to natural populations. This constitutes a portion of the accommodation phase in Darwin's thought. The idea was still only half-formed, however. The final piece of the puzzle was put into place when Darwin read Malthus. He again borrowed an idea: selection pressure created by an overproduction of consumers and a limited supply of resources. He was immediately able to use this new insight to organize practically all of his previous observations into one conceptual system—and equilibrium was once again achieved.

For the next four years Darwin discovered applications of his theory in every realm of the natural world. With each additional piece of evidence that he could include in his theory, his state of equilibrium grew. Equilibrium to disequilibrium and finally back to equilibrium—this was the course of Darwin's thought from 1831 to 1842. Because this process involved more than ten years of his life, it is small wonder that biology students who only read about the process of evolution and Darwin's theory of natural selection in the class

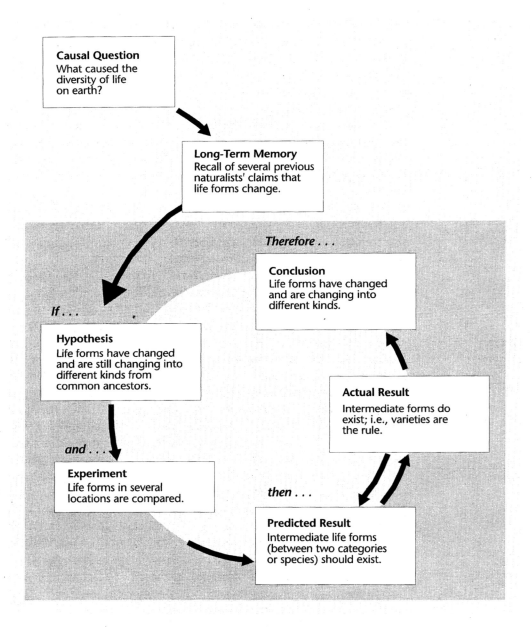

Causal Question
What caused the diversity of life on earth?

Long-Term Memory
Recall of several previous naturalists' claims that life forms change.

Therefore . . .

Conclusion
Life forms have changed and are changing into different kinds.

If . . .

Hypothesis
Life forms have changed and are still changing into different kinds from common ancestors.

Actual Result
Intermediate forms do exist; i.e., varieties are the rule.

and . . .

Experiment
Life forms in several locations are compared.

then . . .

Predicted Result
Intermediate life forms (between two categories or species) should exist.

Figure 3.8a ▾ **Darwin's Thinking Cycles?** These two abductive-deductive thinking cycles may have been used by Charles Darwin to reject creationism and replace it with his theory of evolution. Note that these thinking cycles are not directly initiated with observations but with a search through long-term memory for one or more alternative hypotheses. Thus, theoretical concept construction is hypothetical-deductive rather than inductive-deductive in nature.

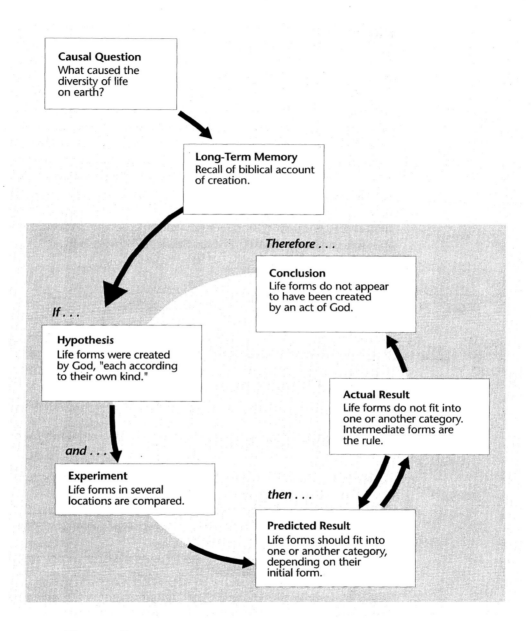

Figure 3.8b

textbook or listen to a lecture on the subject seldom develop anything more than the ability to recall a few isolated facts and half-formed ideas. What then is the answer to the question, How does one construct new theoretical concepts? The answer, of course, is through the processes of abduction and self-regulation.

In summary, the acquisition of declarative knowledge—whether the concepts to be constructed are basically descriptive or theoretical—involves self-regulation and the use of procedural knowledge and is very much a constructive process. Of course, students can memorize in a rote fashion aspects of declarative knowledge, but such learning by rote is seldom long-lasting, and it will not improve procedural knowledge. Consequently, the pedagogical task is to teach in such a way that students participate in the constructive process because doing so improves meaningfulness and retention of the declarative knowledge and increases consciousness and generalizability of the procedural knowledge (Hewson and Hewson, 1984; Posner, Strike, Hewson, and Gertzog, 1982).

▼ PRACTICE IN CLASSIFYING SCIENCE CONCEPTS

To allow you to apply your current understanding of the distinction between descriptive and theoretical concepts and empirical-inductive and hypothetical-deductive thinking patterns, classify the scientific terms in Table 3.1 (pages 98–99). To help you justify your classifications, a slightly edited version of the empirical-inductive and hypothetical-deductive thinking patterns presented earlier is included here.

The empirical-inductive thinking patterns most frequently involved in constructing meaning of scientific terms are:

EI1 understands terms defined with reference to familiar actions and examples that can be observed directly;

EI2 applies conservation reasoning to objects;

EI3 establishes one-to-one correspondences and arranges data in increasing or decreasing sequence; and

EI4 makes simple classifications and successfully relates systems to subsystems, classes to subclasses.

The hypothetical-deductive thinking patterns most frequently involved in constructing meaning of scientific terms are:

HD1 understands terms defined by relationships with hypothetical entities or conditions through abstract relationships such as ratios or mathematical limits;

HD2 imagines all possible combinations of conditions even though not all may be realized in nature;

HD3 identifies the effects of several variables by varying only one at a time;

HD4 recognizes and applies functional relationships, such as direct and inverse proportion; and

HD5 understands the nature of probability and recognizes its implications for experimental design and data analysis.

The differences between these thinking patterns might be summarized as follows: The empirical-inductive patterns apply simple operations to real objects and experiences, but not to hypothesized relationships, hypothesized objectives, or postulated properties. A concept thus can usually be considered descriptive if one can grasp its meaning through direct experience and the use of empirical-inductive thinking patterns. If a term derives its meaning principally from its position within a theoretical system and the use of hypothetical-deductive thinking patterns, then it has to be classified as theoretical. The answers for the first four terms are provided in the table to illustrate how you might refer to the above lists of thinking patterns when you give your reasons.

Questions for Reflection

1. When in your life have you experienced disequilibrium and successfully undergone self-regulation? Can you identify aspects of that experience that were important to your success? If so, what were they?
2. What sorts of things do you think teachers can do to help students successfully self-regulate?

Endnotes

1. Of course, as humans who construct mental representations of the "world out there," we have no way of even knowing if it actually exists. Whether the world out there is real makes no practical difference in behavioral terms. Successful behavior requires us to assume that it exists, even though that assumption may be wrong!

Table 3.1 ▾ **Terms and Thinking Patterns**

Term	Descriptive (D) or Theoretical (T)	Thinking Patterns
1. Succession	D	Defined descriptively through examples of changes in vegetation as a pond is filled with silt. Requires simple classification (EI4) and serial ordering (EI3).
	T	Defined by means of changes in environmental conditions that lead to successful competition of new species of plants with those established earlier under differing conditions (HD1, HD2).
2. Hardy–Weinberg Law	T	Requires thinking about hypothesized systems and entities (genes) (HD1), understanding of probability (HD5) and ability to generate all possible combinations of genotypes (HD2), and ability to apply quantitative proportional relationships (HD4). *Note:* There is an algorithm for solving genetics problems involving the Hardy–Weinberg Law that can lead to correct answers by use of empirical-inductive thinking patterns in extremely simple situations, but with little or no comprehension of the concept involved.
3. Pressure	D	Defined operationally through a barometer reading, with pressure differences defined by a manometer (EI1). Pressures can be compared (EI3).
	T	The usual definition—force per unit area—depends on the force concept (HD1) and on proportions (HD4). Pressure can be used to calculate gas volumes or forces exerted on container surfaces.
	T^+	Pressure is the time-average effect of molecular bombardment of the containing surface (HD1, HD5). This concept derives its meaning from the kinetic-molecular theory, a theoretical system in modern physics.

Table 3.1 ▾ **Terms and Thinking Patterns (continued)**

Term	Descriptive (D) or Theoretical (T)	Thinking Patterns
4. Shadow	D	Can be observed easily and is familiar (EI1). Correspondence of object shape and shadow shape can be established (EI3), as can qualitative size relationships.
	T	Ratio and proportions are used to describe size relations of obstacle and shadow in terms of light source, obstacle, and shadow positions (HD3, HD4).
	T⁺	The concept of shadow is qualified by the diffraction of light according to the wave theory (HD1). This concept's meaning is affected by the theoretical system of the electromagnetic theory of light. *Note:* Introduction of the quantum theory would escalate the conceptual level another step.
5. Digestion		
6. Meiosis		
7. Enzymatic action		
8. Population		
9. Temperature		
10. Acceleration		
11. Chemical equation		
12. Potential energy		

CHAPTER 4

STAGES IN THE DEVELOPMENT OF PROCEDURAL KNOWLEDGE

One of the first scientists to ask questions about the development of procedural knowledge was psychologist Jean Piaget. As a precocious teenager growing up in Switzerland in the early twentieth century, Piaget became deeply interested in the question of how thinking patterns develop. Piaget was influenced by

German philosopher Immanuel Kant, who viewed knowledge acquisition as a complex interaction between our sensory impressions of things and *a priori,* or rational, judgments that do not depend on experience. Although Piaget was sympathetic to many of Kant's views, he quickly became frustrated (to the point of a nervous breakdown) over philosophy's general disdain for empirical testing. To remedy this shortcoming, he embarked on a scientific research program to discover how humans acquire knowledge. He did so by actually studying children as they learn about their world. Hence, the fledgling field of genetic (developmental) epistemology acquired one of its most illustrious members.

The primary purpose of this chapter is to follow in Piaget's footsteps in an attempt to provide a scientific answer to the question, Through what steps, or stages, does procedural knowledge develop? The chapter will take a brief look at Piaget's stages of intellectual development, consider alternatives to his theory, and then closely examine the relationship between procedural and declarative knowledge. A knowledge of stages in the development of procedural knowledge will greatly assist us in selecting and sequencing subject matter to "fit" our students' intellectual capabilities.

▼ PIAGET'S THEORY

A great deal has been written about the development of procedural knowledge (generally referred to as *operative knowledge* by Piagetians) within the Piagetian tradition (e.g., Collea, Fuller, Karplus, Paldy, and Renner, 1975; Collette and Chiappetta, 1986; Inhelder and Piaget, 1958; Karplus et al., 1977). In Piaget's theory the child at birth is in a stage called *sensory-motor.* During this stage, which lasts for approximately 18 months, the child acquires such practical knowledge as the fact that objects continue to exist even when they are out of view (object permanence). The name of the second stage describes the characteristics of the child—*preoperational*—the stage of intellectual development before mental operations appear. In this stage, which persists until around 7 years of age, the child exhibits extreme egocentrism, centers his or her attention only on particular aspects of given objects, events, or situations and does not demonstrate conservation reasoning. In other words, the child's thinking is rigid. The major achievement during this stage is the acquisition of language.

At approximately 7 years of age, the thinking processes of children begin to "thaw out"; they show less rigidity. Piaget calls this stage *concrete operational,* because he believes it is marked by the development of concrete operations. I previously referred to this as the empirical-inductive level. Concrete operations are defined by Piaget as mentally internalized and reversible systems of thought based on manipulations of classes, relations, and quantities of objects. Concrete operational children can now perform what Piaget calls *mental experiments*; they can assimilate data from an experience and mentally arrange and rearrange them. In other words, concrete operational children have a much greater mobility of thought than preoperational children. The name of the concrete stage of development is representative of the type of thinking of this type of learner. As Piaget explains this stage, "The operations involved . . . are called 'concrete' because they relate directly to objects and not yet to verbally stated hypotheses" (Piaget and Inhelder, 1969, p. 100). In other words, the mental operations performed at this stage are "object bound"—operations are initiated by the observable but not by the nonobservable, the imagined, the possible.

The potential for the development of what Piaget calls *formal operational* thought develops between 11 and 15 years of age. For Piaget, the stage of formal operations constitutes the highest level in the development of thinking patterns. A person who has entered that stage of formal thought "is an individual who thinks beyond the present and forms theories about everything, delighting especially in considerations of that which is not" (Piaget, 1966, p. 148).

Presumably, nothing is genetically predetermined in this sequence of development. Rather, as Inhelder and Piaget state, "maturation of the nervous system can do no more than determine the totality of possibilities and impossibilities at a given stage. A particular social environment remains indispensable for the realization of these possibilities" (Inhelder and Piaget, 1958, p. 337). Piaget chose the name *formal operational* for his highest stage of thought because of his belief that the thinking patterns at this stage are isomorphic with rules of formal propositional logic (Piaget, 1957). This position is perhaps the most problematic in Piaget's theory. A long line of research indicates clearly that, although advances in reasoning performance do occur during adolescence, no one, even professional logicians, reasons with logical rules divorced from the subject matter (Griggs, 1983; Lehman, Lempert, and Nisbett, 1988; Nisbett, Fong, Lehman, and Cheng, 1987; Wason and Johnson-Laird, 1972). More will be said about this later. For this reason, we might prefer to abandon Piaget's terminology and adopt new terminology to refer to these differences in childlike and adultlike thought. As previously introduced, the terms *empirical-inductive* (EI) and *hypothetical-deductive* (HD) seem to better capture the key difference, which seems to be that children prefer to initiate reasoning inductively with observations. Children may raise questions and generate answers, yet they have no systematic means of asking themselves if their answers are correct. They must rely on others for this, so when left on their own they simply generate and primarily use ideas for better or for worse. Without such a reflective ability, children confronted with complex tasks simply choose the most obvious solution that pops into their heads and conclude that it is correct without consideration of alternatives and supporting or detracting arguments.

Kuhn, Amsel, and O'Loughlin (1988) reached a similar conclusion regarding the differences between childlike and adultlike thinking. They identified three key abilities that are acquired by some adults. First is the ability to think *about* a theory rather than thinking only with a theory. In other words, the reflective adult considers alternative theories and asks which is the most acceptable. On the other hand, the empirical-inductive thinker does not consider the relative merits and demerits of alternative theories or hypotheses; he or she merely has an explanation and behaves as though it were true. Chamberlain (1897) referred to these uncritically examined, but accepted, explanations as *ruling theories* (see Appendix B).

Second is the ability to consider the evidence to be evaluated as distinct from the theories themselves. For the child, evidence and theory are indistinguishable. In our experience, perhaps the most difficult distinctions to be made in the classroom are those among the words *hypothesis, prediction,* and *evidence* (Lawson, Lawson, and Lawson, 1984). Presumably this is the case because the words are essentially meaningless if one has never before tried to decide between two or from among three or more abductively generated alternative explanations in a hypothetical-deductive fashion and thus has never before considered the role played by predictions and evidence. The third key ability is that of setting aside one's own acceptance (or rejection) of a theory in order to evaluate it objectively in light of its predictions and the evidence.

▼ THE FOUR CARD TASK AND HYPOTHETICAL-DEDUCTIVE THOUGHT

Although Piaget's characterization of adolescent thought in terms of formal operations appears to be incorrect, his characterization of adolescent thought in terms of its hypothetical, as opposed to empirical, nature appears right on target. Consider Wason's well-known Four Card Puzzle (see Figure 4.1) as an example. The puzzle reads as follows:

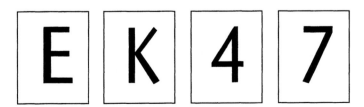

Figure 4.1 ▼ Wason's Four Card Puzzle

Four index cards lay on a table in front of you. You know that each card has a letter printed on one side and a number printed on the other. The cards show E, K, 4, and 7. You are now told this rule: "If a card has a vowel on one side, then it has an even number on the other side." Suppose you want to test this rule to see if it is correct or not correct for these four cards. Which card or cards must be turned over to test the rule?

Most high school students think that the E card and the 4 card must be turned over. They argue that if the E card is turned over, then it could have an odd number on the back and this would break the rule. Therefore, the E card must be checked. They argue that the 4 card should also be turned over because it should have a vowel on the other side, and so on. Of course, the K card is irrelevant because the rule is about vowels, not consonants. Likewise, the 7 card can be ignored for basically the same reason: The rule is about even numbers, not odd numbers.

Is this the way you thought through the puzzle? In point of fact the "correct" answer (based on rules of logic) is to turn over the E card (for the reason stated) and the 7 card. The latter card must be turned over because it may have a vowel on the other side, and vowels with odd numbers break the rule. Thus, both the E and 7 cards could break the rule, whereas no matter what is on the reverse of the K and 4 cards, the rule cannot be broken. When this explanation is given to hypothetical-deductive students, they immediately understand. Consequently, when given a transfer puzzle (e.g., if a card has a triangle on one side, then it has green dots on the other side), they know which cards to turn over (i.e., the triangle and red dots card). But when the explanation is given to the empirical-inductive students, even though they say that they understand, they do not. Consequently, when given the transfer puzzle they persist in turning over the wrong card—the green dots card instead of the red dots card (Lawson, 1987).

The key question then is, why are the hypothetical-deductive students able to understand the need to turn over the red dot card while the empirical-inductive students are not? Probably, the hypothetical-deductive students have previously acquired a general pattern of reasoning that the empirical-inductive students have not yet acquired. That pattern of reasoning begins with what "might be" possible rather than with what is observed. More specifically, there might be a triangle on the other side of the red dots card. If there is a triangle on the other side, then there should be green dots on this side. But there are red dots on this side. Therefore, the rule will have been broken. Compare this reasoning with that needed to select the triangle card: "There is a triangle on this card, so there should be a green dot on the other side. If not, the rule has been broken." The reasoning used to select the triangle card is initiated with the observation that there is a triangle on this card.

▼ **ALGEBRA AND HYPOTHETICAL-DEDUCTIVE THOUGHT**

Algebra is a subject that causes many junior high school and high school students difficulty primarily because of its hypothetical-deductive nature, while many students have not developed the necessary hypothetical-deductive thinking skills to allow its assimilation. The temptation of the empirical-inductive thinker when confronted with algebraic problems is to try to apply some rotely memorized algorithm. A common lament is "If I could only see the pattern. . . . Just tell me the steps. . . . Just show me how to do it so I can do that every time. . . ."

The difficulty, of course, stems from the empirical-inductive student's need to initiate thinking with the known, the observed, the real, and to follow a step-by-step algorithm. In algebra, however, thinking must instead be initiated with the unknown, the unobserved, the possible. Consequently, algebra does not allow for the simple algorithmic solutions to which many students have become accustomed. Consider, for example, the following problem from a typical eighth-grade prealgebra text:

▼ Jim has the exact change to pay for his lunch. He has 3 more nickels than quarters, and he has one dime. The total cost of lunch is $1.15. How many nickels does he have?

What must be done to solve the problem? The student must start by setting x, the unknown, equal to something. But how is a student to decide what x should be? Effective thinking would proceed more or less like this:

Well let's see. What could x be? We have three possibilities: We could make x equal to the number of quarters, the number of dimes, or the number of nickels. We are told that Jim has one dime. This is a "known," therefore, there is no need to set x equal to the number of dimes. That leaves x equal to either the number of quarters or the number of nickels. *If* we set x equal to the number of quarters, then the number of nickels is $x + 3$, because we are told that he has 3 more nickels than quarters. Similarly, if we set x equal to the number of nickels, then the number of quarters is $x - 3$. It really does not matter whether x is the number of quarters or the number of nickels. Either one will work. Therefore I will set up the problem like this:

$$x = \text{number of quarters}$$
$$x + 3 = \text{number of nickels}$$
$$1 = \text{number of dimes}$$

Therefore, $25¢(x) + (1)10¢ + (x + 3)5¢ = 115¢.$

To solve the problem, all I have to do now is multiply through according to the rules. Thus,

$$25x + 10 + 5x + 15 = 115$$
$$25x + 5x + 25 = 115$$
$$30x + 25 = 115$$
$$30x = 90$$
$$x = 3$$

So Jim must have 3 quarters, $3 + 3 = 6$ nickels, and 1 dime. To check, I will plug these numbers into the equation like this:

$$25¢(3) + (1)10¢ + (6)5¢ = 115¢$$
$$75¢ + 10¢ + 30¢ = 115¢$$
$$85¢ + 30¢ = 115¢$$
$$115¢ = 115¢$$ ▼

Notice the hypothetical-deductive thinking pattern that started from the very beginning with the unknown, not the known. To the empirical-inductive, intuitive thinker, starting with the unknown is a foreign idea. So, in a genuinely real sense, the problem is unsolvable for EI thinkers before they ever begin because they are initially at a loss to take this first step.

Consequently, initial encounters with algebraic problem solving create a good deal of disequilibrium among EI thinkers. However, if they listen to hypothetical-deductive explanations from their teachers and more reflective peers about how to set up and solve a variety of problems, and they try problem solving themselves, they may gradually "get the idea" and learn to reason in this way.

Unfortunately, if they do not "get the idea," they will most likely become academic casualties, which happens more often than necessary because few teachers understand why algebra is difficult, even though all teachers recognize that it is. Still fewer teachers know what to do to help the empirical-inductive student make the transition from memorization and an empirical-inductive mode of problem solving to understanding and the necessary hypothetical-deductive mode of problem solving.

▼

A NEW VIEW OF STAGE THEORY

Although Piaget's theoretical characterization of the thinking processes that dominate each stage has been found wanting, developmental stages are empirically real and in need of a new theoretical interpretation. I would like to suggest just such a new interpretation, one based on a look at how patterns of thinking are used across age. The basic premise is that deductive reasoning (at least in some form) is present virtually at birth, thus development does not amount to novel changes in this thinking pattern with age but instead involves novel changes to which that thinking pattern can be applied. In this sense, my view of development is opposite that of Piaget's. We will see how this might work.

Stage 1 (Birth to 18 Months)

Of course, children during the first 18 months of life are not able to generate verbal arguments of the *if . . . and . . . then* form. Nevertheless, experimental evidence suggests that their behavior follows this pattern. Consider, for example, Piaget's famous object permanence task in which an experimenter in full view of the infant hides a ball under one of two covers. Diamond (1990) has shown that infants as young as 5 months of age will reach under the cover for the hidden ball, indicating that they have retained a mental representation of the ball even though it is out of sight. Further, I would argue that such behavior indicates that the infant is thinking in the *if . . . and . . . then* form as follows:

>   *If . . .*   the ball is still where he or she put it (even though I can no longer see it)
>   *and . . .*   I reach under the cover where it was hidden
>   *then . . .*   I will find the ball.

In agreement with Meltzoff (1990), I would term the infant's representation of the ball an *empirical representation* because his or her representation is of an event that has been empirically experienced—that is, the infant actually saw the ball hidden under the cover. (See Figure 4.2.)

Stage 2 (18 Months to 7 Years)

Although infants younger than 18 months are able to solve a simple object permanence task, not until 18 months are they able to solve one in which they must represent what they have not actually experienced. Piaget (1954) invented a hiding task, which he called *serial invisible displacement* to tap this higher-order skill. In this task, the adult hides a ball in his or her hand in view of the infant and then moves the hand under a series of three occluders, dropping the ball under one of them. The infant is not given any indication that the ball has, in fact, been dropped off. Instead, the infant sees the hand emerge at the other side of the occluders. Consequently, the infant will look in the last place he or she saw the ball—the hand—and then must *deduce* that because the ball is not there, but must exist somewhere, it must be in one of the places the hand had traveled before the ball disappeared (see Figure 4.3).

The results of this experiment are that children younger than 18 months look in the hand and no further. They are stumped. However, children older

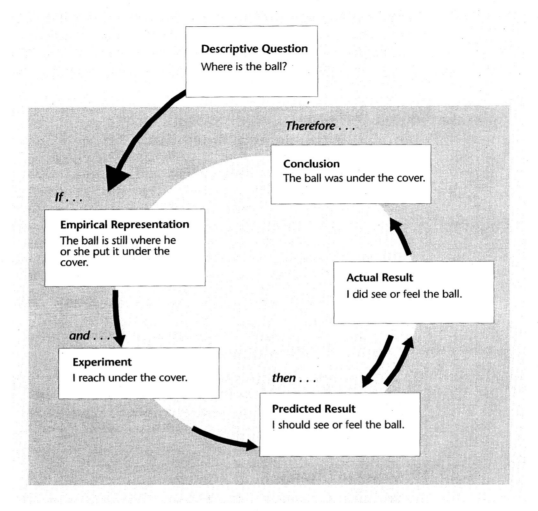

Figure 4.2 ▾ **Stage 1 Preverbal Deductive Thinking.** This *if . . . and . . . then* pattern is applied by children to the empirical representation of a ball that *was* hidden under a cover (birth to 18 months).

than 18 months are able to make the correct deduction and find the ball. Again, the thinking that leads to locating the ball successfully probably takes on the *if . . . and . . . then* deductive pattern:

> *If . . .* the ball is hidden behind one of the occluders
> *and . . .* I lift each in turn
> *then . . .* I will eventually find the ball.

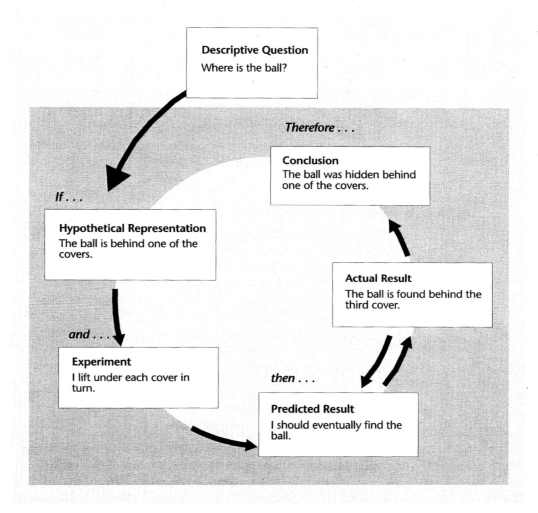

Figure 4.3 ▼ **Stage 2 Preverbal Deductive Thinking.** This *if . . . and . . . then* pattern is applied by children to the hypothetical representation of a ball that *may be* hidden behind one of several covers (18 months to 7 years).

Thus, what separates the first and second stage of development is not the *if . . . and . . . then* pattern of thinking, but the context in which the pattern can be applied. Notice that in this second, more difficult task the child must create and *initiate* thinking with a *hypothetical* rather than *empirical* mental representation. In other words, in this case the representation is of something that the infant has *not* experienced (the ball being dropped off behind one of the occluders). Rather, the infant must generate this hypothetical representation from the task conditions and then use it as his or her starting point for thinking (Meltzoff, 1990). In Meltzoff's words:

> *By 18 months of age there has been the growth of a kind of second-order representational system and a capacity for hypothetical representations. This enables the child to wonder "what if," to contemplate "as if," and to deduce "what must have been" in advance of, and often without, the perceptual evidence. (p. 22)*

Notice that language is not necessary in either type of argument, whether those of Stage 1, which involve empirical representations, or those of Stage 2, which involve hypothetical representations.

Stage 3 (7 Years to Early Adolescence)

During much of Stage 2, the child becomes quite proficient at using language to name and describe objects, events, and situations in his or her environment. The acquisition of language allows for the *if . . . and . . . then* pattern to be applied at a new level—naming, describing, and classifying.

In a recent study by Lawson (1991), the mellinark task and similar tasks were administered to children from 6 to 8 years of age. Carefully sequenced instruction was designed to teach the children how to use the correct pattern of thinking to discover the creatures' relevant attributes. As discussed previously, the pattern of thinking was deductive in nature—that is,

If . . . tiny spots are the key features that make a creature a mellinark

and . . . all of these creatures in Row 1 are mellinarks

then . . . they all should have tiny spots.

None of the thirty 6-year-olds in the Lawson study were able to generate or comprehend this pattern of thinking, whereas fifteen of the thirty 7-year-olds and almost all (twenty-nine of thirty) of the 8-year-olds were. Work reviewed by Dempster (1992) and Levine and Prueitt (1989) indicates that the younger childrens' failure is most likely related to relatively late maturation of the prefrontal cortex. Levine and Prueitt's work even presents a neural model of the shift.

My position is that Stage 3, which begins at age 7, involves use of the *if . . . and . . . then* pattern to name, describe, and classify the objects, events, and situations in the child's environment, all mediated by language. However, there is a distinct limitation to this type of reasoning. Notice that reasoning (like that in Stage 1) is initiated with what the child directly perceives in his or her environment; for example, the child is able to actually see the tiny spots on the creatures in the mellinark task (see Figure 4.4). In this sense, the representations the child uses to initiate thinking are empirical in origin and have been derived by induction, that is, the generalization of specific observations to general classes of objects, events, or situations.

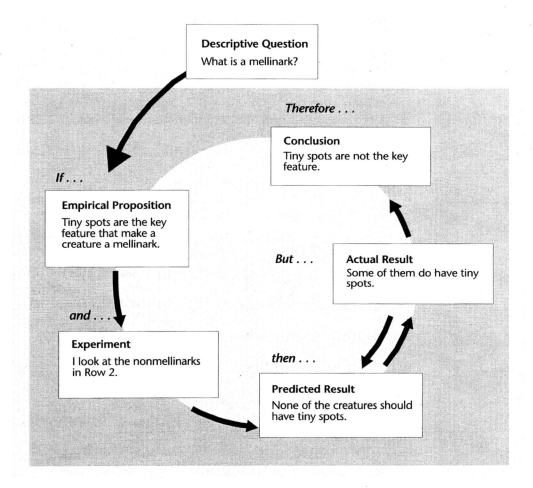

Figure 4.4 ▽ **Stage 3 Verbal Deductive Thinking.** This verbally mediated *if . . . and . . . then* pattern is applied by children to empirical propositions about the observable features of mellinarks and nonmellinarks of Rows 1 and 2 (7 years to early adolescence).

Stage 4 (Early Adolescence and Older)

At roughly 11 to 12 years of age some children become increasingly able to use language to apply the deductive pattern of thinking to "hypothetical" rather than empirical representations. *Hypothetical* here means much the same as when applied to Stage 2 reasoning. The key difference between Stages 4 and 2 is that Stage 4 reasoning is language-mediated, and Stage 2 is not.

Consider, for example, the question raised previously in Chapter 2: How are salmon able to locate successfully the streams of their birth before they spawn? The salmon will not tell us how they do it, and we cannot find out by merely watching the salmon as they head upstream, so answering a question of this sort requires that we generate and test alternative hypotheses about how the salmon *might* accomplish the task. Such a hypothesis-generation process requires the use of abduction, not induction. A relevant abductive-deductive argument would go as follows:

If . . .   salmon navigate by using their eyes
and . . .   we blindfold some of the returning salmon
then . . .   they should not be as successful at finding their home stream as those that are not blindfolded.

Notice again that the *if . . . and . . . then* pattern of the argument is the same as in the previous three stages. The key difference between this Stage 4 thinking and Stage 3 thinking is not the pattern, but what initiates the pattern. Stage 3 thinking is initiated by empirical representations, by induction (the direct perception of environmental stimuli such as that used for the mellinark task). Stage 4 thinking, on the other hand, is initiated by hypothetical representations, by abduction (the process of creating alternative hypotheses) (see Figure 4.5).

The importance of such a shift in thinking cannot be overemphasized. Whereas thinking at Stage 3 is primarily a response to environmental encounters (i.e., reactive), Stage 4 thinking is reflective, self-contained, and proactive. In this sense, it is the only stage that is truly scientific. The epistemology of the Stage 3 thinker is one of observation: What causes events? To find the answer, observe the events. The epistemology of the Stage 4 thinker is vastly different: What causes events? To find the answer, one must first mentally create several possible causes, deduce their implied consequences, and then observe the results of experimental manipulations to support or reject the possibilities. In this sense, Piaget was right in his claim that children's thinking begins with the real while adult thinking begins with the possible. The implication is that, as science teachers, a central challenge is helping students make such a shift in their thinking if they have not already done so.

THE RELATIONSHIP BETWEEN PROCEDURAL AND DECLARATIVE KNOWLEDGE: A CLOSER LOOK

One of the most frequently quoted statements from the field of educational psychology comes from David Ausubel and the opening of his textbook with Novak and Hanesian (1978): "If I had to reduce all of educational psychology to just one principle, it would say this: The most important single factor

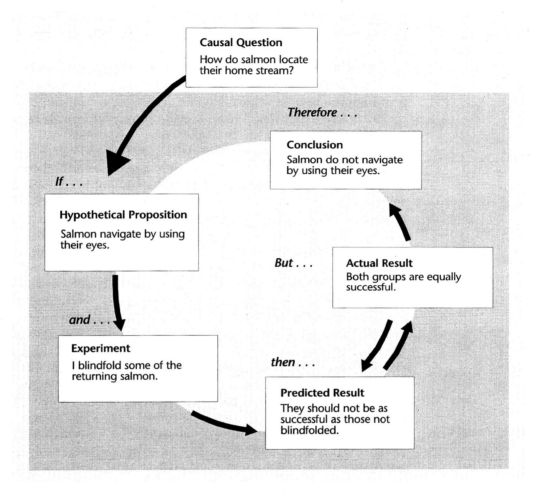

Figure 4.5 ▾ **Stage 4 Verbal Deductive Thinking.** This verbally mediated *if . . . and . . . then* pattern is applied by adolescents and adults to hypothetical propositions about nonobservable means of salmon navigation (early adolescence and older).

influencing learning is what the learner already knows. Ascertain this and teach him accordingly."

The statement can and has been interpreted to imply that the most important "thing" for a teacher to know about his or her students before instruction is what they already know about the subject to be taught. In other words, if you intend to teach about evolution, then you should ascertain the status of your students' prior declarative knowledge of evolution. However, according to Ausubel (1989), the word knows in the above quotation should not be interpreted so narrowly. Rather, it should be interpreted to include both declarative knowledge (e.g., specific knowledge about evolution) and procedural knowledge.

In Ausubel's words, procedural knowledge plays the more fundamental role: "It's involved in everything, while domain-specific declarative knowledge is of importance to new learning only in the specific domain of concern and then only when the prior domain-specific knowledge is made relevant via use of an advance organizer or some other conceptual bridge" (Ausubel, 1989).

Piaget has frequently said much the same thing. In Piaget's words, declarative knowledge structures "are the result of a *construction* and are not given in the objects, since they are dependent on action, not in the subject, since the subject must learn how to coordinate his actions" (Piaget, 1976, p. 13). "To know is to modify, to transform the object, and to understand the process of this transformation, and as a consequence to understand the way the object is constructed" (Piaget, 1964, p. 176). To be able to act, modify, and transform either physically or conceptually implies the presence of some procedural knowledge structures that guides those actions. Thus to *know* requires the presence of procedural knowledge (thinking skills). For example, when does someone "know" the concept of *number?* The developmental answer would be that she knows it when she conserves it—for example, when she recognizes that the number of checkers stays the same even though their arrangement may change. This implies the presence of the procedural operations of thinking back to the start—reversing the action of rearranging, of counting, of (not) adding to, of (not) taking away. Likewise, when does someone "know" a concept such as *ecosystem?* Again, the answer is that he "knows" it when he conserves it—that is, when he recognizes that an ecosystem transformed by being stripped of its first-, second-, and higher-order consumers is still an ecosystem. He recognizes the key property of ecosystems—their ability to recycle materials. Again, procedural operations are implied. As Piaget (1965, p. 2) has stated, "Every notion, whether it be scientific or merely a matter of common sense, presupposes a set of principles of conservation, either explicit or implicit." A person's operative structures (procedural knowledge) determine what can or cannot be meaningfully known (i.e., acted on either physically or mentally).

Suppose, for example, a biology teacher wishes to have students learn the principles of Mendelian genetics. As Walker, Mertens, and Hendrix (1979) correctly point out, understanding principles of genetics requires the use of hypothetical-deductive reasoning patterns. First, students must understand the nature of theoretical models and their relationship to empirical data. Second, the ability to create zygote possibilities given certain frequencies of genes is required. This involves combinatorial thinking. Third, the application of combinatorial thinking results in the generation of certain ratios of gene combinations that, in reality, represent general probability estimates that certain phenotypes will occur. Thus, hypothetical-deductive thinking, combinatorial thinking, and probabilistic thinking are involved in "understanding" and using Mendelian genetics.

This analysis suggests to the developmentalist that a topic such as genetics would present severe comprehension problems for students who have little or no facility with these aspects of reflective hypothetical-deductive thought. Such students, of course, may be quite capable of verbally parroting words and phrases—for example, *gene, dominant, recessive, crossing over*—but this verbal knowledge would be no part of their useful bag of knowledge. Presumably such ideas simply cannot be assimilated because the procedural patterns required for assimilation are either missing or poorly developed. This is why science educators, who have a developmental perspective on teaching, object to the introduction of theoretical concepts such as these to students who are not developmentally "ready" (e.g., Herron, 1978; Lawson and Karplus, 1977; Renner, 1976). Similarly, Inhelder and Piaget (1958) discussed the key distinction between Piaget's formal operational adolescent and his concrete operational child and the consequences for theoretical concept construction:

> *The adolescent differs from the child above all in that he thinks beyond the present. The adolescent is the individual who commits himself to possibilities—although we certainly do not mean to deny that his commitment begins in real-life situations. In other words, the adolescent is the individual who begins to build "systems" or "theories" in the largest sense of the term.*
>
> *The child does not build systems—the child has no powers of reflection—i.e., no second-order thoughts [that] deal critically with his own thinking. No theory can be built without such reflection. (pp. 339–340)*

In other words, it is the second-order reflective procedures of thinking that enable the adolescent to construct theories. It is not the construction of theories that enable the adolescent to develop procedures of critical and reflective thinking. Such a position implies that students who have not developed the hypothetical-deductive thinking skills discussed previously will not be able to comprehend theoretical concepts if they are taught in ways that do not encourage reflective thought—that is, by typical didactic lecture methods. This prediction was tested in high school biology, chemistry, and physics classes by Lawson and Renner (1975).

First, Lawson and Renner constructed final examinations in all three areas. The tests evaluated comprehension of the descriptive and theoretical concepts that had been introduced by the teachers during the year. The researchers then tested the students using a variety of tasks that required hypothetical-deductive thinking skills for success. Based on performance on the tasks, students were classified into developmental stages and substages ranging from early empirical-inductive to fully hypothetical-deductive thought (in Piagetian terms, from early concrete operational to fully formal operational). They were then administered the final exams in their respective disciplines.

Results of the study for the combined classes are shown in Figure 4.6. As predicted, the results showed that none of the EI-level students demonstrated any understanding of the theoretical concepts. This result provides clear support for the Ausubelian and Piagetian hypothesis that hypothetical-deductive thinking skill (a component of procedural knowledge) is necessary for the comprehension of theoretical concepts (a component of declarative knowledge). Notice also that hypothetical-deductive thinking skill seems to help in the comprehension of descriptive concepts. The teaching procedures used in the classrooms were largely expository, which meant that the students were seldom confronted with direct experience in the meaning of any of the terms introduced. Apparently, this procedure, in effect, rendered potentially understandable descriptive concepts meaningless, at least for the EI students.

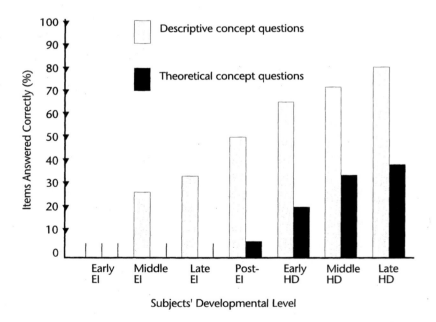

Figure 4.6 ▾ **Comprehension of High School Science.** The graph shows the relationship between the developmental level of a sample of high school science students and their comprehension of descriptive and theoretical science concepts. (After Lawson and Renner, 1975.)

A Return to the Mellinarks

An excellent example of the problems faced by EI students when finding out for themselves the defining attributes of a newly introduced term is provided by the following transcripted interview. Here one student, an empirical-inductive tenth grader, is trying to figure out what a mellinark is (see Figure 3.6 on page 88). Keep in mind that the mellinark concept is descriptive because its defining attributes are observable. Nevertheless, without the student having the ability to reflect on self-generated problem-solving strategies and evidence, even this concept becomes difficult to construct. The relevant part of the interview starts when the student is asked how to test an idea:

Interviewer: Suppose I define a mellinark as being a creature with a tail. How could I test to see if that idea is right or not? Is there any information here that would tell me if that idea is right or wrong?

Student: *You could, um . . . just look to see if the other creatures have the same tails . . . or, I mean . . . characteristics of the creatures . . . with the tails and the points and the dots and stuff to see if they are . . . all the same or close to . . . and then . . . I don't know.*

I: OK, let's look at the second row. We know that none of these are mellinarks. So what would you expect about these with regard to tails? I mean, if it's true that mellinarks are creatures with tails, then what would you expect to find in Row 2 with regard to tails?

S: *They would be some different kind of creature with tails . . . I don't know . . . they would just . . . they don't have the dots on 'em. And then . . . they are more . . . I don't know.*

I: OK. Let's go back. Once again, I'm going to say that mellinarks are creatures with tails and I look down here [Row 2] and I see that this nonmellinark has a tail. See that tail right there? . . .

S: *Yeah . . .*

I: And I know that that is not a mellinark. So I would conclude from that that my definition must be wrong.

S: *Yeah . . . well they could have classified 'em wrong. It could have been a mistake. These would have been up with the other mellinarks.*

I: Yes, that's a possibility. But let's assume that's not the case. Let's assume that they did it right. That is, let's take it as the truth that none of these in Row 2 are mellinarks. So, the other alternative is that I got my ideas wrong. Mellinarks aren't creatures with tails after all, or maybe they do have tails but there is something else in addition to tails that mellinarks have.

S: *OK.*

I: So let's look and see what else there might be. I see that these all have little dots. So maybe a mellinark is a creature with a tail and little dots. Does that seem like a good definition to you?

S: *I think then that Number 1, 2, 5, and 6 on the bottom would all be mellinarks.*

I: OK, they all fit the definition. But let's look at the second row and see if that tells us anything about whether I've got a good definition.

S: *Number 4 could be a mellinark depending upon it's own classification. And Number 6 because they both have tails and they have the dots . . . and Number 1 and 3 . . . they just don't seem to fit in like Number 4 at the bottom . . . but they still have the same tail. . . . I don't know.*

I: OK. But notice once again that we are told that Numbers 4 and 6 are not mellinarks. What does that tell me about my definition?

S: *That they probably interacted with some of the other creatures and they produced mellinarks that you guys didn't think were mellinarks.*

I: Might it tell me that my definition is wrong?

S: *No. . . . It wouldn't tell that I was wrong . . . that is . . . I would just say that . . . oh, yeah . . . they don't have the black solid dots . . . they are just different, I guess.*

The startling aspect of this response is the student's unwillingness or inability to consider that the initial idea might be wrong, even after repeated attempts to get him to do so. ("Might it tell me that my definition is wrong?" "No, . . . It wouldn't tell that I was wrong. . . .") Instead of recognizing, for example, that figures 4 and 6 in Row 2 contradict the statement that mellinarks are creatures defined by the presence of a tail and little dots, the student draws the conclusion that they are indeed mellinarks but that they were put in the wrong row! "They probably interacted with some of the other creatures and they produced mellinarks that you guys didn't think were mellinarks." Thus, instead of using the data to test one proposed definition, this empirical-inductive student modifies the data to be consistent with the definition. Actually, in his mind, the proposal definition is not really a proposal (in the sense of a statement put forth to be tested). Instead, it is a truth.

The second response is that of a transitional student also given the mellinark task. As can be seen, the transitional student has similar difficulties but is much more responsive to suggestions:

S: *To me this is mind-boggling. I don't relate much to this. I'll say Number 4 is a mellinark . . . Number 3 . . . Number 1 is not a mellinark. There is no rhyme or reason to this to me—absolutely none.*

I: Well, let's just take them one at a time. You said 4 is a mellinark.

S: *I guess because it compares to this [Number 4, Row 1]. And that's the only reason, the circle fits in the middle. And this [Number 3, Row 3] relates because it's a rounded figure . . . and some of these [Row 1] are, but some of these [Row 2] aren't. This [Number 1, Row 3] is more of a jagged effect, so I would say it's not a mellinark. These are more straight line. This has a tail on it. I can't even relate to that. I can't figure out what you are getting at, because you see some of both ideas in both of them. Because I can't reason on it, I don't like guessing either.*

I: Well, some people have looked at it this way. Say, for example, that all of these [Row 1] have tails. If a mellinark is a creature with a tail, then you would expect that none of them in Row 2 would have a tail, but some of them do. So the idea is that a mellinark is just a creature with a tail must be wrong.

S: *Uh huh.*

I: So there must be some other reason for being a mellinark.

S: *Yeah, that's what I was looking for—some similar point. If they were all more of a rounder effect, and they were more of a jagged effect or straight lines. But I could not see that—I could not see what you were getting at.*

I: Well, suppose you look for combinations of features. For example, these all have tails and a big dot.

S: *Well, that's true. Maybe the big dot plus a tail is what the mellinark is. Ah! Okay, that makes a little more sense.*

I: Okay, go with that idea for a minute. Does that pan out?

S: *Yeah, I think it does—you get your dot, tail and your mellinark . . . or your dots. Is that what you are saying? Your dots, with the big dot and with the tail. Because you don't see all three on any of these [Row 2] that I can see. Okay . . . so if you put all three combinations, then I would say 1, 2, and 6 [Row 3]. So you had to give me that idea, but after I looked I thought, ah! Heh! heh! heh! But I don't think I could sit here and figure that out. Okay.*

This response is instructive because it again reveals the essential limitation of the nonreflective thinker. In this case, she generated the idea that shape is important as she matched Numbers 4 and 3 in Row 3 with the mellinarks in Row 1, and she matched Number 1 in Row 3 with the first nonmellinark in Row 2. But her uneasiness is apparent—"I can't even relate to that. I can't figure out what you are getting at"—because she is clearly aware that not all the shapes in Row 1 are rounded and not all those in Row 2 are straight: "And this relates because it's a rounded figure . . . and some of these are, but some of these aren't." She still is unable to proceed. In other words, the uneasiness arises because her idea is not confirmed by the data. In fact, it is disconfirmed, and she lacks the reflective skills to know what to do next. Nevertheless, she is aware that something is wrong, but she cannot figure out what to do to correct it: "Because I can't reason on it, I don't like guessing either." She is in what Piaget has referred to as a *state of mental disequilibrium.* Of course, what she should do is reject her proposed definition and try another, but that is precisely the thinking skill (procedural knowledge) that appears to be lacking. Notice, however, that when presented with the correct reasoning pattern, she follows along easily. The problem is not one of comprehension, but one of generation: "But I don't think I could sit here and figure that out."

On the other hand, to the hypothetical-deductive student, generating and testing a definition that gets disconfirmed presents no real problem. The HD student simply generates another, and another, until he or she finds one that is not disconfirmed. Consider, for example, the following response of an HD student:

S: *Numbers 1, 2, and 6 are mellinarks.*

I: OK, how did you figure that out?

S: *Um. Well, the first thing I started looking for was just overall shape, whether it's straight, looks like a dumbbell, but this doesn't really work, because some of these [Row 2] are similar in overall body shape. So I ruled that out. Well, then I said, all of these are spotted [Row 1]. But some of these [Row 2] are spotted, and these aren't mellinarks, so that can't be the only thing. So I looked back at these [Row 1] and noticed that they all have a tail. But some of these have a tail [Row 2], so that can't be the only thing either. And so then I was sort of confused and had to look back. And think about what else it was. Then I saw the big dot. So all of these [Row 1] have all three things, but none of these [Row 2] have all three.*

Notice the pattern of reflective thinking employed. First, the idea that shape is a critical feature is inductively generated, tested, and rejected. The idea that the presence of spots is a critical feature is generated, tested, and rejected. Then she began to consider combinations of features and quickly arrived at a definition that is consistent with all of the data.

Thus, an essential problem of nonreflective empirical-inductive thinkers is that they are able to generate ideas inductively, but they neither seek nor recognize when data exist that disconfirm the ideas or how to proceed when those ideas are recognized as being disconfirmed. Instead of simply rejecting the proposed definition and generating another, they either reject the data or are left with the uneasy sense that all is not right, but without being able to proceed.

The educational implication is that instruction must be designed and implemented in such a way as to help students acquire skill in using the apparently necessary thinking skills. Of course, this does not imply that students who lack these thinking skills are unable to acquire descriptive concepts. The teacher can, for example, tell students that mellinarks are creatures that have one large spot and several small spots and a tail; he or she then can point out the relevant examples and nonexamples. The point is not that such students could not assimilate this instruction and acquire the concept, but that they are not likely to construct the concept on their own.

The issue of appropriate selection and sequence of concepts becomes extremely important. In general, descriptive concepts or descriptive manifestations of theoretical concepts should precede the introduction of theoretical concepts that place severe demands on students' thinking skills (see Chapter 8). The elementary school science program of the Science Curriculum Improvement Study (SCIS) is a good case in point. The early grades introduce the ideas of objects, property, serial order, habitat, and other similarly descriptive concepts. The middle elementary grades introduce more complex concepts such as system and subsystem, variable, food chain, and food web. Still later the concepts of energy source, energy receiver, energy chain, producer, consumer, and community are introduced. Finally, at the sixth-grade level, when some students are beginning to develop some expertise in hypothetical-deductive thought patterns, the more theoretical concepts of electricity, scientific theory, and ecosystem are introduced. The intent is to match the kind of tasks and concepts that students are asked to comprehend in class with the kind of tasks and concepts they are attempting to master in their spontaneous attempts to order and explain their out-of-school world.

A general principle of instruction then is that the demands that the subject matter places on students' reasoning must be analyzed. Only material that is "appropriate" to the developmental level of the learner should be introduced. But what does the term *appropriate* really mean? Surely, if the subject matter selected places no new demands on students' ability to think, then that subject matter would surely not facilitate thinking development. To the developmental science teacher, this result is untenable: One of the major objectives of education is to help students develop their ability to think. In this context, an "appropriate" selection of subject matter means choosing concepts and activities that will challenge but not overwhelm students' thinking skills.

According to the current thesis, thinking skills develop as the child or the adolescent engages in spontaneous attempts to bring coherence to his or her world by seeking answers to self-chosen questions, that is, through self-regulation. As Piaget (1974) put it,

> the child may on occasion be interested in seriating for the sake of seriating, in classifying for the sake of classifying, but, in general, it is when events or phenomena must be explained and goals attained through an organization of causes that operations will be used the most. (p. 17)

▼ HOW DOES HYPOTHETICAL-DEDUCTIVE THOUGHT DEVELOP?

Lawson, Lawson, and Lawson (1984) studied the individual's ability to reflect on the correctness of his or her abductively created hypotheses. They found that this ability results from the internalization of external argumentation patterns that occurs when others' alternative hypotheses are proposed and tested. This hypothesis appears to agree essentially with the earlier thinking of Piaget, who proposed that advanced reasoning developed as a consequence of "the shock of our thoughts coming into contact with others, which produces doubt and the desire to prove" (1928, p. 204). Piaget went on to state:

The social need to share the thought of others and to communicate our own with success is at the root of our need for verification. Proof is the outcome of argument. . . .

Argument is therefore, the backbone of verification. Logical reasoning is an argument [that] we have with ourselves, and [that] produces internally the features of a real argument. (p. 204)

Here we define hypothetical-deductive thought during adolescence as the internal ability to ask oneself questions, generate possible answers, deduce predictions based on those answers, and then sort through the available evidence to verify or reject those answers. Thus, the growing awareness of and ability to use such thought results from attempting to engage in arguments of the same sort with other people and listening to others' arguments in which alternative propositions (hypotheses) are put forward and accepted or rejected as the basis of evidence and reason as opposed to authority or emotion.

This position also seems consistent with that of Vygotsky (1962), who views speech as social in origin and who argues that only with time does it come to have self-directive properties that eventually result in internalized verbalized thought. This position is similar to that of Luria (1961), who holds that the progressive differentiation of language to regulate behavior occurs in four steps: (a) The child learns the meaning of words; (b) language then serves to activate behavior but without limiting it; (c) language then controls behavior by activating or inhibiting communication from an external source; and (d) internalized language then serves as a self-regulating function through instructions to oneself.

Even Piaget (1976) proposed a similar three-level theory of procedural knowledge development. The first level (sensory-motor) is one in which language plays little or no role because it has yet to be acquired. The child learns primarily through sensory-motor activity, and knowledge is action. The second level is characterized by the acquisition of language. The child is able to respond to spoken language and acquire knowledge transmitted from adults who speak the same language. To learn, the child is able to raise questions and have adults respond orally to those questions. Of course, this is not to say that all adult responses are understood; nonetheless, a new and powerful mode of learning is available to the child. The essential limitation of this level is that the use of language as a tool for reflection and as an internal guide to behavior is poorly developed. Thus, thinking at this level is essentially intuitive. The final level begins at the moment when individuals begin to ask questions of themselves. It is through the gradual "internalization" of elements of the language of argumentation that individuals acquire the ability to "talk" to themselves, which is the essence of reflective thought and which allows individuals to test internally alternative hypothetical statements and arrive at internally reasoned decisions to solve problems.

Voss, Greene, Post, and Penner (1983) have characterized advanced think-ing in the social sciences as largely a matter of constructing proposals for action that conform to many of rhetorical argumentation's classical principles. Like-wise, Lawson and Kral (1985) view the process of literary criticism as mainly a process of argumentation using these classical forms.

No distinct age norms are suggested for the passing from empirical-in-ductive thinking to the hypothetical-deductive level, yet there seems to be no biological or psychological reason why a child as young as 8 or 9 years old could not begin to internally reflect on his or her own thoughts given an environment in which such reflective behavior was strongly encouraged. Of course, this represents just a beginning, and one would still require considerably more time and experience to internalize the language of argumentation and develop the associated hypothesis-testing schemes. On the other hand, a dogmatic environ-ment in which the relative merits of ideas are not discussed and rules are strictly and unthinkingly enforced would most likely retard the development of skill in using hypothetical-deductive thought.

Given this view of the development of such thought, the childlike thinker is not conscious of the nature of his or her thought processes; rather, thinking is dominated by context-dependent cues and intuitions. The adultlike thinker, on the other hand, has become conscious of his or her thought patterns and has internalized powerful patterns of argumentation that allow a conscious reflection on the adequacy or inadequacy of alternative possibilities before action. Thus, adult thinking is not based on formal logic, as Piaget claimed, but on the creation of alternative ideas, predictions, evidence, and arguments, all mediated by language.

Argumentation is also likely to cause the initial development of empirical-inductive level thought. However, at this lower level the arguments are not about alternative explanations, but about accurate descriptions and classifica-tions. Consider, for example, the argument presented by Gesell (1940) that occurred between two children ages 4 and 5.

> **Four:** I know that Pontius Pilate is a tree.
>
> **Five:** No, Pontius Pilate is not a tree at all.
>
> **Four:** Yes, it was a tree, because it says: "He suffered under Pontius Pilate," so it must have been a tree.
>
> **Five:** No, I am sure Pontius Pilate was a person and not a tree.
>
> **Four:** I know he was a tree, because he suffered under a tree, a big tree.
>
> **Five:** No, he was a person, but he was a very pontius person. (p. 55)

Here the 4-year-old is attempting to form a descriptive concept of Pontius Pilate and mistakenly believes that the words refer to a tree—a big tree. The 5-year-old, however, provides contradictory feedback to the belief that causes the 4-year-old to rethink his position and eventually get it right. Here the belief testing takes place through dialogue. The belief testing of the reflective-thinking adolescent and adult, on the other hand, can be mediated internally as the reflective hypothetical-deductive thinker creates hypotheses and internally checks them for consistency with other known facts before drawing a conclusion.

Notice that the hypothetical-deductive thinker has "internalized" important patterns of argumentation that the empirical-inductive thinker has not. An important element in this internalization is a process Piaget (1976) has called *reflective abstraction*. Reflective abstraction involves the progression from spontaneous actions to the use of explicit, verbally mediated rules to guide behavior. Reflective abstraction occurs when students are prompted to reflect on their arguments and actions. This reflection is prompted by contradiction from the physical environment or verbally from other people. The result of reflective abstraction is that students gain accurate declarative knowledge and become more aware of and skilled in using the procedures of knowledge acquisition.

▼ DEVELOPING THE PROCEDURE OF CONTROLLED EXPERIMENTATION

To obtain a better understanding of how procedural knowledge at the hypothetical-deductive level develops, consider a specific procedure that is essential for accurately identifying causes of specific events: controlled experimentation. The argument is as follows: When the values of only one input variable vary (i.e., the values of all other input variables remain constant) and the values of the outcome variable (effect) vary, then one can conclude that a specific input variable is a cause of the observed effect. This form of argumentation is known as the *method of differences* (Freeley, 1976; Olsen, 1969; Shurter and Pierce, 1966). Thus, when one obtains a conscious awareness of this procedure, then he or she has developed a powerful mode of action and argumentation.

Researchers have found that young children have little difficulty in determining when a test is "fair" or "not fair" when the variables concerned are familiar (Wollman, 1977). However, they lack a general plan of attack or general strategy to use in setting up "fair comparisons" (i.e., controlled experiments) in unfamiliar situations. In other words, after a test has been performed, they may be able to state if it is fair or not fair (controlled or not controlled) if the variables are familiar; however, they are unable to use this idea as a general guide to behavior. What is lacking is a general verbal rule to serve as an anticipatory guide to behavior.

Ausubel (1964) suggests that it is on children's intuitive feeling of fairness that we can base environmental encounters that will transform their intuitive understanding into conscious, internally mediated verbal rules to guide behavior. A fair question to ask is, Where did this intuitive understanding come from? We have assumed that it is derived from situations in which children make comparisons and attempt to evaluate the validity of those comparisons. For example, suppose two children run a race. When the race is over and one child has lost, he blames the loss on the fact that he was wearing street shoes while his friend wore tennis shoes. He claims that the race was not really a fair test of who the fastest runner was. Other familiar examples would not be difficult to imagine. In other words, the intuitions come from argumentation about the truth or falsity of statements (e.g., "I can run faster than you can." "No, you can't, I can run faster than you"). The point is this: From environmental encounters such as these, children develop intuitive understanding of the procedures involving the control of variables and determining probabilities, proportions, and so forth. What remains is for these intuitions to be transformed into conscious verbal rules so that the child is able to use them as internally mediated problem-solving strategies.

With respect to the strategy of controlling variables, examine the manner in which the intuitions about fairness can be transformed to a conscious verbal rule to guide behavior. This discussion is based on an experiment (Lawson and Wollman, 1976) in which 9- and 13-year-old children, on the basis of initial testing, were unable to demonstrate the ability to control variables in any general sense. After four half-hour training sessions, these same children were clearly able to demonstrate skill in controlling variables systematically and, in most cases, unhesitatingly. Further, as evidence of general skill in using this procedure, their skill transferred to new tasks, both manipulative tasks and pencil-and-paper tasks.

Session 1

The first session began by briefly introducing the child to the intent and format of the training. He or she was told that several different kinds of materials would be used to try to teach him or her how to perform "fair tests." Coupled with the initial use of this term in the context of bouncing tennis balls, this instruction was done to provide an intuitive feel for what the training was all about—in a sense, to provide a "ballpark" in which to work. The materials used in this session were quite familiar to children: three tennis balls (two were relatively bouncy, and one was considerably less bouncy), two square pieces of cardboard, two square pieces of foam rubber, and a table. The child was told that the first problem was to find out which tennis ball was the bounciest. To do this, he or she would instruct the experimenter in how to perform the experiment, and the experimenter would carry out the instructions. Although each session varied somewhat, in general the child would begin by telling the experimenter to take two balls and drop them to see which bounced higher (height of bounce then became the dependent variable). The experimenter would then drop the two balls from different heights (an uncontrolled experiment). The child would respond by saying, "That isn't fair. Drop them from the same height." On the next trial the height would be equalized; however, one ball would be dropped so that it hit the table top while the other ball hit the floor (again, an uncontrolled experiment). This procedure was followed by continually trying to intervene with new uncontrolled variables (spin one ball, push one ball, let one ball hit cardboard or foam rubber). Children were then told that a test was called a "fair test" if all the things (variables) that might make a difference were the same in both balls (except, of course, for the difference in the balls themselves). Each time a test was made in which these variables were not the same was called an "unfair test." Following introduction of those more general statements and terms, several additional examples were given and talked through.

The overall intent of this first session was to allow the students to generate the procedures for testing and then provide contradictions that would force them to reflect on the inadequacies of their chosen procedure. The general verbal rule was also introduced in a context in which it was believed that they could gain initial understanding.

At the onset of the first session, virtually all of the children insisted that to determine which tennis ball was bouncier, the balls must be dropped from the same height and hit the same surface on the floor. In each instance they demonstrated an intuitive feeling that the tests were "not fair" and would respond by saying, "Drop them from the same height," "Make them both hit the floor," "Don't spin one," and so on. After the comparisons with the tennis balls were made, the children were able to accept or reject the tests as fair or unfair, but they were unable to state a general rule or procedure for performing fair tests before a test itself (i.e., to perform a fair test, keep all the factors equal except the one being tested). Not even the most articulate children were able to respond spontaneously by telling the experimenter to have "everything the same" for both balls. Even when they were asked to summarize their instructions without mentioning specific factors, they were initially at a loss for words.

Students had a feeling for evenness, fairness, and symmetry but not a general rule to act as a guide for behavior—that is, they lacked skill in using language to structure their thinking. This phenomenon is very much akin to the experience we all have had when we "know" something is true but just cannot seem to find the words to explain it. The extension of this intuitive understanding to the point where this intuition can be expressed clearly through the use of language and applied successfully to monitor internally one's thinking constitutes the essence of the "development" of procedural knowledge.

Session 2

The second session began by reminding the child of the intent of the training and by pointing out the new materials: six metal rods of varying size, shape, and composition (Inhelder and Piaget, 1958). These were placed on the table, and the child was asked to classify them in as many ways as possible. This was done to determine his or her skill in forming the classes of size, shape, and material and to ensure that these differences in the rods were noted. The rods were then placed into a stationary block of wood, and all of the factors (variables) that might affect the amount of rod bending (the dependent variable) were discussed. The child was then asked to perform "fair tests" to find out if the variables of rod length, thickness, shape, and composition, as well of the amount of weight hung on the ends of the rods, affect how much the rods will bend. Whenever the child performed a test, he or she was asked, "Is this a fair test? Why is it a fair test? Can you be sure that this rod bends more than that one *only* because it is thinner? Is there any other reason (an uncontrolled variable) why it might be bending more?" These questions and others were used to focus the child's attention on all the relevant variables and recognize unambiguous experiments in an attempt to lead him or her to understand the necessity for a procedure that keeps "all factors the same" except the one being tested to determine causal relationships. Several examples and counterexamples were discussed at length. The procedure of controlled experimentation involved in this session was, of course, identical to that of the first; the material (i.e., the context), however, was different.

Session 3

At the outset of the third session, the child was asked to experiment with an apparatus called a whirlybird (Science Curriculum Improvement Study, 1970b). The whirlybird consists of a base that holds a post, at the end of which an arm is attached. When pushed or propelled by a wound rubber band, the arm will spin around like the rotor on a helicopter. Metal weights can be placed at various positions along the arm. The child was briefly shown how the whirlybird worked and was given the task of finding out all of the things (variables) that he or she thought might make a difference in the number of times the arm would spin before it came to rest (the dependent variable). Possible variables included the number of times the rubber band was wound, the number of rubber bands, the number of weights placed on the arm, the position of the weights, how tightly the arm and post were fastened together, and the angle of the base. Following these explorations with the apparatus, the child was asked to perform "fair tests" to prove that the independent variables mentioned actually did make a difference in the number of times the arm would spin. Again, whenever a test was performed children were asked questions that forced them to reflect on their actions: "Is this a fair test? Why is it a fair test? Does it prove that it makes a difference? Why else might the arm spin more times?" (i.e., were all other independent variables held constant?).

The general intent of this session was similar to that of the second session and the fourth and final session. The strategies underlying the questions and materials were identical in all sessions. The symbolic notation (the language used) remained invariant, while transformations in imagery were gained by using materials extending from the familiar to the unfamiliar. Children were given a variety of tasks and were allowed to choose their own procedures for performing those tasks. When mistakes were made, the children were forced to reflect on their procedures and were challenged to correct them.

Session 4

In this session the use of physical materials as the source of activity and discussion was replaced by the use of written problems, which were considered to represent an additional step away from the concrete and toward the abstract level. Probing questions relative to children's understanding of the written situations were asked as in the previous sessions. In a sense, learning by doing was replaced by learning by discussion (language alone). The following two written problems were presented and discussed at length.

▼ **Written Problem 1**
Fifty pieces of various parts of plants were placed in each of five sealed jars of equal size under different conditions of color of light and temperature. At the start of the experiment each jar contained 250 units of carbon dioxide. The amount of carbon dioxide in each jar at the end of the experiment is shown in the table.

Which two jars would you select to make a fair comparison to find out if temperature makes a difference in the amount of carbon dioxide used? ▼

Experimental Conditions and Results

Jar	Plant Type	Plant Part	Color of Light	Temperature (°C)	CO_2*
1	Willow	Leaf	Blue	10	200
2	Maple	Leaf	Purple	23	50
3	Willow	Root	Red	18	300
4	Maple	Stem	Red	23	400
5	Willow	Leaf	Blue	23	150

*In cm in jars at the end of the experiment.

▼ **Written Problem 2**

An experimenter wanted to test the response of mealworms to light and moisture. To do this he set up four boxes as shown in the diagram. He used neon lamps for light and constantly watered pieces of paper in the boxes for moisture. In the center of each box he placed 20 mealworms. One day later he returned to count the number of mealworms that had crawled to the different ends of the boxes.

The diagrams show that mealworms *respond* to (that is, move toward or away from):

a. light but not moisture
b. moisture but not light
c. both light and moisture
d. neither light nor moisture.

Which of the above choices seems most reasonable? Please explain your choice.   ▼

The training sessions clearly resulted in students who indeed had a conscious awareness of the relevant rule. In short, they had internalized the meaning of the argument that, to identify a specific cause, it alone must be varied while other possible causes must be held constant. They also appeared capable of using this understanding.

We presumed (and the results supported this presumption) that for intuitions to manifest themselves in the form of useful linguistic rules (cognitive strategies or forms of argumentation), children need (a) a variety of problems requiring a specific procedure for solution, (b) contradictions to their proposed solutions that force them to attend more closely to what they are or are not doing, and (c) useful terms that remain invariant across transformations

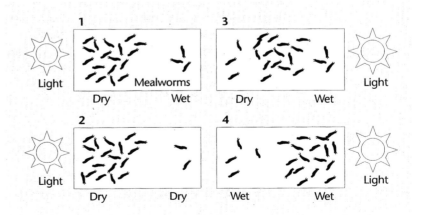

Mealworm Responses to Experimental Conditions

in images—in this instance, the key terms were *fair test* and *unfair test* and additional words that were used to define these terms. This is essentially the position taken by Bruner and Kenney (1970), who studied problem-solving procedures in mathematics. They designed instructional strategies to teach 8-year-old children the mathematical concepts of factoring, the distributive and commutative properties of addition and multiplication, and quadratic function. They summarized their instructional procedures in this way:

> *It begins with instrumental activity, a kind of definition of things by doing. Such operations become represented and summarized in the form of particular images. Finally, and with the help of symbolic notation that remains invariant across transformations in imagery, the learner comes to grasp the formal or abstract properties of the things he is dealing with. (p. 494)*

In other words, this learning begins with physical experience with objects. This experience provokes children with a task and provides them with a mental record of what has been done and seen. Contradictions produced by arguments with others or by the physical world forces a reflection back on the procedures, arguments, and evidence used to generate conclusions. By a closer inspection of the procedures—that is, by noting the differences between the procedures that produced good results and those that produced contradicted results—the child becomes more aware of what he or she should and should not do. The instruction of verbal rules (symbolic notation) also aids in the identification of current procedures in the experiences. Finally, additional experiences that require the same procedure are provided along with the repetition of the invented symbolic notation to allow the student to "reflectively abstract" the procedure from the particular situations. In effect, what is being abstracted is not the relevant properties of specific objects but the procedures and arguments for evaluating the relative truth or falsity of alternative possibilities.

One further point: The older students in the experiment were more successful then the younger students, and although it might be possible to train still younger students (third grade, for example), the task would be considerably more difficult. Several reasons could be suggested for this increased difficulty, not the least of which is that many of the children had seldom, if ever, engaged in external dialogues in which the relevant pattern of thinking and argumentation was used.

Questions for Reflection and Activities

1. Select an excerpt from a middle school or high school science textbook that you think is written entirely at the concrete (empirical-inductive) level. Explain why you made your selection.

2. Select another excerpt that is written entirely at the formal or hypothetical-deductive level. Explain why you made your selection.

3. What, if anything, could be done to make the formal excerpt in Question 2 understandable to empirical-inductive students?

4. Suppose that two nearly identical islands exist in the South Pacific. Approximately 100,000 people live on each island. Island A has remained completely isolated from the outside world and is controlled by an all-powerful king who dictates what people should believe and how they should act. Island B has actively traded goods with peoples of many cultures and belief systems for many years, and thus is knowledgeable of several of the world's often conflicting religious, political, and economic systems. On which island would you expect to find the greater percentage of hypothetical-deductive thinkers? Explain. What are the implications of your answer for the science classroom?

5. With a partner, select a few tasks that appear in Chapter 2, the Classroom Test of Scientific Reasoning (Appendix F), or both. Select two samples of students of various ages. Have your partner administer the tasks to one sample, while you administer the tasks to the other sample. Give the tasks to one student at a time so that they can explain their answers and thinking. Record student responses and classify the answers and explanations into developmental levels. Exchange the answers and explanations of your sample of students with those of your partner. Both you and your partner should now classify these responses. Compare your new classifications with those initially made by your partner. What is your percentage of agreement? Discuss the disagreements to see if you and your partner can reach agreement. On what percentage of responses are you unable to reach agreement? How could you modify your procedures to reduce this percentage in the future?

CHAPTER 5

THE LEARNING CYCLE

This book has argued that use of the constructive process of self-regulation results in the creation or change of declarative knowledge that resides in conceptual systems of various degrees of complexity and abstractness. It also has argued that conscious awareness of the procedures involved in the construction of such knowledge "develops" when *if . . . and . . . then* arguments with others occur that force an individual to reflect on the adequacy of his or her previous declarative knowledge. Conscious verbal rules to guide behavior in new situations develop from such encounters. Thus, development extends the range of effective thinking from familiar to novel situations. We now come to the central issue of this book. How can science instruction be designed and carried out to help students construct and retain useful concepts (declarative knowledge) *and* develop a conscious awareness of effective thinking skills (procedural knowledge) with general applicability?

▼ ESSENTIAL ELEMENTS OF SCIENCE INSTRUCTION

Previous chapters suggest that, when designing lessons to improve both conceptual knowledge and thinking skills, the following elements should be included:

1. Students should explore new phenomena in which they act based on previous beliefs (concepts and conceptual systems), or previous procedures (thinking skills), or both.

2. Those actions should lead to results that are ambiguous or that can be challenged or contradicted. Disequilibrium results, and questions are raised that provoke argumentation and thinking of the *if . . . and . . . then* form. Students then are forced to reflect on the previous beliefs or procedures used to generate the results.

3. Tentative answers or more effective procedures should then be invented by students or introduced by the teacher.

4. Tentative answers or the more effective procedures should now be used to generate new arguments, predictions, or data to allow either the change of old beliefs or the construction of a new belief (concept).

5. To allow the self-regulation to reestablish equilibrium, opportunities should be provided for students to test the extent to which new concepts or procedures can be applied in additional contexts.

Suppose, for example, that students in a biology class are asked to use their previous conceptual knowledge (beliefs) to predict the salinity in which brine shrimp eggs will hatch best; they also must design and conduct an experiment to test their prediction. If students work in teams of two to three, then approximately ten to fifteen sets of class data will be generated. These data can be displayed on the board. Because no specific procedures were given to the groups, the results will vary considerably. This variation in results then allows students to question one another about the procedures used to generate the results. It also provokes disequilibrium in some students because their results are contradictory to their expectations. A long list of differences in procedures can then be generated. For example:

- The hatching vials contained different amounts of water.
- Some vials were capped, others were not.

- The amounts of eggs varied from vial to vial and group to group.
- Some eggs were stirred, others were not.
- Some groups used distilled water, others tap water, salt water, and so on.

Once this list is generated, the students clearly see that these factors should not vary. A better procedure is thereby suggested—that is, a better way to think about the problem is introduced. All of the groups then will follow the same procedure and input variables will be controlled. When this is done, the effect of various concentrations of salt can be separated from the spurious effects of the other variables. Finally, once the new data are obtained, the results are clear and allow students to see whose predictions were and were not correct, and they allow the teacher to introduce the term *optimum range* for the discovered pattern of hatching. For some students, this will help to restore equilibrium; for other students, additional activities may be necessary.

▼ THE LEARNING CYCLE

Given the previously listed essential elements of instruction, which of the following procedures would you select as most effective in teaching about the metabolic activity of an animal such as the water flea of the *Daphnia* genus?

1. Provide the students with live *Daphnia,* thermometers, depression slides, and microscopes. Have the students count the number of heartbeats per minute of the *Daphnia* at three different temperatures: 5, 20, and 35 degrees Celsius (° C). Ask them to plot the number of heartbeats versus the temperature on a sheet of graph paper.

2. Provide the students with live *Daphnia,* thermometers, depression slides, and microscopes, and ask the students

    a. to find out if different temperatures influence the rate of heartbeat and

    b. to explain how variables could account for the differences observed.

3. Explain to the students that temperature has a general effect on the metabolism of invertebrates. Higher temperature means a higher rate, and lower temperature slows down metabolic activity. One rule states that metabolic rate doubles for every 10° C increase in temperature. A "coldblooded animal" such as *Daphnia* is directly influenced by environmental temperature. Now have your students go to the laboratory and use live *Daphnia* to verify that your explanation is correct.

4. Provide students with live *Daphnia,* a hot plate, dexedrin solution, a 5% solution of alcohol, a light source, rulers, thermometers, slides, pH

paper, balances, graph paper, microscopes, a stirring device, and ice cubes. Ask them

a. to investigate the influence of environmental changes on the *Daphnia* heartbeat and

b. to search for quantitative relationships among the variables.

Certainly the resources available to you and the preparation of your students will influence your choice. Compare your selection with the comments below.

1. This approach may be effective for students who are somewhat inexperienced in the process of scientific inquiry, because it is fairly directive. The approach does not spoil student motivation by telling them what they will discover. For more experienced students, however, it may be too directive by limiting the scope of inquiry into only one variable (temperature) and failing to justify the selection of three temperatures; that is, why are only three temperatures selected? And why select 5° C, 20° C, and 35° C?

2. This approach is much like the previous one because it focuses on the effect of a single variable although without specifying which temperatures to use. This increased nondirectiveness is a strength: It is more apt to cause students to think about what they are doing as it forces them to make their own decisions. If improved skill in thinking is a goal, then some nondirectiveness is essential.

3. This approach has little to recommend it because it tells the students what they will find. This has two extremely unfortunate consequences. First, it shifts the motivation for the activity away from the students satisfying their curiosity about nature to satisfying their teacher. Second, it shifts the source of authority about what is correct or incorrect from its natural place in data to an authority figure, namely, the teacher. Regrettably, this approach is too often taken by teachers. However, in science, mental constructions are tested in the empirical world, not in armchairs.

4. Clearly, this is the most nondirective, open-ended approach. It does what approaches 1 and 2 do and more so. For the inexperienced student, this nondirectiveness would be difficult without helpful procedure hints. If frustration is a problem, then these hints can be provided to small groups of students working together, or the entire class can be stopped to discuss ideas of ways to get started. For experienced students, this approach is highly recommended, because it allows for a variety of paths of investigation that allow considerable opportunity to think and make decisions about what to investigate and how best to investigate it.

The recommended approach in 4 and the somewhat more directive approaches in 1 and 2 are examples of exploratory activities on which later conceptual understandings can be built.

In fact, *exploration* is the first phase of the three-phase learning cycle. Initially, these three phases were termed *exploration, invention,* and *discovery* (Karplus and Thier, 1967). More recently, they have been labeled as *exploration, term introduction,* and *concept application* (Lawson, 1988). This book will use these more recent terms.

During exploration, students learn through their own actions and reactions in a new situation. They explore new materials and new ideas with minimal guidance. The new experience should raise questions or complexities that they cannot resolve with their accustomed ways of thinking. In this way, exploration provides the opportunity for students to voice potentially conflicting, or at least partially inadequate, ideas. This can spark debate and an analysis of the reasons for their ideas. That analysis can then lead to an explicit discussion of ways of testing alternative ideas through the generation of predictions. The gathering and analysis of results may then lead to a rejection of some ideas and the retention of others in the cyclic pattern of self-regulation. It also allows for a careful examination of the procedures used in this cyclic process. Exploration should also lead to the identification of a pattern of regularity in the phenomena (e.g., heart rate increases with temperature). Approaches 1 and 2 above are also considered explorations, although for many students they are not as likely to encourage reflective thought as approach 4.

Allowing for initial exploration allows students to begin to interact with the phenomena in a thoroughly personal way that can have a profound effect not only on their observational skills but also on their hypothesis creation and testing skills. In a series of very interesting studies, Wright (1988) examined the effect of intensive instruction on students' skill in making observations of discrepant events and generating and testing alternative hypotheses to explain them. After viewing a discrepant event, students were required to identify seventy-five potentially relevant details of the event and generate five acceptable hypotheses. This intensive exploration activity proved to be extremely effective: Students became much better at creating alternative hypotheses and designing experiments to test them. Wright's use of initial exploration and attention to detail hits at precisely the correct place to prompt the use and development of hypothetical-deductive thinking skills.

The second phase, *term introduction,* starts with the introduction of a new term or terms such as *metabolism, coldblooded,* and *poikilotherm,* which are used to refer to the patterns discovered during exploration. Such terms may be introduced by the teacher, the textbook, a film, or another medium. This step should always follow exploration and relate directly to the pattern discovered during the exploration activity. The lecture in approach 3 could be part of a term introduction session following laboratory activities such as in approach

4. Ideally, students should be encouraged to discover as much of a new pattern as possible before it is revealed to the class, but it would be unrealistic to expect students to discover all of the complex patterns of modern science.

In the last phase of the learning cycle, *concept application,* students apply the new term or thinking pattern to additional examples. After the introduction of coldbloodedness, for instance, concept application might be concerned with determination of the type of metabolism of other invertebrates or of vertebrates such as mice or humans.

The concept application phase is necessary for some students to extend the range of applicability of the new concept. Without a variety of applications, the concept's meaning may remain restricted to the examples used at the time it was initially defined and discussed. Many students may fail either to abstract it from its concrete examples or to generalize it to other situations. In addition, application activities aid students whose conceptual reorganization takes place more slowly than average students or who did not adequately relate the teacher's original explanation to their experiences.

Note that this phase is referred to as *concept application* while the previous phase was labeled *term introduction.* A *concept* has been defined as a mental pattern that is referred to by a verbal label (i.e., a *term*). Thus, a concept is the pattern plus the term. Teachers can introduce terms, but students must perceive the pattern themselves. Therefore, *term introduction* is a better label for the second phase than *concept introduction.* Exploration provides the opportunity for students to discover the pattern. Term introduction provides teachers with the opportunity to introduce the term and students with the opportunity to link the pattern with the term—that is, to construct the concept. Finally, concept application allows students to discover applications (and nonapplications) of the concept in new contexts.

Exploration, term introduction, and concept application often take on a spiral nature such as that shown in Figure 5.1. Exploratory sessions frequently require the application of previous concepts while creating a need for the introduction of the new terms. Term introduction sessions frequently lead to questions that are best answered by giving students opportunities to work on their own to discover applications of the new concept. Concept application activities can provide opportunities to use terms introduced earlier, and they can permit students to explore a new pattern.

The learning cycle is a flexible instructional model. Certainly for young children and for anyone who lacks direct physical experiences with a particular set of phenomena, the exploration phase should involve that direct physical experience. This, however, does not imply that all explorations have to be conducted this way. Indeed, I had the pleasure of taking a history of science course in graduate school taught using learning cycles where the explorations consisted of slide presentations, lectures, and discussions. The class explored various scientists' ideas and activities in this way and only later "invented" the

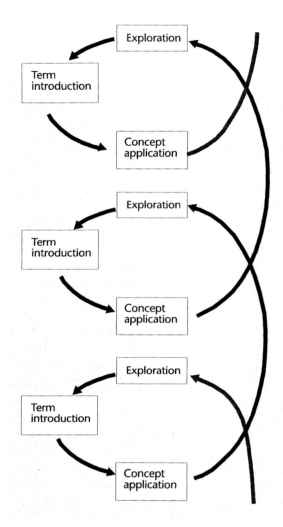

Figure 5.1 ▾ **The Spiral Curriculum.** Learning cycles consist of three phases called *exploration, term introduction,* and *concept application.* When learning cycles are used to create a curriculum, the curriculum takes on a spiral form because previously learned terms and concepts are often applied in subsequent learning cycles.

concept of science. More will be said about the use of different learning formats (e.g., lecture, laboratory, readings, discussions) in different phases of the learning cycle when research into the learning cycle is reviewed in Appendix D. The learning format of the three phases of the learning cycle can be changed, but one cannot change the sequence of the phases or delete any of them. If the sequence is changed or a phase is deleted, then a learning cycle no longer exists.

The main thesis here is that situations that allow students to examine the adequacy of previous beliefs (conceptions) force them to argue about and test those beliefs. This, in turn, can provoke disequilibrium when those beliefs are contradicted and provide the opportunity to construct more appropriate concepts and to become increasingly conscious of and skilled in using the procedures required for concept construction (i.e., thinking patterns and forms of argumentation). The central instructional principle is that correct use of the learning cycle accomplishes this end.

▼ THREE TYPES OF LEARNING CYCLES

Learning cycles can be classified as one of three types: descriptive, empirical-abductive, and hypothetical-deductive. The essential difference among the three is the degree to which students merely attempt to describe nature or explicitly generate and test alternative hypotheses.

The three types of learning cycles represent three points along a continuum from descriptive to experimental science. They place differing demands on student initiative, knowledge, and thinking skills. In terms of student thinking, descriptive learning cycles generally require only empirical-inductive patterns (e.g., seriation, classification, and conservation), while hypothetical-deductive learning cycles demand use of higher-order patterns (e.g., controlling variables, correlational thinking, and hypothetical-deductive thinking). Empirical-abductive learning cycles are intermediate and require empirical-inductive thinking patterns, and generally involve some higher-order patterns.

In descriptive learning cycles, students discover and describe an empirical pattern within a specific context (exploration). The teacher gives it a name (term introduction), and the pattern is then identified in additional contexts (concept application). This type of learning cycle is called *descriptive* because the students and teacher are describing what they observe without attempting to explain their observations. Descriptive learning cycles answer the question "What?" but do not raise the causal question "Why?"

In empirical-abductive learning cycles, students again discover and describe an empirical pattern in a specific context (exploration) but go further by creating possible causes of that pattern. This requires the use of abduction to transfer terms and concepts learned in other contexts to this new context (term introduction). The terms may be introduced by students, the teacher, or both. With the teacher's guidance, the students then sift through the data gathered during the exploration phase to see if the hypothesized causes are consistent with those data and other known phenomena (concept application). In other words, observations are made in a descriptive fashion, although this type of learning cycle goes further to create (through abduction) and initially test causes, hence the name *empirical-abductive*.

The third type of learning cycle, hypothetical-deductive, involves the statement of a causal question to which the students are asked to create alternative explanations. Student time is then devoted to deducing the logical consequences of these explanations and explicitly designing and conducting experiments to test them (exploration). The analysis of experimental results allows for some hypotheses to be rejected, some to be retained, and for terms to be introduced (term introduction). Finally, the relevant concepts and thinking patterns that are involved and discussed may be applied in other situations at a later time (concept application). This type of learning cycles requires the explicit creation and testing of alternative hypotheses through a comparison of logical deductions with empirical results, hence the name *hypothetical-deductive*.

The following steps are used in preparing and then implementing the three types of learning cycles:

1. Descriptive learning cycles
   a. The teacher identifies concept(s) to be taught.
   b. The teacher identifies some phenomenon that involves the pattern on which the concept is based.
   c. *Exploration phase:* The students explore the phenomenon and attempt to discover and describe the pattern.
   d. *Term introduction phase:* The students report their data, and they or their teacher describe the pattern; the teacher then introduces a term or terms to refer to the pattern.
   e. *Concept application phase:* Additional phenomena are discussed or explored that involve the same concept.

2. Empirical-abductive learning cycles
   a. The teacher identifies concept(s) to be taught.
   b. The teacher identifies some phenomenon that involves the pattern on which the concepts are based.
   c. *Exploration phase:* The teacher or students ask a descriptive and a causal question.
   d. Students gather data to answer the descriptive question.
   e. Data to answer the descriptive question are displayed on the board.

f. The descriptive question is answered, and the causal question is raised.

g. Alternative hypotheses are advanced to answer the causal question, and the already gathered data are examined to allow an initial test of the alternatives.

h. *Term introduction phase:* Terms are introduced that relate to the explored phenomenon and to the most likely hypothesized explanation.

i. *Concept application phase:* Additional phenomena are discussed or explored that involve the same concepts.

3. Hypothetical-deductive learning cycles

a. The teacher identifies concept(s) to be taught.

b. The teacher identifies some phenomenon that involves the pattern on which the concepts are based.

c. *Exploration phase:* The students explore a phenomenon that raises the causal question, or the teacher raises the casual question.

d. In a class discussion, hypotheses are advanced, and either students are told to work in groups to deduce implications and design experiments or this step is done in class discussion.

e. The students conduct the experiments.

f. *Term introduction phase:* Data are compared and analyzed, terms are introduced, and conclusions are drawn.

g. *Concept application phase:* Additional phenomena are discussed or explored that involve the same concepts.

Although steps for the development of learning cycles such as these can be suggested, keep in mind that developing good learning cycles is a difficult process. First, of course, is the development of a good idea and a plan of attack as outlined above. Then the plan must be tried out in the classroom. These initial trials will provide important feedback from the students as they work through the lesson. This feedback will lead to improvements in the lesson. Having another teacher in the classroom who can provide feedback is also a good idea. Unfortunately, a trial lesson may be ineffective and thus discarded. But if revisions can be made to make the lesson effective, then they should be included and the plan shared with colleagues. Feedback from their trials will further improve the learning cycle. In this way, a variety of new learning cycles will be developed. Students also can periodically provide important written feedback. After a series of learning cycles, they should be asked to report anonymously on which lessons they liked best and least and why.

Descriptive Learning Cycles

As stated earlier, the three types of learning cycles are not equally effective at generating disequilibrium, argumentation, and the use of thinking patterns to examine alternative conceptions or misconceptions. Basically, descriptive learning cycles are designed to have students observe a small part of the world, discover a pattern, name it, and look for the pattern elsewhere. Little or no disequilibrium may result, because students will most likely not have strong expectations of what will be found. Having students graph a frequency distribution of the length of a sample of seashells will allow introduction of the term *normal distribution* without provoking much argumentation among the students. A descriptive learning cycle into skull structure and function (Chapter 6) allows a teacher to introduce the terms *herbivore, omnivore,* and *carnivore.* It also allows for some student argumentation as they put forth and compare ideas about skull structure and possible diets. Yet seldom are possible cause-and-effect relationships hotly debated, and hard evidence is not sought. Nevertheless, the *if . . . and . . . then* thinking pattern may be used to construct meaning from inductively generated descriptive concepts or abductively generated theoretical concepts.

Empirical-Abductive Learning Cycles

On the other hand, consider the empirical-abductive learning cycle titled "What Causes the Breakdown of Dead Organisms?" that was designed to teach about the process of biological decomposition. During exploration, two questions are raised: (a) What factors affect the rate of breakdown of dead organisms? (b) What causes the breakdown? Students are then challenged to design experiments to answer the first question by testing the effects of a variety of variables such as temperature, amount of water, amount of light, and amount of chemicals such as salt, sugar, alcohol, and antiseptic. Following student experimentation, results are displayed on the board. The results generally reveal that increased temperature and increased amounts of water increase the rate of breakdown, while chemicals such as salt, sugar, and alcohol retard breakdown.

The students are then reminded of the second question: *What* causes the breakdown? Even though they have just observed the growth of large quantities and varieties of molds and bacteria, students invariably respond to this question by answering that heat and water caused the breakdown. "What do you suppose caused the terrible odor? What is that fuzzy black stuff all over the bread? *What* do you suspect the black stuff is doing?" Only after considerable prodding with such questions do one or more students propose that perhaps the molds and bacteria actually cause the breakdown. However, once this hypothesis has been proposed, data can be reexamined to see if they "fit." Because molds and bacteria are living things and all living things presumably require water and a proper temperature for survival, it makes sense that containers with no water or at freezing temperatures would show no breakdown: The growth of molds and bacteria would be slowed or stopped. Likewise, containers with excess chemicals such as salt and alcohol might kill the molds and bacteria. Hence, the data support the hypothesis, and the teacher can then introduce the term *biological decomposition* to label the process just discussed (term introduction). Other examples of biological decomposition or other learning cycles can now be started that allow the idea to be applied to other contexts (concept application).

Why is this learning cycle termed *empirical-abductive?* First, it should be clear that it begins with a look at the empirical world. Further, the students' empirical experiments are not designed with well-formulated hypotheses in mind. For example, they may have a hunch that increased temperature may increase the rate of breakdown, but this idea probably comes from past experience (such as with refrigeration) rather than from a hypothesis about biological decomposition. Second, when asked the question about the actual causes of the breakdown, the students are initially restricted to using *induction,* and they merely induce from their results that water and heat cause the breakdown when, in fact, the results only show a correlational relationship. To go beyond this restricted and incorrect view, students must be given hints and encouraged to think further about the problem until one of them "hits" on the hypothesis that the molds and bacteria are the actual causal agents. Because this "hitting" on the right idea involves abduction (i.e., the use of analogy to borrow ideas from past experience rather than direct observation), not induction, and because the process is necessary to arrive at the desired hypothesis of biological decomposition, we will use the term *empirical-abductive* to refer to learning cycles of this type. In short, any learning cycle that begins with a "What factors affect . . . ?" question and follows by creating a hypothetical cause is an empirical-abductive learning cycle.

Hypothetical-Deductive Learning Cycles

Like empirical-abductive learning cycles, hypothetical-deductive learning cycles require explanation of some phenomenon. This allows the possible creation of alternative conceptions and misconceptions with the resulting argumentation, disequilibrium, and analysis of data to resolve conflict. However, unlike empirical-abductive cycles, hypothetical-deductive cycles call for the creation and explicit testing of alternative hypotheses to explain a phenomenon. In brief, a causal question is raised, and students must propose alternative hypotheses. These, in turn, must be tested through the deduction of predicted consequences and experimentation. This places a heavy burden on student initiative and thinking skills.

Consider, for example, the hypothetical-deductive learning cycle "What Caused the Water to Rise?" described below (also see Chapter 6), which involves the concept of air pressure. Like empirical-abductive learning cycles, it requires students to do more than describe a phenomenon. An explanation is required. Explanation opens the door to many alternative hypotheses (some of which constitute scientific misconceptions). The resulting arguments and analysis of evidence represent a near-perfect example of how hypothetical-deductive learning cycles can be used to promote disequilibrium, the construction of conceptual knowledge, and the development of procedural knowledge.

What Caused the Water to Rise?

To start, students invert a cylinder over a candle burning in a pan of water. They observe that the flame soon goes out and water rises into the cylinder. Two causal questions are posed:

1. Why did the flame go out?
2. Why did the water rise?

Students typically explain that the flame used up the oxygen in the cylinder and left a partial vacuum that "sucked" water in from below. This explanation reveals two misconceptions:

1. Flames destroy matter, producing a partial vacuum.
2. Water rises because of a nonexistent force called *suction*.

Testing these ideas requires use of the hypothetical-deductive pattern of thinking and the isolation and control of variables (see Figure 5.2).

Rising Water in Plants

Consider the question of rising water in plants. Objects are attracted toward the center of the earth by a force called *gravity,* yet water rises in tall trees to the uppermost leaves to allow photosynthesis to take place. What causes the water to rise in spite of downward gravitational force? The following alternative hypotheses (alternative conceptions and misconceptions) are often proposed:

1. Water evaporates from the leaves to create a vacuum that sucks water up.
2. Roots squeeze to push water up through one-way valves in the stem tubes.
3. Capillary action pulls the water up like a paper towel soaks up water.
4. Osmosis pulls water up.

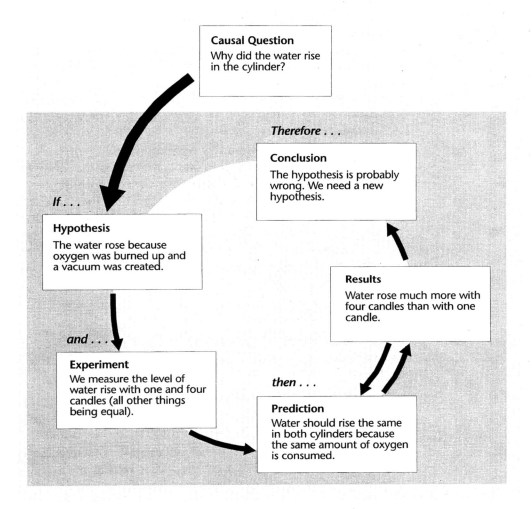

Figure 5.2 ▾ **The Hypothetical-Deductive Thinking Pattern.** The top box represents the key question raised, in this case, "Why did the water rise?" The subsequent hypotheses, experiments, predictions, results, and conclusions follow the hypothetical-deductive *if . . . and . . . then* pattern of thinking and require students to isolate and control independent variables in comparison of water rise with one and four candles. As shown, the initial hypothesis leads to a contradicted prediction and thus should be rejected (reasoning to a contradiction). Students must now create an alternative hypothesis or hypotheses and start over again until they have a hypothesis that is consistent with the data.

Of course, equipment limitations keep some ideas from being tested, but the "leaf evaporation" hypothesis can be tested by comparing water rise in plants with and without leaves. This requires the thinking patterns of isolation and control of variables. The "root squeeze" hypothesis can be tested by comparing water rise in plants with and without roots; the "one-way valve" hypothesis can be tested by comparing water rise in right-side-up and upside-down stems. The results allow students to reject some hypotheses and not others. The surviving hypotheses are considered "correct," for the time being at least, just as in "real" science—which, of course, is precisely what the students are doing. Following the experimentation, terms such as *transpiration* can be introduced and applied elsewhere as with all types of learning cycles (Chapter 6 has more details on this learning cycle).

The question of rising water in plants may reveal misconceptions, but few students would feel strongly committed to any one point of view because it is not likely to be tied to other points of view to which they have strong intellectual or emotional commitments. But consider the case of evolution and special creation. Here commitments often run deep, and thus a hypothetical-deductive learning cycle using the question "Where did present-day life forms come from?" can stir considerable controversy, argumentation, and hypothetical-deductive thought.

The Concept of Evolution

To teach the concept of evolution using a hypothetical-deductive learning cycle, we start again with alternative hypotheses or theories. At least three can be offered:

1. Present-day organisms were all created during a brief period of time by an act of special creation (i.e., by God). Further, organisms were created by God in virtually the same forms as we see them today.
2. Present-day organisms have spontaneously arisen from dead material throughout time. For example, dead, rotting meat will produce fly larvae. Old rags in damp places will produce baby rats.
3. Present-day organisms have gradually evolved from a few simple organisms over vast periods of time.

Students may propose other explanations, but these three should be mentioned. Notice that an interesting thing has happened: What represents the revealed truth for some people—namely, special creation—is treated not as truth, but as simply one of three alternative possibilities. The recognition that alternatives can exist, as opposed to revealed truths, represents a crucial step.

Once the theories have been proposed, they must be tested through prediction, data gathering, and analysis. The theory of spontaneous generation leads to replication or discussion of the classic experiments of Spallanzani, Needham, and Pasteur and to its ultimate rejection (see Chapter 1). The themes of special creation and evolution led to consideration of the processes of geologic sedimentation and fossil formation and to the fossil record. Clearly, the predicted fossil records for the two theories are quite different, even contradictory, in some respects. Special creation predicts a pattern of fossil remains with no fossils in the deepest, oldest sedimentary layers (before special creation) and all forms of simple and complex life in the layer immediately following creation, with the remaining layers up to the surface showing fewer and fewer life forms as some become extinct. Evolution also predicts no life in the deepest, oldest layers (before evolution began), but the next layers should contain very few and only the simplest life forms (e.g., single-cell bacteria, blue-green algae), with the progressively higher, younger layers showing gradually more complex, larger, and more varied life forms.

Students thus have opposing theories with dramatically different predictions. Which is correct? To find out, the students simulate a hike in the Grand Canyon and observe fossils found in six sedimentary layers from the canyon walls. The fossils reveal a pattern like that predicted by the evolution theory and clearly unlike that predicted by the special creation theory. Therefore, the students obtain evidence and arguments in favor of evolution. Subsequent activities allow the concept of evolution to be applied in other contexts. Most certainly one such activity would be a learning cycle into the concept of natural selection.

▼ LEARNING CYCLES AS DIFFERENT PHASES OF DOING SCIENCE

Figure 5.3 summarizes the major differences among the three types of learning cycles. Descriptive learning cycles start with explorations that tell us what happens under specific circumstances in specific contexts. They represent descriptive science. In the context of the candle-burning experiment, they allow us to answer questions such as "How high and how fast will the water rise under varying conditions?" But they stop before the question "What causes the water to rise?" is raised. Empirical-abductive learning cycles include the previous questions but go further and call for causal hypotheses. They include both the question and hypotheses boxes of Figure 5.3 and may use data gathered during the exploration phase initially to test the hypotheses. Hypothetical-deductive learning cycles generally start with a statement of the causal question and proceed to the creation of alternative hypotheses and their testing and thus represent the classical view of experimental science.

Clearly, the three types of learning cycles show some overlap because they represent various phases of the generally continuous and cyclic process of doing science. As is the case with any classification system, some learning cycles

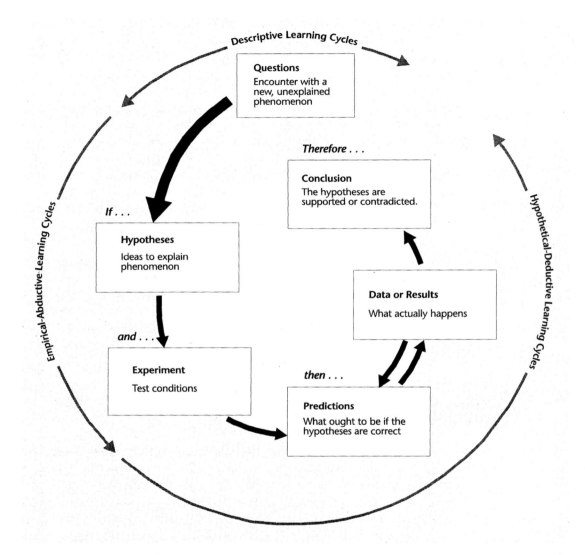

Figure 5.3 ▼ The Major Differences Among the Three Types of Learning Cycles. The primary difference among the three types of learning cycles is the extent of student involvement in describing natural phenomena (descriptive learning cycles) or generating and testing alternative hypotheses to explain natural phenomena. If the students generate but do not explicitly test alternative hypotheses, then the learning cycle is empirical-abductive. If students explicitly test the alternatives, then the learning cycle is hypothetical-deductive.

will be difficult to classify because they will have characteristics of more than one type of learning cycle. Nevertheless, the system should still prove helpful in both instruction and curriculum design.

▼ **A NOTE ON CREATIVITY**

Wallas (1926) described the following four stages of the creative process:

1. Preparation—the stage in which the problem is investigated in all directions.
2. Incubation—the stage of nonconscious thinking about the problem, or when an individual dismisses the problem from his or her conscious mind and attends to something else.
3. Illumination—the stage in which "the happy idea" spontaneously appears.
4. Verification—the stage of conscious and deliberate testing of the new idea.

Torrence (1967) defined creativity as the process of becoming sensitive to problems, deficiencies, gaps in knowledge, missing elements, and disharmonies; identifying the difficulty, searching for solutions, making guesses, or formulating hypotheses and possibly modifying and retesting them; and, finally, communicating the results.

The similarity of Wallas's and Torrence's descriptions of the process of creativity to my description of the constructive self-regulation process detailed earlier is remarkable. Presumably they are one and the same. If so, creativity can be enhanced by giving students the opportunity to use their own minds in answering questions through use of the learning cycle in the classroom. According to Torrence (1967):

Many complain that we do not yet know enough about the factors affecting creative growth. In my opinion, we have known enough about these factors since the time of Socrates and Plato to do a far better job of creative education than is commonly done. Socrates knew that it was important to ask provocative questions and to encourage natural ways of learning. He knew that it was not enough to ask questions that call only for the reproduction of what has been learned. He knew that thinking is a skill that is developed through practice and that it is important to ask questions that require the learner to do something with what he learns—to evaluate it, produce new ideas from it, and recombine it in new ways. (p. 85)

The acquisition of thinking skills, conceptual knowledge, and creativity thus can be fostered if students are given the opportunity through learning cycles to use the process to create and test their own ideas. However, the proper climate for this must be established and maintained. We must accept student ideas, becoming more interested in intellectual invention than in the rightness or wrongness of what is invented. We must cease to form judgments of students' inventions and instead let evidence itself be the judge. As Rogers (1954, p. 147) has pointed out, "When we cease to form judgments of the other individual from our own locus on evaluation, we are fostering creativity."

▼   A NOTE ON INTELLIGENCE AND ACHIEVEMENT

A considerable body of literature has addressed the nature and modifiability of intelligence (e.g., Herrnstein, Jensen, Baron, and Sternberg, 1987). The word *intelligence* is typically defined as the capacity for understanding, for solving problems, making reasonable decisions, and the like. Because these capacities depend on creative and critical thinking skills and an accurate and organized body of concepts, facts, and principles (i.e., both procedural knowledge and declarative knowledge), and because we have just detailed teaching procedures for improving students' thinking skills and conceptual knowledge, we have provided procedures for improving students' intelligence. This does not imply that all aspects of intelligence are modifiable and that all student differences in intellectual aptitude can be erased. Nevertheless, we have considerable reason to believe that past methods of schooling can be considerably improved and learning cycle instruction can indeed make students more intelligent. Further, these improvements in intelligence ought to be manifest in improvements in general academic achievement.

Consider the following test of intelligence and how performance on it might relate to the thinking skills introduced in Chapter 2. The task of the problem solver is to complete the matrix of small figures in the top box in Figure 5.4 by selecting the correct option from the eight options below it.

Before looking at the answer options, examine the left-hand column of the matrix. Notice that the bottom figure is simply a composite of the top and middle figures. Does this pattern also hold true for the second column? A quick inspection reveals that it does. Now examine the top row of the matrix. Notice that the right-hand figure is a combination of the left-hand and middle figures. Does this pattern hold true for the second row? Again, it does. The missing figure is most likely a combination of either the first two figures in the third column or a combination of the first two figures in the third row. Either combination will do and, in fact, both are the same. Thus, the correct answer is most certainly option 7. The thinking pattern just described has been called *additive superimposition* (following Hunt, 1974) because initial figures are mentally added by superimposing them to produce new figures.

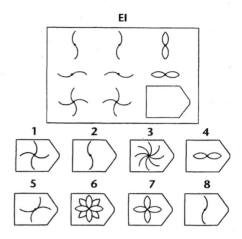

Figure 5.4 ▼ **Matrix Diagram 1**

Now consider Figure 5.5. Again the task of the problem solver is to select the correct option to complete the matrix. Will the superimposition pattern work again? Clearly not. The correct answer is option 5. But if additive superimposition will not work, then what pattern or patterns will? Certainly, the problem has more than one solution, yet consider this strategy: Notice that each figure consists of three parts, a base, a pair of sides, and a top. Consider

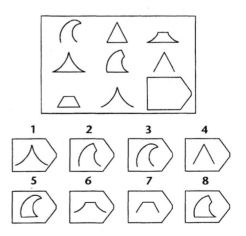

Figure 5.5 ▼ **Matrix Diagram 2**

the base: It varies in being either present or absent. When present, it is straight. Also in each complete row and column are two figures with bases and one without. If we extrapolate this pattern to the third row or the third column, which contain the missing figure, we can readily conclude that the missing figure must have a base. This follows, because the third row and column already contain one figure with a base and one without.

Now consider the sides. In each complete row and column the sides are of one of three types: (a) one convex and one concave, (b) both straight, or (c) both concave. Again, by extrapolating this pattern to the row and column with the missing figure, we can conclude that the missing figure must have one convex and one concave side. This follows because the figures present have either two straight sides or two concave sides.

All that we need to complete the figure is to select the correct top. In the complete rows and columns, the tops are either pointed or flat. In fact, each complete row and column has two pointed tops and one flat top. The row and column with the missing figures have one flat and one pointed top, so the missing figure must have a pointed top. The missing figure must be option 5.

Such a problem-solving procedure involves identifiable thinking patterns. First, clearly the individual figures must be divided into component parts—identification of the variables, as it were. Next, these variables must be separated and considered independently in a systematic search for the pattern followed by each. In short, the identification, separation, and systematic analysis of variables or features will lead to the correct solution. The previously used additive superimposition strategy, which is more perceptual and less analytical, will not work on this more complex problem.

The two problems in Figures 5.4 and 5.5 are part of a series of problems collectively known as the Raven Progressive Matrices Test. Raven, its designer, spoke of the test as a measure of a person's "innate educative ability" (Raven, 1940). Spearman himself considered it to be an appropriate measure of his own g or general intelligence factor (Spearman & Wynn-Jones, 1951). Other psychologists such as Jensen (1972), Vernon (1947), and Vincent (1952) considered the Raven test to be the best and purest measure of g available.

Psychometricians have used the Raven test to measure innate intelligence. For example, a sample of children at a specific age is tested, and the number of correct items each child selects is used to classify him or her as bright, average, or dull. A less complex, but similar, test is constructed for younger children and administered for the same purpose. More complex, but again similar, "advanced" tests are constructed and administered to find out whether older children or adults are bright, average, or dull.

But intelligence can be considered in another way. To the developmentalist, *intelligence* does not refer to some innate ability but to how far along an individual has progressed in the development of certain intellectual skills. Rather than constructing several tests of different complexity, the same test could be used at varying age levels. Administration of the test in this fashion would reveal that as children become older they become more "intelligent." The developmentalist's view of intelligence represents as much of a revolutionary shift in paradigm from that of the psychometrician as did the Copernican shift from a geocentric to a heliocentric solar system. Taking the developmentalist's view of intelligence to heart, the job of educators would be to provide instruction that optimizes the rate of growth in intelligence and to ensure that no student fails to complete the developmental process. More specifically, the job is to help students develop thinking skills such as those needed to solve Raven's Progressive Matrices items—that is, to become more intelligent. When intelligence is viewed in this way, considerable evidence indicates that use of the learning cycle helps students become more intelligent. Much of this evidence is reviewed in Appendix D.

These improvements in reasoning and intelligence might reasonably be expected to show up in improved academic achievement, and indeed this is the case, at least whenever measures of achievement require more than memorization. The Iowa Tests of Educational Development (Science Research Associates, 1970) appear to offer such a measure. According to test developers:

> *The student is required to show his ability to express himself clearly and correctly, to analyze critically materials of the type that educated adults encounter in their reading, and to deal with mathematical problems and concepts. The rote recall of isolated information, such as rules of grammar and dates of historical events, is given little or no emphasis. Rather, the student must interpret and analyze material that is new to him, and apply broad concepts and generalized skills to situations not previously encountered in the classroom, utilizing the working knowledge he has acquired in his studies and in daily life. (pp. 1–2)*

For some Iowa Test items, the overlap in thinking demands is fairly clear. For instance, one item on the reading test requires a student to read about some of Lavoisier's experiments and identify the specific hypothesis being tested, the controls used, and the conclusions drawn. The parallel with the thinking patterns involved in the identification and control of variables is clear. Also, several items on the mathematics test call for the application of proportional thinking, and most of the social studies items require the isolation of variables, a search for cause-and-effect relationships, and the documentation of hypotheses with evidence. For example, one items asks the students to identify the variables most influential in determining the nation's diet:

The diet of a nation is most influenced by:
(A) The race of the people
(B) Tradition, climate, and soil conditions
(C) The population and industrial level
(D) Biological preferences and certain foods

Another item asks students to link a hypothesis with supporting evidence:

Many of the nations that have come into existence since World War II have adopted a socialistic philosophy. This is evidenced by:
(A) Government ownership of major industries
(B) Restriction of emigration and immigration
(C) Existence of a single political party
(D) Imposition of high tariffs

These types of items do seem to require such aspects of hypothetical-deductive thinking as the isolation of variables and the gathering of evidence to support hypotheses. Consequently, high correlations between hypothetical-deductive thinking skills and achievement measured by these tests not only should be expected, but also have been found. For example, one study of ninth-grade students (Lawson, 1982) found high positive correlations between measures of hypothetical-deductive thinking skills and performance on the Iowa Tests for all measured areas of academic achievement: reading, language arts, mathematics, social studies, and science. But, of course, the establishment of a correlation does not necessarily imply a cause-and-effect relationship. This is the key question: If students are taught science using learning cycles for an extended period of time, in which reasoning patterns are improved, does this cause general improvement in academic achievement?

Several studies suggest that the answer is yes. In one key study, Renner, Stafford, Coffia, Kellogg, and Weber (1973) used the Stanford Achievement Test to compare two groups of fifth-grade students that were similar with the exception that one group had been taught science for five years using learning cycles and the other group had learned its science from a textbook. The two groups were tested in mathematics concepts, skills, and applications; word and paragraph meaning; and social studies skills and content. Analysis of the two groups' test scores showed that the learning cycle group outscored the textbook group on every subtest. A statistical comparison of the seven academic areas revealed significant differences between the two groups in mathematics applications, social studies skills, and paragraph meaning. On the other hand, no significant differences were found in mathematical computations and concepts, social studies content, and word meaning.

Of particular interest was Renner et al.'s observation of a thread of commonality where significant differences were found. In the case of mathematics applications, performance on the instrument was determined by ability to apply mathematical knowledge and to think mathematically in practical situations. The stated goal of the social studies skills test is testing "knowledge in action." The paragraph meaning test was said to measure students' ability to understand connected discourse involving varying levels of comprehension. The common thread is that each area requires a level of thought that transcends mere recognition and recall. Apparently, the children who had experience with the learning cycle lessons tended to use the high levels of thinking more effectively than those who had no such experience.

▼ **HISTORICAL PERSPECTIVE: ORIGINS OF THE LEARNING CYCLE**

All people are teachers during some period of their lives whether professional or otherwise. Everyone "knows" something about how to teach. The learning cycle is one method of teaching that purports to be consistent with the way people spontaneously construct knowledge; anyone who has reflected on how to teach effectively has no doubt discovered aspects of the learning cycle. For that reason, we cannot say who first invented the learning cycle as a method of instruction. Indeed, it has probably been invented many times by many teachers even well before Socrates employed his famous method to get his followers to reflect on the inadequacies of their own knowledge. On the other hand, it would be incorrect to conclude that recent theoretical and empirical work offers nothing new. The act of teaching involves procedures and the use of procedural knowledge, which develops not through the abrupt invention of new ideas, but through a gradually increasing awareness or consciousness of those procedures. In a real sense, recent work into inquiry methods of instruction represents not a novel departure from past practices, but a growing awareness of how we should teach and why we should teach in a particular way. Increased awareness should lead to a more consistent use of correct procedures and more effective learning.

The Origins of Inquiry-Oriented Instruction

Early approaches to science instruction in colleges and secondary schools alike consisted mainly of daily recitations from books and lectures. Use of the laboratory was unheard of before the mid-1800s. Physical materials and specimens, if used at all, were used to verify book or lecture information. But by the mid- to late 1800s, laboratory instruction became popular because firsthand observation and manipulation were thought to be useful in "disciplining" the mind.

The idea of mental discipline stemmed from the field of psychology and the then popular theory that (a) human mental behavior was compartmentalized into several "faculties" or abilities such as logic, memorization, and observation; (b) such mental behavior could be enhanced by "exercising" these faculties; and (c) these faculties, when developed, would function in all life situations. This faculty theory was used to justify the use of abstract, meaningless, laborious tasks during instruction to exercise and strengthen students' minds.

Largely through the research of psychologists such as E. L. Thorndike, faculty theory began to lose favor. Consequently, emphasis in schools shifted away from rote tasks and toward efforts to present meaningful information, develop positive attitudes and interests in science, and develop useful reasoning skills. By 1898, U.S. organizations such as the National Education Association were making such modern-sounding recommendations as "The high school work should confine itself to the elements of the subject . . . full illustration of principles, and methods of thought" (Hall and Committee, 1898).

The sentiment to teach students scientific principles, concepts, and thinking skills was even more apparent in the Central Association of Science and Mathematics Teachers' 1910 committee report on secondary education. The report identified the major problems of science teaching as motivation of students, selection of teaching materials, and teaching "the scientific spirit and method" (Galloway, 1910). The committee suggested the following:

1. More emphasis on "reasoning out" than on memorization.
2. More emphasis on developing a problem-raising and problem-solving attitude among students.
3. More applications of the subject matter to personal and social issues.
4. Less coverage of territory; the course should progress no faster than students can go with understanding.

Although teaching methods that emphasized memorization were strongly criticized, no detailed methods were advocated except to suggest that procedures that involved problems or projects offered promise for better class discussions, more active student participation, and more opportunity for "research type" learning.

John Dewey was a vocal advocate of science instruction that emphasized a method of inquiry. Addressing the National Education Association, Dewey (1916) argued that "science is primarily the method of intelligence at work in observation, in inquiry and experimental testing; that, fundamentally, what science means and stands for is simply the best ways yet found out by which human intelligence can do the work it should do, ways that are continuously improved by the very process of use."

But it would take more than forty years before this view of the nature of science would make its way into a large-scale science curriculum movement, or not until the National Science Foundation sponsored curriculum development projects in the late 1950s and early 1960s (see Hurd, 1961). Such inquiry-oriented projects as the Biological Sciences Curriculum Study (BSCS), the Chemical Education Materials Study (CHEM Study), the Science Curriculum Improvement Study (SCIS), the Elementary Science Study (ESS), the Physical

Science Study Committee (PSSC Physics), and the Earth Science Curriculum Project (ESCP) sprang up largely as a reaction to the Soviet Union's perceived superiority in science and mathematics education as evidenced by the successful 1958 launch of Sputnik into space.

Although several of these "alphabet soup projects," as they came to be called, developed excellent inquiry-oriented activities, most failed to generate and articulate a systematic method of instruction, with the notable exception of the SCIS program and its learning cycle method (see below). Most projects only alluded to "discovery," "inquiry," or "problem-solving" approaches, the steps of which were not always made clear to teachers and so sometimes were difficult to implement.

A survey of various teaching methods advocated in science methods textbooks, just before and during this curriculum movement, echoed the emphasis on inquiry. One textbook even included a method called the "learning cycle" (Heiss, Obourn, and Hoffman, 1950). According to the book's authors, their method is based on the sequence of events that Dewey identified in what he called a complete act of thought. The steps in this process were identified as:

1. Sensing the problem or question.
2. Analyzing the problem.
3. Collecting evidence.
4. Interpreting the evidence.
5. Drawing and applying conclusions.

The corresponding steps in the Heiss, Obourn, and Hoffman learning cycle were as follows.

1. Exploring the unit: using demonstrations to raise questions, proposal of hypotheses to answer those questions, and cooperative planning for testing.
2. Experience getting: testing hypotheses, collecting and interpreting data, and drawing conclusions.
3. Organization of learning: preparing outlines and summaries and taking tests.
4. Application of learning: applying new information, concepts, and skills to new situations.

The Heiss, Obourn, and Hoffman learning cycle most closely approximates a hypothetical-deductive learning cycle: It involves the generation of hypotheses and their testing through the deduction of their consequences. If Step 1 of the Heiss, Obourn, and Hoffman learning cycle can include student explorations that raise questions, if Step 3 can include the opportunity for teachers to introduce new terms to label novel aspects of the phenomena experienced by students in Steps 1 or 2, and if organization allows for additional activities to take place with the application phase, then we are probably discussing the same approach and methods.

One variation on this teaching approach has been called the *problem-solving approach* by authors such as Van Deventer (1958) and Anderson, DeVito, Dyris, Kellogg, Kochendorfer, and Weigand (1970). Washton (1967) lists the following sequence of student behaviors in the problem-solving method:

1. Students explore perplexing phenomena and are asked to state a problem or question.
2. Students are encouraged to propose and screen hypotheses.
3. Students design and conduct experiments to test hypotheses.
4. Students organize and analyze the data obtained.
5. Students are guided to formulate a conclusion or sometimes to suspend judgment.

Authors such as Kuslan and Stone (1968), Victor (1989), and Collette and Chiappetta (1986) also identify this approach, but refer to it as the "inquiry" approach. Carin and Sund (1980) refer to it as the "guided discovery" approach. None of these authors before Lawson, Abraham, and Renner (1989) have identified the other learning cycles, namely, the descriptive and empirical-abductive types.

Origins in the SCIS Program

Identification of the modern learning cycle and its three phases in the SCIS program can be traced to the early work of Robert Karplus at the University of California at Berkeley during the late 1950s and early 1960s (*SCIS Newsletter*, No. 1, 1964; Science Curriculum Improvement Study, 1973). To be more precise, its origin can be traced to a day in 1957 when a second-grade student invited her father, Professor Karplus, a physicist at Berkeley, to talk to her class about the family's Wimshurst machine, a device for generating electrical charges. Karplus found the visit enjoyable, and so did the children. The next few months brought other talks on electricity and magnetism to both elementary school and junior high school students. Soon Karplus turned his thoughts to the possibility of developing a program for elementary school science.

With a grant from the National Science Foundation, Karplus prepared and taught three units—"Coordinates," "Force," and "What Am I?"—during the 1959–60 school year. Although the experience proved interesting, analysis of the trial teaching revealed serious student misconceptions and other weaknesses. The experience prompted Karplus to raise a key question: "How can we create a learning experience that achieves a secure connection between the pupil's intuitive attitudes and the concepts of the modern scientific point of view?"

As he taught lessons in a first, second, and fourth grade twice a week during the spring of 1960, Karplus continued to familiarize himself with the points of view children take toward natural phenomena. He also began to develop tentative answers to his question. Following that experience, Karplus was helped by a visit to the research institute of Jean Piaget in Switzerland.

When Karplus returned to the United States in the fall of 1961, he returned to the elementary classroom with a plan to stress learning based on the pupils' own observations and experiences. However, he planned also to help them interpret their observations in a more analytical way than they would without special assistance. During part of that school year, J. Myron Atkin, then a professor of education at the University of Illinois, visited Berkeley to share his views on teaching with Karplus. Together they formulated a theory of *guided discovery* teaching that was implemented in subsequent trial lessons (Atkin and Karplus, 1962).

The Atkin and Karplus guided discovery approach was designed to be analogous to the way in which scientists of the past invented and used new concepts of nature. In their 1962 paper, they offered the example of the ancients' observations and interpretation of the motions of the sun and planets. The geocentric model of the solar system was taken to be a conceptual *invention* following initial observations. The heliocentric concept represents an alternative *invention*. With the help of these inventions, people attempted to *discover* phenomena other than those that led to the initial proposed inventions, phenomena that could be understood using the invention. When successful, these attempts led to reinforcement and refinement of the concept. If the attempts were unsuccessful, they revealed the concept's limits and sometimes led to its replacement. This is the pattern of exploration, invention, and discovery seen in the development of the modern conception of combustion as recounted in Chapter 1.

Atkin and Karplus clearly distinguished between the initial introduction of a new term (invention) and its subsequent verification or extension (discovery). Atkin and Karplus likened the process to the Copernican teacher who instructs students that the sun is at the center of the solar system while almost everyone else in society knows that the earth is at the center. Atkin and Karplus did not introduce the terms *exploration* or *learning cycle* in their 1962 paper, but the phases of invention and discovery were clearly evident in their discussion and example lessons.

During the summer of 1962, Karplus accepted an invitation to work with the Elementary Science Study of Educational Services Incorporated, where it became clear to him that children need time to *explore* an experimental system at their own pace with their own preconceptions. Only after this initial "exploration" is it wise to introduce a more analytical point of view. Armed with this new insight, Karplus tried out the modified approach the following school year in several public school classes near the SCIS's temporary headquarters at the University of Maryland. In 1967 Karplus and Herbert Thier first explicitly stated the three phases of the teaching approach. "The plan of a unit may be seen, therefore, to consist of this sequence: preliminary exploration, invention, and discovery" (Karplus and Thier, 1967, p. 40).

Origins in Biology Education

The learning cycle's origins also can be found in biology education. In 1953, the National Academy of Sciences convened a conference on biology education to examine past teaching practices and suggest alternative approaches. A resulting project was undertaken in the fall of 1956, funded by the National Science Foundation under the direction of Chester Lawson, a geneticist at Michigan State University. The project involved thirty high school and university biology teachers from throughout the country and resulted in a sourcebook of more than 150 laboratory and field activities that were appropriate for use in high school courses (Lawson and Paulson, 1958). Although no explicit statement of teaching method resulted from that work, it provoked Lawson and others to begin a search for such a method. The project also served as the precursor to the well-known Biological Science Curriculum Study (BSCS) project.

Like Karplus, Lawson turned his attention to the history of science for insight into the process of conceptual invention. His book *Language, Thought, and the Human Mind* carefully detailed the nature of scientific invention and identified a general pattern of thought that he referred to as "Belief–Expectation–Test" (Lawson, 1958). This pattern can now be seen to be similar to Karplus and Atkins's pattern of invention and discovery: Conceptual *invention* constitutes a *belief* that in turn leads to an *expectation* to be *tested* in the real world. If one *discovers* confirming evidence, then the invention is retained. If not, then it is rejected in favor of another belief. We saw this pattern of thought in Macbeth's attempt to test the existence of the dagger that appeared before him.

Following work on the biology sourcebook, Lawson carefully reviewed current psychological and neurological research in hopes of developing a comprehensive theory of human learning that would include a model of relevant neurological mechanisms and instructural implications. The theory that resulted from that work stipulated that learning involves (a) attention directed to some undifferentiated "whole," (b) the differentiation of the whole through the identification of its parts, (c) the invention of a pattern by which the parts are interrelated, (d) testing the invented pattern to see if it applies, and (e) use of the new pattern in other similar instances. Lawson's theory would not be published until 1967. His literature search, however, uncovered the Atkin and Karplus (1962) paper, on which he commented: "If we substitute the term 'initial unity' for system, 'differentiation' for the identification of objects within the system, 'pattern or relations' for invention, and 'reinforcement' for discovery, we can see the relation of this teaching approach to our theory of learning" (p. 119).

Obviously, the same pattern of instruction had been independently "invented" by Atkin and Karplus and Lawson. When Karplus, the physicist, needed a biologist to consult in the development of the life sciences portion of the SCIS program, he called Lawson.[1] What began for Lawson as a two-week consultation in the summer of 1965 ended with a ten-year job as director of the SCIS program's life science curriculum. The final product of the SCIS program in the mid-1970s was a kindergarten through sixth grade life science and physical science curriculum based on learning cycles.

Changes in Names: The Phases of the Learning Cycle

The term *learning cycle* does not appear in any of the SCIS program's early publications, although the phases of exploration, invention, and discovery are clearly spelled out (Karplus and Thier, 1967; Science Curriculum Improvement Study, 1973; Jacobson and Kondo, 1968). The term *learning cycle* first appears in the teacher's guides to the SCIS program units beginning around 1970 (e.g., Science Curriculum Improvement Study, 1970a).

The terms *learning cycle, exploration, invention,* and *discovery* continued to be used by Karplus and others through 1975 (e.g., Collea, Fuller, Karplus, Paldy, and Renner, 1975). However, in 1976 and 1977 it became apparent that many teachers were having a difficult time understanding what the terms *invention* and *discovery* were intended to mean in the context of classroom lessons. In a series of 1977 publications, Karplus thus referred to the phases as *exploration, concept introduction,* and *concept application* (e.g., Karplus et al., 1977).

Still other science educators have chosen to modify the terms further. The modified use here of the learning cycle phases as *exploration, term introduction,* and *concept application* is suggested primarily because the names of the phases are intended to convey meanings to teachers (not necessarily to students). Teachers can introduce terms during the second phase of the learning cycle, but they cannot introduce concepts. The concepts must be invented or constructed by students.

▼ THE LEARNING CYCLE IN THE BSCS PROGRAM

Tables 5.1 and 5.2 (pages 164–167) present adapted summaries that were initially created by BSCS of the instructional approach used in recent curricular materials. These are clearly learning cycle approaches, although BSCS divides the exploration phase into *engage* and *explore* stages. The term introduction phase is referred to as the *explain* stage, and the concept application phase as the *elaborate* stage. In addition to these three stages, BSCS includes another called *evaluate*—of course, students and teachers need to evaluate learning, so the addition of this stage is not unique. The only possible difference between the two approaches may come in the use of or need for a separate stage of engagement. Obviously, students must be engaged if learning is to take place. Good explorations can do this by stimulating questions and eliciting connections with past experience. Teacher comments to "set the stage" for the exploration phase, however, are usually a good idea. In short, Tables 5.1 and 5.2 do an excellent job of identifying just what teachers and students should and should not be doing during the different phases of instruction.

▼ THE LEARNING CYCLE IN DRIVER'S CONCEPTUAL CHANGE MODEL

Working primarily with elementary school students, Driver (1989) has conducted detailed investigation into the methods of instruction that can prompt students to explore their preconceptions and modify them in light of new experiences. She offers the model shown in Figure 5.6 as a general teaching sequence to provoke conceptual change. Her sequence and the learning cycle share many features. The phases of orientation, elicitation of ideas, restructuring of ideas, clarification and exchange, and exposure to conflict situations would all be considered as parts of the exploration phase of the learning cycle. Similarly, the construction of new ideas is akin to the learning cycle's term introduction phase. Lastly, Driver's evaluation, application of ideas, and review change in ideas phases are all normal components of the concept application phase of good learning cycles.

▼ KEY POSTULATES

The educational system should help students achieve the following goals:

1. construct sets of meaningful and useful concepts and conceptual systems;

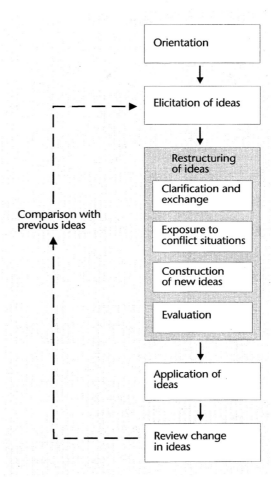

Figure 5.6 ▾ **Driver's General Teaching Sequence.**
The sequence is used to provoke conceptual changes.
From Rosalind Driver in *Adolescent Development in School
Science,* Philip Adey, ed., The Falmer Press, 1989, p. 88. Re-
printed by permission of the author and the publisher.

2. develop skill in using the thinking patterns essential for independent,
   creative, and critical thought; and
3. gain confidence in their ability to apply their knowledge to learn, solve
   problems, and make carefully reasoned decisions.

Table 5.1 ▼ The BSCS Instructional Model: Teacher's Role

Stage of the Instructional Model	Teacher Actions	
	Consistent with Model	*Inconsistent with Model*
Engage	• Creates interest • Generates curiosity • Raises questions • Elicits responses that uncover what the students know or think about the concept or topic	• Explains concepts • Provides definitions and answers • States conclusions • Provides closure • Lectures
Explore	• Encourages students to work together without direct instruction • Observes and listens to student interactions • Asks probing questions to redirect students' investigations when necessary • Provides time for students to puzzle through problems • Acts as consultant for students	• Provides answers • Tells or explains how to work through problems • Provides closure • Tells students that they are wrong • Gives information or facts that solve problems • Leads students step by step to a solution
Explain	• Encourages students to explain concepts and definitions in their own words • Asks for justification (evidence) and clarification from students • Formally provides definitions, explanations, and new labels • Uses students' previous experiences as basis for explaining concepts	• Accepts explanations that have no justification • Neglects to solicit students' explanations • Introduces unrelated concepts or skills

Adapted from *Science & Technology: Investigating Human Dimensions* by BSCS. Copyright 1992 by Biological Science Curriculum Studies. Reprinted with permission of Kendall/Hunt Publishing Company. Originally presented in Trowbridge, L. W., & Bybee, R. W. (1990). *Becoming a secondary school science teacher (fifth edition).* (pp. 320–321). Columbus, OH: Merrill Publishing Co.

Table 5.1 ▽ The BSCS Instructional Model: Teacher's Role (continued)

Stage of the Instructional Model	Teacher Actions	
	Consistent with Model	*Inconsistent with Model*
Elaborate	• Expects students to use formal labels, definitions, and explanations provided previously • Encourages students to apply or extend concepts and skills in new situations • Refers students to existing data and evidence and asks, "What do you already know? Why do you think?" (Exploration strategies apply here also.)	• Provides definitive answers • Tells students that they are wrong • Lectures • Leads students step by step to a solution • Explains how to work through problems
Evaluate	• Observes students as they apply new concepts and skills • Assesses students' knowledge and skills • Looks for evidence that students have changed their thinking or behaviors • Allows students to assess their own learning and group-process skills • Asks open-ended questions such as "Why do you think . . . ? What evidence do you have? What do you know about *x*? How would you explain *x*?"	• Tests vocabulary words, terms, and isolated facts • Introduces new ideas or concepts • Creates ambiguity • Promotes open-ended discussion unrelated to concepts or skills

Table 5.2 ▾ **The BSCS Instructional Model: Student's Role**

Stage of the Instructional Model	Student Actions	
	Consistent with Model	*Inconsistent with Model*
Engage	• Asks questions such as "Why did this happen? What do I already know about this? What can I find out about this?" • Shows interest in the topic	• Asks for the "right" answer • Offers the "right" answer • Insists on answers or explanations • Seeks one solution
Explore	• Thinks freely but within limits of the activity • Tests predictions and hypotheses • Forms new predictions and hypotheses • Tries alternatives and discusses them with others • Records observations and ideas • Suspends judgment	• Passive involvement: Lets others do thinking and exploring • Works quietly with little or no interaction with others (only appropriate when exploring ideas or feelings) • "Plays around" indiscriminately with no goal in mind • Stops with one solution
Explain	• Explains possible solutions or answers to others • Listens critically to others' explanations • Questions others' explanations • Listens to and tries to comprehend explanations offered by teacher • Refers to previous activities • Uses recorded observations in explanations	• Proposes explanations from "thin air" with no relationship to previous experiences • Brings up irrelevant experiences and examples • Accepts explanations without justification • Does not attend to other plausible explanations

Adapted from *Science & Technology: Investigating Human Dimensions* by BSCS. Copyright 1992 by Biological Science Curriculum Studies. Reprinted with permission of Kendall/Hunt Publishing Company. Originally presented in Trowbridge, L. W., & Bybee, R. W. (1990). *Becoming a secondary school science teacher (fifth edition).* (pp. 320–321). Columbus, OH: Merrill Publishing Co.

Table 5.2 ▼ The BSCS Instructional Model: Student's Role (continued)

Stage of the Instructional Model	Student Actions	
	Consistent with Model	*Inconsistent with Model*
Elaborate	• Applies new labels, definitions, explanations, and skills in new but similar situations • Uses previous information to ask questions, propose solutions, make decisions, and design experiments • Draws reasonable conclusions from evidence • Records observations and explanations • Checks for understanding among peers	• "Plays around" with no goal in mind • Ignores previous information or evidence • Draws conclusions from "thin air" • In discussion uses only labels provided by teacher
Evaluate	• Answers open-ended questions by using observations, evidence, and previously accepted explanations • Demonstrates understanding or knowledge of concept or skill • Evaluates his or her own progress and knowledge • Asks related questions that would encourage future investigations	• Draws conclusions without using evidence or previously accepted explanations • Offers only yes or no answers and memorized definitions or explanations as answers • Fails to express satisfactory explanations in his or her own words • Introduces new, irrelevant topics

The preceding pages have presented a theory of knowledge construction and a compatible instructional theory. That instructional theory argues that the most appropriate, perhaps the only, way to accomplish these objectives is to teach in a way that allows students to reveal their prior conceptions and test them in an atmosphere in which ideas are openly proposed, debated, and tested, with the means of testing becoming an explicit focus of classroom attention. Correct use of the learning cycle method allows this to happen. The theory of knowledge construction and its companion instructional theory can be summarized by the following postulates:

A Theory of Knowledge Construction

1. Children and adolescents personally construct beliefs about natural phenomena, some of which differ from currently accepted scientific theory.
2. Alternative beliefs (misconceptions) may be impediments to the construction of scientifically valid beliefs (scientific conceptions).
3. The replacement of alternative beliefs requires the individual to move through a phase in which a mismatch between the alternative belief and the scientific conception provokes a *cognitive conflict* or state of mental *disequilibrium* and the need for *self-regulation.*
4. The improvement of thinking skills (procedural knowledge) arises from situations in which persons state alternative beliefs and engage in verbal exchanges in which arguments are advanced and evidence is sought to resolve the contradiction. Such exchanges provoke people to examine the reasons for their beliefs.
5. Argumentation provides experiences from which particular forms of argumentation (i.e., patterns of thinking) may be internalized.

A Theory of Instruction

1. The learning cycle is a method of instruction that consists of three phases called *exploration, term introduction,* and *concept application.*
2. Use of the learning cycle provides students with the opportunity to reveal alternative beliefs and to argue and test them—that is, to self-regulate and construct more adequate conceptions and develop thinking patterns.
3. The three types of learning cycles—*descriptive, empirical-abductive,* and *hypothetical-deductive*—are not equally effective at provoking self-regulation and improved thinking skills.
4. The essential difference among the three types of learning cycles is the degree to which students either gather data in a purely descrip-

tive fashion or initially set out to explicitly test alternative beliefs (hypotheses).

5. Descriptive learning cycles are designed to have students observe a small part of the world, discover a pattern, name it, and seek the pattern elsewhere. Normally, only descriptive thinking skills are required.

6. Empirical-abductive learning cycles require students to describe and explain a phenomenon; the cycles thus allow for alternative conceptions, argumentation, self-regulation, and the development of higher-order thinking skills.

7. Hypothetical-deductive learning cycles require the immediate and explicit statement of alternative conceptions and hypotheses to explain a phenomenon, as well as higher-order thinking skills to test the alternatives.

▼ SELECTING APPROPRIATE EXPLORATIONS

Perhaps the most crucial aspect of learning cycle instruction is selecting the appropriate exploration activity. To provide a better sense of how this is done, alternatives from general science, biology, chemistry, and physics are provided. Assessments of the appropriateness of each alternative follow.

General Science

Suppose you are beginning your general science course's section on density. Which one of the following activities would you begin with?

1. Present a video in which 1–cubic decimeter blocks of various solid materials are carefully weighed and the volumes of 1-kilogram blocks of the same materials are calculated from the dimensions; in this way, two densities are determined for each material to be compared.

2. Arrange for a laboratory period in which students can use rulers, calipers, graduated cylinders, and balances to determine the volumes and masses of objects of widely differing shapes and various materials; the data will be used to plot a graph of volume versus mass.

3. Discuss students' experiences with floating and sinking objects, including their own bodies when they swim or play in water.

4. Explain with demonstrations how various specimens of material are weighed, how their volumes are found, and how to calculate the density of each material.

5. Arrange for a laboratory period during which pupils will accurately measure the densities of carefully machined blocks and rods of material whose volumes can be calculated easily from linear measurements.

Certainly, the resources available and the preparation of students will influence your choice. Compare the following comments with your own.

1. Videos are popular ways of introducing new topics. In this case, the video presents observations the students might make in the laboratory if they had access to the expensive materials. However, videos should be used after a laboratory period if a laboratory is available. Videos raise questions, provoke inquiry, or present contradictions less effectively than firsthand experiences. Because paying attention to the video preempts their initiative, few students watching a video for the first time would think critically about what they observe. Furthermore, seeing a picture of an object or process does not carry the impact of seeing the object or influencing the process oneself.

2. Such an approach is highly recommended. Students have considerable freedom to use their own judgment, try out their own ideas, and learn from their own mistakes as they gain practical experience with specimens and instruments that they will use later in defining density. A teacher can circulate among the students to diagnose student learning problems and identify their reasoning patterns.

3. Even though this approach involves students with their own experiences, the relationship between density and buoyancy is not so obvious that it will constitute a good exploration activity. Only after density has been defined can the concept be usefully applied in comparing solids and liquids.

4. This direct explanation would be inappropriate for introducing a new topic because it assumes that students have a good grasp of volume, mass, and the concept of ratio.

5. This type of laboratory makes it more difficult for students to ask their own questions and take responsibility for satisfying their own curiosity. The reasons for making careful observations and calculating the density at this time will not be clear to many students. Such a laboratory activity would be more appropriate later in the learning sequence, but even then it might focus more attention on some of the potential errors in measurement.

Biology

You are beginning your biology course's section on evolution. Rank the following ways to begin. Use 1 for most effective and 4 for least effective.

Rank

1. Show a video that traces the evolution of several modern organisms by reviewing fossil evidence, procedures of dating rock strata, and reconstructions of ancient forms of these organisms.

_____

2. Arrange for a trip to a museum where students are free to select exhibits that enable them to observe fossils of ancient organisms, follow the geologic history of the earth, look for relationships between climate changes and changes in populations or organisms, and trace the evolutionary lines of the horse, Darwin's finches, or the skeleton of vertebrates.

_____

3. Provide groups of students with chalk, meter sticks, and a list of important events in geologic and archeologic time as a challenge to construct a timeline that indicates the relative occurrence of these events.

_____

4. Present an explanation of how biotic potential, limiting factors, variation, heredity, and natural selection interact over enormous spans of time to result in the changes in organisms that we call evolution.

_____

5. Provide a laboratory in which students observe, draw, and classify—with the aid of a key—a variety of fossil specimens.

_____

6. Present an explanation concerning the five basic processes recognized by the modern synthetic theory of evolution (gene mutation, changes in chromosome number and structure, genetic recombination, natural selection, and reproductive isolation) and diagram how these interact to result in progressive change.

_____

Certainly the resources available and the preparation of students will influence your choice. Compare the following comments with your own.

1. Videos are popular ways of introducing new topics. In this case the video presents observations the students might make in a museum or laboratory if they had access to the necessary materials. However, videos should be used after a museum visit or work in the lab. Videos

raise questions, provoke inquiry, and present contradictions less effectively than do firsthand experiences. Because paying attention to the video preempts their initiative, few students watching a video for the first time would think critically about what they observe. Furthermore, seeing a picture of an object or process does not have the impact of seeing the object or influencing the process oneself.

2. The second approach is worthwhile as an introductory activity to the difficult topic of evolution. Students have considerable freedom to examine and compare past life forms according to their own interests and curiosity. Their experience and discussions with one another will lead them to ask how old life forms disappeared while newer ones took their place. Seeking answers to this question becomes the aim of the remainder of the course's section on evolution.

3. The third activity can be effective for getting students to appreciate the tremendous span of time in which natural selection operated. As described, the activity is open and allows students initiative, the possibility to make mistakes, and opportunities for self-regulation as they discover contradictions between their preconceived ideas and the lengths of timeline segments. Because of the narrower focus of this activity, it is not as good an introduction to the entire section as the second alternative.

4. The fourth, rather theoretical, approach would be highly inappropriate as the introduction of a new topic because it takes for granted that all students have a good grasp of the five rather difficult concepts.

5. Use of keys for classifying objects can be worthwhile for elementary school pupils because it involves class inclusion, a thinking pattern many children of this age find challenging. However, few older students would be challenged by this activity, and most would not reexamine their thinking patterns.

6. Even though the sixth approach, often taking the form of a lecture, provides a unified picture and appears efficient, it is too abstract for most students and does not provide them with any way to judge the validity of a statement.

Chemistry

You have been asked to develop a laboratory exercise on kinetics for beginning chemistry students. Rank the following procedures in terms of their effectiveness in encouraging student self-regulation; use 1 for most effective and 4 for least effective.

Rank

A. Provide the students with the materials and explicit instructions for an iodine clock reaction involving potassium iodate and potassium bisulfite. Require that they verify the relationship between reaction rate and the concentration of KlO_3.

_____

B. Provide the students with the materials for an iodine clock reaction. Supply a list of possible variables of the system—for example, concentration of KlO_3, concentration of $KHSO_3$, concentration of starch solution, and temperature. Supply a list of possible relationships between variables—for example, the rate is directly proportional to the concentration of any one of the reactants, and the rate is directly proportional to the temperature. Ask the students to identify the most accurate relationships between some of the variables.

_____

C. Provide the students with a variety of chemical systems that exhibit rate determining processes—for example, clock reactions, gas evolution reagents, and combustion reactions. Ask the students to investigate and identify common variables in these systems.

_____

D. Provide the students with materials for the $KHSO_3$–KlO_3 iodine clock reaction. Indicate that a relationship exists between the rate of the reaction and the concentration of KlO_3. Challenge the students to discover the relationship and then to use their data to predict the concentration of KlO_3 required for a 30-minute delay in the appearance of the color.

_____

According to the learning cycle, to induce self-regulation, an introductory period of exploration or openness in a laboratory exercise should be used. Hence, Procedures B and C are superior to A and D. Furthermore, C is more open and exploratory than B. Procedure C may encourage students to examine several aspects of a clock reaction that a teacher might not think important or interesting but which appear important to the students. It enables them to begin where they are in their understanding of chemical reactions and enlarge their concrete experiences with such systems without having the instructor impose his or her own reasoning on the activities. Hence, Procedure C is preferred.

Procedure B also provides considerable openness while directing the students toward variables determined by the instructor. A variant of this procedure would be a good application activity that focuses the activities of the students and makes their efforts more efficient in meeting any content goals. Predictions and expectations before the experiments can be exploited to produce contradictions in the thinking of the students and start them on self-regulation. Extreme cases not tested directly or concretely also can encourage self-regulation. Hence, Procedure D is favored over Procedure A, which has little to recommend it.

The social interactions that occur in the laboratory setting are important for starting self-regulation. Testing one's ideas against the ideas of peers is a profitable way to spend time during the laboratory period. Instructor–student dialogues can be extremely valuable when the instructor asks the student to justify his or her results. Helping students to become aware of their own thinking is a major function of the instructor who wishes to encourage students along the path of self-regulation. The common thinking tools of chemists—such as checking the dimensions or units of an answer, making an order-of-magnitude estimate, and seeing if the answer makes sense at the extreme values of the variables—are aspects of the self-regulation process that can be learned as part of laboratory activities.

Physics

You have been asked to develop a laboratory exercise on the pendulum for beginning physics students. Rank the following procedures for their usefulness in encouraging student self-regulation; use 1 for most effective and 4 for least effective.

Rank

A. Provide the students with a mass on a string. Indicate the variables of the system and suggest that they verify the square-root relationship between the length of the string and the period of oscillation.

_____

B. Provide the students with a mass on a string. Supply a list of possible system variables—for example, angle of swing, mass, length of string, acceleration of gravity, and the period of oscillation. Supply a list of possible relationships between variables—for example, the period oscillation is directly proportional to the mass, and the period is directly proportional to the length of string. Ask the students to identify the relationship(s) that fit the data best.

_____

C. Provide the students with a variety of periodic systems—for example, a cork floating on water, a baseball bat swinging by a hole in its handle, a clock pendulum, a mass on a string, and a uniform metal rod with pivot holes in it. Ask the students to identify system variables and to search for quantitative relationships among variables.

_____

D. Provide the students with a mass on a string. Indicate that for small angles of oscillation a relationship can be found between the length of the string and the period of oscillation. Challenge them to discover the relationship based on their data and then compute the length of string required for a 10-second period.

_____

Procedure C may encourage students to examine several aspects of a swinging object that a teacher might not think important or interesting, but that students may think important. The procedure enables students to begin where they are in their understanding of periodic motion and enlarge their experiences with such systems without having the instructor impose his or her own reasoning on their activities. Hence, C is the preferred procedure.

Procedure B also provides a lot of openness while directing the students toward variables determined by the instructor. A variant of this procedure would be a good application activity because it focuses the students' activities and makes their efforts more efficient when content goals are important. Predictions and expectations before the experiments described in Procedure D can be exploited to produce contradictions in students' thinking and start them on self-regulation. Hence, Procedure D is favored over Procedure A. Quite obviously, Procedure A has little to recommend it because the students are told how the experiment is supposed to turn out before they perform it.

Questions for Reflection and Activities

1. Select a concept or a set of closely related concepts that you expect to teach. Design an exploration activity that is suitable for teaching the concept or concepts. Design a term introduction activity that will follow the exploration. Also list concept application activities to follow.

Endnotes

1. Karplus became aware of Lawson's work through Jack Fishleder, who was on the SCIS staff in 1965 and had been a contributing author to the 1958 Lawson-directed project.

CHAPTER 6

CHARACTERISTICS OF EFFECTIVE SCIENCE INSTRUCTION

The primary purpose of this chapter is to identify and discuss specific characteristics of effective science instruction. The objective is to provide the reader with knowledge of specific teaching strategies needed to become a successful teacher. We begin by listing characteristics of effective lessons and follow with the characteristics of student and teacher behavior and then with questioning techniques. We then turn to examples of how these characteristics can be found

177

in specific science lessons. When considering each item and list, keep in mind that the major objectives of effective science teaching are to help students:

1. develop creative and critical thinking skills or, in the words of the Educational Policies Commission, to develop a command of the "rational powers" and Freedom of the Mind;

2. construct understanding of the major conceptual systems that form the basis of modern scientific thought; and

3. develop the self-confidence to pose questions and problems and to seek answers and solutions.

▼ LESSON CHARACTERISTICS

The following questions will help us identify specific characteristics in lessons that work for or against effective instruction.

1. Does the lesson involve materials or activities that are of interest to students?

Perhaps the primary factor in any investigation and in any classroom is motivation. Before meaningful inquiry can take place, students must be interested and motivated. Thus, it is imperative that the lesson contain materials or activities that appeal to students, stimulating their interest and curiosity.

2. Does the lesson involve materials or activities that lead students to think, question, and discuss meanings?

The central purpose of today's schools—and consequently any science lesson—is to encourage the use and development of thinking skills. For maximum progress toward this goal, students must be confronted with situations that lead them to question, analyze, compare, evaluate, infer, and otherwise use their thinking skills. Activities should be provided that involve students in collecting and analyzing data, raising questions, sharing ideas, questioning findings, and discussing meanings.

3. Does the lesson provide for a variety of levels and paths of investigation to accommodate individual initiatives and direction?

Obviously, not all students in a particular class work at the same pace, are equally interested, or are as intellectually able. Therefore, each lesson must involve some flexibility. Much of this problem is solved when a teacher supplies students with materials and activities that interest them. When students are free to interact with materials and other students, they will automatically do so at their own levels and in their own directions. Teachers should encourage individual initiative and direction.

4. Is the content of the lesson appropriate to the learner's developmental level?

The idea of the learner's developmental level is extremely important in selecting a topic and how it is to be taught. Just how this should be done is the focus of continuing research. The key point, however, is that instruction should be designed to challenge but not overwhelm students' thinking skills. Some disequilibrium is necessary for intellectual development but too much can lead to frustration, loss of motivation, and giving up.

5. Does the lesson involve a concept or concepts that are fundamental to developing an understanding of the discipline's embedded theories?

In selecting content for lessons, teachers need to keep in mind that science instruction should lead students to develop an understanding of the world in which they live. Our understanding of that world is facilitated by the construction of concepts and conceptual systems such as the theory of plate tectonics, kinetic-molecular theory, cell theory, evolution theory, and quantum theory. It is through investigations related to these and other fundamental theories, not through trivial activities or ideas, that students are able to gain insight and understanding. A meaningful evaluation of the lesson from this point of view implies that the evaluator adequately understands the embedded theories of the relevant discipline.

6. Does the amount of reading in the lesson impede the success of a student with limited reading ability?

No science lesson should be planned with an excessive amount of required reading. Although reading is recognized as extremely important, success in science should not depend on it. Generally related assigned readings should come *after* the lesson's exploration and term introduction phases.

7. Are visual and technical aids such as blackboard diagrams, slides, films, videos, or computers used as effective aids or supplements to investigations?

Visual aids such as blackboard diagrams can offer significant help in organizing and synthesizing students' investigative experiences. After initial understanding has been obtained by firsthand experience, films, slides, videos, and other technical devices can serve as effective means of expanding a student's sphere of comprehension and awareness. The visual aids should not, however, serve as substitutions to the firsthand experience. Computers can be used to help gather, organize, and present data, but they should not replace actual experiences with natural phenomena.

▼ CHARACTERISTICS OF STUDENT BEHAVIOR

The clearest indication that inquiry is taking place in a classroom is that students are actively involved in investigations.

   8. Are students making observations or collecting information that raises questions?

Whenever possible, materials should be provided or situations created in which the students are confronted with unexplained events that raise questions. For example, a simple task such as planting seeds can raise many questions. Students can be given seeds, containers, and soil and instructed to plant them in any way they feel is best. After several days have passed and some seeds have grown, many questions present themselves. Why did only some seeds grow? Why are some plants taller than others? Why are some plants greener than others? What are the structures (cotyledons) on the sides of the stems?

   9. Are the students formulating hypotheses, theories, and predictions that aid in answering the questions?

Using the same example as above, student hypotheses may be as follows: Some seeds did not grow because they received too much or too little water, sunlight, space, or fertilizer. Perhaps some did not grow because they became moldy. Some plants are not as green as others because they got too little sunlight. After formulating their hypotheses, students should be encouraged to perform experiments that lead to clearly stated predictions that allow the hypotheses to be tested.

   10. Are the students analyzing, interpreting, and evaluating data individually, in groups, or as a class with the teacher's guidance?

Data produced by investigations should be thoroughly analyzed, interpreted, and evaluated so that students are able to carefully think through the meaning of their results. This can be accomplished in various ways, although generally the younger the students are, the more teacher guidance is needed. A useful device for the interpretation of data (see Criterion 13) is to record them on the classroom chalkboard and then have the entire class discuss their meanings.

   11. Are class conclusions based on the evidence at hand or on the teacher's authority?

For students to develop confidence in the inquiry process and in their ability to inquire, conclusions must be based on the data produced by the investigation, not on the teacher's authority. If the teacher clearly sees that the investigation produced unacceptable results, then a further investigation should be proposed that may produce results contradictory to the original investigation. If this investigation is carried out and contradictory results are obtained, then the class has a real contradiction. In most cases, the only course of action would be to perform both investigations again to determine the source of error. Of course, this is how science usually is done. Things seldom, if ever, go as planned.

▼ CHARACTERISTICS OF TEACHER BEHAVIOR

To be successful in guiding students, a teacher must provide effective direction through stimulation rather than through authority.

12. While investigations are being conducted, is the teacher a fellow investigator?

This, of course, does not mean that the teacher should dominate the investigation. However, he or she should become a fellow investigator, exhibiting enthusiasm and interest in the activities by walking around the room, posing individual questions to stimulate further investigation, and being alert to students who might be having difficulty and need special assistance in getting started. Because the activities and investigations are being conducted by students and most likely have been done before by the teacher, he or she may be tempted to sit back and ignore what the class is doing. This should be resisted. We cannot ask students to be investigators if we are not willing to do so ourselves.

13. Does the teacher act as a classroom secretary when data need to be organized for class analysis?

The primary function of a teacher in the inquiry classroom is that of a guide and organizer. By recording class data on the blackboard or suggesting ways in which data should be recorded, the teacher not only helps students organize their results but also focuses attention on certain aspects of the data to help in their analysis and interpretation.

14. Are new terms introduced only after students have had sufficient direct experience with materials, events, or situations that enable them to comprehend the verbal presentation?

For new terms to be meaningful, they must be mentally linked to some pattern grounded in firsthand experience with the materials and phenomena of the discipline. Introducing the verbal labels of abstract concepts before such experience generally leads to rote memorization, noncomprehension, and poor retention.

15. Does the teacher provide additional materials, experiences, or events that enlarge, refine, and reinforce the meaning of previously introduced terms?

After classroom investigations have brought students comprehension of concepts or new thinking patterns, they should be encouraged to extend their thinking and look for applications of these concepts and patterns whenever possible. Suppose, for example, the classroom investigations have led students to develop the concept of natural selection by simulating the process with colored toothpicks on a lawn. This concept of natural selection is not significant if it only applies to this particular situation. If, however, the students are provided other examples or if they ask for examples, then the concept's meaning and importance are extended. The process of discovering applications and extending conceptual meaning may involve many lessons. In programs such as the Science Curriculum Improvement Study, which develops concepts in a "spiral" fashion, this process is woven through the entire six-year sequence of units. For this reason, Criterion 15 often may not apply to isolated lessons.

16. Does the teacher handle classroom interruptions by calmly, separately, and personally addressing the offending student or students?

A common mistake made by almost all new teachers and a great many experienced teachers is to raise their voices and even yell across a room to reprimand students. This type of teacher behavior, although seemingly successful, seldom has lasting effects. It generally leads to a loss of respect for the teacher and his or her ability to control a classroom. Personally addressing the offending student in a calm and deliberate manner saves the student the embarrassment of being disciplined by the teacher and saves the teacher his or her temper. Specific suggestions for handling a variety of behavior problems from gum chewing to violence and extortion can be found in Sprick (1985).

17. Does the teacher appear confident, calm, and friendly?

These traits—as well as understanding, patience, and a good sense of humor—often make the difference between a successful or unsuccessful lesson, be it inquiry or otherwise.

▼ CHARACTERISTICS OF EFFECTIVE QUESTIONING

To be successful, a teacher uses the method of inquiry in guiding both students and the direction of their investigations and thinking.

18. Does the teacher pose most questions in a divergent or evaluative form?

Divergent and evaluative questions allow a variety of student responses and stimulate creativity and critical thinking. "What might have caused that?" "How would we find out?" "What do you think might have happened to the seeds?"

"How could that idea be tested?" These are *divergent* questions because they have no single answers. They allow for divergent, creative, and critical thinking, and they stimulate discussion. Questions that call for a predetermined answer are *convergent*. This type of question can direct students' attention to specific details of an investigation. Examples include "Which liquid evaporated first?" and "How many *Daphnia* were eaten?"

In addition to being classified as divergent or convergent, questions have been classified into "levels." At the lowest level, the questions require only the recall of specific pieces of information; at the highest level, they require the evaluation of alternative proposals (Bloom, 1956). Bloom's taxonomy has six levels: knowledge, comprehension, application, analysis, synthesis, and evaluation. In general, higher-level questions provoke the use of higher-order thinking patterns and should be used more frequently than lower-level questions.

19. If convergent questions are posed, are they formulated to focus attention on particular aspects of an investigation in which the student is having difficulty?

Convergent questions can be of value in the science classroom if they are used to help a student more carefully analyze a situation, find and correct an error, or clarify a point of confusion. Following this type of questioning, the teacher has the responsibility of asking divergent questions to once again stimulate the student to think in a wider scope.

20. Are the questions phrased directly and simply?

Ambiguous questions lead to confusion and inattention. Keep the question direct and to the point to maximize student response.

21. Does the teacher call on an individual after posing the question?

Calling on an individual before asking questions encourages the rest of the class to disregard the question. If the question is asked first, then the entire class is stimulated to think about the answer. Sometimes a teacher will ask questions and not call on a specific pupil. This procedure leads to a chorus of answers that can occasionally get out of hand and lead to a classroom-control problem.

22. Does the teacher wait at least four to five seconds for an individual's response?

A teacher often asks a question and then does not allow a student to think about his or her response before the teacher calls on another student. This procedure not only is unfair but also does not allow for creative or critical thinking about the question raised. The length of time a teacher allows for individual responses to questions is called *wait time*. Increasing wait time greatly increases the quality of student thinking and the number of student responses.

The teacher also can, and often should, increase the time that he or she waits after a student response. Increasing this second wait time also increases the quality and quantity of student thinking.

23. Does the teacher listen to and accept all sincere student answers as valuable contributions?

Contradictions and discussions over the validity of the answer or data should come from other students and other data rather than the teacher. This procedure not only opens the classroom to free discussion and meaningful inquiry, but also puts the authority for the correctness on the evidence or data, where it belongs.

24. In answering student questions, does the teacher respond by providing additional ideas or information that enable the students to continue their thinking?

Any time the teacher supplies an answer that the student or class could instead answer through an investigation or further thinking, then student thinking and inquiry stops.

The teacher should develop the ability to respond to student questions with more questions and suggestions of possible paths of investigation to enable the students to continue the investigation or thinking. This does not imply that student questions should never receive direct answers. A question such as "What kind of tree is this?" should be answered directly, or the student should be given the means to obtain the information.

25. Did the student and the teacher enjoy the lesson?

People become scientists because they are curious, enjoy their subject matter and their investigations, and enjoy pondering questions. To teach science as something other than an interesting and enjoyable enterprise is unnecessary and a misrepresentation of the enterprise.

▼ EXAMPLE LESSONS

Perhaps the best way to understand how these specific characteristics can be incorporated into instruction is to consider their use in specific lessons. Therefore, we will examine the following four lessons:

- What Can Be Learned from Skulls?
- What Causes the Water to Rise?
- What Causes Water to Rise in Plants?
- How Do Lenses Work?

All four lessons include "Teacher Materials" that could become part of a teacher's guide, and all but the last lesson have "Student Materials" that could become part of a student laboratory book or manual. As you read through each lesson, you may wish to evaluate the lesson by how well it incorporates the twenty-five characteristics of effective instruction introduced above. Additional lessons can be found in Appendix G.

▼▼

WHAT CAN BE LEARNED FROM SKULLS?

Teacher Materials

Synopsis Students observe a variety of vertebrate skulls and attempt to identify the animal, its habitat, and what it eats. Through class discussion, the relationships between skull characteristics and implied functions are explored and the terms *herbivore, omnivore, carnivore, nocturnal, diurnal,* and *niche* are introduced. This is an empirical-abductive learning cycle.

Suggested Time Two class periods

Background Information Vertebrate skulls reveal adaptations for specific functions. Large eye sockets, for example, accommodate the size of eyes that would be needed for nocturnal activity. Eye sockets on the sides of the skull imply a positioning of the eyes for the type of peripheral vision that would be needed by prey animals, whereas a more frontal location implies good depth perception, which would be needed by predatory animals. Teeth also reveal adaptations. Those of herbivores are relatively flat for grinding plant material, while the teeth of carnivores are more pointed and sharper for grasping and tearing flesh.

The purpose of this learning cycle is to provide students with an opportunity to observe skull characteristics and create hypotheses about the animal's food source and habitat (i.e., the place where it lives) and to improve their ability to support or refute ideas through the use of evidence and logical argumentation. It also provides you as teacher with an opportunity to introduce the terms *herbivore, omnivore, carnivore,* and *niche,* where *niche* is defined as an organism's role or function within a biological community.

Teaching Tips *Advance Preparation*

1. Place a different skull at each of ten numbered stations.

Exploration

2. To introduce the lesson, remind students of the work of paleontologists, who are able to infer many things about the lifestyle and habitat of ancient animals from only a few fossil bones. Ask the students for examples of this sort of work and what might be some of the clues that paleontologists use to draw their inferences. Tell students that this lesson will challenge them to create hypotheses about the lifestyle and habitat of a variety of vertebrates by observing the skulls located around the room. They should consider these specific questions: What type of food does each animal eat (e.g., plants, animals, or both)? What evidence exists for that inference (e.g., number, shape, size, and location of teeth)? Is this animal active during the day, night, or both? What is the evidence (e.g., size and location of eye sockets)? Is the animal a predator or prey? Why

(e.g., eyes in front for the depth perception that a predator would need; eyes to the side for the peripheral vision required by prey)? Raise the questions only during the introduction. Do *not* mention specific characteristics and inferences such as sharp teeth means meat eater or eyes front means predator. Let the students discover these on their own. If they are not discovered, you may mention them later during the term introduction discussion.

Term Introduction

3. After students have gathered data on each skull, have them describe the observed differences. Start the discussion by holding up Skull 1. Ask for hypotheses and evidence. Go on to Skull 2 and so on. You may find it helpful to assign each skull to a specific group of students to report their findings and arguments. This allows students to take a more active role in the discussion.

4. As the discussion begins to focus on teeth, write the words the students use to describe them (e.g., *tearing, crushing, grinding*) on the classroom chalkboard.

5. These teeth types will suggest function. Discuss this relationship. At the appropriate time introduce the terms *herbivore, carnivore, omnivore,* and *niche.* Introduce them by giving the definitions first; then state the term. For example, "This animal has sharp teeth that appear to be used for tearing, and it has no flat teeth for grinding. This implies that it eats only animals. An animal that eats other animals is called a *carnivore.*" "An animal that eats only plants is called a *herbivore,*" and so on.

6. Student attention to eye sockets will allow you to introduce the terms *nocturnal* and *diurnal:* "This animal has large eye sockets, which implies that it has large eyes for night vision. An animal that is active during the night is called *nocturnal.*"

Concept Application

7. For concept application, provide opportunities in subsequent class periods for students to examine a variety of bones—for example, birds and fish—in addition to skulls and make inferences from their structure about their functions.

Biological Terms	*Thinking Skills*
nocturnal	accurately describe nature
diurnal	create alternative hypotheses
herbivore	generate logical arguments
carnivore	
omnivore	
niche	

▼▼

WHAT CAN BE LEARNED FROM SKULLS?

Student Materials

Introduction Do we need to see an entire animal to determine where it lives or what it eats? Sometimes we can use bones as clues to gain insight into possible answers to these questions. Observation is a key to understanding. What can be inferred by looking at skulls?

Objectives 1. To infer function and animal behavior from the observation of skull characteristics.
2. To improve your ability to support or refute hypotheses through the use of evidence and logical argumentation.

Materials Ten skulls of 10 different species of vertebrates.

Procedure 1. In your group, go to a station and take approximately 5 minutes to examine the skull carefully.
2. Observe the size and shape of the overall skull as well as other characteristics of the teeth, eye sockets, brain case, and so on. Record interesting observations on the data sheet. Make a sketch if you want.
3. Decide what kind of animal the skull came from, what type of food it ate, and where it might have lived. What characteristics of this skull allow organisms of this type to be successful? What evidence do you have for your hypotheses?
4. Move to the next station when you are ready. (No more than two groups may work at one station simultaneously.)

▲▲

▼▼

WHAT CAUSES THE WATER TO RISE?

Teacher Materials

Synopsis   Students invert a cylinder over a candle burning in a pan of water. They observe that the flame soon goes out and water rises into the cylinder. They then attempt to explain their observations. Testing these explanations leads to new explanations and increased understanding of combustion, air pressure, and the nature of scientific inquiry. This is a hypothetical-deductive learning cycle.

Suggested Time   Two class periods

Background Information   The primary purpose of this learning cycle is to involve students personally in the use of science in an attempt to answer two questions arising from firsthand observation.

    A burning candle is held upright in a pan of water by a small piece of clay. A cylinder is inverted over the candle and placed in the water, and shortly thereafter the candle flame goes out and water rises in the cylinder. These observations raise two major causal questions:

1. Why did the flame go out?
2. Why did the water rise?

    The generally accepted answer to the first question is that the flame "consumed" oxygen in the cylinder to a level at which too little oxygen remained to sustain combustion, thus causing the flame to die. The generally accepted answer to the second question is that the flame heated the air in the cylinder, causing it to expand and forcing some to escape out the bottom. When the flame went out, the remaining air then cooled and contracted, creating a partial vacuum. This partial vacuum is then replaced by water rising into the cylinder until the air pressure pushing on the surface of water inside is equal to the air pressure pushing on the water surface outside.

    This investigation is a particularly good way to introduce students to science as a hypothesis-creating and hypothesis-testing enterprise; the hypotheses they invariably create to answer the second question can be experimentally shown to be inadequate and thus must be modified through the use of both creative and rational thought processes, data gathering, and analysis.

    Students' initial misconceptions generally focus on a theory that states that oxygen is "used up," creating a partial vacuum that "sucks" water into the cylinder. They fail to realize that when oxygen is "burned" it combines with carbon to produce CO_2 rather than being destroyed (hence no partial vacuum can be created in this way). They also fail to understand that a vacuum cannot "suck" anything. Instead, the force that causes the water to rise is a push from the relatively greater number of air molecules hitting the water surface outside the cylinder.

The experiments and discussions will provide you with an opportunity to attempt to modify these misconceptions by introducing more satisfactory theories of combustion and air pressure. More important, it allows you to introduce science as an intellectually stimulating and challenging way of describing and explaining nature.

Teaching Tips   *Exploration*

1. You can either initiate this lesson with a demonstration or let students obtain materials and start on their own.

2. To demonstrate the phenomenon, use Steps 4 and 5 below during the class discussion. If you let the students start on their own, plan on stopping them after 15 to 30 minutes to discuss their observations and ideas.

3. During the discussion, observations and ideas should be listed on the board. The most obvious questions are: Why did the flame go out? Why did the water rise? The most likely explanation to the second question is that because the oxygen was "burned up" the water rose to replace the oxygen that was lost.

Lead the students toward the understanding that this explanation (hypothesis) predicts that varying the number of burning candles will *not* affect the level to which the water will rise. Four candles, for instance, would burn up the available oxygen faster and go out sooner than one candle, but they would not burn up more oxygen, so the water should rise to the same level.

4. Have the students do this experiment and report their results. These will, of course, show that the water level is affected by the number of candles (the more candles, the higher the water level). Their hypothesis, therefore, has been contradicted. At this point, emphasize the need for an alternative explanation and ask students to propose one. If no one has a good alternative, then challenge the students to develop a new explanation as their homework assignment.

5. If someone does propose the "correct" explanation (i.e., the heated air escaped out the bottom, etc.), do not tell the class that it is correct. Instead, treat it as just another hypothesis to be tested. Ask students to think of a way to test the hypothesis. They should realize that the hypothesis leads to the prediction that bubbles should be seen escaping out the bottom of the cylinder. (*Note:* It also leads to the prediction that the number of candles will affect the level of water rise because more candles will heat more air; therefore, more will escape and in turn will be replaced by more water.) Have the students repeat the experiment to see if bubbles are observable. If no one proposes the correct explanation, then propose it yourself. But make sure you do not give the students the impression that this is the correct explanation; it is simply an idea you had that should be tested along with any others that have been generated. The conclusion that it is correct should come only after data have been gathered that are consistent with its predictions (e.g., bubbles; more candles results in a higher water rise; water rises after the flame goes out while the air cools).

Term Introduction

6. After such data have been gathered, carefully repeat your explanation of the phenomenon, introducing the term *air pressure* and the molecular theory of gases, which assumes that air is composed of moving particles that have weight and can bounce into objects (such as water) and push them out of the way. You may wish to discuss the common misconception of suction in this context. The molecular theory implies that, as a force that can suck up water, suction does not exist (i.e., the water is being pushed into the cylinder by moving particles of air rather than being sucked upward by some nonexistent force).

Concept Application

7. To allow students to apply the molecular theory of gases and the concept of air pressure to new situations, provide each group with a piece of rubber tubing, a syringe, a beaker, and a pan of water. Instruct them to invert the beaker in the pan of water and fill it with water in that position with the mouth of the beaker submerged. (Students will probably make futile efforts to force water through the tube and into the beaker before discovering that they must extract the air through the tube.)

8. For their homework assignment, challenge the students to find a way to insert a peeled, hard-boiled egg into a bottle with an opening that is smaller in diameter than the egg. The students must not touch the egg after it has been placed on the opening. (After a small amount of water in the bottle has been heated, you need only place the smaller end of the egg over the opening of the bottle to form a seal. The egg will be forced into the bottle by the greater outside air pressure as the air inside cools.)

9. Unobserved by students, place approximately 1 centimeter of water in a ditto fluid can and boil the water vigorously. Then screw the cap on tightly to form a seal. Place the can on your desk in full view of the students and allow them to witness the can being crushed. Challenge the students to explain their observations using the molecular model of gases and the concept of air pressure.

Chemical Terms	*Thinking Skills*
air pressure	accurately describe nature
molecular theory	state causal questions
of gases	create alternative hypotheses
combustion	plan and conduct controlled experiment
energy transfer	organize and analyze data
	draw and apply conclusions

▼▼

WHAT CAUSES THE WATER TO RISE?

Student Materials

Introduction Often things seem simpler at first glance than they really are. On closer examination the complexity and mystery become more apparent. Discovering and solving these mysteries can be enjoyable and more satisfying than looking for answers in books or asking people who claim to know better than you. There is a way to search for your own answers. It is called science, and it can be fun. We are going to do some now.

Objectives 1. To stimulate curiosity about natural phenomena.
2. To become aware that science is an activity that involves creating hypotheses and predictions to arrive at explanations.

Materials
aluminum pie tins	cylinders (open at one end)
birthday candles	jars (of various shapes and sizes)
matches	beakers or test tubes (or both)
modeling clay	syringes
rubber tubing	

Procedure 1. Select a partner and obtain the materials.
2. Pour some water into the pan. Stand a candle in the pan using the clay for support.
3. Light the candle and put a cylinder, jar, or beaker over the candle so that it covers the candle and sits in the water.
4. What happened?
5. What questions are raised?
6. What possible reasons can you suggest for what happened?
7. Repeat your experiment in a variety of ways to see if you obtain similar or different results. Do your results support or contradict your ideas in Question 6? Explain.

▲▲

▼▼

WHAT CAUSES WATER TO RISE IN PLANTS?

Teacher Materials

Synopsis   Students design and conduct experiments to test hypotheses about causes of water rise in plants by removing plant parts, coating surfaces with petroleum jelly, and so on. This is a hypothetical-deductive learning cycle.

Suggested Time   Two to three class periods

Background Information   The stems of vascular plants contain xylem vessels that conduct water, which rises from the roots to the leaves for use in photosynthesis and other vital cell processes. But what causes water to rise against the physical force of gravity? Apparently, several factors are involved.

One force results from the osmotic movement of water into roots from the soil. This osmotic force, called *root pressure,* is generated at the bottom of the xylem and tends to push water upward. Evidence of this root pressure comes from cut stems that will temporarily bleed fluid after the stems are cut.

Root pressure is also presumably responsible for the occasional appearance of drops of water on the tips of leaves at the vein endings when water loss resulting from evaporation (called *transpiration*) is low and the soil contains a lot of water. This bleeding is called *guttation.*

Root pressure alone, however, is not strong enough to account for the movement of water up a tall tree. Another force or set of forces must be involved. One of these appears to be the cohesion of water molecules. The polarity of water molecules provides an extremely strong attraction among them. Thus, a column of molecules will stick together and exert a "pull" on the top molecules, which results in the rise of the entire column.

But what sort of a pull can exist at the top of the column? Several popular textbooks suggest (even state) that the transpiration of water from the leaves will cause a partial vacuum that can "suck" the water up like a milkshake through a straw. Clearly, however, this cannot be the case because suction as a force does not exist. The force that moves the milkshake up the straw is a push from below because of greater air pressure on the surface of the milkshake outside the straw than on the surface inside the straw. Many of your students most likely will hold this suction misconception.

So what provides the pull? The best answer now appears to involve osmosis and goes as follows: Transpiration of water in leaf cells increases their concentration of solutes and thus increases the osmotic "pull" of extracellular water into the cells such as in nearby xylem tubes. Because the column of water sticks together (because of the cohesive forces of water molecules) the osmotic pull at the top will cause the entire column to rise. This is commonly referred to as the *cohesion theory.*

Although the cohesion theory has gained wide acceptance among plant physiologists, a few problems remain unresolved. The theory requires the maintenance of the water column in the xylem, and yet breaks frequently occur. How the theory can accommodate this contradictory finding is not clear. Another puzzle is how the column of water is first established. Perhaps it "grows" there as the plant grows.

That no single theory solves all the problems should be viewed as a positive aspect of this learning cycle. In a genuine sense, this learning cycle allows students to move quickly to the cutting edge of this area of research.

Expect a variety of hypotheses from your students at the outset. For example, the following alternative hypotheses were proposed by students in a previous class:

1. Water evaporates from the leaves to create a vacuum that sucks water up.
2. Roots squeeze to push water up through one-way valves in the stem tubes.
3. Water's capillary action pulls it up similar to the way it does with a paper towel.
4. Osmosis pulls water up.

Of course, equipment limitations keep some ideas from being tested, but the leaf evaporation hypothesis (number 1 above) can be tested by comparing water rise in plants with and without leaves, requiring the isolation and control of variables. And the root squeeze hypothesis (number 2) can be tested by comparing water rise in plants with and without roots; the one-way valve hypothesis can be tested by comparing water rise in right-side-up and upside-down stems. The results will allow some hypotheses to be rejected but not others. The survivors are considered "correct," for the time being at least, just as in "real" science—which, of course, is precisely what the students will be doing.

Teaching Tips

Exploration

1. Start by posing the problem and calling for the proposal of several hypotheses. These should be listed on the board, followed by a discussion of how students might try to test them. Point out that the strategy they should attempt to follow is to falsify hypotheses rather than attempt to "prove" them. For instance, the one-way valve hypothesis predicts that water will rise in a right-side-up stem but not in an upside-down stem. If water rises equally well in both stems, then the hypothesis must be false. Tell students to test as many hypotheses as they can in the time provided.
2. Advise students to cut stems under water and to keep the stems in water for a minute before performing other manipulations. This procedure prevents air bubbles from blocking the xylem.

Term Introduction

3. At an appropriate time, have students report their experimental designs and results to the class. This can be done in a variety of ways. Select the one that best suits your needs and the amount of time available. One successful approach is to have each group select a spokesperson to present a brief oral report (three to five minutes) and answer questions at the conclusion of the report. After all of the reports are given, you can summarize the major findings and

introduce or reintroduce terms such as *osmosis, transpiration, cohesion,* and *xylem.* Be prepared to deal with the notion of suction. You may not wish to tell students that suction as a force does not exist, but ask them to imagine what goes on at the molecular level when evaporation occurs. Ask them to imagine how a molecule escaping from the water surface could possibly pull those left behind.

Concept Application

4. Tell students that another set of tubes called *phloem tubes* conduct food from the leaves in vascular plants to storage areas such as roots. Challenge the students to propose alternative hypotheses to explain how food travels through the phloem tubes. Challenge them to design and, if possible, conduct experiments to test their ideas.

Biological Terms	*Thinking Skills*
transpiration	accurately describe nature
xylem	create alternative hypotheses
osmosis	generate logical predictions
cohesion	plan and conduct controlled experiments
root pressure	organize and analyze data
guttation	draw and apply conclusions

▼▼

WHAT CAUSES WATER TO RISE IN PLANTS?

Student Materials

Introduction   If you place a piece of a plant such as a stalk of celery (with leaves) in a beaker with colored water, you will soon notice that the colored water somehow moves up through the stalk and into the leaves. Observations such as this suggest that the general pattern of water movement in plants is upward from the roots, through the stem, and to the leaves. But what causes the water to move upward? Clearly, this movement is opposite to the force of gravity, which pulls things down. Do you have any ideas?

Objectives   1. To determine the cause or causes of water rise in plants.
2. To identify some of the structures through which water travels in plant stems.

Materials

food coloring	test tube rack
toluidine blue stain	single-edge razor blade
slides and coverslips	a variety of plants and stems (e.g.,
compound microscope	celery, coleus, bean, onion,
petroleum jelly	sunflower, pyrocantha, palo verde,
	orange, corn, *Impatiens*)
	colored pencils or markers
	test tubes

Procedure   1. List any hypotheses that you and others in the lab may have about the cause of the upward movement of water through plants.
2. Select one partner to work with. Use the materials provided to design experiments to test these hypotheses. In general, you will have to place plants or plant parts into containers partially filled with colored water and wait several minutes to observe the movement or lack of movement of the colored water through the plants. Your plan of attack should be to try to refute (or support) each hypothesis by comparing predicted results with actual results. Use a table to summarize your work for each experiment. Should you include some sort of control? If so, what and why?
3. Were you able to tell precisely where in the plant stem the water was moving? If not, then you may want to make cross sections of stems that have had colored water or stain passing through them. Perhaps the colored water will have stained the water-conducting portion of the stem and it will be visible under the microscope in cross section.
4. Be prepared to report your observations, experimental results, and tentative conclusions to the class near the end of the lab period.

▲▲

▼▼

HOW DO LENSES WORK?

Teacher Materials

Synopsis Students explore the images formed by convex lenses and discover that when the distance between an object and a lens becomes great, the distance between the lens and its upside-down image becomes constant. This is a descriptive learning cycle.

Suggested Time Two class periods

Background Information Light travels in straight lines that may bend when they pass through different materials. When light "rays" pass through a convex lens, the rays bend and actually cross, hence the image created by a convex lens on a surface appears upside down. When the distance between an image-producing object and a lens becomes great, the distance between the lens and the object's upside-down image becomes constant. This distance is called the *focal length* of the lens. An increase in lens thickness causes greater bending of the light rays, hence a decrease in focal length. This inverse relationship is expressed quantitatively as:

$$1/f_c = 1/f_1 + 1/f_2$$

where f_c is the focal length of two lenses in combination with respective focal lengths f_1 and f_2.

Teaching Tips *Exploration*

1. The students are given one convex lens and a white card at the start of the learning cycle and instructed to find out everything they can about the lens and to make and record any measurements they believe to be important. The students generally measure the diameter and sometimes the thickness, and they find that the middle of the lens is its thickest portion. Using the card, the students also find that the lens projects an image onto the card.

2. The students also usually find that the distance between the lens and the image on the card is variable because they are using an object—usually a light bulb—that is relatively close to the lens.

3. Students typically ask questions relative to what would happen if an object were moved a greater distance from (or moved closer to) the lens. They have probably already found that for every distance between the object and the lens there is only one distance at which the image will focus clearly on the card; as the object is moved closer to the lens, eventually the image on the card disappears and the bulb image viewed through the lens becomes larger. That effect provides you with the opportunity to introduce the term *magnification.*

4. After awhile, the students will find that no matter how far they move the object from the lens, the distance between the lens and the object's image becomes relatively constant.

Term Introduction

1. At this point in the investigation, the numerical data that came from the measurements need to be examined. Have the students put their data on the classroom chalkboard. These data will consist of the measurements taken of the image distances and the object distances; if not already done, this is an opportune time to introduce those ideas. Eventually—and not too much time will pass—the students will agree that as the *object distance* gets larger, the *image distance* remains relatively constant. In fact, the students will probably insist that the image distance is constant. The data that the class have collected should be clear on that point before the central term coming from the learning cycle, *focal length,* is introduced.

2. Generally, the concept of a convex lens's focal length can be introduced as follows: When the distance between the object and the lens becomes great, the distance between the lens and its upside-down image becomes constant. That distance is known as the *focal length* of the lens. Physicists usually refer to the object being at an "infinitely great" distance from the lens, but that phrase usually is not meaningful to students—although it will be later if you introduce it now. The phrase probably is not meaningful because during the investigation distances were called "great" and "greater" and not "infinite"; besides, *infinite* is a rather indefinite term.

Concept Application

1. The students are now ready to apply the idea of focal length and that term should be used as frequently as possible during the application phase. There are at least two fruitful directions to follow in this phase of the learning cycle, and you might think of others to use instead of or in addition to the ideas that follow. Generally, it is not good practice to allow the initial application phase of the learning cycle to go on for long. The two applications of the concept can be expressed as questions.

   a. How closely can an object be brought to the lens before its image distance begins to change?

When the image distance begins to change, it is no longer the focal length. At this point, the term *infinity* can—and probably should—be introduced, and the importance of what that infinite distance is being compared to should be explored. All of the discussion should follow the period when measurements are taken and observations are made.

Data can be collected to answer the first question by moving an object closer to and farther away from a convex lens and measuring the distance between the lens and the image projected on the card. Keep in mind that when the object is far away, that distance is the focal length of the lens. So what is really being researched is the relative size of "infinity." The size of "infinity" depends on the thickness of the lens.

One of the purposes of the application phase needs to be reviewed at this point. When new ideas are introduced they are understood well by some students, tentatively by most, and not at all by a few. One principal purpose of the application phase is to increase the number of peer teachers available. Those who understand the concept well can now begin to function in a teaching role and teach both those who have achieved a tentative understanding and those who have no understanding. This new influx of peer teachers allows for several small classes to begin, with results encouraging results. The data collected to answer the first question are numerical, and that type of data generally is easy to explain because of the definite quality of the numbers. Furthermore, supporting conclusions with data is more important than the conclusions themselves. So when evaluating the contributions of students toward the application of a newly introduced idea, the discussion of the data and the nature of the argument are more important than the conclusions reached.

    b. How do the focal lengths of a thick lens and a thin lens compare?

To collect data to answer the second question, two or more lenses can be held together at their edges with tape. The technique allows the students to begin with one lens and add others as they wish, although physicists sometimes disapprove because of the air that is present between the faces of the convex lenses. But the results usually demonstrate that as the lens combination increases in thickness, its focal length becomes shorter. The entire process of securing lenses together is not necessary if lenses of varying thicknesses are available.

2. This lesson has been classified as a descriptive learning cycle primarily because students attempt to describe the numerical relationships among objects, lenses, and images. But clearly the learning cycle can and should go beyond this descriptive phase. If and when students generate models of light rays to explain their observations, the learning cycle becomes empirical-abductive. If alternative models are generated and tested, then the learning cycle becomes hypothetical-deductive.

Physics Terms	*Thinking Skills*
magnification	accurately describe nature
focal length	organize and analyze data
infinity	draw and apply conclusions

▲▲

▼ KEEPING INQUIRY GOING AND "COVERING" CONTENT

Before we leave the issue of specific characteristics of effective science instruction and turn to larger issues of curriculum development, a few additional remarks follow on classroom-management techniques that will keep inquiries going smoothly. Conversations among students or between teacher and students are an important part of the learning process. While participating in experiments, students spontaneously exchange observations and ideas with one another. During term introduction sessions, you introduce and define a new term or a set of related terms. When gathering feedback, you may address a question to a particular student. On other occasions, use discussions in which students report on experimental results, compare observations, and sometimes challenge one another's findings. Many students should participate in these discussions, and you as teacher should avoid controlling the topic or the pace. Encourage the students to give their comments to one another.

If you call attention to disagreement between two findings, then you invite evaluative comments and suggestions that may lead to more meaningful inquiries. However, announcing that one student is right and another wrong rarely leads to more inquiry experiences. Instead, such action encourages students to ask you as the authority figure for the answers, and it reduces their commitment to independent investigation.

The questions you ask and the way in which you ask them will affect the students' work and attitudes. Note the difference between these questions: "What did we study yesterday?" "What did you find out yesterday?" Both questions call for review of a previous activity, but the first only seeks an answer already in the teacher's mind. The second inquires into a student's own experience.

As previously mentioned, a question that aims for a predetermined answer is convergent because of its specific goal. Most questions in multiple-choice tests are convergent (as are many questions asked by some teachers). On the other hand, a question that allows a variety of answers is divergent because it may lead in many directions. Provocative discussion questions are usually of this type.

Suit your questions to your purpose. If you wish to gather feedback about understanding or recall of a certain fact, then ask a convergent question. Often this is best done individually, perhaps while small-group work is in progress. When you are looking for a specific answer, make this clear to the student. If you wish to spark discussion, then ask a divergent question and sit back while several students propose answers. If the students continue their discussion without your leadership, so much the better.

Which of these two questions is divergent? Which is convergent? "What caused the plant to die?" "What might have caused the plant to die?" The first question calls for a specific answer, so it is convergent. The student either knows or does not know the cause, so the question requires no thinking, only recall or guessing the answer already in the teacher's mind. The second question is divergent because it has many potential answers. Notice how it opens the door to student thinking and hypothesis creation and testing. It opens the door to science itself. For inquiry to take place in your classroom, divergent questions must be the norm.

One more important point: Do not forget about wait time! After you have asked a divergent question, be patient and allow plenty of time for student thinking. Most teachers wait less than a second before continuing or answering their own questions. This practice inhibits thinking.

Helping Students Create Hypotheses

Another important aspect of effective science instruction is that it allows for, even demands, that students create their own hypotheses. Getting students to create hypotheses is not always easy. Teachers sometimes remark, "But my students just do not think." Good exploration activities are designed with this in mind and generally will provoke student hypothesis creation with little special effort on your part. Nevertheless, the following are important tips to follow if difficulty arises.

- Make certain the causal question is clear. Write the question(s) on the classroom chalkboard. Even though you may have repeated it several times, some students may still not have heard it.
- Do not ask for one hypothesis. This implies that only one correct answer exists. Instead, ask for *alternative* hypotheses. "What *might* be some reasons for what was observed?" Empirical-abductive learning cycles are designed to have students make observations and gather data *before* asking for hypotheses. Good exploration activities usually provide several "hints" and provoke considerable thinking.
- After raising a question, call on specific students by name. This alerts other students that they also may be called on so they had better think of some answers.
- Do not respond differently to the correct hypothesis if and when it is advanced. Instead, treat it as another possibility and continue to ask for alternatives. This gives the students the correct message that you the teacher are not the arbitrator of what is correct or incorrect. Rather, a hypothesis must be tested before judgment can be made.
- Keep in mind that you are also an investigator, so you also may advance hypotheses. Generally, it is best to offer hypotheses that students can test and find incorrect; however, if no one comes up with the correct answer, then you should. If you get into the habit of advancing a combination

of correct and incorrect hypotheses, then students will learn to treat your ideas just like their own—that is, as ideas to be tested.

- In hypothetical-deductive learning cycles, students are asked to propose alternative hypotheses before data are collected. In some HD investigations, alternative hypotheses are suggested in the introductory material. In others, enough information is provided to elicit ideas most of the time. But if difficulty remains, then briefly describe the data-collection process and ask students to predict what they think might happen. Because students often have intuitions about possible outcomes, this question will spark more discussion. After students have indicated what they think will happen, ask them why they think it will happen. Of course, their answer is their hypothesis. When you find two students with opposite predictions and alternative hypotheses, then you have found precisely what you are looking for. Now the class can proceed to the experiments to test the alternatives.

- Accept all sincere hypotheses as reasonable even when they seem implausible to you. A positive teacher response encourages additional thought, while a negative one may prevent future participation.

- Make sure that your quizzes and tests require use of the process skills used in creating and testing hypotheses. Although this may cause some initial student frustration, do not give in and require only the "facts" on evaluations. Doing so would give the students the wrong message that the facts are more important than the processes. This message minimizes future student participation in the process. More will be said about student evaluation in Chapter 9.

Correcting "Wrong" Conclusions

When you open up the teaching process to "real" inquiries, the possibility exists that students will not discover the correct answers. For some teachers, this possibility poses a genuine concern. This is not to advocate teaching students incorrect conclusions, but students gather data in groups, and ample opportunity exists for a teacher to debunk incorrect data-collection procedures and conclusions. Thus, if correctness lies in the data and one's interpretation of them (as scientists claim it does), then little danger exists for students to venture off with incorrect ideas—especially if you are willing to repeat the data-collection process when results are particularly mixed. And if you emphasize the tentativeness of all conclusions in science, then danger will be reduced even more.

It is better to have students believe in the primacy of the inquiry process than have the teacher or text reveal the correct answer. Doing so may well reduce motivation for future inquiries. Students might ask, "If the teacher was going to tell us the correct answer, why did we bother going through all the trouble to get our own?" Nevertheless, if students have arrived at some incorrect conclusion that they simply cannot live with, then you might consider introducing the current scientifically accepted answer as follows: "You have carefully explored the issue and tentatively concluded such and such. Scientists interested in this problem have done considerably more research on the question and on the basis of this research, they now believe. . . ." This approach allows you to present the correct answer, reemphasizes the notion that answers come from research, and does not seriously undermine the student's own research efforts.

Classroom Control, Motivation, and Seating Arrangements

Classroom control is an important concern for every teacher. Obviously, during the lesson's exploration phase, the teacher is no longer the focus of student attention. Rather, attention is on the phenomenon and on cooperative group interactions. Your job becomes one of moving about the classroom from one group of students to another, providing helpful suggestions or probing questions. To some teachers, this approach may seem to lead to a loss of classroom control, but in reality, good exploration activities when properly introduced increase student interest and motivation, and thus greatly reduce classroom-control problems. No longer are you purveyor of information; you become a fellow investigator of interesting questions and phenomena. Student motivation shifts from an extrinsic desire for a good grade, which only some students view as possible or desirable, to an intrinsic one of satisfying one's curiosity about nature.

Also keep in mind that a teacher maintains classroom control by never addressing the class until he or she has everyone's attention. If you start talking when students are still talking, then you send the clear and unfortunate message that it is acceptable for students to talk while you talk. Finally, a good way to start the class on a positive note each day is to always take class attendance by making eye contact with each student as you call his or her name. This practice personalizes the classroom setting and fosters positive relationships between teacher and students.

Although explorations and many concept application activities require cooperative group work, having students seated next to or facing one another is not the most effective arrangement when you want to lead discussions or introduce new terms. When you want attention focused on group-generated data or on yourself, then students should sit in rows facing forward. This arrangement reduces unwanted and potentially disruptive student interactions. Row seating also should be used during examinations and any other time when you want students to work independently.

In other words, you should select the seating arrangement to match the nature of the classroom activity. A classroom with lab tables in the back and row seating in the front is ideal. Such an arrangement allows the best of both worlds: highly motivating cooperative group explorations and orderly discussions and term introduction sessions.

Covering Content

When first introduced to inquiry teaching, virtually every experienced teacher agrees with its emphasis on creative and critical thinking but has one question. "Will students learn enough content?" The answer is an emphatic *Yes!*

First, remarkably little of what is introduced in the lecture and textbook method is understood and retained. Allowing students to inquire and to construct knowledge facilitates the retention of information and the transfer of thinking skills *and* content.

Second, most nationally distributed standardized achievement tests—such as the Iowa Tests of Educational Development, the Scholastic Aptitude Tests, the new ACT Test of Critical Thinking, and the National Association of Biology Teachers Achievement Test—emphasize reasoning over specific content, so learning cycle students who experience inquiry lessons will outperform students exposed only to lectures and textbooks on these tests. If your district or state has developed its own "fact-oriented" achievement test, work to have it changed so that it is more in line with the national goals of education and these standardized tests.

Third, an inquiry-oriented curriculum introduces and focuses on major scientific theories (see Chapter 8). The major theories serve as conceptual frameworks for the acquisition and retention of information. Approaches that do not emphasize major theories do not provide such frameworks. Thus, although apparently paradoxical, the inquiry approach actually may introduce fewer terms but teach many more concepts. Some teachers who have used the inquiry method have even found that their students outperform lecture and textbook students on tests on content material that they have not even investigated!

Scheduling the Learning Cycles

Because some learning cycles require extended periods for data gathering, which on any one day may only require a few minutes of class time, you will often need to initiate new learning cycles before finishing others. It is not uncommon to have two to three learning cycles in progress at any one time. Instead of leading to student confusion, it is actually an opportunity to provide syntheses of related subject matter. To ensure that class time is used fully, reserve a place on a classroom chalkboard on which to list the day's activities. When students become familiar with this approach, they will often read the board and go right to work without anything at all having to be said.

Questions for Reflection and Activities

1. Select one of the example lessons presented in this chapter or in Appendix G and prepare a lesson plan or set of notes that you can use to teach it. Review the twenty-five characteristics of effective science instruction (see pages 206–208) and describe specifically how they will be incorporated into the lesson.

Inquiry Score Sheet

Criterion	Scale			Criterion Score
The Lesson				
1. Material and activities of interest	0 1 Students are bored.	2 Students are mildly interested.	3 4 Students are strongly interested.	
2. Materials and activities provoke thinking, questioning, and discussion.	0 1 No thinking, questioning, or discussion.	2 50% of students are stimulated to think, question, and discuss.	3 4 All students provoked to think, question, and discuss.	
3. Lesson provides for a variety of levels and paths of investigation.	0 1 Only one level and path of investigation.	2 Some lesson variety.	3 4 All students able to pursue investigation at own levels and own directions.	
4. Content fits learner's intellectual level.	0 1 Content is appropriate for none of the students.	2 Content is appropriate for 50% of students.	3 4 Content is appropriate for all students.	
5. Lesson involves fundamental concept of the discipline.	0 1 Content or ideas are trivial, not tied to developing meaningful understanding.	2 Concept or idea is of secondary significance.	3 4 Key concept or concepts of discipline are addressed.	
6. Reading does not impede lesson success.	0 1 Amount of reading prohibitive to conducting lesson.	2 50% of students hampered by reading difficulty.	3 4 No student hampered by reading difficulty.	
7. Visual aids used as effective supplements.	0 1 Aids used as substitutes for investigative experience.	2 Aids used but somewhat ineffectively.	3 4 Aids used effectively as supplements.	
Student Behavior				
8. Students making observations and collecting data.	0 1 0 25	2 50 Percent of lesson time	3 4 75 100	
9. Students formulate and test hypotheses, models, or predictions.	0 1 0 25	2 50 Percent of lesson time	3 4 75 100	

Inquiry Score Sheet (continued)

Criterion	Scale					Criterion Score
10. Students analyze, interpret, and evaluate data.	0 0	1 25	2 50 Percent of lesson time	3 75	4 100	
11. Class conclusions based on evidence.	0 Conclusions based on teacher authority.	1	2 Conclusions based on some evidence and some teacher authority.	3 All conclusions based on evidence drawn from students' investigations.	4	

Teacher Behavior

Criterion	Scale					Criterion Score
12. Teacher is fellow investigator.	0 No	1	2 50% of time	3	4 Yes	
13. Teacher acts as classroom secretary when data need to be organized.	0 No	1	2 50% of time	3	4 Yes	
14. Term introduced *after* direct experiences.	0 No	1	2 50% of time	3	4 Yes	
15. Opportunities are provided for extending concept meaning.	0 Concept introduced and not referred to again.	1	2 Many examples are mentioned and discussed.	3 Additional lessons enlarge, refine, and reinforce concept's meaning.	4	
16. Teacher calmly handles classroom interruptions.	0 No	1	2 50% of time	3	4 Yes	
17. Teacher appears confident, calm, and friendly.	0 0	1 25	2 50 Percent of lesson time	3 75	4 100	

Questioning Techniques

Criterion	Scale					Criterion Score
18. Majority of teacher questions are divergent.	0 No	1	2 Few divergent questions are used.	3	4 Yes	

Inquiry Score Sheet (continued)

Criterion	Scale					Criterion Score
19. Convergent questions are used effectively.	0 No	1	2 50% of time	3	4 Yes	
20. Questions are phrased directly and simply.	0 No	1	2 50% of time	3	4 Yes	
21. Individuals called on after questions are asked.	0 No	1	2 50% of time	3	4 Yes	
22. Teacher allows sufficient time for student response.	0 No	1	2 50% of time	3	4 Yes	
23. Teacher accepts student answers and opinions.	0 No	1	2 50% of time	3	4 Yes	
24. Teacher responds to questions by providing additional ideas, information, or clues to extend student thinking.	0 No	1	2 50% of time	3	4 Yes	
25. Teacher and students enjoyed lesson.	0 No one enjoyed.	1	2 50% of students enjoyed.	3 All students and teacher enjoyed.	4	

CHAPTER 7

WHY DON'T MORE TEACHERS USE INQUIRY-ORIENTED METHODS?

More than thirty years ago, considerable work was begun to improve science teaching in the United States. Until that time, teaching focused on fact-laden texts and consisted of a sequence of assign, recite, test, and then discuss the test. For many science teachers, little has changed. In a review of science teaching methods and materials, Hurd, Bybee, Kahle, and Yeager (1980) reported the following facts:

- Eighty percent of primary, 90 percent of intermediate, and 50 percent of all teachers base their instruction on a single textbook.
- Almost all questions arise from information in the textbook and most focus on terminology and definitions; teachers rely on and believe in the textbook.
- Students are trained to seek the "right" answers from the textbook.
- Throughout its history, and particularly in the last two decades, science teaching has stressed laboratory instruction. The average textbook has laboratory activities amounting to approximately 40 percent of the curriculum. Still, less than half of all science teachers regularly use laboratory activities, and 25 percent report that they never, or no more than once a month, use laboratory activities.
- The common sequence of instruction is assign, recite, test, and discuss the test, all based on the textbook.

Hurd et al. (1980) summarized their findings in biology as follows:

In short, little evidence exists that inquiry is being used. And further, scant data support the contention that students in biology attain an understanding of scientific inquiry, or that they can use the skills of inquiry. . . . Biology teachers lecture more than 75% of the time, so little time is left for inquiry. (p. 391)

Is the traditional lecture-and-textbook method the best way to teach? Or is the more recent emphasis on inquiry-oriented methods, such as the learning cycle, more effective? To answer this question, Lott (1983) conducted a meta-analysis of thirty-nine studies published from 1957 through 1980 and found that, when compared to the lecture approach, inquiry approaches led to significantly better performance when high levels of thought were considered and to essentially equal performance on low-level cognitive outcomes. Shymansky (1984) also reported the results of a meta-analysis in which traditional versus inquiry-oriented programs were compared. In all, 302 studies were examined, comparing traditional science curricula to what Shymansky called the "new science curricula." These were defined as programs that:

- were developed after 1955;
- emphasized the nature, structure, and processes of science;
- integrated laboratory activities into course discussion; and
- emphasized higher cognitive skills and an appreciation and understanding of the nature of science.

Traditional science curricula were defined as programs that:

- were developed or patterned after a program developed before 1955;
- emphasized knowledge of scientific facts, laws, theories, and applications; and
- used laboratory activities as verification exercises or secondary applications of concepts previously covered in class.

Results of the meta-analysis showed that all of the new curricula proved superior to traditional curricula across all measures of performance. The size of the positive effect was most marked for Biological Sciences Curriculum Study (BSCS) biology. The average BSCS student outscored 84 percent of traditional course students on attitude measures, 81 percent on process skills, 77 percent on analytic skills, and 72 percent on achievement. In short, the Lott and Shymansky analyses provide impressive evidence of the superiority of laboratory-oriented inquiry teaching methods. The obvious question then is, Why are most teachers not using inquiry-oriented methods?

To answer this question, personal interviews were conducted with several experienced science teachers (Costenson and Lawson, 1986). Teachers who clearly preferred the lecture method as well as some who professed to use inquiry methods were interviewed.

Table 7.1 lists the ten most common reasons given by these teachers for not using inquiry, with the first being the most common. We will consider each reason in turn. Are these valid reasons for holding to more traditional but less-effective methods or can the presumed difficulties be overcome?

▼ RESISTANCE TO INQUIRY

Using Table 7.1, we will examine why many teachers do not use inquiry in teaching.

Time and Energy

Some teachers argue that (a) too much time must be devoted to developing good inquiry materials and (b) too much energy must be expended to maintain enthusiasm through five classes each day.

Many expository teachers rely on the text and any prepared materials that accompany such programs. This makes day-to-day preparation relatively easy. The preparation required for inquiry—initially, at least—would be more

Table 7.1 ▼ **Science Teachers' Ten Most Common Reasons for Not Using Inquiry**

1. Time and Energy	• Too much time must be devoted to developing good lessons. • Too much energy must be expended to maintain enthusiasm through five classes each day.
2. Too Slow	• We have district curricula and must cover all of the material. • The students will not cover all that they will need to know.
3. Reading Too Difficult	• The students cannot read the inquiry book.
4. Risk Is Too High	• The administration will not understand what is going on and will think I am doing a poor job. • I am not sure how each unit will turn out.
5. Tracking	• There are no good thinkers left in regular biology.
6. Student Immaturity	• Students are too immature. • Students waste too much time and thus will not learn enough.
7. Teaching Habits	• I've been teaching this way for 15 years, and I cannot change now.
8. Sequential Text	• Inquiry textbooks lock us into the order of the book. • I cannot skip labs because there is too much new material in each.
9. Discomfort	• I feel uncomfortable not being in control of what is going on in my classroom. • Students feel too much discomfort.
10. Too Expensive	• My lab is not equipped for inquiry. • My district will not buy materials needed to maintain an inquiry approach.

time-consuming. But a large teaching staff can implement a learning cycle approach without investing much more time; it can develop a central filing system and a team approach. Unfortunately, for teachers who are not members of large staffs, the process does involve an increased time commitment. However, just as with other teaching styles, once the development has been accomplished, time commitments to the program would decrease significantly each year.

All too often, school districts are unable to deal adequately with the development of curricula, so teachers must develop materials on their own time. This usually causes burnout and a quick switch back to the expository style. Adoption of a BSCS-like program could alleviate some of the problems. Materials such as those developed through smaller-scale National Science Foundation Curriculum Development Projects also can help fill this void. In addition, a learning cycle–based biology program titled *Biology: A Critical-Thinking Approach*

(Lawson, 1994) has recently become available for high school use. The program includes 38 learning cycles and 6 "reasoning modules."

The criticism that inquiry labs require too much energy to teach seems odd. Granted, energy is required to prepare lab materials, but certainly no more than is required for traditional verification labs. Inquiry labs can actually require less energy to teach than either lecture or verification labs because students, once convinced that their data form the basis for classroom conclusions, become motivated and involved in the process, and thus require little supervision beyond an occasional suggestion of ways to begin.

Too Slow

According to some teachers, the inquiry method is too slow. The typical lament is, "We have district curricula and must cover all of the material."

The question here is, "The method is too slow for whom?" The teachers interviewed were all concerned about existing district-wide curricula or the advent of district-wide year-end testing. All felt that both would require strict adherence to an inflexible timetable. Who has the responsibility to develop the curricula? Who has the responsibility for the development of year-end tests? In both cases, the answer is, "The teachers!" Teachers thus can get existing fact-laden curricula changed and develop year-end tests that reflect educationally sound goals. To be required to teach the entire text in one year forces the teacher to instruct at a shallow and superficial level, and such a condition forces students to learn though rote memorization. For example, *Modern Biology* (Towle, 1989) has fifty-three chapters! Given that the typical school year contains only thirty-six weeks, approximately one and one-half chapters must be covered each and every week to complete the book! Obviously, this is an impossible task if a teacher is serious about student understanding and retention. Using inquiry means that the material "covered" is less but that the concepts mastered are more.

When we consider the overall picture of secondary education, teachers may need help in developing curricula that emphasize sound goals. According to the Educational Policies Commission (1961), the central purpose of education is to help students develop the ability to think: "The ability to think cannot be developed or applied without subject matter. There are two bases for choosing the substantive knowledge which pupils should learn. One is the potential of the knowledge for development of rational powers; the other is the relative importance of the knowledge in the life of the pupil and of society" (p. 19). Therefore, if the phase names of mitosis or a list of small-intestine digestive enzymes do not meet these requirements, then why emphasize and why test for them? Szent-Gyorgyi (1964) offered good advice when he quoted

Fouchet, who asked us to take the fire, not the ashes, from the altar of knowledge. Szent-Gyorgyi, however, being of a more earthly disposition, suggested that we eat the meat, not the bones. His remark that teachers, on the whole, have a remarkable preference for bones, especially dry ones, seems apt.

Using the available time, what knowledge should we emphasize? According to most experts, the emphasis should be placed on unifying themes that reflect the structure of the respective disciplines and serve as the framework to help students integrate information (American Association for the Advancement of Science, 1989; Bruner, 1963; Gregor, 1979; National Research Council, 1990). The structure of disciplines is reflected by the embedded theories that guide investigations (Lawson, 1958; Lewis, 1975; Suppes, 1968).

Lewis (1977) has listed major theories that could be introduced in introductory biology courses (see Table 7.2). As discussed in Chapter 1, each theory is composed primarily of a small list of postulates or basic hypotheses that together explain a phenomenon or a set of related phenomena. Such lists, if given to students at the appropriate time (i.e., as summaries *after* the inquiries have taken place), serve to focus both students' and teacher's attention on the relevant ideas; in doing so, the lists can help separate the relevant from the irrelevant and thus reduce the need to "cover" huge amounts of "facts."

Even though lists of embedded theories and basic postulates can reduce the need for long lists of terms and facts, even they tell us little about the central goals of secondary science instruction. In Arizona, for example, a University Board of Regents Task Force has developed guidelines that delineate what the regents believe to be major objectives of secondary science. The report by the Task Force on Laboratory Science (1985) lists nine abilities that every student should master (see Table 7.3). Note that none of these abilities involves any discipline-specific declarative knowledge. What the task force is saying to teachers is that it does not matter *what* content they use, just as long as they use *some* content in an inquiry-oriented method to help students acquire these abilities.

Reading Too Difficult

Many teachers claim that their students cannot read inquiry books. Although the teachers surveyed were unable to articulate precisely why their students had difficulty reading inquiry texts, it may be in part that inquiry texts place greater demands on students' thinking skills. Many high school students are intuitive or empirical-inductive thinkers, whereas scientific inquiry is guided by reflective or hypothetical-deductive reasoning—thus reading about scientific inquiry is difficult. Expository, fact-laden texts place no such demands on student thinking: They only place demands on memorization ability. But challenging students' thinking is far better than taxing their ability to memo-

Table 7.2 ▼ **Theories in General Biology Courses**

Cell Theory

Sexual Reproduction as Theory

Mendel's Theory

Classical Gene Theory

Theory of Descent with Modification

    Subtheories Within the Theory of Descent with Modification

        Examples: Theories of Phylogeny and Classification

                Species Theories

                Geographic Distribution Theories

Theories of the Mechanism of Evolution

        Examples: Theory of Natural Selection

                Synthetic Theory

    Subtheories Within the Theories of the Mechanism of Evolution

        Examples: Theory of Sexual Selection

                Mimicry Theories

                Competitive Exclusion Theory

Theories of the Origin of Life on Earth

        Examples: Coacervate Theory

                Virus Theory

                Proteinoid Theory

Ecology Theories

        Examples: Theory of Biogeochemical Cycles

                Theory of Succession

                Theory of Community Structures

Biochemical Theories

        Examples: Enzyme Theory

                Glycolysis Theory

                Citric Acid Cycle Theory

                Electron Transport Theory

                ATP Theory of Energy Transfer

                DNA Theory of Chromosome Structure and Duplication

                DNA–RNA–Protein Theory of Gene Action

Source: Lewis, 1977

rize, because thinking skills can be improved and are of general use, whereas rote recall of isolated facts has little value.

Certainly, reading difficulties are not confined to inquiry texts. Textbook publishers in recent years have become concerned with book readability. Likewise, districts have spent considerable time developing programs for "below grade-level" readers. Yet with the emphasis on lower reading levels, many

Table 7.3 ▾ **Major Objectives for Laboratory Science**

After completing two years of high school laboratory science, the student should be able to:

1. describe the nature of science;
2. describe the characteristics of a scientific theory;
3. use the metric system and scientific notation;
4. use mathematical relationships to describe observational and experimental results;
5. determine the reasonableness of results through estimation, approximation, and order of magnitude;
6. identify common variables and name specific values for these variables in dynamic and static systems;
7. identify, measure, and conserve key characteristics of objects and substances, including solid and liquid amount, length, area, weight, volume, and density;
8. construct and use theoretical models;
9. generate predictions based on the assumed truth of hypotheses and imagined experimental situations;
10. design and conduct controlled experiments to test hypotheses;
11. recognize information needed to establish the correlation between two variables and the additional information needed to establish cause and effect;
12. demonstrate an ability to categorize or classify objects or data in an organized, logical manner;
13. use appropriate instruments and tools to gather scientific information in a laboratory, field, or library setting;
14. demonstrate a basic understanding of experimental error and its analysis;
15. distinguish between observations and inferences;
16. evaluate evidence in light of the probabilistic nature of phenomena;
17. interpret data and observations for relationships and trends;
18. organize and communicate results from observation and experimentation, both quantitatively through the use of relationships and qualitatively in clear, concise spoken or written language; and
19. function with ambiguity and acceptance of divergent methods of problem solving.

---

expository texts have created comprehension problems. Sentences must be added to explain terms, which creates an additional reading problem:

> *Expository textbooks have frequently been found to contain linguistic flaws, including a lack of unity, cohesion, and semantic elaboration. A primary characteristic of these texts is the limiting of detailed facts with few cohesive ties*

*either among the details or between the facts and the main point they poten-
tially clarify. (Vaughan, 1984, p. 128)*

Expository biology texts make the problem worse by including enormous numbers of terms. Even though *Modern Biology* uses a lower reading
level, as Yager (1983) points out, the 1981 edition includes 17,130 special
biological terms, an average of 23 biological terms per page! Therefore, a
lower reading level does not necessarily lead to better comprehension. In
fact, Armbruster and Anderson (1984) maintain that an expository book is
inconsiderate of the reader. The reader is so overwhelmed by the vast
number of special terms that comprehension is nearly impossible. As mentioned, however, the problem is seldom conceptual. The problem is the
shear weight of terms to be memorized.

Consider in more detail the role of the textbook in developing or retarding
the development of scientific thinking skills. The following passage from
Mader (1985), a traditional expository text, illustrates the point well. With
reference to Mendel's concept of segregation, Mader states:

In interpreting these results, Mendel stated what is now called Mendel's Law of
Segregation. *Mendel concluded that characteristics such as tall or short stems
are determined by discrete factors. Mendel stated that each organism contains
two factors for each trait and that the factors segregate during the formation of
gametes so that each gamete contains only one factor from each pair of factors.*
(p. 135)

We should not need to point out that Mendel stated no such law. More
correctly, the concept of segregation was a hypothesis! Stating it as a law, as
Mader does, leaves the student with the impression that no hypotheses were
needed to guide Mendel's experiments. Rather, the data were simply sitting
around ready to be analyzed for conclusions and summarized as laws. Such
statements leave the student with a distorted view of scientific investigation
and with little understanding of how to participate in the process. Now
consider the more lengthy, but more readable and accurate treatment of
segregation by Starr and Taggart (1978):

Mendel's first set of experiments were monohybrid crosses. . . .
*All of his seeds grew into plants bearing only purple flowers. . . . What had hap-
pened to the white-flower trait? . . . Mendel arrived at an explanation for the results. First he assumed that a hybrid must have two "units" of hereditary material for each trait. Second he assumed that units of heredity do not blend
together but remain distinct. . . . If these assumptions are true, there is only one
possible outcome; each F_1 hybrid offspring must be Aa (carrying units for both
forms of the trait). . . . If Mendel's ideas were not correct, . . . then only the dominant form of the trait would show up in the second generation, . . . If Mendel's
ideas were correct, though, there would have to be about as many recessive as
dominant individuals. . . . This is exactly what happened. (pp. 162–163)*

Note how the Starr and Taggart passage "walks" the reader through Mendel's reasoning and his data from question to hypothesis (assumptions), to predictions, and finally to results and conclusions. This sort of treatment may require more words, and it may be difficult for the empirical-inductive students to follow, but it most certainly affords the reader the opportunity to begin to understand the interplay among questions, ideas, and evidence—which, of course, is at the heart of the scientific enterprise. In contrast, expository treatments serve mainly to obscure and confuse, and they lead to rote memorization.

Consider that reading from an expository book is usually initiated by the teacher rather than by the reader. Inquiry can stimulate readers to find answers to questions—their own questions. This would in turn give the reader an internal locus of control. From classroom experience, it appears that students using the inquiry approach have fewer reading problems than would be expected with an expository approach. As Hill (1967) stated, "There is solid evidence to confirm that the content area textbook, as traditionally used, is less help and possibly more hindrance to the student than commonly assumed" (p. 412). Therefore, the book should be used as a supportive agent for class activities rather than the ultimate source of all that is right or wrong. Thelen (1979) supported this use of a biology text: "The textbook should be used to reinforce, confirm or enrich those concepts that the teacher is responsible for developing. The reader, when provided with sufficient background concerning the new material, should find the textbook easier to read" (p. 463). In other words, the reading should be assigned *after* the inquiry lessons on those topics that have been investigated, not before. In this way reading assignments serve to reinforce and enlarge the already introduced terms.

Risk Too High

Many a teacher has argued that his or her administration will not understand what is going on: "It will think I'm doing a poor job." Furthermore, a teacher may reason, "When using inquiry, I'm not sure how each unit will turn out."

Risk is high when one deviates from the norm. Individual failures tend to be blamed on the method of instruction, and unsympathetic administrators often tend to agree. Leaving the security of the norm thus takes some courage. Yet can our society continue to let teachers risk losing students by boring them day after day with expository teaching? Can teachers continue to risk the trade-off of memorizing unnecessary facts in exchange for good thinking and problem-solving skills? What, then, is really at risk? Surely the modest personal risk is less than that to society if our schools fail to provide students with an education in thinking.

Do teachers using inquiry risk the feeling of not knowing where the class will lead? Yes, but a good inquiry teacher is leading, but not in the traditional sense. The good inquiry teacher is skilled at dealing with the unexpected because he or she knows the subject matter well and how to use the unexpected to provoke further thinking and inquiry. Teachers must not be afraid to say "I do not know" even when they do.

Expository teachers as tellers and inquiry teachers as facilitators are at opposite poles. Traditional teaching, no matter how disguised, is based on what Rogers (1983) has termed the "mug and jug" theory. The teller asks, "How can I make the mug stay still long enough to fill it from my jug of knowledge that I regard as being important?" The facilitator is concerned mostly with climate and asks, "How can I create an atmosphere that will allow my students to be curious, feel free to make mistakes, and feel free to learn from the environment as well as from their fellow students and me?" The proper attitude was described by Chinese philosopher Lao-Tse (Brynner, 1962):

A leader is best
When people barely know he exists,
Not so good when people obey and acclaim him,
Worst when they despise him.
But of a good leader, who talks little,
When his work is done, his aim fulfilled,
They will all say, "We did this ourselves."

Does a teacher risk anything because an administration does not support the inquiry method? Perhaps, but if an administration does not understand, then the teacher's duty is to instruct the administration in the proper use of inquiry in the classroom and to acquaint administrators with the data that show inquiry to be a superior approach to teaching.

Tracking

Some teachers will argue that students cannot do the inquiries because there are no good thinkers left in regular biology; that is, a tracking system often has already placed the more able students in an upper-track curriculum, leaving only transitional and empirical-inductive thinkers in the regular classes. So teachers often ask, "How can this type of class use inquiry?"

The answer might be found in their own districts if their elementary schools are using materials from the Elementary Science Study (ESS) or the Science Curriculum Improvement study (SCIS). These teachers are dealing with nonreflective thinkers every day, yet they use these materials through the inquiry method to develop important science concepts and thinking skills.

The expectations for the lower tracks cannot initially be set too high, and teachers cannot expect the average student initially to function at the hypothetical-deductive level. Knowing that a substantial portion of adolescents and adults are not achieving hypothetical-deductive thought, it becomes important that these lower-tracked students be given the opportunity to develop their thinking skills. A good program should start with descriptive lessons and group experiments and only gradually ask students to design experiments on their own. Teachers should make sure that students are involved personally with each exercise so that they can gain confidence. With this confidence, each student then will be willing to experience some cognitive discomfort while attempting to acquire higher-level thinking skills.

Another approach to the problem exists. If tracking creates instructional problems that inhibit the proper atmosphere for inquiry, then the same people who were involved in its creation can also be involved in its demise: teachers. Nontracked inquiry programs can and do work in many high schools. Inquiry eliminates many of the problems that tracking is supposed to solve. For example, classroom tests for measuring reasoning (e.g., Lawson, 1978; also see Appendix F in this text) can be used for pairing hypothetical-deductive thinkers with empirical-inductive thinkers in laboratory groups, thus letting the learning experiences develop through group dynamics. This gives students an increased chance to achieve course goals. These same students in an expository classroom would have only their text to rely on, thus creating the need for tracking.

Student Immaturity

Sometimes teachers argue that inquiry cannot be used because their students are too immature and waste too much time.

If students are wasting time, that is a problem of classroom management, not the inquiry method. If investigations are at an appropriate level, then interest should be high and participation widespread. Students always have the opportunity not to learn with *any* method, not just with the inquiry method; if the students do not listen to a lecture and keep their mouths shut, then the teacher will not notice their failure to learn.

The nature of an inquiry class does give some students an opportunity to be nonproductive. It then becomes extremely important for each teacher to develop techniques that will maintain participation. Leonard (1980) provides many good suggestions. Using his *extended discretion approach,* students begin with fairly structured inquiries that require little student autonomy. Only gradually is structure decreased and autonomy increased. Inquiry surely means more noise and more mobility, but the argument that high school students are too immature to inquire cannot be taken seriously; elementary school students are surely more immature and yet fully able to participate in inquiry lessons when properly designed and carried out. Again, skeptical secondary school teachers are urged to consult experienced ESS or SCIS teachers in their own or nearby elementary school districts.

Teaching Habits

Occasionally, a teacher will say something such as, "I've been teaching this way for 15 years, and I cannot change now."

When people get stuck in old ruts, change does become difficult, but it presumably remains possible. When confronted with the considerable evidence (Lawson, 1985; Lott, 1983; Shymansky, 1984; see also Appendix D in this text) that expository methods are less effective than inquiry for student attitudes, interest, learning, and intellectual development, teachers should respond accordingly. Most teachers receive little outside help in the development of their teaching style and just have not been exposed to proper inquiry lessons; therefore, they can hardly be expected to teach in that style. All the blame cannot be deferred, however. These same teachers should be members of professional organizations that have communicated the effectiveness of inquiry in the past. It is almost unimaginable that any science teacher has not at least read about inquiry and wondered if it would work for him or her.

With possible increases in federal and state support, many teachers may have the opportunity to experience inquiry firsthand. If no program is available, then these teachers should consider seeking an inquiry teacher and letting him or her help in the development of an inquiry program.

Old dogs *can* learn new tricks, and probably will once they are convinced that the goals and methods of inquiry are more effective. Nevertheless, this is crucial: Teachers tend to teach as they have been taught. Many high school teachers have been taught science in colleges and universities by professors who lecture and by labs that verify. The typical college professor, who serves as a poor role model, must shoulder the major portion of the blame for poor teaching practices in high schools. Efforts to improve instructional methods in high schools must be accompanied by improvements in college teaching. This argument is developed more fully in a wonderful book by Morris Kline, *Why the Professor Can't Teach* (1977). Although Kline's major thesis refers to mathematics instruction, many of his points are applicable to science teaching.

Sequential Text

Another often-heard objection from teachers is that inquiry textbooks lock them into the order of those specific books and that they cannot skip labs because too much new material is presented in each.

Several of the interviewed teachers were concerned about the inflexibility of some inquiry-oriented programs. They felt that because of the programs' central themes and the constant referral to previous material, changing the order of presentation became impossible and too often laboratory investigations were used to introduce new material that was central to the understanding of concepts being developed.

These teachers were unable to delete investigations, if the situation warranted, without losing valuable information. These disadvantages seem highly questionable when compared to the alternative of a disjointed chapter-by-chapter presentation of scientific facts. Without central themes, students are given the impression that the material presented in each chapter in no way relates to others. The study of science becomes an exercise in memorization—so the baby is thrown out with the bathwater!

Many teachers fail to appreciate central themes themselves and fail to see relationships among concepts. Some, for example, require students to memorize steps in the Krebs cycle. More teachers require memorization of the phase names in mitosis and meiosis. What possible purpose can this serve? Teachers have allowed the tail to wag the dog. Teachers and districts should develop their own sound curricula that are independent of any text. The teacher has three responsibilities before classes ever begin:

1. Isolate those theories that provide an accurate and adequate understanding of the discipline.
2. Using an inquiry framework, find laboratory investigations that help develop the theories.
3. Make sure that the investigations are carried out using inquiry.

Once this process is complete, reading—but not necessarily a textbook—should be selected that best meets the goals of the curriculum and that will be used as reference rather than as the center of classroom instruction. This process would develop a better curriculum.

Discomfort for Teachers and Students

Another typical complaint might be, "I do not feel comfortable not being in control of what is going on in my classroom. Students also feel too much discomfort."

After discussing inquiry with the interviewed teachers, it became clear that many did not use inquiry because they felt uncomfortable with the approach. Whether this discomfort was primarily due to inquiry itself or their own general lack of skills in using inquiry was not clear. Possibly those teachers who experience discomfort have limited training in inquiry or have been trained but lost their enthusiasm after they returned to their own districts. Much of this loss could result from lack of support both internally (district) and externally (workshop). No one knows that the teacher is doing a great job. Peer "coaching" and clinical supervision by supervisors may possibly furnish the support needed (Bird and Little, 1985). If such support and gratification are not forthcoming, then the enthusiasm required for inquiry could soon falter, letting the teacher fall back to the expository style.

A third possibility does seem to exist, however: The teachers are more comfortable when they can clearly demonstrate that students know what they are expected to know. Likewise, administrators appreciate objectives that are clearly stated and evaluated. Unfortunately, those objectives that are most easily spelled out, taught, and evaluated are of least value to the student and society; furthermore, the objectives of inquiry cannot be easily spelled out, taught, and evaluated, and thus greater discomfort results. Most certainly, however, the studies reviewed by Lott and Shymansky did clarify these objectives, just as does any sound achievement test. An important task, then, is in training teachers to clearly state, teach, and evaluate higher-order cognitive outcomes.

Usually, discomfort is also felt by high school students, not because inquiry is so difficult, but because in most cases they have not been allowed previously to think for themselves and to make mistakes. As a former student remarked, "The discomfort students might feel could be the pain in their brains finally getting started. It's like having braces. They hurt when they are being tightened, but the final product is a straight brain." The inquiry approach does not allow a student to be an inactive participant as in the expository approach. Being an active participant creates an unfamiliar situation for some, and so the discomfort. If the students are made to believe that their answers are important and not judged right or wrong by teacher or text, then this discomfort soon fades.

For students raised on the inquiry approach in the elementary school—for example, by SCIS or ESS—no such discomfort exists when they face inquiry in high school. In fact, the opposite occurs when inquiry-oriented students meet expository teachers: discomfort and, more telling, student comments that they are no longer doing science in their "science" class.

Teachers should not give up inquiry just because expository schooling typically constitutes most of the students' past experience. Going along with this crowd does not create a better educational atmosphere.

Too Expensive

Finally, teachers may argue that their labs are not equipped for inquiry and that their districts will not buy the materials needed to maintain an inquiry approach.

In many cases, science is being taught in rooms that are not equipped for laboratory work. This seemed to be a problem for those interviewed when considering the learning cycle approach. Surveys have revealed that 40 percent of all science classes are taught in classrooms that were not designed for laboratory use, although only 25 percent of the teachers in those rooms felt the room was inadequate for that purpose (Hurd et al., 1980). Thus, poorly equipped rooms do not seem to be as limiting as some teachers argue. Besides, inquiry does not happen because of furniture: It happens because teachers' and students' minds are at work.

Many teachers feel that the equipment used in the inquiry approach is prohibitively expensive in both start-up and annual maintenance costs. This objection appears valid. The problem may have to be taken to the district level for satisfactory results. Most districts have some funds available; however, administrators often need better directions in how to spend them. Yet teachers also must keep in mind that inquiry can be taught without fancy equipment; it requires creativity on the part of the teacher to find alternative materials. Much inquiry can be achieved with materials just outside the classroom, whether purchased at local stores or brought from students' homes. The outdoors and the world of living things are available to all teachers, and bags of seeds from the grocery store work just as well as those from supply companies—and at a fraction of the cost.

Another former student remarked that while she was in the Peace Corps in Africa, she saw two young boys in ragged, dirty clothes dissecting a lizard on the ground with a rusty razor blade from the trash. Children cannot truly be stopped from inquiring on their own. It costs little and pays a lot if it is also allowed in the classroom.

▼ **CONCLUSION**

None of the above reasons for not using inquiry-oriented lessons is sufficient. However, to implement inquiry in the classroom, three crucial ingredients are needed: (a) teachers must understand the nature of scientific inquiry, (b) they must have sufficient understanding of the structure of their particular disciplines, and (c) they must become skilled in inquiry teaching techniques. Lacking this knowledge and skills, teachers are left with little choice but to teach facts in the less-effective expository way.

Questions for Reflection and Activities

1. Visit one or more middle school or high school classrooms and evaluate the lesson presented in terms of the twenty-five criteria of the Inquiry Scoring Sheet in Chapter 6.

2. If the teacher or teachers score relatively low on the criteria, then interview them to find out why they may oppose using inquiry methods. Compare those reasons with those given in this chapter.

3. If the teacher or teachers score relatively high based on the criteria, then interview them to find out what experience(s) helped them become inquiry-oriented teachers.

CHAPTER 8

PRINCIPLES OF CURRICULUM DEVELOPMENT AND IMPLEMENTATION

This chapter is concerned with principles of curriculum development in which the curriculum intends to (a) teach students the set of central concepts and conceptual systems (theories) that constitute the various disciplines and (b) help students develop their creative and critical thinking skills. We turn first to the issue of teaching concepts and conceptual systems.

▼ CURRICULUM PRINCIPLES: CONCEPT ORGANIZATION AND PRESENTATION

As discussed in Chapter 3, conceptual systems are mental constructions that integrate concepts about the world of human experience. The concepts are about objects and their interactions. For example, the conceptual system called *ecosystem* is first a description of animals, plants, water, sunlight, air, minerals, and so on and then an explanation of how they interact to maintain life on the earth.

Conceptual systems have an internal order in which each concept is related to other concepts in a necessary way. Presumably, such an internal order reflects a similar order in the natural world and thus becomes a description or an explanation of the natural world. Some descriptive concepts within any conceptual system are basic and fundamental, and they represent the system's foundation. Other of the system's concepts, although necessary to understanding the system, are of a second or third order and can be derived from the basic descriptive concepts. For example, to teach the concept of ecosystem depicted in Figure 3.1 (page 70), first-order descriptive concepts such as plants, animals, molds, bacteria, and yeasts should be taught first. From these concepts are derived the second-order descriptive concepts: producers and consumers. The concept of *producers* in an ecosystem refers to all of the plant populations that produce food. The concept of *consumers* refers to all animal populations that eat plants or other animals that eat plant eaters. A third-order descriptive concept is that of *community*, which includes all the populations of plants (producers) and animals (consumers) that live in interdependence in a given area. Finally, the concept of ecosystem can be considered fourth-order because it is defined as the community plus "abiotic environmental factors" in any particular locale.

Any conceptual system can be meaningful to students only to the extent that it is related in their minds to some experience of their own. The beginning of any course that intends to teach new concepts must be an experience with the empirical world, either by direct sensory contact with physical or biological examples or by secondary experiences such as films or descriptions of events or situations to which the students can relate their own experiences.

In teaching a conceptual system, an important task is to identify the system's basic concepts. Each will relate either perceptibly (i.e., descriptive concepts) or imperceptibly (i.e., theoretical concepts) to some phenomena.

Because both types of concepts derive meaning from phenomena directly or indirectly, a student cannot be expected to comprehend a concept's meaning without in some way experiencing the particular phenomenon in question. Further, because conceptual systems are constructed first on a basic description of perceptible phenomena, and only later on imperceptible theoretical concepts, students should begin their conceptual construction with perceptible experience—that is, with phenomena that relate to descriptive concepts. First-order descriptive concepts should precede the introduction of second-order concepts (they are chunked into second-order concepts), which then may be chunked into third-order descriptive concepts and so on. Once this descriptive base is formed, the groundwork has been laid for introducing any system theoretical concepts.

When first presented to introduce the conceptual system's descriptive aspects, the perceptible experiences should be presented in a way that integrates the material to be learned in an undifferentiated way—that is, as an *undifferentiated whole*. Or if a student already understands the descriptive aspects of a theoretical conceptual system, then the basic theoretical concepts can also be initially presented in an integrated fashion as an undifferentiated whole. The basic sequence of instruction is as follows:

1. perceptible phenomena as an undifferentiated whole
2. first-order descriptive concepts
3. second-order descriptive concepts
4. higher-order descriptive concepts
5. theoretical concepts

The Undifferentiated Whole

The concept of an undifferentiated whole may be vague and elusive, but presumably it plays an essential function in meaningful learning, as opposed to memorization of unrelated terms. An *undifferentiated whole* is a mental event that spontaneously results from an interaction of the mind with new sensory input. It becomes differentiated, and the resulting parts become integrated into a new and more complex whole as a result of continued interaction of the individual with the experience that produced the initial sensory input. Perhaps an analogy will clarify the concept.

The undifferentiated whole is a mental event analogous to a zygote, an undifferentiated cell that has the potential to develop into a mature organism. The process of development involves repeated cell divisions, differentiation of parts, and the integration of those parts into a functional biological system. This development requires a suitable environment from which the zygote obtains necessary materials. Likewise, the undifferentiated whole becomes differentiated through mental identification, analysis, and integration of the parts of the initially undifferentiated phenomena.

At least four different types of undifferentiated wholes are of interest. The first type involves the perception of objects; the second involves the perception of some behavior in relation to objects; the third involves the perception of a system of interrelated objects; and the fourth involves the perception of symbols that represent the interrelationships of concepts.

The first type of undifferentiated whole—*perceptual object*—is exemplified by the work of Hebb (1949). Hebb was interested in explaining how infants learned visual perception of objects. Presumably, infants cannot automatically perceive objects; they must learn to do so. As mentioned in Chapter 3, Hebb's data came from Senden's work with congenitally blind people who had gained sight after surgery. They could not identify objects without handling them. They could not visually distinguish a key from a book when both lay on a table, and they could not see any difference between a square and a circle. Only after a long period of practice were they eventually able to distinguish between these shapes and objects.

Although the subjects could not visually identify objects at first, they did see something. Hebb considered that they perceived a primitive unity of *figure-on-ground* that resulted from the interaction of the stimulus pattern with some function of the nervous system. The primitive unity constituted the undifferentiated whole in this situation and functioned as an essential part of learning to perceive an object.

The second type of undifferentiated whole—a behavioral whole—comes from Lewis's description of how a child learns new words (Lewis, 1936). The new words are initially integral parts of behavior patterns, which are at first undifferentiated wholes. Lewis describes an example of such a behavior pattern. When he asked his son, "Where's ballie?" the child turned toward a small white ball, picked it up, and handed it to his father. Lewis commented on this:

> We must first recall that the child's initial response to the phrase "Where's ballie?" was not simply an awareness of the ball, or even merely the turning of his attention to it. His response consisted rather of a series of movements involving the ball, turning towards it, seizing it and presenting it to the speaker, receiving in turn a smile and a word of approbation. (p. 200)

The child has learned a particular behavior that involved his father: the phrase "Where's ballie?" and a particular object. The behavior initiated by "Where's ballie?" and ending with "a smile and a word of approbation" constituted a behavioral whole for the child. The child did not know that the small, round white object was called a *ball* by adults. He did not know the adult meaning of "Where's . . . ," and he did not know that his father was asking a question. He simply carried out a behavior sequence in response to a specific verbal stimulus.

The third type—perception of a system of interrelated objects—comes from SCIS's (1974) life science program. This project developed an elementary school curriculum for the biological and physical sciences. The biological science program is designed to teach an understanding of the ecosystem to first through sixth graders. The program starts in the first grade with the children planting seeds and observing an aquarium that contains sand, water, fish, snails, and various aquatic plants. The choice of the aquarium as a starting place for the investigation of an ecosystem was deliberate. An aquarium is a miniature ecosystem that can be differentiated into parts and the parts interrelated to produce a conceptual system known as an ecosystem.

The aquarium to the first-grade children is similar to the object of Senden's newly sighted patients. The children initially are able to differentiate some parts of the aquarium, but they are blind to many other parts and to practically all of the parts' interrelations. For the children, the aquarium created in their minds a whole that is largely undifferentiated, but which can be differentiated and eventually integrated into a complex conceptual system. However, at the beginning for the first-grade children, the whole is at the preconceptual level because their initial reactions are primarily naming the parts they recognize, such as the fish and the plants, and asking for names of other parts such as the sand.

The fourth type of undifferentiated whole—the perception of symbols that represent the interrelationships of concepts—comes from Snyder and David's *The Principles of Heredity* (1957). These authors present a theoretical conceptual system that involves both descriptive and theoretical concepts. They begin with the descriptive concepts. In the first chapter, they describe examples of heredity and use pedigree charts of human inheritance. In the first part of Chapter 2, they describe Mendel's experiments with heredity in pea plants. In this way, the empirical descriptive foundation is laid out in the beginning for the introduction of the theoretical conceptual system that explains empirical data.

In the latter half of Chapter 2, Snyder and David present the theoretical conceptual system—not the entire system, but the basic descriptive and theoretical concepts (i.e., the basic postulates of Mendelian theory)—to lay a foundation that can be developed into a refined system by the processes of differentiation and integration. This foundation is the undifferentiated whole. In the book it consisted of a diagram (see Figure 8.1 in this text), which depicted the transmission of dominant and recessive genes through three generations, plus definitions of descriptive and theoretical concepts related to the diagram. The rest of the text was an elaboration or modification of the concepts depicted by the diagram.

The whole of Senden's patients was an undifferentiated pattern of an object. The object was on the table; the whole was a vague outline in the

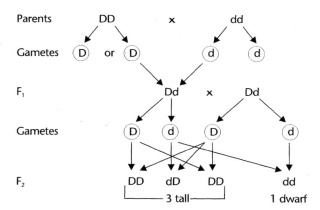

Figure 8.1 ▽ **Gene Transmission.** This diagram serves as a theoretical symbolic undifferentiated whole. The descriptive concepts that were introduced and defined in relation to the diagram were *gamete, zygote,* and *phenotype.* The theoretical concepts that were introduced and defined were *genotypes, heterozygous, homozygous, heterozygote, homozygote, unit character, alleles, recessive gene,* and *dominant gene.* Adapted from *The Principles of Heredity,* Laurence Snyder and Paul David, D.C. Heath and Company, 1957. Reprinted by permission.

patients' minds. Eventually, the patients differentiated and integrated the vague outline to produce a detailed perception of an object.

The whole for Lewis's child was an undifferentiated set of words. The whole for the first graders in the life science program was an undifferentiated pattern of a physical-biological system. The system (aquarium) was on the classroom table; the whole was a vague impression in the pupils' minds. Initially, the children could recognize certain parts such as fish, plants, snails, water, and so on. Presumably, their whole was less vague than that of Senden's patients, yet their initial conception was a long way from the differentiated-integrated conceptual system that they eventually achieved by the end of the sixth year.

The whole for readers of Snyder and David's book on heredity was based on terms, definitions, and relations. The whole consisted of postulates of a theoretical conceptual system that explained a simple case of inheritance in pea plants. This explanation was elaborated, enlarged, or modified in the remainder of the book.

In all four examples, the primary function of the undifferentiated whole was to provide a structure, form, or framework to be later differentiated. It was a form that grew with each additional item of information into a complex object or behavior or an interrelated conceptual system. If the students can be assumed to have had the experiences on which the concepts of the whole are derived, then a verbal presentation of the undifferentiated whole is sufficient. However, if the students cannot be assumed to have had these experiences, then these experiences must be provided, as was the case for Senden's patients and the first-grade students.

Because the whole in each case functioned as a perceptual or conceptual organizer, it is fair to wonder whether the undifferentiated whole is the same as Ausubel's *advance organizer*. It may be. Ausubel (1968) wrote of organizers:

> *The principal strategy advocated in this book for deliberately manipulating cognitive structure so as to enhance proactive facilitation or to minimize proactive inhibition involves the use of appropriately relevant and inclusive introductory materials (organizers) that are maximally clear and stable. These organizers are introduced in advance of the learning material itself and are also presented at a higher level of abstraction, generality, and inclusiveness; and since the substantive content of a given organizer is selected on the basis of their appropriateness for explaining, integrating, and interrelating the material they precede, this strategy simultaneously satisfies the substantive as well as the programming criteria specified above for enhancing the organizational strength of the cognitive structure. . . . In short,* the principal function of the organizer is to bridge the gap between what the learner already knows and what he needs to know before he can successfully learn the task at hand. *(p. 148) (emphasis added)*

This statement suggests that Ausubel's advance organizer is not the same as the undifferentiated whole. For example, Ausubel stated, "These organizers are introduced in advance of the learning material itself and are . . . at a higher level of abstraction, generality, and inclusiveness." Although undifferentiated wholes are introduced early in the course of instruction, they are an integral part of the learning material and are not "introduced in advance of the learning material."

Second, undifferentiated wholes are not necessarily "at a higher level of abstraction, generality, and inclusiveness." Snyder and David's initial description of gene behavior is quite specific and is not more abstract than statements about two-factor crosses or linkage that are made later in the text.

Third, the principal function of an undifferentiated whole is much more than "to bridge the gap between what the learner already knows and what he needs to know."

On the other hand, Ausubel's advance organizer and the undifferentiated whole do have something in common: Both are "selected on the basis of their appropriateness for explaining, integrating, and interrelating the material they precede."

Thus, both differences and similarities are seen between Ausubel's advance organizer and the undifferentiated whole. Nevertheless, one thing seems clear:

Organization of subject matter by some means is essential for meaningful learning.

Returning to the problem of building a curriculum, in addition to being an expert pedagogue, the curriculum developer must be an expert in the discipline, one who can analyze its conceptual systems to discover their basic descriptive concepts and theoretical concepts, and one who can create an undifferentiated whole and present it at the appropriate level so that it will serve to integrate and interrelate the content of the discipline. The developer then must be able to identify first-, second-, and higher-order descriptive and theoretical concepts (if any exist) and introduce them through meaningful inquiries so that concepts can be constructed and chunked with others.

▼ EXAMPLES OF TEACHING CONCEPTUAL SYSTEMS

The Ecosystem

We now examine two examples from biology that illustrate what has been said thus far. The first example is that of the conceptual system known as the *ecosystem*. Figure 3.1 depicted its basic first-, second-, and higher-order descriptive concepts that make up its conceptual system or theory. Ecosystem theory consists of the following basic postulates:

1. Biological communities consist of interacting populations in which energy enters and exits the community and specific inorganic molecules are exchanged between the community and its abiotic environment in a cyclic fashion.

2. An ecosystem consists of the biological community, the abiotic environment, and all their interactions in the particular area being considered.

3. Green plants (the producers) use the energy of sunlight to synthesize from inorganic molecules absorbed from the environment complex organic molecules to be used as a source of food or energy.

4. Food or energy is distributed to other populations in the community (the consumers and decomposers) through many links in food chains and food webs.

5. Food or energy is used by individuals at each feeding level in the food chains; therefore, less and less is available at progressively higher levels, which limits the length of the food chains.

6. Excretion and decomposition are essential processes that return inorganic molecules to the environment for absorption and reuse by producers.

7. Feeding patterns may result in dangerously high concentrations of nonbiodegradable molecules in the bodies of animals at or near the tops of food webs (biological magnification).

This theory or conceptual system derives its meaning from an analysis of the relationships (both qualitative and quantitative) among the various *classes* of objects within the system. Observable objects and organisms such as water, rocks, frogs, and grass must first be organized into classes such as producers, consumers, and environmental factors, and *then* relationships among these classes must be examined. The pattern, or form, of the relationships among these related classes is what constitutes the ecosystem; hence, the ecosystem concept requires understanding of higher-order relationships. How can these relationships become understood by students? Examine some of the learning cycle activities developed by the Science Curriculum Improvement Study that were designed to do just this (SCIS, 1974).

To initiate exploration of the ecosystem, students start with an undifferentiated whole—a complete but simple ecosystem. A plastic box divided into two sections with an aquarium in one section and a terrarium in the other can serve this purpose. The assumption is made that the introduction of a complete but simplified ecosystem in this way sufficiently capitalizes on students' intuitive and partial understandings of living and nonliving systems. In other words, students realize that we need food, water, and air; that cows eat grass; that too much heat can kill plants; and so on. These are the types of intuitive and partial understandings that subsequent activities will differentiate and integrate into an understanding of the ecosystem concept.

First, students are grouped into teams of three to four students, and each group builds its own system. The students plant a variety of seeds in each terrarium, and they add *Anacharis,* a green algae culture, duck weed, and other green plants to their aquariums. A week or so after the plants have begun to grow and the algae populations have increased, *Daphnia,* mealworms, isopods, snails, crickets, tadpoles, or other plant eaters are added to the systems. During this time students observe and record these organisms' feeding relationships and behavior patterns. Animal eaters are then added to the systems, such as guppies, frogs, or chameleons. Again, feeding relationships are observed. The guppies, of course, will eat the *Daphnia,* which ate the algae. The frogs will eat the mealworms, and the chameleons will eat the crickets, which ate the grass seeds, and so on.

During a discussion, the terms *environmental factors* and *environment* are introduced. This is done by having students compare the various systems in the classroom and naming all physical "things" that might affect the organisms in the systems. Students suggest factors such as soil, water, light, air, temperature, the plastic box, and so forth. These factors are listed on the classroom board. Above the list the teacher then writes the phrase *environmental factors* and points out that all the factors taken together make up the organisms' *environment.*

While the plant eaters and animal eaters are being added to the systems, several specific experiments are initiated to examine relationships among the plants and animals of the systems and the environmental factors. These experiments are considered concept application experiences with the descriptive concept of environmental factors. The response of isopods to water, heat, and light can be explored. The effect of various concentrations of salt on the hatching of brine shrimp eggs can be determined. And an interesting way to examine environmental relationships is through experiments that examine the effects of such factors as light, heat, soil, sand, water, and antiseptic solutions on the decomposition rates of various types of plants and animals.

Following several of these experiments and observations of the aquarium–terrarium systems, students are gathered together for a discussion of what they have done and what they have observed. A chart such as that shown in Figure 8.2 (next page) is drawn on the board. The teacher asks students to report the names of the plants that they have in their systems. As the name of each plant is mentioned, it is placed in the appropriate box in the chart. The teacher then asks students to report on which animals ate which plants. The names of the plant eaters are then written on the chart, with an arrow drawn from the plant to the animal indicating the feeding relationships. This, of course, is followed by having the students name the animals that ate other animals. Once the names of all the organisms are written in the chart and the arrows are drawn, the teacher focuses students' attention on sequences of feeding relationships and introduces the term *food chain* to refer to such sequences; the term labels this second-order descriptive concept. The terms *producers, first-order consumers, second-order consumers,* and *decomposers* are also introduced. These terms correspond to sections of the chart; thus classes of organisms with specific feeding relationships are differentiated within the system. Terms to refer to the third-order descriptive concepts of *aquarium community* and *terrarium community* are then written on the board below the chart to indicate that the sum of all such feeding relationships among the classes or organisms in an area (in this case, in the aquarium–terrarium system) is called a *biological community.*

All of these experiences prepare the way for introduction of the term *ecosystem.* Once the chart of the aquarium and terrarium communities is completed, all that remains to be added is the environment. To do this, the teacher asks the students what, other than food, the populations in the community require in order to live. Students should volunteer environmental factors such as those studied previously and perhaps others not already men-

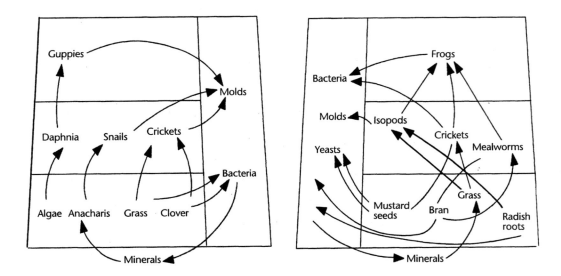

Figure 8.2 ▾ **SCIS Classroom Chart A.** This chart is used to introduce the terms *producers, consumers, decomposer, food chain,* and *biological community.* This chart symbolically represents the laboratory systems. Symbolizing concrete objects and events is a useful step in concept construction. From *Science Teaching and the Development of Reasoning.* Copyright 1974 by the Regents of the University of California. Reprinted by permission.

tioned. All of these factors are then listed on the board, with arrows indicating which populations each factor influences. This is shown in Figure 8.3. The teacher adds the word *environment* to the top of the list and explains that a community interacting with its environment is called an *ecosystem.* The term *ecosystem* is then written at the top of the chart, and term introduction is complete. All of the subordinate concepts can then be chunked together to produce a single higher-order concept: the ecosystem.

At this point, many students have a good grasp of the meaning of the term *ecosystem* and its use, but this is relative only to the phenomena experienced— that is, the actual classroom aquarium–terrarium systems. If instruction were ended at this point, the more general aspects of the concept probably would not be appreciated. In other words, we realize that human beings are a part of an ecosystem; we conceptualize ponds, forests, grasslands, seashores, the ocean floor, and so on as ecosystems. They are, of course, interconnected, but at the same time they can be conceptually isolated. Students are extremely unlikely to abstract the form of this concept and develop this type of understanding unless additional activities involving the ecosystem concept are initiated. These addi-

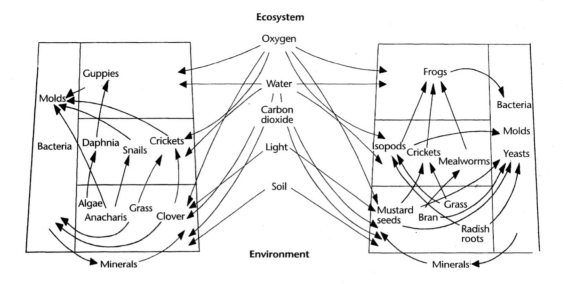

Figure 8.3 ▽ **SCIS Classroom Chart B.** This chart is used to introduce the term *ecosystem.* From *Science Teaching and the Development of Reasoning.* Copyright 1974 by the Regents of the University of California. Reprinted by permission.

tional activities constitute the application phase of instruction. They are essential in enabling students to construct a more general and useful understanding of ecosystems.

How can this type of understanding be constructed? According to the instructional pattern suggested previously, a series of additional activities are needed, all of which involve the same concepts and the same symbolic notation, although in varying contexts. This suggests that we should study other ecosystems, such as forests, rivers, ponds, sandy beaches, rocky intertidal areas, deserts, lawns, and so on. These can be studied through field trips to the actual areas be they 50 miles away or on the school grounds and through films, videos, slides, trips to museums, and perhaps zoos. The language (symbolic notation) used throughout all of these experiences must stay the same. That language, of course, is the terms *environment, producers, consumers, decomposers, population, food chain, food web, community,* and *ecosystem.* This study of a variety of ecosystems and the continued reintroduction of the terms allows the students the opportunity to use the terms in a variety of contexts and to eventually extract the "form" of the concepts from the concrete situations at their own rates.

Evolution and Natural Selection

As another example, the instructional pattern described above will be applied to teaching the conceptual system associated with organic evolution and the process of natural selection. As discussed in Chapter 1, the explanation of evolution by natural selection proposed by Charles Darwin in *Origin of Species* synthesized several previously known but isolated biological and geological ideas. As mentioned, this synthetic theory involved these six basic postulates:

1. *Enormous spans of time* are available for gradual geological and biological change.
2. Given favorable conditions, populations of organisms are capable of exceedingly rapid growth. This potential for rapid expansion in numbers is termed *biotic potential.*
3. Populations seldom reach their potential growth rate because of restricting environmental factors termed *limiting factors.*
4. *Variation* is found among the characteristics of individuals within a species.
5. Some characteristics that contribute to this variation are *heritable.*
6. Individuals with certain characteristics have a better chance of surviving and reproducing than individuals with other characteristics. In other words, there is a *natural selection* of certain characteristics.

The synthesis of these six postulates into an understanding of evolution through natural selection requires that the student transcend the realm of the concrete present and build a theoretical conceptual system. The basic instructional sequence that will allow this to happen again begins with a presentation of the undifferentiated whole. The parts of the whole will then be differentiated by conducting a series of learning cycles involving the concepts of geologic time, biotic potential, limiting factors, variation, heritability, and natural selection.

Introduction of the Whole

The undifferentiated whole in this instance is the idea of gradual change of living things over time (i.e., organic evolution). In the century before Darwin, the evidence that organisms changed through time became increasingly convincing. The fossil record presented a complex and confusing picture to seventeenth- and eighteenth-century naturalists, who generally believed species to be fixed (Green, 1958). By the late eighteenth and early nineteenth centuries, however, men such as Buffon, Lamarck, and Erasmus Darwin (Charles's grandfather) argued that the fossil record implied an evolution or extinction of species. Buffon, for example, in his essay "Animals Common to Both Continents" (1778) seemed to believe that the fate of the mammoth implied evolution of specifics:

> *This species was unquestionably the largest and strongest of all quadrupeds; and since it has disappeared, how many smaller, weaker, and less remarkable species must likewise have perished, without leaving any evidence of their past experience? How many others have undergone such changes, whether from degeneration or improvement, occasioned by the great vicissitudes of the earth and waters, the neglect or cultivation of Nature, the continued influence of favorable or hostile climates, that they are now no longer the same creatures? (in Green, 1958, p. 152)*

Buffon appears to be remarkably close to the idea of evolution through natural selection. For our purposes, however, the key idea is that of change or extinction over time. This is the idea that must initiate the study of natural selection. This is the phenomenon or "whole" that subsequent activities will differentiate. As was the case for the ecosystem, instruction is designed to capitalize on students' previous intuitive and partial understanding of the phenomena under consideration. In this case, initial activities capitalize on students' existing understanding of concepts such as change, death and its various causes, and reproduction.

A study of the fossil record can serve to introduce the whole: the idea of change or extinction over time. Many textbooks and laboratory guides contain suitable activities for studying the fossil record. A learning cycle titled "What Changes Have Occurred in Organisms Through Time?" allows students to discover the evolutionary patterns of several invertebrates and vertebrates (Lawson, 1994). Also, films and slides are available to introduce students to the large number and variety of species that have changed or become extinct. Many museums also have exhibits of past forms of life that would be appropriate for field trips. Of course, most students are familiar with and interested in extinct species such as dinosaurs. The evolution of dinosaurs as shown in Figure 8.4 could provide a worthwhile topic for discussion.

Geologic Time

Students conduct a brief exploration activity to appreciate the vast amounts of time available for gradual change. Table 8.1 (from Lawson and Paulson, 1958) provides many important landmarks in time that can serve as a basis for conducting this activity. Grouped into teams of two or three, students are provided the table of data, paint, chalk, sticks, or other suitable means of marking distances. They are then challenged to construct a time line with a single scale and to place each event from the table in its relative position on the line. The groups will have to decide what distance or time unit they will use. For example, if they choose to make one pace equal to 1,000 years, then they

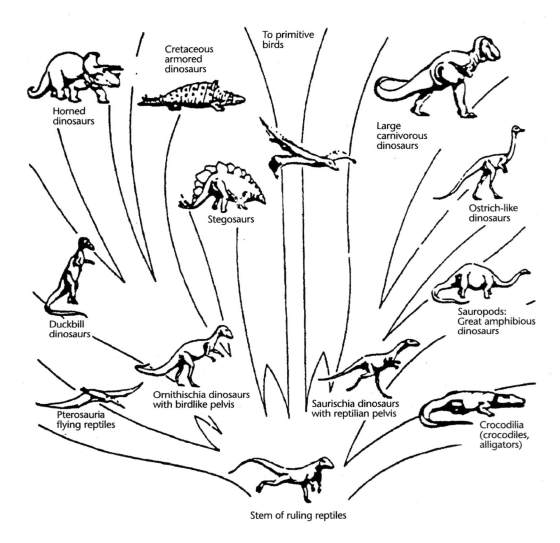

Figure 8.4 ▼ **A Phylogenetic Tree of the Ruling Reptiles.** From the primitive stock came crocodiles, flying reptiles, the two major orders of dinosaurs, and primitive birds. An introduction of this kind to past forms of life should be adequate to provide the initial whole and to set the stage for later investigations. The question presented by these activities is, of course, "How do these changes occur?" This will be answered by exploration in Darwin's six postulates, followed by synthesizing or term introduction lessons and several concept application experiences. The first postulate explored is geologic time.   Reprinted with permission from A. S. Romer, *The Vertebrate Story* (4th ed.), University of Chicago Press, 1959.

Table 8.1 ▼ **Important Landmarks in Time.** Selection of time periods is somewhat arbitrary, thus there is some overlapping. *Note:* Columns do not represent landmarks in chronological order.

Historical	Archaeological	Geological	Astronomical
Beginning of Dark Ages in Europe, A.D. 500	Evidence of ground stone tools, 10,000 B.C.	Marine algae and invertebrates abundant 500 million years ago	Probable origin of our galaxy, 5.5 billion years ago
Discovery of America, 1492	Evidence of permanent dwelling, 7000 B.C.	Age of Fishes, 350–400 million years ago	Probable origin of life, 3.4 billion years ago
Signing of the Magna Carta, A.D. 1215	Evidence of woven garments, 8000 B.C.	Appearance of mammals, 150 million years ago	Probable origin of earth, 4.5 billion years ago
Birth of Christ	Evidence of domestic dogs, 14,000 B.C.	Appearance of amphibians, 300 million years ago	
Fall of Egypt to Alexander, 332 B.C.	Remains of a bow and arrow dated to 11,000 B.C.	Age of Reptiles, 80–250 million years ago	
Beginning of Iron Age, 1500 B.C.	Crude farming tools, 9000 B.C.	First land plants, 360 million years ago	
Korean War, 1952	Chipped stone tools, 18,000 B.C.	First humans appear 1 million years ago	
Writing of U.S. Constitution, 1787	Evidence of humans on North American continent, 17,000 B.C.	Appearance of flowering plants, 160 million years ago	
Development of Egyptian civilizations, 5000–2000 B.C.		Modern human types (Cro-Magnon) appear, 55,000 years ago	
Beginning of Crusades, A.D. 1000			

Source: From Lawson & Paulson, 1958, p. 456.

will have to go outside to construct their time line. Also, they will soon realize that they will be unable to place all of the events on the line, because the distance from the present to the probable origin of life 2 billion years ago would be approximately 1,140 miles! The job of finding a suitable unit and then placing the events along the time line will be challenging. After completing the time line and then discussing various solutions in class, students should be impressed with the tremendous span of time available for evolution since the origin of life.

Biotic Potential

Bacterial populations can be cultured as part of students' initial explorations in the phenomenon of biotic potential. Population sizes are estimated using microscope slides with grids. The growth of the population should be recorded and graphed during the initial period of bacterial population expansion. The resulting data when graphed as in Figure 8.5 show a geometric increase in numbers. The students should extrapolate their data to gain some idea of the possible result if this type of growth continued for an extended length of time. The activity could be combined with similar activities such as the growth of *Drosophila* and yeast populations mentioned below.

An ear of corn can be provided to each pair of students. The number of kernels on each ear is counted and multiplied by the approximate number of ears on one corn plant. In the field, various types of fruits also can be collected. The seeds contained in them are counted and multiplied by the number of fruits per plant to obtain the approximate number of seeds produced by one plant. If female frogs are available for discussion, then the ovaries can be observed and the number of eggs per female estimated.

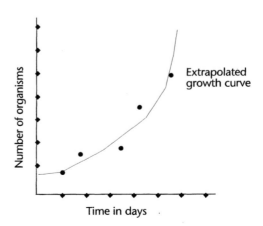

Figure 8.5 ▾ **Exponential Growth of Bacteria Population**

Following these activities, the phrase *biotic potential* is introduced during a classroom discussion. First, the teacher poses the question, "What would happen if all the bacteria, corn kernels, seeds, and frog eggs developed into adults?" The response should be clear: There would be a lot of bacteria, frogs, and corn plants around. The teacher then asks, "What would happen if all of these plants and animals had young that grew up and had young, and this continued for several generations?" The result is obvious. The world would be overrun with these organisms. It is at this point that the teacher introduces the term *biotic potential* to signify a population's capacity for an overwhelming expansion of numbers.

Limiting Factors

The following two exploratory activities serve as a basis from which to introduce the term *limiting factors*. Cultures of *Drosophila* are supplied to each pair of students. Each team has two containers, one small and one large, both containing six flies. Every week for a month or two, the number of flies in both jars is counted and graphed. When the populations have both reached their upper limits and crashed, then the recording and graphing are complete.

Yeast cultures also may be grown in a potato broth prepared by boiling several potatoes in approximately 2,500 milliliters of water. After boiling, the broth is filtered through cheesecloth. Each student is then supplied with a culture dish of broth, to which a small amount of yeast is added until a density of approximately one yeast cell per microscope field is reached. Sugar is then added to the cultures. Each day for the following ten days or so the students estimate the size of their yeast population and plot the data on a graph such as that in Figure 8.6.

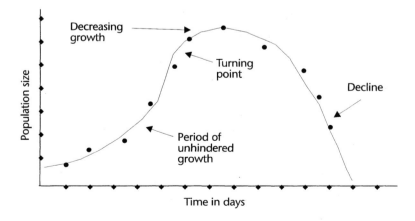

Figure 8.6 ▾ **Growth and Decline of Yeast Population**

After these investigations, a class discussion is held to elicit reasons that students believe the populations did not continue to expand. The students should be able to name such factors as not enough food, the accumulation of toxins, crowding, not enough space, too little oxygen, not enough water, and too many competitors. The teacher should list student ideas on the board. Above the list the teacher then writes the words *limiting factors*. This constitutes the term introduction phase of the investigation.

As concept application experiences designed to extend this concept's applicability, the teacher should give the students the opportunity to name limiting factors of such populations as deer, fox, mountain lions, pelicans, and human beings. Many films and videos are available that depict naturally occurring populations. One or two of these can be shown to allow students additional opportunities to isolate limiting factors.

Variation

Initial exploratory experiences to develop the descriptive concept of variation could include a short field trip to sample and record the lengths of snail shells; leaves on maple, oak, or other suitable trees; and the height of acorns, pine cones, or blades of grass. In the laboratory the length of various kinds of seeds purchased from a grocery store can be measured and recorded. Student heights and weights also can serve as a source of data. The field and laboratory data should be plotted on frequency-versus-size graphs. The approximately normal curves obtained for each sample are then used to introduce the term *variation*.

Heredity

Exploration of this descriptive concept is begun by supplying wild and mutant strains of *Drosophila* to pairs of students. The students are encouraged to examine the flies to determine which characteristics can be used to differentiate the fly types. The students isolate three or four males and three or four females with specific traits and place them into culture bottles to reproduce. The students may choose to cross wild-type males and mutant females, wild-type females and mutant males, wild-type males and females, or mutant males and females.

After mating and the subsequent development of larvae and pupae, the adults should be taken from the containers. In 10 to 12 days from the outset, a new generation of adult flies will emerge. These flies can then be etherized and their particular phenotype determined and compared to that of the parent generation and to others of their own generation. Further crosses can be carried out and ratios of offspring types determined. The purpose of this investigation is to allow students an opportunity to experience and record specific phenotypic traits as they are *inherited* from parent to offspring.

Natural Selection

Stebbins and Allen (1975) describe an activity in which students play the role of birds preying on "toothpick insects." In this activity, a teacher distributes approximately 400 toothpicks to students. One-third of the toothpicks are painted green, one-third are painted yellow, and one-third red. The exact number of each color is recorded.

The toothpicks are then taken by the teacher to a grassy area on the school grounds and spread throughout the area. Students are told to play the role of toothpick-insect–eating birds and then are given five minutes to capture as many insects as possible. The students are then taken to the area to begin the hunt. The captured toothpick insects are taken back to the classroom and counted, and the numbers of green, yellow, and red toothpick insects are compared. Percentages of each color of toothpick insect are then calculated, and the class is asked, "What color insect would you rather be if you had a choice?" An answer and an explanation are obtained. At this point the teacher can introduce the term *natural selection* to explain the process of differential selection of a particular color of toothpick insect. This is the term introduction phase of the investigation into the process of natural selection.

Lawson (1994) contains another learning cycle that simulates natural selection and related phenomena. The first activity, which could be used instead of the toothpick insect activity, uses sets of 100 paper chips of 10 different colors to represent mice. The paper-chip mice are spread randomly over a variety of fabric patterns that simulate various environments. Students here also act as predatory animals, selectively removing mice from their environments. In this experiment a quota is prescribed for each predator to ensure that 25% of the chips remain in the habitat. Following the predation, the surviving chips are removed and grouped according to color. Reproduction of the survivors is then simulated by adding more chips of the same colors to the population. The predation and reproduction processes are then repeated until the resulting population is adapted to its surroundings.

The famous case of industrial melanism can be read about and discussed in class (Kettlewell, 1959). To introduce the theory of evolution through natural selection, the terms *geologic time, biotic potential, limiting factors, variation, heredity,* and *natural selection* are listed on the board. In the following class discussion, students are encouraged to analyze, evaluate, and synthesize these concepts in explaining the process of evolution through natural selection. This could be done in groups of three or four students or perhaps an entire class.

The activities described thus far provide experiences that allow the initial construction of many concepts. They should provide students with an initial understanding of the theory of evolution and the theory of natural selection. The task remaining is to provide additional experiences that involve the same concepts but in varying contexts. This, of course, is the concept application phase, and it is necessary to give students the opportunity to coordinate and abstract properties of the concepts from their physical or biological contexts.

Stebbins and Allen (1975) suggest several other activities that can serve this purpose. They describe means for investigating adaptive radiation, the founder principle, the effect of predator vision, positive selection of flowering plants, mutations, sexual reproduction, selection in predators, and, most important, natural selection and evolution of humans. When conducting such activities, it is imperative that the teacher continue to raise questions that encourage students to reflect on the roles of the various ideas studied. As Stebbins and Allen point out, the limitations of the simulations must be examined. Questions such as the following should be raised and considered.

- How do you think these processes affect human beings today?
- Are we still evolving? If so, in what direction?
- Why was DDT so effective in killing mosquitoes when it was first introduced? Why did it become less effective?
- How did dogs and cats obtain their present forms?

These and other questions are needed to encourage students to think beyond the activities and to begin abstracting the form of the process of evolution through natural selection—that is, to chunk the basic descriptive concepts into the higher-order theoretical conceptual system known as evolution through natural selection.

In summary, the described instructional pattern involves (a) the identification and presentation of an initially undifferentiated whole, (b) the differentiation of the whole through physical experiences leading to identification of its parts and the patterns of relationships among the parts, (c) the introduction of terms (symbolic notation) to label these parts and patterns of relationships, and (d) exploration of new contexts that involve the same patterns. These application experiences provide the student the opportunity to self-regulate and abstract the form of the concepts under consideration from their specific contexts. In other words, learning begins with physical experience with objects, events, and situations. This experience provides the students with a mental record of what they have done and seen. Symbolic notation is then introduced that labels and aids in the identification of patterns in the experiences. Finally, additional experiences that involve the same patterns are provided along with repetition of the introduced terms to allow students to abstract the form of the concepts from the specific phenomena used in their construction.

▼ CURRICULUM PRINCIPLES FOR THE DEVELOPMENT OF THINKING SKILLS

The general objective of any educational system is to transmit the culture of the society. Part of that general objective is the transmission of the accumulated knowledge of that society. No one could argue about the value of such an objective, and a cursory glance at the courses and curricula of U.S. schools would reveal that the schools indeed attempt to achieve this objective. However, as was mentioned in Chapter 1, according to the Educational Policies Commission, one other objective is of primary importance. That objective was called *freedom of mind.* To achieve freedom of mind, one must develop the ability to think and to reason. This ability is of primary importance because no society can be certain that its store of accumulated knowledge is adequate to deal with an ever-changing world. Thus, there must be some means of acquiring new knowledge or of modifying or replacing the misconceptions of the past. For this, the ability to think and reason is necessary. This section will describe curricular principles that will promote the development of important thinking skills and reasoning patterns needed for freedom of mind.

Self-Regulation

As you probably recall, the core idea for development of thinking skills is that teachers must create situations that require students to engage in the self-regulation process described in Chapter 3. Self-regulation is initiated by a contradiction of behavior or of some belief or by a question or problem to which an individual has no answer or solution. A contradiction may be ignored, in which case nothing is accomplished as far as the development of thinking skills is concerned. But if it is not ignored, argumentation ensues. The word *argumentation* is defined as (1) reasoning, discussion; (2) a discussion dealing with a controversial point; (3) a setting forth of reasons together with the conclusion drawn from them; and (4) the premises and conclusions so set forth. Within the self-regulation process, argumentation, whether with oneself or another, leads to searching behavior for some idea or ideas that will resolve the difficulty. These ideas are the hypotheses that must be tested. The testing of these hypotheses leads to the development of explicit methods of testing—the thinking skills and reasoning patterns described earlier. In this way thinking skills develop.

The thesis presented here is that students consciously learn to use the self-regulation process and develop thinking skills as a result of practice. In other words, they must be confronted with contradictions or complexities that they must resolve by their own thinking and data gathering. Chapters 5 and 7 explained the learning cycle method of exploration, term introduction, and application. In this method the teacher provides materials for exploration that are intended to give students new experiences and raise questions and to give the teacher the opportunity to introduce new terms. The application aspect of the method consists of presenting the student with different examples of the same concepts or reasoning patterns in order to reinforce the concepts and thinking skills involved in the lessons.

Special courses designed only of problem-solving situations and devoid of subject matter are not recommended. Ideally, the questions and problems should originate within the framework of study of a discipline. The specific manner in which any teacher can create problem situations depends on the teacher's ingenuity plus the nature of the discipline. At least three possibilities use the learning cycle as the basic instructional method:

1. independent investigations,
2. a historical model, and
3. comparison of contrasting conceptual systems.

Independent Investigations

The independent investigation curricular model, which might be termed the *graduate school model,* can be applied in most natural and social science courses—indeed, in any subject matter in which inquiry takes place. An example from a first-grade class exemplifies the method in the natural sciences. The children were observing and recording events and changes in classroom aquaria that contained aquatic plants, fish, and snails. One day the water in the aquaria near the windows became green with algal bloom. Several children noticed this and asked, "What made the water green?" Instead of answering, the teacher asked the pupils for their own ideas. There were a variety of responses, each of which served as a guide for setting up an experiment. At this age the children were incapable of carefully controlled experimentation, but with the guidance of the teacher they did several experiments from which the children concluded that sunlight was the significant variable.

Any science course that involves the actual manipulation of materials pertinent to the subject matter repeatedly presents the teacher with opportunities for raising questions that can be used as a starting point for the students' own investigations. Depending on how much the students already know and the level of their thinking skills, the investigations can be carried out by the class as a whole, by smaller groups of students, or by individual students. In any case, the questions should be selected with care. They should be difficult enough to pose a real challenge to the students, but they should not be so difficult that they frustrate the students beyond their abilities. A degree of success in the investigative undertaking is essential to maintain interest and motivation. Constant frustration can only discourage students and produce rejection on their part.

Historical Model

The historical approach to creating a curriculum for creative and critical thinking requires a carefully designed program of student investigations. The Harvard Case Histories, which describe the history of the development of several scientific disciplines through the actual investigations carried out by famous scientists, could be used as a model for designing such a curriculum. Each discipline has a history from the first observations of particular phenomena, the first experiments, and continued data collection to the creation of laws and theories that changed over time as new and contradictory data were revealed.

A curriculum that uses the historical model follows the actual history of a discipline's development. The students are introduced to the original questions through exploration of the phenomena that confronted investigators. In this way students obtain original data from which they attempt to generate their own hypotheses. This is followed by hypothesis testing. New data are then obtained that require the students to revise their explanations or create new ones. By judicious collection of data properly correlated with the students' success in deriving, modifying, and creating explanations, the students' growth in thinking skills and in understanding the discipline parallels the discipline's historical development.

Comparing Conceptual Systems

The method of comparing contrasting conceptual systems seems to be particularly suited for the social sciences, which are abundant with conflicting theories. An example is Jerome Bruner's "Man: A Course Study Curriculum," which contrasts different cultures. Various social, economic, and political systems are replete with conflict in the modern world. Different religions and philosophical systems can challenge the student to question, argue, search for evidence, and introduce the concept of value in relation to thinking and decision making (Bruner, 1968).

All three of the above suggested procedures stress one essential ingredient: the students' active intellectual involvement in answering questions. The specific answers the students achieve are only incidental. It is the intellectual process through which they go that gradually develops their thinking skills. These programs have no absolute answers. Teachers are not authorities, but guides to encourage and motivate students to apply their own thinking skills and thus aid their development.

The notion of stages of intellectual development discussed previously is critical in the context of selecting topics and questions for student investigation. For instance, consider the task of having young children try to construct theoretical concepts such as genes or atoms. Such a task would be difficult on four counts. First, few children have enough experience with the phenomena that require explanation using these theoretical concepts. Second, the concepts derive their meaning not so much from the phenomena as from their relationships with other theoretical concepts and their positions within theoretical conceptual systems. Third, young children have yet to develop the hypothetical-deductive reasoning patterns needed to construct theoretical conceptual systems (see Chapter 4). Fourth and finally, the task of explaining these phenomena is totally unrelated to the intellectual tasks they face each day in spontaneously attempting to understand their world. They are still trying to classify, seriate, and describe their environment before generating meaningful causal relationships within that experience. Although not impossible, to have them go beyond this and attempt the task of explaining some scientific phenomenon is so unrelated to their normal intellectual activities that the experience would be practically devoid of meaning and could do little or nothing to promote thinking skill development. The presentation of such abstract explanations may, in fact, encourage rote memorization and thus actively retard intellectual development. To promote the development of thinking skills, the classroom tasks must correspond generally with the sorts of challenges that children face in their spontaneous attempts to order and explain their world.

▼ TEXTBOOK USE AND SELECTION

The textbook is an integral part of the science curriculum for many teachers. This is regrettable for several reasons, most important of which is that the majority are poorly written, too dense with terms, and of little help to students in developing an understanding of the nature of science. Recall Yager's finding that *Modern Biology* includes 17,130 special biological terms with an average of 23 special terms per page (Yager, 1983)! Needless to say, this is far too many terms for the high school student to assimilate with any meaning. The inevitable result is rote memorization, frustration, or outright intellectual dropout. If such a textbook is to be used at all in a learning cycle curriculum, its readings must come *after* the exploration and term introduction phases of the learning cycle. In other words, text reading should be a part of the concept application phase, if they are to be assigned at all.

Few textbooks are written with the learning cycle approach in mind. Perhaps the best of the available texts that attempt to emphasize scientific reasoning is J. J. W. Baker and G. E. Allen's *The Study of Biology* from Addison-Wesley. Regrettably, this text is written for a year-long college course. Also regrettable is that more recent editions of the text have de-emphasized the history of science and scientific reasoning at the expense of encyclopedic coverage. Ironically, the now out-of-print first edition (1967) is superior to the more recent editions in this respect. The following passage from the first edition (p. 74) well illustrates how Baker and Allen emphasize the thinking involved in investigating one aspect of the photosynthesis process:

> *Clues leading to the solution of a problem in one area of biological research are often provided by investigations in a slightly different area. So it was with plant photosynthesis. The Dutch-born microbiologist C. B. Van Neil had been studying photosynthesis in purple sulfur bacteria. Like the cells containing chlorophyll in green plants, these bacteria use light energy to synthesize carbohydrate materials. However, purple sulfur bacteria use hydrogen sulfide (H_2S) instead of water. This fact suggests a deduction which might determine the origin of the oxygen given off by green plants during photosynthesis.*

> *Hypothesis: If . . .*   *the oxygen released by plants during photosynthesis comes from the carbon dioxide molecule, . . .*

> *Prediction: then . . .*   *the purple sulfur bacteria will release oxygen as a result of their photosynthetic activity.*

> *On the other hand,*

> *Hypothesis: If . . .*   *the oxygen released by plants during photosynthesis comes from a water molecule, . . .*

> *Prediction: then . . .*   *the purple sulfur bacteria will release sulfur as a result of their photosynthetic activity. (p. 174)*

Note how Baker and Allen explicitly state alternative hypotheses and predictions. For students who have not yet become fully conscious of this hypothetical-deductive mode of thinking and who are not aware of the difference between a hypothesis and a prediction, this treatment of the thinking process can be helpful.

With these points in mind, Mayer and Barufaldi (1988), through the National Center for Science Education, offer the following ten guidelines in selecting a text:[*]

> 1. *Beware the encyclopedic text, the one that purports to "cover" the discipline, the one that is proud of mentioning every conceivable aspect of the subject. No textbook can do so and no student should be asked to memorize such wealth*

*From "Textbook Chooser's Guide," by W. V. Mayer and J. P. Barufaldi, The National Center for Science Education, 1988. Reprinted by permission.

of detail. Instead, consider if the text fairly presents the major concepts of the discipline and provides examples to illuminate them. The adequate development of selected major principles is more likely positively to affect the student than are reams of nugatory details.

2. *Beware of any text that emphasizes memorization of vocabulary. Students are expected to learn new words when confronted by a new discipline, but page after page containing bold faced or italicized words to be defined and memorized constitute a dull exercise not exemplifying either disciplinary concepts or the nature of science. Selected useful and meaningful vocabulary can be an inestimable aid in broadening understanding. Concentration on words for the sake of words is a pedestrian and non-illuminating activity.*

3. *Beware of the text that does not read well. One written in short choppy sentences that develop detail but not ideas is quite likely to be used by the student to uncover only a snippet of information. The text should provide a narrative of inquiry rather than a rhetoric of conclusions. Paragraphs and chapters are not to be watertight entities unrelated to what has gone before or to what will come. Rather, the text should build on previous information and serve to develop a basis for intellectual growth as the student proceeds through the book.*

A text should not be merely a passive reading experience. A text written merely to tell a student something is unlikely to be as effective as one designed to be interactive, eliciting responses from the student by requiring activity related to the subject under consideration.

4. *Beware of the dogmatic textbook. Science is an ever-changing body of data constantly refined on the basis of new evidence. Texts that present the corpus of science as a fixed and unchanging mass of evidence do not prepare students to live in a world where change may be the only constant. However, it is as unrepresentative of science as is dogmatism, to equivocate to the point where students are left with the impression that science is a body of untested hypotheses, guesses, and ever-changing data bases.*

5. *Beware of the text as the sole source of biological information. The textbook must be regarded as an introduction to science that provides alternative avenues for learning. Activities should be included that will expand the student's horizons and send students to other sources of information on the topic. The text should be teaching the student how to learn and should include activities for independent information gathering.*

6. *Beware of the text that does not explicate the nature of science. One of the major reasons students take science courses is to become acquainted with science as a way of knowing. The processes of science should permeate the textbook and not be confined to an isolated chapter or paragraph on what is erroneously referred to as "the scientific method." Rather, examples of the investigatory nature of*

science that delineate its processes, its successes, and its limitations should appear in every chapter, if not on every page. Eliminate from consideration textbooks that present science as a process of uncertainty. Statements such as "some scientists believe" and "Many scientists agree" present science as a guessing game whose issues are decided by vote. Scientists conclude on the basis of data, and their conclusions are valid at a given point. Science is not a consensus activity [or] a random guess process, and texts that present it as such do a disservice to the discipline and to the students attempting to understand it.

7. *Beware the text that does not clearly elucidate the role of controlled experiment, hypothesis formulation, and theory in science. These are basic intellectual tools of the scientist, and their proper use has led science to its great contributions. If the status of experimental data, the testing of hypotheses and the process of theory formation are presented in a muddled and confusing fashion, the student will be denied access to the processes of science.*

8. *Beware of the bland textbook, the one written in such a way as to eliminate controversial or contentious issues and the one that presents biology simply as a fixed body of non-applicable data. The nature of scientific controversy should be presented. Current biological problems still unresolved should be discussed. Students should be encouraged to analyze, synthesize, and evaluate evidence for and against a given hypothesis.*

9. *Beware the textbook that emphasizes only one aspect of the discipline—one that presents biology only in terms of morphology and systematics, for example, and ignores other and perhaps more applicable aspects of the discipline. No text can present all aspects of the subject, but each acceptable text should present some alternative patterns within the discipline and include, for biology, such topics such as ecology, genetics, growth and development, evolution, and behavior as major activities subsumed under the head of biology.*

Further, science should not be presented as an enterprise operating in isolation from society and technology. The interrelationships of science with social and technological aspects should permeate the text.

10. *Beware the classical textbook, one that leaves the student with an impression that science is a retrospective exercise. A textbook that does not deal in some measure with current problems is not preparing students for the future they will face or for the issues with which they will have to deal as voting citizens. Modern discoveries should be included.*

Mayer and Barufaldi emphasize that too many terms to be memorized not only dull the mind but also the spirit. As an example, consider the following passage from *Modern Biology* (Towle, 1989). Whenever a special biological term is used, I have replaced it with one of my own italicized terms.

Phases of *Sisotim*

The fourth event in the *llec* cycle, a continuous process that scientists divide into four phases: *orpphase, atemphase, amayllopphase,* and *oletphase.* As you read, keep in mind that *sisotim* produces two identical *llecs* with the same number of *emosomorhcs* as the parent *llec.*

Orpphase is the first phase of *sisotim. Orpphase* can be subdivided into three steps. During early *orpphase,* the *nitamorhc* coils and forms *emosomorhcs.* Simultaneously both the *suloelcun* and the *raelcun* membrane break down and disappear. In organisms other than plants two dark cylindrical bodies, called *eloirtnecs (ZELO-eert-NES),* move away from each other, going toward opposite ends, or *elops,* of the *llec.* (p. 132)

Did you understand the passage? Now your task is to memorize the terms (and a lot more) so that you can pass a recall-based test on what you have read. Are you motivated to learn more terms? Are you surprised that such text-based instruction turns students away from science? I'm not.

▼ **USING FIELD TRIPS TO ENCOURAGE SELF-REGULATION**

Field trips can serve a vital purpose in the science curriculum. Student motivation and excitement are usually high and so students are apt to learn and retain more on field trips than in the classroom. Likewise, many phenomena can be explored in the field that simply cannot be brought into the classroom or laboratory. In terms of the learning cycle, fieldwork can serve as the exploration phase, with the term introduction and application phases occurring in the classroom. In some instances, the first two phases, or perhaps even initial applications, can take place in the field.

Before considering a learning cycle approach to fieldwork, consider some approaches to introducing fieldwork in an intertidal zone. Rank the following lesson plans in terms of how you perceive their effectiveness in promoting self-regulation for your students. Use 1 for most effective and 4 for least effective.

Rank

A. Provide students with rulers and run a transect from the upper to lower zones in the intertidal area. Have students measure and record the shell sizes of *Tegula funebralis* (a common West Coast snail) found along the transect. Have the students plot size-versus-frequency graphs for all of the snails measured.

_____

B. Provide the students with rulers, quadrats, and a map of the intertidal area and have them measure and record *Tegula* shell sizes and determine the density of the snails from three locations in the intertidal area: the lower, middle, and upper zones. Then ask the students to search for quantitative relationships among the variables and to explain these relationships in light of other observations and general ecological concepts.

C. Explain to the students that interspecific competition affects population characteristics of many species. For example, the snail *Tegula funebralis* is common in the intertidal area. The older, larger snails are found in the lower zone, whereas the younger, smaller snails live in the upper zone. Tell the students that this is so because their food source (algae) is more abundant in the lower zone; however, the starfish *Pisaster*, which preys on the snails, lives in the lower zone. Because the smaller snails are unable to move fast enough to escape the starfish, they must remain in the upper zone. Now have your students go to the intertidal area and collect data to verify your explanation.

D. Provide students with rulers, thermometers, identification keys, quadrats, and a map of the intertidal area and have them select an abundant population in the area, identify interesting variables with respect to individual organisms and the population's distribution, and search for quantitative relationships among these variables.

According to the learning cycle method, an introductory period of exploration or openness is recommended to induce self-regulation. Hence, Procedures B and D are the most likely ways to initiate student questioning and self-regulation. Procedure D may be more effective than B for the students who are already applying hypothetical-deductive patterns. It is more open and allows students to examine interesting phenomena that you may not have anticipated. However, Procedure D affords little guidance and may not be as effective for less-skilled reasoners as the somewhat more structured Procedure B. The choice of openness or structure depends on the students' thinking skills and their past experiences with this kind of instruction.

Procedure A provides students with direct experience. As it is presented, however, it is not likely to initiate self-regulation because it is a highly directive "cookbook." Self-regulation could be initiated if the plotted data raised questions that were related to previous partial understandings.

Unfortunately, Procedure C is much like the kind of labs and fieldwork that many teachers conduct. Because the students already know what the data are supposed to show, no self-regulation and intellectual development are likely to occur. Further, it encourages a reliance on authority rather than on evidence and initiative. This is a good way to "turn off" students.

An Example of Student Field Work

The following example of a field investigation shows how one pair of college students explored a rocky intertidal area and the types of alternative hypotheses they arrived at to explain their data. As you read their report, look closely for evidence of hypothetical-deductive thinking patterns. Also look for evidence of self-regulation with respect to data and various ecological ideas and experiments the students were given. Below is the students' assignment.

▿▿

A Field Trip to the Intertidal Area

Purpose: To examine ecological relationships of intertidal organisms.

Equipment: Rulers, quadrats, thermometers, notebook, pencil, map identification key.

Procedure: Select a partner with whom you can work. Take 30–50 minutes to explore the various types of organisms that live in the intertidal area. Then choose an abundant population in the area, identify interesting variables with respect to the individuals of the population and the population's distribution, and search for quantitative relationships among these variables. Keep a record of your data.

Subsequent to the fieldwork, your findings and analyses should be reported and handed in. You will be given three weeks to complete your report.

John R. Brown
Julie B. Shayer

Tegula Population Study

Introduction

The population we selected to study was the *Tegula funebralis* population found at Sunset Bay, Oregon. Quadrats (80 x 20 cm) were used to sample the number of snails per quadrat, as well as the size of each snail. We noticed that the small snails seemed to be in the upper zones while the larger snails were in the lower zone. Since the snails are so abundant, we decided also to obtain a fairly large sample and plot a graph of its age versus frequency distribution. This should give us an indication of the population's state of growth or decline (similar to the salamander population mentioned in the textbook).

Conclusions and Discussion of *Tegula* Results

The graphs seem to show that the *Tegula* population is increasing and decreasing approximately every 8 to 10 years. The growth period approaches an exponential growth, characteristic of organisms in an unlimited environment, and then it declines suddenly.

These crashes could be attributed to severe environmental conditions each 8 to 10 years, but the oscillations appear to be truly cyclic, so this is most unlikely. (Sunspots could also be considered, of course!)

A density-dependent mechanism could be responsible. As the population grows too large, some density-dependent factor acts to reduce the population. If the population falls below a certain level, the density-dependent processes fade and the population builds up. Such a system would result in regular oscillations. However, in our case the oscillations appear to be too great for this model to hold.

Intraspecific competition in the *Tegula* population for a limited resource could be a cause of the oscillations. This could result in rather violent oscillation.

A more likely cause of the oscillations is interspecific competition between some predator, e.g., starfish, on the prey—*Tegula*. A model for this type of competition states that as the predator population increases, it consumes a larger number of prey until the prey population begins to decline. As the numbers of prey decline, the predators have less and less food, so their population declines. In time the number of predators is so small because of starvation that the prey are left free to increase in numbers and so on. This cycle may continue indefinitely.

It seems likely that the starfish can capture the smaller snails more easily than the larger ones. The larger the snail, the faster it can move to escape the predator.

Size and Distribution Data for *Tegula,* Sunset Bay			
Size (mm)	Frequency	Number of Snails	Number of Quadrats
1.1–1.2	1	0	108
1.2–1.3	0	1	51
1.3–1.4	1	2	20
1.4–1.5	1	3	10
1.5–1.6	1	4	14
1.6–1.7	10	5	8
1.7–1.8	30	6	4
1.8–1.9	30	7	2
1.9–2.0	41	8	3
2.0–2.1	48	9	2
2.1–2.2	49	10	1
2.2–2.3	35	11	0
2.3–2.4	33	12	1
2.4–2.5	41	13	0
2.5–2.6	49	14	1
2.6–2.7	38	15	0
2.7–2.8	29	16	0
2.8–2.9	28	17	1
2.9–3.0	15	21	1
3.0–3.1	10	26	1
3.1–3.2	2	48	1

To show this hypothesis correct or incorrect, information about the age distribution of the predator of *Tegula* would be needed. If oscillations occurred that coincided with the ones for *Tegula,* then the hypothesis would be supported. It is clear that additional information about the snails' life cycle, as well as its daily activities, would be needed as a starting point for additional research.

One final alternative, which perhaps is the best explanation, is that the snails and their food source are in a cyclic relation. The snails' food supply is depleted when the snail population is up, therefore a fall in population results with a subsequent rise in food supply. This idea also has its drawbacks. No obvious answer is available without additional research.

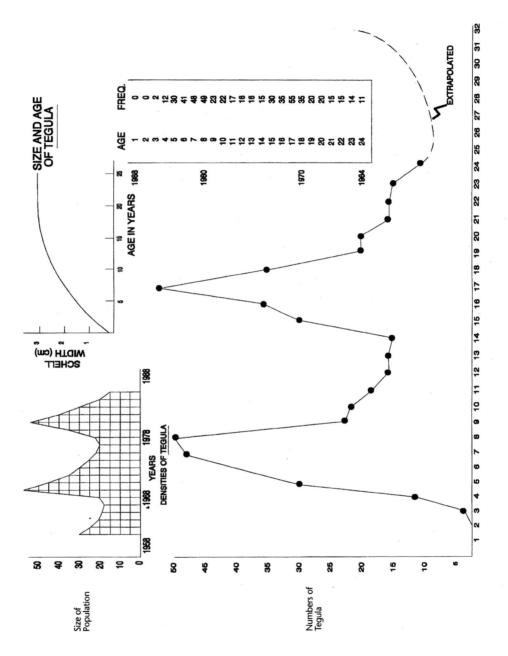

Age Distribution of Tegula (Years)

Comments and Questions About Student Work

Certainly, the field activity should be considered part of the exploration phase of this investigation. Lectures and textbook readings about ecological concepts also can be considered part of the exploration phase in this case. These are explorations because the instructor was perceptive and allowed the students considerable time to integrate abstract readings and lectures with concrete experiences before requesting some final product. This integration process is a fundamental part of self-regulation.

1. What evidences did you find of hypothetical-deductive thinking in the students' work?
2. What are some of the students' alternative hypotheses following their explorations and data gathering?
3. Do you think the students have reached a state of equilibrium in their thinking about the oscillations in the snail population size?
4. What sort of additional evidence or experimentation do the students seem to ask for at the end of their report?

Questions for Reflection

1. Identify the basic theories (conceptual systems) that you think should be taught in your course (e.g., high school biology, eighth-grade physical science, high school physics). On a large sheet of paper, create a diagram (i.e., a concept map) that shows the primary relationships among the major concepts.
2. What relationship, if any, does your diagram have with the levels of organization of atoms → molecules → cells → organs → organisms → populations → communities → ecosystems → biosphere → planet → solar system → galaxy → universe?
3. In what way(s) does your diagram reflect hierarchical relationships?
4. In what order should the basic concepts or theories be taught in your course? Why?
5. Obviously, it makes no sense to introduce all 17,130 of the special biological terms that Yager found in *Modern Biology* to your students. But some terms should be introduced. How will you decide which to introduce and which to ignore? What selection criteria does the Educational Policies Commission recommend? (See Appendix A).
6. Select a textbook and use the National Center for Science Education guidelines to evaluate its appropriateness for use.

CHAPTER 9

STUDENT ASSESSMENT

An educational setting that seeks to develop student thinking skills should select the procedures that will be used to assess student work with great care to ensure that they are compatible. Students may adjust with relative ease to a program that encourages them to question, debate, and seek answers to questions and to resolve issues. However, if they are not assessed on this aspect of instruction, only on the amount of information they can remember, then they will quickly perceive that the stated goal of developing thinking skills is insincere. This in turn will lead to a loss of interest in inquiry and an abrupt return to memorization.

In this chapter we will discuss procedures that will assess the extent to which thinking skills have been acquired and can be applied. We also discuss the use of written assignments, including homework problems, that aim to encourage the development of thinking skills and the construction of concepts. We start with a look at test items.

▼ CLASSIFYING TEST ITEMS

Below are eighteen test items. Read the items from your specific subject area and think about how you would respond. Even if you do not know the answers (which is not important), think about what information you would need or what thinking patterns you would use to solve the problems. On the basis of what you have learned to this point, classify the problems as requiring:

1. only the recall of specific facts,
2. an empirical-inductive thinking pattern, or
3. a hypothetical-deductive thinking pattern.

My own classification will follow.

Biology

▼ **Item 1**

The stages in the life cycle of a house fly are, in order,

a. larva–egg–pupa–adult
b. pupa–larva–egg–adult
c. pupa–egg–larva–adult
d. egg–larva–adult–pupa
e. egg–larva–pupa–adult   ▼

▼ **Item 2**

Fifty pieces of various parts of plants were placed in each of five sealed containers of equal size. When the experiment began, each jar contained 250 units of CO_2. The amount of CO_2 in each jar at the end of two days is shown in Table 9.1.

On the basis of the data in the table, a fair test of the amount of CO_2 used per day at two different temperatures could be made by comparing which jars?

_____

Please explain why you chose those jars.

_____

_____   ▼

Table 9.1 ▼ **Carbon Dioxide Use by Various Plant Species**

Container	Plant	Plant Part	Light Color	Temp. (° C)	CO_2 Remaining
1	Willow	Leaf	Blue	10	200
2	Maple	Leaf	Purple	23	50
3	Willow	Root	Red	18	300
4	Maple	Stem	Red	23	400
5	Willow	Leaf	Blue	23	150

▼ **Item 3**

In the early spring some chemical poison was dumped into a pond. It killed all of the molds, bacteria, yeasts, and other types of decomposers. By the end of the summer, some members of the pond's bass population died. The most likely reason for their death is that:

a. the poison that killed the decomposers also killed the bass.

b. the bass had used the decomposers as a food source; because their food was no longer available, the bass starved.

c. the bass ate the poisoned decomposers and poisoned themselves.

d. the dead decomposers could no longer recycle nutrients, so the productivity of the pond dropped to almost zero.

Please explain your choice. ▼

▼ **Item 4**

In the city zoo are 6 lions, 12 seals, 10 zebras, 6 bears, 535 birds, and 55 horses. These are examples of:

a. ecosystems

b. food chains

c. biomes

d. populations ▼

Geology

▼ **Item 5**

Magnetic poles are usually named

a. anode and cathode

b. north and south

c. east and west

d. plus and minus

e. red and blue   ▼

▼ **Item 6**

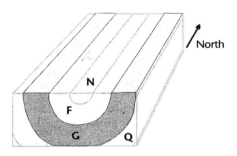

Of the labeled beds in the block diagram, the correct order from *oldest* to *youngest* is:

a. NFGQ

b. FQGN

c. QGFN

d. GNFQ

Please explain your choice.   ▼

▼ **Item 7**

Use the diagram on page 265 and data below to answer the next question.

Data

- a, b, c, d, and e are sedimentary beds.
- Y and Z are igneous rocks.
- All rocks adjacent to Y and Z appear to be chemically altered.
- Y contains radioactive material that has been dated at 40 million years old.
- b contains igneous rock material that has been dated at 200 million years old.

a. Rock c is younger than b and older than Z.

b. Rock b is younger than Z and older than a.

c. Rock a is older than Z and younger than Y.

The diagram is
a cross section
of rock layers.

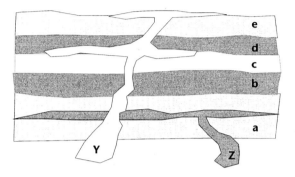

d. Rock c is older than b and older than Z.

e. Rock Z is younger than a and older than Y.

Please explain your choice.   ▼

▼ **Item 8**

A geologist finds a sandstone bed 1,000 feet in thickness. She notes the size of the sand particles and, by studying the patterns of deposition, determines that the sandstone bed was deposited by stream action. She finds a stream that is carrying particles of the same size and depositing the particles in the same patterns. This stream averages deposits of 1 foot of sand every 10 years. The geologist concludes that the sandstone bed was deposited over a period of at least 10,000 years. Which of the geologist's assumptions below is or are probably valid?

a. Streams carried particles in the past as they do today.

b. Particles being deposited today are similar to particles deposited in the past.

c. The deposition of the sandstone bed was continuous and constant.

d. Gravity and climate acted on streams in the past as they do today.

e. Three of the above are probably valid.

Please explain your choice.   ▼

Chemistry

▼ Item 9

The type of bond most often found in carbon compounds is the

a. metallic bond

b. covalent bond

c. ionic bond

d. james bond

e. cohesive bond. ▼

▼ Item 10

According to kinetic theory, the rate of diffusion of a high–molecular-weight gas is slower than the rate of diffusion of a low–molecular-weight gas. Which of the following can you conclude?

a. If both are released at the same time and place, perfume vapor with a molecular weight of 360 will be smelled before onion vapor with a molecular weight of 720.

b. The higher the molecular weight of a gas, the sooner an equilibrium state is reached in a closed system.

c. Onion vapor is more offensive than perfume vapor.

d. If both are released at the same time and place, perfume vapor with a molecular weight of 360 will be smelled after onion vapor with a molecular weight of 720. ▼

▼ Item 11

The relative rates of diffusion of two gases under ideal conditions are inversely proportional to the square roots of their molecular weights. In a test comparing diffusion of onion vapor (molecular weight 720) and perfume vapor (molecular weight 360), the onion vapor is detected approximately 6 seconds after its release. How long after release would you expect perfume vapor to be detected?

a. 3 sec.

b. 4 sec.

c. 5 sec.

d. 9 sec.

e. 12 sec. ▼

▼ Item 12

How many atoms are there in one molecule of this substance?

$$(NH_4)_2TiO(C_4O_4)_2 \cdot H_2O$$ ▼

▼ Item 13

Balance this equation, which involves the new elements X and Z:

$$2\,H_2XO_3 + A\,H_3ZO_3 \rightarrow B\,HX + C\,H_3ZO_4 + D\,H_2O$$

The coefficient C is:

a. 1
b. 2
c. 3
d. 4
e. 5.

▼

Physics

▼ **Item 14**

The term *wave period* is defined as:

a. the distance a particle is displaced from its point of rest.

b. the length of time required for a particle to make a complete vibration.

c. the number of complete vibrations per second.

d. the time rate of change of distance in a given direction. ▼

▼ **Item 15**

During part of an automobile race, four cars were timed as they traveled around the track. Arrange the cars in order from fastest to slowest given the following data.

• Car A takes 85 seconds for two laps.
• Car B takes 125 seconds for three laps.
• Car C takes 70 seconds for two laps.
• Car D takes 74 seconds for two laps.

Fastest: _____

Second: _____

Third: _____

Fourth: _____ ▼

▼ **Item 16**

An object falling from rest near the surface of the earth moves through the distance *s* in the time *t*. These variables are related by the equation $s = 1/2gt^2$, where *g* is the acceleration of gravity. Circle the points where the particle will be at $t = 2$ sec. and at $t = 3$ sec., given the marked points at $t = 0$ sec. and $t = 1$ sec.

• $t = 0$ sec.
• $t = 1$ sec.
•
•
•
•
•
•
•
•
•
• ▼

▼ Item 17

Which of the following pairs of vectors has the resultant of the smallest magnitude?

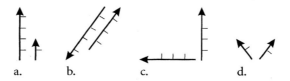

Please explain how you found your answer. ▼

▼ Item 18

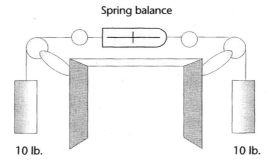

The diagram shows two weights connected to a scale by strings passing over two pulleys. What is the reading of the scale? ▼

▼ EMPIRICAL-INDUCTIVE AND HYPOTHETICAL-DEDUCTIVE TEST ITEMS

Test items can be classified as either empirical-inductive (EI) or hypothetical-deductive (HD) according to the thinking patterns required to respond successfully without guessing. Using the patterns described in Chapter 2 and restated below in somewhat different form, I concluded that Items 1 and 3 are EI and Items 2 and 4 are HD.

Items are EI if successful response requires the student to do the following:

EI1   classify observations; relate systems to subsystems, classes to subclasses;

EI2   apply conservation reasoning to objects;

EI3   establish one-to-one correspondences or serially order a set of observations;

EI4   understand and apply descriptive concepts—that is, concepts defined in terms of familiar objects, events, or situations; and

EI5   apply a memorized algorithm or formula.

Items are categorized as HD if successful response requires the student to do the following:

HD1   understand and apply theoretical concepts—that is, concepts that derive their meaning from inferences rather than from direct experience; use theories and idealized models to interpret data;

HD2   use combinatorial thinking;

HD3   identify functional relationships and apply proportional thinking;

HD4   understand the general necessity for the control of variables and recognize hidden assumptions; and

HD5   recognize the implications of probability for experimental design and data analysis.

Item 1 was classified into category (1) because it involves knowledge of a sequence. The student either knows or does not know the proper sequence; reasoning is not required. Item 2 was classified as hypothetical-deductive because the student must recognize ambiguous and unambiguous experimental conditions—that is, understand what constitutes controlled experimental conditions (HD5).

Item 3 was classified as hypothetical-deductive because correct response requires understanding the relationships among the concepts of producers, decomposers, and consumers in the nutrient cycle of a pond ecosystem (HD1). The item also involves drawing an inference based on an understanding of these relationships. Item 4 was considered to involve only empirical-inductive thinking patterns because the concept of population can be understood in terms of experiences with familiar objects (EI4).

Item 5, like Item 1, is a category (1) item because knowledge of a convention is required, and nothing more.

Item 6 was classified as EI: It requires the student to recall that older layers of sediment are deposited first (EI1) and to order serially the observations (EI3 and EI4). Item 7 also involves serial ordering a set of observations (EI3). Although the problem involves a more complicated application of thinking patterns, it does not demand HD thinking. The item is classified as EI. If, however, the alternative given the students were not so directive, then the problem could require HD thought because careful analysis of combinations of layers and ages (HD2) would be required. Item 8 was considered HD; it requires the student to recognize hidden assumptions (HD4) and understand the geologist's concept application of an invalid assumption (HD1 and HD4). Item 9 involves knowledge only, so it falls into category (1). Although a good understanding of the kinetic theory certainly depends on hypothetical-deductive thought, Item 10 was classified as EI because it requires the student only to order serially the given data (EI3). Two inversions from the given data are needed, however—high weight → slow rate and slow rate → long time—which ultimately lead to a direct correspondence: lower weight → shorter time. Item 11, on the other hand, requires the student to apply an inverse-square-root relationship, an HD reasoning pattern (HD3).

Item 12 was classified as EI because the correct response involves merely applying certain facts and well-defined rules about chemical formulas and using them to manipulate symbols (EI5). Item 13 was classified as HD because it requires a systematic overall approach to analysis and comparison of the various combinations and possibilities (HD2). It also requires hypothetical-deductive reasoning as in "B has to be 2 because there are two atoms of X, A equals C because of conservation of Z atoms," and so on.

Item 14 requires a knowledge of a definition but no reasoning and therefore falls into category (1). Item 15 was classified as EI: It requires the student to establish a correspondence between time and speed (EI3). Car B requires an adjustment of time by proportional thinking, an HD pattern (HD3). Students who successfully explain this show some evidence of HD thought.

Item 16 was classified as HD because it requires the application of an algebraic formula to an unusual graphical representation of the motion (HD3). Item 17 was classified as EI; it can be solved by the simple algorithm of graphic vector addition (EI4, EI5), although the explanation may reveal HD thought by its thoroughness. Item 18 is HD. It requires the student to suppress the impulse toward using vector addition of forces and to apply the action–reaction principle instead (HD1). Justifying how the correct answer of 10 pounds is derived can be difficult even for a physics teacher.

Many of the items asked students to describe their reasons for their answer choice. Asking them to justify answers can be an important part of a test, a part that particularly emphasizes the use of thinking patterns in an identifiable way. Thus, if selection of the correct answer is only partially justified, then the student's thinking can be probed further to find out whether the correct answer was a lucky guess or the result of effective thinking. Conversely, although some items require only EI thinking for success, an analysis of student responses could indicate the use of HD thinking. In view of these advantages, teachers are urged to include a few test items that require justification and for which students are allowed more time, possibly four to five minutes for each question. Do not use too many of such items, because they can create grading problems and take a relatively long time to answer.

As mentioned in Chapter 6, Bloom (1956) developed a method of classifying test items that is similar to that used here. Basically, the Bloom taxonomy classifies items into one of six levels: knowledge, comprehension, application, analysis, synthesis, and evaluation.

In general, any item at the knowledge level of Bloom's taxonomy would require no thinking patterns or only EI thinking patterns for successful response. Although items on this level may involve abstract theories or idealized models, the student need only *recall* the names of such theories. He or she need not use them in a way that would imply that they were understood.

Items classified into Bloom's comprehension or application levels may require either EI or HD thought, depending on the nature of the concept being assessed.

Test items on the analysis, synthesis, and evaluation levels all involve HD thinking patterns; they require elements such as:

- recognizing unstated assumptions,
- checking consistency of hypotheses with given information and assumptions,
- comprehending interrelationships among ideas, and
- comparing major theories and generalizations.

▼ USING TEST ITEMS TO ENCOURAGE SELF-REGULATION

How can knowledge of the thinking patterns involved in responding to test items help you use these items to encourage self-regulation? First, if your stated goals are to teach science concepts *and* help students develop hypothetical-deductive thinking patterns, then you should not only present students with problems that encourage HD thinking in the classroom or laboratory, but also include problems of this type on tests. Students quickly learn that test items reveal what a teacher really believes is important. Tests therefore *must* include items that challenge students' ability to think. This line of reasoning, however, leads to a fundamental problem.

Unfortunately, because some students initially reason at the empirical-inductive level, such a test will include items that such students almost certainly will miss. But eliminating this type of item completely would be wrong. A line of attack more conducive to self-regulation and intellectual growth would be to (a) include a few HD items, (b) discuss the answers to these items after the test, (c) discuss similar items during class time, (d) use some as thought-provoking homework assignments (see the next section), and (e) award grades at least partially on the basis of improvement during the semester.

Suppose that laboratory and classroom activities invite the use of thinking patterns that are required to understand controlled experimentation. The subsequent test should include several items that evaluate the extent to which students have become able to reason in this way. Not only should test items be included that refer to the materials used in the laboratory activities, but also items that involve new and unfamiliar materials should be included. These allow you to evaluate the extent to which the developing thinking patterns can be generalized to new situations. Hypothetical-deductive thinking patterns will become generally useful only after students have gradually thought through a wide variety of specific situations that invite the use of HD thought. If used properly, test items can aid in this process.

Although most of the previous example questions are of the multiple-choice type, also consider other types of exam questions. For example, provide a paragraph or two on an examination that contains partially true or partially false statements. Have the students defend those statements (or even parts of statements) that they believe to be accurate and refute those statements that they believe to be inaccurate in light of their knowledge and understanding of the discipline. Or provide data on examinations. Ask students to create alternative hypotheses about the data. Then, in light of their current knowledge and understanding, have them describe how they would go about testing their hypotheses. Also effective is allowing students to work in small groups on examination questions of the type just described. Students as individuals or in groups also might be given paragraphs that describe perplexing situations (e.g., current political, economic, and ecological issues) that do not allow for absolute answers. They could then be asked to offer their assessment of the situation and perhaps propose a course of action to arrive at an optimal solution.

Additional examples of appropriate assessment procedures are certainly possible. The point is simply this: Students can become motivated to inquire. After all, this is the behavior that governed a large part of their lives before they enrolled in school. However, if students are not assessed on the basis of their willingness and ability to inquire and their ability to think, and instead are assessed solely on the amount of content they have stored, then they will quickly learn that stored knowledge is valued more than the intellectual processes needed to construct that knowledge. This will lead them to stop inquiring and thereby stop their intellectual development.

In summary, test items should assess not only specific knowledge, but also descriptive and theoretical conceptual understanding, and they should assess the extent to which important thinking patterns have been developed and are generalized. In this way, tests will serve as both a means of assessment and valuable learning experiences that can significantly aid the self-regulation process.

▼ USING HOMEWORK PROBLEMS TO ENCOURAGE SELF-REGULATION

In part, Chapter 3 discussed the general process of self-regulation, the process that presumably results in the construction of new conceptual knowledge and the refinement and extension of thinking patterns. Homework problems can be used to provoke self-regulation provided the following two elements are present:

1. Problems must be chosen so that students can partially but not completely understand them in terms of old ideas (i.e., a moderate state of disequilibrium must result from the problem).
2. Students must be given sufficient time to grapple with the new situation and put the ideas together themselves, even though appropriate "hints" might be provided to direct their thinking.

An important facet then in selecting problems that encourage self-regulation is to obtain a careful match between what the students know and the kind of problem they are asked to work through. In the ideal situation, the problems are challenging but the students feels that they can be solved. The hypothesis is that a challenging but solvable problem will place students in an initial state of disequilibrium. However, through their own efforts at bringing together what they have done in the laboratory, read in the textbook, heard in lectures, learned from experience, and obtained from teacher or peer discussions, they will gradually organize their thinking about this information and successfully solve the problem. This success will then establish a new and more stable equilibrium. The new state of equilibrium will be one with increased understanding of the subject matter and increased problem-solving capability. Before we examine examples of the kind of problem that can initiate self-regulation, the deficiencies of standard homework problems will be discussed.

What Is Wrong with Typical Homework Problems?

Typical homework problems seldom require students to examine their thinking, make comparisons, and raise questions that are actually crucial to scientific inquiry. These problems usually require students to apply a fact, an equation, or sometimes two or three equations to obtain a solution. Students quickly come to realize that the name of this game is "Can you recall the correct fact?" or "Can you discover the correct equation?" This is a game of recognition—a sort of matching process that requires little thought. Although this process can be important, little if any self-regulation takes place in this way. Typical homework problems do not require the student to think about:

1. the data of the problem,
2. the approach to the problem,
3. the tacit assumptions of a problem-solving strategy,
4. the physical arguments involved in the problem as opposed to the mathematical ones, and
5. the statement of a problem.

The Data of the Problem

Usually, just the right amount of data are provided, no more, no less. Real situations, however, provide a dearth or superfluity of information, and the problem becomes one of discovering what is relevant.

The Approach to the Problem

Approaching the problem usually is determined by the chapter heading. For example, if a mechanics problem can be solved by Lagrange's equations, Newton's laws, or energy conservation, then the choice is dictated by irrelevant considerations—for example, the problem comes from the chapter on Lagrange's equations. Yet students must learn that many approaches may seem reasonable and that the problem is that of deciding whether one is particularly appropriate.

A Problem-Solving Strategy's Tacit Assumptions

Students frequently are presented problems that would require deciding on a specific solution strategy in real life—for example, deciding between using Boyle's law or the Van der Waals equation. This decision is usually made *for* rather than *by* the student.

Physical Arguments Rather than Mathematical Arguments

Too often problems are only exercises in using mathematical tools (a necessary exercise) without ever demanding that the student either arrive at or qualitatively justify the mathematical result by physical (phenomenological) arguments that use both principles and order-of-magnitude calculations. Indeed, the physical or intuitive argument often precedes the mathematical in real research.

The Statement of a Problem

Problems are tailored to fit the text when, in fact, the real problem is doing the tailoring by conceptualizing a real situation in terms of a model. This involves all of the preceding points.

How to Encourage Self-Regulation

Keep in mind the following eight suggestions when designing, discussing, using, and scoring homework problems to encourage self-regulation:

1. Use open-ended problems—that is, problems with no single solution—to encourage thinking. They are often excellent tools.

2. Use problems that present an apparent paradox; the disequilibrium they produce can initiate self-regulation. By their nature, paradox problems are generally short and incisive. Problems that are numerically or analytically simple, yet incisive and illuminating in content, are particularly useful.

3. To encourage self-regulation, ask students to record and hand in all of the various ideas they tried and found unsuccessful as well as the ones that were successful in arriving at the problem solution. Discussions of these steps in an atmosphere that recognizes these ideas as not only worthwhile but also necessary clues students in to the fact that "real" problems *should* and indeed *must* involve a certain amount of trial and error, albeit informed trial and error.

4. Have students search for necessary data so that they examine their conceptualization of the problem. Either give superfluous data or omit necessary data. To account for the latter, students should have to make plausible assumptions or introduce suitable symbols for quantities that are needed to solve the problem.

5. Require students to diagram the situation. To do so, students must think deeply about the spatial relationships of the interacting objects,

and they may find discrepancies when they compare their preconceptions with the diagram.

6. Provide for a "problem clinic" or tutorial service where students can get help with problems while they are solving them and before they must be turned in. Interaction with other people can be both helpful and even necessary if students are to conceptualize and then critically analyze their own thinking.

7. For problems designed to engage students over a period of several days or weeks, consult with them several times to discuss their approaches.

   a. An initial approach may seem reasonable and yet be known in advance as inappropriate. Do *not* intervene at this point; let the students discover for themselves why the approach will not work.

   b. Discuss alternative approaches both when the initial approach is appropriate and when it is reasonable but not appropriate. In either case, let the students first discover which approach will work. Then discuss alternatives, even if the first approach worked. Students may accept inappropriate alternatives as reasonable and then discover on their own why they are not.

   c. Discuss both semiquantitative (order-of-magnitude) and qualitative arguments that anticipate the outcome of more rigorous approaches. Limiting cases should be used as a check when solutions to simpler problems are already known.

   d. Discuss alternatives to an inappropriate and overly time-consuming approach. Overall, students should get a feel for the general considerations that are appropriate in choosing and comparing strategies—in effect, a feeling for the process of inquiry—from the teacher.

8. Remind students that a premature glance at a solution will surely affect their conception of the problem and distort the problem-solving procedure. And solutions (numerical or algebraic) should be provided for all problems (not just the "odd-numbered" ones). Knowing the solution can provide stimulating feedback *after* the student has completed and carried through a formulation of a solution.

Examples of Physical Science Homework Problems

▼ **Problem 1**

The net force on the spring scale in the diagram is zero, so how can the scale register a nonzero reading? What does the scale register? Because it is pulled down by 10 pounds on each side, why does it not show 20 pounds?

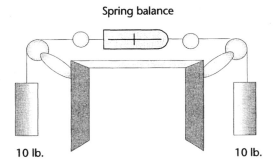

Spring balance

Spring balance and suspended weights

Comment: This example, which is especially useful when associated with a demonstration, illustrates how a little knowledge can go a wrong way. At first, concepts are only vaguely grasped and thus overextended. Here we obviously have two forces whose sum is equal to zero, yet the scale does not read zero. Or we might think that each force contributes 10 lb. of tension to the scale to give 20 lb. These two approaches use unrestricted (overextended) concepts that must be coordinated through self-regulation with other concepts (for example, free-body diagrams and action–reaction) to resolve the discrepancy. ▼

▼ **Problem 2**

A capacitor and resistor are connected as in the circuit shown on page 279. The values are $C = 250$ μμf, $R = 10,000$ Ω, and $E = 400$ V. Initially the switch is closed and then it is opened suddenly. Use two methods to calculate the energy dissipated in the resistor after the switch is opened. Do both methods give the same result? Should they give the same result? If so, why? If not, why not?

Comment: This problem calls for two quantitative analyses of the same situation. If the student is able to think of two methods of solution and obtain the same answer using both methods, then no disequilibrium will result. However, if two different answers are obtained, then the student should check his or her work. The discrepancy may be resolved quickly if the source of the difference is an error in calculation. If, however, the difference results from difficulty in conceptualization, then the check will promote self-regulation. ▼

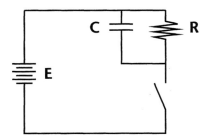

This circuit diagram shows a capacitor, resistor, switch, and battery.

▼ Problem 3
The gas temperature at one level of the upper atmosphere is approximately 1,000° K. The temperature at the surface of a burning match is equivalent. A person in the upper atmosphere, however, would be very cold. How can that be?

Comment: This problem presents a paradox, because 1,000° K is an extremely high temperature and yet the upper atmosphere is cold. Resolution through self-regulation leads to a more scientific and less everyday notion of the relationship between temperature and "cold" or "hot."   ▼

▼ Problem 4
A glass is exactly full of water at 0° C and has an ice cube floating in it. When the ice melts (still at 0° C), the water will not overflow, because the ice displaced a volume of water equal to the volume of the water into which the ice melted. So far so good. Now consider some fine points. In what *direction*—slight overflow or the opposite—would each of the following conditions affect the result? Give only the *direction*.

a. The ice cube contained grains of sand.

b. The ice cube contained air bubbles.

c. The water (and the glass) were not at 0°, but because of its alcoholic content, the ice has density less than that of water.

Comment: This problem originally appeared in an article by Richard Crane (1969). Along with others in that article, it is an excellent problem that will promote self-regulation. Several problems that appeared in a second article by Crane (1970) also are thought-provoking and should encourage self-regulation.   ▼

▼ Problem 5
If internal energy is partly molecular motion, what is the difference between a hot golf ball sitting on a tee and a cold golf ball rapidly moving off the tee?

Comment: Of course, the molecular motion part of internal energy refers to *random* motion. Thus, self-regulation refines or sharpens a global or relatively diffuse concept. Students typically assimilate only parts of a concept at first. By provoking the students to discover or recover all parts, the problem allows the concept to become more sharply defined. ▼

▼ **Problem 6**

When a cylinder that is open at one end is placed over a burning candle sitting in a container of water, the candle's flame goes out and water rises into the cylinder. Why does the flame go out and why does the water rise? *Note:* Not all observations are mentioned in the description. What other observations would you make in looking at the phenomenon? Obtain the necessary materials and try the experiment for yourself. Run the experiment and vary the number of candles used, the amount of water in the container, the size and shape of the cylinder, the speed at which you place the cylinder over the candle, and anything else you can imagine.

Comment: This problem is one that often yields a quick but erroneous solution. Most students hypothesize that the candle goes out because it burns up all of the oxygen in the cylinder and the water then enters to replace the oxygen. Selected items of information or questions could be supplied at this point to provoke students to abandon this idea and continue their search. For example: "What is produced when a flame consumes oxygen? Two burning candles make more water rise than one. Small bubbles were observed escaping from the bottom of the cylinder. Why might this have occurred?" These observations contradict the initial explanation and should provoke disequilibrium. Once other explanations are offered, they can be analyzed to determine their suitability. They may lead some students to try the experiment to collect more data. Explanations then can be evaluated for their compatibility with data and physical conditions. ▼

▼ **Problem 7**

Everyone "knows" that to win a tug of war, a team has to pull harder than the other team. What everyone does not know is that both teams actually pull equally hard, even the winning team. Under these circumstances, short of the other team just letting go, how can one team ever win?

Comment: Obviously, one normally thinks that good teams pull harder than poor teams and this is why they win. This problem makes one apply the free-body diagram method and the action–reaction idea to resolve a problem already believed solved by common sense but now made to appear strange. This nonroutine use of physics concepts makes it more likely that they will *not* be overlooked in the future. ▼

▼ **Problem 8**

Polishing surfaces reduces friction between them unless they are polished extremely well, in which case friction increases. How can that be true?

Comment: One never expects polishing to increase friction. Resolving this paradox leads to better understanding of the relation of macroscopic effects to microscopic phenomena—for example, friction to microscopic and molecular interaction. ▼

▼ **Problem 9**

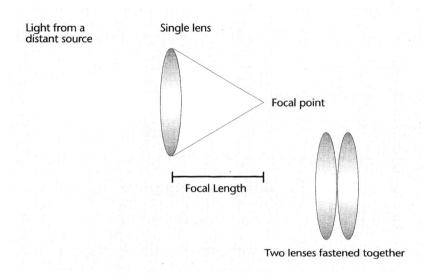

The diagram of the convex lens on the left shows focal point and focal length. On the right are two convex lenses fastened together.

   a. On the left side of the diagram, the focal lengths of two identical thin, convex lenses are the same and measured to be 20 cm each ($F_1 = 20$ cm, $F_2 = 20$ cm). The two lenses are placed next to each other as shown on the right and taped together only at their edges. The focal length of this combination is 10 cm ($F_c = 20$ cm). Write an equation that gives the focal length of a lens combination that consists of two lenses having identical focal lengths.

   b. One of the 20-cm focal length lenses is replaced by one 5 cm long ($F_3 = 5$ cm). The focal length of the resulting combination is measured at 4 cm. Write an equation that can calculate the focal length of a lens combination that consists of two lenses of unequal focal lengths.

   c. Now check your two equations. Are they the same? Do you think they should be the same. If so, why? If not, why not? If you believe they should be the same but you have two different equations, then rethink the problem and reduce the two situations to one equation.

Comment: Students generally will solve parts a and b with little difficulty. However, they will seldom write an equation that is general enough to account for both situations. The suggestion in part c that the equations should be the same, the student's own intuitive feeling that a general equation could be found, and the original incompatible equations should produce disequilibrium and provoke the student to rethink the problem.   ▼

▼ **Problem 10**

A student measures her weight by climbing onto the large platform of a big spring scale. She steps to one side and notices that just as she started to do this, the scale registers less than her weight. Before she can puzzle this through, she notices that just as she completes the step, the scale registers more than her weight. If nothing is wrong with the scale, what is going on?

Comment: "Weight is weight is weight," a famous poet might have said. So how can a scale read less than one's weight? Worse, how can it also read more? Still worse, if it is not the scale that must be fixed, then how am I, the student, to fix my ideas? ▼

▼ **Problem 11**

A brick is supported by String A from the ceiling, and another string, B, is attached to the bottom of the brick. If you give a sudden jerk to B it will break, but if you pull on B steadily, A will break. The force is the same both ways, so how could this occur?

Comment: To be most effective, this problem should be demonstrated. Anything actually seen makes a much greater and longer-lasting impression than anything simply heard or read about. This comment, of course, applies to other problems as well. Because the student is used to thinking in temporal terms, she or he will think that force is force and so equal forces have equal effects. So how can the string break in one instance and not in the other? Again, common sense conflicts with observation, and this use of physics to set the world straight is likely to be retained.

▼ **Problem 12**

We all know that water expands when it freezes into ice. Will putting ice under pressure cause it to melt? Explain using LeChatelier's principle. (Use diagrams, simple equations, and plenty of discussion with other students to solve this problem.)

Comment: This problem provokes the student not only to carefully consider the molecular configuration of water and ice and the effect of increased pressure on this configuration, but also to synthesize this understanding with what previously is likely to be only a vaguely understood and highly abstract principle of equilibrium. The use of diagrams, equations, and peer discussion are helpful in the conceptual differentiation and integration that is central to self-regulation. ▼

▼ **Problem 13**

Eratosthenes of Alexandria (273–192 B.C.) assumed that the earth is spherical and that the sun is so far away that its rays strike the earth parallel to one another. With the following information, he accurately computed the distance around the earth:

a. The distance between the cities of Alexandria and Syene is 800 kilometers.

b. Alexandria is directly north of Syene.

c. At noon on June 21, a post casts no shadow at Syene (*note:* the post is pointing toward the center of the earth).

d. At noon on June 21, a similar post casts a shadow at Alexandria (this post also points directly toward the earth's center).

e. Lines drawn from the posts to the center of the earth have an intersecting angle of 7 degrees.

See if you can do what Eratosthenes did and figure out the distance around the earth.

Comment: This classic problem not only requires that students apply hypothetical-deductive thinking, but also involves proportional thinking and the use of diagrams. Because of these complexities, the task should not be seen as one in which all students are expected to generate a "correct" solution, but one in which a variety of approaches are compared and constructed and their merits explored.   ▼

Examples of Biological Science Homework Problems

▼ Problem 14

How long does mitosis take? The life span of a cell is the period of time from its formation to the time it completes division to form two new daughter cells. This period is called the cell's *generation* time. By observing living cells, biologists have determined the generation time for a variety of cell types. If we know the generation time, we can determine how long a cell spends in mitosis. Given that 100 cells are observed in the field under a microscope and 50 are undergoing mitosis and also knowing that the generation time is 2 hours, approximately how long does it take the cells to undergo mitosis? After you have arrived at an answer, reflect on your procedure. Try to write an equation that expresses the numerical relationships; use the following:

$$N_o = \text{total number of cells observed}$$
$$t_m = \text{time spent in mitosis}$$
$$N_m = \text{number of cells observed in mitosis}$$
$$T_{gt} = \text{generation time}$$

Express the relationship below:

Comment: Like the previous problem, this one involves proportional relationships and hypothetical-deductive thought. Seldom are biology students asked to think quantitatively and to generate general equations. Although the demands on student self-regulation may be great, the effort should pay off in terms of a better understanding of specific biological concepts and an increased understanding of the relationship between mathematics and science.   ▼

Table 9.2 ▾ Data Testing Smell Hypothesis

		Recapture Site	
	Capture Site	*Stream A*	*Stream B*
Plugged Noses	Stream A	39	12
	Stream B	16	3
No Plugged Noses	Stream A	46	0
	Stream B	8	19

▾ **Problem 15**

To test the hypothesis that salmon use their sense of smell to return home, several salmon from two streams were captured and tagged. The noses of some fish were plugged and all of the fish were transported downstream and placed back into the water below the fork where the two streams joined. The fish were then recaptured after they swam back upstream. Table 9.2 displays the experimental data. Do the data support the hypothesis? Explain.

Comment: Obviously, both hypothetical-deductive and correlational thinking are required here. This sort of problem provides an excellent opportunity for self-regulation with respect to these thinking patterns. Having students explain their thinking allows them to argue about the meaning of the data as well as the adequacy or inadequacy of the experimental design.   ▾

▾ **Problem 16**

Evidence has been obtained to support the hypothesis that a gene is a segment of the DNA molecule that is capable of coding for the manufacture of protein molecules. How long a segment of DNA would be needed to code for any specific protein? *Hint:* Assume that DNA consists of various sequences of just four different bases: A, T, G, and C. Assume also that protein molecules consist of chains of amino acid molecules and 20 different kinds of amino acids exist. Protein molecules thus differ from one another in the number and sequence of their amino acids. This implies that the DNA code would have to be larger than a single base (or a single letter). If the code consisted of a single letter (only four are available) then we could code for only four different amino acids. But we have 20 amino acids, so the code must contain at least two bases (two letters). Would a two-letter code work? How many different amino acids could a two-letter code specify? How about a three-letter code? What about more?

Comment: Generating all possible combinations of code units, of course, requires combinatorial thinking. Again, the approach the teacher should take is to provide students with the opportunity to compare their problem approaches and argue for and against their alternatives. Let argumentation and self-regulation be the goal rather than the attainment of a single "correct" answer. ▼

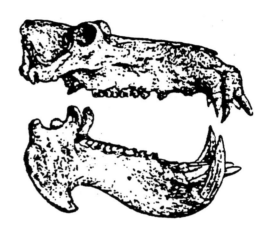

▼ **Problem 17**
Carefully observe the illustration and reflect on your previous laboratory work to answer the following questions.

a. What do you believe the function of the back teeth to be? Why?

b. What do you believe the function of the front teeth to be? Why?

c. Explain why you think this animal is a herbivore, a carnivore, or an omnivore?

d. Note the position of the eye orbits. How might this positioning be useful to this animal?

e. Can you think of other animals that also have this type of eye positioning?

f. Do you believe this animal to be terrestrial, aquatic, amphibious, or adapted for flight? Why?

g. The actual skull is approximately sixteen times larger than the illustration. What animal do you think it is? Why?

Comment: This problem is primarily an opportunity for students to apply what they have learned about skull adaptations. However, the final question (g) requires a careful search through memory as well as an element of hypothetical-deductive thinking. The problem is fun, especially if the students are not told the "real" answer. What animal do you think it is? Why? ▼

▼ **Problem 18**

Regions of relatively stable climax communities that cover many miles of land are sometimes referred to as *biomes*. Consult reference material and list the world's major terrestrial biomes and their primary locations. Your reference source probably indicates that the state of Arizona is part of the desert biome. But, in fact, all of the world's major biomes except for tropical rainforest can be found in Arizona. How can this be? In other words, what conditions must exist in Arizona to allow for the existence of such a wide range of climax communities? Explain in general terms how these conditions influence the plants that dominate the various communities.

Comment: For students who live in mountainous regions this problem should cause little disequilibration. However, for those not accustomed to changes in elevation and its dramatic effects on community structure, this problem provides an excellent opportunity to juxtapose the effects of elevation and latitude. It also provokes students to challenge the oversimplified biome diagrams found in most textbooks. ▼

▼ **Problem 19**

Experiments such as the one described by Stanley Miller indicate that no special supernatural processes or powers are necessary to get simple inorganic molecules to combine into larger and more complex organic molecules. Apparently, an energy supply is all that is needed for many of these small inorganic molecules to accumulate in one place. This starts molecular collisions until the small molecules "spontaneously" combine. In a sense, then, this theory of the origin of life involves the idea of *spontaneous generation*. But the experiments of Redi, Spallanzani, and Pasteur argued that the theory of spontaneous generation is wrong. Instead, the theory of biogenesis is correct. Are the theories of biogenesis and the origin of life on earth contradictory or not? Explain.

Comment: This is an excellent problem because it provokes students to think deeply about several key ideas, including some that may be strongly held. One may be special creation, which relies on a spontaneous generation of sorts. The required self-regulation on the part of some students may be considerable. With this in mind, make sure that you use the problem to stimulate discussion, debate, and so on, but do not demand closure on the students' part. ▼

▼ Problem 20

The eye color of the imaginary grizzly gronk population of the White Mountains varies. Some gronks have purple eyes, some have white eyes, and some have orange eyes. Professor Greengenes has discovered that whenever two purple-eyed gronks mate, they always produce purple-eyed offspring. Likewise, whenever two orange-eyed gronks mate, they always produce orange-eyed gronks. But when white-eyed gronks mate, they are able to produce offspring with three colors of eyes.

a. Use aspects of Mendelian theory to explain how eye color is determined among gronks. (For example, What is the genotype of the white-eyed gronks? How can they mate to reproduce offspring of all three colors of eyes?)

b. Use your theory to predict the phenotypic ratio of offspring if purple-eyed and white-eyed gronks were mated.

Comment: This problem involves several elements of scientific reasoning, such as hypothetical-deductive thinking, proportional thinking, and probabilistic thinking. You may need to provide some students with the hypothetical-deductive "hint" of starting by generating several ideas about what the genotype might be, and then proceed from these to the empirical reality stated in the problem. Of course, this idea of starting from the hypothetical and reasoning to the "real" is precisely the opposite of the way many students are accustomed to reasoning. The problem thus requires a considerable amount of self-regulation. As with most problems of this type, giving students the opportunity to share ideas and discuss their thinking is an excellent way to help them develop more advanced thinking patterns.   ▼

▼ **WRITTEN WORK**

In addition to exams and homework problems, students should be given the opportunity to prepare and submit written reports. Writing forces students to reflect on past experiences and partially understood ideas and to synthesize them into coherent wholes. In this way writing provides an excellent impetus for self-regulation. Perhaps the most common written report in the sciences is the lab report, the classroom equivalent of the scientific research paper that scientists prepare and publish in scientific journals. The lab report should be structured in the same way as a scientific research paper by including sections devoted to the causal question raised, the alternative explanations proposed, the experimental procedures, the predicted results, the actual results, and a discussion of the results, including a statement of the conclusion or conclusions drawn. Students can be required to submit such a report based on specific labs conducted in class that included these elements or they can be required to design and conduct research at home that includes these elements. Preparing such a report will be particularly challenging for students who start the year as empirical-inductive thinkers. The resulting disequilibrium and self-regulation can go a long way toward helping these students become hypothetical-deductive thinkers. The following are more specific guidelines to help students in preparing their lab reports.

Lab Report Guidelines

During the semester you will be required to submit a detailed lab report based on one or more of your investigations. The following information will help you with the format of the paper. Note that you will be graded on content (e.g., creativity, reasoning, experimentation) *and* style (e.g., grammar, spelling, neatness). Divide the report into the following sections.

Causal Question

In the first section state the causal question you are addressing. Include an introduction that consists of any background information your reader might need and a discussion of why the question is scientifically important or interesting.

Alternative Hypotheses (Explanations)

In the second section present the alternative hypotheses (at least two) that you will be testing. Be sure that your proposed explanations can be tested with the facilities at our disposal. For example, suppose you hypothesize that water rises in plants because there are little pumps in the roots or one-way valves in the stems. These are reasonable hypotheses. To test them, you must be able to imagine and conduct an experiment that yields expected results (predictions) and actual results (your data). Your hypotheses must be testable.

Experimental Procedure

This next section describes what you did to test your proposed explanations. Include a diagram of your setup and enough verbal description so that someone unfamiliar with your experiment could repeat it. State your independent variable (the factor that you manipulate) and your dependent variable (what you are measuring) for each experimental design. Be certain that you have designed controlled experiments and that you have enough data to differentiate random variations from "real" variations; in other words, you may need to repeat your experiment several times.

Expected Results (Predictions)

Your expected results (predictions) are derived from your proposed explanations (hypotheses) and your experimental design. To generate a prediction, we assume for the purpose of investigation that the explanation is correct. In this section of the report, the prediction may be stated as part of an *If–then* statement. The *If* portion is essentially a restatement of your proposed explanation. An explicit *and* portion represents your experiment, and a *then* portion states the results you expect to find if your proposed explanation is correct. For example:

> *If* there are pumps in the roots of plants that allow water to rise (proposed explanation),
>
> *and* we cut off the roots of a group of experimental plants while not cutting off the roots of a second group of plants (experiment),
>
> *then* we would expect that those plants with intact roots would show a greater water rise than those plants without roots (prediction).

Important Note: The *If–then* statement is simply a convenient way to illustrate the relationship among proposed explanation, experiment, and expected results. A hypothesis does not have to include the word *if,* and a prediction does not have to start with *then.* You cannot differentiate hypotheses from predictions just by looking for these cue words, because they frequently are omitted. You must understand the difference between them.

Actual Results

This section presents the actual results of your experiment. Your data should be quantitative and presented in tables or graphs (or both). Clearly label each axis on graphs, and columns and rows on tables. Also include a verbal discussion of major results.

Discussion and Conclusion

This section identifies trends in your data and discusses whether these trends agree or disagree with predictions derived from your proposed explanations. You may discuss any suggestive qualitative observations, explain any anomalous results, and suggest possible improvements in your experimental design. In conclusion, you should decide whether to accept or reject your hypotheses based on the results of your experiments. Do your actual results agree with your expected results? If so, then the hypotheses have been supported. If you decide to reject your proposed explanations, you may be able to suggest additional (post hoc) explanations at this time. Do your results suggest any further investigations of interest? If so, briefly discuss them.

The One-Page Lab Report

Although the lengthy lab report just described is an excellent way to provoke students to reflect on the process of doing science, you probably will not want to require such reports for every lab. A much shorter one-page report that includes all of the major elements of scientific thought can be prepared and graded with relative ease. Because the one-page version (Figure 9.1) includes the major elements of scientific thought, it can prod students to use hypothetical-deductive thought. To complete the report, students only need to fill in the boxes with the appropriate sentences. Figure 9.2 provides an example.

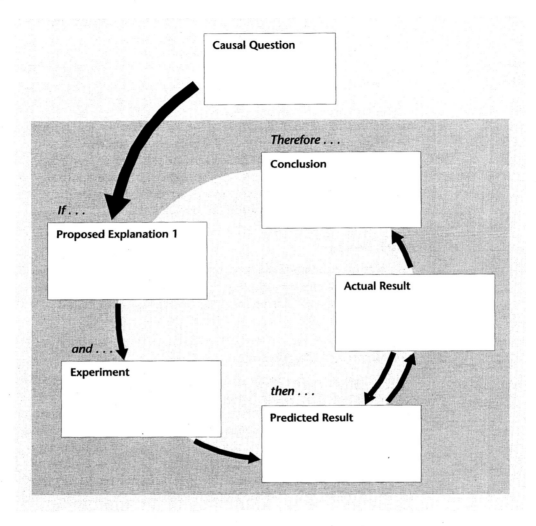

Figure 9.1 ▾ One-Page Lab Report

Science Fair Projects

The learning cycle classroom is devoted to doing science. Observations are made, questions are raised, hypotheses are created, experiments are conducted, and so on. The beauty of teaching science in this way is that the students are working as a large team of scientists would, with ideas shared, discussed, and debated. Consequently, no single student shoulders all of the

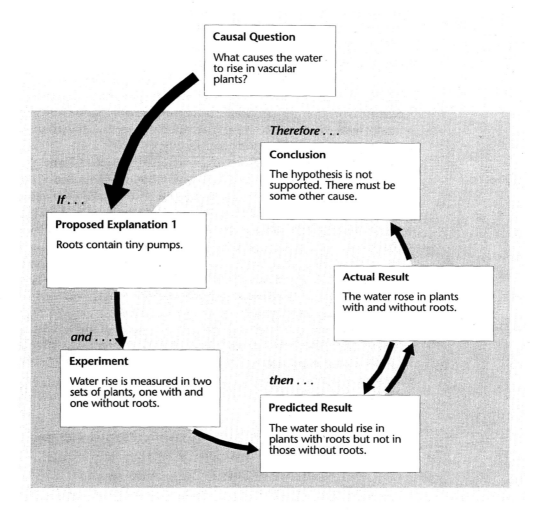

Figure 9.2 ▾ **Use of One-Page Lab Report.** This report details the experiment on water rise in plants.

responsibility for the progress made by the team. In a real sense, the total of the classroom activity is much greater than the sum of its parts.

The drawbacks to this team approach to science learning include some students who may not fully participate in the process and some who may follow the classroom investigations fairly well but who discover that they do not understand the process particularly well when left on their own to carry out an investigation. For this reason, having students prepare their own lab reports, even when the labs were conducted by teams, is a good idea. Of course, an even more demanding task is to have individual students derive their own questions, create their own alternative hypotheses, and conduct their own investigations. This, of course, is the role of the science fair project. Obviously, a science fair is not needed to have students conduct and report on their own investigations. Indeed, a wonderful activity would be to have students report their findings to the class in much the same way that scientists present findings to their peers at scientific conventions. However, the key point, whether or not a science fair is actually held, is to make certain that students are challenged to conduct their own investigations and report their results.

In keeping with the nature of science, projects can be one of three types: descriptive, empirical-abductive, or hypothetical-deductive. The *descriptive* project investigates an aspect of nature and reports what patterns, if any, were found. The *empirical-abductive* project includes not only a descriptive element but also the student's subsequent explanations (hypotheses or theories) for the patterns found. For example, if the student has raised the question, "What factors affect the role of breakdown of dead organisms?" and has discovered that organisms break down best in hot and wet conditions, they should then generate (abduce) one or more possible explanations for this result. Finally, the *hypothetical-deductive* project requires the student to raise a causal question, propose alternative hypotheses, plan experiments to allow the deduction of expected (predicted) results, and then carry them out to discover which if any hypotheses are supported. Obviously, this type of project places greater demands on student thinking skills than do either of the other two types.

Picking a reasonable question to investigate is not easy. Consider the following possibilities:

1. How do the number of coils of wire of an electromagnet affect the number of paper clips it can attract?
2. How do giraffes sleep?
3. How do different kinds of light affect the growth of a lima bean plant?
4. What elements react best in a nuclear fusion reactor?
5. Does age affect a person's reaction time?
6. What are the travel patterns of an ant colony?
7. How are locations for oil exploration determined?
8. Do mealworms react to sounds?
9. How do galaxies move?
10. What room designs provide the best musical sounds?
11. What causes water to rise in plant stems?

Clearly, Questions 2, 4, 7, and 9 are inappropriate because they cannot be investigated personally by students. The purpose of the project should *not* be to look up information in the library. Questions 1, 3, 5, 6, 8, and 10 could each form the basis of either a descriptive or an empirical-abductive project. Finally, because Question 11 is causal, it lends itself best to a hypothetical-deductive project. This is the most demanding type of project but the one with the greatest payoff in terms of encouraging self-regulation and the development of thinking skills.

A problem that many students have in conducting hypothetical-deductive projects is that they confuse hypotheses with predictions. This problem often stems from a lack of hypothetical-deductive thinking skills, although it also may result from the confusion of poor instruction. Consider, for example, Figure 9.3 (page 294), which has been reproduced from a set of guidelines on science fair projects given to students. Look closely at the example hypothesis, which states: "Plants grow best in potting soil." Is this a hypothesis (a tentative explanation)? No, it is a prediction, and the suggested project is not hypothetical-deductive. Instead, it is descriptive project or possibly an empirical-abductive one if, in fact, the predicted result occurs and a legitimate reason (hypothesis) is proposed. A legitimate reason, however, cannot be that the student has observed plants in the past that grew best in potting soils and so, by extrapolation (induction), these new plants should do as well. Notice that this induction merely extrapolates from past experience and proposes no insight into why potting soil is best.

What follows is a legitimate hypothesis to be tested: Potting soil contains more nutrients needed for plant growth than does sand. To test this hypothesis, we can do one or both of two things. We either take nutrients out of the potting soil or add nutrients to the sand (or both). If the hypothesis is correct, then we predict (deduce) (a) that plants will grow worse in nutrient-deficient potting soil (as compared to nutrient-rich potting soil, all other variables held constant) and (b) that plants will grow better in nutrient-enriched sand (as compared to normal sand, all other variables held constant). How would you test the hypothesis that potting soil retains moisture needed for plant growth better than sand? To test this hypothesis, you must vary water-retention ability while holding all other independent variables (possible causes or hypotheses) constant.

In summary, although they are well intentioned, most teachers—and even science fair judges—do not understand the process of alternative hypothesis testing and experimental design well enough to encourage or reward students to generate and test actual alternative hypotheses. Most science fair projects are tired descriptions or demonstrations of scientific principles rather than real science. How many more times will we see the exploding volcano at the science fair? Science fairs can be worthwhile, but to be of most value they should include all of the essential elements of doing hypothetical-deductive science that were presented in the preceding section on lab report guidelines.

Looking at a Science Project

Directions: This is a sample of a science project at a science fair. Study this display carefully and answer the questions below the picture.

Problem
**Does soil affect
the growth of plants?**

Hypothesis
**Plants grow best
in potting soil.**

Experiment

potting   water   sand
soil

Each plant receives same
amount of water and light.

Results

potting   water   sand
soil

Conclusion
Plants grow best in
potting soil.

What are the headings? _____

What does this project try to prove? _____

What are words in the project that you would like to know more about? _____

Figure 9.3 ▾ **Science Fair Project.** The teacher who prepared these science fair guidelines has confused hypotheses and predictions and has incorrectly implied that scientific experiments can prove hypotheses.

Portfolio Assessment

Having students collect and file their course work in a notebook or folder has been a commonly used strategy ever since teachers began looking for ways to assess student progress. These collections of assembled papers, lab reports, quizzes, class notes, and exams have recently been called *portfolios* (e.g., Collins, 1990). Portfolios can be collected periodically and evaluated in one or more ways by the teacher. A perceived advantage of portfolio assessment is that it may enable the teacher to better assess student progress over time. A possible disadvantage in awarding grades is that the portfolios and perhaps the teacher place too much emphasis on neatness and organization skills and not enough on real enthusiasm and understanding of the science.

Questions for Reflection

To provide you with more experience in classifying test items, consider the following test items. Classify them into one of the three categories—(1) recall of specific facts, (2) empirical-inductive thinking, or (3) hypothetical-deductive thinking—by using the criteria provided along with any that you have developed.

1. In a population of butterflies, wing coloration is determined by one pair of alleles (W and w). The dominant allele makes up 60% of all the alleles in the population.
    a. With respect to this characteristic, how many different genotypes are there?
    b. What percentage of each is present in the population?
    Please explain your choice.

    Your reasons (please refer to EI1 through HD5) (circle one).

    Recall   Empirical-Inductive   Hypothetical-Deductive

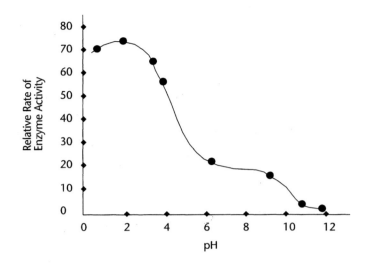

2. The enzyme graphed above will work best in:
   a. an acid medium
   b. an alkaline medium
   c. a neutral medium
   d. a carbohydrate medium.
   Please explain your choice.

   Your reasons (please refer to EI1 through HD5) (circle one).

   Recall   Empirical-Inductive   Hypothetical-Deductive

3. A meandering river with steep valley walls and no flood plain would be considered:
   a. young.
   b. mature.
   c. old.
   d. rejuvenated.
   Please explain your choice.

   Your reasons (please refer to EI1 through HD5) (circle one).

   Recall   Empirical-Inductive   Hypothetical-Deductive

4. A chemist places 3.0 moles of $H_2(g)$, and 4.5 moles of $CO_2(g)$ in an empty reaction vessel and maintains the temperature at 100° C as equilibrium is established. Analysis of the mixture indicates that 2.0 moles of $CO(g)$ and

2.0 moles of $H_2O(g)$ are present. How much hydrogen, $H_2(g)$, is present at equilibrium?

a. 1.0 mole
b. 1.5 moles
c. 2.0 moles
d. 2.5 moles
e. 3.0 moles

Please explain your choice.

Your reasons (please refer to EI1 through HD5) (circle one).

Recall   Empirical-Inductive   Hypothetical-Deductive

5. When an unknown gas is bubbled through clear lime water, $Ca(OH)_2$, a white precipitate forms. The gas can be assumed to be carbon dioxide provided that:

a. all the following are true.
b. no other gas forms a white precipitate in lime water.
c. the gas does not react chemically with the lime water.
d. no other substance gives a white precipitate with CO_2.
e. there is no marked change in the temperature of the lime water.

Please explain your choice.

Your reasons (please refer to EI1 through HD5) (circle one).

Recall   Empirical-Inductive   Hypothetical-Deductive

6. Weathering processes on the moon:

a. should be similar to those on the earth, assuming the principle of uniformity holds everywhere in the universe.
b. should be more severe than on earth because of extreme temperature changes.
c. should be quite different than on earth because of the lack of free oxygen and water on the moon.
d. should be similar to those on earth because the rocks on the moon are so chemically and structurally similar to those of the earth.

Please explain your choice.

Your reasons (please refer to EI1 through HD5) (circle one).

Recall   Empirical-Inductive   Hypothetical-Deductive

7. Newton's law of gravitation is expressed as $F = G\,Mm/d^2$, where F is the force, M and m are two masses, G is a constant, and d represents the

distance between the two masses. Assuming that M and m as well as G remain the same, which of the following graphs shows how the force changes when the distance between the masses varies?

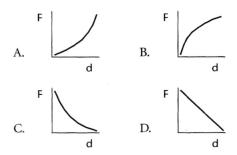

Please explain your choice.

Your reasons (please refer to EI1 through HD5) (circle one).

Recall   Empirical-Inductive   Hypothetical-Deductive

8. What is the displacement of a car that travels at a steady speed of 40 km/hr for 3 hours on a straight road?
   a. 43 km
   b. 120 km
   c. 13.3 km
   d. More information is needed.
   Please explain your choice.

   Your reasons (please refer to EI1 through HD5) (circle one).

   Recall   Empirical-Inductive   Hypothetical-Deductive

9. Galileo investigated the problem of the acceleration of falling bodies by rolling balls down smooth planes inclined at increasing angle because he had no means of determining very short intervals of time. From the data obtained, he extrapolated for the case of free fall. Which of the following is an assumption implicit in the extrapolation?
   a. Air resistance is negligible in free fall.
   b. Objects fall with constant acceleration.
   c. The acceleration observed with the inclined plane is the same as that involved in free fall.
   d. The planes are frictionless.

e. A vertical plane and one that is nearly so have almost the same effect on the ball.

Please explain your choice.

Your reasons (please refer to EI1 through HD5) (circle one).

Recall   Empirical-Inductive   Hypothetical-Deductive

10. Charles Darwin's famous book *The Origin of Species* was first published in what year?
    a. 1750
    b. 1801
    c. 1859
    d. 1954

Please explain your choice.

Your reasons (please refer to EI1 through HD5) (circle one).

Recall   Empirical-Inductive   Hypothetical-Deductive

11. Students who are predominantly empirical-inductive thinkers will experience disequilibrium when confronted with test items and written assignments that require hypothetical-deductive thought. What strategies can help this situation on tests and quizzes? On written assignments?

12. Obtain a test that has been administered recently to a group of middle school or high school students and analyze the items in terms of the level of thinking required.

CHAPTER 10

DIRECTIONS FOR FUTURE RESEARCH AND DEVELOPMENT

The learning cycle is an exceptionally flexible inquiry-oriented method of instruction that has been shown effective at improving students' attitudes toward science, their conceptual knowledge, and their general thinking skills. For many teachers, it is not only a good way, but also the only way to teach science. Indeed, it may be the single most effective way to teach any subject matter in which concept construction is a goal. This is not to imply that

300

additional research into the learning cycle is not needed. Rather, in the Kuhnian sense, the learning cycle represents a "paradigm" for instruction (Kuhn, 1970). A considerable amount of "normal science" remains to be done to test the cycle's limits of effectiveness and to fine-tune its use in different disciplines, with different types of students, and with different technologies. One does not need to be a professional researcher with a Ph.D. to direct or participate in such research. In that spirit, what follows is a brief look at a variety of issues about which secondary school science teachers should know and be able to research in their own classrooms. The issues deserve attention to ensure that the general method of the learning cycle can be most effectively implemented in specific areas.

▼ CONCEPTIONS AND MISCONCEPTIONS

A highly productive area of research has developed in recent years that aims to learn more about the conceptual knowledge that students bring to the classroom. Much of this research has focused on identifying what have been termed "misconceptions," which are defined as conceptions that are inconsistent with or even contradictory to modern scientific views (e.g., Arnaudin and Mintzes, 1985; Brumby, 1984; Champagne, Klopfer, and Anderson, 1980; Clement, 1982; Driver, 1981; Halloun and Hestenes, 1985; Minstrell, 1982; Piburn, Baker, and Treagust, 1988; Simpson and Marek, 1988; Stewart, 1982). Some misconceptions are deeply rooted and quite instructor-resistant. *Misconception* is a widely used term, but *alternative conception* may be a better label because all conceptions are merely personal attempts to construct models of external processes; therefore, no two are the same and none is a perfectly adequate representation. Further, the label *alternative conception* does not have the negative connotation that *misconception* does.

In the context of inquiry-oriented instruction—that is, the learning cycle—students' alternative conceptions are hypotheses to be tested. In this way they are integral in prompting investigations and argumentation and thus to be sought and discussed rather than avoided. A fertile area of research is thus the identification of alternative conceptions in different areas of science. A careful review of the history of science should prove helpful in this regard (Wandersee, 1986). Along with their identification, a taxonomy of alternative conceptions also may be useful if based on their origins. For example, the idea of special creation has its origin in religion, whereas the ideas that gravity pulls heavy objects faster to earth than light objects and that we are capable of pulling liquids up through a straw both have origins in personal experience.

Some alternative conceptions have origins in defective classroom instruction, while others may derive from students' lack of thinking skills or cognitive deficiencies or differences. An obvious goal of instruction is to help students construct more appropriate conceptions, and to reach this goal depends in large part on identifying the nature of the alternative conception and its source (Anamvah-Mensah, 1987; Smith and Anderson, 1987).

Lawson and Thompson (1988), for example, found that a sample of empirical-inductive seventh graders held more misconceptions about genetics and natural selection than did their hypothetical-deductive peers. Lawson and Weser (1990) found the same thing in a sample of college students. They found also that the empirical-inductive college students were less likely to surrender their misconceptions than their hypothetical-deductive classmates. Lawson and Weser suggested that this was because the empirical-inductive students did not have sufficient hypothetical-deductive thinking skills to consider adequately the alternative conceptions, available evidence, and arguments in favor of the scientific conceptions; as a result, they were less likely to modify previous unsatisfactory beliefs.

Individual student differences, other than thinking skills, are also of potential interest. Cognitive styles, preferences, and a variety of other presumably socially derived individual difference variables may have profound influence on concept change and concept construction (Okebukola and Jegede, 1988; Staver and Walberg, 1986). Clearly, higher-order concepts are complex, and their construction requires the coordination of a relatively large number of separate pieces of information. In some cases students may not have sufficient mental capacity to coordinate this information, so alternative instructional approaches may need to be explored (Niaz, 1988).

Novak's notion of concept mapping (Lehman, Carter, and Kahle, 1985; Novak, Gowin, and Johansen, 1983) is potentially productive, as is Anderson and Smith's (1986) notion of conceptual change teaching; both should be explored in conjunction with these issues. A variety of aptitude-treatment interaction studies are suggested, much like those reviewed previously by Renner, Abraham, and Birnie (1983, 1985, 1988). Finally, researchers will need to continually refine their methods for evaluating students' concepts and thinking skills, as well as changes in their concepts and skills (Finley, 1986).

In summary, future research on student misconceptions and conceptual change should be designed to answer three general questions:

1. What sorts of alternative conceptions do students bring with them to the classroom?
2. What are the sources of these alternative conceptions, their generality, stability, and ease of modification?
3. How can learning cycles or other instructional methods be designed to modify or replace these conceptions effectively for different types of students?

For a recent meta-analysis of the conceptual change literature in reading education and science education, see Guzzetti, Snyder, Glass, and Gamas (1993).

▼ MOTIVATION AND ASSESSMENT

Learning cycle inquiry instruction relies on students' intrinsic motivation to fuel their participation in learning activities. Events occur, data are gathered, and questions are raised, all of which are designed to be mildly disequilibrating and thereby arouse student curiosity. The point of such activities is to find answers to satisfy curiosity rather than obtain an extrinsic reward such as a good grade. Lepper, Greene, and Nisbett (1973) found that children who were given extrinsic rewards for performing an initially interesting activity actually lost interest in the activity, while nonrewarded children retained their interest. The inquiry instruction thus appears to rely properly on intrinsic motivation. But school systems generally require that student progress be assessed and grades awarded. How should this be done?

The notion of mastery learning may be useful to explore, although it is not without problems. Certainly, we want students to "master" both declarative and procedural knowledge. Unfortunately, the hardest things to master are those that take the most time (e.g., higher-order thinking skills), and if we demand mastery too soon, we may simply frustrate students and ourselves. Too often, the end result is that we give up and resign ourselves to mastery of the trivial. Clearly, both theoretical and empirical work need to be done to resolve these and related issues.

▼ COOPERATIVE LEARNING

Many of the learning cycle's exploration and application phase activities are conducted by students working in small groups of two to three. Students need to communicate with one another and cooperate to design and conduct experiments, gather data, and the like; the learning cycle thus includes many elements of cooperative learning as described by Johnson and Johnson (1975). Johnson (1976), found that sixth-grade students in inquiry-oriented science classes perceived those classes to be more cooperative than their textbook classes. They also voiced a distinct preference for cooperation. Many studies have reported various attitude and achievement benefits to cooperative modes, but, as with all complex instructional interactions, identifying which factor or factors are responsible for those benefits is difficult (Capie and Tobin, 1981; Humphreys, Johnson, and Johnson, 1975; Johnson and Johnson, 1979; Lazarowitz, Hertz, Baird, and Bowlden, 1988; Sharan, 1980; Slavin, 1980).

Optimal ways of establishing laboratory groups have been investigated specifically in the context of inquiry instruction. Lawrenz and Munch (1984, 1985) taught a physical science course for preservice teachers and established three types of lab groups based on reasoning skill levels: homogeneously grouped, heterogeneously grouped, and student choice. The researchers found the homogeneous grouping to be best in terms of student gains in reasoning skills and content achievement. Their results imply that students learn best when they interact with others at or near their own level of thinking. This finding appears to contradict the notion that more able peers can serve as effective classroom teaching assistants. Instead of assisting other group members in learning new material and skills, perhaps such assistants only take over and tell others what to do. Clearly, careful research needs to explore the complexities of the group dynamics in learning cycle activities to arrive at appropriate guidelines (Tobin and Gallagher, 1987).

SEQUENCING AND SELECTING CONTENT

The learning cycle is an approach to lesson planning. Each lesson to teach a concept or group of closely related concepts is initiated with an exploration activity into the phenomenon from which the concept directly or indirectly derives meaning. Because concepts build on one another to form conceptual systems, some should be taught before others. The learning cycle approach does not specifically address these larger curriculum development issues, so key questions remain. In what order should related concepts be taught? How should individual inquiries be sequenced to produce optimal learning? These were the questions addressed in Chapter 8.

Gagné (1970) has long advocated careful task analyses and the construction of learning hierarchies in which subtasks are mastered one at a time and later assembled to allow solution of complex tasks or to comprehend complex concepts. But what motivates students while they learn the subtasks? Should biology students be told, for example, that they must learn concepts of atomic structure because they will need to know them later? Or should the metric system be taught before its use? If these ideas and skills are needed later, then why not teach them later?

Considerable research has been conducted into Ausubel's notion of using advance organizers to precede and help coordinate later instruction. The results of research into advance organizers are mixed, and the idea itself is unclear to many (Lott, 1983). What are advance organizers, and should they be used? If so, how? Chapter 8 suggested that instruction should proceed from the whole to its parts. As discussed, this idea seems similar to Ausubel's but perhaps the opposite of the Gagnéan approach. General ideas such as those need to be made more specific to allow for their satisfactory testing and resolution in the context of learning cycles.

What content should be taught and at what level? Some work has been done to identify intellectually appropriate content for students of various ages and intellectual abilities (Shayer and Adey, 1981). The SCIS curriculum is perhaps the best example of articulating student intellectual capabilities with content. The curriculum begins with a careful descriptive look at objects and their properties and only later explores theoretical notions such as light, magnetism, energy flow, and ecosystem dynamics. This progression from de-scriptive to theoretical science mirrors children's intellectual development as they progress from childhood empirical-inductive and intuitive skills to more abstract early adolescent hypothetical-deductive skills. However, many text-book approaches still attempt to teach very young children about theoretical entities such as atoms and energy. More research could be aimed at specifically finding out the consequences of such instruction. If found largely futile, then it should be modified or eliminated.

Recall that we have classified learning cycles into three types—descriptive, empirical-abductive, and hypothetical-deductive—which require differing types of student thinking skills. The descriptive cycles use descriptive skills, while the hypothetical-deductive cycles require more advanced hypothetical-deductive skills. The empirical-abductive cycles require intermediate skills. This idea has led researchers such as Kim (1988) to suggest that instruction at the elementary level should be through descriptive and empirical-abductive cycles. The SCIS program, however, does not do this.

Although the SCIS developers did not identify the three types of learning cycles, they clearly exist in the program, and a variety of types occur at all levels. The first-grade organisms unit, for example, includes a learning cycle that explores the question, "What caused the black stuff on the bottom of the aquarium?" After this causal question is raised, students assemble to generate possible answers (i.e., alternative hypotheses). Their ideas concern such aquar-ium organisms as fish, plants, and snails. The students then set out to design and conduct an experiment to test their ideas. To do this, the fish, plants, and snails are isolated in new aquariums to see in which aquarium the black stuff appears. In this way the students clearly propose and test alternative hypothe-ses—as in hypothetical-deductive learning cycles. Furthermore, their attempts are generally quite successful.

Note, however, that student hypotheses are based on familiar experiences and do not involve the imagination of theoretical entities. And another key element—the teacher—is involved in the lesson. Clearly, he or she is guiding the students as they work in one large group to generate ideas and design their experiments. Perhaps the key variables across age are not the type of inquiry that should be used but the extent to which students must rely on experience or imagination and work in groups with teacher guidance or individually. Leonard's work on discretionary capacity seems relevant to this last point (Leonard, 1980). Leonard's idea is to design instruction so that it gradually increases the burden on students to carry out their work *after* the teacher has provided sufficient group activities to teach students the skills needed for that work. Some inquiry along these lines has been conducted, but additional research would be worthwhile.

▼ THE ROLE OF ANALOGY

The theory of concept construction introduced earlier argued that theoretical concepts are formed through analogical reasoning (i.e., abduction). This suggests that analogies can play a crucial role in instruction, particularly when the concepts under consideration are theoretical and complex. Consider, for instance, the theoretical concept of natural selection. This is indeed a complex idea because it involves the integration of previously constructed concepts such as biotic potential, limiting factors, heredity, variation, long spans of time, and a struggle for survival. Needless to say, it took the keen intellects and considerable efforts of a Charles Darwin and an Alfred Wallace to put these ideas together to explain the evolution of species. Because few, if any, of our students are as intellectually able, experienced, and motivated as Darwin and Wallace, how can they be expected to construct an idea of this complexity? Of course, the answer lies in our ability as teachers to guide students in the appropriate directions. Darwin and Wallace did not have such guidance. But in precisely what directions should students be guided? Inquiries can be developed and taught to help students construct the subordinate concepts of biotic potential, limiting factors, heredity, variation, and long spans of time. But how can the struggle for survival be taught in the classroom? And how can its integration with prior concepts be facilitated? The answer may lie in the use of the appropriate analogy. Recall that Darwin claimed that a key moment in his thinking was when he saw the similarity between his own experiences with artificial selection of domestic animals and the natural world: When he "saw" that the same selective process could occur in both places, he presumably had the necessary framework to assimilate the subordinate concepts and "invent" the concept of natural selection.

Unfortunately, most of our students will not have personal experiences with artificial selection, so it may not be an effective analogy. Another must be found. In this case, as discussed in Chapter 8, one analogy appears to work quite well: the simulation in which students play the role of predatory birds capturing and eating toothpick insects (Stebbins and Allen, 1975). In that simulation, the predatory birds capture and eat "animals" represented by paper chips of various colors. Over three generations of this selection process, the color of the prey population changes to "fit" the environment in which it lives (a particular piece of fabric). Students thus simulate the process of selection in the classroom and can, like Darwin, borrow this pattern and apply it to nature to understand the process of natural selection.

The theory of the role of analogy in concept construction and the success of this type of lesson suggests that research might identify other useful analogies and devise learning cycles in which they are used to teach complex theoretical ideas. Clearly, a careful examination of the history of science could be helpful in this endeavor. Gabel and Samuel (1986), for example, investigated the role of analogies in solving molarity problems in chemistry, and Clement (1986) investigated analogies' roles in explaining Newtonian mechanics. Several other examples can be found in a special 1993 issue of the *Journal of Research in Science Teaching* (volume 30, number 9), which was devoted to the use of analogy in science teaching.

▼ RETENTION AND TRANSFER OF THINKING SKILLS

Most studies of the effectiveness of the learning cycle method have been relatively short in duration. The notable exceptions (e.g., Renner et al., 1973) have been conducted with SCIS students who have studied science through learning cycles for as many as six or seven years. These studies have shown transfer of performance gains in thinking to academic areas as diverse as mathematics, social studies, and reading. However, the ultimate goal of instructional approaches such as the learning cycle is to improve thinking skills that will transfer to tasks outside of the school environment. Do more able reasoners make more informed decisions about political issues? Do more able reasoners influence their children more in the direction of rational thought? Do they become more personally involved in social issues? Do they reject pseudoscientific positions in favor of more empirically supported positions?

The retention and transfer issue is indeed complex and difficult to research. In general, it can be approached in steps. First, is the learning cycle better than other approaches at teaching thinking skills that were the explicit focus of instruction? Research strongly suggests that this is so. Second, is the learning cycle better than other approaches at teaching thinking skills that were *not* the explicit focus of instruction? Again, research suggests that this is so. Third, do the improved thinking skills transfer to other academic subjects? The answer to this question appears to be "yes." Fourth, are the improvements in thinking skills lasting? A clear answer to this question is more difficult to obtain because it requires longitudinal data. Clearly, studies of this sort are needed. Fifth, do lasting improvements (if they exist) translate into improved academic performance and improved performance in "real" life? Note that improvements in academic performance would be expected to occur only when that academic performance requires thinking skills. Many "advanced" courses obviously are not really advanced at all: They simply require the memorization of huge numbers of facts and place little, if any, demand on higher-order thinking skills. One might well predict that the more able thinkers would be "turned off" by such courses and do poorly. None of this means that research cannot investigate these issues, only that such research will indeed be difficult, particularly because appropriate dependent measures of success will be difficult to identify.

Previous research into some of these issues has suggested future trends. Lawson (1985) reviewed programs designed to teach higher-order reasoning skills and concluded that more diverse and longer-duration instruction generally was slower in producing *specific* gains (e.g., Fuller's ADAPT program at Nebraska) than were short-term efforts to teach *specific* thinking skills (e.g., Seigler, Liebert, and Liebert, 1973), but that the slowly acquired gains were more general because they involved a greater variety of skills that were applicable in a greater variety of contexts. This result seems reasonable: More diverse and longer-term instruction more closely approximates the out-of-school experiences that contribute to intellectual development. The suggested research study is one in which students are raised on a diet of learning cycles in all disciplines in, say, kindergarten through twelfth grade, and are compared to those raised by more traditional means.

▼ TEACHING CONTENT VERSUS PROCESS

Virtually everyone who first hears about the learning cycle method wonders if it allows for a sufficient number of concepts to be taught. The notions that students bring their own conceptual baggage to the classroom and that they are active agents in constructing their own knowledge imply that the teacher cannot simply "cover" topic after topic in rapid succession through the lecture method and achieve much student understanding. Consequently, the number of concepts and facts "covered" must be reduced. But another implication is that this reduced coverage is more than compensated for by increased understanding and retention. The key issue is one of deciding just what content, from among the vast available supply, teachers should attempt to teach.

Textbooks are of little help: Many textbook authors and most publishers are primarily in the business of making money, and the way to do this is to satisfy as many teachers as possible by loading a text with as many topics as possible. As a result, we now have textbooks that give students not only headaches, but also backaches.

Lewis (1988) suggests a solution to this problem. Recall that individual concepts reside in conceptual systems. In the sciences, of course, these conceptual systems are *theories*. A finite set of embedded (scientifically accepted) theories exist in each science, and each theory consists of a finite set of postulates. Therefore, much of what exists in textbooks can be ignored as unimportant provided we identify and teach the embedded theories of each science and their key postulates. Because the postulates define the concepts, learning cycles would be designed to teach those key concepts in the appropriate areas. These ideas should be implemented and researched in the future. For example, *Biology: A Critical-Thinking Approach, Student Readings,* the readings book for high school students that accompanies Lawson (1994), is only 137 pages long but introduces the postulates of 29 basic biological theories.

▼ TEXTBOOKS

What role should textbooks play in the learning cycle? Earlier it was suggested that textbooks be used only during the concept application phase, although little research has explicitly investigated this issue. In one study, however, Abraham and Renner (1984) substituted reading material in chemistry for the exploration phase and found that this adversely affected poor reasoners but not more able reasoners. But neither group of students preferred reading as a substitute for the laboratory in the exploration phase.

As suggested in the previous section, a new type of text could be researched and developed that deals only with specific theories and their postulates. That text material also could be written according to learning cycle phases. In other words, the author would first raise questions, describe observations, and present data. Then he or she would discuss patterns and introduce terms. Finally, applications of the concepts in other contexts would be discussed. Such an approach of phenomenon first and idea second is clearly different from the common practice of using key terms as section headings and then defining them after their introduction. Use of the learning cycle in text passages may prompt better understanding and retention and better engage students' use of "metacognitive" skills (Holliday, 1988).

▼ NEW TECHNOLOGIES

Considerable science education interest can be found now in new technologies such as microcomputers and videodiscs (Berger, Pintrich, and Stemmer, 1987; Brasell, 1987; diSessa, 1987; Ellis and Kuerbis, 1988; Good, 1987; Hawkins and Pea, 1987; Heath, White, Berlin, and Park, 1987; Mokros and Tinker, 1987; Nachmias and Linn, 1987; Reif, 1987; Rivers and Vockell, 1987; Sherwood, Kinzer, Bransford, and Franks, 1987; Ulerick, Bybee, and Ellis, 1988). Science, however, requires contact with nature, so these new technologies are unlikely ever to replace the hands-on activities of learning cycles. On the other hand, new technologies can provide useful additions to the learning cycle, in theory at least. The learning cycle itself can be used as a guide to help develop effective use of these technologies. One appropriate use of the technologies is in the concept application phase of the cycle where simulations and the like could be used to extend and refine the usefulness of terms previously introduced. For example, the simulation of genetic crosses over many generations or the simulation of ecological trends over many years or even centuries can be easily accomplished with computers. Simulations also could be used in the exploration phase when the phenomena of interest cannot be directly experienced given the normal classroom constraints. Many other uses are sure to be found (e.g., to help plot data gathered during explorations or to present other data bases for analysis). These issues can easily serve as settings for future research.

Consistent with the learning cycle approach, Thomas and Hooper (1991) classify the use of simulations into three categories: *experiencing, informing,* and *reinforcing* or *integrating.* Like explorations, experiencing simulations are used to (a) provide motivation, (b) provide an organizing structure, (c) serve as a concrete example, or (d) expose misconceptions and areas of knowledge deficiency. Like the term introduction phase of the learning cycle, informing simulations serve as a means of initial formal exposure to a topic. In the Thomas and Hooper scheme, reinforcing simulations allow students to apply the new knowledge in the same context in which it was learned; integrating simulations enable the knowledge to be integrated into functional units and assimilated with other units so that the knowledge can be useful. These obviously are functions of concept application activities in the learning cycle.

▼ TEACHER EDUCATION AND PROFESSIONAL GROWTH

Chapter 7 discussed Hurd, Bybee, Kahle, and Yeager's (1980) national survey results, which indicated that less than 25% of science teachers use learning cycles or similar "inquiry" methods. Given the clear and convincing evidence in favor of the learning cycle method, why do so few teachers use it? Recall the ten reasons teachers commonly give for not using inquiry? Among the most frequently cited reasons were that too much time must be devoted to developing good materials and that the approach is too slow to "cover" the typical district curriculum. However, research on this issue clearly shows that rapid "coverage" of material does not lead to its assimilation, and so it is unsuccessful. Ironically, programs that attempt to cover large numbers of concepts do just that: "cover" the concepts, where *cover* is defined precisely as it is in the dictionary—that is, to conceal from view.

Certainly real problems exist that must be solved in specific instances, but none of the teachers' ten most common reasons alone or in combination need prevent implementation of the learning cycle. To do so on a wider scale, however, will require curriculum development and major preservice and in-service teacher-education efforts. Obviously, for kindergarten through sixth-grade teachers, SCIS and Elementary Science Study (ESS) materials are available for immediate use. The availability of high-quality learning cycle materials, appropriate curriculum guides, and comprehensive tests at other grade levels is more problematic. Various science educators have developed materials appropriate to the high school level, and some programs, as mentioned earlier, have been developed at the college level, but the publication and distribution of such materials has been a problem because of their nontraditional nature. Nevertheless, teachers need to be made aware of their existence and the advantages they offer. They also must be educated to use the materials properly. Given that teachers generally teach as they have been taught and that they are typically taught science with the traditional lecture method, discovering and implementing ways of using new materials warrants further research. Here we might do well to consider teacher-education and dissemination efforts in other countries. In Japan, for example, a much more centralized, systematic, and extensive in-service teacher-education program exists that appears in many ways to be more effective than our generally disjointed and haphazard methods.

To keep abreast of current research and development in a particular field, a teacher should belong to and actively participate in one or more of the following organizations. Each publishes a journal (as noted) and holds annual meetings in various locations around the country. The journals and meetings are an excellent source of current thinking.

1. American Association for the Advancement of Science: *Science*
2. American Association of Physics Teachers: *American Journal of Physics* and *The Physics Teacher*
3. American Chemical Society: *Journal of Chemical Education*
4. Association for the Education of Teachers in Science (AETS): *Science Education*

5. National Association of Biology Teachers: *The American Biology Teacher*
6. National Association of Geology Teachers: *Journal of Geology Education*
7. National Association for Research in Science Teaching: *Journal of Research in Science Teaching*
8. National Science Teachers Association: *The Science Teacher, Science and Children,* and *Journal of College Science Teaching*

▼ OTHER CURRENTLY POPULAR METHODS

There never has been or ever is likely to be a shortage of teaching methods studies comparing Brand X and Brand Y. A few of the more recent methods are mastery learning, outcome-based education, and Hunter's essential elements of instruction (Hunter, 1982). The basic notion behind mastery learning is that all students are capable of acquiring and should acquire key ideas and skills (i.e., master them) before they move on to the next topic. Hunter's approach appears even more simplistic. She argues correctly that good instruction includes a few essential elements, but she incorrectly concludes that these elements are things such as teaching one objective at a time and telling the students beforehand precisely what they are supposed to learn.

The most regrettable result of mastery approaches to the teaching and learning process is that they often degenerate into teaching only the simplest facts. This happens because students are unable to "master" higher-order thinking skills or construct complex concepts in a short time, and so they are dropped. The Hunter approach is more problematic than the mastery approach because it denies the dual goal of every science lesson: to teach concepts and improve thinking skills. Further, telling students precisely what they are supposed to learn robs the lesson of its inquiry nature and thereby limits or eliminates curiosity, which is the most powerful source of motivation in science. The Hunter approach also appears to contradict directly the notion that the child actively constructs his or her knowledge, which is a basic tenet of the learning cycle method. Nevertheless, some educators (e.g., Granger, 1988) have attempted a synthesis of the Hunter and learning cycle approaches. Perhaps a closer look is in order; beyond these apparent contradictions there may be common ground that will strengthen both approaches.

▼ PROJECT 2061

To improve science teaching in grades K through 12, the American Association for the Advancement of Science (1989) and the National Science Foundation are now sponsoring a large-scale, grassroots curriculum development and implementation project called Project 2061. The project selected its name from the year that Halley's Comet next comes closest to the earth. The name is meant to convey a long-term and viable commitment to science curriculum reform. One central purpose of the curricular materials that Project 2061 hopes to develop is *scientific literacy* for all Americans. In the project's words:

> A scientifically literate person uses scientific knowledge and scientific ways of thinking for individual and social purposes. Scientific habits of mind can help people in every walk of life to deal sensibly with problems that often involve evidence, quantitative considerations, logical arguments, and uncertainty; without the ability to think critically and independently, citizens are easy prey to dogmatists, flimflam artists, and purveyors of simple solutions to complex problems. (p. 13)

To educate students so that they attain such literacy, Project 2061 advocates the use of learning and teaching principles that are consistent with the nature of scientific inquiry. The project lists the following six principles of learning:

1. Learning is not necessarily the outcome of teaching.
2. What students learn is influenced by existing ideas.
3. Progression in learning is usually from the concrete to the abstract.
4. People learn to do well only what they practice doing.
5. Effective learning by students requires feedback.
6. Expectations affect performance.

The project also lists the following five principles of teaching:

1. Teaching should be consistent with the nature of scientific inquiry.
   - Start with questions about nature.
   - Engage students actively.
   - Concentrate on the collection and use of evidence.
   - Provide historical perspectives.
   - Insist on clear expression.
   - Use a team approach.
   - Do not separate knowing from finding out.
   - De-emphasize the memorization of technical vocabulary.
2. Science teaching should reflect scientific values.
   - Welcome curiosity.

- Reward creativity.
- Encourage a spirit of healthy questioning.
- Avoid dogmatism.
- Promote aesthetic responses.

3. Science teaching should aim to counteract learning anxieties.
   - Build on success.
   - Provide abundant experience in using tools.
   - Support the roles of girls and minorities in science.
   - Emphasize group learning.
4. Science teaching should extend beyond the school.
5. Teaching should take its time.

These principles have been derived from a careful, thoughtful, and thorough review of the research literature from science learning and teaching by a large and diverse group of some of the best and brightest scientists and educators in this country. The principles should be taken seriously by science teachers. Further details about Project 2061—including an excellent discussion of which concepts and conceptual systems in the sciences, mathematics, and related technological fields should be taught to students through these principles—can be found in *Project 2061: Science for All Americans* (American Association for the Advancement of Science, 1989) and in *Benchmarks for Science Literacy* (American Association for the Advancement of Science, 1993). Obviously, the teaching methods advocated in this text are in the same spirit as those advocated by the AAAS.

▼ INTEGRATING SOCIAL AND TECHNOLOGICAL ISSUES

The science–technology–society (STS) movement has recently been and will continue to be an influential and highly visible movement in science education (Aikenhead, 1980; Bybee, 1987; Fensham, 1987; Yager, 1984). The movement's basic intent is to integrate technological and societal issues into the science classroom.

The intent is very much in keeping with the aims of Project 2061. Indeed, the latter describes seven key aspects of human society that can be fruitfully explored using the methods of scientific investigation:

1. cultural effects on human behavior,
2. the organization and behavior of groups,
3. the process of social change,
4. social trade-offs,

5. forms of political and economic organization,
6. mechanisms for resolving conflict among groups and individuals, and
7. national and international social systems.

In the area of technological advances, Project 2061 urges attention to eight basic technological areas: agriculture, materials, manufacturing, energy sources, energy use, communication, information processing, and health technology. Some science educators have taken the STS movement so to heart that they appear to be advocating curriculum reform in which key social and technological issues provide the primary focus of instruction. For example, units of instruction can be developed around the energy crisis, the greenhouse effect, oil spills, and so on. In such a curriculum, science concepts are taught when necessary to understand aspects of the social or technological issues. This may be appropriate on occasion, but as a general strategy for science curriculum development it is misguided for essentially three reasons. First, few teachers are expert in or knowledgeable enough to be able to make such an integration work. Second, the nature of the science curriculum would have to be modified whenever a new crisis arises. And third, a better way already exists: integrate relevant social and technological issues into the science curriculum as part of the concept application phase of learning cycles, which have the exploration and understanding of nature as their primary objective.

This approach puts the motivation for science instruction where it naturally resides—in the natural human curiosity to understand the world. Once this understanding has been obtained in the sense of pure science, it can be applied to social and technological issues in the sense of applied science. Indeed, this is the normal historical relationship between science and technology. Consequently, the suggested approach would be, for example, to *explore* patterns of inheritance, *introduce* concepts of Mendelian and molecular genetics, and *discover* how these concepts apply to the field of genetic engineering (i.e., follow the exploration, term introduction, and concept application phases of the learning cycle). Or students in a chemistry class can *explore* the question, "What's in water?" The teacher could then *introduce* such concepts as hardness, polarity, and solubility; the concepts could then be *applied* to issues of water pollution.

Advocating the learning cycle approach for integrating the social and technological does not imply that such issues do not influence pure science. Indeed they do, although beyond the obvious influence that instruments such as the microscope and the telescope have had on biology and astronomy, these influences generally are subtle and beyond the experience of most secondary school students. These subtle issues thus are better left for college graduate-level courses in the history or philosophy of science. In short, the position advocated here is to design the curriculum around the principles presented in

Chapter 8 and to integrate social and technological issues with the science rather than the other way around.

The Committee on High School Biology Education of the National Research Council raises a fourth objection to science courses offered under the STS label (National Research Council, 1990). In the committee's words:

> *We are concerned that courses offered as "science, technology, and society" (STS) usually do not follow a study of basic sciences. Instead, they typically replace basic science courses, [which results in] . . . a lack of scientific breadth needed to study interdisciplinary topics more than superficially. (p. 88)*

To avoid creating a STS curriculum in which students fail to acquire the scientific declarative and procedural knowledge needed in addressing societal issues, the council takes a position similar to the learning cycle approach in which the basic science is taught first and applied second. More specifically, the council proposes an interdisciplinary "capstone" course that would be offered in a student's final year of high school. The course would consider current major scientific, technological, and societal problems.

▼ TESTING

Most standardized aptitude and achievement tests (e.g., the Scholastic Aptitude Test, the Iowa Tests of Educational Development, and the American College Testing Program) attempt to assess general knowledge and thinking skills. The American College Testing Program, for example, is developing a new test of critical thinking that includes items in four main categories: recognizing an argument's elements, analyzing its structure, evaluating the argument, and extending it (American College Testing Program, 1988). On the skills required for success on their tests, Science Research Associates (1970), makers of the Iowa Tests, has said, "the student must interpret and analyze material that is new to him, and apply broad concepts and generalized skills to situations not previously encountered in the classroom" (pp. 1–2).

In other words, most standardized tests at the national level correctly attempt to assess broad concepts and general thinking skills. Regrettably, many local districts have set up committees to develop district-level tests in specific disciplines that are far less imaginative. In some cases, the tests only measure rote recall of isolated facts. Such tests are counterproductive to the learning cycle method's efforts toward developing and teaching. Whether this is simply a policy issue or one open to research is not clear. One learning cycle teacher, however, reported that her students outperformed those of traditional teachers in her school on a fact-oriented, district-developed biology test. Her students even did better on topics that she did not teach! Perhaps improved thinking skills generalize to previously unsuspected areas.

▼ THEORETICAL ISSUES AND A PROBLEM WITH "SOCIAL" CONSTRUCTIVISM

The following theoretical issues will continue to affect instruction and help us refine our own view of the learning cycle:

1. better descriptions of general thinking skills (Yap and Yeany, 1988);
2. the role played by specific content in the use of thinking skills (Griggs, 1983; Lehmann, Lempert, and Nisbett, 1988; Linn, Pulos, and Gans, 1981; Staver, 1986);
3. principles of neural modeling, information processing, and memory (Anderson, 1992; Grossberg, 1982; Lawson, 1986; Lawson and Lawson, 1993);
4. the nature of intelligence and its potential modifiability (Herrnstein, Jensen, Baron, and Sternberg, 1987; Sternberg, 1985); and
5. the nature of social interactions and language during various phases of the learning cycle (Glasson and Lalik, 1993).

These theoretical issues are extremely interesting and important. They will surely add precision to our ability to design effective instruction in the future. For example, with respect to the fifth issue, the Glasson and Lalik (1993) article proposes the use of a "language-oriented" learning cycle based on a learning theory that they call "social constructivism." Their article suggests a social constructivist theory consisting of seven basic postulates:

1. To learn, people must actively construct knowledge by identifying and testing existing understandings, interpreting meanings of experiences, and adjusting knowledge frameworks accordingly.

2. Language can be used to stimulate cognitive activity as people use language to represent current understandings as well as processes by which they develop those understandings.

3. Initially, a child's speech and action are part of one and the same complex psychological function.

4. The more complex the action demanded by the situation, and the less direct its solution, the greater the importance of speech in the operation as a whole.

5. The development of higher psychological functions such as logical memory and concept formation occur as a slow and sometimes incomplete process of internalization.

6. Patterns identified during the learning process are mental constructions of the learner that reflect the purposes, experiences, and perspectives of that learner.

7. Patterns constructed during the learning process are not attributes of external phenomena.

A reasoned evaluation of current evidence supports the first six postulates. Consequently, the Glasson and Lalik language-oriented learning cycle has many features that should prove effective in the classroom. The seventh postulate, however, has a serious flaw that could have unfortunate consequences if one takes the postulate seriously. In fact, it—or closely related postulates—appears to be shared by others who advocate one or another version of "social" constructivism. For example, Guba and Lincoln (1989, p. 84) state that constructivists believe "that there exist multiple, socially constructed realities ungoverned by any natural laws, causal or otherwise." And Roth (1993) claims that "an ontology of a real and objective world independent of our human ways to categorize this world . . . is incompatible with constructivism." Accordingly, discourse within the scientific community "is viewed as the most important mechanism for testing knowledge claims" (Prawit, 1991, p. 742).

Why is this position in error and why does it matter? First, the constructivist proposal that patterns are constructed during the learning process is correct. But do these patterns exist only in the learner's mind as claimed by social constructivists? There appear to be four possibilities. For example, patterns constructed during the learning process exist:

1. only in the learner's mind,
2. only in external phenomena,
3. in neither the learner's mind nor external phenomena, or
4. in the learner's mind *and* in external phenomena.

The second and third positions most likely are not true. As Descartes said, "I think, therefore I am." Regarding external patterns, for example, a pattern exists of periods of light and dark. Night follows day, which follows night, which follows day, and so on. Presumably, everyone has "constructed" such a pattern. Does it exist only in our minds as the first position would claim? Or does this and other patterns—such as winter follows fall, which follows summer, which follows spring—also exist in the "world out there" as claimed by the fourth position?

To the constructivist, the "world out there" and any patterns detected in it are mental constructions, just as dreams are mental constructions. Therefore, we must admit to the possibility that the "world out there" and any perceived patterns in it are merely mental constructions that do not really exist "out there." Fortunately, we can test the first and fourth positions. For example, to test the claim that our mental constructions of automobiles traveling at high speeds on freeways do not really exist, all we need do is dress in black pants and shirt, travel to a busy freeway at night, and stand in the fast lane. If we are killed by one of those imaginary mental constructions, then we have obtained evidence that contradicts the first position and supports the fourth. On the other hand, if the mentally constructed automobiles pass through and leave us unharmed, then we have evidence that supports the first position and contradicts the fourth.

Of course, even if we are killed, we have not *proven* that automobiles exist. After all, if we were to repeat the experiment, we might obtain different results. Nevertheless, the bottom line here is survival. Humans construct and test many alternative realities. The ultimate test of those invented realities is not "how they play in discussions in Peoria," as claimed by social constructivists, but how well their deduced consequences match external patterns. Thus, even though we cannot *prove* that speeding automobiles are real, we assume that they are and we get out of the way. Social constructivists do as well. Consequently, even though we cannot prove that the "world out there" and our constructed patterns in that external world really exist, we quite naturally assume that they do. To do otherwise not only is not reasonable, but also is not science.

Further, and this is the key point about science teaching, if we adopt the view that the "world out there" does not really exist, then we lose our most basic way of testing alternative hypotheses; as a consequence, we lose our most effective way of developing student thinking skills. Simply put, to test mental constructions—that is, alternative hypotheses—we must do more than merely talk about them as a group of philosophers might. We must deduce their consequences and test them against the cold reality of the "world out there." In other words, we must do science.

▼ CONCLUSION

As reviewed in Appendix D, a considerable amount of research has supported the notion that correct use of the learning cycle in the science classroom is effective in helping students obtain the stated objectives. More research remains to be done to explore various facets of the learning cycle and to extend and test its effectiveness in new areas and for longer periods of time. Also, future theoretical work in the field of neuroscience and new technologies probably will aid our understanding and ability to teach effectively. Although these improvements will help to fine-tune the learning cycle method (Hestenes, 1987), they probably will not alter its fundamental role and importance because learning cycle instruction follows the way in which humans spontaneously construct knowledge. This pattern of learning may be made more explicit by educational theorists and researchers in the future, but it will not be changed unless the human mind evolves a different means of learning.

Questions for Reflection and Activities

1. How can student "misconceptions" be used as "alternative hypotheses" in learning cycles designed to answer causal questions?

2. Select a scientific concept or set of related concepts that have important implications and applications to societal issues and design a learning cycle in which these social issues are addressed during the application phase.

3. In what ways might new technologies be used to improve science instruction? In what ways might they actually make instruction less effective?

4. Design a research study to test alternative hypotheses about the most effective ways to establish cooperative classroom groups. Conduct the study if possible and submit a written report of your findings to a journal devoted to science education research.

5. Design a second research study to test alternative hypotheses about another aspect of science instruction. Conduct and report the results of this study as well.

6. According to the Educational Policies Commission (see Appendix A), two basic criteria should be used to decide what substantive knowledge—that is, subject-matter–specific declarative knowledge, domain-specific concepts—should be taught. The first criterion is the potential of the knowledge for the development of rational powers (i.e., thinking skills); the second is the relative importance of the knowledge in the lives of the student and society. With these criteria in mind, select a science concept or set of related concepts that you think should be taught at some specific grade or grades. Design a learning cycle to teach the concepts. Write it up using the format in the example learning cycles that appear in Chapter 5 and Appendix G. Submit your write-up, including both student and teacher materials, to your course instructor so that he or she can suggest improvements and share your write-up with other interested students. Use the following criteria in preparing your write-up.

LEARNING CYCLE WRITE-UP CRITERIA

General

1. Is the proper format used?
2. Are proper grammar, punctuation, and spelling used?
3. Do sentences contain unnecessary words? If so, delete them.
4. Is each sentence clear? Are sentences and paragraphs in the correct order?
5. Does the title represent the key descriptive or causal question? For example, "What kinds of . . . are there?" "What will happen if . . . ?" "What variables affect . . . ?" "What might be the cause of . . . ?"

Student Material

6. Does the student introduction engage the students' interest? Is it a "grabber"? Are major questions clear? Is the introduction well "motivated"?
7. Are the objectives clear? Do they represent process goals?
8. Is the list of materials complete? Does it contain enough materials to allow for a variety of paths of exploration? For example, does it allow observation or manipulation of several objects, events, or situations? testing of several independent variables? testing of several alternative hypotheses?
9. Are the procedures clear? Will the students have a clear idea of what questions they are trying to answer? The students should not be told how to answer the questions. In general, the procedures should be minimal. Cookbook procedures are to be avoided. Students may, however, be told how to perform specific techniques if those techniques are particularly difficult or potentially dangerous without guidance.
10. Is space provided for students to record data?
11. Are five to ten study questions included? Assume that the questions will be assigned after the term introduction phase. Some questions should be divergent and thought-provoking. Some should call for the application of the newly introduced concepts to new contexts. If the learning cycle involves the testing of alternative hypotheses, one question should require the explication of this process.

Teacher Material

12. Are the major terms that will be introduced identified?
13. Does the synopsis provide a brief but clear overview of what the students will do? Does it indicate the type of learning cycle? That is, does it use descriptive (looks for patterns in nature), empirical-abductive (finds patterns and tries to explain them by generating hypotheses), or hypothetical-deductive (tests alternative hypotheses) thought?
14. Does the background section clearly introduce and define the key scientific terms involved in the lesson? Does it state in general terms how key

terms are to be introduced? Assume that the reader is an intelligent but inexperienced teacher.

15. Do the teacher tips provide *detailed* suggestions as to how to conduct the lesson? That is, do they suggest how to engage the students' interest? how to guide the explorations? when and how to hold class discussions? how to collect, display, and analyze data? how to introduce each term? how to initiate the application phase?

16. Are the key scientific terms and thinking skills involved in the lesson listed? The list of thinking skills should include some or all of the following:

> accurately describe nature
> state causal questions
> generate alternative hypotheses
> generate logical predictions
> plan and conduct experiments
> organize and analyze data
> draw and apply conclusions

17. Have at least five multiple-choice test questions been included? Are all questions above the knowledge level? That is, do they test comprehension, application, analysis, synthesis, or evaluation?

18. Do the test questions include at least four (and preferably five) alternative answer choices? None of the choices should include "All of the above," "None of the above," and so on. Are the correct answers marked?

19. Do some of the questions require use of the thinking skills involved in the lesson?

Before Submission

20. Have you had at least two other people read and critique your learning cycle? Have you carefully considered their suggestions and made all appropriate changes?

21. Have you carefully edited and rewritten your write-up at least *five* times before submission?

CHAPTER 11

NEUROLOGICAL MODELS OF SELF-REGULATION AND INSTRUCTIONAL METHODS

Chapters 1 through 10 introduced and discussed the basic postulates of learning cycle instructional theory, and they suggested possible directions for future research and development. At this point, you should be ready to begin implementing the theory in your classroom. Although you certainly will have some initial successes, do not let the inevitable setback deter you. Most teachers find that considerable trial and error are required for them to become skilled at directing the learning cycle classroom. But once they have become skilled, they cannot imagine teaching any other way. Chapters 11 and 12 go beyond the basics and can be omitted from an undergraduate course on teaching methods. However, their topics—neurological models of learning and the role of logical and analogical thinking in knowledge construction—are critically important from a theoretical perspective and should be of interest to both advanced students and experienced teachers.

The processes of self-regulation and its component of reflective abstraction are key to the development of thinking skills and concept construction. As a theoretical concept, self-regulation had its origin in Piaget's early thinking. Perhaps his most detailed explication of its process can be found in Piaget (1971a). Although his general notion of self-regulation has won many advocates and seems intuitively reasonable to most of them, it carries a serious theoretical weakness: Although based on a valid biological analogue—namely, genetic assimilation (see Lawson, 1982b)—it remains only an analogy. To move our understanding beyond analogical arguments of this sort, obviously we must actually understand how the brain functions, because ultimately it is the brain that constructs and stores our knowledge.

A considerable amount of progress toward this understanding has been made during the past twenty years or so in the related fields of neural physiology and neural modeling. We now turn our attention to that work with a brief introduction to general brain anatomy and neurological signaling. This introduction will be followed by a neurological explanation of the psychological process of self-regulation. The primary intent of this chapter is to provide a theoretical rationale for self-regulation and for learning cycle instruction at the level of neural anatomy and physiology.

▼ BASIC NEUROLOGICAL PRINCIPLES[*]

General Brain Anatomy

Figure 11.1's side view of the human brain shows the spinal cord, brain stem, and cerebral cortex. In general, the cortex is divided into a frontal portion, which is made of neurons that control motor output, and a rear portion, which receives sensory input.

The thalamus is a relay center at the top of the brain stem that relays signals from the sense receptors to the sensory cortex. All sensory input except smell passes through one of twenty-nine thalamic regions on its way to the cortex. One of the most important nuclei is the *lateral geniculate nucleus*

---

[*]The following explication of neurological principles previously appeared in Lawson (1986).

Figure 11.1 ▾ **General Brain Anatomy.** This diagram shows the location of key structures involved in neural modeling.

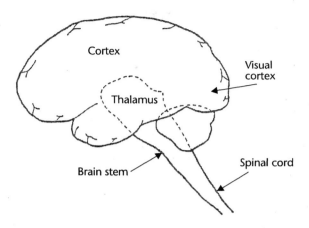

(LGN), the relay station of the optic tract from the retina to the visual cortex (see Figure 11.2).

At the center of the brain stem from just below the thalamus down to the medulla (the lowest segment of the brain stem) is the reticular formation. The reticular formation is believed to play a key role in nerve networks by serving

Figure 11.2 ▾ **Optic Tract.** The sensory input path runs from both retinas to the LGN near the center of the brain to the visual cortex at the rear of the brain.

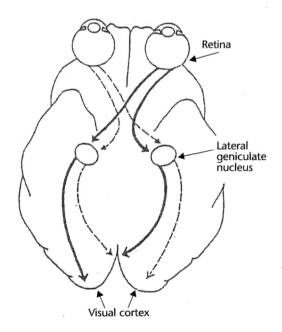

as a source of nonspecific arousal. In the inner surface of the deep cleft between the two brain hemispheres lies the hypothalamus, the apparent source of specific drive dipoles such as fear–relief and hunger–satisfaction that also play a key role in neural modeling.

Neuronal Signals

The basic unit of the functioning nervous system is the nerve cell or neuron. Although many types of neurons exist, they all share the characteristics exemplified by the pyramid cells found in the cerebral cortex (shown in Figure 11.3).

Pyramid cells consist of four basic parts: a cell body, a set of dendrites, an axon or axons, and a set of terminal knobs. The dendrites and the cell body are capable of receiving electrical signals from axons of other neurons. The axons (which may branch) conduct signals away from the cell body. When stimulated by incoming signals, the terminal knobs open small packets of chemical transmitter that, if released in sufficient quantity, cause the signal to pass across the gap or synapse to the next neuron.

Figure 11.3 ▾ **The Pyramid Cell of the Cerebral Cortex and Its Major Parts**

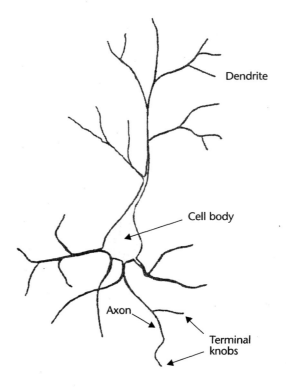

A nonfiring neuron has a slightly negative electric potential across the cell membrane (approximately −70 millivolts, or mV), which is termed its *resting potential.* Incoming signals can be either excitatory or inhibitory; they modify the resting potential in an additive fashion and thus induce what is termed the cell's *generating potential.* When the generating potential exceeds a certain threshold, a spike or action potential is generated in the cell body and travels down the axons.

The action potential travels at a constant velocity with an amplitude of up to approximately 50 mV. Signals are emitted in bursts of varying frequency, depending on the level of neural depolarization. Apparently, all of the information in the signal depends on the pulse frequency of the bursts.

An important point is that neurons appear to arrange themselves in distinct layers or slabs within various substructures of the brain. Consider, for example, the arrangement of neurons in the visual system. Light is received by an initial layer of photoreceptors in the retina. Excitation of retinal cells fires signals along the optic nerve to a layer of neurons located in the lateral geniculate nucleus. Cells of this nucleus then process their signals and in turn relay signals to a third layer of cells in the visual cortex at the back of the brain (see Figure 11.2). From the visual cortex, signals are transmitted back to the LGN and to additional layers of neurons for further processing. The signals returned to the LGN play a particularly significant role by allowing the system to compare incoming signals with expectations acquired from previous learning. More will be said about this later (also see Grossberg, 1982, especially pp. 8–15). An excellent discussion of neural anatomy that is relevant to learning and memory also can be found in Mishkin and Appenzeller (1987).

▼ GENERAL PRINCIPLES OF NETWORK MODELING

Table 11.1 (after Hestenes, 1983) lists crucial components and variables of neurons and layers of neurons as well as their physiological and psychological interpretation in Grossberg's theory.

Consider the ith neuron in a collection of interacting neurons. The average generating potential of the ith neuron at node V_i is signified by X_i, the stimulus or short-term memory (STM) trace. This activity can be sustained by a feedback loop; thus, Grossberg makes STM the property of any neuron where activity is sustained for a specific period of time. STM is *not,* as commonly interpreted in cognitive psychology, a single undetermined location in the brain into which a limited amount of information can be put and temporarily stored.

The signal that propagates along the axon or axons (designated e_{ij}) from node V_i to synapse knob N_{ij} is signified by S_{ij}. The signal is, of course, a function

Table 11.1 ▽ **Neuron Components and Variables**

	Node	Directed Axon Pathway	Synaptic Knob	
Components	V_i	e_{ij}	N_{ij}	V_j
Variables	X_i	S_{ij}	Z_{ij}	X_j

	Variable	Physiological Interpretation	Psychological Interpretation
Activity	X_i	Average generating potential	Stimulus trace or STM trace
Signal	S_{ij}	Average firing frequency	Sampling or performance signal
Synaptic strength	Z_{ij}	Transmitter release rate	LTM trace

After Hestenes, 1983.

of the activity X_i at node V_i. The final extremely important neural variable is the synaptic strength, Z_{ij}, of knob N_{ij}. The tentative physiological interpretation of Z_{ij} is the average rate of transmitter release at the synapse. In effect, Z_{ij} represents how easily signals down e_{ij} can cause V_j to fire. If signals are able to get the knob to release a lot of transmitter (a large value for Z_{ij}), then signals are sent across the synapse and the next cell in line (V_j) fires. If signals are unable to get the knob to release much transmitter (a small value for Z_{ij}), then signals will not cause V_j to fire. Increases in Z_{ij} represent modification of knobs to allow transmission of signals among neurons. Thus, Z_{ij} becomes the location of long-term changes in systems of neurons—that is, the system's long-term memory (LTM). In this way learning is considered to be a biochemical modification of synaptic strengths. As with STM, Grossberg's theory makes LTM a property of neuron connections rather than a specific single location in the brain.

Equations of Variable Interactions

Grossberg has proposed equations to describe the basic interaction of these variables. Of particular significance are equations that describe changes in X_i

and Z_{ij}—that is, changes in short-term and long-term memory, respectively. In general, for a network with n nodes, these equations are of the form:

$$\dot{x}_i = -A_i\, x_i + \sum_{k=1}^{n} S_{ki}\, Z_{ki} - \sum_{k=1}^{n} C_{ki} + I_i\,(t) \tag{11.1}$$

$$\dot{Z}_{ij} = -\, B_{ij}\, Z_{ij} + S_{ij}{}'\,[X_j]^+ \tag{11.2}$$

where overdots represent a time derivative, and $i, j = 1, 2, \ldots n$.

The equations describe what is necessary to drive a change in activity of V_i (i.e., $\dot{X}_i$) and a change in rate of transmitter release at knob N_{ij} (i.e., $\dot{Z}_{ij}$). Equation 11.1 is referred to as the *activity equation* of node V_i because it describes factors that influence changes in STM. Equation 11.2 is referred to as the *learning equation* because it describes the elements .needed to produce changes in LTM.

Consider first the terms in Equation 11.1. As mentioned, X_i represents the initial level of activity of nodes V_i. The term A_i represents a passive decay constant that is inherent in any dissipative system. The sign is negative, indicating a drop in activity of V_i across time as a result of the product of A_i and X_i. In other words, if V_i receives no additional input or feedback from itself, then the activity stops. The term $S_{ki}\, Z_{ki}$ represents inputs (S_{ki}) to nodes V_i from prior cells in the system mediated by their respective synaptic strengths (Z_{ki}). The positive sign indicates that these signals act to stimulate or increase the activity of cells V_i. These inputs are additive, hence their summation. The C_{ki} term represents inhibitory node–node interactions of the network, thus the negative sign. Recall that inputs to neurons can be excitatory or inhibitory. The final term, I_i, represents inputs to V_i from sources outside the network (i.e., neurons other than those in slab V_k).

Equation 11.2, the learning equation, describes the conditions necessary to modify the synaptic strength of knobs N_{ij}. The term Z_{ij} represents initial synaptic strength; B_{ij} is a decay constant, thus the term $B_{ij}\, Z_{ij}$ is a forgetting or decay term. $S_{ij}{}'\,[X_j]^+$ can be considered the learning term because it drives increases in Z_{ij}. $S_{ij}{}'$ is the signal that has passed from node V_i to knob N_{ij}. The prime simply indicates that the initial signal, S_{ij}, was perhaps slightly altered as it passed down e_{ij}. The term $[X_j]^+$ represents the level of activity at postsynaptic nodes V_j that exceeds firing threshold. Only activity above threshold can cause changes in Z_{ij}.

In short, the learning term indicates that for information to be stored in LTM, two events must occur simultaneously. First, signals must be received at N_{ij}. Second, nodes V_j must be receiving inputs from other sources that cause them to fire. When these two events drive activity at N_{ij} above a specified constant of decay, then the Z_{ij}s will increase—that is, the network learns.

▼ ## LEARNING IN A SIMPLE NEURAL CIRCUIT: CLASSICAL CONDITIONING

Learning in Grossberg's theory occurs when synaptic strengths (Z_{ij}) increase—that is, when transmitter release rate increases and makes transmission of signals from one neuron to the next easier. Learning is, in effect, an increase in the number of connections among neurons that are "operative." So to have a "mental structure" become more complex, transmitter release rates must increase at many knobs so that the signals can be easily transmitted across synapses that were previously inoperative. This view reveals the sense in which nativists are "correct": If we equate mental structures with already present but inoperative synapses, then the mental structures are present before any specific experience. The view also reveals how constructivists are "correct": For the synapses to become operative, experience is necessary to "strengthen" some of the connections. Just how can experience do this?

Consider Pavlov's classical conditioning experiment in which a dog is stimulated by the sound of a bell to salivate. Recall that when Pavlov first rang a bell, the dog, as expected, did not salivate. However, after repeated simultaneous presentation of food (which initially caused salivation) and bell ringing, the ringing alone was able to cause the dog to salivate.

In Pavlovian terms, the food is the *unconditioned stimulus* (US). Salivation on presentation of the food is the *unconditioned response* (UCR), and the bell is the *conditioned stimulus* (CS). In general terms, Pavlov's experiment showed that when a conditioned stimulus (a bell) is repeatedly presented with an unconditioned stimulus (food) it will eventually evoke the unconditioned response (salivation) by itself.

How is the unconditioned stimulus able to do this? Figure 11.4 shows how Grossberg uses his principles to construct a simple neural network that is capable of explaining classical conditioning. The network can be depicted as just three cells—A, B, and C—each of which actually represents many neurons of types A, B, and C, respectively.

Initial presentation of food causes cell C to fire. This creates a signal down its axon that, because of prior learning (i.e., a relatively large Z_{CB}), causes the signal to be transmitted to cell B. Cell B fires, and the dog salivates. At the outset, ringing of the bell causes cell A to fire and send signals toward cell B, but when the signal reaches knob N_{AB}, its synaptic strength, Z_{AB}, is not initially large enough to cause B to fire. The dog does not salivate. However, when the bell and the food are paired, cell A can learn to fire cell B according to Equation 11.2. The firing of cell A results in a large S'_{AB}, while the appearance of food results in a large $E[X_B]^+$. Therefore, the product $S'_{AB}[X_B]^+$ is sufficiently large to drive an increase in Z_{AB} to the point at which it alone can cause node V_B to fire and evoke salivation. Food is no longer needed. The dog has learned to

Figure 11.4 ▽ **Classical Conditioning in a Simple Neural Network.** Cells A, B, and C represent layers of neurons.

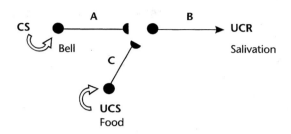

salivate at the ringing of a bell. The key point for neural modeling theory is that learning is driven by simultaneous activity of pre- and postsynaptic neurons—in this case, the activity of cells A and B.

▼ LEARNING IN HUMANS: A MORE COMPLEX NETWORK

The Basic Pattern of Knowledge Construction

How might Grossberg's principles be applied to account for learning in humans? Consider the simple behavior of a human infant learning to orient a bottle to suck milk. We will use Grossberg's principles to deal with the increase in complexity. Such a step is necessary because it will provide a model of simple learning on which we can begin to visualize neural events that may be involved in self-regulation and higher-order cognition.

The behavior of interest was reported by Jean Piaget, who was observing his son Laurent (between ages seven and nine months). Piaget (1954) reports as follows:

> *From 0:7 (0) until 0:9 (4) Laurent is subjected to a series of tests, either before the meal or at any other time, to see if he can turn the bottle over and find the nipple when he does not see it. The experiment yields absolutely constant results; if Laurent sees the nipple he brings it to his mouth, but if he does not see it he makes no attempt to turn the bottle over. The object, therefore, has no reverse side or, to put it differently, it is not three dimensional. Nevertheless Laurent expects to see the nipple appear and evidently in this hope he assiduously sucks the wrong end of the bottle. (p. 31)*

Laurent's initial behavior consisted of lifting and sucking whether or not the nipple was oriented properly. Apparently, Laurent does not notice the differences between the bottle's bottom and top or he does not know how to modify his behavior to account for the presentation of the bottom. Thanks to his father, Laurent has a problem.

To construct a neural model of Laurent's behavior, we need to be clear on just what new behavior (knowledge) Laurent must construct. At the outset, he knew how to flip the bottle to orient it properly for sucking, provided the nipple was visible. He also knew how to bring the bottle to his mouth and to suck. What he lacked was the ability to flip the bottle *before* lifting and sucking when only the bottom was visible. This was the behavior that needed to be constructed. How was it constructed?

Again, we return to Piaget's experiment. On the sixth day of the experiment, when the bottom of the bottle was given to Laurent, "he looks at it, sucks it (hence tries to suck glass!), rejects it, examines it again, sucks it again, etc., four or five times in succession" (p. 127). Piaget then held the bottle in front of Laurent to allow him to look at both ends simultaneously. Although his glare oscillated between the bottle top and bottom, when the bottom was presented to Laurent again he still tried to suck the wrong end.

The bottom of the bottle was given to Laurent on the eleventh, seventeenth, and twenty-first days of the experiment. Each time he simply lifted and began sucking the wrong end. But by the thirtieth day he "no longer tries to suck the glass as before, but pushes the bottle away, crying" (p. 128). When the bottle was moved a little farther away, "he looks at both ends *very* attentively and stops crying" (p. 128).

Finally, two months and ten days after the start of the experiment, when the bottom of the bottle was given to Laurent he was successful in flipping it over first: "[H]e immediately displaces the wrong end with a quick stroke of the hand, while *looking* beforehand in the direction of the nipple. He therefore obviously knows that the extremity he seeks is at the reverse end of the object" (pp. 163–164).

Laurent's learning behavior, although relatively simple, follows a pattern of learning. That pattern consists of an initially successful behavior driven in part by a response to an external stimulus and in part by an internal drive (in this case, hunger). The initially successful behavior is contradicted when it is misapplied beyond the situation in which it was constructed. This leads to frustration (reminiscent of Piaget's concept of disequilibrium) and, in neural modeling terms, an eventual shutting down of the internal drive coupled with a nonspecific arousal that causes the child to stop the incorrect behavior and attend more closely to the external stimulus that initially provoked the behavior. Attention, once aroused, allows the child to notice previously ignored cues or relationships among the cues, which in turn allows him or her to couple those cues with modified behavior to deal successfully with the new situation. Hence, a new procedure has been actively constructed. Let us see how this can happen at the level of neurons.

The Neural Network

Figure 11.5 depicts a neural network (after Grossberg, 1982, Chap. 6) that might drive this learning. In general, CS_i represents the ith conditioned stimulus among possible stimuli that excites cell population U_{i1} in the sensory cortex. Input to U_{i1} has already passed through slabs of neurons (specifically, the retina and the LGN); in this specific case, CS_1 represents the undifferentiated pattern of visual inputs from Laurent's bottle (i.e., either top or bottom). In response to CS_i, U_{i1} sends signals to another slab of neurons in the motor cortex, U_{i2}, called the Brodmann area 4, located at the top of the brain (Albus, 1981, pp. 89–90) as well as to all populations of arousal cells for specific drives (probably located in the hypothalamus; see Grossman, 1967). Because in this case hunger is the drive of interest, CS_i will be generally limited to arousal of the cell populations that increase the hunger drive, Ah^+, and those that decrease the hunger drive, Ah^- (see Grossberg, 1982, pp. 259–262 for a discussion of the pairing of cue with appropriate drives). Populations Ah^+ and Ah^- then send

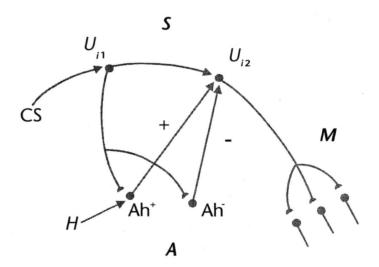

Figure 11.5 ▾ **Minimal Network for Response.** This diagram shows the minimal network that would model the initiation of the lifting and sucking response when cued by the appearance of the bottle (CS). Cell populations in the sensory cortex (U_{i2}) send excitatory input to excitatory arousal cells (Ah^+) and inhibitory arousal cells (Ah^-). The hunger drive (H), coupled with excitation from CS, causes U_{i2} to fire and initiate the motor response. S represents the sensory system, A the arousal system, and M the motor control system.

signals to U_{i2}. Finally, and only when excited by signals from U_{i1} and excitatory signals from Ah^+, U_{i2} will fire and send signals to M (the motor cells controlling the behavioral response), which releases the conditioned response: the lifting and sucking of the bottle.

Notice that this sequence of several events causes the synaptic weights at the Ah^+ and U_{i2} layers to increase because pre- and postsynaptic activity occurs at both layers, thus conditioning the behavior of lifting and sucking to the appearance of the bottle when the child is hungry. In this way, this minimal network can explain the initiation of Laurent's behavior. Now how can it explain its termination after satisfaction of the hunger drive?

The Rebound from Hunger to Satisfaction

Intake of food gradually reduces the activity of Ah^+ cells, which in turn causes a "rebound" or activation of Ah^- cells that itself inhibits activity at U_{i2}, thereby stopping the motor response. Precisely how does the satisfaction of hunger at Ah^+ generate a rebound of activity at Ah^-? The simplest version of the neural rebound mechanism, referred to as a *dipole,* is shown in Figure 11.6.

An internally generated and persistent input, *I,* stimulates both the $Ah^+$and the Ah^- channels. This input will drive the rebound at Ah^- when the hunger-derived input, *H,* is shut off. When Laurent is hungry, inputs *I* and *H* sum and create a signal along e_{13} (i.e., from V_1 to V_3). A smaller signal is also set along e_{24} by *I* alone. At the synaptic knobs N_{13} (i.e., the knob connecting V_1 to V_3) and N_{24}, transmitter is produced at a fixed rate, although it is, of course, used more rapidly at N_{13} than at N_{24}. Signals emitted by V_3 exceed those emitted by V_4. Because these signals compete subtractively at V_5 and V_6, only the output from V_5 is positive, hence producing a positive incentive to drive feeding behavior.

When hunger is reduced and the hunger drive stops, the network exhibits a rebound because of the relative depletion of transmitter at N_{13}. This occurs because input *I* to both V_1 and V_2 is the same, but signals leaving N_{24} are now stronger than those leaving N_{13} (the result of varying levels of transmitter). The subtractive effect thus causes a firing of V_6 that causes feeding behavior to stop, because of its inhibitory effect on U_{i2}.

Stopping Feeding Behavior Resulting from Frustration

We also need a mechanism to stop feeding while the hunger drive persists. Again the dipole is involved. A nonspecific *orienting arousal* (OA) source is also required (see Figure 11.6). In general, unexpected feedback to the sense receptors causes a decrease in input to U_{i1}, Ah^+, and Ah^- to the point at which activity at U_{i2} falls below threshold and the motor behavior is stopped. A

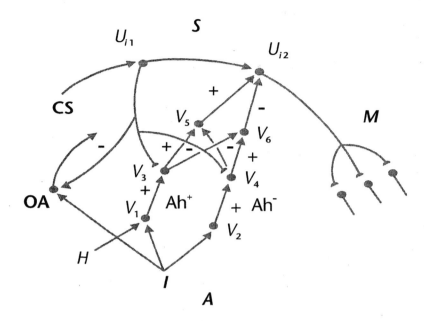

Figure 11.6 ▾ **Hypothesized Network.** This diagram might explain the stopping of feeding behavior when the hunger drive, *H,* is reduced. *I* represents a tonic, persistent input from the arousal system. Cell populations V_1 though V_6 represent the dipole system responsible for the rebound from hunger to satisfaction when *H* is reduced. OA is a source of nonspecific orienting arousal.

decrease in activity at U_{i1} also will cause a decrease in inhibitory output to the nonspecific OA cells (probably in the reticular formation). With inhibition shut down, the orienting arousal cells fire and provoke a motor response of cue search. Simply put, unexpected events are arousing. Once the maladaptive behavior is extinguished, attention can be focused on the situation and the problem solver—Laurent, in this case—is free to attend to previously ignored cues. Recall Laurent's behavior on the thirtieth day of Piaget's experiment: Laurent "no longer tries to suck the glass as before, but pushes the bottle away, crying" (p. 128). Further, when the bottle was moved a little farther away, "he looks at both ends *very* attentively and stops crying" (p. 128). A key question then is, "How do unexpected events cause a decrease in input to U_{i1}?"

Match and Mismatch of Input with Expectations: Adaptive Resonance

A detailed answer to the previous question is beyond the scope of this chapter (see Grossberg, 1982, pp. 8–14 and 262–265, for details). In general, however, we can show that the suppression of specific input and the activation of nonspecific arousal depends on the layer-like configuration of neurons and feedback expectancies. Consider a pattern of sensory representations to the visual system (i.e., the retina). The retina consists of a layer of retinal cells, V_1, $V_2, \ldots, V_n$, each of which has an activity, $X_1(t), X_2(t), \ldots, X_n(t)$, at every time t because of inputs $I_i(t)$ from an external source. At every time t, the input drives a pattern of activity $X(t) = X_1(t), X_2(t), \ldots, X_n(t)$ across the layer. From the retina, the pattern of activity is sent to the LGN, where it excites another layer of cells $V_1, V_2, \ldots, V_n$ and also sends inhibitory signals to the nonspecific arousal source (see Figure 11.7). In this way, nonspecific arousal is initially turned off by the input.

Following Grossberg, the field of excitation in the LGN will be referred to as $F^{(1)}$. Now suppose that, because of previous experience, the pattern of activity, X_1, at $F^{(1)}$ causes a firing of another pattern, X_2, at $F^{(2)}$, where X_2 may be the next pattern to follow X_1 in a sequence of events previously recorded and $F^{(2)}$ is another layer of cells that, in this case, would be in the visual cortex. We would then expect X_2 to occur when X_1 excites cells in the LGN. Suppose further that the pattern X_2 at $F^{(2)}$ is now fed back to the LGN to be compared with the retinal input following X_1. This would allow the two patterns to be compared. In effect, the present is compared with an expectation. If the two patterns match, then an individual sees what he or she expects to see. This allows an uninterrupted processing of input and a continued quenching of nonspecific arousal. Grossberg refers to the match of input with expectations as an *adaptive resonance*.

But suppose the new input to $F^{(1)}$ does not match the expected pattern X_2 from $F^{(2)}$. Mismatch occurs, which causes activity at $F^{(1)}$ to be turned off; this in turn shuts off the inhibitory output to the nonspecific arousal source and turns on nonspecific arousal as well as initiates an internal search for a new pattern at $F^{(2)}$ that will match X_1. If no match can be found, new cells will be used that can record the new neural sensory input.

The previous discussion can explain the shutdown of maladaptive behavior even in the presence of a continued hunger drive. But why did it take so many contradictions to extinguish that behavior? The answer lies partially in the fact that, on many trials, Laurent's behavior actually was not maladaptive. It was successful before the start of Piaget's experiment. Further, it was successful on the many trials during the experiment when Laurent was allowed to feed in his normal way. On these trials the synaptic strengths of Ah^+ and U_{i2} continued to be increased while fired by C_{i1} (the top of the bottle). On the other hand, when his behavior was frustrated, the sensory representation of the bottom of the bottle (C_{i2}) active at U_{i1} during the Ah^- rebound is being conditioned to Ah^-. The *net* feedback from Ah^+ to U_{i1} (either directly to U_{i2} or by way of U_{i2}) will be smaller than when behavior is always successful. As

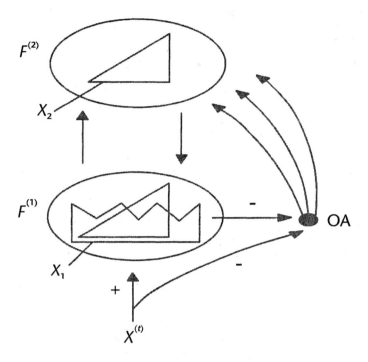

Figure 11.7 ▼ **Match and Mismatch of Activity Patterns.** This diagram shows activity on successive layers of neurons in the brain (after Grossberg, 1982). Input $X(t)$ excites a pattern of activity at $F^{(1)}$ and inhibits nonspecific orienting arousal (OA). The pattern X_1 at $F^{(1)}$ excites pattern X_2 at $F^{(2)}$ which feeds back to $F^{(1)}$. A mismatch causes quenching of activity at $F^{(1)}$ and shuts off inhibition of OA, which is then free to excite $F^{(2)}$ to search for another pattern to match input.

Piaget's experiment continued, the C_{i2} projections to Ah^- became stronger until finally, on the thirtieth day, they dominated the $C_{i1} \rightarrow Ah^+$ projections and Laurent stopped attempting to lift and suck the bottle when the bottom was presented. At last he is free to construct new connections. His incorrect behavior has been extinguished, and nonspecific arousal cells are firing to allow him to search for important sensory cues previously ignored.

What Laurent must learn is to flip the bottle when the bottom of the bottle is visible. The bottom is the important cue to be linked with flipping. According to the theory, to provoke this learning the neural activity in the cells responsible for recognizing the bottom of the bottle must be sustained in STM while the motor act of flipping occurs. Nonspecific arousal serves as the source drive to provoke a variety of behaviors (e.g., turning and flipping the bottle), so when

Laurent hits on the act of flipping while he is either paying attention to the relevant visual cues or they are stored in STM, the situation allows the required learning to take place. Note how this neurological account of knowledge construction is analogous in many ways to the biological process of genetic assimilation (see Lawson, 1982b).

Again consider Figure 11.6. In this case, let U_{i1} represent the pattern of excitation in the sensory cortex provoked by sight of the bottom of the bottle. If this pattern remains active in STM during the act of flipping (see Grossberg, 1982, pp. 247–250 for mechanisms), the synaptic strengths of the sensory pattern playing at the nonspecific orienting arousal center (firing because of nonspecific arousal) are strengthened. The sensory pattern from U_{i1} plus the nonspecific arousal provides pre- and postsynaptic activity that drives increases in the Z_{ij}s. This in turn fires the OA $\rightarrow U_{i2}$ pathway. In this way, U_{i2}, the cells responsible for the flipping of the bottle, receive inputs from U_{i1} (the bottom of the bottle) and from the orienting arousal source, which also causes increases in synaptic strengths. In other words, the network allows the child to link, or condition, the sight of the bottom of the bottle with the behavioral response of flipping. Flipping the bottle when the bottom is seen was the behavior that had to be constructed. Performance of the behavior resulted in the sight of the nipple, which, of course, has previously been conditioned to the act of lifting and sucking. Flipping thereby becomes linked to lifting and sucking. With each repetition of the above sequence, the appropriate synaptic strengths increase until the act takes place with considerable ease.

Laurent thus has actively solved his problem, and the network has become more complex by the strengthening of synaptic connections. As with Pavlov's dog, an increase in complexity of the neural networks (mental structures) has resulted, and this increase has not been due to the unfolding of innate ideas (in Fodor's sense)—unless we consider the presence of prewired synaptic connections as innate ideas.

▼ EXTENSION OF NETWORK CHARACTERISTICS TO HIGHER LEVELS OF LEARNING

Data on the deployment of advanced reasoning indicate that the percentage of students who successfully use advanced strategies increases gradually with age (Lawson, Karplus, & Adi, 1978). These advances cannot be attributed to direct teaching, because the increases either come much later than the direct teaching that could have led to success (e.g., proportional thinking) or come without the benefit of any direct teaching (e.g., correlational thinking) (Lawson and Bealer, 1984). For the sake of simplicity, we restrict our discussion to problems of proportional thinking because they seem to evoke the most consistent and smallest class of student responses. We further restrict the discussion to just one problem of proportional thinking: the Pouring Water Task (Suarez and Rhonheimer, 1974).

As adapted by Lawson, Karplus, and Adi (1978), the Pouring Water Task requires the student to predict how high water will rise when poured from one cylinder into another. Students are shown that water at mark 4 in a wide cylinder rises to mark 6 when poured into a narrow cylinder. They must then predict how high water at mark 6 in the wide cylinder will rise when poured into the narrow cylinder. Student responses vary, but each typically falls into one of four categories:

1. additive strategy—for example, water rose from 4 to 6 ($4 + 2 = 6$), so it will rise from 6 to 8 ($6 + 2 = 8$);
2. qualitative guess—for example, the water will rise to approximately 10;
3. additive proportions strategy—for example, the water will rise to 9 because the ratio is 2 to 3 and $2 + 2 + 2 = 6$ in narrow, while $3 + 3 + 3 = 9$ in the wide; and
4. proportions strategy—for example, $2/3 = 4/6 = 6/x$, $x = 9$.

Again, for the sake of simplicity we consider only two of these strategies—additive and proportions—because they appear to reflect the most naive and the most sophisticated strategies, respectively.

The typical naive response to the task of the child using the additive strategy is 8, and the typical sophisticated response of the adolescent using the proportions strategy is 9. The central question thus becomes, "How does the shift from use of the additive strategy to use of the proportions strategy during adolescence come about?" It comes about in basically the same manner that Laurent used to learn to flip his bottle. The child who responds to the Pouring Water Task with the additive strategy is like Laurent when he responds to the bottom of the bottle by lifting and sucking. The neural modeling problem is one of modeling the shift from an additive to a proportions strategy, just as we modeled the shift from immediate lifting and sucking to a modified response of flipping and only then lifting and sucking. To the naive child problem solver, the Pouring Water Task presents problem cues, just as the bottle presented cues to Laurent. The difficulty is that these cues set off the wrong response—the additive response. In other words, by analogy with the neural network involved in Laurent's shift in behavior, we assume that the problem cues (CS_1) combine with some internal drive to solve the task and the UCR, the additive response controlled by some U_{i2} in the motor cortex.

For children younger than perhaps age 10 or 11, responding to quantitative problems by use of addition or subtraction (or both) is indeed a common strategy and one that often leads to success. They do, of course, know how to multiply and divide, and many can solve textbook proportions problems, but using the proportions strategy (which uses multiplication or division) seldom occurs to them, just as it did not occur to Laurent to flip the bottle before lifting and sucking (at least during the first thirty-nine days of Piaget's experiment). Laurent's motor behavior had been successful in the past, and he had no reason to believe it would not continue to be so. Indeed, many children who use the additive strategy are quite certain that they have solved the problem correctly.

How then do additive reasoners come to recognize the limitations of their thinking? And once they do, how do they learn to deploy the correct proportions strategy? The steps in that process are seen as follows:

1. indiscriminate use of the additive strategy to solve additive *and* multiplicative problems;

2. contradictory and unexpected (i.e., negative) feedback after using the additive strategy to solve multiplicative problems, which eventually leads to terminating its use in a knee-jerk fashion;

3. initiation of nonspecific orienting arousal, which provokes an external search for problem cues and an internal search through memory for successful strategies that can be linked to those cues;

4. selection of cues and the construction of a new strategy that appears successful;

5. repeated positive feedback from the successful use of the constructed strategy; and

6. the acquisition of an internal system of strategy monitoring to allow a check for consistency or contradiction, which results in the matching of problem cues with appropriate strategies in future situations.

We will consider each step in turn.

Initiating and Terminating Problem-Solving Behavior

Figure 11.8 shows a hypothesized minimal neural network (analogous to that previously derived to account for Laurent's behavior) that may account for some of the characteristics of the problem-solving behavior in question. The figure assumes that some problem-solving drive (P) exists and functions to stimulate arousal cells Ap^+. Although the physical basis of specific drives such as hunger and fear are well known, the very existence of a "problem-solving drive" is entirely speculative. Let CS_i represent problem cues from the Pouring Water Task that initially evoke use of the additive strategy. Specific problem cues of the task fire U_{i1} cells in the sensory cortex that in turn send that pattern of activity to arousal cells, which are also being stimulated by the hypothesized problem-solving drive, P, to arousal cells Ap^+. Because of previous conditioning, this activity feeds to U_{i2} (also activated by U_{i1}), which represents neural activity to initiate the motor response of addition in this case.

In this way, problem cues (CS_i) from the Pouring Water Task are initially conditioned to additive behavior. Perhaps the key cue is that the water previously rose "two more" marks when poured into the narrow cylinder (an absolute difference). Other cues, such as the relative difference of the water levels (narrow cylinder $= 1\frac{1}{2} \times$ the height of the wide cylinder), are ignored. Just as Laurent's feeding behavior was terminated by satisfaction of the hunger drive, the student's problem-solving behavior is terminated by reduction of the problem-solving drive, P, when a solution has been generated. When input from P stops, the tonic input, I, to both Ap^+ and Ap^- causes a rebound at Ap^- that quickly inhibits U_{i2} activity to stop problem-solving behavior.

Terminating the Additive Strategy Because of Contradiction

A student using the additive strategy to generate a response of 8 to the Pouring Water Task fully expects that this answer is correct, just as Laurent expected to get milk when he sucked the bottom of the bottle. As we saw in the case of Laurent, the unexpected feedback from an incorrect answer eventually ends the

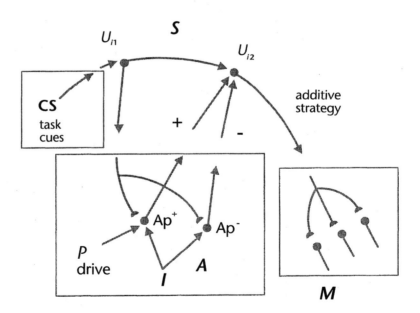

Figure 11.8 ▾ **Components of Hypothesized Neural Network.** This network combines sensory cues from the Pouring Water Task (CS) with an internal problem-solving drive (P) from the arousal system (A) to fire activity at U_{i2}, which initiates use of the additive strategy in the motor control system (M).

conditioned motor response in similar situations and the turning on of non-specific arousal, which will cause closer inspection of the problem cues and a search for a more effective strategy.

What form can this contradiction take? Certainly, missing problems on a math test could be one form. Yet that feedback normally occurs well after the act of problem solving has been terminated, so it would most likely lose effectiveness in focusing attention on the problem. A seemingly more effective source of feedback, at least on the Pouring Water Task, would be to have the student actually pour the water after predicting 8. The rise of water to mark 9 presents immediate contradictory feedback that could produce the desired effect. A crucial point, however, is that a single contradiction, no matter its source, probably is not sufficient to shut down the additive strategy. Recall that Laurent required many trials before he stopped bringing the bottom of the bottle to his mouth to suck. A possible reason for this is that the student's use of the additive strategy does not always lead to contradiction. In many problem situations, addition and subtraction are the correct operations. Even if they are not correct, the student may not discover they are wrong for many days, if ever.

Sensory input from additive problems (C_{i1}) to the Ap^+ channel linked to the additive strategy (U_{i2}) thus would continue to be strengthened in some situations. When using the additive strategy leads to contradictions, the sensory input from proportions problems (C_{i2}) leads to Ap^-, and so the $C_{i2} \rightarrow Ap^-$ channel would be conditioned. As students who use the additive strategy meet continued contradictions, the C_{i2} projections to Ap^- would become stronger than the C_{i1} projections to Ap^+ until they eventually dominate and the student no longer responds unthinkingly to quantitative problems of this sort.

Orienting Arousal and the Search for a New Strategy

Only when the unthinking use of the additive strategy has been extinguished and nonspecific arousal is sufficient can the sort of problem inspection and strategy search occur that will lead to successful conditioning of the C_{i2} input to the proportions strategy. How might this occur?

Again, consider the example of Laurent learning to flip his bottle prior to lifting and sucking. What seems to be required in the case of proportional thinking is to link C_{i2} input (multiplicative cues from the proportions problem) to the U_{i2} motor response of the proportion strategy. In other words, input C_{i2} at $F^{(1)}$ must match $F^{(2)}$ feedback. This would not appear difficult: It seems to simply require that it occur to the student to use multiplication or division instead of addition or subtraction in the presence of C_{i2} input and nonspecific arousal (see Figure 11.6). But this is not the entire story. A student so conditioned may respond to additive problems with a proportions strategy if he or she is not sufficiently aware of the problem cues that suggest which strategy to use!

Feedback and Internal Monitoring of Problem Solving

How then do we resolve the problem of reliably matching cues with reasoning strategies? This, of course, is a central question. The following answer may suffice. When confronted with a quantitative problem, certain key words or concrete referents are conditioned to strategies (as stated above). For example, the word *twice* suggests a multiplicative relationship. The word *more* suggests an additive relationship. However, because these cues are not always reliable, the problem solver must initiate a strategy to determine its consequences, or its probable consequences if it is carried out completely, and then compare those consequences with other known information about the problem situation. If this leads to an internal contradiction, then that strategy must be incorrect and another tried. In this case, internal contradiction would mean that an adaptive resonance has not been found between input and expectations. This would lead to an immediate termination of the $S \rightarrow Ap^+$ input, which drives a rebound at Ap^- to terminate that strategy and provoke excitation of nonspecific arousal and a search through LTM for another strategy.

For example, in the Pouring Water Task, using the additive strategy would lead one to predict that water at mark 2 in the narrow cylinder would rise to mark 0 when poured into the wide cylinder. The water disappears! This is impossible, so the additive strategy must be wrong because it leads to contradictory feedback. Or consider the following problem:

John is 6 years old, and his sister Linda is 8. When John is twice as old as he is now, how old will Linda be? The word *twice* may suggest that we multiply $6 \times 2 = 12$ to get John's age and thus multiply $8 \times 2 = 16$ to get Linda's age (many students do this after a lesson on proportions). Of course, this is wrong: We all know that Linda cannot age at a rate faster than John! Thus, if one internally monitors the tentative solution, an internal contradiction results that shuts down S input to U_{i1}, Ap^+, and U_{i2}, supporting the proportions strategy. This strategy is given up: It failed to obtain an adaptive resonance. A new one is searched for in LTM, found, and then tried until solution expectancies no longer generate internal contradictions. In this way internal reasoning and internal contradiction are used to match problem cues to problem strategies. This novel qualitative thinking process presumably takes place when students have learned a variety of problem cues and solution strategies and are left on their own to match cues with strategies.

To summarize, the advanced problem solver appears to have at his or her disposal the memory record of a variety of problem cues, a variety of problem strategies, and a general mode of operation that says, "Try the various strategies available until you get one that does not produce internal contradictions." Thus, the key difference between the additive thinking child and the proportional thinking adolescent is not the strategies they possess—both types of individuals are capable of using both types of strategies—but that the child unthinkingly initiates a strategy and then fails to internally check its consequences for consistency with other known data (e.g., water does not disappear when poured from one container to another), while the adolescent unthinkingly initiates a strategy and (this is new) checks its results for possible contradictions. If contradictions are found (if an adaptive resonance is not found), a new strategy is tried until no contradictions are discovered. This key difference may arise because the adolescent has gradually become aware of the fallacy of automatically "jumping to conclusions" while the younger child has not. A novel behavior with emergent properties thus has arisen neither by direct assimilation of environmental input nor by the maturation of innate structures. It has arisen by the construction of novel combinations of already present, but previously unlinked, problem-solving behaviors and problem cues founded on the neurological elements with the capacity to form new interrelationships after certain patterns of stimulation.

▼ INSTRUCTIONAL IMPLICATIONS

The proposed model of neural processing and self-regulation clarifies why the normal curriculum is insufficient to provoke many students to construct the skills needed to deal successfully with problems of the Pouring Water type. Students learn strategies, but they are seldom confronted with the diversity of problems needed to provoke the sort of close inspection of problem cues needed to link cues with strategies and tentative results with implied consequences. Obviously, students must be taught to add, subtract, multiply, and divide. There is little reason to suppose, however, that they need to know, for example, that "the product of the means equals the product of the extremes."

In short, what is acquired in school lessons is insufficient. This statement is reminiscent of Piaget's position regarding the role of teaching in intellectual development. He has long insisted that direct teaching is insufficient because direct teaching seldom if ever affords the possibility for self-regulation (Piaget, 1964). Unfortunately, as previously mentioned, Piaget's model of psychological self-regulation is based on evolutionary rather than neurological concepts. The current theory, although most certainly too simplistic to account for the details of advanced problem solving, nevertheless suggests neurological mechanisms that may be involved in some aspects of the self-regulation and knowledge-construction process.

Consider the child's initial use of the additive strategy in a knee-jerk fashion as an instance of the immediate assimilation and processing of input by previously constructed mental structures (strategies). This is the Piagetian state of equilibrium. The individual is satisfied by his or her response and not intellectually aroused. But suppose repeated attempts at using that strategy lead to contradiction. At the neurological level, this could speculatively be interpreted as the $S \to Ap^+$ channel being weakened and the $S \to Ap^-$ channel being strengthened until it dominates and nonspecific orienting arousal is turned on and searching behavior is initiated to construct an appropriate response to solve the problem. This is the state of disequilibrium. Finally, through internal trial-and-error search behavior (see Grossberg, 1982, pp. 14–15), a closer inspection of the phenomena, or both, a successful behavior pattern is constructed—that is, new neural connections are formed by increases in the synaptic strengths of the pathways from the input stimulus to the output response. This constitutes accommodation of mental structures, construction of more complex behavior, and resolution of the problem. In Piagetian terms, it restores equilibrium, although at a more sophisticated, emergent level.

Having seen one sequence of events in the successful deployment of proportional thinking, we can now determine why some students never construct that ability.

First, if prerequisite strategies and knowledge are not in place they cannot be used. By analogy, Laurent already knew how to flip his bottle: That was not the problem. Instead, it was to connect the flipping with the appearance of the bottom of the bottle. Likewise, the problem for most adolescents is not that they do not know how to multiply and divide or have not "learned" that the "product of the means equals the product of the extremes." Rather, the problem is that they have failed to link the appropriate operations with the appropriate problem cues.

Second, students must be confronted with many diverse problem-solving opportunities that provide the necessary contradictions to their use of the additive strategy. Without feedback and contradiction, the necessary arousal will not occur. Thus, even if students are told to use "proportions" to solve the problems, they are unlikely to do so in transfer situations because use of the old incorrect strategy has not been extinguished.

The previous discussion, although related most directly to the gradual development of proportional thinking, does not necessarily preclude its direct teaching. For example, with respect to the Pouring Water Task, direct contradiction of the additive strategy can be obtained simply by pouring the water from the wide to the narrow cylinder and noting the rise to mark 9 instead of mark 8. Other problems with similar contradictory feedback can be utilized. We would expect this type of instruction to be highly effective, yet teachers and curriculum developers must continue to remind themselves of the remaining limiting factor—namely, the student. No matter how potentially interesting the material may seem to the teacher, it is the student who must be aroused by the contradictory feedback to relinquish an incorrect strategy and begin the search for a new one! Sufficient arousal may be difficult to achieve in the impersonal classroom setting, particularly if the problems bear little resemblance to problems of personal importance. Further, short-term direct teaching is probably insufficient to promote the construction of the internal monitoring system needed to match problem cues to solution strategies in novel situations. Long-term efforts are needed to accomplish this.

SELF-REGULATION, CONSTRUCTIVISM, AND THE LEARNING PARADOX

The process of self-regulation described by Piaget and as previously detailed at the level of neural mechanisms clearly implies that knowledge acquisition is a process in which the learner actively constructs his or her knowledge. As described previously, this view has become known as *constructivism* (see Piaget, 1977a, 1977b; Resnick, 1980; Wittrock, 1974). Constructivism stands in marked opposition to the empiricist doctrine that complex knowledge is directly assimilated from the environment. It also contradicts the nativist doctrine that innate structures exist that spontaneously unfold with maturation (Chomsky and Fodor in Piattelli-Palmerini, 1980). According to Bereiter (1985), however, a fundamental theoretical problem exists with constructivism. As Bereiter sees it, constructivist theory offers no satisfactory account of how the learner guided only by simple cognitive structures can generate more complex structures that allow new behaviors with distinctive properties. Bereiter asks, "How can a structure generate another structure more complex than itself?" (p. 204). To him, it would not seem possible for a simple self-generating system to become more complex without some external ladder or rope to climb, which presumably does not exist. Consequently, we are left with what has been called the "learning paradox" (Pascual-Leone, 1976, 1980).

How can the learning paradox be resolved? How can simple procedures guided by simple cognitive structures generate more complex procedures with novel properties that are not present in the initial procedures without reverting to empiricism or nativism? Recently, Lawson and Staver (1989) proposed a solution to the learning paradox based in part on the concept of emergent properties and in part on the neural modeling principles just discussed. What follows is a recapitulation of the Lawson and Staver proposal.

Emergent Properties in the Natural Sciences

Emergent properties are defined as qualitatively unique properties of an object or a system of interacting objects that are derived from a unique combination or configuration of the system's component parts and are not easily predictable from knowledge of the parts. Consider, for example, graphite and diamond, two substances composed only of carbon atoms. In graphite, the carbon atoms are arranged in layers that slide easily past one another, giving graphite a soft, greasy feel and an opaque, black appearance. Diamond can be produced from graphite under extremely high temperature and pressure, which alter the arrangement of the carbon atoms. In diamond, each carbon atom is bonded to four others in a three-dimensional structure. This three-dimensional array contains no layers and makes diamond an exceptionally hard and brittle crystalline material. Thus its properties are emergent from those of graphite. By analogy with the learning paradox, its emergent properties do *not* rise from novel parts, but from a novel arrangement of the *same* parts.

Several examples of emergent properties exist in the biological sciences. Consider evolution. The properties of all living things—from the simplest single-celled bacterium to the most complex multicellular organism—depend on deoxyribonucleic acid (DNA) molecules, which provide the blueprints for the construction of all living things. Bacterial DNA and human DNA differ not in kind, but in the amount and arrangement of their constituent parts (nucleotides). Evolution has progressed from the single-celled, bacteria-like organisms of the primordial soup to modern complex multicellular organisms. Those organisms possess qualitatively unique emergent properties (e.g., bilateral symmetry, limbs, brains, leaves) and behavior (e.g., conducting photosynthesis, capturing prey, speaking, reasoning) that have developed from the unique combination of the component parts of DNA molecules, *not* from novel components!

Developmental biology offers many examples of emergent properties. Although *preformism* (the idea that if we see something develop from the egg, then it must have been there all the time but in an invisible form) was a popular theory in the seventeenth and eighteenth centuries, it has long since been abandoned. Initially, the human infant is but a single fertilized egg cell. During the course of embryological development, the zygote divides to form billions of cells in novel combinations with novel shapes, sizes, and functions, which together bestow on the fetus new structures such as a heart, lungs, a brain, eyes, and legs. These structures allow the organism to carry out novel behaviors, not the least of which is to begin to sustain life independent of its mother.

Emergent Properties in Cognition

Suppose that the construction of more complex behaviors with novel properties takes place in an analogous way to these physical and biological examples of emergent properties. Perhaps the learner initially possesses simple innate structures (Chomsky and Fodor in Piattelli-Palmerini, 1980) or perhaps the learner possesses innate functions (Piaget in Piattelli-Palmerini, 1980). Selection of either position leads to the same end because innate functions must be guided by innate structures. The essential task of the learner, then, is to construct qualitatively different emergent behaviors out of unique combinations of those initially given parts. Viewed in this way, qualitatively novel "developments" arise from combinations of preexisting simple structures.

The current view thus endows the learner with innate capabilities that allow initial learning to take place, but the view also claims that nativism alone does not result in distinctive behaviors. Rather, the learner actively constructs novel combinations, thereby giving rise to a new level of behavior. The key idea is that properties of thought emerge that are qualitatively different from those that came before. But how might this occur? To answer this question, we must consider the individual parts and how they combine. In the case of cognition, as has been seen, the individual parts are neurons. To resolve the learning paradox, two conditions must be met. First, we must determine whether the individual parts—in this case, individual neurons—can and do organize themselves into more complex combinations given only normal environmental stimulation and their inherent fundamental and structural properties. Second, we must find out whether cognitive development consists of the emergence of new behaviors with properties not previously exhibited—that is, with emergent properties. Having shown these two factors to be true, the learning paradox, theoretically, is resolved at a general level. For a more convincing argument, however, we must find out how specific novel combinations of neurons combine to produce specific behaviors with specific emergent properties. Of course, our current knowledge of neural anatomy and cognition do not allow such specificity. At present, we shall be satisfied if the first and second points can be explicated, leaving the specific details for future research.

In fact, the solution of the learning paradox rests primarily on the first factor, because no one would seriously argue that cognitive development does not involve the acquisition of behaviors with emergent properties. For example, the newborn is unable to move about, eat, or drink successfully without considerable parental assistance. Yet during the infant's first one to two years of life, effective sensory motor behaviors to do these tasks are acquired. Next acquired is the ability to use sounds to describe and communicate effectively with others about what is seen, heard, smelled, and felt. Still later comes the ability to use language to invent and test ideas about unseen causes of perceived events. All of these behaviors were not present in previous stages of development, so they constitute behaviors with emergent properties. In essence, the Lawson and Staver argument is that all of these behaviors depend on neural activity and all new neural activity involves not new sorts of neurons, but novel combinations of the same sorts of neurons—just like changing graphite to diamond involves transforming one arrangement of carbon atoms into another.

The question then is, "Given normal environmental stimulation, do individual neurons, like individual atoms of carbon or individual cells of an embryo, spontaneously form functional relationships with one another that allow the organism to perform behaviors with emergent properties?" Lawson and Staver believe the answer is yes. To explain how they arrived at this answer, we must return to the basic principles of neural modeling theory.

A Return to Classical Conditioning

Recall that learning in Grossberg's theory occurs when synaptic strengths (Z_{ij}s) increase—that is, when transmitter release rate increases and makes transmission of signals from one neuron to the next easier. Hence learning is, in effect, an increase in the number of connections among neurons (i.e., an increase in complexity). Presumably, the structural connections already exist, but they are not functional until the transmitter release rates at certain terminal knobs increase above a specified threshold. Thus, to have a "mental structure" become more complex, transmitter release rates must increase at many knobs so that the signals can be easily transmitted across synapses that were previously there but inoperative. As stated before, this view reveals in what sense nativists are correct. If we equate mental structures with already present but inoperative synapses, then the mental structures are present before any specific experience. The view also reveals how constructivists are correct. For the synapses to become functional, experience is necessary to "strengthen" some of the connections. We return now to Pavlov's classical conditioning experiment to see just how experience can do this.

When Pavlov first rang the bell, the dog as expected did not salivate. However, after repeated simultaneous presentation of food and bell ringing, the ringing alone was eventually able to cause the dog to salivate. Pavlov's experiment showed that a repeatedly presented conditioned stimulus (a bell) presented simultaneously with an unconditioned stimulus (food) will eventually evoke an unconditioned response (salivation) by itself.

Grossberg used his principles to construct a simple neural network capable of explaining classical conditioning. Initial presentation of food caused cell C to fire, which created a signal down its axon, which, because of prior learning, caused the signal to be transmitted to cell B. Cell B fired, and the dog salivated. At the outset, ringing of the bell caused cell A to fire and send signals toward cell B. However, when the signal reached knob N_{AB}, its synaptic strength Z_{AB} was not initially large enough to cause B to fire. The dog did not salivate. However, when the bell and the food were paired, cell A learned to fire cell B, according to Grossberg's learning equation. The firing of cell A resulted in a large S'_{AB}, while the appearance of food resulted in a large $[X_B]^+$. Thus, the product $S'_{AB}[X_B]^+$ was sufficiently large to drive an increase in Z_{AB} to the point at which it alone caused node N_B to fire and evoke salivation. Food was no longer needed. The dog had learned to salivate at the ringing of a bell. The key point in terms of neural modeling theory was that learning is driven by simultaneous activity of pre- and postsynaptic neurons—in this case, activity of cells A and B. From the point of view of constructivism, the key point is that learning results from novel combinations of the basic elements of the brain, not from the production of new elements.

No homunculus controls this increase in complexity (i.e., new functional connections between cell A and cell B); rather, the increase results from the simultaneous ringing of the bell and the appearance of the food. The bell evokes presynaptic activity at cell A, and the food evokes postsynaptic activity at cell B, thus transmitter release rate at synapse A–B increases. A new functional connection has been made. The system has become functionally more complex because of its own "nature" *and* its experience.

This shows in principle how neural networks "spontaneously" become functionally more complex. Resolution of the learning paradox requires only that these sorts of spontaneous increases in neural network complexity allow for novel behaviors with emergent properties. As previously mentioned, future research still must explicate the specific details of just which specific new functional connections lead to which specific behaviors and specific emergent properties.

Questions for Reflection

1. Why do the neurological principles presented in this chapter imply that the development of hypothetical-deductive thinking patterns is a long-term process that involves considerable trial and error and disequilibrium? (*Hint:* Why did it take so long for Laurent to learn to flip his bottle before sucking?)
2. "Teaching is not telling." In what sense is the saying accurate? Can "telling" ever be helpful in the learning process? If so, under what conditions?
3. What do you think is the most important behavior that emerges as a consequence of the development of hypothetical-deductive thinking patterns? Explain.

CHAPTER 12

THE ROLE OF LOGICAL AND ANALOGICAL THINKING IN KNOWLEDGE CONSTRUCTION

The primary purpose of this chapter is to continue the theoretical discussion of self-regulation and the knowledge construction process initiated in Chapter 11.

Two general modes of reasoning, often referred to as *logical thinking* and *analogical thinking,* have been of considerable interest to psychologists and educators for many years. The key question we will address is this: What role do logical and analogical thinking play in knowledge construction? Of course, previous chapters have partially addressed this question. This chapter will readdress the question and take a closer look, including a neurological explanation of why analogies can play a significant role in learning.

▼ THE ROLE OF LOGIC

Clearly, even if possible, a faithful recording of external events is not sufficient to account for all of human cognition. If we note, for example, that John is older than Mike and that Mike is older than Beth, then it only seems "logical" that John *must* be older than Beth. We can quickly draw this obvious conclusion even though John's and Beth's absolute ages are not given. Rather we were able to *deduce* the correct conclusion by using our powers of reason. Without these powers—that is, our inferential ability—knowledge construction would be severely restricted. For many people, including Piaget, logic and reasoning amount to one and the same thing. Indeed, early logicians studied logic because it was supposed to be the discipline involved in discovering effective patterns of thinking. Inhelder and Piaget (1958) advanced one of the strongest statements with regard to the role of logic in advanced thinking when they stated, "Reasoning is nothing more than the propositional calculus itself" (p. 301). Other statements by Piaget reflect his belief that logical operations, once acquired, allow an individual to reason with the logical form of propositions regardless of context. For example, "concrete operations fail to constitute a formal logic; they are incompletely formalized since form has not *yet* been divorced from subject matter" (Piaget, 1957, p. 17).

Similarly, Inhelder and Piaget (1958) argued that the formal stage is reached when a coordination is achieved "between a set of operations of diverse kinds and that the form be liberated from particular contents" (pp. 331–332). Unfortunately for this view, a long line of research beginning with the work of Wason and others clearly reveals that form is not completely liberated from content in "logical" reasoning (see Cheng and Holyoak, 1985; Evans, 1982; Griggs and Cox, 1982; Johnson-Laird, 1983; Markovits, 1984, 1985; Overton, Ward, Black, Noveck, and O'Brien, 1987; Wason, 1966; Wason and Johnson-Laird, 1972). Even Piaget (1972) came to admit that content might play a significant role in formal reasoning. However, he failed to offer any suggestions as to how his theory would have to be modified to account for such a result. More recently, Cheng and Holyoak (1985) argued that people possess general schemes of permission, causation, obligation, and so on that relate to particular classes of events from experience. Johnson-Laird (1983) sees reasoning as even more tied to specific events and argues that reasoning involves constructing representations of particular events described by sets of specific premises. He used the phrase "mental models" to refer to these representations.

In basic agreement with more recent authors, the essential feature of advanced reasoning appears to be not logic but the tendency of the thinker to initiate reasoning with one or more specific antecedent conditions (Markovits, 1984, 1985), or if the individual is unable to imagine more than one antecedent condition, then at least he or she is aware that more than one is possible, so conclusions drawn are tempered by this possibility. Presumably, knowledge of specific antecedent conditions (multiple hypotheses) arises from previously constructed mental models of specific situations, as proposed by Johnson-Laird (1983), while the general tendency to search for multiple hypotheses arises by generalization from a variety of particular situations in which this has turned out to be the case. This proposed view of advanced reasoning will be referred to as the *multiple-hypothesis theory.*

Two Common Forms of Logic

Although the multiple-hypothesis theory of advanced reasoning is not based on the use of abstract forms of logic, we must begin with a discussion of two basic logical forms to explain just what the theory is and how it can be tested. But before discussing those forms of logic, we begin with a brief exploration activity, one that requires you to complete seven "tasks." Each task consists of four statements. Consider each statement to be true. If a conclusion can reasonably be drawn from the statements, then write the conclusion in the blank. If no conclusion can reasonably be drawn, then write "No conclusion" in the blank.

Task 1. The Square

1. If a drawing is a square, then it has four sides. This drawing is a square, therefore _____.
2. If a drawing is a square, then it has four sides. This drawing is not a square, therefore _____.
3. If a drawing is a square, then it has four sides. This drawing has four sides, therefore _____.
4. If a drawing is a square, then it has four sides. This drawing does not have four sides, therefore _____.

Task 2. High School Graduate

1. If a person has successfully completed high school degree requirements, then he or she is a high school graduate. John has successfully completed high school degree requirements, therefore _____.

2. If a person has successfully completed high school degree requirements, then he or she is a high school graduate. Linda has not successfully completed high school degree requirements, therefore _____.

3. If a person has successfully completed high school degree requirements, then he or she is a high school graduate. Kathy is a high school graduate, therefore _____.

4. If a person has successfully completed high school degree requirements, then he or she is a high school graduate. Joe is not a high school graduate, therefore _____.

Task 3. The Gas Tank

1. If the car is running, then gas is in the tank. The car is running, therefore _____.

2. If the car is running, then gas is in the tank. The car is not running, therefore _____.

3. If the car is running, then gas is in the tank. Gas in the tank, therefore _____.

4. If the car is running, then gas is in the tank. No gas is in the tank, therefore _____.

Task 4. Driver's License

1. If a person has a valid driver's license, then he or she may legally drive a car. Sam has a valid driver's license, therefore _____.

2. If a person has a valid driver's license, then he or she may legally drive a car. Bob does not have a valid driver's license, therefore _____.

3. If a person has a valid driver's license, then he or she may legally drive a car. Gloria may legally drive a car, therefore _____.

4. If a person has a valid driver's license, then he or she may legally drive a car. Beth may not legally drive a car, therefore _____.

Task 5. The Rose Bowl

1. If the Arizona State University (ASU) football team plays in the Rose Bowl game, then John will be in Pasadena on New Year's Day. The ASU team is playing in the Rose Bowl game, therefore _____.

2. If the ASU football team plays in the Rose Bowl game, then John will be in Pasadena on New Year's Day. The ASU football team is not playing in the Rose Bowl game, therefore _____.

3. If the ASU football team plays in the Rose Bowl game, then John will be in Pasadena on New Year's Day. John was in Pasadena on New Year's Day, therefore _____.

4. If the ASU football team plays in the Rose Bowl game, then John will be in Pasadena on New Year's Day. John was not in Pasadena on New Year's day, therefore _____.

Task 6. Monkey's Uncle

1. If Hitler was a great man, then I am a monkey's uncle. Hitler was a great man, therefore _____.

2. If Hitler was a great man, then I am a monkey's uncle. Hitler was not a great man, therefore _____.

3. If Hitler was a great man, then I am a monkey's uncle. I am a monkey's uncle, therefore _____.

4. If Hitler was a great man, then I am a monkey's uncle. I am not a monkey's uncle, therefore _____.

Task 7. The Four Cards

1. If an E is on the front of a card, then a 4 is on the back. An E is on the front of this card, therefore _____.

2. If an E is on the front of a card, then a 4 is on the back. An E is not on the front of this card, therefore _____.

3. If an E is on the front of a card, then a 4 is on the back. A 4 is on the back of this card, therefore _____.

4. If an E is on the front of a card, then a 4 is on the back. A 4 is not on the back of this card, therefore _____.

You may find comparing your answers with those of one or two other people interesting. Determining the "correct" answers is by no means simple, but we should start by considering the two abstract forms of logic referred to as the *conditional* (that is, *if . . . then*) and the *biconditional* (or *if and only if*). Specific forms of conditional logic are as follows:

1. $p \supset q, p \therefore q$ (this form is termed *modus ponens*)
2. $p \supset q, \bar{q} \therefore \bar{p}$ (this form is known as *modus tollens*)

For example, suppose p refers to the statement "A drawing is a square"; $\bar{p}$ refers to its negative, that is, "A drawing is *not* a square"; q refers to the statement "It has four sides"; $\bar{q}$ refers to its negative, that is, "It does *not* have four sides"; the symbol $\supset$ means "implies"; and the symbol $\therefore$ means "therefore." Consequently, an example of use of the logical rule of modus ponens ($p \supset q, p \therefore q$) would be, "If a drawing is a square, then it has four sides." This means that the "logically" correct answer to Task 1, Statement 1, following the rule of modus ponens is "it has four sides." Application of the rule of modus tollens ($p \supset q, \bar{q} \therefore \bar{p}$) to Statement 4 of Task 1 would be, "If a drawing is a square, then it has four sides." This drawing does not have four sides, therefore "it is not a square."

Two presumed misapplications of conditional logic are:

3. $p \supset q, \bar{p} \therefore \bar{q}$ (the conclusion of $\bar{q}$ is referred to as the fallacy of *denying the antecedent*)

4. $p \supset q, q \therefore p$ (the conclusion of p is referred to as the logical fallacy of *affirming the consequent*)

Again with reference to Task 1, consider Statement 2. If we were to conclude in that statement, "This drawing is not a square, therefore it does not have four sides," we would be committing the fallacy of *denying the antecedent*. Drawings that are not squares may still have four sides (e.g., rectangles, trapezoids). And lastly, if we were to conclude for Statement 3, "This drawing has four sides, therefore it is a square," we would be committing the fallacy of *affirming the consequent*.

The corresponding forms of biconditional logic are as follows:

1. $p \equiv q, p \therefore q$
2. $p \equiv q, \bar{p} \therefore \bar{q}$
3. $p \equiv q, q \therefore p$
4. $p \equiv q, \bar{q} \therefore \bar{p}$

In his logic textbook, Copi (1972) identified six types of conditional statements, each of which corresponds to a different sense of the *If . . . then* construction, so that each asserts a different type of implication. The following statements from Tasks 1 through 6 represent the six types; all follow precisely the same *If . . . then* form.

1. If a drawing is a square, *then* it has four sides.
2. If a person has successfully completed high school degree requirements, *then* he or she is a high school graduate.
3. If the car is running, *then* gas is in the tank.
4. If a person has a valid driver's license, *then* he or she may legally drive a car.
5. If the ASU football team plays in the Rose Bowl game, *then* John will be in Pasadena on New Year's Day.
6. If Hitler was a great man, *then* I am a monkey's uncle.

Clearly, the six conditional statements are of the same "logical" form, yet they vary in context. In Statement 1, the consequent follows logically from the antecedent by virtue of the fact that squares are a subclass of a class of drawings that have four sides, and thus must have properties of that class. Another subclass called rectangles also exists that has four but unequal sides. In Statement 2, on the other hand, the consequent follows from its antecedent by the very definition of the term *graduate,* which means one who has completed the degree requirements. The consequent of Statement 3 does not follow from its antecedent either by logic alone or by definition. Here the connection is an empirical one of a necessary but not sufficient cause. The car cannot run without gas in the tank, but gas alone is not sufficient to get the car running. Statement 4 also involves necessary conditions; however, here the condition of having a valid driver's license is not only necessary but also sufficient to allow one to drive a car (assuming the person is not drunk or otherwise impaired). Statement 5 does not involve causal relationships of the type implied in Statements 3 or 4; it simply reports a decision on the part of John to behave a certain way under certain circumstances. Finally, Statement 6 differs from the previous five statements in that no "real" connection between the antecedent and consequent is suggested. Rather, this sort of conditional is often used as an emphatic or humorous method of denying the antecedent by way of modus tollens. Clearly, the speaker is not a monkey's uncle, therefore Hitler must not have been a great man. These six conditional statements will be referred to respectively as (1) class membership, (2) definitional, (3) necessary but not sufficient cause, (4) necessary and sufficient cause, (5) decisional, and (6) material. Although these conditional statements appear similar to Cheng and Holyoak's pragmatic reasoning schemes, no claim is made that they actually constitute six different reasoning schemes.

A seventh type of *If . . . then* statement has appeared in the psychological literature that does not fit any of these categories. It was first investigated by Wason (1966). Wason's *If . . . then* statement, which is part of his Four Card Puzzle, reads as follows: "*If* a card has a vowel on one side, *then* it has an even number on the other side." Because there exists no nonarbitrary reason for this connection between vowels and even numbers to be asserted, this seventh form will be referred to as *arbitrary.* This is an important point and could well explain why the Four Card Puzzle elicits such a wide range of responses from adults. In other words, because the puzzle does not contain any nonarbitrary information about the nature of the connection between the antecedent and the consequent, the subject may be unable to decide what sort of connection (e.g., causal, decisional, definitional) it is supposed to hold.

The seven previous logic tasks involved these seven types of conditional statements. The four sentences of each task corresponded to the four possible conditions (i.e., p, $\bar{p}$, q, $\bar{q}$). If we use the standard rules of conditional logic (modus ponens and modus tollens) to guide reasoning on each of the seven tasks, we reach identical conclusions for all tasks. For Question 1 of Task 1 (the square), for example, we would reason with the form $p \supset q, p \therefore q$, and conclude that "the drawing has four sides." For Question 2, the reasoning would follow the form $p \supset q, \bar{p} \therefore q$ or $\bar{q}$, and we would conclude that "no conclusion can be reached." Question 3 should lead to the same conclusion as 2 when we follow reasoning of the form $p \supset q, q \therefore p$ or $\bar{p}$, and we would conclude that "no conclusion can be reached." Finally, Question 4 reasoning would be of the form $p \supset q, \bar{q} \therefore \bar{p}$, and we would conclude that "the drawing is not a square."

Thus, Piaget's initial position, which claimed that adult reasoning follows logical form regardless of context, would lead to the prediction that persons identified as formal operational by performance on Piagetian tests of formal reasoning would draw the same inferences on all seven tasks because the form of each task is identical. However, previous research and a further analysis of the seven tasks allows us to anticipate the results of such a test. Consider, for instance, application of the conditional rules of inference to the definitional Task 2 (high school graduate) and the necessary and sufficient Task 4 (driver's license). Although these two tasks follow the same logical form as the others, the context would seem to dictate that the reader draw a different set of conclusions. Use of modus ponens in Question 1 on Task 2, for example, would lead appropriately to the conclusion that "John is a high school graduate." Also use of modus tollens in Question 4 would lead appropriately to the conclusion that "Joe has not successfully completed high school degree requirements." These conclusions are of the same form as the other tasks. But Questions 2 and 3 probably also could be answered "correctly" with a biconditional interpretation of the relationships between p and q (i.e., $p \equiv q$) by virtue of the fact that the relationship is a definitional one—that is, someone who has successfully completed high school degree requirements *is* a high school graduate and vice versa. Therefore, Question 2 states that Linda has not successfully completed high school degree requirements, therefore "she is not a high school graduate." Is this conclusion unreasonable? Probably not. Of course, we can think of situations that could render this conclusion false (e.g., Linda did not complete the requirements, but she performed a few "favors" for the principal, who awarded her the degree), but these situations are beyond the meaning normally associated with the phrase "high school graduate." In other words, the "correct" conclusions in the definitional situation and in the necessary and sufficient conditions of Task 4 (driver's license) could well be of the biconditional form. In this way, context clearly appears to affect reasoning; the view that a formal operational person reasons with the form of arguments regardless of their context appears wrong, at least when dealing with these types of implications.

But what about the contexts actually cause one's inferences to shift from a conditional to a biconditional form? As mentioned previously, the multiple-hypothesis theory would argue that the answer lies in an individual's ability to conceive of alternative antecedent conditions (or alternative hypotheses). Given $p \supset q$, can the thinker imagine other antecedent conditions that could reasonably lead to q? If the thinker *can* imagine other antecedent conditions, then his or her inferences look like those of someone using conditional logic. If not, then the inferences look like those of someone using biconditional logic. Again consider the high school graduate task. Can antecedent conditions other than "completing high school requirements" lead an individual to become a high school graduate? Possibly, as just discussed, but it requires considerable effort. Therefore, for most people p implies q and q implies p. Contrast this to the causal gas tank task. Given $p \supset q$ (if the car is running, then gas is in the tank), are there other occasions (conditions) when gas might be in the tank? Suppose, for example, that gas is in the tank, but the ignition has not been turned on. This would prevent that car from running. Thus, when confronted with the incomplete argument, "If the car is running, then there is gas in the tank. The car is not running, therefore . . . ," one can easily avoid the incorrect conclusion that no gas is in the tank by simply imagining that the ignition has not been turned on.

More specifically, the context of the task should affect the pattern of inferences drawn (i.e., conditional or biconditional) to answer a question because some contexts make it easier (or more difficult) for the thinker to imagine alternative antecedents. When alternative antecedents are easy to imagine, the inference pattern will most likely be that of the conditional. When antecedents are difficult to imagine, the inference pattern will most likely be that of the biconditional. This implies that when alternative antecedent conditions do not exist, affirming the consequent and denying the antecedent are not logical fallacies (Johnson-Laird, 1983, pp. 52–53).

More specifically for the seven tasks, we could ask the following questions about alternative antecedent conditions (the questions are listed, by and large, in order of ease of generation of alternatives as judged by me and a group of graduate students):

1. Can I imagine a reason, other than no gas in the tank, that could keep the car from running? Answer: Yes. The ignition is not turned on.
2. Can I imagine drawings, other than squares, that have four sides? Yes. Rectangles are not squares, but they have four sides.
3. Can I imagine a reason, other than ASU playing in the Rose Bowl Game, that could get John to Pasadena on New Year's day? Answer: Yes. He may be there to visit friends.
4. Can I imagine letters, other than E's, that could have 4's on their backs? Answer: Yes. There may be an A on the front.
5. Can I imagine a situation, other than Hitler being a great man, that could cause me to be a monkey's uncle? Answer: This question is

difficult to answer because it is not really a "serious" question. Hitler being a great man could not really cause someone to be a monkey's uncle in the first place. But if one is willing to accept this, then they may be willing to accept alternatives as well.

6. Can I imagine conditions, other than having a valid driver's license, that would enable me to legally drive a car? Answer: Possibly there are, but they are not apparent, so we will answer no.

7. Are there conditions, other than completing high school degree requirements, that would enable someone to become a high school graduate? Answer: Possibly there are, but they are not obvious, so we will answer no.

Presumably, as an individual progresses from Questions 1 to 7, alternative antecedent conditions become increasingly hard to imagine. Alternatives seem to come easily to mind in the gas tank situation, but only with considerable difficulty in the monkey's uncle context and perhaps not at all in the driver's license and high school graduation contexts. Therefore, a subject should respond to the earlier tasks with an inference pattern like that of a person using conditional logic; and he or she should respond to the later tasks with an inference pattern like that of a person using biconditional logic. This result thus would support this view:

The context of the task influences the inference patterns that an individual uses in its solution, and the context effect results from the extent to which he or she is able to use his or her knowledge of the context to generate alternative hypotheses and antecedent conditions that could lead to the imagined consequent.

This position differs from the popular "familiarity" hypothesis, which suggests that the subject's familiarity with the context is crucial in determining his or her reasoning patterns (Griggs and Cox, 1982). All normal adults are assumed to be familiar with the contexts used in all seven of the tasks but will nevertheless draw different inferences, depending on whether the context facilitates or restricts the generation of alternative hypotheses. The multiple-hypothesis theory also goes beyond the Johnson–Laird mental model hypothesis in that, although it argues that reasoning is based on use of specific mental representations (not the use of abstract forms of logic), a key factor that determines the ultimate form of the inferences (i.e., conditional or biconditional) is a person's knowledge of alternative antecedent conditions. The multiple-hypothesis theory goes beyond the Cheng and Holyoak (1985) pragmatic reasoning scheme hypothesis for the same reason.

The Multiple-Hypothesis Theory of Hypothetical-Deductive Thought: Key Elements

Table 12.1 and Figure 12.1 summarize key elements of the multiple-hypothesis theory. The table shows two types of mental representations. In the first type, only one antecedent condition, p (the left-most solid circle) is linked through past experience (the solid line) with one consequent q (the solid circle on the right). The inferences that result from using such a mental representation follow the form of the biconditional. The argument is not that the reasoner is using biconditional reasoning, but that the thinker is reasoning about the specific mental representation; this is in agreement with Johnson-Laird (1983). The form of the reasoning is that of the biconditional *because of* the nature of the representation. For example, if p represents the antecedent condition of "completing high school degree requirements" and q represents the status of being "a high school graduate" and if no other antecedent conditions can be imagined, then it follows that if an individual completes high school degree requirements, then he or she is a high school graduate ($p \therefore q$); and if an individual is a high school graduate, then he or she must have completed the degree requirements ($q \therefore p$). Likewise, if an individual has not completed the requirements, then he or she is not a graduate ($\bar{p} \therefore \bar{q}$) and vice versa ($\bar{q} \therefore \bar{p}$).

In the second type of representation, two antecedent conditions (o and p) are linked to one consequent q. Because of the nature of this more complex representation, the pattern of inferences drawn is that of the conditional. For example, suppose o represents the alternative antecedent condition that "one has not completed high school degree requirements, but instead has done special favors for the school principal." Suppose that p represents the condition of "completing high school degree requirements." In this case, both conditions are linked to the consequent q of "being a high school graduate." Now there are two ways to become a high school graduate, thus it follows that $o \therefore q$ or $p \therefore q$. However, if we are told that Sue is a high school graduate (q), we do not know how she became one; therefore, given q, no conclusion regarding o or p can be drawn. Likewise, given $\bar{o}$, q or $\bar{q}$ may follow because we are not informed about p (i.e., $\bar{o} \therefore$ no conclusion). Finally, if we are told that Sue is not a graduate ($\bar{q}$), then we may conclude that she has neither completed the requirements nor done special favors for the principal (i.e., $\bar{q} \therefore \bar{p} \cdot \bar{o}$).

As another example, consider the conditional statement "If the car is running, then there is gas in the tank." Given the statement that "the car is not running ($\bar{p}$)," what conclusions should be drawn? If someone's mental representation merely associates gas (q) with running (p) and no gas ($\bar{q}$) with not running ($\bar{p}$), then one would incorrectly conclude that no gas is in the tank ($\bar{p} \therefore \bar{q}$). On the other hand if someone is able to imagine at least two reasons why the car may not be running—for example, no gas ($\bar{q}$) and ignition not turned

Table 12.1 ▼ **Mental Representations.** Specific situations are shown with one and two antecedent conditions and the inferences that result from each type.

Mental Representations	Resulting Inferences	
One Antecedent Condition		
p ——— q	$p \therefore q$ $q \therefore p$	$p \therefore \bar{q}$ $q \therefore \bar{p}$
Two Antecedent Conditions		
o and p → q	$o \therefore q$ $p \therefore q$ $q \therefore$ no conclusion	$o \therefore$ no conclusion $p \therefore$ no conclusion $q \therefore p \cdot o$

on ($\bar{o}$)—then reasoning takes the form of the conditional, and the conclusion is that no conclusion follows.

Figure 12.1 depicts how three levels of intellectual development can arise as a consequence of the nature of an individual's mental representations and from a generalization of the more complex type. At Level 1, only mental representations with one antecedent condition exist, thus all inferences take the form of the biconditional. At Level 2, the child's increased experiences have produced many types of mental representations that vary from situation to situation, so the resulting form of inferences (biconditional or conditional) varies by situation, depending on whether alternative antecedent conditions are imagined. Finally, the Level 3 thinker has constructed a more general representation that can be applied to all situations; in effect, this allows him or her to argue that "even though I may be able to think of only one antecedent condition, I know from past experience that in most situations other possibilities exist, so I had better look for some before I jump to a hasty conclusion." Therefore, at Level 3, most reasoning takes the form of the conditional.

Testing the Alternatives

As we recall, Piaget's theory states that adult formal operational people reason through conditional statements regardless of their context. To test the alternative multiple-hypothesis theory of hypothetical-deductive thinking, 922 college students were administered a test that allowed them to be classified as *concrete, transitional,* and *formal* thinkers as defined by Piaget's theory. The

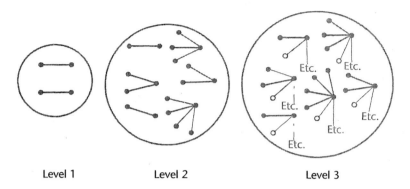

Level 1   Level 2   Level 3

Figure 12.1 ▼ **Levels of Intellectual Development.** This diagram represents intellectual development as types of mental representations. At Level 1, only mental representations of specific situations with one antecedent condition exist, so inferences are biconditional. At Level 2, mental representations exist for specific situations with differing numbers of antecedents, so the pattern of inferences drawn (biconditional or conditional) depends on the specific situation. At Level 3, the reasoner has constructed the knowledge that alternatives probably exist, even when these are not easily imagined (these are represented by the open circles). The reasoning thus becomes hypothetical-deductive as the person seeks alternatives; if found, the inferences drawn take the form of the conditional.

seven "logic" tasks were then randomly distributed so that each student received just one task (Lawson, 1991). Under these conditions, Piagetian theory led to the prediction that formal operational subjects would respond similarly using conditional logic to each task because of their similar logical form. The multiple-hypothesis theory, on the other hand, led to the prediction that responses should vary from task to task depending on the extent to which the context suggests alternative antecedent conditions. More specifically, the multiple-hypothesis theory predicted that:

- The percentage of conditional responses should significantly decrease from Task 1 to Task 7. (See the previous seven questions for the predicted task order.)
- The percentage of biconditional responses should significantly increase from Task 1 to Task 7.
- Further, multiple-hypothesis theory argues that Piagetian tests of formal operational reasoning actually measure whether a person has constructed a general approach to reasoning, which tells him or her to seek alternative antecedent conditions even when none may be obvious. Therefore, sub-

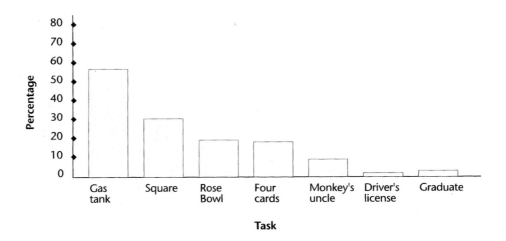

Figure 12.2 ▾ **Subjects Drawing Inferences with Conditional Logic Pattern on Each Task (Percentage)**

jects who have been classified as formal operational should respond with a greater proportion of inferences of the conditional form than subjects classified as transitional or concrete operational on each logic task.

Figure 12.2 shows the percentage of subjects responding to the seven tasks with the conditional form for all questions (i.e., Question 1 ∴ q, Question 2 no conclusion, Question 3 no conclusion, Question 4 ∴ p). The percentages ranged from 56.7% on the gas tank task to 1.9% on the driver's license task.

Figure 12.3 shows the percentage of subjects who responded to the seven logic tasks with the biconditional form for all questions (i.e., Question 1 ∴ q, Question 2 ∴ $\bar{q}$, Question 3 ∴ p, Question 4 ∴ $\bar{q}$). Again, the percentages varied widely from task to task. Only 17.1% of the subjects' responses followed the biconditional pattern on the gas tank task, while 76.4% of responses did so on the driver's license task. Results fit the pattern predicted by the multiple-hypothesis theory, which argued that task context influences the thinking used because context is able to evoke alternative antecedents. The task for which alternatives were assumed to be the easiest to generate (the gas tank) did indeed elicit the greatest percentage of inferences of the conditional form (and least percentage of the biconditional form), while the tasks that were assumed to be the most difficult to imagine alternatives (the driver's license and the graduate) elicited the least percentage of inferences of the conditional form (and the greatest use of the biconditional form).

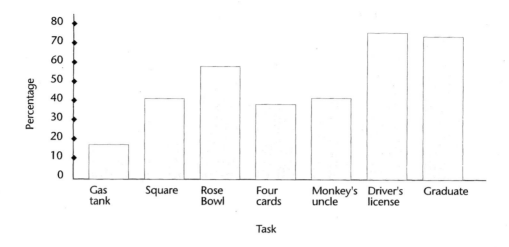

Figure 12.3 ▼ **Subjects Drawing Inferences with Biconditional Logic Pattern on Each Task (Percentage)**

Figure 12.4 shows the percentage of subjects at each Piagetian developmental level (concrete, transitional, formal) that drew inferences with the conditional pattern on each task. Note two trends. First, as predicted by the multiple-hypothesis theory, the formal subjects tended to respond more frequently with the conditional pattern than the other two groups. Group differences reached significance ($p < .05$) on two of the tasks (the square, $\chi^2 = 10.1$, $p = .006$; monkey's uncle, $\chi^2 = 6.6$, $p = .035$). For the gas tank, Rose Bowl, four cards, driver's license and the graduate tasks, the respective χ^2 values and probability levels were $\chi^2 = 4.5$, $p = .11$; $\chi^2 = 3.1$, $p = .22$; $\chi^2 = 3.5$, $p = .17$; $\chi^2 = 3.4$, $p = .18$; and $\chi^2 = .4$, $p = .81$. Second, the formal operational subjects did not consistently draw inferences that followed the conditional pattern from task to task (the percentage varied from 65.5% on the gas tank task to 1.7% on the driver's license task). This indicates a strong context effect. Students identified as formal operational thus do *not* appear to be reasoning with context-free rules of conditional logic.

Conclusions and Recommendations

The results lead to two major conclusions. First, specific contexts influence the pattern of inferences that an individual draws (conditional or biconditional), presumably because the contexts facilitate or restrict the ability to imagine alternative antecedent conditions. When someone is able to imagine reason-

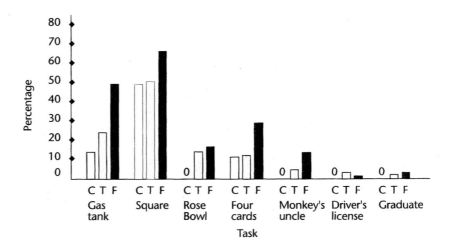

Figure 12.4 ▾ Subjects Drawing Inferences with Biconditional Logic Pattern on Each Task (Percentage). The Piagetian levels: C = concrete, T = transitional, and F = formal.

able alternatives, the pattern of inferences drawn is similar in form to that of conditional logic. When someone is unable to imagine reasonable alternatives, the pattern of inferences is similar in form to that of biconditional logic (Markovits, 1984, 1985). Second, the more skilled reasoners (as identified by performance on the Piagetian reasoning items) responded more often with the conditional response pattern than did their less-skilled peers. Hence, the study's general conclusion is that task context influences the pattern of inferences that someone draws (conditional or biconditional), but that a general (context-free) thinking ability exists that consists primarily of a propensity to consider alternatives. In other words, some people seem to have a general rule to guide thinking, but instead of being a logical rule, it is of the sort that says, "Before I jump to a hasty conclusion [i.e., $p \therefore q, \overline{p} \therefore \overline{q}, q \therefore p, \overline{q} \therefore \overline{p}$], are there alternative antecedent conditions that would render a hasty conclusion false? If so, then I cannot draw a conclusion." In other words, the context influences an individual's conclusions based on an ability to imagine alternatives within specific contexts given the general propensity to look for them.

So rather than the construction of a new set of logical operations, adolescent intellectual development can be viewed primarily as the construction of a general disposition to consider alternative possibilities and the construction of accompanying hypothesis-testing schemes that allow an individual to process evidence to choose among the alternatives (e.g., control of variables, correlational thinking, probabilistic thinking). Lawson and Hegebush (1985), for instance, found that in causal contexts, young children showed little interest or awareness of cause-and-effect relationships. Older children, however, were aware of causal relationships but tended to restrict their thinking to one cause for one effect (inferences of the biconditional form were frequently drawn), whereas adolescents were more likely to generate multiple possible causes. Apparently, some adolescents and adults move beyond this restricted view and become aware of multiple causes for specific effects in specific contexts and, indeed, construct a general disposition (a habit of mind) that leads them to probe deeply for alternatives even when the alternatives are not thrust on them by circumstances (hence, a frequent avoidance of drawing inferences of the biconditional form).

▼ A NEUROLOGICAL EXPLANATION OF MEMORY AND ANALOGICAL THINKING

Although the use of context-free forms of logic such as modus ponens and modus tollens appear to play little or no role in reasoning, the process of abduction or analogical reasoning seems to be absolutely essential for scientific insight. Consequently, considerable interest now exists in the psychology of analogical transfer—that is, the use of analogies to solve novel problems and to construct generalized rules or concepts. This section will present a neurological level theory of memory and analogical transfer based in part on Grossberg's neural modeling principles presented earlier. Although he has not directly confronted the issue of analogical transfer, his principles of neural networks and his theory of human memory can provide a framework in which we can understand how analogical transfer occurs and why it plays a central role in human learning and memory.

The central question that must be addressed is this: What causes some but not all experiences to find their way into long-term memory (LTM)? Grossberg's answer is contained in a general way in his learning equation, which was presented and discussed in Chapter 11 in the context of the self-regulation process. We will return to the learning equation again because it provides the key to understanding memory in general and, more specifically, the role of analogy in facilitating the transfer of information from short-term memory (STM) to long-term memory. We begin the discussion by describing an experience I had while I visited a Japanese science classroom. That experience will serve to more sharply focus the issue.

During the visit, a teacher and his students discussed the results of an experiment that investigated the role of a variety of factors on seed growth. The teacher organized the students' comments in words and diagrams on the chalkboard. The students were enthusiastic, and the teacher wrote clearly on the board. The experiment was familiar, but my inability to understand spoken or written Japanese made comprehension of the discussion difficult.

At the conclusion of the lesson, our visiting group adjourned to the school principal's office for a traditional cup of tea. I then realized that I had observed a very good lesson and should attempt to make a few notes, including a record of what the teacher had written on the board. Predictably, I was able to reconstruct some, but not all, of what had been written. Recalling the relative position of the major items on the board was easy. The diagram of the seeds and their container, the numbers 1 and 2, letters A and B, and the question mark were all easily recalled. But recalling the shapes of the Japanese symbols and words was impossible. To be more specific, a symbol shaped like ? was recalled easily, but a symbol such as 木 was not. Why?

You may be saying to yourself, "This is not the least bit surprising. Familiar English language elements were recalled, while unfamiliar Japanese language elements were forgotten. Because the observer does not speak or write in Japanese, this is entirely predictable." Agreed! Clearly, this can be predicted based on past experiences that we all have had in trying to remember familiar and unfamiliar items. But how can this be explained at the neurological level? After all, all of the stimuli on the board were clear, and all could have easily been copied at the time. The questions then are: Why does an individual remember items that are familiar and forget items that are not? What precisely does "familiar" mean in neurological terms? And how does familiarity facilitate transfer into long-term memory?

Recall that Grossberg's learning equation (11.2), stated as

$$\dot{Z}_{ij} = B_{ij} + S_{ij} [X_j]^+$$

describes conditions necessary to modify the synaptic strength of knobs N_{ij}. The term Z_{ij} represents initial synaptic strength; B_{ij} is a decay constant, thus the term $B_{ij} Z_{ij}$ is the forgetting term. $S_{ij}[X_j]^+$ is the learning term because it drives increases in Z_{ij}. S_{ij} is the strength signal that has passed from node V_i to knob N_{ij}. The term $[X_j]^+$ represents the level of activity at postsynaptic nodes V_j that exceed firing threshold. The learning term indicates that for information to be stored in LTM, two events must occur simultaneously. First, signals must be received at N_{ij}. Second, nodes V_j must be receiving inputs that cause them to fire. When these two events drive activity at N_{ij} above a specified constant of decay, the Z_{ij}s will increase.

Adaptive Resonance

Adaptive resonance is a crucial component of transferring information to LTM. As we know, the brain is able to process a continuous stream of changing stimuli and constantly modify behavior accordingly. This implies that a mechanism exists to match input with expectations from previous experience and to select alternative expectations when a mismatch occurs. Grossberg's model for such a mechanism was shown in Figure 11.7.

Following Grossberg, the field of excitation on a particular slab of neurons was referred to as $F^{(1)}$, while the field at the next slab was referred to as $F^{(2)}$. Suppose that, because of previous experience, a pattern of activity, P_1, at $F^{(1)}$ causes a firing of a pattern P_2 at $F^{(2)}$, where P_2 could be a single neuron; P_2 then excites a pattern P on $F^{(1)}$. The pattern P is compared with the input following P_1. P is the expectation. P will be P_1 in a static scene and the pattern to follow P_1 in a temporal sequence. If the two patterns match, then we see what we expect to see. This allows an uninterrupted processing of input and a continued quenching of nonspecific arousal. Recall that the match of input with expectations is referred to as an *adaptive resonance*. An individual is only aware of patterns that enter the resonant state. Unless resonance occurs, no coding in LTM will take place. This is because only in the resonant state is there both pre- and postsynaptic excitation of the cells at $F^{(1)}$.

Now suppose the new input to $F^{(1)}$ does not match the expected pattern P from $F^{(2)}$. Mismatch occurs, and this causes activity at $F^{(1)}$ to be turned off by lateral inhibition, which in turn shuts off the inhibitory output to the nonspecific arousal source. This turns on nonspecific arousal and initiates an internal search for a new pattern at $F^{(2)}$ that will match P_1.

Such a series of events explains how information is processed across time. The important point is that stimuli are considered "familiar" if a memory record of them exists at $F^{(2)}$ such that the pattern of excitation sent back to $F^{(1)}$ matches the incoming pattern. If they do not match, then the incoming stimuli are unfamiliar, and orienting arousal is turned on to allow an unconscious search for another pattern. If no such match is obtained (as in the case of looking at an unfamiliar Japanese symbol), then no coding in LTM will take place unless attention is directed more closely at the object in question. Directing attention at the unfamiliar object will boost an individual's presynaptic activity and may eventually allow a recording of the sensory input into a set of previously uncommitted cells. (For details, see Grossberg, 1982, especially pp. 29–31.)

Grossberg's theory of adaptive resonance is a general explanation of how input patterns find their way into LTM. That theory must be extended at this point. In general, the theory of analogical transfer that is proposed here describes specific neural processes that greatly facilitate coding of new experi-

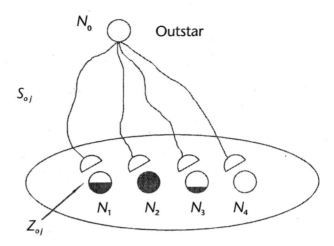

Figure 12.5 ▽ **Active Outstar.** The darkened neurons represent active neurons. The darker the cell, the more active it is. If the outstar is sampling the slab during this activity, then the synaptic strengths of each synaptic knob will tend to mirror the activity of the cell (as in Figure 12.6). The more active the cell, the more the synaptic strength will grow.

ences in LTM. However, before we discuss the role that analogy plays, we must look more closely at the way neurons function to recall and reproduce patterns.

Outstars and Instars: Fundamental Units

Grossberg has identified the *outstar* as the underlying neural mechanism for reproduction and recall of patterns. It is a neuron whose cell body lies in one slab of interconnected neurons with a set of synaptic knobs that connect it to a set of cell bodies embedded in a lower slab of neurons (see Figure 12.5). The outstar is a fundamental functional unit able to learn and reproduce a pattern. Understanding how outstars accomplish this is central to understanding how appropriate analogies can greatly enhance learning.

The outstar in Figure 12.5 is actively firing impulses down its axon to a lower slab of neurons that are simultaneously receiving a pattern of input from a still lower slab of neurons or perhaps from the environment (e.g., a pattern of visual input on the retina). In the figure, the darkened neurons represent active neurons; the darker the cell body, the more active it is (i.e., the more input it is receiving, hence the more frequently it is firing). When the outstar N_o is firing and the signals S_{oj} are reaching the slab when the pattern is, the

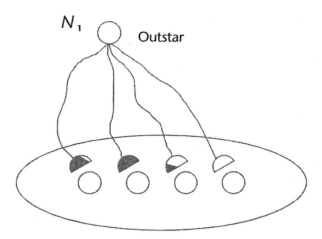

Figure 12.6 ▼ **Less Active Outstar.** The darkened synaptic knobs represent the synaptic strength after the outstar has sampled the slab long enough to learn the pattern. The synapses shown have learned the pattern they have sampled in Figure 12.5.

synaptic strengths Z_{oj} will grow. An important consequence of this change in synaptic strengths is that when the pattern of activity on the slab is gone, the outstar is able to *reproduce* the pattern whenever it fires again. When the outstar fires repeatedly, synapses with high synaptic strength will cause their associated cells to become quite active, and cells with low synaptic strength will be less active, just as they were when the slab was being sampled. In this manner, the pattern will reappear (see Figure 12.6).

Not only are slabs of neurons connected by axons from higher slabs, as depicted in Figures 12.5 and 12.6, but also the neuron cell bodies on the input slab have axons that connect them to the cell bodies of higher slabs. As depicted in Figure 12.7, a pattern of activity on a lower slab is mirrored by the rate of transmitter release in the synapses leading to the cell bodies on the higher slab. Thus, when the pattern is active on the lower slab and when the cell body on the higher slab (the outstar) is active, these synaptic strengths will increase in a fashion that mirrors that pattern of activity. Consequently, if the pattern appears again, the outstar will fire. In this sense, the outstar has remembered the pattern. An important point is that a "sufficient" period of time is needed for the outstar (the neuron on the higher slab) to learn the pattern. We shall see later that analogy can play a key role by reducing this period of time, thus making learning possible when it would otherwise not occur.

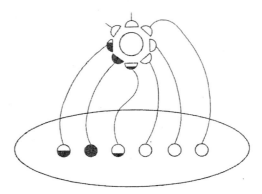

Figure 12.7 ▼ **Instar and Learned Firing Pattern.** The darkened cells are active; the darker they are, the more active. If the cell above is then fired, the synaptic strengths will grow via Grossberg's learning equation. The synaptic strengths of other cells decay. In this fashion, the synapses (the instar) learn the pattern that has fired the cell on which they impinge. If this pattern appears again as part of an input, then the synaptic strengths of the instar will cause the cell to fire.

The activity depicted in Figure 12.7 is of such functional importance that Grossberg has given it a name: the *instar*. The instar is actually the set of synaptic weights associated with the synaptic knobs connected to a neuron. If a pattern fires a neuron repeatedly, then that pattern will reappear as part of the instar of that neuron.

To summarize, the synaptic strengths of an outstar align themselves to an input. The outstar is then able to reproduce the input. If an outstar, or a collection of outstars, is not aligned to an input, then that input cannot be reproduced unless it is presented again. Thus, it will not be remembered. The important point is this: If an outstar is not present, then a pattern cannot be reproduced and thus it cannot be remembered. In the example of the Japanese classroom, the Japanese symbols could not be reproduced because an outstar (or outstars) necessary to reproduce them did not exist. We conclude, therefore, that outstars must be present for recall to occur.

Having said this, keep in mind that actual input patterns, such as those on the retina, are never exactly the same. We do not look the same when we awake as we did when we went to bed, but we do "recognize" ourselves nevertheless. Grossberg's theory of adaptive resonance shows how this can be accomplished. Adaptive resonance is a method by which slabs of neurons can interact with one another to find a best fit. Suppose that Slab 1 is presented with an image. That image will have several features—that is, it will consist of several patterns.

Each pattern (or feature) that has been learned will trigger an outstar in Slab 2. The outstars triggered in Slab 2 will fire in turn on Slab 1. Patterns that have been correctly triggered will reproduce the pattern that triggered them. If all is correct, or "close," then a best fit has been found. A nonmatching pattern causes a search for a different outstar associated with a different pattern. Grossberg's theory of adaptive resonance includes a detailed description of this search for a best fit.

The Outstar as a Mechanism for Chunking

Before we discuss the role of analogy in facilitating learning, one more neurological mechanism needs to be in place. That mechanism deals with the well-known psychological phenomenon of *chunking,* which was referred to earlier in the context of concept construction. Chunking has an interesting place in the literature of psychology. Miller's "magic number 7," plus or minus 2, refers to the fact that it is almost universally true that people can only remember seven unrelated units of data (without using memory tricks or aids) (Miller, 1956). This may be why telephone numbers are seven digits long. But clearly we all construct concepts (patterns) that contain far more information than seven "units." A mental process thus must occur in which previously unrelated pieces of input are grouped or "chunked" together to produce higher-order chunks (units of thought). As previously mentioned, this implied process is known as chunking (Simon, 1974).

Grossberg has hypothesized that the outstar is the anatomical or functional unit that makes chunking possible. An outstar sampling a slab can group a set of neurons that are firing at the same time. To do this, the outstar must merely fire at a rate that is fast enough to allow the synaptic strengths at its synapses to mirror the activity of the neurons being grouped (or chunked). For adaptive resonance to occur, the neurons being chunked must fire the outstar. In this sense, the purpose of an outstar is to form a chunk and later to identify the chunk once it has been formed.

An architecture known as *on-center, off-surround* (OCOS) plays an important part in the process of chunk formation. OCOS is sometimes referred to as "winner-take-all" architecture. In OCOS architecture, active cells excite nearby cells and inhibit those that are farther away. Because OCOS cells excite nearby cells, those that are close together will excite one another. The result is hot spots of active cells close together that inhibit cells farther away. The cells within the hot spots sample the slab and become the outstars that learn the pattern. Thus, the cells in a pattern in Slab 1 become the cells that will excite a hot spot, and the cells in the hot spot become the outstars that learn the pattern.

Chunking can be either temporal or spatial. For example, a spoken word is the sequential chunk of neural activity required to produce the word; a heard word is the sequential pattern of sounds that have been identified as that word.

The OCOS architecture can force a winner (a hot spot) on the sampling slab and thus force chunking to occur in either the spatial or the temporal case.

If the outstar is indeed the biological mechanism that is the basis for chunking, then Miller's magic number 7 must have some physical relationship to the outstar architecture. What might this be? Physical limits probably are associated with the activity of cells, their rates of decay, and the spread of axonal trees. This is purely speculation, but only so many hot spots can exist on a slab, so some limit must exist, and an excited neuron can continue to fire for only a certain length of time. Constraints such as these should force a physical limit on the size of a chunk.

The Neural Basis for Analogy

An analogy consists of objects, events, or situations that share features (or patterns) in common—that is, they are similar in one or more ways. We shall show that shared features have a significant neural impact. We implicitly assume that *similar* features will have the same sort of impact. The heart of the argument will be the discovery that chunks with similar *or* shared features reinforce one another, and in a significant manner, by forming feedback loops. These feedback loops cause the activity of the sampling outstars (i.e., the codes that are sampling the new to-be-learned patterns) to grow exponentially as the feedback loop is forming. Such an exponential increase in cell activity is significant for two reasons. First, it causes rapid sampling, which means fast learning (or learning period, because slow learning and no learning are often synonymous). Second, exponential growth of activity is important because cells on an OCOS slab compete with one another, and those that become active first are able to quench less active cells. A specific example of analogical transfer will be used to explicate these points.

Analogy Facilitates Learning: An Example

When I was in seventh grade, my mathematics teacher introduced the word *perpendicular* and the symbol $\perp$ to refer to two lines that intersect at a 90° angle. The teacher wanted us to remember the word and the symbol (and, of course, their meaning), so when he introduced the word and the symbol, he also introduced the words *pup in da cooler*. The teacher intuitively believed that the introduction of these similar sounding words and the images they would evoke in our minds would aid in recall. The words not only brought out a few laughs from my classmates but also worked extremely well. To this day, I cannot think of the word *perpendicular* or the symbol $\perp$ without *pup in da cooler* following close behind. The words *perpendicular* and *pup in da cooler* are quite similar. The letters are similar, of course, and so are the chunks. We shall focus on each of

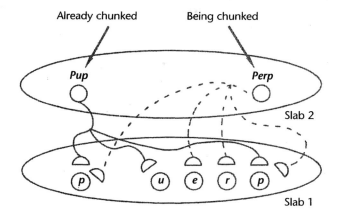

Figure 12.8 ▾ **Chunks Sharing Features.** Pup chunks the features (the phonemes) "beginning *p* sound," "*uh* sound," and "ending *p* sound." *Perp* chunks the same beginning and ending *p* sounds.

these facets because they make the example analogous to analogies that share similarities at different levels.

Assume that the word *pup* is an already constructed chunk in LTM, and the word *perp* represents a to-be-learned chunk. Having *pup* as an active chunk in LTM will speed the learning of *perp*. Similarly, hearing the words *pup in da cooler* will speed the learning of *perpendicular* because they share features in common.

Basic auditory features (or patterns) are called *phonemes,* although we can simplify the discussion by assuming that letters are the basic auditory patterns, the phonemes. Merely replace the "letter" with "phoneme" to provide a more technically correct version of the following discussion. In brief, when *perpendicular* is spoken, much of the neural activity present in the STM of the words *pup in da cooler* remains active because the two words sound much the same. The shared features remain active, and they will cause chunking to occur, which will make it possible to quickly learn the word *perpendicular.*

To explain how shared features cause chunking of new input to occur, consider the neural model depicted in Figure 12.8. The word *perp* is heard. The sound presents input to Slab 1 as shown and in turn activates the chunk for *pup* already stored in LTM on Slab 2. In other words, the sound *perp* creates neural activity on Slab 1 and a hot spot of neural activity on Slab 2. We thus have the outstar representing the chunk *pup* (on Slab 2) feeding the beginning and ending letters *p,* which remain active on Slab 1. These letters begin to form a

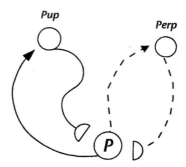

Figure 12.9 ▽ **A Forming Feedback Loop.** The arrows indicate portions of in-stars. A signal travels from *pup* to *p* (as part of an outstar), then along the dashed arrow from *p* to *perp*, back to *p* along the dashed line, and from there along the arrow back to *pup*. The dashed lines indicate an instar (from *p* to *perp*) and an outstar (from *perp* to *p*) during formation.

portion of an instar connected to the hot spot on Slab 2 that will chunk *perp*. This neural activity will create a feedback loop from *pup* on Slab 2 to *p* on Slab 1, then to *perp* on Slab 2, and back again (see Figure 12.9). This feedback loop will greatly increase the activity of the Slab 2 neuron *perp,* and this increased activity will make it much easier for the chunk (the outstar) *perp* to form.

Slab 2 has neurons that chunk each syllable: *pup, in, da, coo,* and *ler.* A Slab 3 also exists, and on it is a single neuron that will chunk the five syllables: *pup, in, da, coo, ler.* Again, feedback loops are involved. As shown in Figure 12.10, multiple feedback loops connect the neurons on Slab 3, chunking the words *pup in da cooler* and *perpendicular* with each other through neurons on lower slabs (e.g., *pup in da cooler* on Slab 3 to *in* on Slab 2, to *perpendicular* on Slab 3, then back to *in* on Slab 2, and from there back to *pup in da cooler* on Slab 3). Another feedback loop forms from *pup in da cooler* on Slab 3 to *pup* on Slab 2, to *p* on Slab 1, then to *perp* on Slab 2; from there to *perpendicular* on Slab 3, back to *perp* on Slab 2, back to *p* on Slab 1, to *pup* on Slab 2, and finally to *pup in da cooler* on Slab 3. Other similar feedback loops also form.

An Emergent, Self-Organizing Control System

How the symbol ⊥ is learned has not yet been explained. Consequently, this section will show that the shared features that exist between *pup in da cooler* and *perpendicular* are responsible for creating an emergent neural control system that can greatly increase the speed at which ⊥ is learned.

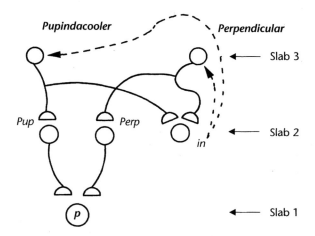

Figure 12.10 ▾ **Multiple Feedback Loops.** These loops connect the neurons on Slab 3 that chunk the words *pup in da cooler* and *perpendicular*. One feedback loop begins at *pup in da cooler,* then goes to *in,* to *perpendicular,* back to *in,* and from there back to *pup in da cooler.* Another feedback loop is *pup in da cooler* to *pup,* to *p,* then to *perp,* and from there to *perpendicular,* back to *perp,* back to *p,* to *pup,* and finally to *pup in da cooler.* Others exist as well. The instars from *p* to *perp,* from *perp* to *perpendicular,* and from *p* to *pup* and *pup* to *pup in da cooler* are not shown.

The section begins with two simple alternative configurations to the emergent neural control system and then introduces the control system itself. Why the neural control system is such an improvement over the alternatives, and why it is able to increase so greatly the rate of learning will be explained.

Figure 12.11 depicts the first simple alternative in which *perp* represents the word *perpendicular,* which is to be associated with the recall of the $\perp$ symbol. A and C each represent a neuron or, in the OCOS architecture, a small group of neurons that mutually excite one another. A is the neuron, or group of neurons, that are active in the auditory neural subsystem when the word *perpendicular* is spoken. This group of neurons either chunks or will chunk this word. C is a neuron that will sample the area of the visual system that contains the symbol $\perp$; it will be the neuron that will chunk this symbol if the learning is successful.

The neural excitation of neurons A and C will result in the association of the word *perpendicular* with the symbol $\perp$. If the association is successful, the word *perpendicular* will cause the recall of the symbol. The activity of A could be considered chunking enhancement. This is because C is a sampling cell, and

Figure 12.11 ▼ **Perp Associated with ⊥**

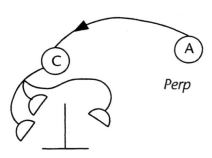

Perp

its activity will result in the formation of a chunk, a set of features that will be grouped together. Activity of the cell A will help to increase the sampling rate of C, and thus the ability of C to chunk (or construct concepts). The problem with the configuration in Figure 12.11 is that the activity of cell C depends solely on the activity of A. Thus, unless A is extremely active or repeated many times, the learning that C is attempting will not take place.

Figure 12.12 extends Figure 12.11. In this configuration, two words, *pup* and *perp*, activate neuron C, which will thus be twice as excited as in the previous case (provided $X_A = X_B$ and $Z_{AC} = Z_{BC}$). This configuration is an improvement over Figure 12.11, but it still does not allow for large-scale boosts in neural activity.

Figure 12.13 shows the emergent self-organizing neural control system that can cause large-scale boosts in activity. In fact, it can cause the sampling rate of C to increase exponentially. As shown, neurons A and B form a feedback loop. Presumably, this is the neural mechanism that an analogy produces. Because neurons A and B of the control structure form a feedback loop, as they

Figure 12.12 ▼ **Activation by an Extension.** Two words—*pup* and *perp*—activate neuron C. The neuron will be excited twice as much as in Figure 12.11, provided that $X_A = X_B$ and $Z_{AC} = Z_{BC}$.

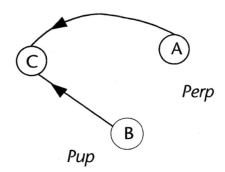

Perp

Pup

Figure 12.13 ▼ **Self-Organizing Neural Control System.** This system can cause the sampling rate of C to increase exponentially because neurons A and B form a lateral feedback loop.

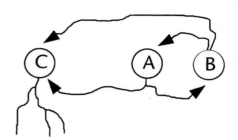

fire, each will increase the rate at which the other fires. A increases the firing rate S_{BA} of B, and B increases the firing rate S_{AB} of A, and the sampling rate of C initially grows exponentially.

In the architecture presented in Figure 12.13, the signal S_{AB}, which travels down the axon leaving A, travels to both B and C. Thus, $S_{AB} = S_{AC}$. In the same fashion, $S_{AB} = S_{BC}$. An increase in S_{AB} and S_{BA} thereby also results in an increase in S_{AC} and S_{BC}. The signals to C from A and B are a by-product of this architecture. The feedback loop from A to B and back again to A (see Figure 12.14) emerges when the organism is presented with data that cause A and B to fire at the same time. As a by-product, other regions are also flooded with neural excitation. The neurons chunking *pup* and *perp* are such an A and B. If the region they flood is a winner-take-all region, then a C will emerge, become strongly excited, and be able to learn the symbol ⊥. *Perp* will be associated with ⊥, and if C's axonal tree also reaches the auditory cortex, then ⊥ will be associated with *perp.*

The Control System Drives Learning the Symbol ⊥

To say that the control system drives learning ⊥ means that the system determines the rate at which the learning will occur. To understand why the analogy controls the rate of learning, notice in the sampling-rate equation that, even if Z_{AC} is small, if $S_{BA} \cdot Z_{BA}$ is large, then $d/dt\,(X_C)$, the sampling rate of C will be large. This is interesting, because $S_{BA} \cdot Z_{BA}$ will be large if the association between A and B is strong. Thus, the analogy, the signals between A and B, drive the learning of the symbol ⊥.

The shared features within the input data *pup in da cooler* and *perpendicular* caused the control system (neurons A and B and the feedback loop they form) to arise. A represents the neuron chunking the word *pup in dacooler*; B represents the neuron chunking *perpendicular*. The system arose because the shared features caused the chunking to occur. As mentioned before, chunking principally occurred because the shared features caused an exponential growth

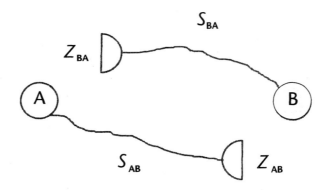

Figure 12.14 ▾ **Components of the Feedback Loop**

in neural activity. This rapid rise in activity allowed the chunks to form. Therefore, the input data, the neural ability to chunk, and the exponential growth associated with feedback caused the control system to emerge. (For mathematical demonstrations of these points, see Lawson and Lawson, 1993.)

A Return to the Japanese Classroom

In summary, the example of learning the word *perpendicular* and its mathematical symbol have natural explanations within hierarchical neural networks. A proposed network to explain why the Japanese symbol could not easily be recalled also would consist of a hierarchy of slabs. The first slab of this network would be of neurons activated by line segments tilted (or oriented) in a specific direction. The second slab would consist of cells (outstars) that chunk neurons in the first slab. If a neuron on the second slab has chunked the neurons on the first that are activated by the Japanese symbol, then that symbol can be recalled by activating that neuron. If no neuron has previously chunked the Japanese symbol, then the symbol cannot be recalled unless presynaptic activity associated with the symbol receives a considerable boost.

The neural models that have been presented suggest that analogies can greatly facilitate learning and memory. So how could an analogy be used to help recall a symbol such as the Japanese symbol 木? According to the theory, the correct approach would be to try to imagine something "like" the symbol. For example, it might remind you of the three crosses at Christ's crucifixion, with the middle cross taller than the other two. As has been demonstrated, activation of these similar images already stored in LTM greatly increases postsynaptic neural activity; according to Grossberg's learning equation, this allows for storage of the new input in LTM. Of course, we may not be able to generate a satisfactory analogy, image, or set of images, in which case we would have to resort to the more tedious task of describing the symbol: It has three vertical lines attached to a horizontal line, and so on. Provided that patterns for these terms exist in memory at $F^{(2)}$, this procedure will work, but it requires considerable effort to describe all of the relevant variables. This effort, in fact, is a method for maintaining relevant portions of the image in STM so that chunking can occur. In this way we have a neurological account of why "a picture is worth a thousand words." The images are far superior because the relevant features are already linked in the analogous image. Of course, if irrelevant features are linked, then the analogy will be misleading. The *pup in da cooler* and *perpendicular* example was meant to demonstrate the manner in which analogy can speed learning by incorporating relevant features shared by new ideas and those already known.

Summary

The two examples we have addressed—forgetting the Japanese symbol and learning the word *perpendicular* and its mathematical symbol—have natural explanations within a hierarchical neural network. The explanation of the first example used a hierarchical network with two slabs. The second example used a hierarchical network with three slabs. The network proposed to describe the behavior exhibited in the first example explained why the Japanese symbol could not be recalled easily. The first slab of this network was a slab of neurons activated by line segments tilted (or oriented) in a specific direction. The second slab consisted of cells (outstars) that chunked neurons in the first slab. If a neuron on the second slab has chunked the neurons on the first that are activated by the Japanese symbol, then that symbol can be recalled by activating that neuron. If no neuron has chunked the Japanese symbol, then it cannot be recalled unless presynaptic activity associated with the symbol receives a considerable boost.

The first slab of the three-slab network consisted of cells activated by phonemes, sounds that are building blocks of speech, much as oriented lines can be used as building blocks for line images. The third slab chunks neurons active on the second slab. These chunks become words such as *pup in da cooler* and *perpendicular*. The second example demonstrates that similar activity on the second slab (activity such as that created by *pup* and *perp*) can create feedback loops between elements on the slab (between the neurons chunking *pup* and *perp*). The feedback loops greatly increase the neural postsynaptic activity and thus increase the ability to chunk and therefore to learn.

▼ **INTEGRATING PHILOSOPHY, NEURAL MODELING, SCIENTIFIC INSIGHT, AND INSTRUCTION**

We conclude by integrating specific aspects of philosophy, neural modeling, scientific insight, and instruction. Chapter 11 included a brief discussion of two opposing philosophical views of knowledge acquisition, namely, empiricism and nativism. At this point, a look back at these two philosophical views should prove instructive. Recall Grossberg's learning equation,

$$\dot{Z}_{ij} = B_{ij}\,Z_{ij} + S_{ij}[X_j]^+$$

The equation claims that novel experiences will make their way into LTM when the product of neural activity resulting from incoming stimuli (i.e., the presynaptic activity S_{ij}) times the neural activity resulting from already established connections in the brain (i.e, the postsynaptic activity $[X_j]^+$) exceeds current synaptic strength (Z_{ij}) times a decay constant (B_{ij}). This implies that novel information can enter LTM in at least two different ways. First, the incoming signal (S_{ij}) can be boosted so much that little postsynaptic activity ($[X_{ij}]^+$) is necessary to drive the product of S_{ij} and $[X_j]^+$ high enough to increase the Z_{ij}s significantly. We all have experienced trying to memorize information, such as the names of all the states and their capitals, by simply repeating the words over and over again. This repetition presumably boosts the presynaptic incoming signals high enough for the connections to be eventually made (i.e., for the Z_{ij}s to increase sufficiently). In this way, some experiences *can* make their way directly into LTM. Highly emotionally charged situations also boost presynaptic activity so that "one-shot" learning is possible in some circumstances. In this sense, the empiricist doctrine that claims that knowledge is directly assimilated from the environment is correct.

But recall our discussion of trying to recall the question mark and the Japanese symbol after the visit to the Japanese science classroom. The question mark was easily recalled, while the Japanese symbol was just as easily forgotten. Presumably, this was because the incoming signals from the question mark (the presynaptic signals, S_{ij}) were "greeted" in the brain by postsynaptic activity ($[X_j]^+$) because of a memory record of question marks seen in the past. The product of S_{ij} and $[X_j]^+$ thus was great enough to cause the transmitter release rates of the relevant neurons to increase to the extent that a new set of functional connections was formed. On the other hand, the incoming signals from the Japanese symbol were not "greeted" by comparable postsynaptic activity because no prior memory record of the Japanese symbol existed. Therefore, no change in transmitter release rate at those neurons occurred. Hence, when attention was directed away from the board and when the incoming signals from the Japanese symbol decayed, the symbol was forgotten.

In this sense, Piaget's contention that an individual must have a preexisting mental structure to assimilate experience is correct. The nativist position that requires the existence of prior knowledge structures also can be viewed as partially correct in the sense that previous "ideas" must be present for the experiences to make their way into the mind. Of course, the nativists then incorrectly conclude that these prior ideas must be innate because they could not come from experience. But even though empiricists and nativists can rightly claim to be partially correct, neither side has recognized both key terms of Grossberg's learning equation—namely, the S_{ij} and $[X_{ij}]^+$—and neither side has properly included the role of behavior and the process of adaptive resonance.

Of course, to get new experiences into LTM, we need not always rely on the boosting of presynaptic activity. Instead, we can use clever mnemonic techniques that will boost postsynaptic activity. Suppose, for example, that you have just met someone for the first time, and he tells you his name is "Bill." One strategy for recalling his name would be to repeat the name "Bill" over and over again, hoping to boost the S_{ij}s so that a permanent record is stored in LTM. Although this procedure might work, a much easier way is to ask yourself, "Who else do I know with the name 'Bill'?" Most likely, only a moment's reflection will lead to recalling another Bill, at which point a whole host of memories linked to this other Bill will be triggered. You recall his last name, his face, his wife, and a variety of experiences that you have shared with this other Bill. The net effect of this reminiscence is that the postsynaptic activity associated with the neuron or neurons associated with the name "Bill" are given a huge boost of activity (i.e., the $[X_{ij}]^+$s associated with "Bill" increase). Therefore, when you look at the new Bill, the S_{ij}s that are active in STM from this experience are "greeted" by the large $[X_{ij}]^+$s resulting from the postsynaptic activity associated with the name Bill and all of those previous experiences from LTM. Consequently, the transmitter release rates (Z_{ij}s) increase, and a new functional connection is made so that the next time you see the new Bill, his name will be recalled from LTM.

The use of analogy to boost postsynaptic activity amounts to much the same thing. Instead of using the same name and associated memories from LTM to boost postsynaptic activity, an analogous word or experience can be used to boost the postsynaptic activity. As we have seen, this allows feedback loops to form that lead to an exponential increase in postsynaptic activity. This idea gives us a neural level explanation for scientific insight, and it also suggests an extremely valuable teaching device.

The process of abduction, or analogical reasoning, was first introduced in Chapter 1's discussion of Charles Darwin and his use of analogy to describe the process of natural selection. Darwin used analogical reasoning when he explained the evolution of species as a process *like* the artificial selection of domestic plants and animals. He used the term *natural selection* to label this hypothetical analogous process in nature. The scientific inventions of others such as Kepler, Mendel, Coulomb, and Kekulè also can be viewed as the products of analogical reasoning or abduction. The list of analogies in science is long; as Pierce (see Hanson, 1958) stated, perhaps not overzealously, "all the ideas of science come to it by way of Abduction" (p. 85).

Our discussion of neural models reveals why this is so. Consider Darwin's words from his autobiography as quoted in the editor's preface of *Voyage of the Beagle* (1962): "Innumerable well-observed facts were stored in the minds of naturalists ready to take their proper places as soon as any theory which would receive them was sufficiently explained" (p. xxii).

Two points must be made. First, for Darwin himself the key event in his invention of natural selection as the mechanism for evolution occurred when he "saw" that the evolutionary process in nature was analogous to the process of artificial selection in domestic breeding. In neural terms, for Darwin to invent natural selection, he needed the postsynaptic neural activity of his experiences with artificial selection boosted at the same time that he was contemplating these "innumerable observed facts" that were also stored in his memory. When these two sets of memory records were boosted simultaneously—that is, when both presynaptic activity, the S_{ij}s, and postsynaptic activity, the $[X_{ij}]^+$s were boosted—a new set of connections was formed. When Darwin became conscious of these new connections, he felt the moment of insight, the Eureka experience. Second, as reflected by Darwin's words, other informed naturalists also will come easily to put innumerable facts in their proper places once the relevant pattern is presented to them.

Of course, Darwin was interested in teaching other naturalists about the process of natural selection. But suppose we wish to teach students about the great theoretical ideas of science, such as natural selection? How can students come to understand these ideas? The answer, predictably, is to use the same process that lead to their invention in the first place, that is, by analogy. In neurological terms, the familiar analogy that is presented orally by the teacher sets off in the students' brains the postsynaptic pattern of activity, the boosted $[X_{ij}]^+$s that can be matched with presynaptic S_{ij}s to allow the new connections to be made. Without such a match, no "understanding" will occur, and transfer to LTM will not take place. Here, understanding is defined neurologically as the resonant state that occurs when the pattern driven from LTM matches that derived from the environment.

One final point. The preceding discussion has omitted one possibly crucial element. Recall that the young Charles Darwin began his explorations as a believer in special creation. Before he could even begin to wonder about the causes of evolution, he had to become convinced that his initial belief in special creation was wrong and that evolution, in fact, does occur. When old ideas must be changed before new ones can be assimilated, the more complex and time-consuming process of self-regulation must occur. This implies that the truly effective teacher not only must know the subject matter well enough to be able to present all of the puzzle pieces and the patterns that will enable the students to put those pieces together, but also must know the contradictory patterns that students may bring to class and how to open their minds so that they become willing and able to wrestle successfully with the scientific and ascientific alternatives and the evidence. Only then will students emerge as persons stocked not only with valid conceptual knowledge, but also with the procedural skills that allow old and perhaps inappropriate ideas to be evaluated carefully and the process of self-regulation to proceed. In other words, the primary goal of instruction is not merely to teach concepts, but to teach students how to change old concepts and construct new ones when appropriate.

Questions for Reflection and Activities

1. In what way(s) are the three reasoning levels of the multiple-hypothesis theory of advanced reasoning similar to or different from the thinkers described by Chamberlain in "The Method of Multiple Working Hypotheses"? (See Appendix B.)
2. Would learning rules of logic help someone become a better reasoner? Explain.
3. Explain in neurological terms why analogies aid recall and retention.
4. Why has analogical reasoning played such a large role in scientific discovery?
5. What role can analogical reasoning play in science classrooms?
6. Design a learning cycle that includes one or more analogies and is suitable for teaching a theoretical concept.

THE CENTRAL PURPOSE OF AMERICAN EDUCATION

Educational Policies Commission

Part I: Education in the American Society

In any democracy education is closely bound to the wishes of the people, but the strength of this bond in America has been unique. The American people have traditionally regarded education as a means for improving themselves and their society. Whenever an objective has been judged desirable for the individual or the society, it has tended to be accepted as a valid concern of the school. The American commitment to the free society—to individual dignity, to personal liberty, to equality of opportunity—has set the frame in which the American school grew. The basic American value, respect for the individual, has led to one of the major charges which the American people have placed on their schools: to foster that development of individual capacities which will enable each human being to become the best person he is capable of becoming.

The schools have been designed also to serve society's needs. The political order depends on responsible participation of individual citizens; hence the schools have been concerned with good citizenship. The economic order depends on ability and willingness to work!

Source: This article is taken from *The Central Purpose of American Education* (Washington, D.C.: National Education Association, 1961).

hence the schools have taught vocational skills. The general morality depends on choices made by individuals; hence the schools have cultivated moral habits and upright character.

Educational authorities have tended to share and support these broad concepts of educational purposes. Two of the best known definitions of purposes were formulated by educators in 1918 and 1938. The first definition, by the Commission on the Reorganization of Secondary Education, proposed for the school a set of seven cardinal objectives: health, command of fundamental processes, worthy home membership, vocational competence, effective citizenship, worthy use of leisure, and ethical character. The second definition, by the Educational Policies Commission, developed a number of objectives under four headings: self-realization, human relationship, economic efficiency, and civic responsibility.

The American school must be concerned with all these objectives if it is to serve all of American life. That these are desirable objectives is clear. Yet they place before the school a problem of immense scope, for neither the schools nor the pupils have the time or energy to engage in all the activities which will fully achieve all these goals. Choices among possible activities are inevitable and are constantly being made in and for every school. But there is no consensus regarding a basis for making these choices. The need, therefore, is for a principle which will enable the school to identify its necessary and appropriate contributions to individual development and the needs of society.

Furthermore, education does not cease when the pupil leaves the school. No school fully achieves any pupil's goals in the relatively short time he spends in the classroom. The school seeks rather to equip the pupil to achieve them for himself. Thus the search for a definition of the school's necessary contribution entails an understanding of the ways individuals and societies choose and achieve their goals. Because the school must serve both individuals and the society at large in achieving their goals, and because the principal goal of the American society remains freedom, the requirements of freedom set the frame within which the school can discover the central focus of its own efforts.

The freedom which exalts the individual, and by which the worth of the society is judged, has many dimensions. It means freedom from undue governmental restraints; it means equality in political participation. It means the right to earn and own property and decide its disposition. It means equal access to just processes of law. It means the right to worship according to one's conscience.

Institutional safeguards are a necessary condition for freedom. They are not, however, sufficient to make man free. Freedom requires that citizens act responsibly in all ways. It cannot be preserved in a society whose citizens do not value freedom. Thus belief in freedom is essential to maintenance of freedom. The basis of this belief cannot be laid by mere indoctrination in principles of freedom. The ability to recite the values of a free society does not guarantee commitment to those values. Active belief in those values depends on awareness of them and of their role in life. The person who best supports these values is one who has examined them, who understands their function in his life and in the society at large, and who accepts them as worthy of his own support. For such a person these values are consciously held and consciously approved.

The conditions necessary for freedom include the social institutions which protect freedom and the personal commitment which gives it force. Both of these conditions rest on one condition within the individuals who compose a free society. This is freedom of the mind.

Freedom of the mind is a condition which each individual must develop for himself. In this sense, no man is born free. A free society has the obligation to create circumstances in which all individuals may have opportunity and encouragements to attain freedom of the mind. If this goal is to be achieved, its requirements must be specified.

To be free, a man must be capable of basing his choices and actions on understandings which he himself achieves and on values which he examines for himself. He must be aware of the bases on which he accepts propositions as true. He must understand the values by which he lives, the assumptions on which they rest, and the consequences to which they lead. He must recognize that others may have different values. He must be capable of analyzing the situation in which he finds himself and of developing solutions to the problem before him. He must be able to perceive and understand the events of his life and time and the forces that influence and shape those events. He must recognize and accept the practical limitations which time and circumstance place on his choices. The free man, in short, has a rational grasp of himself, his surroundings, and the relation between them.

To be free, a man must be capable of basing his choices and actions on understandings which he himself achieves and on values which he examines for himself. He must be aware of the bases on which he accepts propositions as true.

He has the freedom to think and choose, and that freedom must have its roots in conditions both within and around the individual. Society's dual role is to guarantee the necessary environment and to develop the necessary individual strength. That individual strength springs from a thinking, aware mind, a mind that possesses the capacity to achieve aesthetic sensitivity and moral responsibility, an enlightened mind. These qualities occur in a wide diversity of patterns in different individuals. It is the contention of this essay that central to all of them, nurturing them and being nurtured by them, are the rational powers of man.

The Central Role of the Rational Powers

The cultivated powers of the free mind have always been basic in achieving freedom. The powers of the free mind are many. In addition to the rational powers, there are those which relate to the aesthetic, the moral, and the religious. There is a unique, central role for the rational powers of an individual, however, for upon them depends his ability to achieve his personal goals and to fulfill his obligations to society.

These powers involve the processes of recalling and imagining, classifying and generalizing, comparing and evaluating, analyzing and synthesizing, and deducing and inferring. These processes enable one to apply logic and the available evidence to his ideas, attitudes, and actions, and to pursue better whatever goals he may have.

This is not to say that the rational powers are all of life or all of the mind, but they are the essence of the ability to think. A thinking person is aware that all persons, himself included, are both rational and nonrational, that each person perceives events through the screen of his own personality, and that he must take account of his personality in evaluating his perceptions. The rational processes, moreover, make intelligent choices possible. Through them a person can become aware of the bases of choice in his values and of the circum-

stances of choice in his environment. Thus they are broadly applicable in life, and they provide a solid basis for competence in all the areas with which the school has traditionally been concerned.

These powers involve the processes of recalling and imagining, classifying and generalizing, comparing and evaluating, analyzing and synthesizing, and deducing and inferring. These processes enable one to apply logic and the available evidence to his ideas, attitudes, and actions, and to pursue better whatever goals he may have.

This is not to say that the rational powers are all of life or all of the mind, but they are the essence of the ability to think. The traditionally accepted obligation of the school to teach the *fundamental processes*—an obligation stressed in the 1918 and 1938 statements of educational purposes—is obviously directed toward the development of the ability to think. Each of the school's other traditional objectives can be better achieved as pupils develop this ability and learn to apply it to all the problems that face them.

Health, for example, depends upon a reasoned awareness of the value of mental and physical fitness and of the means by which it may be developed and maintained. Fitness is not merely a function of living and acting; it requires that the individual understand the connection among health, nutrition, activity, and environment, and that he take action to improve his mental and physical condition.

Worthy home membership in the modern age demands substantial knowledge of the role that the home and community play in human development. The person who understands the bases of his own judgments recognizes the home as the source from which most individuals develop most of the standards and values they apply in their lives. He is intelligently aware of the role of emotion in his own life and in the lives of others. His knowledge of the importance of the home environment in the formation of personality enables him to make reasoned judgments about his domestic behavior.

More than ever before, and for an ever-increasing proportion of the population, *vocational competence* requires developed rational capacities. The march of technology and science in the modern society progressively eliminates the positions open to low-level talents. The man able to use only his hands is at a growing disadvantage as compared with the man who can also use his head. Today even the simplest use of hands is coming to require the simultaneous employment of the mind.

> *The march of technology and science in the modern society progressively eliminates the positions open to low-level talents. The man able to use only his hands is at a growing disadvantage. . . .*

Effective citizenship is impossible without the ability to think. The good citizen, the one who contributes effectively and responsibly to the management of the public business in a free society, can fill his role only if he is aware of the values of his society. Moreover, the course of events in modern life is such that many of the factors which influence an individual's civic life are increasingly remote from him. His own firsthand experience is no longer an adequate basis for judgment. He must have in addition the intellectual means to study events, to relate his values to them, and to make wise decisions as to his own actions. He must also be skilled in the process of communication and must understand both the potentialities and the limitations of communication among individuals and groups.

The worthy use of leisure is related to the individual's knowledge, understanding, and capacity to choose, from among all the activities to which his time can be devoted, those which contribute to the achievement of his purposes and to the satisfaction of his needs. On these bases, the individual can become aware of the external pressures which compete for his attention, moderate the influence of these pressures, and make wise choices for himself. His recreation, ranging from hobbies to sports to intellectual activity pursued for its own sake, can conform to his own concepts of constructive use of time.

The development of *ethical character* depends upon commitment to values; it depends also upon the ability to reason sensitively and responsibly with respect to those values in specific situations. Character is misunderstood if thought of as mere conformity to standards imposed by external authority. In a free society, ethics, morality, and character have meaning to the extent that they represent affirmative, thoughtful choices by individuals. The ability to make these choices depends on awareness of values and of their role in life. The home and the church begin to shape the child's values long before he goes to school. And a person who grows up in the American society inevitably acquires many values from his daily pattern of living. American children at the age of six, for example, usually have a firm commitment to the concept of fair play. This is a value which relates directly to such broad democratic concepts as justice and human worth and dignity. But the extension of this commitment to these broader democratic values will not occur unless the child becomes aware of its implications for his own behavior, and this awareness demands the ability to think.

A person who understands and appreciates his own values is most likely to act on them. He learns that his values are of great moment for himself, and he can look objectively and sympathetically at the values held by others. Thus, by critical thinking, he can deepen his respect for the importance of values and strengthen his sense of responsibility.

The man who seeks to understand himself understands also that other human beings have much in common with him. His understanding of the possibilities which exist within a human being strengthens his concept of the respect due every man. He recognizes the web which relates him to other men and perceives the necessity for responsible behavior. The person whose rational powers are not well developed can, at best, learn habitual responses and ways of conforming which may insure that he is not a detriment to his society. But, lacking the insight that he might have achieved, his capacity to contribute will inevitably be less than it might have become.

> *The person whose rational powers are not well developed can, at best, learn habitual responses and ways of conforming which may insure that he is not a detriment to his society. But, lacking the insight that he might have achieved, his capacity to contribute will inevitably be less than it might have become.*

Development of the ability to reason can lead also to dedication to the values which inhere in rationality: commitment to honesty, accuracy, and personal reliability; respect for the intellect and for the intellectual life; devotion to the expansion of knowledge. A man who thinks can understand the importance of this ability. He is likely to value the rational potentials of mankind as essential to a worthy life.

Thus the rational powers are central to all the other qualities of the human spirit. These powers flourish in a humane and morally responsible context and contribute to the entire personality. The rational powers are to the entire human spirit as the hub is to the wheel.

These powers are indispensable to a full and worthy life. The person in whom—for whatever reason—they are not well developed is increasingly handicapped in modern society. He may be able to satisfy minimal social standards, but he will inevitably lack his full measure of dignity because his incapacity limits his stature to less than he might otherwise attain. Only to the extent that an individual can realize his potentials, especially the development of his ability to think, can he fully achieve for himself the dignity that goes with freedom.

A person with developed rational powers has the means to be aware of all facets of his existence. In this sense he can live to the fullest. He can escape captivity to his emotions and irrational states. He can enrich his emotional life and direct it toward ever higher standards of taste and enjoyment. He can enjoy the political and economic freedoms of the democratic society. He can free himself from the bondage of ignorance and unawareness. He can make of himself a free man.

The Changes in Man's Understanding and Power

The foregoing analysis of human freedom and review of the central role of the rational powers in enabling a person to achieve his own goals demonstrate the critical importance of developing those powers. Their importance is also demonstrated by an analysis of the great changes in the world.

Many profound changes are occurring in the world today, but there is a fundamental force contributing to all of them. That force is the expanding role accorded in modern life to the rational powers of man. By using these powers to increase his knowledge, man is attempting to solve the riddles of life, space, and time which have long intrigued him. By using these powers to develop sources of new energy and means of communication, he is moving into interplanetary space. By using these powers to make a smaller world and larger weapons, he is creating new needs for international organization and understanding. By using these powers to alleviate disease and poverty, he is lowering death rates and expanding populations. By using these powers to create and use a new technology, he is achieving undreamed affluence, so that in some societies distribution has become a greater problem than production.

While man is using the powers of his mind to solve old riddles, he is creating new ones. Basic assumptions upon which mankind has long operated are being challenged or demolished. The age-old resignation to poverty and inferior status for the masses of humanity is being replaced by a drive for a life of dignity for all. Yet, just as man achieves a higher hope for all mankind, he sees also the opening of a grim age in which expansion of the power to create is matched by a perhaps greater enlargement of the power to destroy.

As man sees his power expand, he is coming to realize that the common sense which he accumulates from his own experience is not a sufficient guide to the understanding of the events in his own life or of the nature of the physical world. And, with combined uneasiness and exultation, he senses that his whole way of looking at life may be challenged in a time when men are returning from space.

Through the ages, man has accepted many kinds of propositions as truth, or at least as bases sufficient for action. Some propositions have been accepted on grounds of superstition; some on grounds of decree, dogma, or custom; some on humanistic, aesthetic, or religious grounds; some on common sense. Today, the role of knowledge derived from rational inquiry is growing. For this there are several reasons.

In the first place, knowledge so derived has proved to be man's most efficient weapon for achieving power over his environment. It prevails because it works.

More than effectiveness, however, is involved. There is high credibility in a proposition which can be arrived at or tested by persons other than those who advance it. Modesty, too, is inherent in rational inquiry, for it is an attempt to free explanations of phenomena and events from subjective preference and human authority, and to subject such explanations to validation through experience. Einstein's concept of the curvature of space cannot be demonstrated to the naked eye and may offend common sense; but persons who cannot apply the mathematics necessary to comprehend the concept can still accept it. They do this, not on Einstein's authority, but on their awareness that he used rational methods to achieve it and that those who possess the ability and facilities have tested its rational consistency and empirical validity.

In recent decades, man has greatly accelerated his systematic efforts to gain insight through rational inquiry. In the physical and biological sciences and in mathematics, where he has most successfully applied these methods, he has in a short time accumulated a vast fund of knowledge so reliable as to give him power he has never before had to understand, to predict, and to act. That is why attempts are constantly being made to apply these methods to additional areas of learning and human behavior.

The rapid increase in man's ability to understand and change the world and himself has resulted from increased application of his powers of thought. These powers have proved to be his most potent resource, and, as such, the likely key to his future.

The Central Purpose of the School

The rational powers of the human mind have always been basic in establishing and preserving freedom. In furthering personal and social effectiveness they are becoming more important than ever. They are central to individual dignity, human progress, and national survival.

> *The rapid increase in man's ability to understand and change the world and himself has resulted from increased application of his powers of thought.*

The individual with developed rational powers can share deeply in the freedoms his society offers and can contribute most to the preservation of those freedoms. At the same time, he will have the best chance of understanding and contributing to the great events of his time. And the society which best develops the rational potentials of its people, along with their intuitive and aesthetic capabilities, will have the best chance of flourishing in the future. To help every person develop those powers is therefore a profoundly important objective and one which increases in importance with the passage of time. By pursuing this objective, the school can enhance spiritual and aesthetic values and the other cardinal purposes which it has traditionally served and must continue to serve.

The purpose which runs through and strengthens all other educational purposes—the common thread of education—is the development of the ability to think. This is the central purpose to which the school must be oriented if it is to accomplish either its traditional tasks or those newly accentuated by recent changes in the world. To say that it is central is not to say that it is the sole purpose or in all circumstances the most important purpose, but that it must be a pervasive concern in the world of the school. Many agencies contribute to achieving educational objectives, but this particular objective will not be generally attained unless the school focuses on it. In this context, therefore, the development of every student's rational powers must be recognized as centrally important.

Part II: Achieving the Central Purpose

It is no easy matter to adopt school programs to this central purpose. To make an enduring change in a mind which has already had some years of experience is among the most complex of all human enterprises. Although the school's obligation to develop the ability to think is widely accepted, there is much uncertainty as to the procedures most likely to achieve that objective. There is a great need to learn more than is now known about how men think, what

rationality and creativity are, how they can be strengthened, and how the opportunities of the school can best be employed to develop whatever rational potential a child may have.

The Need for Further Research

Development of rational powers is unfortunately an area of relative neglect in research. The emphasis of recent research has been on the conditions under which learning occurs and on the pathological aspects of learning in specific situations. The psychology of thinking itself is not well understood. The process of inference, for example, can be described as a leap from a given body of data to a conclusion suggested but not guaranteed by the data, and therefore in need of validation. Although the logic of this process may be thus stated, its psychology remains little known. Considerable research would need to be done before one could, with reasonable assurance, design a program of study that would develop the ability to make valid inference.

> *The purpose which runs through and strengthens all other educational purposes—the common thread of education—is the development of the ability to think.*

Research by Thorndike, Woodworth, Cattell, James, and others disproved early theories of faculty psychology and mental discipline. But these psychologists did not fully develop a theory of the processes by which knowledge and skills are transferred to new situations and reorganized in new generalizations. Yet such transfer and reorganization obviously occur.

Another gap in research on learning relates to apparent inability, or very low ability, to deal with high-level abstractions. Some pupils appear to lack potential for significant development of the rational powers. Yet, except perhaps in cases of physical damage to the brain, the reasons for this apparent lack are not understood. Psychological studies increasingly reveal unsuspected potential for growth in the development of human beings. Abilities sometimes appear to vary with environment. What is needed is an understanding of the influence of early environment on the susceptibility of the rational powers to development. Ways might then be found to overcome the effects of inadequate early environment.

There is no known upper limit to human ability, and much of what people are capable of doing with their minds is probably unknown today. In this sense, it can hardly be said that any person has ever done the best he can. Research might make possible for all people constantly higher levels of aspiration and attainment.

Thus, in the general area of the development of the ability to think, there is a field for new research of the greatest importance. It is essential that those who have responsibility for management and policy determination in education commit themselves to expansion of such research and to the application of the fruits of this research. This is the context in which the significant answers to such issues as educational must be sought and given. A new emphasis on this field by educational research may be expected to yield great dividends to the individual citizen and to the nation as a whole. And it would endow with greater substance America's belief in freedom and equal opportunity.

Prerequisites of Rationality

The school must be guided, in pursuing its central purpose or any other purposes, by certain conditions which are known to be basic to significant mental development. The school has responsibility to establish and maintain these conditions.

One of them is physical health. The sick or poorly nourished pupil, the pupil suffering from poor hearing or vision, is hampered in learning. An adequate physical basis for intellectual life must be assured.

Mental health is also of profound importance. With it, the pupil can have that desire and respect for learning which promote the satisfactory development of his capacity for effective mental performance. Without it, the likelihood of such development is drastically reduced, if not rendered impossible. The pupil who is unduly apprehensive, is hampered in his learning; and he frequently hampers the learning of others. As the child is helped to view himself and the society in a healthy way, to develop self-discipline, and to feel secure in his relationships, he becomes better able to respond positively to the school.

It is a responsibility of the society to identify and combat the forces which militate against healthy growth; but the school must also deal with the pupil as he is. Rapport must be established with every pupil, and when emotional maladjustment impedes progress or when motivation is lacking, the school must help him cope with his personal difficulties. It must create the conditions in which the school experience can mean something to him. This may require starting from programs with limited use of the higher intellectual processes and planning for him a sequence of stimulating activities to engage and expand his interests and progressively to raise the level at which he is able to attack problems.

This may require starting from programs with limited use of the higher intellectual processes and planning for him a sequence of stimulating activities to engage and expand his interests and progressively to raise the level at which he is able to attack problems.

The school must be guided in all things by a recognition of human individuality. Each pupil is unique. He is different in background, in interests, moods, and tastes. This uniqueness deeply affects his learning, for he can react to the school only in terms of the person he is. No two pupils necessarily learn the same thing from a common learning experience. The school must not only recognize differences among pupils; it must deal with each pupil as an individual.

While the development of rational powers is central among the several important purposes of the schools provided for all youth, the ability to utilize such opportunity varies considerably. The schools must meet the needs of those who are handicapped in their rational powers by cultural deprivation, low levels of family aspiration, or severely limited endowment. Hence, to take account of these and other individual needs and differences, the schools must and should vary the relative emphasis they place on the development of rational powers among their other important purposes.

Developing Rational Powers

Although research has not yet yielded a firm base for planning programs to develop intellectual power, the research which has been done, combined with the experience of teachers, does provide some guidance.

The school which develops the ability to think is itself a place where thought is respected and where the humane value; implicit in rationality are honored. It has an atmosphere conducive to thinking, and it rewards its pupils for progress toward the goals that it values. Such a school consciously strives to develop its pupils' rational powers. It achieves its goals because it aims directly at them.

The rational powers of any person are developed gradually and continuously as and when he uses them successfully. There is no evidence that they can be developed in any other way. They do not emerge quickly or without effort. The learner of any age, therefore, must have the desire to develop his ability to think. Motivation of this sort rests on feelings of personal adequacy and is reinforced by successful experience. Thus the learner must be encouraged in his early efforts to grapple with

problems that engage his rational abilities at their current level of development, and he must experience success in these efforts.

The rational powers of any person are developed gradually and continuously as and when he uses them successfully. There is no evidence that they can be developed in any other way.

The teacher has the critical role in enabling the student to achieve these successes, selecting problems which are within his grasp, providing clues and cues to their solution, suggesting alternative ways to think about them and assessing continuously the progress of the pupil and the degree of difficulty of the problems before him. Good teaching can help students to learn to think clearly. But his can be done only by careful selection of teaching procedures deliberately adapted to each learner.

Choice as to methods and means of developing the ability to think is necessarily in the hands of the individual teacher. Professional and lay assistance may be brought into the classroom, but the intimate awareness of changes in pupils which permits evaluation of progress cannot be possessed by persons who have only limited or irregular contact with the pupils. It is therefore crucial that the teacher possess a thorough knowledge of the material to be taught, a mature mastery of a variety of teaching procedures, an understanding of his pupils, and the quality of judgment that will enable him to blend all in making decisions.

Study of an abstract subject like mathematics or philosophy, in and of itself, does not necessarily enhance rational powers, and it is possible that experiences in areas which appear to have little connection may in fact make a substantial contribution to rational development. As a case in point, the abilities involved in perceiving and recognizing pattern in a mass of abstract data are of considerable importance in learning to analyze, deduce, or infer. These abilities may be developed in the course of mathematical study; but they may be developed as well through experiences in aesthetic, humanistic, and practical fields, which also involve perception of form and design. Music, for example, challenges the listener to perceive elements of form within the abstract. Similarly, vocational subjects may engage the rational powers of pupils.

Also, there is a highly creative aspect in the processes of thought. All the higher mental processes involve more than simple awareness of facts; they depend also on the ability to conceive what might be as well as what is, to construct mental images in new and original ways. Experiences in literature and the arts may well make a large contribution to these abilities than studies usually assumed to develop abstract thinking.

Further, the processes of thought demand the ability to integrate perceptions of objective phenomena with judgments of value in which subjective emotional commitments are important elements. Perceptions of the feelings of individuals—one's own and those of others— also provide data for the processes of thought. There is no assurance that the ability to perceive or to integrate these varied elements is acquired by abstract study alone.

No particular body of knowledge will of itself develop the ability to think clearly. The development of this ability depends instead on methods that encourage the transfer of learning from one context to another and the reorganization of things learned. The child can transfer learning when he is challenged to give thought to the solution of new problems, problems in which he becomes interested because they are within his range of comprehension, problems that make him strive to use fully his developed and developing abilities.

Although the substance of knowledge does not of itself convey intellectual power, it is the raw material of thought. The ability to think cannot be developed or applied without subject matter. There are two bases for choosing the substantive knowledge which pupils should learn. One is the potential of the knowledge for development of rational powers, the other is the relative importance of the knowledge in the life of the pupil and of society.

The ability to think cannot be developed or applied without subject matter. There are two bases for choosing the substantive knowledge which pupils should learn. One is the potential of the knowledge for development of rational powers, the other is the relative importance of the knowledge in the life of the pupil and of society.

The social sciences, for example, provide an excellent opportunity to acquire knowledge which is of considerable importance in daily living and simultaneously to improve the ability to analyze, compare, generalize, and evaluate information. Individual and social interests alike require that the citizen understand the nature and traditions of the free society and that he have skill and insight in studying the issues which his society faces. This requires the tools of the historian, economist, political scientist, sociologist, geographer, and anthropologist. The pupil who learns to use these tools and to integrate the insights to which they lead will improve his ability to think wisely about social problems and to acquire information of significance to himself and his society. He will also develop a sense of the complexity of society and the difficulties which lie in the path of those who would understand it and meet its problems.

The school must foster not only desire and respect for knowledge but also the inquiring spirit. It must encourage the pupil to ask: "How do I know?" as well as "What do I know?" Consequently, the school must help the pupil grasp some of the main methods—the strategies of inquiry—by which man has sought to extend his knowledge and understanding of the world. This requires emphasis on the strategies that have proved most successful. The students should, for example, develop some understanding of the methods of inquiry characteristic of the natural and social sciences. Educators, working with experts in the various disciplines, should choose content on the basis of its appropriateness for developing in pupils of various ages understanding of the various strategies of inquiry.

Application of these strategies of inquiry has led not only to substantive knowledge of the object world, but also to insights into the nature of reality and of the place of man in the general scheme of things. The free mind is aware of these insights: the astronomers' view of the vastness of space, the physicist's view of the almost infinitesimal, the biologist's view of endless change, the geologist's view of the infinity of time, the historian's view of continuity, the anthropologist's view of human variation.

In acquainting students with the strategies of inquiry, the teacher can further their ability to identify and qualify generalizations, to recognize statements which are not and perhaps cannot be supported by data, to move from data to appropriate generalizations, and to project new hypotheses.

> *The free mind is aware of these insights: the astronomers' view of the vastness of space, the physicist's view of the almost infinitesimal, the biologist's view of endless change, the geologist's view of the infinity of time, the historian's view of continuity, the anthropologist's view of human variation.*

Emphasis on the strategies of inquiry can have the additional effects of arousing appreciation of the competence and work of the masters of these fields of learning and of contributing to the ability to reach the decisions required by responsible citizenship today.

In addition to seeking development of the specific rational powers, the school must help the student extend the areas of his life to which he applies them. Thus the school goes beyond the experiences which develop thinking to encourage the student to think about his environment and himself, to use his mind to make of himself a good citizen and contributing person. Through his ability to perceive form and design he can appreciate the role of beauty in his life. His awareness of his values and his reasoned commitment of them provide him with a basis for looking objectively at his own values and those of others and thus for achieving a moral life. The school should encourage the student to live the life of dignity which rationality fosters.

Part III: Conclusion

Individual freedom and effectiveness and the progress of the society require the development of every citizen's rational powers. Among the many important purposes of American schools the fostering of that development must be central.

Man has already transformed his world by using his mind. As he expands the application of rational methods to problems old and new, and as people in growing numbers are enabled to contribute to such endeavors, man will increase his ability to understand, to act, and to alter his environment. Where these developments will lead cannot be foretold.

Man has before him the possibility of a new level of greatness, a new realization of human dignity and effectiveness. The instrument which will realize this possibility is that kind of education which frees the mind and enables it to contribute to a full and worthy life. To achieve this goal is the high hope of the nation and the central challenge to its schools.

THE METHOD OF MULTIPLE WORKING HYPOTHESES

T. C. Chamberlain

With this method the dangers of parental affection
for a favorite theory can be circumvented.

As methods of study constitute the leading theme of our session, I have chosen as a subject in measurable consonance the method of multiple working hypotheses in its application to investigation, instruction, and citizenship.

There are two fundamental classes of study. The one consists in attempting to following by close imitation the processes of previous thinkers, or to acquire by memorizing the results of their investigations. It is merely secondary, imitative, or acquisitive study. The other class is primary or creative study. In it the effort is to think independently, or at least individually, in the endeavor to discover new truth, or to make new combinations of truth, or at least to develop an individualized aggregation of truth. The endeavor is to think for one's self, whether the thinking lies wholly in the fields of previous thought or not. It is not necessary to this habit of study that the subject-material should be new; but the process of thought and its

results must be individual and independent, not the mere following of previous lines of thought ending in predetermined results. The demonstration of a problem in Euclid precisely as laid down is an illustration of the former; the demonstration of the same proposition by a method of one's own or in a manner distinctively individual is an illustration of the latter; both lying entirely within the realm of the known and the old.

> *There are two fundamental classes of study. The one consists in attempting to following by close imitation the processes of previous thinkers, or to acquire by memorizing the results of their investigations. It is merely secondary, imitative, or acquisitive study. The other class is primary or creative study.*

Creative study, however, finds its largest application in those subjects in which, while much is known, more remains to be known. Such are the fields which we, as naturalists, cultivate; and we are gathered for the purpose of developing improved methods lying largely

"The Method of Multiple Working Hypotheses," *Science,* Vol. 148 (May 7, 1965), pp. 754–759. Copyright 1965 by the American Association for the Advancement of Science. Reprinted by permission. (Originally published in 1898.)

in the creative phase of study, though not wholly so.

Intellectual methods have taken three phases in the history of progress thus far. What may be the evolutions of the future it may not be prudent to forecast. Naturally the methods we now urge seem the highest attainable. These three methods may be designated, first, the method of the ruling theory; second, the method of the working hypothesis; and, third, the method of multiple working hypotheses.

In the earlier days of intellectual development the sphere of knowledge was limited, and was more nearly within the compass of a single individual; and of knowing, or at least seeming to know, all that was known as a justification of their claims. So, also, there grew up an expectancy on the part of the multitude that the wise and the learned would explain whatever new thing presented itself. Thus pride and ambition on the one hand, and expectancy on the other, developed the putative wise man whose knowledge boxed the compass, and whose acumen found an explanation for every new puzzle which presented itself. This disposition has propagated itself and has come down to our time as an intellectual predilection, though the compassing of the entire horizon of knowledge has long since been an abandoned affection. As in the earlier days, so still, it is the habit of some to hastily conjure up an explanation for every new phenomenon that presents itself. Interpretation rushes to the forefront as the chief obligation pressing upon the putative wise man. Laudable as the effort at explanation is in itself, it is to be condemned when it runs before a serious inquiry into the phenomenon itself. A dominant disposition to find out what is, should precede and crowd aside the question, commendable at a later stage, "How came this so?" First full facts, then interpretations.

It is the habit of some to hastily conjure up an explanation for every new phenomenon that presents itself.

Premature Theories

The habit of precipitate explanation leads rapidly on to the development of tentative theories. The explanation offered for a given phenomenon is naturally, under the impulse of self-consistency, offered for like phenomena as they present themselves and there is soon developed a general theory explanatory of a large class of phenomena similar to the original one. This general theory may not be supported by any further considerations than those which were involved in the first hasty inspection. For a time it is likely to be held in a tentative way with a measure of candor. With this tentative spirit and measurable candor, the mind satisfies its moral sense, and deceives itself with the thought that it is proceeding cautiously and impartially toward the goal of ultimate truth. It fails to recognize that no amount of provisional holding of a theory, so long as the view is limited and the investigation partial, justifies an ultimate conviction. It is not the slowness with which conclusions are arrived at that should give satisfaction to the moral sense, but the thoroughness, the completeness, and all-sidedness, the impartiality, of the investigation.

It is in this tentative stage that the affections enter with their blinding influence. Love was long since represented as blind, and what is true in the personal realm is measurably true in the intellectual realm. Important as the intellectual affections are as stimuli and as rewards, they are nevertheless dangerous factors which menace the integrity of the intellectual processes. The moment one has offered an original explanation for a phenomenon which seems satisfactory, that moment affection for his intellectual child springs into existence; and as the explanation grows into a definite theory, his parental affections cluster about his intellectual offspring, and it grows more and more dear to him, so that, while he holds it seemingly tentative, it is still lovingly tentative, and not impartially tentative. So soon as this parental affection takes possession of the mind, there is a rapid passage to the adoption of the theory. There is an unconscious selection and magnifying of the phenomena that fall into harmony with the theory and support it, and an unconscious neglect of those that fail of coincidence. The mind lingers with pleasure upon the facts that fall happily into the embrace of the theory, and feels a natural coldness toward those that seem refractory. Instinctively there is a special searching-out of phenomena that support it, for the mind is led by its desires. There springs up, also, an unconscious pressing of the theory to make it fit the facts, and a pressing of the facts to make them fit the theory. When these biasing tendencies set in, the mind rapidly degenerates into the partiality of paternalism. The search for facts, the observation of phenomena and their interpretation, are all dominated by affection for the favored theory until it appears to its author or its advocate to have been overwhelmingly established. The theory then rapidly rises to the ruling position, and investigation, observation, and interpretation are controlled and directed by it. From an unduly favored child, it readily becomes master and leads its author whithersoever it will. The subsequent history of that mind in respect to that theme is but the progressive dominance of a ruling idea.

The moment one has offered an original explanation for a phenomenon which seems satisfactory, that moment affection for his intellectual child springs into existence;

Briefly summed up, the evolution is this: a premature explanation passes into a tentative theory, then into an adopted theory, and then into a ruling theory.

When the last stage has been reached, unless the theory happens, perchance, to be the true one, all hope of the best results is gone. To be sure, truth may be brought forth by an investigator dominated by a false ruling idea. His very errors may indeed stimulate investigation on the part of others. But the condition is an unfortunate one. Dust and chaff are mingled with the grain in what should be a winnowing process.

Ruling Theories Linger

As previously implied, the method of the ruling theory occupied a chief place during the infancy of investigation. It is an expression of the natural infantile tendencies of the mind, though in this case applied to its higher activities, for in the earlier stages of development the feeling are relatively greater than in later stages.

Unfortunately it did not wholly pass away with the infancy of investigation, but has lingered along in individual instances to the present day, and finds illustration in universally learned men and pseudo-scientists of our time.

The defects of the method are obvious, and its errors great. If I were to name the central psychological fault, I should say that it was the admission of intellectual affection to the place that should be dominated by impartial intellectual rectitude.

So long as intellectual interest dealt chiefly with the intangible, so long it was possible for this habit of thought to survive, and to maintain its dominance, because the phenomena themselves, being largely subjective, were plastic in the hands of the ruling idea; but so soon as investigation turned itself earnestly to an inquiry into natural phenomena, whose manifestations are tangible, whose properties are rigid, whose laws are rigorous, the defects of the method became manifest, and an effort at reformation ensued. The first great endeavor was repressive. The advocates of reform insisted that theorizing should be restrained, and efforts directed to the simple determination of facts. The effort was to make scientific study factitious instead of casual. Because theorizing in narrow lines had led to manifest evils, theorizing was to be condemned. The reformation urged was not the proper control and utilization of theoretical effort, but its suppression.

We do not need to go backward more than twenty years to find ourselves in the midst of this attempted reformation. Its weakness lay in its narrowness and its restrictiveness. There is no nobler aspiration of the human intellect than desire to compass the cause of things. The disposition to find explanations and to develop theories is laudable in itself. It is only its ill use that is reprehensible. The vitality of study quickly disappears when the object sought is a mere collocation of dead unmeaning facts.

> *There is no nobler aspiration of the human intellect than desire to compass the cause of things. The disposition to find explanations and to develop theories is laudable in itself. It is only its ill use that is reprehensible. The vitality of study quickly disappears when the object sought is a mere collocation of dead unmeaning facts.*

The inefficiency of this simply repressive reformation becoming apparent, improvement was sought in the method of the working hypothesis. This is affirmed to be *the* scientific method of the day, but to this I take exception. The working hypothesis differs from the ruling theory in that it is used as a means of determining facts, and has for its chief function the suggestion of lines of inquiry; the inquiry being made, not for the sake of the hypothesis, but for the sake of facts. Under the method of the ruling theory, the stimulus was directed to the finding of facts for the support of the theory. Under the working hypothesis, the facts are sought for the purpose of ultimate induction and demonstration, the hypothesis being but a means for the more ready development of facts and of their relations, and the arrangement and preservation of material for the final induction.

It will be observed that the distinction is not a sharp one, and that a working hypothesis may with the utmost ease degenerate into a ruling theory, and the demonstration of the one may become a ruling passion as much as of the other.

A Family of Hypotheses

Conscientiously followed, the method of the working hypothesis is a marked improvement upon the method of the ruling theory; but it has its defects, defects which are perhaps best expressed by the ease with which the hypothesis becomes a controlling idea. To guard against this, the method of multiple working hypotheses is urged. It differs from the former method in the multiple character of its genetic conceptions and of its tentative interpretations. It is directed against the radical defect of the two other methods; namely, the partiality of intellectual parentage. The effort is to bring up into view every rational explanation of new phenomena, and to develop every tenable hypothesis respecting their cause and history. The investigator thus becomes the parent of a family of hypotheses; and, by his parental relation to all, he is forbidden to fasten his affections unduly upon any one. In the nature of the case, the danger that springs from affection is counteracted, and therein is a radical difference between this method and the two preceding. The investigator at the outset puts himself in cordial sympathy and in parental relations (of adoption, if not of authorship) with every hypothesis that is at all applicable to the case under investigation. Having thus neutralized the partialities of his emotional nature, he proceeds with a certain natural and enforced erectness of mental attitude to the investigation, knowing well that some of his intellectual children will die before maturity, yet feeling that several of them may survive the results of final investigation, since it is often the outcome of inquiry that several causes are found to be involved instead of a single one. In following a single hypothesis, the mind is presumably led to a single explanatory conception. But an adequate explanation often involves the co-ordination of several agencies, which enter into the combined result in varying proportions. The true explanation is therefore necessarily complex. Such complex explanations of phenomena are specially encouraged by the method of multiple hypotheses, and constitute one of its chief merits. We are so prone to attribute a phenomenon to a single cause, that, when we find an agency present, we are liable to rest satisfied therewith, and fail to recognize that it is but one factor, and perchance a minor factor, in the accomplishment of the total result. Take for illustration the mooted question of the origin of the Great Lake basins. We have this, that, and the other hypothesis urged by different students as the cause of these great excavations; and all of these are urged with force and with fact, urged justly to a certain degree. It is practically demonstrable that these basins were river-valleys antecedent to the glacial incursion, and that they owe their origin in part to the pre-existence of those valleys and to the blocking-up of their outlets. And so this view of their origin is urged with a certain truthfulness. So, again, it is demonstrable that they were occupied by great lobes of ice, which excavated them to a marked degree, and therefore the theory of glacial excavation finds support in fact. I think it is furthermore demonstrable that the earth's crust beneath these basins was flexed downward, and that they owe a part of their origin to crust deformation. But to my judgement neither the one more than the other, nor the third, constitutes an adequate explanation of the phenomena. All these must be taken together, and possibly they must be supplemented by other agencies. The problem, therefore, is the determination not only of the participation, but of the measure and the extent, of each of these agencies in the production of the complex result. This is not likely to be accomplished by one whose working hypothesis is preglacial erosion, or crust deformation, but by one whose staff of working hypothesis embraces all of these and any other agency which can be rationally conceived to have taken part in the phenomena.

Conscientiously followed, the method of the working hypothesis is a marked improvement upon the method of the ruling theory; but it has its defects, defects which are perhaps best expressed by the ease with which the hypothesis becomes a controlling idea. To guard against this, the method of multiple working hypotheses is urged.

A special merit of the method is, that by its very nature it promotes thoroughness. The value of a working hypothesis lies largely in its suggestiveness of lines of inquiry that might otherwise be overlooked. Facts that are trivial in themselves are brought into significance by their bearings upon the hypothesis; and by their causal indications. As an illustration, it is only necessary to cite the phenomenal influence which the Darwinian hypothesis has exerted upon the investigations of the past two decades. But a single working hypothesis may lead investigation along a given line to the neglect of others equally important; and thus, while inquiry is promoted in certain quarters, the investigation lacks in completeness. But if all rational hypotheses relating to a subject are worked co-equally, thoroughness is the presumptive result, in the very nature of the case.

In the use of the multiple method, the reaction of one hypothesis upon another tends to amplify the recognized scope of each, and their mutual conflicts whet the discriminative edge of each. The analytic process, the development and demonstration of criteria, and the sharpening of discrimination, receive powerful impulse from the co-ordinate working of several hypotheses.

Fertility in processes is also the natural outcome of the method. Each hypothesis suggests its own criteria, its own means of proof, its own methods of developing the truth; and if a group of hypotheses encompass the subject on all sides, the total outcome of means and of methods is full and rich.

The use of the method leads to certain peculiar habits of mind which deserve passing notice, since as a factor of education its disciplinary value is one of importance. When faithfully pursued for a period of years, it develops a habit of thought analogous to the method itself, which may be designated a habit of parallel or complex thought. Instead of a simple succession of thought in linear order, the procedure is complex, and the mind appears to become possessed of the power of simultaneous vision from different standpoints. Phenomena appear to become capable of being viewed analytically and synthetically at once. It is not altogether unlike the study of a landscape, from which there comes into the mind myriads of lines of intelligence, which are received and coordinated simultaneously, producing a complex impression which is recorded and studied directly in its complexity. My description of this process is confessedly inadequate, and the affirmation of it as a fact would doubtless challenge dispute at the hands of psychologists of the old school; but I address myself to naturalists who I think can respond to its verity from their own experience.

The use of the method leads to certain peculiar habits of mind which deserve passing notice, since as a factor of education its disciplinary value is one of importance. When faithfully pursued for a period of years, it develops a habit of thought analogous to the method itself, which may be designated a habit of parallel or complex thought.

Drawbacks of the Method

The method has, however, its disadvantages. No good thing is without its drawbacks; and this very habit of mind, while an invaluable acquisition for purposes of investigation, introduces difficulties in expression. It is obvious, upon consideration, that this method of thought is impossible of verbal expression. We cannot put into words more than a single line of thought at the same time; and even in that the order of expression must be conformed to the idiosyncrasies of the language, and the rate must be relatively slow. When the habit of complex thought is not highly developed, there is usually a leading line to which others are subordinate, and the difficulty of expression does not rise to serious proportions; but when the method of simultaneous vision along different lines is developed so that the thoughts running in different channels are nearly equivalent, there is an obvious embarrassment in selection and a disinclination to make the attempt. Furthermore, the impossibility of expressing the mental operation in words leads to their disuse in the silent process of thought, and hence words and thoughts lose that close association which they are accustomed to maintain with those whose silent as well as spoken thoughts run in linear verbal courses. There is therefore, a certain predisposition on the part of the practitioner of this method to taciturnity.

We encounter an analogous difficulty in the use of the method with young students. It is far easier, and I think in general more interesting, for them to argue a theory or accept a simple interpretation than to recognize and evaluate the several factors which the true elucidation may require. To illustrate: it is more to their taste to be taught that the Great Lake basins were scooped out by glaciers than to be urged to conceive of three or more great agencies working successively or simultaneously, and to estimate how much was accomplished by each of these agencies. The complex and the quantitative do not fascinate the young student as they do the veteran investigator.

Multiple Hypotheses and Practical Affairs

It has not been our custom to think of the method of working hypotheses as applicable to instruction or to the practical affairs of life. We have usually regarded it as but a method of science. But I believe its application to practical affairs has a value coordinate with the importance of the affairs themselves. I refer especially to those inquiries and inspections that precede the coming-out of an enterprise rather than to its actual execution. The methods that are superior in scientific investigation should likewise be superior in those investigations that are the necessary antecedent to an intelligent conduct of affairs. But I can dwell only briefly on this phase of the subject.

In education, as in investigation, it has been much the practice to work a theory. The search for instructional methods has often proceeded on the presumption that there is a definite patent process through which all students might be put and come out with results of maximum excellence; and hence pedagogical inquiry in the past has very largely concerned itself with the inquiry, "What is the best method?" rather than with the inquiry "What are the special values of different methods, and what are their several advantageous applicabilities in the varied work of instruction?" The past doctrine has been largely the doctrine of pedagogical uniformitarianism. But the faculties and functions of the mind are almost, if not quite, as varied as the properties and functions of matter; and it is perhaps not less absurd to assume that any specific method of instructional procedure is more effective than all others, under any and all applicable to all the phenomena of nature. As there is an endless variety of mental processes and combinations and an indefinite number of orders of procedure the advantage of different methods under different conditions is almost axiomatic. This being granted, there is presented to the teacher the problem of selection and of adaptation to meet the needs of any specific issue that may present itself. It is important, therefore, that the teacher shall have in mind a full array of possible conditions and states of mind which may be presented, in order that, when any one of these shall become an actual

case, he may recognize it, and be ready for the emergency.

Just as the investigator armed with many working hypotheses is more likely to see the true nature and significance of phenomena when they present themselves, so the instructor equipped with a full panoply of hypotheses ready for application more readily recognizes the actuality of the situation, more accurately measures its significance, and more appropriately applies the methods which the case calls for.

---

so the instructor equipped with a full panoply of hypotheses ready for application more readily recognizes the actuality of the situation, more accurately measures its significance, and more appropriately applies the methods which the case calls for.

The application of the method of multiple hypotheses to the varied affairs of life is almost as protean as the phases of that life itself, but certain general aspects may be taken as typical of the whole. What I have just said respecting the application of the method to instruction may apply, with a simple change of terms, to almost any other endeavor which we are called upon to undertake. We enter upon an enterprise in most cases without full knowledge of all the factors that will enter into it, or all of the possible phases which it may develop. It is therefore of the utmost importance to be prepared to rightly comprehend the nature, bearings, and influence of such unforeseen elements when they shall definitely present themselves as actualities. If our vision is narrowed by a preconceived theory as to what will happen, we are almost certain to misinterpret the facts and to misjudge the issue. If, on the other hand, we have in mind hypothetical forecasts of the various contingencies that may arise, we shall be the more likely to recognize the true facts when they do present themselves. Instead of being biased by the anticipation of a given phase, the mind is rendered open and alert by the anticipation of many phases, and is free not only, but is predisposed, to recognized correctly the one which does appear. The method has a further good effect. The mind, having anticipated the possible phases which may arise has prepared itself for action under any one that may come up, and it is therefore ready-armed, and is predisposed to act in the line appropriate to the event. It has not set itself rigidly in a fixed purpose, which it is predisposed to follow without regard to contingencies. It has not nailed down the helm and predetermined to run a specific course, whether rocks lie in the path or not; but, with the helm in hand, it is ready to veer the ship according as danger or advantage discovers itself.

It is true, there are often advantages in pursuing a fixed predetermined course without regard to obstacles or adverse conditions. Simple dogged resolution is sometimes the salvation of an enterprise; but, while glorious successes have been thus snatched from the very brink of disaster, overwhelming calamity has in other cases followed upon this course, when a reasonable regard for the unanticipated elements would have led to success. So there is to be set over against the great achievements that follow on dogged adherence great disasters which are equally its result.

Danger of Vacillation

The tendency of the mind, accustomed to work through multiple hypotheses, is to sway to one line of policy or another, according as the balance of evidence shall incline. This is the soul and essence of the method. It is in general the true method. Nevertheless there is a danger that this yielding to evidence may degenerate into unwarranted vacillation. It is not always possible for the mind to balance evidence with exact equipoise, and to determine, in the midst of the execution of an enterprise, what is the measure of probability on the one side or the other; and as difficulties

present themselves, there is a danger of being biased by them and of swerving from the course that was really the true one. Certain limitations are therefore to be placed upon the application of the method, for it must be remembered that a poorer line of policy consistently adhered to may bring better results than a vacillation between better policies.

Nevertheless there is a danger that this yielding to evidence may degenerate into unwarranted vacillation.

There is another and closely allied danger in the application of the method. In its highest development it presumes a mind supremely sensitive to every grain of evidence. Like a pair of delicately poised scales, every added particle on the one side or the other produces its effect in oscillation. But such a pair of delicately poised scales, every added particle on the one side or the other produces its effect in oscillation. But such a pair of scales may be altogether too sensitive to be of practical value in the rough affairs of life. The balances of the exact chemist are too delicate for the weighing-out of coarse commodities. Despatch may be more important than accuracy. So it is possible for the mind to be too much concerned with the nice balancings of evidence, and to oscillate too much and too long in the endeavor to reach exact results. It may be better, in the gross affairs of life, to be less precise and more prompt. Quick decisions, though they may contain a grain of error, are oftentimes better than precise decisions at the expense of time.

The method has a special beneficent application to our social and civic relations. Into these relations there enter, as great factors, our judgment of others, our discernment of the nature of their acts, and our interpretation of their motives and purposes. The method of multiple hypotheses, in its application here, stands in decided contrast to the method of the ruling theory or of the simple working hypothesis. The primitive habit is to interpret the acts of others on the basis of a theory. Childhood's unconscious theory is that the good are good, and the bad are bad. From the good the child expects nothing but good; from the bad, nothing but bad. To expect a good act from the bad, or a bad act from the good, is radically at variance with childhood's mental methods. Unfortunately in our social and civic affairs too many of our fellow-citizens have never outgrown the ruling theory of their childhood.

Many have advanced a step farther, and employ a method analogous to that of the working hypothesis. A certain presumption is made to attach to the acts of their fellow-beings, and that which they see is seen in the light of that presumption, and that which they construe is construed in the light of that presumption. They do not go to the lengths of childhood's method by assuming positively that the good are wholly good, and the bad wholly bad; but there is a strong presumption in their minds that he concerning whom they have an ill opinion will act from corresponding motives. It requires positive evidence to overthrow the influence of the working hypothesis.

The method of multiple hypotheses assumes broadly that the acts of a fellow-being may be diverse in their nature, their motives, their purposes, and hence in their whole moral character; that they may be good though the dominant character be bad; that they may be bad though the dominant character be good; that they may be partly good and partly bad, as is the fact in the greater number of the complex activities of a human being. Under the method of multiple hypotheses, it is the first effort of the mind to see truly what the act is, unbeclouded by the presumption that this or that has been done because it accords with our ruling theory or our working hypothesis. Assuming that acts of similar general aspect may readily take any one of several different phases, the mind is freer to see accurately what has actually been done. So, again, in our interpretations of motives and purposes, the method

assumes that these may have been any one of many, and the first duty is to ascertain which of possible motives and purposes actually prompted this individual action. Going with this effort there is a predisposition to balance all evidence fairly, and to accept that interpretation to which the weight of evidence inclines, not that which simply fits our working hypothesis or our dominant theory. The outcome, therefore, is better and truer observation and juster and more righteous interpretation.

> *Going with this effort there is a predisposition to balance all evidence fairly, and to accept that interpretation to which the weight of evidence inclines, not that which simply fits our working hypothesis or our dominant theory. The outcome, therefore, is better and truer observation and juster and more righteous interpretation.*

Imperfections of Knowledge

There is a third result of great importance. The imperfections of our knowledge are more likely to be detected, for there will be less confidence in its completeness in proportion as there is a broad comprehension of the possibilities of varied action, under similar circumstances and with similar appearances. So, also, there will be a less inclination to misapply evidence; for, several constructions being definitely in mind, the indices of the one motive are less liable to be mistaken for the indices of another.

The total outcome is great care in ascertaining the facts, and greater discrimination and caution in drawing conclusions. I am confident, therefore, that the general application of this method to the affairs of social and civic life would go far to remove those misunderstandings, misjudgments and misrepresentation which constitute so pervasive an evil in our social and our political atmospheres, the source of immeasurable suffering to the best and most sensitive souls. The misobservations, the misstatements, the misinterpretations, of life may cause less gross suffering than some other evils; but they, being more universal and more subtle, pain. The remedy lies, indeed, partly in charity, but more largely in correct intellectual habits, in a predominant, ever-present disposition to see things as they are, and to judge them in the full light of an unbiased weighing of evidence applied to all possible constructions, accompanied by a withholding of judgment when the evidence is insufficient to justify conclusions.

> *I am confident, therefore, that the general application of this method to the affairs of social and civic life would go far to remove those misunderstandings, misjudgments and misrepresentation which constitute so pervasive an evil in our social and our political atmospheres, the source of immeasurable suffering to the best and most sensitive souls.*

I believe that one of the greatest moral reforms that lies immediately before us consists in the general introduction into social and civic life of that habit of mental procedure which is known in investigation as the method of multiple working hypotheses.

APPENDIX C

WHAT IS SCIENCE?

R. P. Feynmen

I thank Mr. DeRose for the opportunity to join you science teachers. I also am a science teacher. I have much experience only in teaching graduate students in physics, and as a result of that experience I know that I don't know how to teach.

I am sure that you who are real teachers working at the bottom level of this hierarchy of teachers, instructors of teachers, experts on curricula, also are sure that you, too, don't know how to do it; otherwise you wouldn't bother to come to the Convention.

The subject "What Is Science?" is not my choice. It was Mr. DeRose's subject. But I would like to say that I think that "What Is Science?" is not at all equivalent to "how to teach science," and I must call that to your attention for two reasons. In the first place, from the way that I am preparing to give this lecture, it may seem that I am trying to tell you how to teach science—I am not at all in any way, because I don't know anything about small children. I have one, so I know that I don't know. The other is I think that most of you (because there is so much talk and so many papers and so many experts in the field) have some kind of a feeling of lack of self-confidence. In some ways you are always being lec-

Paper presented at Fourteenth Annual Convention, National Science Teachers Association (April 1–5, 1966), New York City.

tured on how things are not going too well and how you should learn to teach better. I am not going to berate you for the bad work you are doing and indicate how it can definitely be improved; that is not my intention.

As a matter of fact, we have very good students coming into Caltech, and during the years we found them getting better and better. Now how it is done, I don't know. I wonder if you know. I don't want to interfere with the system; it's very good.

Only two days ago we had a conference in which we decided that we don't have to teach a course in elementary quantum mechanics in the graduate school anymore. When I was a student, they didn't even have a course in quantum mechanics in the graduate school; it was considered too difficult a subject. When I first started to teach, we had one. Now we teach it to undergraduates. We discover now that we don't have to have elementary quantum mechanics for graduates from other schools. Why is it getting pushed down? Because we are able to teach better in the university and that is because the students coming up are better trained.

What is science? Of course you all must know, if you teach it. That's common sense. What can I say? If you don't know, every teacher's edition of every textbook gives a complete discussion of the subject. There is some kind of distorted distillation and watered-down and mixed-up words of Francis Bacon from some centuries ago, words which then were supposed to be the deep philosophy of science. But one of the greatest experimental scientists of the time who was really doing something, William Harvey, said that what Bacon said science was, was the science that a lord chancellor would do. He spoke of making observations, but omitted the vital factor of judgment about what to observe and what to pay attention to.

And so what science is, is not what the philosophers have said it is and certainly not what the teacher editions say it is. What it is, is a problem which I set for myself after I said I would give this talk.

After some time I was reminded of a little poem.

A centipede was happy quite, until a toad in fun
Said, "Pray, which leg comes after which?"
This raised his doubts to such a pitch
He fell distracted in the ditch
Not knowing how to run.

All my life, I have been doing science and known what it was, but what I have come to tell you—which foot comes after which—I am unable to do, and furthermore, I am worried by the analogy with the poem, that when I go home I will no longer be able to do any research.

There have been a lot of attempts by the various press reporters to get some kind of a capsule of this talk; I prepared it only a little time ago, so it was impossible; but I can see them all rushing out now to write some sort of headline which says: "The Professor called the President of NSTA a toad."

Under these circumstances of the difficulty of the subject, and my dislike of philosophical exposition, I will present it in a very unusual way. I am just going to tell you how I learned what science is. That's a little bit childish. I learned it as a child. I have had it in my blood from the beginning. And I would like to tell you how it got in. This sounds as though I am trying to tell you how to teach, but that is not my intention. I'm going to tell you what science is like by how I learned what science is like.

My father did it to me. When my mother was carrying me, it is reported—I am not directly a aware of the conversation—my father said that "If it's a boy, he'll be a scientist." How did he do it? He never told me I should be a scientist. He was not a scientist; he was a businessman, a sales manager of a uniform company, but he read about science and loved it.

When I was very young the earliest story I know when I still ate in a high chair, my father would play a game with me after dinner. He had bought a whole lot of old rectangular bathroom floor tiles from some place in Long Island City. We set them up on end, one next to the other, and I was allowed to push the end and watch the whole thing go down. So far so good.

Next, the game improved. The tiles were different colors, I must put one white, two blues, one white, two blues, and another white and then two blues—I may want to put another blue, but it must be a white. You recognize already the usual insidious cleverness; first delight him in play, and then slowly inject material of educational value!

Well, my mother, who is a much more feeling woman, began to realize the insidiousness of his efforts and said, "Mel, please let the poor child put a blue tile if he wants to." My father said, "No, I want him to pay attention to the patterns. It is the only thing I can do that is mathematics at this earliest level." If I were giving a talk on "what is mathematics." I would have already answered you. Mathematics is looking for patterns. (The fact is that this education had some effect. We have a direct experiment test, at the time I got to kindergarten, we had weaving in those days. They've taken it out; it's too difficult for children. We used to weave colored paper though vertical strips and make patterns. The kindergarten teacher was so amazed that she sent a special letter home to report that this child was very unusual, because he seemed to be able to figure out ahead of time what pattern he was going to get, and made amazingly intricate patterns. So the tile game did do something to me.)

> *If I were giving a talk on "what is mathematics," I would have already answered you. Mathematics is looking for patterns.*

I would like to report other evidence that mathematics is only patterns. When I was at Cornell, I was rather fascinated by the student body, which seems to me was a dilute mixture of some sensible people in a big mass of dumb people studying home economics, etc., including lots of girls. I used to sit in the cafeteria with the students and eat and try to overhear their conversations and see if there was one intelligent word coming out. You can imagine my surprise when I discovered a tremendous thing, it seemed to me.

I listened to a conversation between two girls, and one was explaining that if you want to make a straight line, you see, you go over a certain number to the right for each row you go up, that is, if you go over each time the same amount when you go up a row, you make a straight line. A deep principle of analytic geometry! It went on. I was rather amused.

She went on and said, "Suppose you have another line coming in from the other side and you want to figure out where they are going to intersect. Suppose on one line you go over two to the right for every one you go up, and the other line goes over three to the right every one that it goes up and they start twenty steps apart," etc.—I was flabbergasted. She figured out where the intersection was! It turned out that one girl was explaining to the other how to knit argyle socks.

Now I will go on with my own experience as a youngster in mathematics. Another thing that my father told me—and I can't quite explain it, because it was more an emotion than a telling—was that the ratio of the circumfer-

ence to the diameter of all circles was always the same, no matter what the size. That didn't seem to me too unobvious, but the ratio had some marvelous property. That was a wonderful number, a deep number, pi. There was a mystery about this number that I didn't quite understand as a youth, but this was a great thing, and the result was that I looked for pi everywhere.

When I was learning later in school how to make the decimals for fractions, and how to make 3 1/8, I wrote 3.125, and thinking I recognized a friend, wrote that it equals pi, the ratio of circumference to diameter of a circle. The teacher corrected it to 3.1416.

I illustrate these things to show an influence. The idea that there is a mystery, that there is a wonder about the number was important to me, not what the number was. Very much later when I was doing experiments in the laboratory—I mean my own home laboratory—fiddling around—no, excuse me, I didn't do experiments; I never did; I fiddled around. I made ratios and gadgets. I fiddled around. Gradually through books and manuals I began to discover there were formulas applicable to electricity relating the current and resistance, and so on. One day, looking at the formulas in some book or other, I discovered a formula for the frequency of a resonant circuit which was 2π LC where L is the inductance and C the capitance of the circuit. And there was pi, and where was the circle? You laugh, but I was very serious then. Pi was a thing with circles, and here is pi coming out of an electric circuit. Where was the circle? Do you who laughed know how that π comes about?

I have to love the thing. I have to look for it. I have to think about it. And then I realized, of course, that the coils are made in circles. About a half year later, I found another book which gave the inductance of round coils and square coils and there were other pi's in those formulas. I began to think about it again, and I realized that the pi did not come from the circular coils. I understand it better now; but in my heart I still don't quite know where that circle is, where that pi comes from.

When I was still pretty young—I don't know how old exactly—I had a ball in a wagon I was pulling, and I noticed something, and so I ran up to my father to say that when I pull the wagon, the ball runs to the back, and when I am running with the wagon and stop, the ball runs to the front. Why?

How would you answer?

He said, "That, nobody knows!" He said "It's very general, though, it happens all the time to anything; anything that is moving tends to keep moving; anything standing still tries to maintain that condition. If you look close you will see the ball does not run to the back of the wagon when you start from standing still. It moves forward a bit too, but not as fast as the wagon. The back of the wagon catches up with the ball which has trouble getting started moving. It's called inertia, that principle." I did run back to check and sure enough the ball didn't go backwards.

He put the difference between what we know and what we call it very distinctly.

Regarding this business about names and words, I would tell you another story. We used to go up to the Catskill Mountains for vacations. In New York, you go to the Catskill Mountains for vacations. The poor husbands had to go to work during the week, but they would come rushing out for weekends and stay with the families. On the weekends, my father would take me for walks in the woods. He often took me for walks and we learned all about nature, and so on, in the process. But the other children, friends of mine, also wanted to go and tried to get my father to take them. He didn't want to, because he said I was more advanced. I'm not trying to tell you how to teach, because what my father was doing was with a class of just one student; if he had a class of more than one, he was incapable of doing it.

So we went alone for our walk in the woods. But mothers were very powerful in those days, as they are now, and they convinced other fa-

thers that they had to take their own sons out for walks in the woods on Sunday afternoon. The next day, Monday, we were playing in the fields and this boy said to me, "See that bird standing on the wheat there? What's the name of it?" I said, "I haven't got the slightest idea." He said, "It's a brown-throated thrush. Your father doesn't teach you much about science."

I smiled to myself, because my father had already taught me that that doesn't tell me anything about the bird. He taught me "See the bird? It's a brown-throated thrush, but in Germany it's called a Halzenflugel, and in Chinese they call it a chung ling—and even if you know all those names for it, you still know nothing about the bird. You only know something about people; what they call that bird.

He put the difference between what we know and what we call it very distinctly.

Now that thrush sings, and teaches its young to fly, and flies so many miles away during the summer across the country, and nobody knows how it finds its way, and so forth. There is a difference between the name of the thing and what goes on.

The result of this is that I cannot remember anybody's name, and when people discuss physics with me, they are often exasperated when they say "the Fitz-Cronin effect" and I ask "What is the effect?" I can't remember the name.

I would like to say a word or two—may I interrupt my little tale—about words and definitions, because it is necessary to learn the words. It is not science. That doesn't mean just because it is not science that we don't have to teach the words. We are not talking about what to teach; we are talking about what science is. It is not science to know how to change centigrade to Fahrenheit. It's necessary, but it is not exactly science. In the same sense, if you were discussing what art is, you wouldn't say art is the knowledge of the fact that a 3-B pencil is softer than a 2-H pencil. It's a distinct difference. That doesn't mean an art teacher shouldn't teach that, or that an artist gets along very well if he doesn't know that. Actually, you can find out in a minute by trying it; but that's a scientific way that art teachers may not think of explaining.

In order to talk to each other, we have to have words, and that's all right. It's a very good idea to try to see the difference, and it's a good idea to know when we are teaching the tools of science, such as words.

To make my point still clearer, I shall pick out a certain science book to criticize unfavorably, which is unfair, because I am sure that with little ingenuity, I can find equally unfavorable things to say about others.

There is a first-grade science book which, in the first lesson of the first grade, begins in an unfortunate manner to teach science, because it starts off on the wrong idea of what science is. There is a picture of a dog, a windable toy dog, and a hand comes to the winder, and then the dog is able to move. Under the last picture it says, "What makes it move?" Later on, there is a picture of a real dog and the question "What makes it move?" Then there is a picture of a motor bike and the question "What makes it move?" and so on.

I though at first they were getting ready to tell what science was going to be about: physics, biology, chemistry. But that wasn't it. The answer was in the teachers' edition of the book; the answer I was trying to learn is that energy makes it move.

Now energy is a very subtle concept. It is very, very difficult to get right. What I mean by that is it is not easy to understand energy well enough to use it right, so that you can deduce something correctly using the energy idea. It is beyond the first grade. It would be equally well to say that God makes it move, or spirit makes it move, or movability makes it move. (In fact, it is equally well to say that energy makes it stop.)

Look at it this way: That's only the definition of energy. It should be reversed. We might say when something can move that it has energy in it, but not that what makes it move is energy. This is a very subtle difference. It's the same with the inertia proposition. Perhaps I can make the difference a little clearer this way:

If you ask a child what makes the toy dog move; if you ask an ordinary human being what makes a toy dog move, that is what you should think about. The answer is that you would up the spring; it tries to unwind and pushes the gear around... what a good way to begin a science course. Take apart the toy; see how it works. See the cleverness of the gears; see the ratchets. Learn something about the toy, the way the toy is put together, the ingenuity of people, devising the ratchets and other things. That's good. The question is fine. The answer is a little unfortunate, because what they were trying to do is teach a definition to what is energy. But nothing whatever is learned.

Suppose a student would say, "I don't think energy makes it move." Where does the discussion go from there?

I finally figured out a way to test whether you have taught an idea or a definition. Test it this way: You say, "Without using the new word which you have just learned, try to rephrase what you have just learned in your own language. Without using the word 'energy' tell me what you know now about the dog's motion. You cannot. So you learned nothing except the definition. You learned nothing about science. That may be all right. You may not want to learn something about science right away. You have to learn definitions." But for the very first lesson is that not possibly destructive?

I finally figured out a way to test whether you have taught an idea or a definition. Test it this way: You say, "Without using the new word which you have just learned, try to rephrase what you have learned in your own language."

I think for lesson number one to learn a mystic formula for answering questions is very bad. The book has some others—"Gravity makes it fall," "The soles of you shoes wear out because of friction." Shoe leather wears out because it rubs against the sidewalk and the little notches and bumps on the sidewalk grab pieces and pull them off. To simply say that it is because of friction is sad, because it's not science.

My father dealt a little bit with energy and used the term after I got a little bit of the idea about it. What he would have done I know, because he did in fact essentially the same thing—though not the same example of the toy dog. He would say, "It moves because the sun is shining" if he wanted to give the same lesson. I would say, "No. What has that to do with the sun shining? It moved because I wound up the springs."

"And why, my friend, are you able to move to wind up the spring?"

"I eat."

"What, my friend, do you eat?"

"I eat plants."

"And how do they grow?"

"They grow because the sun is shining."

And it is the same with the dog. What about gasoline? Accumulated energy of the sun which is captured by plants and preserved in the ground. Other examples end with the sun. And so the same idea about the world that our textbook is driving at is phrased in a very exciting way. All the things that we see that are moving are moving because the sun is shining. It does explain the relationship of one source of energy to another, and it can be denied by the child. He could say, "I don't think it is on account of the sun shining," and you can start a discussion. So there is a different. (Later I could challenge him with the tides, and what makes the earth turn, and have my hand on a mystery again.)

That is just an example of the difference between definitions (which are necessary) and science. The only objection in this particular case was that it was the first lesson. It must certainly come in later, telling you what energy is, but not to such a simple question as "What makes a dog move?" A child should be given a child's answer. "Open it up; let's look at it."

During those walks in the woods, I learned a great deal. In the case of the birds, for example—I already mentioned migration, but I will give you another example of birds in the woods. Instead of naming them, my father would say, "Look, notice that the bird is always pecking in its feathers. It pecks a lot in its feathers. Why do you think it pecks the feathers?"

I guessed it's because the feathers are ruffled, and he's trying to straighten them out. He said "Okay, when would the feathers get ruffled, or how would they get ruffled?"

"When he flies. When he walks around, it's okay; but when he flies it ruffles the feathers."

Then he would say, "You would guess then when the bird just landed he would have to peck more at his feathers than after he has straightened them out and he's just been walking around the ground for a while. Okay; let's look."

So we would look, and we would watch, and it turned out, as far as I could make out, that the bird pecked about as much and as often no matter how long he was walking on the ground and not just directly after flight.

So my guess was wrong, and I couldn't guess the right reason. My father revealed the reason.

It is that the birds have lice. There is a little flake that comes off the feather, my father taught me, stuff that can be eaten, and the louse eats it. And then on the louse, there is a little bit of wax in the joints between the sections of the leg that oozes out, and there is a mite that lives in there that can eat that wax. Now the mite has such a good source of food that it doesn't digest it too well, so far from the rear end there comes a liquid that has too much sugar, and in that sugar lives a tiny creature, etc.

The facts are not correct. The spirit is correct. First I learned about parasitism, one on the other, on the other.

Second, he went on to say that in the world whenever there is any source of something that could be eaten to make life go, some form of life finds a way to make use of that source; and that each little bit of left-over stuff is eaten by something.

Now the point of this is that the result of observation, even if I were unable to come to the ultimate conclusion, was a wonderful piece of gold, with a marvelous result. It was something marvelous.

Suppose I were told to observe, to make a list, to write down, to do this, to look, and when I wrote my list down it was filled with 130 other lists in the back of a notebook. I would learn that the result of observation is relatively dull, that nothing much comes of it.

I think it is very important—at least it was to me—that if you are going to teach people to make observations, you should show that something wonderful can come from them. I learned then what science was about. It was patience. If you looked, and you watched, and you paid attention, you got a great reward from it (although possibly not every time). As a result, when I became a more mature man, I would painstakingly, hour after hour, for years, work on problems—sometimes many years, sometimes shorter times—many of them failing, lots of stuff going into the waster-basket; but every once in a while there was the gold of a new understanding that I had learned to expect when I was a kid: The result of observation. For I did not learn that observation was not worthwhile.

Incidentally, in the forest we learned other things. We would go for walks and see all the regular things, and talk about many things; about the growing plants, the struggle of the trees for light, how they try to get as high as they can, and; to solve the problem of getting water higher than 35 or 40 feet, the little plants on the ground that look for the little bits of light that come through all that growth, and so forth.

One day after we had seen all this, my father took me to the forest again and said, "In all this time we have been looking at the forest we have only seen half of what is going on, exactly half."

I said, "What do you mean?"

He said, "We have been looking at how all these things grow; but for each bit of growth there must be the same amount of decay; otherwise the materials would be consumed forever. Dead trees would lie there having used up all the stuff from the air, and the ground, and it wouldn't get back into the ground or the air and nothing else could grow, because there is not material available. There must be for each bit of growth exactly the same amount of decay."

Suppose I were told to observe, to make a list, to write down, to do this, to look, and when I wrote my list down it was filled with 130 other lists in the back of a notebook. I would learn that the result of observation is relatively dull, that nothing much comes of it.

There then followed many walks in the woods during which we broke up old stumps, saw funny bugs and funguses growing—he couldn't show me bacteria—but we saw the softening effects, and so on. I say the forest as a process of the constant turning of materials.

There were many such things, descriptions of things, in odd ways. He often started to talk about a thing like this: "Suppose a man from Mars were to come down and look at the world." It's a very good way to look at the world. For example, when I was playing with my electric trains, he told me that there is a great wheel being turned by water which is connected by filaments of copper which spread out and spread out in all directions; then there are little wheels, and all those little wheels turn when the big wheel turns. The relation between them is only that there is copper and iron, nothing else, no moving parts. You turn one wheel here, and all the little wheels all over the place turn, and your train is one of them. It was a wonderful world my father told me about.

You might wonder what he got out of it all. I went to MIT. I went to Princeton. I came home, and he said, "Now you've got a science education. I have always wanted to know something that I have never understood; and so, my son, I want you to explain it to me." I said "Yes."

He said, "I understand that they say that light is emitted from an atom when it goes from one state to another, from an excited state to a state of lower energy."

I said, "That's right."

"And light is a kind of particle, a photon, I think they call it."

"Yes."

"So if the photon comes out of the atom when it goes from the excited to the lower state, the photon must have been in the atom in the exited state."

I said, "Well, no."

He said, "Well, how do you look at it so you can think of a particle photon coming out without it's having been in there in the excited state?"

I thought a few minutes, and I said, "I'm sorry; I don't know. I can't explain it to you."

He was very disappointed after all these years and years of trying to teach me something, that it came out with such poor results.

What science is, I think, may be something like this: There was on this planet an evolution of life to the stage that there were evolved animals which are intelligent. I don't mean just human beings, but animals which play and which can learn something from experience (like cats). But at this stage each animal would have to learn from its own experience. They gradually developed until some animal could learn from experience more rapidly and could even learn from another's experience by watching, or one could show the other, or he saw what the other one did. So there came a possi-

bility that all might learn it, but the transference was inefficient and they would die, and maybe the one who learned it died too before he could pass it on to others.

The question is, is it possible to learn more rapidly what somebody learned from some accident than the rate at which the thing is begin forgotten, either because of bad memory or because of the death of the learner or inventor?

So there came a time, perhaps, when for some species the rate at which learning was increased reached such a pitch that suddenly a completely new thing happened: things could be learned by one animal, passed on to another, and another fast enough that it was not lost to the race. Thus became possible an accumulation of knowledge of the race.

This has been called time-binding. I don't know who first called it this. At any rate, we have here some samples of those animals, sitting here trying to bind one experience to another, and each on trying to learn from the other.

This phenomenon of having a memory for the race, of having an accumulated knowledge passable from one generation to another, was new in the world. But it had a disease in it. It was possible to pass on mistaken ideas. It was possible to pass on ideas which were not profitable for the race. The race has ideas, but they are not necessarily profitable.

So there came a time in which the ideas although accumulated very slowly, were all accumulations not only of practical and useful things, but great accumulations of all types of prejudices and strange and odd beliefs.

> *So there came a time in which the ideas although accumulated very slowly, were all accumulations not only of practical and useful things, but great accumulations of all types of prejudices and strange and odd beliefs.*

Then a way of avoiding the disease was discovered. This is no doubt what is being passed from the past is in fact true, and to try to find out ab initio, again from experience, what the situation is, rather than trusting the experience of the past in the form in which it is passed down. And that is what science is; the result of the discovery that it is worthwhile to recheck by new direct experience, and not necessarily trusting the race experience from the past. I see it that way. That is my best definition.

I would like to remind you all of things that you know very well in order to give you a little enthusiasm. In religion, the moral lessons are taught, but they are not just taught once—you are inspired again and again, and I think it is necessary to inspire again and again, and to remember the value of science for children, for grownups, and everybody else, in several ways; not only that we will become better citizens, more able a control nature, and so on. There are other things.

There is the value of the world view created by science. There is the beauty and the wonder of the world that is discovered through the results of these new experiences. That is to say, the wonders of the content which I just reminded you of; that things move because the sun is shining, which is a deep idea, very strange and wonderful. Yet, not everything moves because the sun is shining. The earth rotates independent of the sun's shining. The nuclear reactions recently produced energy on the earth, a new source. Probably volcanoes are generally moved from a source difference from the sun's shining.

The world looks so different to one who has learned science. For example, the trees are made of air, primarily. When they are burned, they go back to air, and in the flaming head is released the flaming heat of the sun which was bound in to convert the air into a tree, and in the ash is the small remnant of the part which did not come from the air, that came from the soil, earth, instead.

These are beautiful things, and the content of science is wonderfully full of them. They are very inspiring, and they can be used to inspire others.

Another of the qualities of science is that it teaches the value of rational thought, as well as the importance of freedom of thought; the positive results that come from doubting that the lessons are all true. You must here distinguish—especially in teaching—the science from the forms or procedures that are sometimes used in developing science. It is easy to say, "We write, experiment, and observe, and do this or that." You can copy that form exactly. But great religions are dissipated by following form without remembering the direct content of the teaching of the great leaders. In the same way, it is possible to follow form and call it science, but that is pseudo-science. In this way, we all suffer from the kind of tyranny we have today in the many institutions that have come under the influence of pseudo-scientific advisers.

We have many studies in teaching, for example, in which people make observations, make lists, do statistics, and so on, but these do not thereby become established science, established knowledge. They are merely an imitative form of science—analogous to the South Sea island airfields, radio towers, etc., made out of wood. The islanders expect a great airplane to arrive. They even build wooden airplanes of the same shape as they see in the foreigners' airfields around them, but strangely enough, their wooden planes do not fly. The result of this pseudo-scientific imitation is to produce experts, which many of you are. You teachers who are really teaching children at the bottom of the heap can maybe doubt the experts once in a while. Learn from science that you must doubt the experts. As a matter of fact, I can also define science another way: Science is the belief in the ignorance of experts.

When someone says, "Science teaches such and such," he is using the word incorrectly. Science doesn't teach anything; experience teaches it. If they say to you, "Science has shown such and such," you might ask, "How does science show it? How did the scientists find out? How? What? Where?" It should not be "Science has shown," but, "This experiment, this effect, has shown." Any of you have as much right as anyone else, upon hearing about the experiments (but be patient and listen to all the evidence) to judge whether a sensible conclusion has been arrived at.

In a field which is so complicated that true science is not yet able to get anywhere, we have to rely on a kind of old-fashioned wisdom, a kind of definite straightforwardness. I am trying to inspire the teacher at the bottom to have some hope, and some self-confidence in common sense, and natural intelligence. The experts who are leading you may be wrong.

I have probably ruined the system, and the students that are coming into Caltech no longer will be any good. I think we live in an unscientific age in which almost all the buffeting of communications and television words, books, and so on are unscientific. That doesn't mean they are bad, but they are unscientific. As a result, there is a considerable amount of intellectual tyranny in the name of science.

Finally, with regard to this time-binding, a man cannot live beyond the grave. Each generation that discovers something from its experience must pass that on, but it must pass that on with a delicate balance of respect and disrespect, so that the race (now that it is aware of the disease to which it is liable) does not inflict its errors too rigidly on its youth, but it does pass on the accumulated wisdom, plus the wisdom that it may not be wisdom.

It is necessary to teach both to accept and to reject the past with a kind of balance that takes considerable skill. Science alone of all the subjects contains within itself the lesson of the danger of belief in the infallibility of the greatest teachers of the preceding generation.

APPENDIX D

RESEARCH ON THE LEARNING CYCLE

A. E. Lawson, M. R. Abraham, and J. W. Renner

Overview

The following review is concerned with research into the learning cycle approach to instruction. The review will be divided into four sections. Most of the original research on the learning cycle was concerned with the Science Curriculum Improvement Study (SCIS) program because this was the first program to explicitly use the learning cycle as an approach to instruction and curriculum development. The first section of the review will discuss this research. After the original development of SCIS, some instructional researchers and curriculum developers saw great promise in using the learning cycle as a general instructional strategy. The second section reviews research on these programs. Since the learning cycle is a global strategy made up of many factors, it has become apparent in recent years that a profitable approach is to research the effect of the various factors within the learning cycle. This research makes up the third section of this review. Finally, two large-scale studies concerning the use of the learning cycle in

From *A Theory of Instruction: Using the Learning Cycle to Teach Science Concepts and Thinking Skills* (Cincinnati, Ohio: National Association for Research in Science Teaching, 1989), Chapter 6.

high school physics and chemistry will be reviewed in the fourth section.

Research on SCIS

A large amount of research has been produced related to the SCIS program. Much of this research evaluated the general effectiveness of the program. Quite a few studies investigated various aspects of intellectual development of students at various ages. Some of the studies focused on the effect of the program on attitudes, and achievement as well. Since the program was designed with the learning cycle as an instructional strategy, the studies are, in effect, *de facto* investigations of the effectiveness of the learning cycle method.

Affective Domain

Brown (1973) studied the effect of six years of exposure to SCIS science. He found the SCIS program superior in developing positive attitudes towards science of middle-class children when compared to non-SCIS textbook-based programs. In a study comparing the SCIS *Systems and Subsystems* unit versus a non-SCIS unit, Allen (1973a) found that slightly better motivation could be attributed to the 87 third-grade students in the SCIS program.

Malcolm (1976) studied the effect of science programs on self-concept. He used subjects from eight elementary classes ranging from grades three through six. After eighteen weeks of exposure he found SCIS produced higher levels of self-concept in the areas of intellect and school status than did a non-SCIS textbook-based atmosphere. Brown, Weber and Renner (1975), Krockover and Malcolm (1976) and Haan (1978) found superior attitudes in students exposed to the SCIS program. Hendricks (1978) also found affective domain gains in SCIS students. When he studied 247 fifth-grade rural disadvantaged students, he found more positive attitudes, a greater preference toward science, and greater curiosity towards science among students after twelve weeks of science in the SCIS program than those in a non-SCIS program. Lowery, Bowyer and Padilla (1980) studied the effect of six years of SCIS on 110 middle-class rural-suburban elementary students. They found that after six years of SCIS, attitudes toward science and experimentation were more positive for the SCIS students than those in a textbook program.

Although an occasional study (i.e., Hofman, 1977) found no relationship between the SCIS program and student attitudes, by far the bulk of the studies comparing SCIS to non-SCIS programs found superior affective domain scores in favor of SCIS.

Achievement in Content and Process Skills

Many of the studies looking at the effect of the instructional methods associated with the SCIS program assessed student achievement content and process learning. One of the stated goals of the SCIS program was the development of scientific literacy where scientific literacy involves both content acquisition and process skills development (i.e., both declarative and procedural knowledge).

Thier (1965) used interview techniques to investigate the effects of the Material Objects unit on 60 first graders. He found the SCIS group had superior skill in describing objects by their properties than non-SCIS students. SCIS students also showed superior skill in describing similarities and differences between different forms of the same substance. Finally, SCIS students exhibited greater skill in observing an experiment and describing what happened.

Allen carried out a large scale longitudinal study of the SCIS program and its effect upon elementary school children. In the first of a series of articles, Allen (1967) studied the classification abilities of 190 elementary schoolers in grades 2–4. Half the subjects were exposed to SCIS while the remaining lacked an SCIS experience. Allen found no difference between SCIS and non-SCIS students in their skill in classifying. He concluded that the middle-class students in his sample received enough experiences with classification in their home environment so that the additional experiences in the SCIS program did little to improve this skill. In looking at 300 first-grade students, Allen (1971) found evidence of the superiority of the SCIS students over non-SCIS students in their skill in describing an object using specific property words. Property works that were used in the SCIS program were applied to new situations giving evidence of specific transfer. A small amount of general transfer was evidenced by the use of non-SCIS property words being utilized. After a second year of SCIS, the same students continued to show evidence of having learned the content associated with the SCIS program (Allen, 1972). Ninety percent of the SCIS students demonstrated understanding the concepts of "interaction." After a third year of the longitudinal study, SCIS students were found to be more skilled in identifying experimental variables and recognizing change than non-SCIS students (Allen, 1973b).

In another large scale evaluation of the SCIS program, Renner and colleagues conducted a number of studies to investigate variables associated with achievement (Renner, Stafford, Coffia, Kellogg and Weber, 1973). The first study researched the relationship between the learning activities of the *Material Objects* unit and conservation skills of first graders. The conservation of number, weight, liquid and solid amount, length and area were assessed. The *Material Objects* students were compared with those who studied science from a textbook and were found to exhibit far more conservation responses. Thus, the data supported the conclusion that the rate of attainment of reasoning skills, as measured by Piaget-type conservation tasks, was significantly enhanced by the experiences provided by the first-grade *Material Objects* unit of the SCIS program.

The second Renner et al. study examined elementary science students who had been exposed to SCIS for at least four years and compared them to students who had been taught science using a textbook for the same length of time. The study used an instrument constructed to measure students' skill in the processes of observing, classifying, measuring, experimenting, interpreting and predicting. The results showed that the SCIS program was superior to the textbook program in leading children to develop and use these process skills in science.

The third Renner et al. study looked at the transfer of process skills developed in the SCIS program to other areas of the curriculum. The Stanford Achievement Test was administered to SCIS and non-SCIS groups during the fifth grade. Scores in mathematics concepts, skills, and applications, as well as word meaning and paragraph meaning were obtained, as were data concerning achievement in social studies skills and content. Forty-six students who had utilized the SCIS program for five years comprised the experimental group. Sixty-nine students who used a textbook-based science curriculum comprised the control group. Analysis of the scores of the two groups on the Stanford

Achievement Test showed that the experimental group outscored the control group on every subtest. A statistical comparison of the seven academic areas revealed significant differences between the two groups in mathematics applications, social studies skills, and paragraph meaning. On the other hand, no significant differences were found in mathematical computations and concepts, social studies content, and word meaning.

Of particular interest was Renner et al.'s observation of a thread of commonality in the areas where differences were determined. In the case of mathematics applications, performance on the instrument was determined by ability to apply mathematical knowledge and to think mathematically in practical situations. The social studies skills test has a stated goal of testing "knowledge in action." The paragraph meaning test was said to measure the students' ability to understand connected discourse involving varying levels of comprehension. The thread of commonality, then, was that each area requires a level of thought that transcends mere recognition and recall. Apparently, children who have had experience with SCIS units tended to utilize the high levels of thinking more effectively than those who have not had this experience.

The fourth Renner et al. study looked at the transfer of the basic skills developed by the SCIS program to those necessary to the learning of reading. First-grade students studying the *Material Objects* unit were used to study the effect of SCIS as a reading readiness program. The experimental group experienced the *Material Objects* unit for several periods a day and did not have any experiences with a reading readiness program. The students in the control group had a learning experience provided by a commercial reading readiness program. The reading readiness of both groups was evaluated with the Metropolitan Reading Readiness Test at the beginning of the school year and six weeks later. Students in the experimental group showed greater gains in five of the six subtest areas. They outperformed the control group in Word Meaning, Listening, Matching, Alphabet, and Numbers. They were outgained by the control group only on the Copying subtest.

Brown, Weber and Renner (1975) compared SCIS students with non-SCIS students and found the SCIS students had superior attainment of scientific processes. Also, using a measure of attitudes towards science and scientists, they found no significant difference between the attitudes of the SCIS students and those of professional scientists. Thus, they concluded that SCIS was successful in its goal of developing scientific literacy with elementary school students.

Linn and Thier (1975) conducted a nationwide survey of the effectiveness of the *Energy Sources* fifth-grade unit in teaching the reasoning involved in compensating variables. In all, 2290 fifth- and eighth-grade students were involved. Forty-seven fifth-grade classes from seven states in which *Energy Sources* had been taught were considered the experimental group. Performance of students in those classes was compared to performance of students in 36 control classes in which *Energy Sources* was not taught. Nine eighth-grade classes that had not had *Energy Sources* were also involved in the study. Posttest performance on tasks requiring the identification and compensation of variables revealed substantial superiority of the experimental group students in both rural and non-rural settings. As expected, the eighth-grade students performed better than either group of fifth-grade students but the experimental group fifth-graders performed more like the eighth-graders than the controls of their own age group.

Bowyer (1976) studied the development of scientific literacy in 521 rural sixth grade students. Sixty-five percent of the students were exposed to the SCIS program for six years. An instrument based on nine Piaget-type tasks

was developed. Students showed significant gains in (1) skill in recognizing and describing variables, (2) skill in determining relative position, (3) skill in predicting and explaining the temperatures in energy transfer, and (4) skill in understanding the concept of solution and evaporation. Bowyer used these results as evidence of gains in scientific literacy.

Several researchers investigated the transfer of skills gained in SCIS to other areas of the curriculum. Brown (1973) found that six years of SCIS was superior in producing figural creativity than non-SCIS textbook approaches. Maxwell (1974) studied 102 kindergarten students exposed to eight weeks (20 minutes per day, five days per week) of science. He found that SCIS kindergarten students studying the *Material Objects* unit had significantly greater gains in reading readiness and language facility over non-SCIS students. In a study of the content analysis of textual material, TaFoya (1976) found SCIS materials to have greater potential in developing inquiry skills than textbook approaches. Nussbaum (1979) studied 44 third-grade students in Jerusalem, Israel. He found that the SCIS *Relativity* unit was effective in teaching the concept of "space." Furthermore, he found this learning was lasting and generalizable. He also found some evidence of slight advances in Piagetian developmental level. Horn (1980), in examining eighteen classes of first-grade students, found that the SCIS *Material Objects* unit had no more effect than traditional text materials in contributing to new vocabulary and comprehension of text.

Teacher Variables

As was the case with many of the curriculum projects produced in the 1960's, a massive teacher education program accompanied the development of the SCIS curriculum. As a consequence, much research was done investigating the effectiveness and nature of these teacher training programs. Because some of this research was associated with how teachers utilize the learning cycle approach, some insight into learning cycle variables can be seen in this research.

Moon (1969), Porterfield (1969), and Wilson (1969) found that when teaching, SCIS teachers behaved differently. Their questioning behavior using SCIS focused on higher-order, more open-ended questions rather than fact-oriented questions. Moon (1969) studied 32 elementary school teachers. Sixteen were trained in a three-week SCIS workshop. As a result of either the workshop or the use of the SCIS materials, the SCIS teachers used higher-order questions than the non-SCIS teachers. Porterfield (1969) studied sixteen second- and fourth-grade teachers trained in SCIS and compared their questioning behavior with those of sixteen non-SCIS second- and fourth-grade teachers. It was found that non-SCIS teachers use more recognition and recall questions while the SCIS teachers asked more questions requiring translation, interpretation, analysis, synthesis, and evaluation. Wilson (1969) analyzed the questions asked of 30 first-through sixth-grade teachers. Half the sample was SCIS trained and showed a greater propensity for asking skill-type questions emphasizing observation, measurement, interpretation, and prediction. The non-SCIS teachers were more prone to ask comprehension questions. Similar results were found by Eaton (1974). This researcher studied the teaching practices of 42 elementary school teachers and 120 of their fourth-, fifth- and sixth-grade students. Twenty-three of these teachers were exposed to a 17-day SCIS workshop and used the SCIS program. It was found that when SCIS teachers were compared with textbook teachers, they were more open-minded, asked higher-level questions, and had pupils with greater science achievement in science processes.

Lawlor (1974) found that students of SCIS trained teachers had better attitudes towards science. Using interaction analysis, Simmons (1974) studied a random sample of 224 teachers and found that SCIS teachers practiced less dominant behaviors and were more student-oriented than non-SCIS teachers. Finally, Kyle (1985) found that SCIS teachers spent a good deal more time teaching science than teachers not trained to teach SCIS.

All of this indicates that SCIS teachers are more likely to have the skills necessary to interact successfully with students as required by the various phases of a learning cycle. This might, in part, explain the success of the SCIS program.

Summary

Although much of the research cited above can be criticized for comparing the SCIS program with an ill-defined "non-SCIS" approach, there still is much evidence to indicate that SCIS was and is an effective elementary science program that has great benefits in promoting students' attitudes and content and process skill achievement. The point should be made, however, that much of this research is not solely an evaluation of the learning cycle approach but rather the evaluation of SCIS, a curriculum project that has many characteristics including use of the learning cycle. In other words, it may be that some other aspect of the program besides, or in addition to, the learning cycle is responsible for its success. For example, In some cases it may be that the effectiveness of a laboratory versus a non-laboratory approach is being evaluated. That is, the effectiveness of the SCIS program may be due more to the fact that a laboratory, or hands-on, approach is superior to a non-laboratory approach. As a consequence, the research reviewed thus far tells us that the SCIS program is effective, but it does not tell us specifically why.

Learning Cycle Research

As a result of the success of the SCIS program, many science educators saw the learning cycle as a useful model for instruction and curriculum development. Consequently, other groups developed curricula using the learning cycle for science programs at different levels. The research reported in this section is concerned with the investigations of the effectiveness of these individually developed learning cycle curricula.

Attitudes

As it was true of the SCIS program, research groups found that students using the learning cycle often had more positive attitudes toward science and science instruction when using the learning cycle approach than with other approaches usually identified as "traditional." Campbell (1977), for example, found beginning college physics students exposed to a learning cycle approach had better attitudes toward laboratory work than students exposed to a traditional approach. Fifty-five students were exposed to ten laboratory lessons in order to learn physics content. Although there was no significant difference between the groups in learning physics concepts, this research found the learning cycle group had more positive attitudes towards laboratory work, scored somewhat higher on a laboratory final exam, and were not as likely to withdraw from the course.

Davis (1978), using 132 selected fifth- and sixth-grade students exposed to 120 minutes of science for nine weeks, found that learning cycle lessons produced more positive attitudes toward science than either lecture/discussion lessons or verification laboratory approaches. Bishop (1980) found that an eight-lesson planetarium unit taught to three classes of eighth-grade students using the learning cycle developed more positive attitudes than a more traditional planetarium approach. The experimental group enjoyed the unit more and scored better on an achievement test. Although the examples here are not extensive they are parallel and consistent with the results found from the SCIS experience.

Content Achievement

Campbell (1977) compared the effectiveness of the learning cycle approach to conducting physics laboratory activities plus the personalized system of instruction (PSI) to the more traditional lecture-lab-recitation method of college freshman physics teaching. Campbell found the learning cycle and PSI approach to be significantly better than the traditional approach in provoking students to utilize formal reasoning patterns. Students had a more positive attitude (as mentioned previously) and significantly fewer of them dropped out of the learning cycle/PSI course as well. Content achievement was not significantly different between the two approaches.

In the Davis (1978) study cited previously, it was shown that students had a more positive attitude towards science and better understanding of the nature of science using the learning cycle approach. However, this study found no difference in content achievement among three approaches investigated. Bishop (1980) showed that learning cycle students had greater posttest and delayed posttest retention of content than students with traditional planetarium instruction; however, neither group showed mastery of the astronomy concepts being taught. In a five-week unit, Vermont (1985) found no difference between the learning cycle approach and a lecture/laboratory strategy in the learning of the mole concept and the altering of misconceptions related to that concept by 60 college chemistry students.

Schneider and Renner (1980) compared two methods of teaching physical science concepts to 48 ninth-grade students over a one-semester period. One method, labeled *formal instruction*, followed a traditional pattern of lecture, motion pictures, filmstrips, textbook readings, questions and problems, supervised study and demonstrations. The second method, labeled *concrete instruction*, followed the learning cycle approach. Results showed the concrete instruction method was superior to the formal method in content achievement on both immediate and delayed posttests.

Ambiguous results were obtained in a study using 256 college chemistry students by Ward and Herron (1980). In this study learning cycle activities were developed for three experiments in a college chemistry course. Each experiment required approximately three hours to complete. The three experiments (chromatography of a felt tip pen, activity series, and chemical interactions) all required formal schema (propositional, proportional and combinatorial reasoning). Ward and Herron found that the learning cycle approach was clearly superior to the traditional approach in one of the three experiments. In the other two they found no differences. They suggested three possible reasons for these ambiguous results: (1) the limited time spent on the activities of the experiment, (2) flaws in the achievement test used, and (3) suspicion that the teaching assistants who taught the course were not following the guidelines for the learning cycle.

Purser and Renner (1983), using groups of 68 and 67 ninth- and tenth-grade biology students, taught a full eight-month course comparing learning cycle and traditional approaches. They found that for concepts requiring concrete thought, the learning cycle showed definite superiority over the traditional approach. However, for concepts requiring formal thought, the learning cycle approach was no more effective than the traditional approach with their sample of mostly concrete and transitional students.

Saunders and Shepardson (1987) compared what they called "formal" versus "concrete" instructional strategies during a nine-month study of sixth-grade science. The formal approach was characterized by oral and written language activities whereas the concrete approach was defined according to learning cycle parameters. Using groups of 57 and 58 students, Sanders and Shepardson found definite superiority of the learning cycle approach over the formal approach in science achievement.

Thinking Skills

A large amount of research on the learning cycle has investigated the effect that it has on the development of thinking skills. In most cases, *thinking skills* were investigated in the context of Piaget's theory of concrete and formal operational reasoning and were measured using Piagetian-type tasks.

McKinnon and Renner (1971) studied the thinking skills of 131 college freshmen. Approximately one-half of the freshmen were put in an inquiry-oriented science course using the learning cycle approach and the other half served as controls. Significantly greater gains in reasoning were found in the learning cycle group. Similarly, Renner and Lawson (1975) studied 37 college freshmen elementary education majors. Twenty of these were put in an inquiry-oriented learning cycle science class, and the remaining 17 were placed in the traditional physics for elementary education course. The learning cycle class was found to be superior in producing gains in reasoning.

Carlson (1975) studied 133 students enrolled in college introductory physical science. Sixty-six students were trained in formal reasoning using inquiry-oriented instruction that was consistent with the learning cycle approach. The balance of the students served as a control group. This research found the inquiry approach was superior in effecting improvements in formal thinking skills over a non-inquiry approaches.

In a study using 65 high school biology students, Lawson, Blake and Nordland (1975) found that the learning cycle approach was superior to a traditional approach in teaching the skill of controlling variables. However, the skill was not transferable. As a consequence, they concluded that, consistent with Piagetian theory, even the learning cycle used over a short time was not effective in helping students acquire generalizable controlling variables skill. However, Lawson and Wollman (1976), as discussed previously, were successful in teaching 32 fifth- and 32 seventh-grade students to control variables in such a way that the skill transferred to novel tasks. The main difference between the Lawson, Blake and Nordland (1975) approach and the Lawson and Wollman (1976) approach was that the individual training sessions used by Lawson and Wollman allowed for more individual feedback to students' self-generated experimental procedures. This individual feedback was much better at prompting students to reflect on the adequacies and inadequacies of their procedures and to become more aware of those procedures. Lawson and Snitgen (1982) found, during a one-semester college biology class for 72 preservice teachers, that when use of the learning cycle was extended and augmented with special instructional components to directly teach formal reasoning, transferable gains in formal reasoning could be obtained in the classroom setting.

Renner and Paske (1977) compared two forms of one-semester physics instruction for nonscience majors at the University of Oklahoma. The "concrete" mode of instruction followed the learning cycle approach while the "formal" mode followed the traditional lecture-demonstration approach. Students in both groups were pre- and posttested with measures of formal reasoning and the Watson-Glaser Critical Thinking Appraisal. Posttesting also included an attitude survey and a content examination. Three sections were taught by the concrete mode while one section was taught by the formal mode. The concrete instruction sections performed consistently better than the formal section on the content examination and were generally pleased with their instruction, while the formal section was generally dissatisfied with its instruction. Greater gains and fewer losses were made on the Watson-Glaser by the concrete sections. They also showed greater gains on the formal tasks from the low to high concrete levels and from high concrete to low formal levels; however, the formal section showed greater gains from the low to high formal level. This result suggests that inquiry-oriented instruction is more effective at producing reasoning gains for concrete students but for students with some expertise in formal

reasoning, further progress is better attained by traditional methods.

Tomlinson-Keasey and Eisert (1977a) reported results of the evaluation of the ADAPT project at the University of Nebraska. ADAPT is an interdisciplinary project based upon Piagetian principles to help college students develop formal reasoning. Instruction in English, history, economics, physics, anthropology, and mathematics was patterned after the learning cycle. A pencil-paper inventory of formal reasoning, administered prior to and following the freshman year, revealed significant differences in favor of the ADAPT group over two control groups. A follow-up study during the sophomore year indicated significant differences in favor of the ADAPT group on the Watson-Glaser Critical Thinking Appraisal (Tomlinson-Keasey and Eisert, 1977b).

Wollman and Lawson (1978) found that 28 seventh-grade students in an "active" group, subjected to 30-40 minute training sessions, which used an inductive learning cycle approach and manipulatives, were superior to those in a "verbal" group which did not use manipulatives, in acquiring skill in using proportional reasoning.

The Schneider and Renner (1980) study cited previously also investigated their ninth-grade physical science course's ability to promote formal reasoning. The learning cycle approach (called concrete instruction) was found to be superior in promoting formal reasoning as assessed by a battery of manipulative tasks. The superiority of the concrete instruction group persisted on the delayed posttests (three months later). One might argue that this superiority does not reflect a real difference in reasoning skill as the concrete instruction students interacted with manipulative materials while the formal group did not. However, this argument is weakened considerably by the finding that the concrete instruction group also evidenced greater gains on a nonmanipulative test of I.Q. (the Short Form of Academic Aptitude). Thus support was obtained for the hypothesis that the learning cycle approach not only improves understanding of science content, but can effect general advances in reasoning skills and academic aptitude as well.

Finally, Saunders and Shepardson (1987) found that sixth-grade students instructed with the learning cycle approach over a semester showed a greater percentage gain from the concrete to the formal stage than students taught using a "formal" instructional methodology.

Summary

Although some of the research reported here is subject to the criticism of comparing the learning cycle approach with a less well-defined instructional strategy (i.e., "non-learning cycle"), many of the studies reported here use comparisons between the learning cycle and more well-defined approaches. When taken in combination with the research reported previously on the SCIS program, several observations can be made. The learning cycle approach appears to have considerable promise in areas of encouraging positive attitudes toward science and science instruction, developing better content achievement by students, and improving general thinking skills. It has showed superiority over other approaches, especially those that involve reading and demonstration-lecture activities. Nevertheless, these studies, like those cited previously, fail to identify precisely what factor or factors associated with the learning cycle are responsible for this superiority.

Research on Aspects of the Learning Cycle

As mentioned, much of the research reported in the previous two sections is subject to the criticism that comparisons of global instructional strategies, such as the learning cycle, even with well-defined "traditional" approaches, do not identify the specific cause or causes of any outcomes of the instructional methods. The approaches are so different, it is agreed, that general studies may not isolate the critical variables that account for the results. Studies are needed of specific aspects of instruction that characterize or define the learning cycle.

To this end, Story and Brown (1979) found more positive attitudes with hands-on materials versus similar, but non-hands-on instruction and Raghubir (1979) found that a laboratory/investigation strategy, where laboratory preceded discussion, had a greater effect on learning and attitudes for twelfth-grade biology students than a laboratory/lecture strategy where the laboratory was used in a verification or deductive mode.

Abraham (1982) conducted a study using college chemistry students designed to identify the differences between "inquiry" laboratories (using the laboratory to introduce concepts, as is done in the learning cycle) and "verification" laboratories (using the laboratory to confirm or verify a concept presented prior to the laboratory). The nature of these two laboratory types was investigated using a Q-sort type instrument consisting of 25 statements describing various characteristics of laboratory activities. Students ranked the 25 statements according to how accurately they characterized the laboratory. Abraham then used these characterizations to distinguish between the laboratory types as perceived by the students exposed to the inquiry, learning cycle and verification formats. Using discriminant analysis, a set of statements used by students to distinguish between the inquiry and verification laboratory types was identified.

The following statements were ranked significantly higher by the verification group.

1. The instructor is concerned with the correctness of data.
2. The instructor lectures to the whole class.
3. During laboratory the students record information requested by the instructor.
4. Laboratory experiments develop skill in the techniques or procedures of chemistry.

5. Students usually know the general outcome of the experiment before doing the experiment.

The following statements were ranked significantly higher by the inquiry, learning cycle laboratory group.

1. Students were asked to design their own experiments.
2. The instructor requires students to explain why certain things happen.
3. Laboratory reports require students to use evidence to back up their conclusions.
4. Students propose their own explanations for observed phenomena.

From this information it can be seen that laboratory activities used in a learning cycle manner are characterized by students as being associated with experimentation, explanation, observation, and the use of evidence. In contrast, laboratory activities used in a verification or traditional mode are usually associated with correctness, lecture, following instruction, and the development of specific laboratory techniques.

In a meta-analysis of 39 studies, Lott (1983) compared inductive and deductive teaching approaches. Although Lott found no main effects between the two approaches, several interactive effects were apparent. First, the inductive approach had a more positive effect on intermediate level students, and was superior when higher levels of thought and outcome demands were required. Second, students in smaller classes, numbering 17 to 26, performed better when experiencing the inductive approach. As the size of the class increased, performance differences, when compared to the deductive approach, decreased. Finally, the inductive approach functioned better when it was part of complete program opposed to isolated units of instruction. These conclusions may explain some of the ambiguous results of the previously cited research.

Lott's analysis suggests that the learning cycle may be especially effective with concrete operational learners in the Piagetian sense. This may be because "formal" learners are better able to compensate for and are, therefore, more tolerant of less-effective instructional approaches. The learning cycle may be more effective with smaller classes because important interactions among students and the teacher during the exploration phase and during discussions, in which data are analyzed, are more difficult to control when class size becomes large. Students may become isolated from the instruction and the instructional materials in larger classes and become confused. Perhaps the learning cycle is more effective as a total program than in isolated instructional units because students need time to become activated to the techniques of inquiry learning. Finally, the learning cycle may be more effective in learning complex and non-intuitive concepts, because self-evident concepts do not require the intense examination of ideas facilitated by the learning cycle. As a consequence, traditional instruction appears to be just as effective as the learning cycle in teaching self-evident concepts.

Finally, Ivins (1986) compared the effect of two instructional sequences involving science laboratory activities. One of these used an inductive approach to instruction and the other used a deductive approach. Here *inductive* means that the laboratory precedes term introduction as is the case in the learning cycle, and *deductive* means the reverse. Using 103 seventh-grade earth science students, Ivins found the inductive approach created greater achievement and retention of content.

Research on Phases of the Learning Cycle in Chemistry and Physics

Instruction designed to teach scientific concepts can generally be thought of as involving three elements: (1) identification of a pattern of regularity in the environment; (2) discussion of the pattern and the introduction of a term to refer to the pattern; and (3) identification of the "concept" in new situations. Thus, instructional strategies can be characterized as a combination of one or more of these elements, taken in a specific sequence, utilizing different formats of presentation. Taking this view, there are three variables which define different instructional strategies designed to teach concepts: (1) the sequence variable, (2) the necessity variable, and (3) the format variable. When judging the effectiveness of different instructional strategies, the research question boils down to how does the order, existence of the three elements of instruction, and form affect construction?

Two large scale multiexperiment studies were carried out to investigate instruction in terms of these three variables. Specific lessons in high school chemistry and physics were modified in order to do this. Nine experiments in chemistry and eight experiments in physics were carried out over a period of one year. Class observations, case studies, achievement tests and attitude inventories were utilized to assess the effect of varying instructional parameters on the achievement and attitudes of students. A large proportion of the 62 physics students were "formal operational" in the Piagetian sense, while the 159 chemistry students were an even mix of "formal" and "concrete operational." The detailed results of these studies can be found in two reports (Renner, Abraham and Birnie, 1983; Abraham and Renner, 1984) and three research papers (Abraham and Renner, 1986; Renner, Abraham and Birnie, 1985; 1988).

The Sequence Variable

One of the differences between the learning cycle approach and traditional approaches is the sequence of the phases of instruction. In the typical traditional approach, students first are *informed* of what they are expected to learn. The informing is accomplished via a textbook, a lecture, or some other media which discusses the idea to be learned. Next, the idea is *verified* for the student by demonstrating that it is true. In science, the laboratory is often used for this purpose. Finally, the student answers questions, works problems, or engages in some form of *practice* with the new idea. The "inform-verify-practice" sequence of phases corresponds roughly to the three instructional phases of the learning cycle with the sequence of the first two phases reversed (cf., Renner, 1982).

Other instructional approaches could also be simulated by altering the sequence of these phases of instruction. Six sequences of the three phases of the learning cycle are possible. However, noting the specific patterns associated with the three phases allows us to reduce their number somewhat. Going from the exploration phase to the term introduction phase is basically inductive in nature, whereas doing the reverse is basically deductive in nature. In fact, any activity which precedes the term introduction phase would be inductive, and any activity which follows the term introduction phase would be deductive. The exploration and application phases, therefore, function according to their position in the sequence. As a consequence, the sequence question can be refined to a question of the position of the term introduction phase. Therefore, the critical factor to be considered when assessing the effect of the sequence of instructional phases is the position of the term introduction phase. Is it first, second, or third?

The research investigating the sequence of the learning cycle phases was conducted in four separate experiments and the conclusions reached were different for the sample of physics students and the sample of chemistry students. Those conclusions were as follows:

For physics students (Renner, Abraham and Birnie, 1983):

1. The sequence of the phases is unimportant for achievement if all three phases are taught.

2. The students believe that the sequence of the phases is important to how they learn physics and prefer the learning cycle sequence. In particular, the students do not like to discuss a concept until they have gathered their own data from an experiment.

For chemistry students (Abraham and Renner, 1984):

1. "Concrete operational" learners learn review concepts (concepts which were originally taught at an earlier grade) better with sequences which have the term introduction phase last.

2. "Formal operational" learners learn review concepts better with sequences which have the term introduction phase first.

3. All learners learn new concepts better with sequences which have term introduction as the second phase.

4. Students have a more positive attitude towards (preference for) term introduction after the first phase (i.e., either second or third).

The apparent discrepancies between the physics and chemistry samples might be explained by the higher percentage of students who are skilled in formal reasoning in the physics sample. These students might be better able to compensate for the varying sequences of the phases. The above observations can also be seen as consistent with the observations by Lott (1983) concerning inductive versus deductive approaches to instruction. According to Lott, inductive approaches (i.e., learning cycle approaches) are more effective for intermediate level students (like those of the chemistry group). For more accomplished thinkers, the instructional strategy is less important. Also according to Lott, inductive approaches are more effective when greater intellectual demands are placed on students. This would be the case when new concepts are being studied. It would not be as likely to be the case when review concepts are being studied.

The Necessity Variable

Some instructional strategies imply that not all three elements of instruction are necessary. For example, if the exploration phase of a learning cycle were omitted, one would be left with a lesson which began with the introduction of new terms, followed by readings and problems to be solved requiring understanding of the concept(s) implied by the terms introduced. This corresponds to a widely used instructional strategy. Abraham and Renner (1984) and Renner, Abraham, and Birnie (1983) used two strategies to investigate the necessity of the three phases of the learning cycle. The first was to teach lessons that were missing one of the three phases and to compare student attitude and achievement with that of students taught with lessons consisting of all three phases. The second was to vary the sequence of the three phases in lessons taught to different classes and then to test the students after each phase. By comparing the assessment data collected after each phase, Renner, Abraham and Birnie were able to simulate one, two, and three phase lessons. The following conclusions were based on six experiments investigating the necessity variable.

1. In general, all three phases of a learning cycle are necessary for the optimum learning of concepts.

2. Students prefer complete learning cycles, i.e., those with all three phases.

3. Students have negative feelings toward learning cycles which have long and/or complex application phases.

4. The combination of the exploration and term introduction phases is more effective than the term introduction phase alone.

5. The application phase can sometimes substitute for term introduction if this phase includes the use of the term or terms used to refer to the concept.

The Format Variable

Different formats of instruction are commonly used in science lessons. Laboratory, discussion, demonstration, lecture, and reading are probably the most commonly utilized formats at the high school and introductory college levels. The learning cycle typically uses what could be described as a laboratory/discussion format; however, it should be noted that explorations may involve readings and other non-manipulative activities. Seven experiments were conducted which investigated the effect that formats of instruction have on the learning and attitudes of students. The formats investigated were laboratory, discussion, demonstration, lecture, and reading. As was previously the case, the conclusions reached were different for the physics and chemistry students.

For physics students (Renner, Abraham and Birnie, 1983):

1. The format in which the students experienced the phases of the learning cycle did not influence their content knowledge.

2. Students believe they learn more physics content more easily if they first use laboratory apparatus to gather data, discuss the meaning of the data, and have experiences which expand the meaning of the concept.

3. When most of the members of a group have reached the "formal" stage, they can profit from instruction that is not given at an experimental level. However, when students' data from the laboratory are not used as the principle source for building concepts, and reading about or being told about the concepts are substituted for laboratory experience, the students do not like it and become bored quickly.

For chemistry students (Abraham and Renner, 1984):

1. The laboratory format is superior to lecture or reading formats in content achievement for "concrete operational" students.

2. The reading format is effective for "formal operational" students, but ineffective for "concrete operational" students in content achievement.

3. In attitude, the laboratory format is thought of most positively and the reading format is thought of most negatively by students.

4. To be effective, the laboratory format must be used in conjunction with discussions as in the normal learning cycle sequence.

5. The laboratory must provide clear data leading to the concept in order to be effective.

Summary

Research supports the conclusion that instructional strategies utilized to teach science concepts are most effective when they consist of activities which serve three functions: (1) explore and identify a pattern of regularity in the environment, (2) discuss the pattern and introduce a term to refer to that pattern, and (3) discover/apply the concept in new situations. The learning cycle approach is an effective instructional strategy for at least two reasons. First, it utilizes all three of these activities; and second, it uses them in the correct sequence. It should be noted that the sequence, data then concept, is the reverse of the common instructional practice of using the laboratory as a verification of the concept (i.e., concept then data).

The format of each phase of instruction is dictated by the role that the phase plays. The exploration phase is best suited to investigate nature and discover patterns of regularity. The laboratory format has been shown to be most effective in that role, at least for high school students. The term introduction phase is best suited to discuss data, clarify a pattern and give it a name. A class discussion format has been shown to be most effective for this. The application phase is best suited to reinforce, extend, review, or apply the concept. Because of its varying roles, a number of formats can be utilized during this phase (laboratory, demonstration, readings, problem sets, etc.).

In summary, the learning cycle has many advantages over traditional instructional approaches especially when the development of thinking skills is an important goal. Since many studies have shown that a large proportion of the secondary and college population have poorly developed thinking skills, it seems reasonable to conclude that the learning cycle deserves more widespread implementation in science classrooms.

TEACHING AND THE EXPANDING KNOWLEDGE

A. Szent-Gyorgyi

The simplification that comes with expanding knowledge enables teaching to encompass this knowledge.

Our attempt to harmonize teaching with expanding—or rather exploding—knowledge would be hopeless should growth not entail simplification. I will dwell on this sunny side. Knowledge is a sacred cow, and my problem will be how we can milk her while keeping clear of her horns.

One of my reasons for being optimistic is that the foundations of nature are simple. This was brought home to me many years ago when I joined the Institute for Advanced Studies in Princeton. I did this in the hope that by rubbing elbows with those great atomic physicists and mathematicians I would learn something about living matters. But as soon as I revealed that in any living system there are more than two electrons, the physicists would not speak to me. With all their computers they could not say what the third electron might do. The remarkable thing is that it knows exactly what to do. So that little electron knows something that all the wise men of Princeton don't, and this can only be something very simple. Nature, basically, must be much simpler than she looks to us. She looks to us like a coded letter for which we have no code. To the degree to which our methods become less clumsy and more adequate and we find out nature's code, things must become not only clearer but very much simpler, too.

Science tends to generalize, and generalization means simplification. My own science, biology, is today not only very much richer than it was in my student days, but is simpler, too. Then it was horribly complex, being fragmented into a great number of isolated principles. Today these are all fused into one single complex with the atomic model in its center. Cosmology, quantum mechanics, DNA and genetics, are all, more or less, parts of one and the same story—a most wonderful simplification. And generalizations are also more satisfying to the mind than details. We, in our teaching, should place more emphasis on generalizations than on details. Of course, details and generalization can be reached only from details, while it is the generalization which gives value and interest to the detail.

> *Science tends to generalize, and generalization means simplification. My own science, biology, is today not only very much richer than it was in my student days, but is simpler, too.*

After this preamble I would like to make a few general remarks, first, about the main instrument of teaching, books. There is a widely spread misconception about the nature of books which contain knowledge. It is thought that such books are something the contents of which have to be crammed into our heads. I think the opposite is closer to the truth. Books are there to keep the knowledge in while we use our heads for something better. Books may also be a better place for such knowledge. In my own head any book-knowledge has a half-life of a few weeks. So I leave knowledge, for safekeeping, to books and libraries and go fishing, sometimes for fish, sometimes for new knowledge.

Books are there to keep the knowledge in while we use our heads for something better.

I know that I am shockingly ignorant. I could take exams in college but could not pass any of them. Worse than that: I treasure my ignorance; I feel snug in it. It does not cloud my naiveté, my simplicity of mind, my ability to marvel childishly at nature and recognize a miracle even if I see it every day. If, with my 71 years, I am still digging on the fringes of knowledge, I owe it to the childish attitude. "Blessed are the pure in heart, for they shall see God," says the Bible. "For they can understand Nature," say I.

I do not want to be misunderstood—I do not depreciate knowledge, and I have worked long and hard to know something of all fields of science related to biology. Without them I could do no research. But I have retained only what I need for an understanding, an intuitive grasp, and in order to know in which book to find what. This was fun, and we must have fun, or else our work is no good.

My next remark is about time relations. The time spent in school is relatively short compared to the time thereafter. I am stressing this because it is widely thought that everything we have to know to do our job well we have to learn in school. This is wrong because, during the long time which follows school, we are apt to forget, anyway, what we have learned there, while we have ample time for study. In fact, most of us have to learn all our lives, and it was with gray hair that I took up the study of quantum mechanics, myself. So what the school has to do, in the first place, is to make us learn how to learn, to whet our appetites for knowledge, to teach us the delight of doing a job well and the excitement of creativity, to teach us to love what we do, and to help us to find what we love to do.

My friend Gerard quoted Fouchet as advising us to take from the altar of knowledge the fire, not the ashes. Being of more earthly disposition, I would advise you to take the meat, not the bones. Teachers, on the whole, have a remarkable preference for bones, especially dry ones. Of course, bones are important, and now and then we all like to suck a bit on them, but only after having eaten the meat. What I mean to say is that we must not *learn* things, we must *live* things. This is true for almost everything. Shakespeare and all of literature must be *lived*, music, paintings, and sculptures have to be *made*, dramas have to be *acted*. This is even true for history: we should live through it, through the spirit of the various periods, instead of storing their data. I am glad to say that this trend—to live things—is becoming evident even in the teaching of science. The most recent trend is not to *teach* the simpler laws of nature, but to make our students *discover* them for themselves in simple experiments. Of course, I know data are important. They may be even interesting, but only after we have consumed the meat, the substance. After this we may even become curious about them and retain them. But taught before this they are just dull, and they dull, if not kill, the spirit.

It is a widely spread opinion that memorizing will not hurt, that knowledge does no harm. I am afraid it may. Dead knowledge dulls the spirit, fills the stomach without nourishing the body. The mind is not a bottomless pit, and if we put in one thing we might have to leave out another. By a more live teaching we can fill the soul and reserve the mind for the really important things. We may even spare time we need for expanding subjects.

Such teaching, which fills both the soul and the mind, may help man to meet one of his most formidable problems, what to do with himself. The most advanced societies, like ours, can already produce more than they can consume, and with advancing automation the discrepancy is increasingly rapidly. We try to meet the challenge by producing useless things, like armaments. But this is no final answer. In the end we will have to work less. But then, what will we do with ourselves. Lives cannot be left empty. Man needs excitement and challenge, and in an affluent society everything is within easy reach. And boredom is dangerous, for it can easily make a society seek excitement in political adventure and in brinkmanship, following irresponsible and ignorant leaders. Our own society has recently shown alarming signs of this trend. In a world where atomic bombs can fly from one end to the other in seconds, this is tantamount to suicide. By teaching live arts and science, the school could open up the endless horizons and challenges of intellectual and artistic life and make whole life an exciting adventure. I believe that in our teaching not only must details and generalizations be in balance, but our whole teaching must be balanced with general human values.

I want to conclude with a few remarks on single subjects, first, science. Science has two aspects: it has to be part of any education, of humanistic culture. But we also have to teach science as preparation for jobs. If we distinguish sharply between these two aspects then the talk about the "two cultures" will lose its meaning.

A last remark I want to make is about the teaching of history, not only because it is the most important subject, but also because I still have in my nostrils the acid smell of my own sweat which I produced when learning its data. History has two chapters: National History and World History. National history is a kind of family affair and I will not speak about it. But what is world history? In its essence it is the story of man, how he rose from his animal status to his present elevation. This is a fascinating story and is linked to a limited number of creative men, its heroes, who created new knowledge, new moral or ethical values, or new beauty. Opposing this positive side of history there is a negative, destructive side linked to the names of kings, barons, generals, and dictators who, with their greed and lust for power, made wars, fought battles, and mostly created misery, destroying what other men had built. These are the heroes of the history we teach at present as world history. Not only is this history negative and lopsided, it is false, too, for it omits the lice, rats, malnutrition, and epidemics which had more to do with the course of things than generals and kings, as Zineser ably pointed out. The world history we teach should also be more truthful and include the stench, dirt, callousness, and misery of past ages, to teach us to appreciate progress and what we have. We need not falsify history; history has a tendency to falsify itself, because only the living return from the battlefield to tell stories. If the dead could return but once and tell about their ignominious end, history and politics would be different today. A truer history would also be simpler.

As the barriers between the various sciences have disappeared, so the barriers between science and humanities may gradually melt away. Dating through physical methods has become a method of research in history, while x-ray spectra and microanalysis have become tools in the study of painting. I hope that the achievements of human psychology may help us, also, to rewrite human history in a more unified and translucent form.

The story of man's progress is not linked to any period, nation, creed, or color, and could teach to our youngsters a wider human solidarity. This they will badly need when rebuilding political and human relations, making them compatible with survival.

In spite of its many chapters, our teaching has, essentially, but one object, the production of men who can fill their shoes and stand erect with their eyes on the wider horizons. This makes the school, on any level, into the most important public institution and the teacher into the most important public figure. As we teach today, so the morrow will be.

APPENDIX F

CLASSROOM TEST OF SCIENTIFIC REASONING

Directions to Students:

!!DO NOT OPEN THIS BOOKLET UNTIL YOU ARE TOLD TO DO SO!!

This is a test of your ability to apply aspects of scientific and mathematical reasoning to analyze a situation, make a prediction, or solve a problem. In some test items you will be asked to show your work, or explain your answer, or both. Try to answer as completely as you can in the spaces provided. On some items these explanations are more important than your actual answer. When the item lists answers, circle the best answer and explain your selection. *If you do not fully understand what is being asked in an item, please ask the test administrator for clarification.*

Classroom Test of Scientific Reasoning

Item 1   Suppose you are given two balls of clay of equal size and shape. The two balls are also of equal weight. One of the balls is flattened into a pancake-shaped piece. Which of these statements is correct?

(a) The ball weighs more than the pancake-shaped piece.

(b) The two pieces weigh the same.

(c) The pancake-shaped piece weighs more than the ball.

Please explain your selection.

Item 2   The two cylinders in the drawing to the right are filled to the same level with water. The cylinders are identical in size and shape. Also shown are two marbles, one made of glass and one made of steel. The marbles are the same size, but the steel one is much heavier than the glass one.

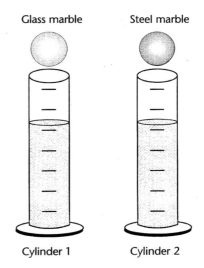

Glass marble   Steel marble

Cylinder 1   Cylinder 2

When the glass marble is put into Cylinder 1, it sinks to the bottom and the water level rises to the 6th mark. If we put the steel marble into Cylinder 2, then the water will rise

(a) to a lower level than it did in Cylinder 1.

(b) to a higher level than it did in Cylinder 1.

(c) to the same level as it did in Cylinder 1.

Please explain your selection.

Item 3 Note the wide and narrow cylinders to the right, which have equally spaced marks on them. Water is poured into the wide cylinder up to the 4th mark (see A).

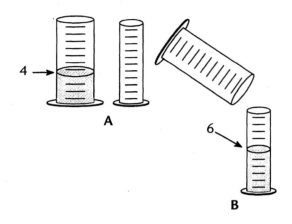

This water rises to the 6th mark when poured into the narrow cylinder (see B). Water is now poured into the wide cylinder up to the 6th mark. How high would this water rise if it were poured into the empty narrow cylinder?

Please show (or explain) how you arrived at your answer.

Item 4 Water is now poured into the narrow cylinder (described in Question 3 above) up to the 11th mark. How high would this water rise if it were poured into the empty wide cylinder?

Answer:

Please show (or explain) how you arrived at your answer.

Item 5   The drawing at right shows three strings hanging from a bar. The strings have metal weights attached to their ends. String 1 and String 3 are the same length. String 2 is shorter. A 10-unit weight is attached to the end of String 1. A 10-unit weight is also attached to the end of String 2. A 5-unit weight is attached to the end of String 3. The strings (and attached weights) can be swung back and forth, and the time it takes for the strings and weights to make a complete swing can be timed. Suppose you wanted to find out whether length of string has an effect on the time it takes to swing back and forth. Which strings would you use to find out?

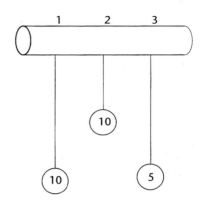

Answer:

Please explain why you choose those strings.

Item 6   Suppose you wanted to find out whether the amount of weight attached to the end of a string has an effect on the time it takes for a string to swing back and forth. Which of the strings in Question 5 above would you use to find out?

Answer:

Please explain why you chose those strings.

Item 7 Twenty flies are placed in each of four glass tubes shown in the drawing. The tubes are sealed. Tubes I and II are partially covered with black paper; Tubes III and IV are not covered. The tubes are suspended in midair by strings as shown and then exposed to red light for five minutes. The number of flies in the uncovered part of each tube is shown in the drawing.

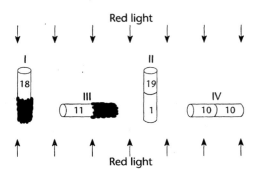

This experiment shows that flies respond to (*respond* means to move toward or away from):

(a) red light but not to gravity.

(b) gravity but not to red light.

(c) both red light and gravity.

(d) neither red light nor gravity.

Please explain your selection.

Item 8 In a second experiment, blue light was used instead of red. The results are shown in the drawing. These data show that flies respond to (respond means to move toward or away from):

(a) blue light but not to gravity.

(b) gravity but not to blue light.

(c) both blue light and gravity.

(d) neither blue light nor gravity.

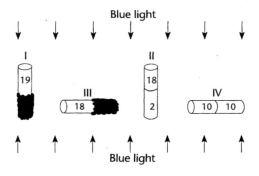

Please explain your selection.

Item 9 Six square pieces of wood are put into a cloth bag and mixed. The six pieces are identical in size and shape, but three pieces are red and three are yellow. Suppose someone reaches into the bag without looking and pulls out one piece. What are the chances that the piece is red?

Answer:

Please show (or explain) how you arrived at your answer.

Item 10 Three red square pieces of wood, four yellow square pieces, and five blue square pieces are put into a cloth bag. Four red round pieces, two yellow round pieces, and three blue round pieces are also put into the bag. All the pieces are then mixed. Suppose someone reaches into the bag—without looking and without feeling for a particular shape piece—and pulls out one piece. What are the chances that the piece is a red or blue circle?

Answer:

Please show (or explain) how you arrived at your answer.

Item 11 The drawing to the right shows a box with a light bulb and four buttons numbered 1, 2, 3, and 4. The bulb will light when the correct button is pushed or the correct combination of buttons are pushed at the same time. Your problem is to figure out which button or buttons must be pushed to light the bulb. Make a list of all the buttons and all the combinations of buttons you would push to figure out how to make the bulb light.

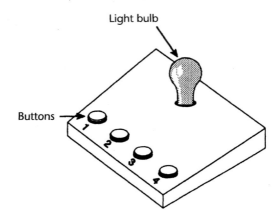

Light bulb

Buttons

Item 12 The fish in the drawing above were caught by a fisherman, who noticed that some of the fish were big and some were small. Also some had wide stripes, and others had narrow stripes. This made the fisherman wonder if there was a relation between the size of the fish and the width of their stripes.

Do you think there is a relation between the size of the fish and the width of their stripes?

(a) Yes

(b) No

Please explain your choice:

Answers and Thinking Pattern Assessed

Item 1 (b) The two pieces weigh the same because no clay has been added or taken away. (Conservation of weight)

Item 2 (c) The water will rise to the same level in both cylinders because the marbles have the same volume and thus displace the same amount of water. (Conservation of displaced volume)

Item 3 The water will rise to the 9th mark. The relationship is proportional: 4/6 = 6/9. (Proportional thinking)

Item 4 The water will rise to 7⅓ marks in the wide cylinder. The same proportional relationship holds as in Question 3 above: 4/6 = 7.33/11. (Advanced proportional thinking)

Item 5 Strings 1 and 2 should be used. They vary in length but not in weight, therefore any observed difference in time would be the result of the variation in length. (Identification and control of variables)

Item 6 Strings 1 and 3 should be used. They vary in weight but not in length, therefore any observed difference in time would be the result of weight variation. (Identification and control of variables)

Item 7 (b) Tube III shows a response to gravity, because the majority of flies (19/20) are at the top, even though the amount of red light is the same at either end. A comparison of Tubes II and IV reveals no significant difference in fly distribution (i.e., 11 to 9 versus 10 to 10), therefore the amount of red light appears to have no effect on the flies. (Isolation and control of variables, probabilistic thinking)

Item 8 (c) Tube III shows a response to gravity as above. A comparison of Tubes II and IV reveals a significant difference in fly distribution that is not likely to result from chance alone (i.e., 18 to 2 versus 10 to 10), therefore the amount of blue light appears to have an effect on the flies. (Isolation and control of variables, probabilistic thinking)

Item 9 3/6 or 1/2. Of these pieces, 3 of 6 or 1 of 2 are red. (Probabilistic and proportional thinking)

Item 10 Seven of the 21 pieces are red or blue circles, so the chances are 7 of 21 or 1 of 3. (Probabilistic and proportional thinking)

Item 11 1, 2, 3, 4, 12, 13, 14, 23, 24, 34, 123, 124, 134, 234, 1234. There are 15 different combinations. (Combinatorial thinking)

Item 12 (b, no) There appears to be no relationship between fish size (large and small) and stripe width (wide and narrow), because the ratio of wide to narrow stripe is the same on both sizes of fish (3 to 4 among the large fish and 9 to 12—that is, 3 to 4—among the small fish. For a relation to exist, there would need to be, for example, mostly wide stripes on the large fish and mostly small stripes on the small fish or vice versa. (Correlational thinking)

Scoring

Responses on each item should be scored as correct or incorrect. To be considered correct, the student should select the correct answer and provide a reasonable explanation. Of course, explanations others than those given may be considered reasonable and should be scored as correct. Total scores of 0–4 indicate empirical-inductive thinking. Scores of 5–8 are transitional, and scores of 9–12 indicate the use of hypothetical-deductive level thinking.

APPENDIX G

LEARNING CYCLES

Teacher Material
Electrolysis of Water
Law of Definite Proportions
Atomic Theory

Learning Cycle 1

Is Water a "Pure" Substance?

Synopsis   To test the postulate of ancient Greek theory that claims that water is a "pure" substance, students pass electricity through water to see if it decomposes. The electricity causes the water to bubble, and the bubbles are collected in test tubes. Students use flame tests to determine that the gases are not identical, suggesting that water is not a pure substance but consists of at least two different substances in a 2-to-1 ratio. Thus, evidence is obtained that allows introduction of the *law of definite proportions* and *atomic theory*. This is a hypothetical-deductive learning cycle.

Suggested Time   Two or three class periods

Background Information   The ancient Greek four-substance theory consists of the following postulates:
1. Everything in the universe consists of one of four basic pure substances or various combinations of the four.
2. The four substances are fire, air, water, and earth.
3. Each of the four pure substances has its own "natural" place.
4. The natural place of fire is above air, which is above water, which is above earth.

The experimental result that gas bubbles are formed at both electrodes when electricity passes through water suggests that water can be broken down; hence, it is not a pure substance (see figure below).

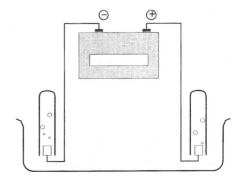

Further, the different gas reactions to flame tests suggests that the gases are not the same "type." Instead, water appears to be composed of two different and simpler substances, thus contradicting the postulate that air is a pure substance. Twice as much of one type of gas is formed, which supports the theory that substances are made of indivisible particles (atoms) that combine with other atoms in simple units (molecules). The results further suggest that water is composed of units that consist of two of one type of atom for every one of the other type of atom. Chemists have named the first gas *hydrogen* and the second *oxygen*. Hence, water appears to consist of molecules of two hydrogen atoms for every one oxygen atom.

The reaction that takes place when water is decomposed by a flow of electricity is called an *electrolysis reaction*. Electrolysis reactions are produced in *electrolytic cells*, which consist of two electrodes in an aqueous solution. The cell is driven by a battery (or some other source of direct electrical current). The battery acts as an electron source, adding electrons to one electrode and withdrawing them from the other. Withdrawing electrons from an electrode gives it a positive charge, while adding electrons to an electrode gives it a negative charge.

The positive electrode (*anode*) attracts negative ions. The negative electrode (*cathode*) attracts positive ions. The decomposition reaction at each electrode is as follows:

$$\text{Cathode:} \quad 4H_2O + 4e^- \rightarrow 2H_2 + 4OH^-$$
$$\text{Anode:} \quad 2H_2O \rightarrow 4H^+ + O_2 + 4e^-$$

$$\text{Overall reaction:} \quad 6H_2O \rightarrow 2H_2 + \underline{O_2 + 4H^+ + 4OH^-}$$
$$4H_2O$$

Canceling $4H_2O$ from both sides gives:

$$2H_2O \rightarrow 2H_2 + O_2$$

Use of a 5% solution of H_2SO_4, which acts as a catalyst, increases the electrical conductivity of the water to expedite gas production. The H_2SO_4 solution should be prepared and presented as "water." Electrolysis occurs in tap water but proceeds more slowly without the H_2SO_4. Distilled water is such a poor electrolyte that no visible gas production occurs.

Initially, the student experiments are only designed to test one postulate of the four-substance theory—that is, "Water is a pure substance." The postulate "Fire is a pure substance" is not tested. However, as mentioned, the result that two "types" of gases (airs) are collected and identified contradicts the postulate that air is pure. On the other hand, bubbles of air rising in water supports the postulate that the natural place of air is above water.

In addition to testing some of the postulates of the ancient Greek theory, this investigation enables students to:

a. use the 2-to-1 ratio of volume of hydrogen to oxygen gas to introduce atomic theory and to propose a 2-to-1 ratio of atoms, to generate the formula H_2O, and to use this as an example of the law of definite proportions.

b. use the experimental results to introduce the terms *molecule, compound,* and *element.*

c. identify hydrogen and oxygen with their respective chemical symbols. A symbol may be one capital letter (such as H) or one capital and a second, lowercase letter (such as Na).

d. identify reactants and products in chemical reactions.

e. assemble models of atoms showing reactants and products in chemical reactions.

f. use subscripts to indicate the number of atoms in a molecule.

g. recognize that the "2" in symbols, such as 2HCl, represents two molecules of HCl.

Teaching Tips   *Advance Preparation*

1. Use a 5% solution of sulfuric acid (H_2SO_4) to prepare the "water" for the students' experiments: Add 27 milliliters (ml) of concentrated H_2SO_4 to 950 ml of tap water. **CAUTION:** *Add acid to water slowly.* An alternate conducting solution can be made by dissolving 50 grams of Na_2SO_4 in 950 ml of water.

2. Atomic models may be made of toothpicks and Styrofoam balls, marshmallows, and so on. If they are available, commercial models have an advantage: They are color-coded and have the correct number of holes needed for correct bonding.

Engagement

1. The ancient Greek four-substance theory, including the postulate that each substance has its own "natural" place (see Study Question 1), should be introduced and discussed. Mention several observations that it can explain, including the postulate that each of the four substances has its own "natural" location (see Study Question 2). Convince students that the theory makes some sense and should be taken seriously. For example, we observe that flames tend to rise in the air. Why? Because flames consist of fire and the natural place for fire is above air. Note that the prime example of fire is the sun. Where is the sun? It is above the air—just where it should be, according to the theory!

Exploration

1. Have one electricity-conducting apparatus assembled (but not connected electrically) so that students can observe the proper setup. It would be preferable to cover the portion of the nichrome wire outside the test tube with heat-shrink tubing to prevent electrolysis products from escaping from the test tubes.

2. After the students' initial observations and recording of data, assemble the class for a discussion. (Leave the apparatus running.) Ask students what they saw—for example, bubbles formed, gas was collected, one tube has more gas.

Record observations on the classroom chalkboard. Two major questions should be addressed. (a) How can the observations be explained? (b) Do the observations support or contradict the claim that water is a fundamental pure substance? that air is a pure substance? that the natural place of air is above water?

3. Students should understand that results tend to contradict the claims that water and air are pure substances, because it appears that the water is separating to form two gases (two new substances). (By the way, how do we know that air is a substance in the first place? Does it have weight? Does it take up space?) But how much of each gas is there and are the gases *really* different? How could we tell?

Using a tube of air in water, demonstrate how to use a grease pencil to mark the level of gas in the tube and how to remove a test tube and test the gas using a burning or glowing splint. Send students back to their stations to measure the volume of gases and to test the gases with a burning splint.

They should discover that one of the gases causes the glowing splint to "pop," while the other gas makes the splint burst into flame. These observations provide evidence that the gases are different. But are they *pure* substances? Or could they also be broken down into still simpler substances? At this point, you can introduce another ancient Greek theory that claims that all substances consist of tiny, unseen, indivisible particles called *atoms*. Thus, the question becomes, "Are the two gases made of two different kinds of atoms?"

4. To attempt to answer this question, have students list their measured values on the board for volumes of the "popping gas" and the "burning gas." Ask, "How we can compare all of these different values?" The students should calculate a class average for each gas and generate a ratio. Most likely this will be close to 2:1. Ask, "What, if anything, does this 'small whole-number ratio' tell us about the nature of the two gases?" Write the following argument on the board:

If . . . the two gases are made of two different types of atoms (i.e., indivisible particles) that are linked together in small groups in the water (e.g., one atom of the popping gas linked to one atom of the burning gas, or two atoms of the popping gas linked to one atom of the burning gas, or vice versa),

and . . . the volumes of the two gases are compared,

then . . . the volumes should be equal or there should be twice as much of one type of gas as the other.

Because the actual class ratio is 2:1 (or close to it), the claim that atoms exist and that the two gases are made of two different types of these atoms has been supported. Tell students that many other gases separate in these small whole-number ratios, which provides more evidence that supports the atomic theory Chemists have found these simple ratios so often that they have coined the phras "law of definite proportions" to describe the phenomenon.

Term Introduction

1. We thus seem to have evidence to support the idea that water consists of two kinds of atoms, with one kind of atom twice as numerous as the other. Because we appear to have discovered something new—that is, two different kinds of atoms—we should give them names. Of course, we could name them anything we choose, but we should name them the same thing that chemists have already named them: *hydrogen* for the popping gas and *oxygen* for the burning gas. Therefore, water appears to consist of units of two hydrogen atoms combined with one oxygen atom. Chemists call these imagined units *molecules*.

2. Explain that chemists use "models" to help them visualize what might be happening at the invisible level of these imagined atoms and molecules. Instruct the students to "play chemist" and see if they can determine what might be occurring by using one color of ball to represent the imagined hydrogen atoms and a different color of ball to represent imagined oxygen atoms. Have students try to model the reaction "Water reacts with electricity to produce two volumes of hydrogen for every one volume of oxygen." Allow students approximately 10 minutes to explore this reaction using the atomic models.

3. Discuss the results of the students' modeling and explain how chemists use abbreviations to write reactions such as the one below. Explain that some types of atoms have one capital letter as a symbol, such as "H" for hydrogen. When a type of atom uses two letters, such as "Na" for sodium, the first letter is always capitalized and the second letter is always lowercase.

   Water reacts to give 2 volumes hydrogen and 1 volume oxygen

   $$H_2O \rightarrow 2H + 1 O$$

   or

   $$2H_2O \rightarrow 2H_2 + 1 O_2$$

4. Point out that *both reactions fit the 2-to-1 ratio of hydrogen to oxygen.* Our data cannot determine which, if either, is correct. Nevertheless, experiments done by chemists have supported the idea that these gases occur in H–H and O–O units called *diatomic molecules* (show models).

5. Now introduce and define the terms *element, compound, reaction, chemical equation, reactants,* and *products* in the context of the students' experiments and modeling. (The smallest particles that make up substances are *atoms.* Two or more atoms combine to form *molecules.* A molecule is the smallest part of a substance that retains the properties of that substance. Substances that contain only one type of atom are called *elements.* A *compound* is a substance formed from two or more different elements, always combined in a fixed ratio.) You may wish to organize these definitions using a "tree," such as the one on the next page.

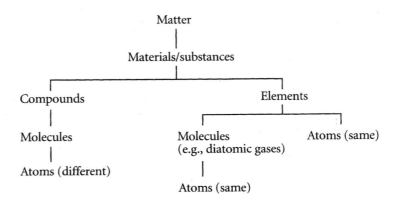

Concept Application

1. Have students do the Additional Activity, using models to better understand chemical reactions.

Chemical Terms	**Thinking Skills**
atom	accurately describe nature
molecule	generate alternative hypotheses
element	plan and conduct experiments
reaction	generate logical predictions
chemical equation	organize and analyze data
reactants	draw and apply conclusions
compound	
products	
diatomic molecule	

Sample Test Questions

Use the following key to answer Questions 1 through 7.
   a. Supports the ancient Greek four-substance theory
   b. Supports the atomic theory
   c. Supports neither theory

1. Bubbles are seen rising in water. (a)
2. Water is wet. (c)
3. Water can be separated into two different gases. (b)
4. When water separates, twice as much of one type of gas is produced as the other type of gas. (b)
5. Metals sink in water. (a)
6. Fire is hot. (c)
7. The sun appears high above the sky. (a)

8. Which of the following could *not* be a symbol for a newly discovered element?

   a. Cq
   b. Di
   c. Z
   *d. ZT

Questions 9 through 13 refer to the reaction

$$N_2(g) + 3H_2(g) \rightarrow 2NH_3$$

9. What is or are the product(s)?

   a. $N_2(g)$
   b. $3H_2(g)$
   *c. $2NH_3$
   d. all of the above
   e. a and b

10. What is or are the reactant(s)?

    a. $N_2(g)$
    b. $3H_2(g)$
    c. $2NH3(g)$
    d. all of the above
    *e. a and b

11. How many molecules are in $2NH_3$?

    a. 1
    *b. 2
    c. 3
    d. 5
    e. 6

12. How many atoms of hydrogen are in $2NH_3$?

    a. 1
    b. 2
    c. 3
    d. 5
    *e. 6

13. How many atoms of nitrogen are in $2NH_3$?

    a. 1
    *b. 2
    c. 3
    d. 5
    e. 6

Learning Cycle 1

Is Water a "Pure" Substance?

Introduction   Water is one of the most common, familiar, and important substances known. Without it, life does not exist. But what exactly *is* water? The ancient Greeks believed that water was one of four basic "types" of substances. According to ancient Greek theory, everything in the universe consists of four basic substances called *fire, air, water,* and *earth.* According to the theory, these four substances are "pure" because they cannot be broken apart to form still simpler substances. In other words, fire, air, water, and earth are *the* basic building blocks of the universe, and everything consists of one or more of these substances.

The purpose of this investigation is to test aspects of this theory by exploring the nature of water. Is water a pure substance? Or does water consist of some combination of still more basic substances that were unknown to the ancient Greeks?

Objectives   1. To test aspects of the ancient Greek four-substance theory, which claims, among other things, that water is a pure substance.

2. To introduce atomic theory and to model the interactions of atoms during several chemical reactions.

Materials   *1 600-ml beaker*   *matches*
2 medium test tubes   *wood splints*
1 9-volt battery   *atomic model set*
2 test leads with alligator clips   *grease pencil*
2 pieces of nichrome wire   *metric ruler*
water supplied by the teacher

Procedure   1. With your partner, examine the apparatus set up by your teacher. The apparatus uses a battery as a source of electricity that passes through a sample of water.

2. Using the materials provided, set up a similar apparatus at your lab station. Use the water supplied by your teacher.

3. To start electricity flowing, hook one alligator clip to the positive end of your battery and the other to the negative end. But before you start, think about what might happen to the water. Consider the following argument:

If . . .   the ancient Greeks are correct that water is a pure substance that cannot be broken apart,

and . . .   electricity passes through a sample of water,

then . . .   the electricity should have no effect on the water—that is, the water should not break apart.

On the other hand,

> *If* . . . water is a combination of simpler substances,
>
> *and* . . . electricity passes through a sample of water,
>
> *then* . . . the electricity may cause the water to break apart into simpler substances.

Which of these possible results do you think will occur?

_____

Other than what you may have been told, what reason(s) do you have for your answer?

_____

4. Hook up the wires and allow the electricity to flow through the water for at least 5 minutes. While you wait, record as many observations as you can below.

_____

_____

_____

_____

5. With your lab partner, discuss the meaning of your observations, particularly in light of the previous arguments and possible results. Be ready to share your observations, arguments, and tentative conclusions with the class. Use the space below to record important points that you discuss.

_____

_____

_____

_____

6. Record results of the flame test below. What do the results imply about the nature of the gases?

_____

_____

_____

_____

7. Measure and record the amount of each type of gas produced in your experiment.

_____

_____

_____

_____

8. What is the ratio of the volumes of the two gases based on the class average?

_____

What does this ratio suggest about the nature of the two gases, the nature of air, and the nature of water?

_____

_____

_____

_____

Additional Activity

Atoms are so small that they cannot be seen without sophisticated electron microscopes. However, chemists can better visualize atoms and molecules and their interactions by manipulating atomic models.

1. Use atomic models to model reactions a through f depicted below.
2. To do so, you will first need to select the correct "atoms." Then build one or more molecules (as needed) of each substance until the number of atoms is the same in the reactants and products. *Do not* break apart reactant molecules (models) to make product molecules (models).
3. Leave models intact on both sides of the equation. The volumes of gases react in small whole-number ratios. Notice that these same ratios may be thought of as the ratios in which the molecules react.
4. Use the space provided to draw a three-dimensional representation of each molecule in the equation and have your teacher check your models before you continue to the next equation.

a. water(l) $\rightarrow$ 1 volume of oxygen gas + 2 volumes of hydrogen gas

_____ $H_2O(l) \rightarrow$ _____ $O_2(g) +$ _____ $H_2(g)$

b. 1 volume of hydrogen gas + 1 volume of chlorine gas $\rightarrow$ 2 volumes of hydrogen chloride gas

_____ $H_2(g) +$ _____ $Cl_2(g) \rightarrow$ _____ $HCl(g)$

c. 1 volume of methane gas + 2 volumes of oxygen gas → 1 volume of dioxide gas + 2 volumes of water vapor

_____ $CH_4(g)$ + _____ $O_2(g)$ → _____ $CO_2(g)$ + _____ $H_2O(l)$

d. 1 volume of nitrogen gas + 3 volumes of hydrogen gas → 2 volumes of ammonia gas

_____ $N_2(g)$ + _____ $H_2(g)$ → _____ $NH_3(g)$

e. 2 volumes of sulfur dioxide + 1 volume of oxygen gas → 2 volumes of sulfur trioxide

_____ $SO_2(g)$ + _____ $O_2(g)$ → _____ $SO_3(g)$

f. 1 volume of oxygen gas + 2 volumes of hydrogen gas → ?

_____ $O_2(g)$ + _____ $H_2(g)$ → _____ _____

Study Questions   1. Do the results of your experiment and those of your classmates support or contradict the ancient Greek theory that claims that the universe consists of fire, air, water, and earth? Explain. (*Hint:* The ancient Greek theory also claims that each of the four substances has its own "natural" location: fire above air, air above water, water above earth. The theory thus explains, for example, why heavy objects—earths—fall in air or sink in water. They are returning to their natural places.)

_____

_____

_____

_____

2. Do the results of the experiments support or contradict the part of the theory that claims that water is a "pure" substance? Explain.

_____

_____

_____

_____

3. Do the results of your experiments support or contradict the part of the theory that claims that air is a pure substance? Explain.

_____

_____

_____

_____

4. What is the name given by chemists to the "popping" gas? to the "burning" gas?

_____

_____

_____

_____

5. What is the difference in the meaning of the following pairs of chemical symbols:

   a. Co and CO
   b. Si and SI
   c. Cs and CS

6. Draw a diagram that shows the difference between H and H_2.

7. Draw a diagram of O_2 and H_2O.

8. Use the terms *atom(s), molecule(s), diatomic, element,* and *compound* with reference to O_2 and H_2O.

_____

_____

_____

_____

9. Use the following reaction:

$$H_2(g) + Cl_2(g) \rightarrow 2HCl(g)$$

   a. Identify the reactant(s).
   b. Identify the product(s).
   c. What does the symbol "(g)" mean?
   d. What does the "2" in H_2 mean?

10. Explain the meaning of the *law of definite proportions* and give an example.

_____

_____

_____

_____

_____

_____

_____

11. Generate a hypothesis for how electricity flowing through water causes the hydrogen and oxygen atoms to separate.

_____

_____

_____

_____

_____

_____

_____

_____

Teacher Material
Independent Variables
Dependent Variables
Alternative Hypotheses
Predictions

Learning Cycle 2

What Happens When Food Coloring and Detergent Are Put in Milk?

Synopsis Students explore several variables that effect the swirling of milk when food coloring and liquid detergent are added. Students then generate and test alternative hypotheses to explain the swirling. This is a hypothetical-deductive learning cycle.

Suggested Time Two or three class periods

Background Information When small amounts of certain types of liquid detergents are put in milk, the milk starts to swirl. The swirling is very apparent when drops of food coloring are added. The cause(s) of the swirling is not fully understood by chemists. Thus, the primary purpose of this investigation is not to arrive at a single "correct" explanation for the swirling, but to introduce students to the process of generating and testing alternative hypothetical (nonobservable) explanations. Any discussion of specific chemical concepts is a bonus and will vary according to student interest and discovery.

Hypothetical explanations are generated by the creative borrowing of ideas from past experience to try to explain a new experience. The nonobservable explanations, referred to as *hypotheses,* are then tested through the use of experiments in which the hypotheses are assumed to be true so that specific expected observable results (predictions) can be deduced and compared with observable experimental results. When an observed experimental result matches a predicted result, we can conclude that the hypothesis that led to the predicted result has been supported. When an experimental result does *not* match a predicted result, then we can conclude that the hypothesis has *not* been supported.

The following is believed to be known about the substances involved in this investigation and may be helpful in constructing hypotheses for the swirling:

- Detergents are typically composed of three chemicals: 47% phosphates, 16% bleaches, and 37% linear alkylsulfonate (LAS). The phosphates bond with metals such as Ca and Mg. This bonding prevents them from bonding with LAS, which would cause them to precipitate out as soap scum and thus eliminate their effectiveness. LAS is a surface-active agent with a nonpolar hydrocarbon chain that is soluble in fats and oils. LAS also has a polar sulfonate group that sticks out of the oil droplets, thus making oil droplets soluble in water.

$$CH_3(CH_2)_9 - \underset{\underset{CH_3}{|}}{\overset{\overset{H}{|}}{C}} - \underset{}{\bigcirc} - \underset{\underset{O}{|}}{\overset{\overset{O}{|}}{S}} - O^- \ Na^+$$

- Fats and oils are triglycerides. At room temperature, fats are solids and oils are liquids. Oils are nonpolar hydrocarbons that detergents render soluble because of the long hydrocarbon end of a detergent.

$$CH_3(CH_2)_4\text{-}CH\text{=}CH\text{-}CH_2\text{-}CH\text{=}CH\text{-}(CH_2)_7COCH_2$$
$$CH_3(CH_2)_4\text{-}CH\text{=}CH\text{-}CH_2\text{-}CH\text{=}CH\text{-}(CH_2)_7COCH$$
$$CH_3(CH_2)_4\text{-}CH\text{=}CH\text{-}CH_2\text{-}CH\text{=}CH\text{-}(CH_2)_7COCH_2$$

- Food colorings are polar compounds that are water soluble.
- Lactose (milk sugar) is found in concentrations of 2% to 6% in milk.
- Casein, a phosphoprotein, is one of the chief constituents of milk and cheese and is used in the manufacture of plastics and glues.

Teaching Tips   *Engagement*

1. Observation of the phenomenon provides sufficient engagement for this investigation.

Exploration

1. Initially, provide only 2% milk and one type of detergent, but do not start with Dawn or Joy, because these produce little or no swirling.

2. As students observe and record their observations, they will begin to ask for different types of milk, detergent, food coloring, dishes, oils, and so on. Be prepared to supply as many items as possible. Here is a sample list of possibilities:

Detergents	Milk	Other
Sunlight	skim	vegetable oil
Dawn	1%	mineral oil
Ivory	2%	motor oil
Palmolive	whole (4%)	ink
Ajax	half and half	lump calcium
Joy	cream	albumin
Dove	lactose	
generic	nonfat dry milk	
	casein (milk protein)	
	condensed	
	nondairy creamer	
dropping pipettes	ethyl alcohol	ring stand with ring

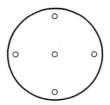

Special Notes:

    a. The ring stand is provided for students who wish to look at the swirling from underneath.

    b. Many of these items are found at home and can be tested by the students as a homework project.

    c. The Dawn and Joy detergent brands should be included at this time because, as mentioned, they do not work well. This result should provoke students to wonder why. Sunlight works very well.

    d. Provide plenty of petri dishes: Students like to run several experiments at once and compare results.

    e. Another experiment that students can try at home is to emulsify vegetable oil in water using a blender. Other materials to test using a blender are egg albumin (egg white) in water, and lactose (milk sugar) in water.

    f. Use glass instead of plastic droppers to make cleanup easier.

    g. Nonfat milk actually contains 1 gram of butter fat.

Term Introduction

1. Summarize students' results and ideas on the board by writing them down in three columns for (a) observations, (b) hypotheses, and (c) experimental predictions. Do not label the columns at the outset. Rather, simply ask students to report their observations, their tentative explanations, and how they thought their experiments should have turned out. The items in the second and third columns should be matched so that the second column lists a specific hypothesis and the corresponding item in the third column lists the experimental prediction that was derived from the hypothesis; for example,

If . . .	swirling is caused by heat	*then* . . .	temperature should rise.
If . . .	swirling is caused by high density	*then* . . .	other objects of high density should produce swirling.
If . . .	swirling is caused by fat molecules in the milk	*then* . . .	nonfat milk should not swirl.

2. Once the three columns are complete, ask students for suggestions as to what terms should be used to label the columns. They will most likely suggest that the first column be labeled "Observations," at which point you should agree and write it at the top of the column.

3. Now ask for suggestions for a term or terms to label the second column. When a student suggests the term "Hypotheses," you should agree and write "Alternative Hypotheses" at the top of the second column. You should define the term *hypothesis* as a tentative, but not directly observable, explanation for some phenomenon—that is, a tentative answer to a causal question. We have a list of alternative hypotheses here because we have several different (alternative) explanations.

4. Now ask for suggested labels for the third column. This one will be more difficult. Students may suggest "Experiment" or perhaps "Expected Result." Even if no one suggests the term *prediction,* you should introduce it and write "Prediction" at the top of the third column. Define *prediction* as the "expected or predicted result" of a particular experiment given that the hypothesis being tested is assumed to be correct. This would be a good time to distinguish between the terms *hypothesis* and *prediction.* (*Note:* In previous courses, many students may have been taught erroneously that predictions are the same as hypotheses. This can cause considerable confusion.)

Here are examples of possible student observations:

a. Food coloring first pushed to the outside edge of the dish.
b. Food coloring moves from the edge, underneath, and is pulled toward the center.
c. Movement eventually stops and starts again when more detergent is added.
d. When it stops, everything moves back toward the center at the surface.
e. When a thin layer of milk is placed in a dish and detergent is placed in the center, the milk is repelled.
f. The higher the fat content, the slower the movement.
g. Nothing happens when pure water is used.
h. When powdered detergent is used, there are many centers of movement.
i. Nothing happens with pure oils.
i. Dawn and Joy do nothing or are extremely slow.
k. Sunlight is fast.

Here are examples of possible student hypotheses:

a. Heat produced convection currents.
b. Detergent broke the surface tension.
c. Movement was produced by a combination of the higher density of the detergent and subsequent diffusion of the dyes.
d. Detergent and milk repel one another.
e. Detergent and coloring attract one another.
f. Fat inhibits the reaction.
g. Detergent reacts with milk protein (casein).
h. Detergent reacts with milk sugar (lactose).
i. Detergent reacts with vitamin D.
j. Detergent reacts in milk fat.
k. The force of the detergent drop falling into the milk forms waves.

Here are examples of student hypotheses followed by specific predictions:

a. If a convection cell is caused by heat, then a temperature rise should be detected.

b. If surface tension is the cause, then milk and water should behave similarly.

c. If surface tension was caused by higher density, then any other object of higher density should cause a similar result.

d. If milk and detergent repel one another, then any time small amounts come in contact, they should remain separate.

e. If detergent and color attract one another, then detergent and dye alone produce a similar result.

f. If fat inhibits the reaction, then as the fat content increases, the rate of movement should be lower.

g, h, i., j. If detergent reacts with milk protein, milk sugar, vitamin D, or milk fat, then varying the amounts of these molecules should cause different rates of swirling.

k. If force is a factor, then drops from different heights should cause different rates of swirling.

5. Introduce the terms *independent variable* and *dependent variable* in the same manner as above by first asking for examples of factors that were different from one experiment to the next. Label the factors that the students changed—such as the type of milk, the amount of milk, the type of detergent—as the *independent variables*, that is, the factors that independently varied among experiments. Also introduce the term *values* to refer to specific "amounts" of these variables; for example, 1% and 2% milk; 15 ml and 30 ml of milk; and Ivory, Dawn, and Palmolive. The term *dependent variable* can be introduced as a factor that depends on changes in an independent variable: in this case, the rate of swirling or the length of time before the swirling stops. Alternative terms for independent and dependent variables that are sometimes better understood are *input and outcome variables, cause and effect, change and response,* and *what you did and what happened.*

6. From previous science classes, students should be familiar with the concept of a *controlled experiment*—that is, an experiment in which the values of only one independent variable are allowed to vary. Nevertheless, take this opportunity to review this most important idea. In this context, a controlled experiment to test the possible effect of fat content in milk would compare 1%, 2%, and 4% milk using the same type of dish, the same type of detergent, the same type and color of food coloring, the same drop size, and so on.

7. Discuss which, if any, of the alternative hypotheses are supported or not supported by the students' experimental results. Point out that hypotheses are neither proven nor disproven. Positive results cannot prove a hypothesis, because some other hypothesis could have predicted the same result. Negative results cannot disprove a hypothesis, because the experiment might have contained an uncontrolled variable.

3. A controlled variable in this experiment was the
   a. rate of swirling.
   b. concentration of fat.
   c. length of time the mixture swirled.
   *d. type of detergent.

4. The results of this experiment
   a. prove the hypothesis true.
   b. disprove the hypothesis.
   *c. support the hypothesis.
   d. do not support the hypothesis.

5. The statement that the swirling is caused by a reaction between fat molecules in milk and detergent molecules is
   a. a prediction.
   *b. a hypothesis.
   c. a result.
   d. a causal question.
   e. an experiment.

6. The statement that the rate of swirling should increase with increased fat concentration is
   *a. a prediction.
   b. a hypothesis.
   c. a result.
   d. a causal question.
   e. an experiment.

7. The statement that the rate of swirling increased with increased fat concentration is
   a. a prediction.
   b. a hypothesis.
   *c. a result.
   d. an experiment.
   e. a conclusion.

Questions 8 through 10 refer to the following experiment:

Another group of students thought that a chemical reaction occurred that increased the temperature of the milk. They thought that the temperature rise created a convection current. To test this idea, they compared the temperature in two dishes of milk ten minutes after adding a drop of detergent to one of the dishes.

The statement that the temperature of the milk in the dish with the detergent should be higher than in the dish without the detergent is
   a. a prediction.
   . a hypothesis.

    c. a result.
    d. an experiment.
    e. a conclusion.

9. The primary independent variable being tested is the
    a. length of time.
    b. chemical reaction.
    c. swirling.
  *d. amount of detergent added.
    e. temperature of the milk.

10. The dependent variable in this experiment is the
    a. length of time.
    b. chemical reaction.
    c. swirling.
    d. amount of detergent added.
  *e. temperature of the milk.

Learning Cycle 2

What Happens When Food Coloring and Detergent Are Put in Milk?

Introduction   When drops of food coloring and detergent are put in milk, a strange phenomenon occurs. In this investigation, you will have an opportunity to explore this phenomenon and generate and test possible explanations.

Objectives
1. To investigate variables that affect the strange phenomenon.
2. To generate and test possible explanations for the strange phenomenon.

Materials   *various kinds of milk*   *glass droppers*
various kinds of liquid detergent   *various colors of food coloring*
petri dishes   *measuring devices*

Procedure
1. Pour some milk in a petri dish. Near the outside edge, carefully add four drops of food coloring to the milk. The drops should be of different colors and an equal distance from one another.
2. Place one drop of detergent in the center of the milk and observe what happens.
3. Conduct several additional trials to discover variables that have an effect on the movement. Keep a record of what you did and your results in the space below.

4. Generate at least three alternative explanations for your observations.

_____

_____

_____

_____

5. Test each of your explanations and be prepared to describe your results and their implications during a class discussion. Use the space below to record results.

Study Questions

1. List the independent variables that you found to have an effect on the movement of the liquids. List two values for each variable.

Independent Variables   **Values**

_____

_____

_____

_____

_____

_____

_____

2. What was the primary dependent variable in your experiments?

_____

_____

3. In what sense are controlled experiments better than uncontrolled experiments?

_____

_____

_____

4. In testing the effect of the variables listed in Question 1, did you conduct controlled experiments? _____. Select one variable and explain why you think you either did or did not conduct a controlled experiment.

_____

_____

_____

5. In science, tentative explanations are called *hypotheses*. What three hypotheses did you or others generate for the movement of the liquids?

_____

_____

_____

6. How do hypotheses differ from *predictions*?

_____

_____

_____

_____

7. In general, how are predictions used to test hypotheses?

_____

_____

_____

_____

8. Which of the hypotheses stated in Question 5 were not supported experimentally? Explain.

_____

_____

_____

_____

9. Which of the hypotheses stated in Question 5, if any, were supported experimentally? Explain.

_____

_____

_____

_____

Teacher Material
Density of Solids
Graphing

Learning Cycle 3

How Were Alien Monoliths Sorted?

Synopsis   Using a variety of procedures, students measure the mass and volume of several monoliths that were discovered on an archaeological expedition in Burma in an attempt to discover a method for sorting the monoliths and saving young Indiana Smith from the wrath of the expedition leader. Density is the monoliths' only distinguishing property. The students are given the task of inventing a way to graph this property. This is a descriptive learning cycle.

Suggested Time   Two class periods

Background
Information   The primary purpose of this investigation is to provide students with an opportunity to discover that metals (the monoliths) can be distinguished from one another by their density. All of the metals are painted the same color (black) but vary in length, cross-sectional shape, and weight. All metals of the same type have the same weight-to-volume ratio. When students graph the weight versus the volume of several samples of the same type of metal, they should discover that the points all fall along a straight line. This discovery will provide the opportunity to introduce the term *density* to label this constant weight-to-volume ratio, which is characteristic of each type of metal.

The metals for the investigation can be obtained from several sources. Aluminum rods can be found in any chemical supply catalog. Hardware stores sell copper tubing and rods, aluminum conduit, and iron pipe. Scraps of copper and iron can be obtained from plumbers. Electricians often have aluminum.

You will need to take various rods and tubes, cut them into different lengths, and paint them completely black. You will need enough so that groups of students start with at least four monoliths of varying lengths, thicknesses, and types.

Students typically weigh the cylinders and measure lengths and diameters. Some use water displacement to determine volume, while others may calculate volume from the dimensions. Eventually, all will have to use water displacement to accommodate the hollow tubes.

The density of the monoliths will be calculated from the information on the graphs. After graphing the points for all of the different monoliths, a pattern develops that indicates the linear relationship between the monoliths' weight and volume.

Teaching Tips   *Engagement*
The video clip from *2001: A Space Odyssey,* which shows the opening sequence of apes moving around a monolith, could be shown to students. Use the map that is

included when presenting the story found in the introduction. For added atmosphere, you might wear an Indiana Jones or a Chinese hat.

Exploration

1. A key opening question might be, "What did the archaeologists measure that was used for their sorting?" Discuss the students' suggestions—for example, weight, length, diameter, shape, area, and volume—but be careful not to give too much guidance at the outset. Allow students to explore several variables.

2. Once the data have been gathered, list all of the variable names at the top of the board and have students record their data underneath. The next question, of course, is, "How can we use these data to distinguish among the monoliths?" Challenge students to use the data to construct graphs that might reveal patterns that could in turn reveal an answer. The graphing can be assigned as homework.

Term Introduction

1. The next day, have students display their graphs and any discovered patterns. If necessary, lead them to construct a graph of weight (mass) on the vertical or y axis versus volume on the horizontal or x axis. This graph could be drawn on a transparency or on a large chalkboard or whiteboard grid. Using this graph, draw the lines of best fit that represent different monolith materials.

2. Have the students divide the mass by the volume for three different points on each line. They will notice that the obtained value for each point will be nearly identical. Tell them that this number represents a constant property of each metal that is called the metal's *density*. Make sure that they note that each metal has its own density value. Also point out that density is sometimes referred to as a *compound* variable because its determination requires the prior determination of two other variables (weight and volume). Also point out that for comparative purposes, densities are usually given in units of grams per milliliter of material (g/ml).

3. Have students use a reference book to compare their calculated densities to known densities of the elements in order to identify the monoliths' composition.

Concept Application

1. Students can be given cylinders or irregularly shaped samples of new materials and challenged to identify their composition.

2. The additional activity is included in the student guide as another application of the concept of density.

   Students need to cut the aluminum into a shape that can be used to determine the area, such as a square, a triangle, or a circle. They already know the density of aluminum, so by measuring the mass and area of their samples, they can determine the thickness (height) of each type of aluminum foil.

For a square or rectangular piece of foil:

$$\text{volume} = \text{length} \times \text{width} \times \text{height}$$
$$\text{density} = \text{mass/volume}$$

Height is the unknown.

Dimensional height analysis (in centimeters, or cm):

$$\frac{cm^3}{\text{Density (g)}\;\Big|\;\text{Length (cm)}\;\Big|\;\text{Width (cm)}\;\Big|} \;\frac{\Big|\;\text{Mass (g)}}{\Big|} = \text{Height}$$

For a circular piece of foil:

$$\text{volume} = \pi r^2 h$$
$$\text{density} = \text{mass/volume}$$

Height is the unknown.

Dimensional height (cm) analysis:

$$\frac{cm^3}{\text{Density (g)}\;\Big|\;\;\pi\;\;\Big|\;\;r^2\,(cm^2)\;\Big|} \;\frac{\Big|\;\text{Mass (g)}}{\Big|} = \text{Height}$$

For a triangular piece of foil (right triangle):

$$\text{volume} = \tfrac{1}{2}\,\text{base} \times \text{height} \times \text{height}$$
$$\text{density} = \text{mass/volume}$$

Height is the unknown.

Dimensional height (cm) analysis:

$$\frac{cm^3}{\text{Density (g)}\;\Big|\;\tfrac{1}{2}\,\text{Base (cm)}\;\Big|\;\text{Height (cm)}\;\Big|} \;\frac{\Big|\;\text{Mass (g)}}{\Big|} = \text{Height}$$

Chemical Terms
density
compound variable

Thinking Skills
accurately describe nature
organize and analyze data
draw and apply conclusions

Sample Test Questions

1. A block of wood 105 cm × 0.051 m × 62 mm, weighs 2.72 kg. What is the density of the wood expressed in grams per cubic centimeter?
   a. 8.2×10^{-3} g/cm^3
   b. 8.2×10^{-2} g/cm^3
   *c. 0.82 g/cm^3
   d. 8.2 g/cm^3
   e. 82 g/cm^3

2. Iron has a density of 7.86 g/cm^3 at 20° C. What is the length of an iron sheet 2.00 cm thick and 120.00 cm wide at 20° C with a mass of 50.0 kg?
   a. 9.4×10^7 cm
   b. 1.5×10^6 cm
   c. 1,638 cm
   d. 53 cm
   *e. 26.5 cm

3. Several irregularly shaped pieces of zinc weighing 30.0 g are dropped into a graduated cylinder containing 20.0 cm^3 of water. The water level rises to 24.2 cm^3. What is the density of the zinc?
   *a. 7.1 g/cm^3
   b. 1.2 g/cm^3
   c. 1.5 g/cm^3
   d. 0.8 g/cm^3
   e. 0.67 g/cm^3

4. What is the volume in liters (l) occupied by 50.0 kg of ethanol at 20° C? The density of ethanol at 20° C is 0.789 g/cm^3.
   a. 39,450 l
   *b. 63.4 l
   c. 39.5 l
   d. 63,400 l
   e. 1,267 l

5. The mass of a cube of iron is 355 g. What is the mass of a cube of lead that has the same dimensions? (Density of lead = 11.4 g/cm^3; density of iron = 7.87 g/cm^3.)
   a. 0.0019 g
   b. 3.18×10^4 g
   c. 245 g
   d. 3.14×10^{-5} g
   *e. 514 g

The graph presented on the next page was produced by a group of students trying to determine the identity of several metals. Use the graph and the table below to answer Questions 6 through 11.

Name	Symbol	Density (g/cm^3)
Aluminum	Al	2.70
Iron	Fe	7.86
Copper	Cu	8.92
Lead	Pb	11.34
Mercury	Hg	13.59
Gold	Au	19.3

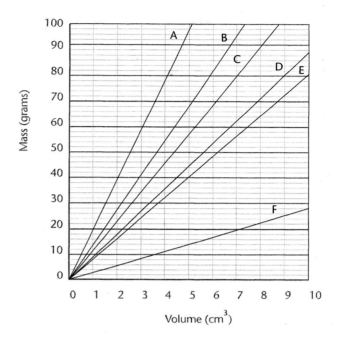

6. What is the identity of element "C"?
   a. Al
   b. Au
   c. Cu
   *d. Pb
   e. Fe

7. What is the relationship described by the graph for "F"?
   a. hyperbola
   *b. linear, positive slope
   c. parabola
   d. linear, negative slope
   e. nonlinear, thermodynamic

8. If you had 15 cm^3 of each of these metals, which would have a mass of 133.8 grams?
   a. Al
   b. Fe
   *c. Cu
   d. Pb
   e. Au

9. A gold nugget was found with a volume of 147.3 cm^3. How much would this nugget be worth at current values? (Use a value of $370 per troy ounce; 1 troy oz. = 31 grams.)
    a. $87,000
    b. $1,500
    c. $32,000,000
    d. $4.04
    *e. $34,000

10. If the line for "C" continued until it hit a volume of 14 cm^3, what would the mass of the metal be?
    a. 810 g
    b. 1.23 g
    c. 2.66 g
    *d. 159 g
    e. Cannot be determined from the information provided.

11. If you placed all of the following metals in a beaker of Hg, which would float?
    a. Pb, Cu, Au, Fe
    b. Al, Cu, Pb, Au
    c. Au, Fe, Pb, Al
    d. Al, Au, Fe, Cu
    *e. Pb, Fe, Cu, Al

Learning Cycle 3

How Were Alien Monoliths Sorted?

Introduction An excavation was recently undertaken by a team of archaeologists near Tin Mountain in Burma on the road to Mandalay. Several strange black monoliths, possibly of alien origin, were uncovered. The team of archaeologists painstakingly measured, sorted, and carefully boxed the monoliths for removal from the site.

When Indiana Smith, a young archaeological apprentice, was carrying some of the boxes back to camp, he was attacked by a rampaging Burma boar. In his effort to flee, Smith dropped the boxes and ran, barely escaping with his life.

Later, on returning to recover the monoliths, Smith discovered that the boxes had been smashed and the monoliths scattered over a large area. The chief archaeologist was furious with Smith for being so careless. He told Smith that he had better find a way to sort the monoliths back into their original groups or be severely reprimanded. Indiana Smith is requesting your chemical expertise to save him from the chief's wrath.

Objectives
1. To generate and carry out a reliable procedure for sorting the monoliths into separate groups.
2. To invent a way to display graphically the difference(s) among the groups of monoliths.
3. To apply this procedure to identify other solids.

Materials *several black monoliths of possible alien origin*   *equipment as requested by students*

Procedure
1. With your partner, generate a procedure for reliably sorting the monoliths into separate groups. List the primary steps in your procedure.

_____

_____

_____

_____

_____

_____

_____

_____

_____

_____

2. Produce a list of equipment that you need to carry out your procedure. Include a purpose for each requested piece of equipment.

   Piece of Equipment   **Purpose**

   _____

   _____

   _____

   _____

   _____

3. Obtain several black monoliths and carry out your procedure. Record your results.

4. After you have obtained data for your monoliths, exchange monoliths with other groups until you have data on at least 12 monoliths.

5. Use the graph paper provided to graph your data. Try several methods of graphing the data until you arrive at what you think is the best method to display difference(s) between the groups of monoliths. Be prepared to share your graphs with the class.

Additional Activity A local consumer group led by Al Khoa and his brother-in-law Ray Nolds, is concerned that people are being ripped off by aluminum foil manufacturers. Al and Ray claim that, although people are being charged twice as much for heavy duty aluminum foil than for regular aluminum foil, there is not a large enough difference in the thickness of the two types to justify the difference in price. As scientific experts, you and your partner have been called in to provide evidence to help settle the dispute.

Given samples of heavy duty and regular aluminum foil and knowing that the density of aluminum is 2.7g/ml, devise and carry out a procedure to obtain that evidence.

Record the steps in your procedure.

_____

_____

_____

_____

_____

Record your results and calculations.

Transfer your results and calculations to butcher paper or whiteboard and be prepared to discuss them during a class discussion.

Study Questions

1. Propose at least three possible molecular-level explanations for why different types of metals have different densities; that is, what might be some of the differences in the nature or arrangements of their atoms and molecules that make them more or less dense?

2. A block of wood 100 cm × 0.088 × 74 mm weighs 5.9 kg. What is its density in grams per cubic centimeter? per ml?

3. Iron has a density of 7.86 g/cm^3 at 20° C. What is the length of a sheet of iron 3.00 cm thick and 95 cm wide?

4. The weight of a cube of iron is 555 g. What is the weight of a similarly sized cube of lead? (The density of lead = 11.4 g/cm^3; density of iron = 7.78 g/cm^3.)

5. Would you expect that lines on the mass versus volume graphs constructed in this investigation would all intersect the x and y axes at zero? Explain.

6. Would you expect that lines on the graphs in Question 6 would ever be curved? Explain.

7. Would you expect to find parallel lines on such graphs? Explain.

▼▼▼

Teacher Material
Energy
Energy Transfer
Potential and Kinetic Energy

Learning Cycle 4

What Is Energy?

Synopsis   Students experiment with Newton spheres, pendulums, and several additional systems that illustrate different sources of energy and energy transfer. After initial explorations, the students generate causal questions and alternative hypotheses to explain the nature and transfer of energy from one part of the system (the energy source) to the other (the energy receiver). A definition of energy in terms of motion, stored motion, and the transfer of motion is derived. This is an empirical-abductive learning cycle.

Suggested Time   Two class periods

Background Information   The universe consists of objects that often move relative to one another. This movement may result in collisions between objects and changes in the directions of their movements or their sticking to each other, in which case the relative movements are stopped or "captured" and stored. This stored motion may be "released" if the "bonded" objects are struck by another moving object or objects.

Historically, *energy* has been defined as the ability to do "work." *Work* involves the movement of an object from one place to another. Through this investigation, students gain an understanding of energy as motion and "stored" motion that can be released to cause other things to move—that is, to do work. The terms *potential energy* and *kinetic energy* are introduced to label stored energy and the energy of motion, respectively.

The word *energy* is derived from the Greek *energos*, meaning active or at work. The units used to express energy are typically the *joule* and the *calorie*. The term *power* is related to but not synonymous with *energy*. Thus, the terms are often confused. *Power* is a compound variable that expresses the amount of work done or energy released over a period of time. The units for the expression of power are *joules/sec* and *watts*.

One basic assumption made about energy is that it can be neither created nor destroyed; it is transferred from object to object. The object that is the source of transferred energy is the *energy source*. The object that receives the energy is the *energy receiver*. For instance, the generation of electricity by the turning of a generator by steam produced by nuclear reaction involves the transfer of motion from subatomic particles in uranium (the energy source) ultimately to the electrons in a copper wire (the energy receiver) by way of a series of intermediate objects.

Teaching Tips   *Advance Preparation*

1. The apparatus for Part 1 (Newton spheres or balancing balls) may be purchased from most science equipment catalogs (e.g., Edmund Scientific Company. Telephone 1-609-573-6250. Medium size $4.95; large size $22.95).

Engagement

1. To help the students start thinking about objects colliding with one another, raise examples of currently or recently popular dances. One such dance from the 1970s was known as the "Bump," because partners literally bumped each other. The dance faded from popularity quickly, possibly because of the considerable energy needed to perform it. Asking the class to name current dances that are similar to the bump would be an appropriate way to provoke student thinking about objects moving, colliding, and using energy. Similar dances from the early 1990s might be slam dancing or moshing.

Exploration: Part 1

1. If you are unable to obtain a class set of Newton spheres, then one demonstration apparatus may be used. In this instance, you should involve the students as much as possible in the demonstration. Each student or group of students could be challenged to identify a different variable. Then have that student or group actually perform the test. As each variable is tested, all of the students can record observations. Another alternative would be to let students build their own apparatuses at home.

2. Write student observations on the board. Their observations for Part 1 may include:
   a. What is done to one side happens to the other side.
   b. The balls in the middle do not move.
   c. The higher the ball is pulled back on one side, the higher the ball rises on the other side.
   d. Repeated collisions cause the balls to heat up.

3. The students will generate causal questions based on their observations. Write these on the board. For example:
   a. Why do the middle balls not move?
   b. Why do the balls heat up?
   c. Why does one released ball on the right cause one ball on the left to rise, while two released balls on the right cause two balls to rise on the left, and so on?
   d. Why does one ball pulled back 6 inches and released cause the ball at the opposite end to rise approximately 6 inches rather than cause two balls at the opposite end to rise 3 inches each?
   e. Why do two balls pulled back 6 inches cause the two balls at the opposite end to rise 6 inches rather than cause one ball to rise 12 inches?

4. At this point, you may want to discuss students' alternative hypotheses or have the students proceed to Part 2 before such a discussion. Either way, the discussion should encourage students to think about what might be happening to the individual atoms or molecules of the apparently stationary middle balls during the time the observable motion of the end balls is being transferred through. This investigation does not explicitly ask students to test their hypotheses, but students may want to discuss how some of them could be tested.

Exploration: Part 2

5. String works better than fishing line for the apparatus in Part 2. The ring stands will need to be weighed down (by books, etc.). The string can be tied to anything (e.g., a chair leg), provided it is kept level and tight. If 1-inch or smaller washers are used, initial trials may require two or more washers. The swings of the washer will be the smoothest if the washer is pulled back just short of horizontal. The washers should hang down the same length, and the pendulums should be approximately 3 inches apart for the best transfer of motion from one pendulum to the other.

6. Variables that students should test include the following:
   a. the number of washers
   b. the length of the string(s)
   c. the number of pendulums
   d. the distance between pendulums
   e. the tightness of the horizontal string.

7. Encourage students to be patient. Most systems require several minutes to complete the cycle of energy transfer from one pendulum to the other. With the two-pendulum system, energy can transfer back and forth several times before the system transfers all of its motion to the air, table, and so on and stops swinging.

Term Introduction

1. Initiate the term introduction discussion by comparing observations in Parts 1 and 2. In both parts, students will clearly observe motion and the transfer of that motion from one object, through an apparently stationary object, to another object that receives the motion. Introduce the terms *motion source, motion receiver,* and *motion transfer* to refer to these objects and their interactions.

2. Ask students to derive a definition for the term *energy* in these contexts. At this point, they should be able to understand that, apart from the objects and their motion, nothing else is involved. In other words, no separate substance exists that could be called *energy*. Hence, the best definition for the term *energy* is motion, provided we allow that this motion can be stored, as would be the case when a sphere or washer is drawn back and held in the air before being released. Consequently, you can introduce the terms *energy source,*

energy transfer, energy receiver, and *stored energy,* where the terms *motion* and *energy* are understood to be synonymous.

3. Introduce the term *potential energy* to refer to motion or energy that is stored, and introduce the term *kinetic energy* to refer to motion or energy that is not stored—that is, energy that is in the act of doing work, is being transferred, is being "used," or has been "released."

4. Of course, the truly interesting causal questions, such as those listed in Tip 3 of the exploration phase, are not answered in this investigation. Nevertheless, they should be raised and, as mentioned, possible molecular-level hypotheses should be generated and discussed.

Concept Application

1. The discussion can continue with several additional examples of energy sources, transfers, and so on. For example, the movement of someone's arm comes from the movement (energy) of their muscles. The movement (energy) of a paper airplane comes from the movement (energy) of someone's hand and arm. The movement (energy) of a slamming door comes from the movement (energy) of air molecules in a sudden gust of wind. The movement of a flame from a burning piece of wood comes from the potential energy stored in the wood.

2. Part 3 can now be used to apply these concepts to several new contexts. The definition of energy as motion will be reinforced as students identify the source of motion in several objects.

3. For Part 3, you will need to obtain materials that exemplify several different energy sources for the ten stations. Here is a list of possible materials:

rubber band	paper clips
glow sticks	canister of metal BBs
blocks of wood	fruit battery
electrical circuits	photon globe
magnets	epsom salts and distilled water
calcium chloride and distilled water	sodium hydroxide and distilled water *(wear goggles)*

The rubber band can be repeatedly stretched back and forth, and students can detect temperature change by placing it on their nose or forehead. Similarly, the paper clip can be bent back and forth and the temperature increase noted. Wood blocks can be rubbed against each other, and the canister of copper BBs also can be shaken to note a temperature rise and energy transfer.

Epsom salts, calcium chloride, sodium hydroxide, and water all produce chemical reactions that are accompanied by temperature change. Each solution should consist of a few crystals of the solid mixed with approximately 10 ml of distilled water.

Electrons as an energy source are demonstrated by means of the "fruit battery," wherein a citrus fruit is used to drive a circuit. Use two pieces of ordinary wire. Connect one wire (clip, wrap, or solder) to a nickel, and one wire to a penny. Connect the other end of each wire to a low-voltage light bulb (an LED works well). Insert the nickel and the penny into a citrus fruit. The light (or LED) should turn on, showing a complete circuit.

The photon globe exemplifies light as an energy source. They are available at science novelty shops or through science catalogs. An emergency glow stick (commonly found at camping stores) will also work.

After the students have visited each station, discuss their observations and their answers to the questions posed in the student guide.

Chemical Terms	**Thinking Skills**
energy	accurately describe nature
energy transfer	state causal questions
energy source	generate alternative hypotheses
energy receiver	plan and conduct experiments
potential energy	draw and apply conclusions
kinetic energy	

Sample Test Questions

1. You rub the metal edge of your ruler on your shoe or desk. Then you sneak up behind the geek on the other side of the room, placing the metal edge on his or her forearm. Much to your delight, the metal burns your victim. From the following choices, what was the probable source of energy for the burn?

   *a. atoms or molecules in the metal edge
   b. air molecules
   c. molecules in your hand
   d. molecules in his skin
   e. light

2. In Question 1, as you heat the metal strip of the ruler with your shoe, which of the following is the energy receiver?

   a. your shoe
   b. the geek's forearm
   c. your hand
   *d. the metal strip

3. In Question 1, as you heat the metal strip of the ruler with your shoe, which of the following is the energy source?

   a. your shoe
   b. the geek's forearm
   *c. your hand
   d. the metal strip

4. You have been playing air hockey for hours on end. Every time the "puck" comes out for you to put into play again, it seems to be hotter than before. From the following choices, what is the primary energy source for the puck's increased temperature?

a. the table
b. air molecules
*c. the paddles
d. your hand
e. molecules in the puck

5. Which of the following best explains what is happening when the one metal ball swings down, strikes others in a row, and only the last ball in the row flies off the other end?

a. A magnetic field forces the last ball on the end to repel the other balls.
b. The balls in the middle actually are heavier and would move if the outside balls had the same mass.
c. The balls in the middle are glued together.
*d. The motion from the first ball is transferred through the middle balls to the last ball.

6. Which best explains what is happening in the washer and pendulum experiment?

a. The washers are attracting and repelling each other through a magnetic force.
*b. The swinging washer is transferring motion to the stationary washer.
c. The swinging washer is causing air currents that blow on the other washer, causing it to move.
d. No one knows why the washers move in the first place.
e. The washer hitting the air causes friction that heats up the washer, increasing its temperature.

7. Energy can be defined as:

a. things that give off heat.
b. a substance.
*c. motion.
d. things that burn.
e. a rise in temperature.

8. A piece of copper metal is pushed into a grapefruit. The metal is attached to a wire that is attached to a light bulb. A second wire comes from the light bulb and is attached to a piece of nickel. This metal is inserted into the other side of the grapefruit. The light bulb glows. In this experiment, which two sources of energy are most likely?

a. subatomic particles and light
b. electrons and light
c. molecules and subatomic particles
*d. molecules and electrons
e. electrons and subatomic particles

9. Which of the following is an appropriate experiment to find out whether the grapefruit is the only source of energy?

a. insert metal strips into the grapefruit
*b. insert wires (without metal strips) into the grapefruit
c. do not insert metal strips into the grapefruit
d. insert a light bulb directly into the grapefruit without wires or metal

10. Drawing a metal ball on a string back 6 inches and holding it in the air before its release and collision with a stationary metal ball on a string increases
   *a. the first ball's potential energy.
   b. the first ball's kinetic energy.
   c. the first ball's potential *and* kinetic energy.
   d. neither potential nor kinetic energy in the first ball.

11. Releasing the first ball in Question 10 increases
   a. its potential energy.
   *b. its kinetic energy.
   c. both its potential and kinetic energy.
   d. neither its potential nor its kinetic energy.

Student Material

Learning Cycle 4

What Is Energy?

Introduction   You probably know that you obtain the energy needed to sustain life from the food you eat. Eat Cheerios! It gives you "go power." Or perhaps you have been told that you "better eat your Wheaties." As far back as 300 B.C. people have been wondering about, talking about, and writing about food and energy.

   The ancient Greeks believed that energy was a substance that could be passed from one object to another. Is energy a substance? Can it be transferred from one object to another? What *is* energy? In this investigation, you will explore a variety of phenomena in an attempt to understand what energy is and how "it" can be transferred from one object to another.

Objectives   1.   To derive a meaningful definition of the term *energy*.
   2.   To investigate how energy can be transferred from one object or system to another.
   3.   To identify a variety of different sources of energy.

Materials

Part 1	Part 2	Part 3
steel ball apparatus	*string*	*10 stations exhibiting a*
	2 large washers (1 inch)	*variety of energy*
	2 ring stands	*sources*
	scissors	

Procedure   *Part 1*

   1.   Obtain the apparatus shown in Diagram A.

Diagram A

2. Observe what happens when one or more balls are pulled away from the others and released. Repeat the experiment several times, changing one variable at a time. Record your observations.

_____

_____

_____

_____

3. Generate and record causal questions and possible alternative explanations for what you observed.

Causal Questions

_____

_____

_____

_____

Alternative Hypotheses

_____

_____

_____

_____

Procedure *Part 2*

4. Set up an apparatus as shown in Diagram B.

Diagram B

5. Pull one washer back while keeping the string tight. Release the washer, making sure that it does not hit the other washer. Repeat the experiment several times, changing one variable at a time. Record your observations.

_____

_____

_____

_____

6. Be prepared to share your observations and ideas from Parts 1 and 2 during a class discussion. Record any new ideas or tentative conclusions following that discussion.

_____

_____

_____

_____

Procedure *Part 3*

7. For Part 3, 10 stations will be located throughout the lab. With your partner, spend a few minutes exploring the materials at each station. At each station use the object(s) in some way(s) to produce a transfer of energy. Then try to answer these questions:
   a. What was the source of energy?
   b. Where did the energy end up? That is, what was the energy receiver?
   c. Through what was the energy transferred?
   d. What evidence is there that energy was transferred?

Station 1

_____

_____

_____

_____

Station 2

_____

_____

_____

_____

Station 3

_____

_____

_____

_____

Station 4

_____

_____

_____

_____

Station 5

_____

_____

_____

_____

Station 6

_____

_____

_____

_____

Station 7

_____

_____

_____

_____

Station 8

_____

_____

_____

_____

Station 9

_____

_____

_____

_____

Station 10

_____

_____

_____

_____

Study Questions

1. What observations were common to your experiments in Parts 1 and 2?

2. Based on your observations and interpretations, propose a definition for the term _energy._

3. Do your experiments support or contradict the idea that energy is a substance? Explain.

4. What were the independent and dependent variables in your experiments in Parts 1 and 2?

5. Name as many different types of energy sources as you can.

6. For each type of energy source mentioned in Question 5, describe how energy can be transferred from the source to a receiver.

7. For each of the systems explored in Parts 1 and 2, name the energy source, the method of transfer, and the energy receiver.

Teacher Material
Diffusion
Temperature
Equilibrium

Learning Cycle 5

What Causes Molecules to Move?

Synopsis   Students add food coloring to water and observe it spread. They then experiment to test the effect of several independent variables on the rate of spread. Results are collectively analyzed and explained using kinetic-molecular theory. The terms *diffusion, heat, temperature, entropy,* and *equilibrium* are introduced and defined in the context of the experiments and their results. This is an empirical-abductive learning cycle.

Suggested Time   Two class periods

Background   Moving molecules disperse throughout a medium of other types of molecules
Information   because of collisions with those other molecules and themselves so that the molecules travel from areas in which they are initially at high concentrations to areas in which they are initially at low concentrations. Net movement is from areas of high concentration to low concentration simply because in areas of high concentration there is a greater probability of any one particle hitting like particles and therefore bouncing away. This random movement toward areas of lower concentration is called *diffusion.* Through successive collisions, the molecules undergoing diffusion are dispersed evenly throughout the medium. If the diffusing molecules are colored, the color will eventually become uniform throughout, signifying that all regions have approximately the same number of molecules. Thus, an *equilibrium* of molecular motion is reached such that the net motion of molecules in any particular direction stops.

The nature of the path that diffusing molecules take influences their rate of spread. In a gas, for example, the molecules are extremely far apart, so fewer collisions enable the molecules to travel in fairly straight paths and diffuse more quickly. In liquids, the molecules are much closer together, so many more collisions slow diffusion.

Whether diffusion is taking place in a gas or in a liquid, four independent variables influence diffusion rate. The first is the size of the diffusing molecule. If the molecule itself is large, then the chances for collisions increase. This is particularly true in liquids where many collisions occur. Larger molecules also are affected by gravity to a greater extent. This would cause a gas to stay lower to the ground and diffuse upward at a lower rate (CO_2 is an example of a gas weighing more than air; the gas diffuses slowly upward).

The second variable is the size of the molecules making up the medium. If these molecules are large, there is a greater chance of collisions. The diffusing molecules thus change direction many times before equilibrium is established and rate is slowed.

The third variable is concentration of the molecules involved. In a gas, the more tightly the medium molecules are pushed together, the greater the chance of collisions. In this way, diffusion slows. The higher the number of diffusing molecules dissolved in a liquid, the greater the chance of collision and slower diffusion.

The fourth variable is the speed of the diffusing molecules. Molecular speed is closely linked to molecular size. The larger the molecule, the slower it moves. Hence, the diffusion of large molecules is slower than the diffusion of small molecules. Molecular speed can be increased when the molecules are hit by something, as when they are heated. Heating simply means that the energy or motion of external molecules or photons has been transferred to the molecules in question so that they move faster. The greater the energy or motion transferred, the faster the molecules of both the diffusing material and the medium move. The increased speed of the molecules produces more collisions, but this is offset by the greater speed of the molecules, so the rate of diffusion increases.

The process of diffusion results in the random distribution of the molecules in question. In a sense, diffusion results in an increase in the disorder or randomness of the system. The term *entropy* is sometimes used to label this randomness. In other words, diffusion results in a decrease in the order and an increase in the entropy of a system. The tendency of molecules is to diffuse—that is, go from more orderly to less orderly states. Hence, we can state the general conclusion that without the input of energy, the entropy of systems increases.

Diffusion is an extremely important process in living things, because it plays a part in the movement of needed molecules to, into, and through cells. Diffusion also plays a part in the movement of waste molecules out of and away from cells.

Teaching Tips   *Advance Preparation*

1. Provide students with information on the molecular weights of the dyes used in this investigation. A list of food coloring formulas and molecular weights is provided on the next page. Many companies use only a few of these to produce the coloring they desire. The list will allow you to estimate the relative weights of the colorings you use. Larger bottles of Schilling food coloring provide specific FD&C numbers. However, these numbers do not indicate absolute weights because the mixing proportions are not included. One way to determine relative weight is to time the descent of the colorings in a 100-ml graduated cylinder. The slower the time, the lighter the coloring. In general, yellow is the lightest, followed by red, green, and blue. The estimated weights, or the relative weights, should be given to the students as part of their materials.

Dye	Molecular formula	Molecular weight
FD&C Blue No. 1	$C_{37}H_{34}N_2Na_2O_9S_3$	792.85
FD&C Blue No. 2	$C_{16}H_8N_2Na_2O_8S_2$	466.37
FD&C Green No. 1	$C_{37}H_{35}N_2NaO_6S_2$	690.80
FD&C Green No. 2	$C_{37}H_{35}N_2Na_2O_9S_3$	792.85
FD&C Green No. 3	$C_{37}H_{34}N_2Na_2O_{10}S_3$	808.85
FD&C Red No. 1	$C_{19}H_{16}N_2Na_2O_7S_2$	494.46
FD&C Red No. 2	$C_{20}H_{11}N_2Na_3O_{10}S_3$	604.49
FD&C Red No. 3	$C_{20}H_6I_4Na_2O_5$	879.92
FD&C Red No. 4	$C_{18}H_{14}N_2Na_2O_7S_2$	480.42
FD&C Red No. 32	$C_{18}H_{16}N_2O$	276.32
FD&C Red No. 40	$C_{18}H_{14}N_2Na_2O_8S_2$	496.42
FD&C Yellow No. 1	$C_{10}H_4N_2Na_2O_8S$	358.19
FD&C Yellow No. 3	$C_{16}H_{13}N_3$	247.29
FD&C Yellow No. 4	$C_{17}H_{15}N_3$	261.31
FD&C Yellow No. 5	$C_{16}H_9N_4Na_3O_9S_2$	534.39
FD&C Yellow No. 6	$C_{16}H_{10}N_2Na_2O_7S_2$	452.37

Engagement

1. You may wish to start by spraying air freshener or strong perfume into the air. Ask the students to raise their hands when they smell the odor. Stronger odors also may be used; for example, butyric acid smells like rancid butter. Simply opening a bottle of butyric acid is enough to allow the odor to spread. Some teachers also have used skunk scent. Be careful if you use this odor: It is quite strong and tends to linger. Simply opening a small bottle is enough to get a response from the students. (You may have to hunt around for skunk scent. Some hunting stores carry it.) The central question raised by the demonstration, of course, is, "What causes the smell to travel?"

Exploration

1. During the exploration, remind students to conduct controlled experiments and challenge them to think about why the color is spreading. Descriptive questions that may be raised include:
   a. What is the effect of water temperature on the rate of dye spread?
   b. What is the effect of dye molecule weight on rate of spread?
   c. What is the effect of the type of liquid (e.g., salt water, sugar water, oil) on the dye's rate of spread?
   d. What is the effect of the amount of dye on the rate of spread?
   e. What is the effect of gravity—that is, where the dye is placed (top or side)—on the rate of spread?

2. After groups of students have conducted their experiments (see Student Material section), have the class record data on the board. First, list all of the independent variables tested (see table below). Plus and minus signs and zeros then can be used to record data. For example, if a group found that an increase

in water temperature increased the rate of spread (a direct relationship), then it should record a plus next to the word *temperature.* If it found an inverse relationship between an independent and the dependent variable, then it should record a minus sign. And if it found that a particular independent variable had no effect, then it should record a zero.

Variables Tested   Effect on Diffusion

1. water temperature

_____

2. dye molecular weight and size

_____

3. amount of dye

_____

4. place dye added

_____

5. corn oil

_____

6. saltwater

_____

7. sugar water

_____

3. Students should also present graphs of their temperature experiments. The graphs can be enlarged on butcher paper or whiteboards for display. The graphs are likely to show some differences that should spark discussion. These differences will be due to differences in experimental procedure. Students also may confuse rate of color fall with the rate of color spread. To separate the rate of fall from the rate of spread, replace the 100-ml graduated cylinders with plastic petri dishes. A piece of graph paper can be cut to fit inside the lid of the petri dish. The bottom of the petri dish is then placed inside the lid on top of the graph paper. The graph paper is effectively sandwiched between the two plastic pieces. The petri dish then can be filled with water and cooled by placing it on ice or heated by placing it on hot water. An alternative method would be to pour cold and hot water into petri dishes. However, the water will cool or warm rather quickly using this method. A drop of detergent can be dropped into the petri dishes to break the surface tension of the water and allow the food coloring to spread at one level.

4. The differences in opinion about temperature effects are good catalysts in producing alternative hypotheses. Ask students, "Why do you think your graph is correct?" This will cause them to think about why the dye moved.

Term Introduction

1. After the data have been recorded on the board, they should be summarized and discussed. Trends should reveal that higher temperature increases the rate of spread, as does the amount of dye, although molecular size and rate are inversely related. Also, mediums such as saltwater, sugar water, and corn oil slow the rate of spread.

2. Remind students of the central causal question—"What causes molecules to move?"—and ask for hypotheses in light of the results; for example, "Can you generate an explanation for why the dye molecules spread that is consistent with the current results?" To start, you may need to focus on the relationship between temperature and rate of spread. Once a student suggests that temperature is a measure of the amount of motion of the molecules, you can pick up on this suggestion by asking, "If the molecules are moving faster in the hotter water, then why should that lead to faster spread?" Students should be able to reply that the faster molecules will produce more collisions and thereby bump the dye molecules around more, causing them to spread faster.

3. Press students to explain also the other relationships found. For example, they may understand that larger molecules move more slowly than smaller ones by using a ball analogy—that is, moving golf balls by hitting them with a stick is a lot easier than moving bowling balls with the same stick.

4. Some students may hold the misconception that heat is some "thing" that gets added when materials are heated. Make clear that the current explanation is different. When molecules are heated, they are merely being hit by some external agent so that they end up moving more rapidly. Temperature is merely a quantitative measure of the amount of this motion. Also note that temperature is the average amount of motion in the system and only the molecules that hit the thermometer are measured.

5. The term *diffusion* should be introduced at this time to label the phenomenon under consideration. Another analogy may be introduced by using a beaker half-filled with white jelly beans. Add a handful of green jelly beans and ask the students to describe how this is similar to their dye-and-water experiment. They should be able to tell you that the white jelly beans represent the water and the green jelly beans represent the dye. Shaking the beaker represents the increased motion of the molecules from the action of heating. Diffusion can be defined then as the random movement of molecules moving from a place of higher concentration to a place of lower concentration.

6. Finally, the terms *equilibrium* and *entropy* can be introduced and defined in the context of the current phenomenon.

Concept Application

1. Have students relate the movement of food coloring to that of perfume or other airborne odors. Make sure the students discuss the role of all the variables that were investigated for food coloring.

2. Have students predict the outcome of a reaction between HCl and NH_3. This may be easily shown through the following demonstration. In a burette tube, place one drop of HCl at one end and ammonium hydroxide at the other. Close the ends of each side with stoppers. A white cloud will form when the gases come into contact with one another. The students should be able to predict where the white solid will occur in the tube. (Because HCl is much heavier, it will move more slowly. The reaction should occur closer to the hydrochloric acid than to the ammonia.) This event may be quantified by using the equation $\frac{1}{2}mv^2$ of ammonia = $\frac{1}{2}mv^2$ of HCl.

3. Have students list the sorts of molecules that must diffuse into and out of living things and list locations where this diffusion is most likely to take place.

Chemical Terms	Thinking Skills
diffusion	accurately describe nature
temperature	plan and conduct experiments
heating	generate alternative hypotheses
entropy	organize and analyze data
equilibrium	draw and apply conclusions

Sample Test Questions

1. Which is the best definition of the term *diffusion*?
   a. It is the process by which molecules spread into a vacuum.
   b. It is the process by which two liquids mix.
   c. It is the process by which two liquids dissolve into one another.
   *d. It is the process by which molecules move from an area of higher to lower concentration.

2. What is meant by the term *temperature*?
   a. It is the amount of energy in molecules.
   b. It is the level mercury attains in a thermometer.
   *c. It is the amount of molecular motion.
   d. It is the level of potential energy in the thermometer.

3. Which statement supports the hypothesis that heating increases molecular motion?
   a. Solids eventually melt when heated.
   b. Colored materials spread more rapidly when heated.
   c. Liquids eventually boil when heated.
   d. The temperatures of materials rise when heated.
   *e. All of the above.

4. Of the examples below, which best illustrates entropy?
   a. Bricks are put together to form a building.
   b. A person eats a sandwich to gain energy.
   c. A tree grows larger with each passing year.
   *d. A car burns gasoline and heats the engine.

5. CO_2 and H_2 gases diffuse through a room at 20° C. Which one will diffuse the fastest? Why?
   a. CO_2 will diffuse faster, because it is denser than air and will not interact as well.
   b. CO_2 will diffuse faster, because it has a greater mass than H_2 and is able to push away air molecules.
   *c. H_2 diffuses faster, because it is lighter and faster than CO_2.
   d. H_2 diffuses faster, because it is smaller and able to avoid the air molecules.

6. Which of the following gases should diffuse at the fastest rate?
   *a. NH_3
   b. HCl
   c. H_2O
   d. CO_2

7. A variable that may be tested for its effect on diffusion rate is the molecular weight of the diffusing molecules. Which of the following procedures best tests for this variable?
   a. Place drops of two dyes with different molecular weights into a beaker of water. The dye that reaches the bottom first diffuses more quickly.
   b. Place drops of two dyes with different molecular weights into two beakers at different temperatures. Measure the diffusion rates.
   c. Place drops of two dyes with different molecular weights into two beakers containing different liquids. Measure the diffusion rates.
   *d. Place drops of two dyes with different molecular weights into two beakers of water at 0° C. Measure the diffusion rates.

Learning Cycle 5

What Causes Molecules to Move?

Introduction You walk into a crowded room. Somehow, you know the one you love is there. It is not that person's face or the sound of his or her laugh that draws you near, it is "That Special Smell," the unisex perfume cologne, available at drug stores near you at $3.50 a quart. We all have experienced the smell of strong perfume or cologne as we walk past people. But how does the smell get from those people to your nose?

Because it is difficult to experiment with unseen smells, in this investigation we will use food coloring and several liquids to determine variables that may affect the rate of movement of dye molecules. Our results may provide clues to help us explain why molecules move from one side of a room to another, from one place in a liquid to other places, and from one location inside living things to other places.

Objectives 1. To discover and record the effect of several independent variables on the rate of movement of food coloring in liquids.

2. To generate one or more hypotheses to explain how molecules travel through liquids, gases, and living things.

3. To test the hypotheses first by comparing their predicted consequences with our previous results.

Materials *various colors of food coloring*   *100-ml graduated cylinders*
petri dishes   *matches*
ice   *stopwatches or a clock with second hand*
salt   *sugar*
corn oil   *thermometers*
glass funnels   *micropipets*

Procedure 1. With your lab partner, pour 50 ml of water into a 100-ml graduated cylinder. Add one drop of one color of food coloring to the water. Observe and record what happens.

_____

_____

_____

2. Consult the materials list for ideas of independent variables that might affect the rate of movement of dye molecules throughout liquids. What variables do you think might make a difference? Why?

Independent Variable   Possible Reason

_____

_____

_____

_____

_____

3. Conduct a controlled experiment to test the effect of water temperature on the rate of dye movement. Use at least three different water temperatures. Do not heat water in graduated cylinders, because they break when heated. Record your data below. When finished, graph your data, comparing the time it took the dye to spread with the water temperature.

_____

_____

_____

_____

4. Conduct controlled experiments to determine the effect of at least two other independent variables on the rate of movement. Prepare graphs, tables, or both to display the results.

Study Questions

1. When you tested the effect of temperature, did you perform a controlled experiment? Explain.

_____

_____

_____

_____

2. Which of the independent variables tested made a difference in the rate of dye spread? Use kinetic-molecular theory to explain why each made a difference.

_____

_____

_____

_____

3. Define the word *heating* in terms of molecular motion.

   _____

   _____

   _____

   _____

4. What is the difference between heating something and its temperature?

   _____

   _____

   _____

   _____

5. Define the words *equilibrium* and *diffusion* in terms of molecular motion.

   _____

   _____

   _____

   _____

6. Explain why perfume molecules travel from one person's skin to another person's nose.

   _____

   _____

   _____

   _____

7. Explain why oxygen molecules will diffuse from your lungs into your bloodstream and why carbon dioxide molecules will diffuse in the opposite direction. (*Hint:* Suppose you have an open box sitting on a table. The bottom of the box is partially covered with marbles. All of the marbles on the left side are white, while all of those on the right are blue. What will happen to the marbles when the box is shaken? Will all the white ones stay on the left side? Will all the blue ones stay on the right?)

   _____

   _____

   _____

   _____

8. What would happen to the motion of molecules on earth if the sun burned out? Explain?

_____

_____

_____

_____

Learning Cycle 6

How Does Cell Structure Relate to Function?

Synopsis   Students view ten numbered but unnamed prepared slides of various plant and animal cells and tissues. They observe and draw structures and speculate about possible functions. This is an empirical-abductive learning cycle.

Suggested Time   Two to three class periods

Background Information   Cells in multicellular organisms exhibit structural differences that allow them to perform a variety of functions. Sometimes these functions can be inferred from examination of their structural characteristics. Slides of cells will illustrate this point. Nerve cells are elongated to facilitate their function as conduits of electrical impulses. Red blood cells have a smooth oval shape to ease their passage through narrow vessels in the circulatory system. Sperm cells have a tail that serves as a means of locomotion. Epithelium cells, which make up the outer layer of skin, are flat and scale-like and appear to be stacked much like shingles protecting a house from weather. The large, rounded form of fat cells allows the storage of excess materials.

A group of similar cells providing a common function is called a *tissue*. Sometimes the cells within specific tissues are arranged in ways that also facilitate function. Slides of the following tissues illustrate this. The cells of arteries and veins are arranged to produce tubes to allow the passage of blood. The walls of the artery are thicker than those of veins, allowing the arteries to withstand greater pressure. Tissue from the inner lining of the small intestine is highly convoluted, providing increased surface area to maximize absorption. A leaf cross section shows upper and lower epidermal cell layers that have thick cell walls and no chloroplasts and serve as a protective function. Between these layers, the chlorenchyma cells contain chloroplasts, which provide the capacity to produce food. Finally, a cross section of a stem reveals vascular cells that make up small tubes that allow the transport of food and water.

This learning cycle is designed to familiarize students with the broad range of cell and tissue characteristics and to promote insight into the relationships among the characteristics and the functions for which they are designed.

Teaching Tips   *Advance Preparation*

1. Suggested prepared unlabeled slides may include:

longitudinal section of neuron	artery cross section
blood	vein cross section

sperm	small intestine
stratified squamous epithelium	variety of leaf types both monocot
adipose tissue	and dicot stem (cross sections)

Exploration

2. You may wish to introduce the investigation by discussing the examples presented in the introduction to the student material and by asking students for additional examples of structure–function relationships.

Term Introduction

3. Using student drawings on the blackboard, a projection microscope, or 35-mm slides, present each slide image. Initiate a discussion by telling the students what organism and where in the organism the various cells are from, but do *not* tell them their "correct" functions. These functions are not important at this time, and introducing the correct answers will only undermine future attempts at getting students involved in inquiry. The "correct" answers are those that make the most sense based on the available evidence. For each cell type, ask students to present hypothesized functions and their reasons. You might also wish to ask what additional evidence might be needed to support or refute their hypothesized functions. You also can present some of this evidence yourself, provided you do not suggest that the issue of cell function is entirely resolved. If you wish, introduce names of specific tissue types, such as epithelium and chlorenchyma, but do not stress the names and do not ask students to memorize them.

Concept Application

4. No specific application activities are included at this time, although any subsequent learning cycles that investigate cell structure and function will allow application of the concepts introduced here. For example, see the next learning cycle, "How Do Multicellular Organisms Grow?"

Biological Terms	**Thinking Skills**
cell structure	accurately describe nature
cell function	state causal questions
cell diversity	create alternative hypotheses
tissues	generate logical predictions
	organize and analyze data
	draw and apply conclusions

Sample Test Questions For Questions 1 through 5, use cell shape to match the animal cells labeled A–E in the figure at the top of page 505 with their functions.

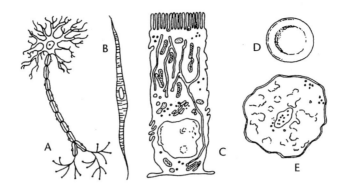

1. D A cell travels around the body in tubes to transport molecules that enter and exit the cell through its cell membrane.
2. A A cell picks up electrical signals from other cells and transmits a common signal to other cells.
3. B A cell is capable of constricting lengthwise to move structures such as bones.
4. E A cell is found in skin and can expand and contract to change skin color.
5. C A cell is found on the inside of the intestinal wall and absorbs food molecules from the digestive tract.

Questions 6 through 10 refer to the following diagram of a leaf cross section. Use the cell's size, shape, and location to match it with its function.

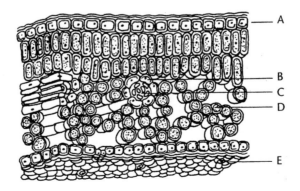

6. E Cells expand and contract to increase or decrease the size of the opening between them, which regulates the passage of air in and out of the leaf.

7. A Cells are covered on top with a waxy substance that does not allow water to pass through easily.

8. C Cells function primarily to conduct molecules of food or water from one part of the plant to another.

9. D Cells absorb light, air, and water to produce food.

10. B Cells surround food- and water-conducting cells and may serve to regulate movement of various types of molecules.

Student Material

Learning Cycle 6

How Does Cell Structure Relate to Function?

Introduction   Buildings come in several shapes and sizes and vary widely in their materials of construction. These differences are sometimes the result of owner preferences, but usually form, size, and materials follow function. For example, a house is designed differently than a theater or a store because they have quite different functions. Likewise, a house in Alaska requires more insulation than one in Hawaii and may have to be made of different materials.

Are analogous structural and functional differences found among the cells of organisms? Cells in multicellular organisms are most certainly located in many different places. Are they also designed differently? If so, in what ways? How might these differences relate to cell function?

In this investigation you will have an opportunity to observe several cell types, note their structural characteristics, and try to infer functions. In other words, we are going to explore possible relationships between cell structure and function.

Objectives   1. To observe the structure of several diverse types of cells found in a variety of organisms and attempt to create alternative hypotheses about their functions.

2. To compare observations and hypotheses and discuss ways in which some of the hypotheses might be tested.

Materials   *unlabeled slides of a variety of cells*   *compound light microscopes*
   and tissues   *stereomicroscopes*
scalpels or razor blades   *carrots*

Procedure   1. Select a partner to work with.

2. Using the appropriate microscope, observe the 12 numbered specimens, noting the cell size, shape, and any other characteristics that might provide clues as to cell function. Speculate as to cell function based on structure and relationships with other cells on the slide. In other words, try to answer this question for each type of cell: What is the function of this cell? Make drawings of your observations on the data sheet that include slide number, appearance, possible function(s), and your reasons for the hypothesized functions.

Data Sheet

Slide 1

Magnification:

_____

Possible functions:

_____

Reasons:

_____

_____

_____

Slide 2

Magnification:

_____

Possible functions:

_____

Reasons:

_____

_____

_____

Slide 3

Magnification:

_____

Possible functions:

_____

Reasons:

_____

_____

_____

Slide 4

Magnification:

_____

Possible functions:

_____

Reasons:

_____

_____

_____

Slide 5

Magnification:

_____

Possible functions:

_____

Reasons:

_____

_____

_____

Slide 6

Magnification:

_____

Possible functions:

_____

Reasons:

_____

_____

_____

Slide 7

Magnification:

_____

Possible functions:

_____

Reasons:

_____

_____

_____

Slide 8

Magnification:

_____

Possible functions:

_____

Reasons:

_____

_____

_____

Slide 9

Magnification:

_____

Possible functions:

_____

Reasons:

_____

_____

_____

Slide 10

Magnification:

_____

Possible functions:

_____

Reasons:

_____

_____

_____

Slide 11

Magnification:

_____

Possible functions:

_____

Reasons:

_____

_____

_____

Slide 12

Magnification:

_____

Possible functions:

_____

Reasons:

_____

_____

_____

3. Now join another pair of students to compare and discuss your observations and alternative hypotheses about possible functions. Note agreements or disagreements and be prepared to discuss your ideas and arguments in a class discussion.

4. During a class discussion, your instructor will tell you where each specimen came from. Write this information next to each slide number in the blanks below. Is this information consistent or inconsistent with your hypothesized functions? Explain for each specimen.

Slide 1

_____

Consistent or inconsistent?

_____

Explain.

_____

_____

_____

_____

Slide 2

_____

Consistent or inconsistent?

_____

Explain.

_____

_____

_____

_____

Slide 3

_____

Consistent or inconsistent?

_____

Explain.

_____

_____

_____

_____

Slide 4

_____

Consistent or inconsistent?

_____

Explain.

_____

_____

_____

_____

Slide 5

_____

Consistent or inconsistent?

_____

Explain.

_____

_____

_____

_____

Slide 6

_____

Consistent or inconsistent?

_____

Explain.

_____

_____

_____

_____

Slide 7

Consistent or inconsistent?

Explain.

Slide 8

Consistent or inconsistent?

Explain.

Slide 9

Consistent or inconsistent?

Explain.

Slide 10

_____

Consistent or inconsistent?

_____

Explain.

_____

_____

_____

_____

Slide 11

_____

Consistent or inconsistent?

_____

Explain.

_____

_____

_____

_____

Slide 12

_____

Consistent or inconsistent?

_____

Explain.

_____

_____

_____

_____

5. If time permits, obtain a cross-sectional slice of carrot and place it in water. Use a stereomicroscope to identify as many types of tissues as you can. Sketch them below and generate alternative hypotheses about possible functions. Store the cross section overnight in a cool location. Observe your carrot cross section again the next day. Do your observations support or contradict your original hypotheses? Explain.

_____

_____

_____

_____

Study Questions

1. Define the term *tissue* and give examples of three types of tissues found in animals and three types found in plants.

_____

_____

_____

_____

2. Cells exhibit considerable variation. List several ways in which cells vary.

_____

_____

_____

_____

3. List functions that might be best accomplished by cells with the variations listed in Question 2. Provide a reason for each hypothesized structure–function relationship.

_____

_____

_____

_____

Learning Cycle 7

How Do Multicellular Organisms Grow?

Synopsis   Students generate alternative hypotheses to account for growth in multicellular organisms and observe prepared slides of growing tissues (e.g., onion root tip or stems) to test their hypotheses. Support is obtained for the hypotheses for increase in cell size and cell division. Students then attempt to generate a correct sequence of phases in the division process. A time-lapse film of a single living cell undergoing division is shown to help students decide which proposed sequence is correct. Appropriate terms are introduced by the teacher when needed. This is a hypothetical-deductive learning cycle.

Suggested Time   Two to three class periods

Background Information   In multicellular organisms, growth results primarily from the addition of new cells and increases in the size of existing cells. In plants, growth takes place because of cell division and enlargement only in specific locations such as the tips of roots, stems, and in a zone just beneath the surface. Root growth takes place because of rapid cell division in a zone just behind the tip. Farther up the root, cell division becomes much less frequent, and most growth results from cell elongation.

Growth in plant stems is similar to that in the root: The tip of the stem consists of a zone of rapidly dividing cells. The cells just below that zone elongate and mature into the differentiated cells of the stem. Growth in both length and diameter of cells in the stem may last quite a bit longer than in the root.

At the onset of cell division in both plants and animals, the cell nucleus appears as a dark but nondescript object somewhere near the center of the cell. As division proceeds, structures in the cytoplasm, such as mitochondria and plastids (in plants), begin to duplicate themselves and migrate to separate locations within the cell. Such structures have their own DNA and can duplicate without the aid of nuclear DNA.

The process of duplication of cell parts, other than the nucleus, is called *cytokinesis*. Although cytokinesis is important, the crucial aspect of cell division concerns the cell nucleus, because it contains the major portion of the cell's DNA located in the chromosomes. Thus, the essential task of cell division is to ensure that each new daughter cell receives a full set of chromosomes. To do this, the chromosomes must duplicate themselves and then divide and migrate to two separate locations. This process is called *mitosis*.

The first noticeable change around the nucleus before chromosome duplication is that the tiny centrosome that lies just outside of the nucleus divides into two parts that move to opposite sides of the nucleus. As they move, fibers begin to form and stretch between the centrosomes. The nuclear membrane begins to disintegrate and disappear. The nuclear DNA duplicates and begins to coil up like a spring.

The duplicated and coiled DNA molecules appear as two strands connected at one small point in the middle. The two stranded coiled DNA molecules are the *chromosomes*. Each strand of a chromosome is referred to as a *chromatid*. The point at which the chromatids are attached to one another is called the *centromere*. Many of these double-stranded chromosomes are present.

The chromosomes then arrange themselves on a plane across the center of the cell right between the two centrosomes. Fibers from the centrosomes attach to the center of the chromosomes at the centromeres. After the fibers are attached, they appear to shorten and pull the chromatids in opposite directions. This separates the chromatids. As they migrate to opposite sides of the cell, they bend at the center. Once the chromatids reach the opposite sides of the cell, they begin to uncoil. The fibers begin to disintegrate, and a nuclear membrane begins to form around each batch of chromatids. The centrosomes remain just outside the newly formed nucleus.

At this point, each new nucleus has exactly the same number and kind of chromatids (now called *chromosomes* once again). The duplication of the nucleus thus is complete. Cell division is complete as soon as a furrow that begins to develop in the cell membrane deepens and gradually separates the cell in two. The end result is two new cells with nuclei identical to that of the parent cell. The entire process of cell division including cytokinesis and mitosis can take as few as 30 minutes or as many as several hours.

The process of *meiosis* as it takes place in the sex cells of multicellular organisms is slightly more complicated. First, chromosomes duplicate from, say, a diploid number of eight to sixteen. Then the sixteen chromosomes divide into two groups of eight in each of two newly formed cells. Then the two cells with eight chromosomes each divide to produce four cells with four chromosomes each (the haploid number). These cells with the haploid number of chromosomes are called *gametes* (usually egg and sperm cells).

When the gametes fuse, the chromosomes from each cell pair up, and the original diploid chromosome number (eight in this case) is restored. The resulting fused cell with the full complement of chromosomes is called the *zygote*.

Although the dividing cells viewed by the students in this learning cycle will not reveal all of these events of cell division, they will reveal the major structures and their major changes and challenge students' ability to make careful observations and use what they see to support or refute the alternative hypotheses that have been proposed.

Teaching Tips   *Introduction*

1. Initiate the investigation with reference to the introductory paragraph in the student material. Write the question "How do multicellular organisms grow?" on the board and encourage students to speculate about possible mechanisms; for example, "What *might* be occurring at the cellular level to account for the

increase in size?" This part of the lab should resemble a brainstorming session in which any and all ideas are viewed as acceptable and are written on the board and labeled as "alternative hypotheses." Stress that the class is only considering possibilities at this point. Evaluation of the alternative hypotheses will come later when actual plant and animal tissues are observed.

Exploration

2. Students should already know the names of obvious cell structures (e.g., cell membrane, cell wall, cytoplasm, nucleus) from previous labs. If not, these terms should be introduced after initial observations have been made.

3. During exploration, tell the students that they are observing slides of a growing root tip (etc.), but do *not* mention the process of cell elongation or cell division at this time. The students' job during exploration is to think about what their hypotheses lead them to expect to find and then observe carefully to see if those expectations are confirmed. For example, if they have hypothesized that growth takes place because of the increase in amount of space between adjacent cells, then they should expect (predict) to see more space between the cells in older portions of the stems and roots (i.e., those areas farther away from the tips). Likewise, if they have hypothesized that growth takes place because of an increase in cell size, then the prediction follows that cells farther away from the tips should be larger than those near the tips. On the other hand, if they think that growth occurs solely because of the increase in numbers of cells, then no obvious differences in cell size are predicted. It may be helpful to discuss these predictions before the students make their initial observations.

4. If students have trouble locating relevant differences or deciding what to look for to test their ideas, stop the class and use a quick drawing on the board to help them locate the area of the slide for best viewing. You also may need to discuss specific hypotheses and predictions as stated above if you have not already done so. You may want to cue students to look for changes in the thread-like structures near the cell's center and introduce the term *chromosome* at this time to refer to those structures. You also may want to challenge students to see if they can figure out a way to determine whether the observed differences among the cells are the result of differences in cell types or differences within one type of cell that is undergoing some sort of change.

5. After students have observed those of other students, hold a class discussion to answer the following questions: What hypotheses have been supported or contradicted? What are the major differences among the observed cells? Also discuss student responses to the question posed under procedure Step 5. If a student hypothesizes that we are observing a sequence of changes of a single cell type, ask how this idea might be tested. If no student advances this hypothesis, then you will have to advance it yourself.

6. Before showing the film loop on cell division (*Mitosis: A Single Topic Inquiry Film,* Biological Sciences Curriculum Study, 1967) compare the various sequences that students have generated to discover similarities and differences.

7. Show the film loop as a source of evidence to discover which of the hypothesized sequences seems most correct.

Term Introduction

8. The term *cell elongation* should be introduced after the students have discovered the elongated cells that appear on the root tip and stem slides.

9. After deciding which sequence of cell changes seems most correct, introduce the term *mitosis* to refer to the replication of chromosomes during the cell division process.

10. Avoid showing students visual materials that emphasize stage names and discrete steps. Emphasize cell division and mitosis as dynamic processes.

Concept Application

11. Have students work through the study questions, or the additional activities, or both. One of these provides an opportunity to view and discuss the process of meiosis as an extension of the cell division process in which the number of chromosomes is reduced to one-half of its original number in the resulting egg and sperm cells.

12. The relevant text reading should be assigned.

Biological Terms	**Thinking Skills**
cell division	accurately describe nature
cell elongation	create alternative hypotheses
mitosis	generate logical predictions
meiosis	organize and analyze data
	draw and apply conclusions

Sample Test Questions

1. Examining the cells in a slide of an onion root tip, one student generated the hypothesis that the cells are really three different "types" of cells that perform different functions. Another student generated the alternative hypothesis that the cells are really one "type" of cell that is undergoing cell division. She thought the differences in appearance reflected different points of time in the division process. Which of the following predictions would logically follow from the first student's hypothesis?

    a. The three "types" of cells should be located next to each other.
    *b. Time-lapse photography of the cells should show no change in appearance of one "type" of cell into another "type."
    c. The three "types" of cells should not be located next to one another.

   d. Time-lapse photography of the cells should show a change in appearance of one "type" of cell into another.

   e. The size of the cells should not vary over time.

2. Which of the predictions in Question 1 above would logically follow from the second student's hypothesis?

   a. The three "types" of cells should be located next to each other.

   b. Time-lapse photography of the cells should show no change in appearance of one "type" of cell into another.

   c. The three "types" of cells should not be located next to one another.

*d. Time-lapse photography of the cells should show a change in appearance of one "type" of cell into another.

   e. The size of the cells should not vary over time.

The next six questions are based on the following key to cell division processes. Use the key to classify each statement.

KEY:

A. Mitosis

B. Meiosis

C. Both mitosis and meiosis

D. Neither mitosis nor meiosis

3. B The resulting cell contains one chromosome of each pair.

4. B The resulting cells could be egg cells.

5. B This type of division prevents an increase in number of chromosomes from generation to generation.

6. C There is pairing of each chromosome and its opposite member.

7. C Each chromosome duplicates itself.

8. A Each daughter cell contains the same kind and number of chromosomes as the parent cell.

Learning Cycle 7

How Do Multicellular Organisms Grow?

Introduction   Two characteristics of living things are (1) they are composed of cells and (2) they grow. But how do multicellular organisms grow? What might happen to the cells or the spaces between cells in the growing parts of plants and animals?

In this investigation, you will have an opportunity to make microscopic observations of the cells of one or more rapidly growing plant and animal tissues to test alternative hypotheses that you and other students in the lab generate. The goal is to discover which alternatives are and are not supported.

Objectives   1.   To observe and record differences among cells in growing portions of plants and animals.

2.   To test alternative hypotheses that attempt to explain growth in multicellular organisms.

Materials   *prepared slides of growing portions of*   *string*
plants (e.g., onion root tip or stem)   *yarn*
and animals (blastulas of whitefish   *red and white pipe cleaners*
or Ascaris)   *microscope*
film loop, Mitosis   *lens paper*
slide projector   *35-mm slides of meiotic sequence*

Procedure   1.   What might be going on at the cellular level to cause multicellular organisms to increase in size? Perhaps growth results from an increase in the size of individual cells—that is, younger or smaller organisms have smaller cells, while older or larger organisms have larger cells. This seems like a reasonable hypothesis. Participate in a class discussion to generate as many alternative hypotheses as possible. List the alternatives below.

_____

_____

_____

_____

2.   The figure at the top of page 526 shows the outline of an onion plant's rapidly growing root tip. The direction of growth is downward, so it may be safe to assume that newer cells are near the tip, while older cells are farther up the root. Assuming this to be the case and that the hypothesis that growth results from increases in cell size (stated above) is correct, draw what the cells in the

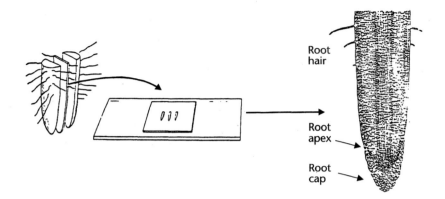

lower and upper portions of the root tip *should* look like. Your drawing represents your *predicted* result based on the "increase in cell size" hypothesis.

Note: If the actual cell sizes look like these predicted cell sizes, then the hypothesis has been supported. If they do not, then the hypothesis has *not* been supported.

3. Make microscopic observations of the tissues and cells of your specimen(s) to answer the following questions:
   a. What differences in cell size, structure, and spacing exist?
   b. What areas appear to be the youngest and the oldest?
   c. Do your observations support or fail to support any of your alternative hypotheses? Be prepared to explain.

4. While observing the slides, clearly draw any differences you see among the cells. On the root tip slide pay particular attention to possible differences in cell size in different locations of the root tip. Also note possible differences in thread-like structures in the cell nuclei. These are called *chromosomes*. Make as many drawings as you like below. Label all obvious cell structures.

5. Enlarge your drawings on a large sheet of paper. These should be big and clear enough so all students can see them when the drawings are posted on the board or wall.

6. Carefully observe all of the other students' drawings. Which hypotheses are supported and not supported? Explain.

_____

_____

_____

_____

7. On the root tip slide, do you think we are looking at many types of cells or at one type of cell that is going through changes? Explain.

_____

_____

_____

_____

8. If you think the cells are going through changes, number your drawings in an order that might reflect the sequence of those changes. Sketch that sequence below.

9. What additional evidence would be needed to test the hypothesis that the onion root tip cells are undergoing division?

_____

_____

_____

10. Compare your hypothesized sequence of changes from Question 8 with the changes in chromosome appearance shown in the film. Does the film provide evidence for or against the cell division hypothesis? Explain.

_____

_____

_____

Application Questions

1. How long does mitosis take? The life span of a cell is the period of time from when the cell was formed to the time it completes division to form two new daughter cells. This time period is called the cell's *generation time.* By observing living cells, biologists have determined the generation time for a variety of cell types. If we know the generation time, we can determine how long a cell spends in mitosis. Given that 100 cells are observed in the field under a microscope and 50 of these cells are undergoing mitosis and also knowing that the generation time is 2 hours, approximately how long does it take the cells to undergo mitosis? After you have arrived at an answer, reflect on your procedure. Try to write an equation expressing the numerical relationships. Use the following variables:

   - N_o for total number of cells observed
   - t_m for time spent in mitosis
   - N_m for number of cell observed in mitosis
   - T_{gt} for generation time

   Express the relationship below:

   _____

   _____

   _____

   _____

2. Now that you have a method for estimating time spent in mitosis, try to apply that method to the data below for onion root tip cells:

   - $N_m = 16$ cells
   - $N_o = 642$ cells
   - $T_{gt} = 22$ hours

   a. How long does an onion root tip cell spend in mitosis (t_m)? _____. Show your calculations in the space below and express your answer in hours and minutes.

   b. What fraction of an onion root tip cell's life span is spent in mitosis? Show your calculations in the space below.

   c. What percentage of an onion root tip cell's life is spent in mitosis? Show your calculations in the space below.

3. Observe replicating cells of whitefish or *Ascaris*. Are there any differences in the processes of cell replication between these animal cells and the onion? If so, briefly describe them.

    _____

    _____

    _____

    _____

4. Set up a cell model using string for cell and nuclear membranes; yarn for uncoiled, unreplicated chromosomes; and red and white pipe cleaners for replicated chromosomes. Move the cell parts around on your table to simulate the process of mitosis. Practice so you will be able to demonstrate the process to others.

5. You probably know that you have the same number of chromosomes as each of your parents. Propose ways in which sperm and egg cells can be created so that their fusion results in a new individual whose cells have the same number of chromosomes as the parents. The actual process in which this occurs is called *meiosis*. View a set of 35-mm slides of meiosis or reduction division to answer the following questions:
    a. What happens to the number of chromosomes in the nuclei of the sex cells that are produced?
    b. How many chromosome divisions occurred in the sex cell formation?
    c. How many new cells are formed at the end of this process?
    d. When during the process did chromosome replication take place?
    e. In the cells of living organisms, chromosomes occur in look-alike pairs called *homologous chromosomes*. Propose a possible reason for this.

6. Obtain some germinating seeds and use ink to place equally spaced marks along the length of the growing root. According to our hypotheses, most of the growth near the root tip occurs as a result of cell division, while most of the growth farther back from the tip occurs because of cell elongation. If we assume that these hypotheses are correct, then what would you predict will happen to the spaces between adjacent marks as the root continues to grow? Observe root growth for the next week or so to find out whether your predictions are confirmed.

Human karyotype

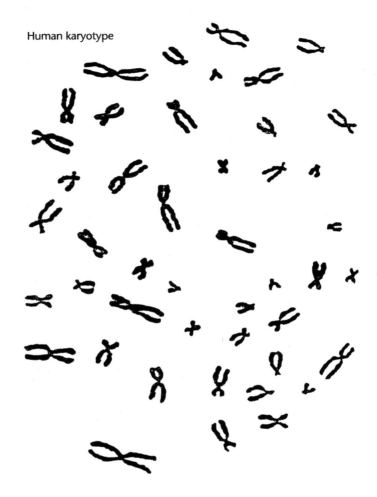

7. The figure above closely resembles an actual photograph of a set of replicated human chromosomes. Cut out the chromosomes and try arranging them in patterns. When you have arranged them in a pattern that makes sense to you, tape or glue them onto your paper. Under your arrangement, explain why you arranged this chromosome *karyotype* the way that you did.

Learning Cycle 8

**What Happens to Molecules
During Chemical Breakdown?**

Synopsis   Students design and conduct an experiment to test alternative hypotheses about what happens to liver and hydrogen peroxide molecules when they are combined. After results are analyzed, the terms *catalyst, enzymes,* and *endothermic* and *exothermic reactions* are introduced. This is a hypothetical-deductive learning cycle.

Suggested Time   Two class periods

Background
Information

Many chemicals speed up reactions between other chemicals. A mixture of hydrogen and oxygen, for example, does not react; but if a spark (activation energy) is provided, the mixture will explode. The same explosion will occur if a small piece of platinum is added. After the reaction is over, the platinum will still be present and unchanged.

A substance such as platinum that speeds up a chemical reaction but is itself unchanged when the reaction is over (even though it may have been temporarily altered during the reaction) is known as a *catalyst.* A catalyst affects only the rate of reaction—that is, it simply speeds up a reaction that already is thermodynamically possible. Catalysts decrease the activation energy needed for a reaction to take place by increasing the number of reacting molecules that are energetic enough to react. The catalyst does this by orienting the reactants to each other in such a way that important internal bonds are weakened, thus making them easy to break (e.g., by being struck by other molecules) and allowing new bonds to form (e.g., by striking and sticking to other molecules).

An inorganic catalyst such as platinum is rather unselective about the reactions it speeds up. Living things contain a huge variety of large globular proteins that act as catalysts. These organic catalysts are called *enzymes.*

One such enzyme, which is investigated in this learning cycle, is produced by liver cells. The enzyme increases the rate of breakdown of hydrogen peroxide (H_2O_2) to water (H_2O) and oxygen (O_2). When students add liver to hydrogen peroxide, bubbles of a gas (oxygen) can be seen immediately in the liquid, and the solution heats up rapidly because of the increased motion of the split molecules. Of course, students do not know which molecules are reacting, nor do they know that the liver molecules are not altered during the reaction. Nevertheless, the introduction to the lab presents several alternative hypotheses for the students to test. Through experimentation, they discover that old hydrogen peroxide and old liver do not react but that new hydrogen peroxide and old liver *do* react, suggesting that the liver contains molecules that facilitate a change in the hydrogen peroxide, which is not itself altered. This conclusion allows you to introduce the term *enzyme* to refer to a type of organic catalyst that speeds up a reaction but remains unchanged at the reaction's completion. The observation that the reaction produces heat allows you to introduce the term *exothermic reaction* (i.e., a chemical reaction that increases the temperature of the reactants as opposed to an *endothermic reaction,* which decreases the temperature) as you discuss the reasons for the rise in temperature.

Teaching Tips   *Exploration*

1. When the introductory reaction takes place, have students note the increase in temperature. Introduce the term *exothermic reaction* for any reactions that give off heat. Challenge students to think of reasons for the temperature increase (e.g., "Molecules of O_2 are given off and hit the inner surface of the test tube, which causes the glass molecules to move and strike your fingers, which causes the molecules of your skin to move more rapidly, which is perceived as an increase in temperature").

2. A procedure to test two of the hypotheses presented is as follows:

   Use two test tubes and a small piece of liver. With a glass rod, push the liver to the bottom of one of the tubes. Put the tube in the rack and add 2 ml hydrogen peroxide. (You may have to keep pushing the liver down with the glass rod.) Allow the reaction to continue until all bubbling stops. Stir gently with the glass rod until the bubbles disappear. Pour this reaction liquid into the other test tube. Put another piece of liver (of the same size) into this liquid. Observe. Pour 2 ml hydrogen peroxide on the liver in the first tube.

   The liquid remaining from the original reaction and the new piece of liver should show no reaction. The liquid is water, not hydrogen peroxide. The older liver will still react with fresh hydrogen peroxide because the enzymes have not changed. Only the hydrogen peroxide has changed. If the peroxide had not changed, a reaction between the liver and the liquid remaining from the original reaction should have taken place. Do not tell this to your students: You want them to think of ways to test the hypotheses. However, you can provide helpful hints.

3. After students have performed their experiments collect the results on the board. These might be listed as follows:

   a. new liver + new H_2O2 $\rightarrow$ +, +, +, etc.
   b. old liver + new H_2O2 $\rightarrow$ +, +, +, etc.
   c. old liver + old H_2O2 $\rightarrow$ −, −, −, etc.
   d. new liver + old H_2O2 $\rightarrow$ −, −, −, etc.

   The plus sign (+) indicates the production of bubbles, and the minus sign (−) indicates no bubbles.

4. Select a student to summarize the results and initiate a discussion of which hypothesis or hypotheses are supported. Challenge students to propose an explanation at the molecular level for their observations.

Term Introduction

5. To introduce the terms *catalyst* and *enzyme,* summarize the results as follows: "Whenever molecules interact in such a way that one type of molecule is changed—such as the hydrogen peroxide—but the other is not changed—such as those from the liver—we call the unchanged molecule a *catalyst.* When the catalyst happens to be a molecule produced by a living thing—that is, an organic molecule—it is called an *enzyme,* and the reaction is called an *enzymatic reaction.* Catalysts and enzymes function to speed up chemical changes, in this case, the change of hydrogen peroxide to water and oxygen."

6. Some students may protest that the appearance of the liver does change during the reaction with H_2O_2. Do not ignore this observation: It is valid. Challenge them to explain the change. You may wish to suggest that the liver probably contains many types of molecules, some of which do not change (i.e., the enzyme) and some of which do. You also may have to acknowledge that the enzymes actually may change some during the reaction but certainly not at the rate of the other molecules.

Concept Application

7. Students should be encouraged to think of other examples of catalysts and enzymes. Relevant textbook readings also should be assigned at this time.

Biological Terms	**Thinking Skills**
catalyst	accurately describe nature
enzyme	state causal questions
exothermic reaction	create alternative hypotheses
endothermic reaction	generate logical predictions
	plan and conduct experiments
	organize and analyze data
	draw and apply conclusions

Sample Test Questions

The first three items refer to the following experiment:

One gram of freshly ground liver was placed in a test tube with 1 ml of hydrogen peroxide (H_2O_2). A gas formed in the tube and was tested with a glowing splint. The splint burst into flame, identifying the gas as oxygen (O_2). A gram of ground liver then was boiled. When fresh hydrogen peroxide was added to the boiled liver, no gas formed. Ground liver treated with strong acid or base produced results similar to those obtained with boiled water.

1. A prediction about enzyme activity in liver is being tested. The prediction is that this activity should be destroyed by
   a. acids, bases, boiling, and hydrogen peroxide.
   b. acids, bases, and hydrogen peroxide.
   *c. acids, bases, and boiling.
   d. grinding the liver.

2. One of the test tubes was the control for these experiments. It was the tube containing

   a. heated liver and hydrogen peroxide.

  *b. freshly ground liver and hydrogen peroxide.

   c. liver treated with base.

   d. liver treated with acid.

3. Suppose the substance that broke down the hydrogen peroxide were an enzyme. It could

   a. not be recovered because it had been destroyed.

   b. not be recovered because it was used up.

   c. be recovered from the acid solution.

  *d. be recovered from the liver after gas had formed.

The next four questions refer to the following experimental results:

Four experiments were conducted in four separate test tubes. Bubbles were seen in some of the test tubes as indicated in the table below.

Test Tube No.	Contents of Test Tube	Results
1	new liver + new hydrogen peroxide	bubbles
2	old liver + new hydrogen peroxide	bubbles
3	old liver + old hydrogen peroxide	no bubbles
4	new liver + old hydrogen peroxide	no bubbles

4. Suppose the hypothesis is advanced that molecules in the liver change but those in hydrogen peroxide do not change when the two substances are mixed. What predicted outcome results from this hypothesis and experiment? The mixture in

   a. tube 3 should produce bubbles.

   b. tube 1 should not produce bubbles.

  *c. tube 4 should produce bubbles.

   d. tube 4 should not produce bubbles.

   e. tube 2 should produce bubbles.

5. Because bubbles were produced only in test tubes 1 and 2, the hypothesis in Question 4 has

   a. been supported.

  *b. been contradicted.

   c. not been tested.

6. Suppose an alternative hypothesis is advanced that molecules in the liver do not change but that those in hydrogen peroxide do change when the two substances are mixed. What predicted outcome results from this hypothesis and experiment? The mixture in

   a. tube 1 should not produce bubbles.

  *b. tube 2 should produce bubbles.

    c. tube 2 should not produce bubbles.

    d. tube 3 should produce bubbles.

    e. tube 4 should produce bubbles.

7. Because bubbles were produced only in test tubes 1 and 2, the hypothesis in Question 6 has

    *a. been supported.

    b. been contradicted.

    c. not been tested.

▼▼

Student Material

Learning Cycle 8

What Happens to Molecules During Chemical Breakdown?

Introduction One of the more common household chemicals consists of hydrogen peroxide molecules (H_2O_2). You can pour it in cuts, in ears, on hair, wherever. What would happen if you drank it (please don't try to find out) or fed it to your dog? What would it do to you or Fido's internal organs? One animal organ that is easy to obtain is beef liver. Conduct the following test to determine what happens when hydrogen peroxide molecules come into contact with beef liver. Put 20 drops of hydrogen peroxide in a small test tube. Hold the tube and add a small piece of liver about the size of a bean seed. What happens to the liver? the hydrogen peroxide? your hand? Record your observations.

Objective 1. To test alternative hypotheses concerning the interaction of liver and hydrogen peroxide molecules when they are combined.

Materials *raw liver* *medicine dropper*
graduated cylinder *hydrogen peroxide (H_2O_2)*
test tubes *test tube rack*
glass stirring rods *scissors*

Procedure 1. When you added the liver to the H_2O_2 molecules, what happened to the liver? The H_2O_2 molecules? To your hand?

_____

_____

_____

_____

_____

2. The following are three possible accounts of what happened to the liver and hydrogen peroxide. List any other alternative hypotheses that you can think of. Be prepared to discuss these and your ideas in class.
   a. The molecules in liver and hydrogen peroxide both changed to form a new substance (new types of molecules).
   b. The hydrogen peroxide molecules changed, but the liver molecules did not.
   c. The liver molecules changed, but the hydrogen peroxide molecules did not.

3. Which of the above do you suspect might be the best explanation? Explain.

_____

_____

_____

_____

_____

4. Try to think of an experimental design that could determine which explanation(s) is correct. What are the expected (predicted) results of your hypotheses and experiments? Be prepared to compare your ideas with others in a class discussion. Record your ideas.

_____

_____

_____

_____

_____

5. Carry out your experiment(s). Record your results.

_____

_____

_____

_____

_____

Study Questions

1. State the alternative hypotheses tested by your design. State the expected results generated from your hypotheses and experimental designs.
2. Do the data support the hypotheses proposed? Explain.
3. Has your experiment allowed you to eliminate other possible explanations? Explain.
4. What might have caused the temperature to increase during the reaction?
5. Did you conduct a controlled experiment? Explain.
6. What were the independent and dependent variables in your experiment?
7. Define the terms _catalyst_ and _enzyme_. How do enzymatic reactions differ from nonenzymatic chemical reactions?
8. How do chemical reactions differ from simple mixing of molecules?

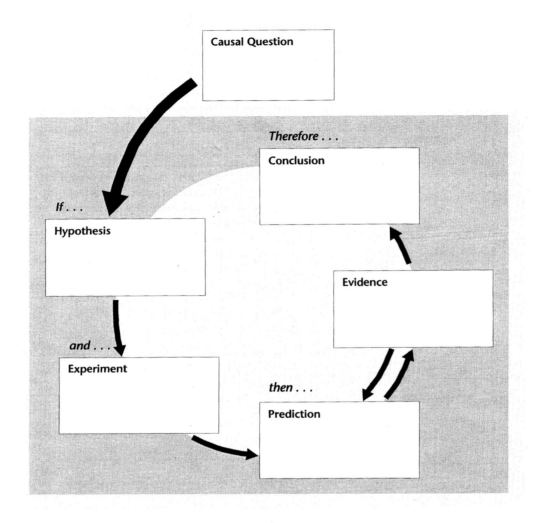

9. Draw an enlarged version of the diagram above on a sheet of paper and fill in the boxes and blanks with one causal question, hypothesis, experiment, expected results, actual results, and conclusion from this investigation.

Teacher Material
Flower Structure
Flower Function

Learning Cycle 9

What Is the Structure and Function of Flowers?

Synopsis   Students explore a variety of individual flowers and attempt to construct a model of a typical flower. Names for identified structures are introduced. Functions for these structures also may be introduced or they may be the subject for optional experimentation. In this option, students generate alternative hypotheses about the possible functions of the various observed parts. They then design and conduct controlled experiments to test their hypotheses. This is either a descriptive or a hypothetical-deductive learning cycle, depending on usage.

Suggested Time
- One and one-half to three class periods, depending on optional work
- Out-of-class time for optional follow-up experiments

Background Information   The following parts can be observed in many types of flowering plants:

a. Pollen grain
b. Ovary
c. Ovule
d. Egg (not observable)
e. Micropyle (not observable)
f. Stigma
g. Anther
h. Style
i. Filament
j. Petals
k. Sepals

The parts will vary in number and exact structure, depending on the species.

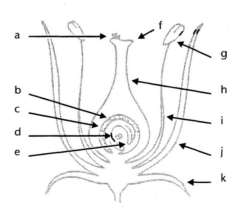

The following functions should be introduced if the experiment option is not used.

Stamen: "male" organ of a flower; subdivided into filament and anther

Filament: stalk-like portion of stamen; elevates anther for pollen distribution

Anther: pollen-producing portion of stamen

Pistil: "female" organ of a flower; subdivided into stigma, style, and ovary

Stigma: sticky top portion of pistil; adheres to pollen

Style: elongated stalk-like portion of pistil; provides passage for fertilization of ovules

Ovary: swollen lower portion of pistil: contains ovule(s); sometimes develops to form fruit

Ovule: structure within ovary; develops to form seed(s)

Petal: often large, colorful portion of floral envelope; usually functions to attract pollinators

Sepal: often green bract underlying petals; usually functions to enclose flower in bud stage.

Teaching Tips   *Advance Preparation*

1. For free or inexpensive flowers, contact local growers, wholesale nurseries, mortuaries, and cemeteries. They are often happy to provide flowers for educational purposes. Many flowers can be collected near the school or brought by students from home.

Term Introduction

2. Construct a model of the typical observations made by the class. Rely strictly on the observations made by class members. A single composite can be made by (a) observing large sketches made by students on butcher paper or (b) listening to student descriptions and making a corresponding sketch on the board. "Because most people saw these parts, we should have some name to commonly call them." Introduce names for the observed parts at this time.

Concept Application

3. Question students as to the possible reasons or causes for the variations of flower structure they observed.

4. If you prefer to have students use the functions of flower parts as the topic of experimentation, direct students to follow the optional procedure section of the student guide.

5. Students may grow plants in the classroom or school greenhouse or adopt a plant that is growing on campus.

6. Plant possibilities:

    a. If students adopt plants on campus, make sure the plants go through an easily studied flower-to-fruit cycle in a reasonable amount of time.

b. Students also may plant seeds, bulbs, or bedding plants that complete flowering and fruit formation in a reasonable amount of time, or they could use Wisconsin™ Fast Plants, which are available from Carolina Biological Supplies, 2700 York Road, Burlington, NC 27215-3398; 1-800-334-5551. The plants, *Brassica rapa,* complete their life cycle in approximately 35 days.

c. If you need more information on available plants that are suitable for this activity, consult your local nursery, a county agricultural extension agent, or garden books on your local area.

d. Some suggested plants:

Perennial	**Annuals or Bulbs**
flowering shrubs	peas
flowering trees	tulips
stone fruit trees	lilies
citrus	amaryllis
olive	cabbage
pyracantha	lettuce

Biological Terms	**Thinking Skills**
pistil	accurately describe nature
stamens	state causal questions
anther	generate alternative hypotheses
petal	generate logical predictions
sepal	plan and conduct experiments
pollen	organize and analyze data
ovary	draw and apply conclusions
ovules	
stigma	
style	
seeds	

▼▼

Student Material

Learning Cycle 9

What Is the Structure and Function of Flowers?

Introduction　All of us have seen many types of flowers of various sizes and colors from a variety of plants. But have you ever looked closely at the parts of flowers? Do all flowers have the same parts? What do the various flower parts look like? What are they for? In this investigation, you will closely examine a variety of flowers to look for similarities and differences in their parts and to diagram the parts of a "typical" flower. You also may be able to conduct an experiment to test ideas about what the parts do.

Objectives　1. To discover the parts of a flower.

2. To diagram the parts of a typical flower.

3. To generate and discuss alternative hypotheses about functions of flower parts.

4. (Optional)　To design and conduct experiments to test alternative hypotheses.

Materials　*dissecting probe*　　　　　　　　　*compound or dissecting microscope*
variety of flowers　　　　　　　　*potting soil*
metric rulers　　　　　　　　　　*potting containers*
cutting surface　　　　　　　　　*forceps*
razor blades　　　　　　　　　　*fertilizer*
hand lens　　　　　　　　　　　*microscope slides*
　　　　　　　　　　　　　　　　plant growth lights
　　　　　　　　　　　　　　　　cover slips
　　　　　　　　　　　　　　　　plant cuttings
　　　　　　　　　　　　　　　　pipet dropper
　　　　　　　　　　　　　　　　seeds or small plants

---

*optional

Procedure　1. Observe and examine a flowering plant.

a. Describe how the flowers are attached to the plant.

b. In what ways does the flower appear to be similar to or different from the rest of the plant?

c. Do all of the flowers on the plant look the same? Describe any differences.

2. Obtain and carefully examine flowers from various plants. Carefully dissect the flowers, noting similarities and differences in structure. Sketch your observations.

3. Using the information you have observed, draw what you think represents a typical flower. Make the flower structures large and clear.

4. Through class discussion, label by name all parts of your typical flower.

5. In a class discussion, generate hypothesized functions for the observed flower parts.

   a. What evidence exists to support these hypothesized functions?

   b. Write at least two alternative hypotheses for the function of each typical flower part.

6. Design an experiment to test your hypothesized functions. Limit your investigation(s) to one or two structures.

7. Discuss your experimental design with your teacher.

8. Provide your teacher with a copy of your alternative hypotheses, experimental procedure, expected results, and location and name of your experimental plants.

9. Conduct your experiment. Keep records of your procedure, observations, data, and conclusions.

10. You are required to submit a report on your experiment.

    a. You must include the following.

       I. Question(s)
       II. Alternative hypotheses
       III. Procedure
       IV. Expected results
       V. Actual results (data)
       VI. Discussion
       VII. Conclusion

    In your conclusion, you should be able to answer the question, "Why do plants produce flowers?"

    b. Did you conduct a controlled experiment? Explain.

Study Questions

1. Are there such things as male flowers? female flowers? flowers that are *both* male and female? If so, how are they similar? different? Provide examples of each type, if possible.

2. Select one typical flower part that you have not experimented with previously. Describe its structure and state two possible functions. What experimental evidence suggests that the structures actually function in one or more of the ways that you state? If you know of no evidence, describe an experiment to test the hypothesized functions.

Learning Cycle 10

Why Do Liquids Evaporate at Different Rates?

Synopsis Students use molecular models and structural drawings as the basis for generating hypotheses and predicting the order in which four colorless chemicals will evaporate. They then measure the rates of evaporation to test their hypotheses. After their results are analyzed, which generally contradicts their initial hypotheses, they are introduced to the terms *volatility* and *polarity*; alternative hypotheses are then proposed and tested. This is a hypothetical-deductive learning cycle.

Suggested Time One to two class periods

Background Information This lab exercise investigates variables that affect the evaporation rates of acetone, propanol, methanol, and water. *Evaporation* is the change of phase from a liquid to a gas as molecules at the liquid's surface acquire enough kinetic energy to escape into the vapor state. The energy required for this phase change ultimately comes from the surrounding environment. All other things being equal, the more energy needed to separate molecules and send them into the vapor state, the lower the rate of evaporation.

In general, the tendency for a liquid to evaporate, known as *volatility*, is determined by two factors: molecular weight and intermolecular forces. Heavy molecules require more energy to be sent into the vapor state than do light ones. Thus, methane (CH_4; molecular weight 18 atomic mass units [amu]) is so volatile that it is a gas at room temperature, while octane (C_8H_{18}; molecular weight 114 amu) is a liquid at the same temperature.

The molecular weight (or size) hypothesis is among the first to be advanced by students and is at least partially supported by the data (i.e., methanol is lighter or smaller than propanol and evaporates faster). However, water (molecular weight 18 amu) is lighter and smaller than the other liquids and evaporates *more slowly* than the heavier molecules. This result contradicts the molecular weight hypothesis and indicates that some other variable or variables play a role.

The other variable is a class of interactions collectively referred to as *intermolecular forces*. Ionic attraction, van der Waals forces, and hydrogen bonding are examples of intermolecular forces. In this activity, intermolecular forces are exemplified by *polarity*, which is the presence in a molecule (or part of a molecule) of a slight separation of positive and negative electrical charge resulting from an unequal sharing of electrons in one or more covalent bonds. Polar molecules are attracted to one another because of electromagnetic forces acting among these positive and negative "poles." The net effect is that liquids made of polar molecules have low volatility because of the "stickiness" of their molecules.

Polarity in a molecule comes about because of a property of elements called electronegativity. *Electronegativity* refers to the tendency of an atom to attract electrons when in a covalent bond with another atom. Oxygen is an element with a rather high electronegativity. When oxygen forms a covalent bond with an element of relatively low electronegativity (such as hydrogen), an unequal sharing of negatively charged electrons exists in that molecule. The diagram below, which represents water, illustrates this phenomenon.

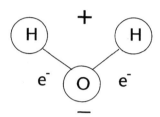

When oxygen forms a bond with an element whose electronegativity is closer to its own (such as carbon), electrons are more equally shared. When electron sharing is unequal, a molecule has polar character; when electron sharing is equal (or when the inequality is perfectly symmetrical), a molecule is nonpolar.

The data from this lab can be interpreted in light of the above discussion. Although small in size, water contains two oxygen–hydrogen bonds (see the diagram in Advance Preparation below). These bonds, in which electron sharing is unequal because of a large difference in electronegativity, produce a highly polar molecule. Therefore, water molecules must gain a large amount of energy before they can be separated from one another and sent into the vapor phase. Water has an extremely low volatility. Acetone, on the other hand, contains no oxygen–hydrogen bonds and thus is quite nonpolar. Far less energy is needed to evaporate acetone molecules, so acetone is extremely volatile. The two alcohols each contain a single oxygen–hydrogen bond, therefore their polarities are equal to each other and are intermediate between water and acetone. Because of the equivalence in polarity, the smaller alcohol and methanol molecules have a higher volatility than the larger propanol molecules.

Using this sort of reasoning, students should be able to rank evaporation rates for any set of organic molecules. The concept of polarity can be extended to include its effects on boiling point temperature, equilibrium, vapor pressure, and solubility.

Teaching Tips   *Advance Preparation*

1. Before class, draw the following molecular structures on the board.

H H   H
| | |
H—C—C—C—C—H
| | ‖ |
H H O H
acetone

H H H
| | |
H—C—C—C—O—H
| | |
H H H
propanol

H
|
H—C—O—H
|
H
methanol

H
|
O—H
water

Engagement

1. Summarize the introduction in the student lab guide in your own words. You might ask students to identify liquids that, in their experience, evaporate quickly. Responses may include nail polish remover (acetone), paint thinner, and gasoline. Pose the question, "Why do liquids evaporate at different rates?"

Exploration

2. Have students each copy the molecular structures onto their data sheet. Have them form teams of two or three to build the models. They should compare their models with other groups to check accuracy.

3. After they have completed model building, have the students predict the ranking of liquids in terms of evaporation rates. The most common prediction will be that water will evaporate fastest, while propanol will evaporate slowest.

4. Write some of the predictions on the board but do not evaluate them at this time.

5. For each prediction, ask students to explain why they made that prediction. When they give a reason, point out that this is their hypothesis.

6. Have students perform the evaporation experiment and record their results. Monitor students to help them generate controlled experiments (e.g., keep them from blowing or fanning liquids, show them how to control the size of drops, and so on).

   CAUTION: Do not use the white ceramic spot plates for evaporation; it is extremely difficult to tell exactly when evaporation is complete.

   Take note of any major differences in the procedures used from group to group. Procedural differences can have a profound effect on measured evaporation rate for a given liquid.

7. Have students record their three trial times for each liquid on the board. Draw a table on the board to organize the large amounts of data.

Term Introduction

1. Initiate a discussion on how to arrive at a consensus about the rankings. Point out any differences in the rankings and discuss procedures that may have led to these differences. For instance, a group that consistently (or even inconsistently) fanned its drops will have shorter evaporation times. This can be a

good opportunity to review the ideas of controlling variables, experimental error, and between-group variation and within-group variation. Nevertheless, the pattern in the data should be extremely clear, and students should not have to repeat the experiment.

2. Encourage the class to evaluate its hypotheses in light of the data. Hypotheses and the aspect of the data that contradict them are:

Hypotheses	**Contradicting Data**
Size of molecule	Smallest molecule evaporates at the lowest rate.
Presence of a double bond	No data contradict this hypothesis.
Weight of molecules	Higher weight (acetone) evaporates most quickly.
	Lowest weight (water) evaporates most slowly.
Alphabetized ranking	No data contradict this hypothesis, but names of substances are arbitrary.
Straight-chain versus bent-chain structure	Acetone has straight-chain form and evaporates quickly.
	Propanol has same form and evaporates relatively slowly.
Amount of hydrogen around molecule	Acetone has more hydrogen than methanol but evaporates faster.
	Acetone has fewer than water, but evaporates faster.
Only liquids with carbon atoms evaporate.	Water eventually does evaporate.
Intermolecular forces	Not contradicted, but requires elaboration.

Two hypotheses are supported by the data. The size hypothesis is supported by the observation that methanol, a smaller molecule, evaporates more quickly than does propanol. This comparison represents a controlled experiment because the polarity of these two molecules is equivalent. The intermolecular force hypothesis is supported by comparing the evaporation rates of propanol and acetone. This represents a controlled experiment because molecular size is substantially similar, but their evaporation rates are quite different. This suggests some other force (in this case, polarity) is at work.

3. Begin the discussion by introducing the term *volatility* as follows: "Some molecules have the tendency to go from the liquid state to the gaseous state more easily than others—that is, they evaporate more easily. Those that evaporate more easily (more quickly) are said to be more volatile than those that evaporate more slowly." Throughout the rest of the discussion, use the term whenever appropriate.

4. Because students have previously been introduced to electronegativity, the term *polarity* should be relatively easy to introduce as follows: "Atoms with a

higher electronegativity tend to pull shared electrons toward them, causing an unequal distribution of electrons around the molecule. This unequal distribution gives the molecule a positive end and a negative end (or 'pole'). This aspect of a molecule is called *polarity*. The more unequal the distribution, the more polar the molecule." You can use the idea of a magnet to help the students visualize this concept.

5. Tell the students that O–H bonds are very polar, while C–O bonds are only somewhat polar and C–H bonds are not at all polar. Have the students use this information to determine the relative polarities of the four types of molecules. Then have them combine this ranking with the ranking based on molecular size to try to explain the observed evaporation rates.

Concept Application

1. Provide students with drawings or models of new liquids and have them predict their evaporation ranking. Then have the students perform an experiment to test their predictions. Provide space on the table for these new data. Other possible liquids include ethanol, diethyl ether, 1-butanol, and methylethyl ketone. The structures for these molecules in order of volatility are:

methyethyl
ketone
1

diethyl
ether
2

ethanol
3

1-butanol
4

Chemical Terms	Thinking Skills
volatility	accurately describe nature
polarity	state causal questions
intermolecular forces	generate alternative hypotheses
electronegativity	generate logical predictions
	plan and conduct experiments
	analyze data
	draw and apply conclusions

Sample Test Questions

1. Susan noticed that water evaporates at a lower rate than acetone. She also noticed that acetone has carbon, while water does not. She used this information to guess that propanol also will evaporate quickly. Susan's statement is

   a. a hypothesis.
   *b. a prediction.
   c. an observation.
   d. a conclusion.

   For Questions 2 through 4, consider the diagrams representing the molecules of four liquids.

2. A student could use the four liquids to conduct a controlled experiment to test the effect of evaporation rate on

   *a. molecular size.
   b. polarity.
   c. the presence of carbon.
   d. the presence of oxygen.

3. Which of the liquids should have the highest volatility?

   a. 1
   b. 2
   c. 3
   *d. 4

4. You are now provided with a new liquid whose molecular structure is

To test the effect of polarity on volatility, you should compare this liquid's evaporation rate with which of the above four liquids?

*a. 1
 b. 2
 c. 3
 d. 4

5. A "polar" molecule is one that
   a. contains carbon–carbon bonds.
   b. contains a double bond.
   *c. contains an unequal electron distribution.
   d. contains water.

6. A liquid that evaporates quickly is most likely composed of molecules that are
   *a. nonpolar.
   b. quite large.
   c. nonvolatile.
   d. ionic.

For Questions 7 through 10, refer to the diagrams representing the molecules of these four liquids.

```
      H  H     H  H                    H  H  H  H  H
      |  |     |  |                    |  |  |  |  |
   H– C– C– C– C– C–H               H– C– C– C– C– C– O– H
      |  |  ‖  |  |                    |  |  |  |  |
      H  H  O  H  H                    H  H  H  H  H

      1                                2


      H  H
      |  |
   H– C– C– O– H                        H
      |  |                              |
      H  H                              O– H

      3                                4
```

7. Which two liquids, when compared, represent a controlled experiment of the effect of polarity on evaporation rate?
   *a. 1 and 2
    b. 2 and 3
    c. 3 and 4
    d. 1 and 4

8. Which two liquids, when compared, represent a controlled experiment of the effect of molecular size on evaporation rate?

     a. 1 and 2
  *b. 2 and 3
     c. 3 and 4
     d. 1 and 4

9. Which drawing represents the most polar liquid?
     a. 1
     b. 2
     c. 3
  *d. 4

10. Which drawing represents the least polar liquid?
  *a. 1
     b. 2
     c. 3
     d. 4

Learning Cycle 10

Why Do Liquids Evaporate at Different Rates?

Introduction   Have you ever had a sunburn or high fever? Perhaps you used rubbing alcohol to help cool your skin. The alcohol works because it evaporates quickly and lowers skin temperature. Putting water on your skin also will work, but not as well. Both liquids look the same, yet there must be some difference between them to explain the difference in evaporation rates. In this investigation, we will attempt to discover why liquids evaporate at different rates.

Objectives   1. To measure the evaporation rates of four colorless liquids.

2. To generate and test alternative hypotheses about the differences in the four liquids' evaporation rates.

3. To use your hypotheses to predict the evaporation rates of several additional liquids.

Materials   *distilled water (H_2O)*   *spot plates and watch glasses*
acetone (C_3H_6O)   *droppers*
methanol (CH_3OH)   *watch or clock with second hand*
propanol (C_3H_7OH)   *molecular model kits*
Additional liquids will be supplied later.

Procedure   1. Copy each molecular structure from the board into the boxes below. Using the molecular model kits, build models of water, acetone, propanol, and methanol.

Water

Acetone

Propanol

Methanol

2. Based on the properties of the model molecules, try to predict the four liquids'
    order of evaporation. Be prepared to share the reasons for your predictions in
    a class discussion. These reasons are your initial hypotheses.

    Predicted order of evaporation:

    First

    _____

    Second

    _____

    Third

    _____

    Fourth

    _____

    Reason(s) for this predicted order:

    _____

    _____

    _____

3. Conduct controlled experiments to determine how long each liquid takes to
    evaporate. Do at least three trials for each liquid and record your results in the
    data table.

4. Rank the liquids' rates of evaporation 1 (fastest) through 4 (slowest) and
    record your ranking on a class data table.

Data Table				
	Time (in seconds)			
Liquid	*Trial 1*	*Trial 2*	*Trial 3*	*Trial 4*
Water				
Acetone				
Acetone				
Propanol				
Methanol				

5. Is your observed ranking the same as your predicted ranking? If so, you have obtained support for your initial hypothesis. If your initial hypothesis was not supported by the results, then generate at least two alternate hypotheses to account for your results. Be prepared to present your data and discuss your alternative hypotheses with the class.

Alternative hypotheses:

_____

_____

_____

_____

6. Following the class discussion, you will be given additional liquids. Knowing what you now know about variables that affect evaporation rates, predict the order in which these liquids will evaporate. Conduct controlled experiments with sufficient replicates to test your prediction.

Predicted order of evaporation:

First

_____

Second

_____

Third

_____

Fourth

_____

Reason(s) for this predicted order:

_____

_____

_____

_____

Study Questions   1. What molecular variables do you think affect the evaporation rates of liquids? What is your evidence?
2. What environmental variables (external to the liquid) do you think affect evaporation rates? What is your evidence?

3. Suppose that you are given a clear liquid of unknown molecular size. Describe a controlled experiment to determine whether the molecules in the liquid are polar.

4. Some people mistakenly associate the term *volatility* with explosiveness. The term correctly refers to the tendency of a liquid to evaporate. Generate a hypothesis to explain how the mistaken association may have come about.

5. Describe a controlled experiment to test the hypothesis you generated in Question 4. Assuming that your hypothesis is correct, state the predicted result of your experiment.

▼▼▼

Teacher Material
Organic Evolution

Learning Cycle 11

What Changes Have Occurred in Organisms Through Time?

Synopsis Students explore the fossils found in six rock layers of the Grand Canyon, each of which represents a different period in geologic time, to determine the fossils' characteristics and to search for patterns in the history of life on earth. Trends in the fossil record are discussed, and various hypotheses to account for these trends are proposed and evaluated by the students. Terms relating to evolutionary patterns and earth history are introduced (e.g., *organic evolution, adaptive radiation,* and *extinction*). This is an empirical-abductive learning cycle.

Suggested Time
- One to one and one-half class periods for fossil exploration
- One-half period for students to find patterns, class discussion, and creating and discussing hypotheses
- One-half class period for introducing terms
- One or more periods for concept application

Background Information The theory of organic evolution (i.e., the idea that species change across time) is a cornerstone of modern biology because it conceptually ties together many varied observations. The idea that species evolved had been suggested by others before Charles Darwin's *The Origin of Species* was published, yet Darwin was the first to spell out major postulates of evolutionary theory clearly as follows:

1. All life evolved from one simple kind of organism.
2. Each species, fossil or living, arose from another species that preceded it in time.
3. Evolutionary changes were gradual and of long duration.
4. Each species originated in a single geographic location.
5. Over long periods of time, new genera, new families, new orders, new classes, and new phyla arose by a continuation of the kind of evolution that produced new species (that is, *adaptive radiation*).
6. The greater the similarity between two groups of organisms, the closer their relationship and the closer in geologic time their common ancestral group.
7. Extinction of old forms (species, etc.) is a consequence of the production of new forms or of environmental change.
8. Once a species or other group has become extinct, it never reappears.

9. Evolution continues today in generally the same manner as during preceding geologic eras.

10. The geologic record is extremely sketchy.

In *The Origin of Species,* Darwin clearly recognized that he was describing two theories: "evolution or descent with modification" and "natural selection." This learning cycle allows you to introduce the theory of evolution.

Teaching Tips *Advance Preparation*

1. At the end of this Teacher Material are illustrations of fossils to use in the six fossil layers needed for this investigation. If you cannot obtain fossil kits, then you can cut up these layer sheets and allow the students to use them instead (with the names and dates removed). The fossil kits are preferred, and the 50 plastic fossil molds that make up the kits can be obtained by ordering individual or partial fossil sets from various biological and earth science supplies. The plastic fossil models used in this investigation were ordered from Carolina Biological Supplies, 2700 York Road, Burlington, NC 27215-3398; 1-800-334-5551.

2. Each fossil kit has fossils that represent six geological time periods. The fossils selected for this investigation demonstrate characteristics true of the fossil record. In general, these fossils reflect (from oldest to youngest):
   - a progression from simple to complex
   - a general size increase of fossils
   - a general increase in diversity
   - continuity of some life forms through several time periods
   - disappearance of extinction of some life forms

   These patterns are revealed in Figure 1 on page 558.

3. Each fossil picture is identified by a letter set in the lower-left corner; for example, L–A represents Layer L and a fossil belonging to A.

Exploration

4. Assign students to work in groups of sizes appropriate to the number of fossil kits you have for the class.

5. Show students a diagram of rock strata and explain that the fossils in each kit were found in the six corresponding rock layers. Also point out that no fossils were found in the seventh and bottom layer (Layer 6).

6. Have students obtain the kits and begin their observations. You may want to call their attention to the list of questions at Step 3 in the procedure section before they begin.

7. When students begin Step 4 in the procedure section, you may need to explain what is meant by a family tree and provide an example such as that at the bottom of the next page. Ask the students to make a "fossil family tree" using this pattern.

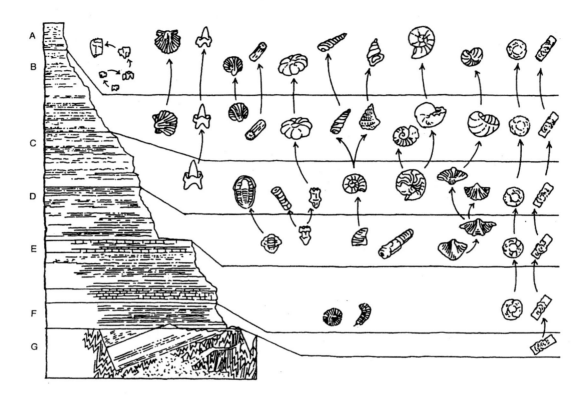

Figure 1 ▾ Fossil Relationships

Term Introduction

8. With reference to the students' diagrams on the board, engage the class in a discussion of its data.

9. Ask students which layer they believe to be the youngest and oldest, and why. Introduce the terms *superposition*, *relative dating*, *fossilization*, and *extinction*

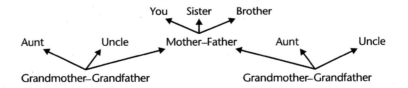

Family tree pattern

with reference to the data. Tell students that scientists have performed radio-active-isotope dating on the rock strata to determine absolute dates.

10. Now ask the class what patterns it found by comparing the different life forms in the respective layers. Students probably will have noted several of the patterns listed in Step 2 of the procedure section. If not, you may have to lead them a little. These patterns should be diagrammed on the board.

11. Ask students to propose hypotheses to account for the existence of these patterns in the fossil record. If they do not understand, lead them with questions such as, "What are some possible ways to account for how these organisms got here on earth? What are some ways to account for their appearance and disappearance in the fossil record at these times?" List all suggested hypotheses on the board.

12. Now ask the class to consider each hypothesis, one at a time, and evaluate how well it is supported or weakened by the data from the fossil record. Introduce and discuss the term *organic evolution.*

Concept Application

13. You may wish to show a video or, on your own, cover some other area of evidence that supports the theory of organic evolution, notably comparative anatomy, comparative embryology, comparative biochemistry, chromosomal similarities, and so on.

14. Another approach you may wish to consider is to explain how scientists "test a theory" by making predictions concerning what they will find when they do experiments or research new areas. Have your students make predictions based on what patterns they think they would find if they could compare the proteins, DNA, or internal anatomy of closely related organisms and distantly related organisms.

15. If you do not choose to cover other areas of evidence at this time, you may want to try one or more of the following as an application:
    - View the BSCS film loop *Fossil Interpretation.*
    - Have your students research the evolutionary sequence of a living organism—for example, horse, human, or elephant.
    - Arrange for a field trip to a local fossil bed or museum.

16. Two pencil-and-paper activities follow; these also can be used as applications.

Activity A
Figure 2 (page 560) illustrates geometric forms from eight successive layers. The oldest, at the base, represents the lowermost layer in the sequence and contains the simplest shapes. Younger layers yield newer or specialized figures, until the youngest figures are encountered in the topmost layer (H). This investigation shows the ideas of divergent evolution, parallel evolution, convergent evolution, and radiation. In several cases, there is no single correct answer.

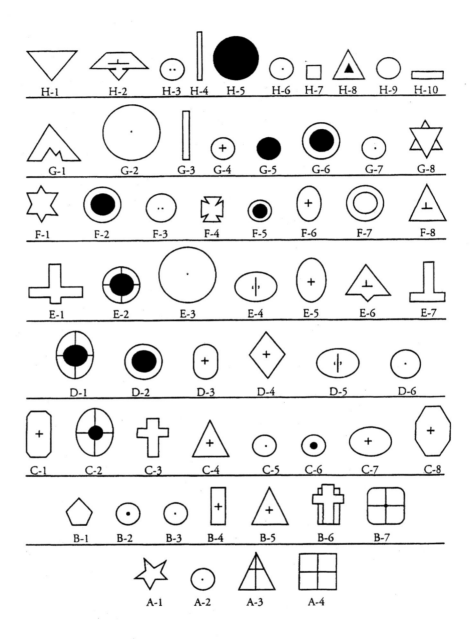

Figure 2 ▼ Geometric Shapes. These shapes simulate the kinds of fossils found in eight stratigraphic intervals. They are to be used in a problem that shows evolutionary patterns and phylogenetic trends.

Examples:

a. Begin with the oldest layer (A) and work upward, connecting by pencil lines the likely related figures, layer by layer.

b. Cut the figures apart, rearranging them into patterns.

c. Connect the various figures with arrows to show trends. Indicate the relationships; show which ones became extinct, changed, or remained constant.

Activity B

Figure 3 (page 562) shows ten geologic layers of graptolite fossils, with the oldest at bottom and the youngest at top. The entire sequence represents fossils found in rocks of the upper Cambrian or lower Ordovician periods and continuing into the Devonian. Graptolites are an extinct group whose exact relationship to modern animals is not known but whose characteristics evolved rapidly through geologic time.

a. Establish possible linkages for the various graptolites shown by using a series of arrows to connect related fossils or by cutting the sketches apart and rearranging them into related sequences. Be careful to keep the fossils in their correct layer when rearranging.

b. Locate with numbers and letters possible examples of parallel evolution, convergent evolution, and divergent evolution.

Biological Terms
organic evolution
fossilization
speciation
adaptive radiation
sedimentation
rock dating
extinction
convergent evolution
divergent evolution
parallel evolution

Thinking Skills
accurately describe nature
state causal questions
create alternative hypotheses
generate logical predictions
organize and analyze data
draw and apply conclusions

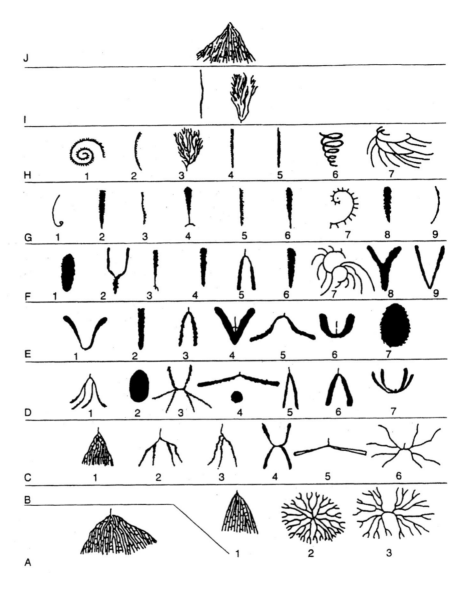

Figure 3 ▼ Graptolite Occurrences. The diagram shows graptolite occurrences for ten consecutive stratigraphic horizons. They are used in reconstructing phylogenetic trends.

**Sample Test
Questions**

1. What is the basis for this chart?

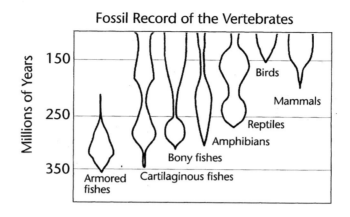

Fossil Record of the Vertebrates

a. the age of fossil mammals
b. the origin of life
c. carbon dating of the earth's strata
d. numbers and geologic ages of fossil species

2. "After an animal group has originated, it tends to develop many kinds." This statement would be classed as

a. a problem.
b. data.
c. a result.
*d. an interpretation.

3. What appears to be the most recent group of animals to have come into existence?

a. reptiles
b. mammals
c. bony fishes
*d. birds

4. The number of kinds of organisms in a group is a measure of successful adaptation. Which group of fish appears to have been the most successful?

a. armored fishes
b. cartilaginous fishes
*c. bony fishes
d. All groups are equally successful.

5. On the same basis, which of the following groups appears to have been the least successful?

   a. bony fishes
 *b. armored fishes
   c. birds
   d. mammals

6. If we were to assume that species do not change, we would expect to find

   a. the simplest fossils in the oldest rocks.
   b. the simplest fossils in the newest rocks.
 *c. the same kind of fossils in old and new rocks.
   d. no fossils in any rocks.

7. Over many years, the uplifting of a mountain range separates a species into two separate populations. After many generations, members of two populations brought together are no longer able to interbreed. This process is called

   a. parallel evolution.
   b. convergent evolution.
   c. convergent radiant evolution.
   d. retrogressive evolution.
 *e. divergent evolution.

d. What might the environment have been like in which the fossilized organism lived? What evidence do you have that is consistent with your hypothesis?
e. How do the fossils differ from one layer to the next?
f. Are similar fossils found in more than one layer?
g. What trends are revealed by a comparison of fossils (or lack of fossils) from one layer to the next?
h. What alternative hypotheses can you propose to explain these trends?

Fossil Layer A

Collenia Algae-Bacteria (Cenozoic) L-A	**Carcharodon** CHORDATA, Pisces (shark tooth; Tertiary-Miocene) L-A	**Medusian** Jellyfish (Cenozoic) L-A	**Merychippus** CHORDATA, Mammalia (horse tooth; Tertiary-Miocene) L-A$_3$
Equus CHORDATA, Mammalia (horse tooth; Quaternary) L-A$_1$	**Tetragramme agassizi** ECHINODERMATA, Echinoidea (sea urchin; Cretaceous L-A	**Turritella alticostata** MOLLUSCA, Gastropoda (Tertiary) L-A	**Venericardia robustus** MOLLUSCA, Pelecypoda (clam; Tertiary-Quaternary L-A
Pecten jeffersonius MOLLUSCA, Pelecypoda (scallop; Tertiary-Quaternary) L-A	**Littorina** MOLLUSCA, Gastropoda (snail; Paleozoic to Recent) L-A	**Hyracotherium** CHORDATA, Mammalia (horse tooth; Eocene) L-A$_5$	**Lytoceras** MOLLUSCA, Cephalopoda (Jurassic-Cretaceous) L-A
Oleneothyris hariani BRACHIOPODA (Cretaceous) L-A	**Fish Bone** CHORDATA (Quaternary) L-A	**Pilohippus** CHORDATA, Mammalia (horse tooth; Pliocene) L-A$_2$	**Mesohippus** CHORDATA, Mammalia (horse tooth; Oligocene) L-A$_4$

Fossil Layer B

Collenia Algae-Bacteria (Tertiary) **L-B**	**Carcharodon** CHORDATA, Pisces (shark tooth; Tertiary-Miocene) **L-B**	**Tetragramme agassizi** ECHINODERMATA, Echinoidea (sea urchin; Cretaceous) **L-B**	**Medusina** Jellyfish (Cretaceous) **L-B**
Turritella alticostata MOLLUSCA, Gastropoda (Tertiary) **L-B**	**Venericardia robustus** MOLLUSCA, Pelecypoda (clam; Tertiary-Quaternary) **L-B**	**Meekoceras gracilitatis** MOLLUSCA, Cephalopoda (Triassic) **L-B**	**Pleurotomoria** MOLLUSCA, Gastropoda (snail; Jurassic) **L-B**
Acanthoscaphites MOLLUSCA, Cephalopoda (Cretaceous) **L-B**	**Oleneothyris hariani** BRACHIOPODA (Cretaceous) **L-B**	**Fish Vertebra** CHORDATA, Bony Fish (Triassic) **L-B**	**Pecten jeffersonius** MOLLUSCA, Pelecypoda (scallop; Tertiary-Quaternary) **L-B**

5. Replace the fossils on the butcher paper with pictures of fossils (available from your teacher). Tape the pictures to the butcher paper to produce a poster of your "fossil family tree."

6. Tape your fossil family tree to the board or a wall and be prepared to talk about your observed trends and those of your classmates in a class discussion.

Study Questions

1. What can be learned about living organisms by studying fossils?

2. Some fossils found in the lower layers are not found in the upper layers. Give two possible explanations for this observation.

3. Some fossils found in upper layers are not found in lower layers. Give two possible explanations for this observation.

4. Fossils are relatively rare. Give possible reasons why this is true.

5. Coal has been discovered at Antarctica. Give a possible explanation that could account for this discovery.

Fossil Layer C

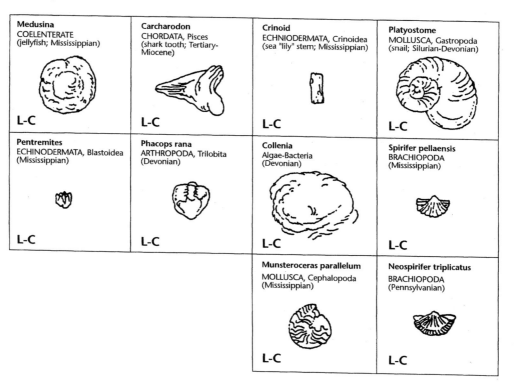

Medusina COELENTERATE (jellyfish; Mississippian)	**Carcharodon** CHORDATA, Pisces (shark tooth; Tertiary-Miocene)	**Crinoid** ECHNIODERMATA, Crinoidea (sea "lily" stem; Mississippian)	**Platyostome** MOLLUSCA, Gastropoda (snail; Silurian-Devonian)
L-C	L-C	L-C	L-C
Pentremites ECHINODERMATA, Blastoidea (Mississippian)	**Phacops rana** ARTHROPODA, Trilobita (Devonian)	**Collenia** Algae-Bacteria (Devonian)	**Spirifer pellaensis** BRACHIOPODA (Mississippian)
L-C	L-C	L-C	L-C
		Munsteroceras parallelum MOLLUSCA, Cephalopoda (Mississippian)	**Neospirifer triplicatus** BRACHIOPODA (Pennsylvanian)
		L-C	L-C

Fossil Layer D

Michelinoceras sociale MOLLUSCA, Cephalopoda (Ordovician)	**Mucrospirifer thedfordensis** BRACHIOPODA (Devonian)	**Medusina** COELENTERATA (jellyfish; Devonian)	**Flexicalymene meeki** ARTHROPODA, Trilobita (Silurian)
L-D	L-D	L-D	L-D
Maciurites MOLLUSCA, Gastropoda (snail; Ordovician)	**Eospirifer radiatus** BRACHIOPODA (Silurian)	**Collenia** Algae-Bacteria (chirt; Devonian)	**Codaster** ECHINODERMATA (blastoid; Silurian)
L-D	L-D	L-D	L-D

Fossil Layer E

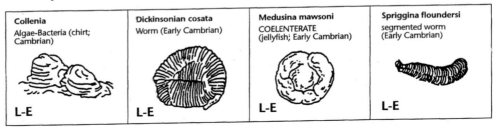

Fossil Layer F

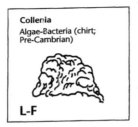

Fossil Layer G

No fossils found in this layer
L-G

6. If we were to assume that organisms have not changed across time, what would the fossil record look like?

7. What patterns would the fossil record reflect if all organisms were created at roughly the same point in time?

8. Draw an enlarged version of the diagram on page 571 on a sheet of paper and fill in the boxes and blanks with one causal question, hypothesis, experiment, expected results, actual results, and conclusion from this investigation.

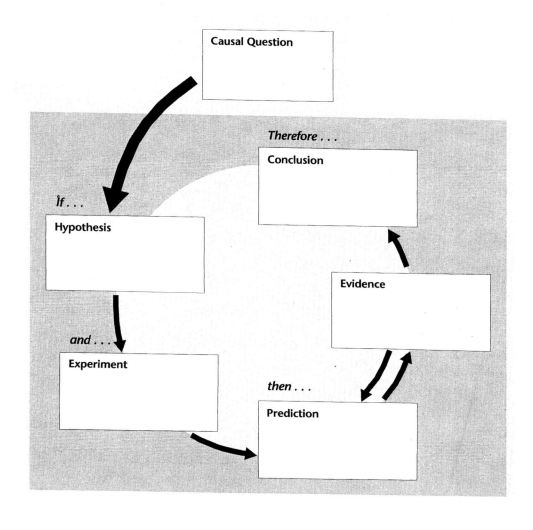

REFERENCES

Abraham, M. R. (1982). A descriptive instrument for use in investigating science laboratories. *Journal of Research in Science Teaching, 19*(2): 155–165.

Abraham, M. R., and Renner, J. W. (1986). The sequence of learning cycle activities in high school chemistry. *Journal of Research in Science Teaching, 23*(2): 121–143.

Abraham, M. R., and Renner, J. W. (1984). *Sequencing language and activities in teaching high school chemistry*. A report to the National Science Foundation (Vol. 241, p. 267). Norman: University of Oklahoma.

Aikenhead, G. S. (1980). *Science in Social Issues: Implication for Teaching*. Toronto: Science Council of Canada.

Albus, J. S. (1981). *Brains, Behavior, and Robotics*. Peterborough, NH: BYTE Books.

Allen, L. R. (1973a). An evaluation of children's performance in certain cognitive, affective, and motivational aspects of the Systems and Subsystems unit of the Science Curriculum Improvement Study elementary science program. *Journal of Research in Science Teaching, 10*(2): 125–134.

Allen, L. R. (1973b). An examination of the ability of third-grade children from the Science Curriculum Improvement Study elementary science program to identify experimental variables and to recognize change. *Science Education, 57*(2): 135–151.

Allen, L. R. (1972). An evaluation of children's performance on certain cognitive, affective, and motivational aspects of the Interaction unit of the Science Curriculum Improvement Study. *Journal of Research in Science Teaching, 9*(2): 167–173.

Allen, L. R. (1971). An examination of the ability of first graders from the science cirriculum study program to describe an object by its properties. *Science Education, 55*(1): 61–67.

Allen, L. R. (1967). An examination of the classification ability of children who have been exposed to one of the "new" elementary science programs. *Dissertation Abstracts, 28*(7): 2591A.

American Association for the Advancement of Science (1993). *Benchmarks for Science Literacy*. New York: Oxford University Press.

American Association for the Advancement of Science (1989). *Project 2061: Science for All Americans*. Washington, DC: Author.

American College Testing Program (1988). *Item Writer's Guide for the Collegiate Assessment of Academic Proficiency Critical Thinking Test*. Iowa City, IA: Author.

Anamvah-Mensah, J. (1987). Comments on plants as producers: A case study of elementary science teaching. *Journal of Research in Science Teaching, 24*(8): 769–770.

Anderson, C. W., and Smith, E. R. (1986). Teaching science. In V. Koehler (Ed.), *The Educator's Handbook: A Research Perspective*. New York: Longman.

Anderson, J. R. (1980). *Cognitive Psychology and Its Implications*. San Francisco: W. H. Freeman.

Anderson, R. D., DeVito, A., Dyril, O. E., Kellogg, M., Kochendorfer, L., and Weigand, J. (1970). *Developing Children's Thinking Through Science*. Englewood Cliffs, NJ: Prentice-Hall.

Anderson, J. R., and Thompson, R. (1989). Use of analogy in a production system architecture. In S. Vosniadou and A. Ortony (Eds.), *Similarity and Analogical Reasoning*. London: Cambridge University Press.

Anderson, O. R. (1992). Some interrelationships between constructivist models of learning and current neurobiological theory, with implications for science education. *Journal of Research in Science Teaching, 29*(10): 1037–1058.

Armbruster, B. B., and Anderson, T. S. (1984). Mapping: Representing informative text diagrammatically. In C. D. Holly and D. F. Dansereau (Eds.), *Spatial Learning Strategies*. New York: Academic Press.

Arnaudin, M. W., and Mintzes, J. J. (1985). Students' alternative conceptions of the human circulatory system: A cross-age study. *Science Education, 69*(5): 721–733.

Atkin, J. M., and Karplus, R. (1962). Discovery or invention? *Science Teacher, 29*(5): 45.

Ausubel, D. P. (1989, September). Personal communication.

Ausubel, D. P. (1979). Education for rational thinking: A critique. In A. E. Lawson (Ed.), *The Psychology of Teaching for Thinking and Creativity*. AETS 1980 Yearbook. Columbus, OH: ERIC/SMEAC.

Ausubel, D. P. (1964). The transition from concrete to abstract cognitive functioning: Theoretical issues and implications for education. *Journal of Research in Science Teaching, 2*(4): 261–266.

Ausubel, D. P. (1963). *The Psychology of Meaningful Verbal Learning*. New York: Grune & Stratton.

Ausubel, D. P., Novak, J. D., and Hanesian, H. (1968). *Educational Psychology: A Cognitive View* (2nd ed.). New York: Holt, Rinehart & Winston.

Baker, J. J. W., and Allen, G. E. (1977). *The Study of Biology*. (3rd ed.). Reading, MA: Addison-Wesley.

Baker, J. J. W., and Allen, G. E. (1967). *The Study of Biology*. Reading, MA: Addison-Wesley.

Barnhart, C. L. (Ed.). (1953). *The American College Dictionary*. New York: Harper & Brothers.

Bereiter, C. (1985). Toward a solution of the learning paradox. *Review of Educational Research, 55*(2): 201–226.

Berger, C. F., Pintrich, P. R., and Stemmer, P. M. (1987). Cognitive consequences of student estimation on linear and logarithmic scales. *Journal of Research in Science Teaching, 24*(5): 437–450.

Biological Sciences Curriculum Study. (1992). *Science & Technology: Investigating Human Dimensions*. Dubuque, IA: Kendall/Hunt.

Bird, T., and Little, J. (1985). *Organizing schools for improvement*. Far West Laboratory, San Francisco. Presented at Spring Conference of Arizona chapter of ASCD.

Bishop, J. E. (1980). The development and testing of a participatory planetarium unit employing projective astronomy concepts and utilizing the Karplus learning cycle, student model manipulation and student drawing with eighth-grade students. *Dissertation Abstracts, 41*(3): 1010A.

Blasi, A., and Hoeffel, E. C. (1974). Adolescence and formal operations. *Human Development, 17*: 344–363.

Bloom, B. S. (Ed.). (1956). *Taxonomy of Educational Objectives: Cognitive Domain*. New York: Longmans, Green & Company.

Bolton, N. (1977). *Concept Formation*. Oxford: Pergamon Press.

Bourne, L. E. (1966). *Human Conceptual Behavior*. Boston: Allyn & Bacon.

Bowyer, J. A. B. (1976). Science Curriculum Improvement Study and the development of scientific literacy. *Dissertation Abstracts, 37*(1): 107A.

Brasell, H. (1987). The effect of real-time laboratory graphing on learning graphic representations of distance and velocity. *Journal of Research in Science Teaching, 24*(4): 385–395.

Bringuier, J. (1980). *Conversations with Jean Piaget*. Chicago: University of Chicago Press.

Brown, T. W. (1973). The influence of the Science Curriculum Improvement Study on affective process development and creative thinking. *Dissertation Abstracts, 34*(6): 3175A.

Brown, T. W., Weber, M. C., and Renner, J. W. (1975). Research on the development of scientific literacy. *Science and Children, 12*(4): 13–15.

Brum, G. D., and McKane, L. K. (1989). *Biology: Exploring Life.* New York: John Wiley & Sons.

Brumby, M. N. (1984). Misconceptions about the concept of natural selection by medical biology students. *Science Education, 68*(4): 493–503.

Bruner, J. S. (1968). *Toward a Theory of Instruction,* New York: W. W. Norton.

Bruner, J. S. (1963). *The Process of Education.* Cambridge, MA: Harvard University Press.

Bruner, J. S., and Kenney, H. J. (1970). Representation and mathematics learning. In W. Kessen and C. Kuhlman (Eds.), *Cognitive Development in Children.* Chicago: University of Chicago Press.

Brynner, W. (Trans.). (1962). *From the Way of Life According to Lao-Tse.* New York: Capricorn Books.

Bunge, M. (1967). *Scientific Research II: The Search for Truth.* New York: Springer-Verlag.

Burmester, M. A. (1952). Behavior involved in critical aspects of scientific thinking. *Science Education, 36*(5): 259–263.

Bybee, R. W. (1987). Science education and the Science-Technology-Society (S.T.S.) theme. *Science Education, 71*(5): 667–683.

Campbell, T. C. (1977). An evaluation of a learning cycle intervention strategy for enhancing the use of formal operational thought by beginning college physics students. *Dissertation Abstracts, 38*(7): 3903A.

Capie, W., and Tobin, K. G. (1981). Pupil engagement in learning tasks: A fertile area for research in science teaching. *Journal of Research in Science Teaching, 18*(5): 409–417.

Carbonell, J. G. (1986). Learning by analogy: Formulating and generalizing plans from past experience. In R. Michalski, J. G. Carbonell, and T. M. Mitchell (Eds.), *Machine Learning: An Artificial Intelligence Approach.* Palo Alto, CA: Tioga Press.

Carin, A. A., and Sund, R. B. (1980). *Teaching Modern Science* (3rd ed.). Columbus, OH: Charles E. Merrill.

Carlson, D. A. (1975). Training in formal reasoning abilities provided by the inquiry role approach and achievement on the Piagetian formal operational level. *Dissertation Abstracts, 36*(11): 7368A.

Caro, T. M. (1986a). The function of stotting: A review of the hypotheses. *Animal Behavior, 34:* 649–662.

Caro, T. M. (1986b). The function of stotting in Thompson's gazelles: Some tests of the predictions. *Animal Behavior, 34:* 663–684.

Case, R. (1972). Learning and Development: A Neo-Piagetian Interpretation. *Human Development, 15:* 339–358.

Catrambone, R., and Holyoak, K. J. (1985). *The function of schemas in analogical problem solving.* Presentation to the American Psychological Association, Los Angeles, CA.

Chamberlain, T. C. (1965). The method of multiple working hypotheses. *Science, 148:* 754–759, 1965. Originally published 1897.

Champagne, A. B., Klopfer, L. E., and Anderson, J. H. (1980). Factors influencing learning of classical mechanics. *American Journal of Physics, 48*(12): 1074–1079.

Cheng, P. W., and Holyoak, K. J. (1985). Pragmatic reasoning schemas. *Cognitive Psychology, 17:* 391–416.

Clausen, J., Keck, D., and Hiesey, W. (1948). *Carnegie Institute, Washington, Publication 581.*

Clement, J. (1986, July). *Misconceptions in mechanics and an attempt to remediate them: The use of analogies and anchoring intuitions.* Presentation to the NSF Conference on the Psychology of Physics Problem Solving, Bank Street College.

Clement, J. (1982). Students' perceptions in introductory mechanics. *American Journal of Physics, 50*(1): 60–71.

Collea, F. P., Fuller, R. G., Karplus, R., Paldy, L. G., and Renner, J. W. (1975). *Physics Teaching and the Development of Reasoning.* Stony Brook: American Association of Physics Teachers.

Collette, A. T., and Chiappetta, E. L. (1986). *Science Instruction in the Middle and Secondary Schools*. Columbus, OH: Charles E. Merrill.

Collins, A. (1990). Portfolios for assessing student learning in science: A new name for familiar idea? In A. B. Champagne, B. E Lovitts, and B. J. Calinger (Eds.), *Assessment in the Service of Instruction* (pp. 157–166). Washington, DC: American Association for the Advancement of Science.

Conant, J. B. (1951). *Science and Common Sense*. New Haven, CT: Yale University Press.

Copi, I. M. (1972). *Introduction to Logic* (4th ed.). New York: Macmillan.

Costenson, K., and Lawson, A. E. (1986). Why isn't inquiry used in more classrooms? *Amerian Biology Teacher, 48*(3): 150–158.

Crane, H. R. (1970). Problems for introductory physics. *The Physics Teacher, 8:* 182.

Crane, H. R. (1969). Problems for introductory physics. *The Physics Teacher, 7:* 371.

Creager, J. C. (1975). Plaudits for Piaget—and some implications for teachers. *American Biology Teacher, 37*(8): 463.

Darwin, C. (1963). *On the Origin of Species*. Lechtworth, England: Aldine Press.

Darwin, C. (1962). *The Voyage of the Beagle* (L. Engel, Ed.). Garden City, NY: American Museum of Natural History and Doubleday.

Dashiell, J. F. (1949). *Fundamentals of General Psychology* (3rd ed.). New York: Houghton Mifflin.

Davis, J. O. (1978). The effects of three approaches to science instruction on the science achievement, understanding, and attitudes of selected fifth and sixth grade students. *Dissertation Abstracts, 39:* 211A.

Dempster, F. N. (1992). Resistance to interference: Developmental changes in a basic processing mechanism. *Developmental Review, 12,* 45–57.

Dewey, J. (1971). *How We Think*. Chicago: Henry Regnery Co. Originally published 1910.

Dewey, J. (1916). Method in science teaching. *General Science Quarterly, 1:* 3.

Diamond, A. (1990). The development and neural bases of inhibitory control in reaching in human infants and infant monkeys. In A. Diamond (Ed.), *The Development and Neural Basis of Higher Cognitive Functions*. New York: Academy of Sciences.

diSessa, A. A. (1987). The third revolution in computers and education. *Journal of Research in Science Teaching, 24*(4): 343–368.

Driver, R. (1989). Changing conceptions. In P. Adey, J. Bliss, J. Head, and M. Shayer (Eds.), *Adolescent Development and School Science*. London: Falmer Press.

Driver, R. (1981). Pupils' alternative frameworks in science. *European Journal of Science Education, 3*(1): 93–101.

Eaton, D. (1974). An investigation of the effects of an in-service workshop designed to implement the Science Curriculum Improvement Study upon selected teacher–pupil behavior and perceptions. *Dissertation Abstracts, 35*(4): 2096A.

Educational Policies Commission. (1966). *Education and the Spirit of Science*. Washington, DC: National Education Association.

Educational Policies Commission. (1961). *The Central Purpose of American Education*. Washington, DC: National Education Association.

Ehrlich, P. R., Holm, R. W., and Parnell, D. R. (1974). *The Process of Evolution* (2nd ed.). New York: McGraw-Hill.

Elementary Science Study (1974). *Attribute Games and Problems*. New York: McGraw-Hill.

Elkind, D. (1961). Children's discovery of the conservation of mass, weight, and volume: Piaget replication study II. *Journal of Genetic Psychology, 98:* 219–227.

Ellis, J. D., and Kuerbis, P. J. (1988, April). *A model for implementing microcomputers in science teaching*. Presentation to the National Association for Research in Science Teaching, St. Louis, MO.

Evans, J. B. S. (1982). *The Psychology of Deductive Reasoning*. London: Routledge & Kegan Paul.

Fensham, P. J. (1987). Physical science, society and technology: A case study in the sociology of knowledge. In K. Riquarts (Ed.), *Science and Technology Education and the Quality of Life*. Proceeding of the 4th International Symposium on World Trends in Science and Technology Education (Vol. 2, pp. 714–723). Kiel, Germany.

Lawson, A. E., Nordland, F. H., and Kahle, J. B. (1975). Levels of intellectual development and reading ability in disadvantaged students and the teaching of science. *Science Education, 59*(1): 113–126.

Lawson, A. E., and Renner, J. W. (1975a). Piagetian theory and biology teaching. *American Biology Teacher, 37*(6): 336.

Lawson, A. E., and Renner, J. W. (1975b). Relationship of science subject matter and the developmental level of the learner. *Journal of Research in Science Teaching, 12*(4): 347–358.

Lawson, A. E., and Renner, J. W. (1974). A quantitative analysis of responses to Piagetian tasks and its implications for curriculum. *Science Education, 58*(4): 545–560.

Lawson, A. E., and Snitgen, D. (1982). Teaching formal reasoning in a college biology course for pre-service teachers. *Journal of Research in Science Teaching, 19*(3): 233–248.

Lawson, A. E., and Staver, J. R. (1989). Toward a solution of the learning paradox: Emergent properties and neurological principles of constructivism. *Instructional Science, 18:* 169–177.

Lawson, A. E., and Thompson, L. D. (1988). Formal reasoning ability and misconceptions concerning genetics and natural selection. *Journal of Research in Science Teaching, 25*(9): 733–746.

Lawson, A. E., and Weser, J. (1990). The rejection of nonscientific beliefs about life: The effects of instruction and reasoning skills. *Journal of Research in Science Teaching, 27*(6): 589–606.

Lawson, A. E. and Wollman, W. T. (1977). Cognitive level, cognitive style and value judgment. *Science Education, 61*(3): 397–407.

Lawson, A. E., and Wollman, W. T. (1976). Encouraging the transition from concrete to formal cognitive functioning—an experiment. *Journal of Research in Science Teaching, 13*(5): 413–430.

Lawson, C. A. (1967). *Brain Mechanisms and Human Learning.* Boston: Houghton-Mifflin.

Lawson, C. A. (1958) *Language, Thought, and the Human Mind.* East Lansing: Michigan State University Press.

Lawson, C. A., and Paulson, R. E. (Eds.) (1958). *Laboratory and Field Studies in Biology: A Source Book for Secondary Schools.* New York: Holt, Rinehart & Winston.

Lawson, D. I., and Lawson, A. E. (1993). Neural principles of memory and a neural theory of analogical insight. *Journal of Research in Science Teaching, 30*(9), 1327–1348.

Lazarowitz, R., Hertz, R. L., Baird, J. H., and Bowlden, V. (1988). Academic achievement and on-task behavior of high school biology students instructed in a cooperative small investigative group. *Science Education, 72*(4): 475–487.

Lehman, D. R., Lempert, R. O., and Nisbett, R. E. (1988). The effects of graduate training on reasoning. *American Psychologist, 43*(6): 431–442.

Lehman, J. D., Carter, C., and Kahle, J. B. (1985). Concept mapping, vee mapping, and achievement: Result of a field study with black high school students. *Journal of Research in Science Teaching, 22*(7): 663–673.

Leighton, R. B. (1964). *The Feynman Lectures on Physics—Exercises.* Palo Alto, CA: Addison-Wesley.

Leonard, W. H. (1980). Using the extended discretion approach to biology laboratory investigation. *American Biology Teacher, 42*(7): 338.

Lepper, M. R., Greene, D., and Nisbett, R. E. (1973). Undermining children's intrinsic interest with extrinsic reward: A test of the "overjustification" hypothesis. *Journal of Personality and Social Psychology, 28*(1): 129–137.

Levine, D. S., and Prueitt, P. S. (1989). Modeling some effects of frontal lobe damage: Novelty and perseveration. *Neural Networks, 2:* 103–116.

Lewis, M. M. (1936). *Infant Speech: A Study of the Beginnings of Language.* Harcourt, Brace & Co.

Lewis, R. W. (1988). Biology: A hypothetico-deductive science. *American Biology Teacher, 50*(6): 362–367.

Lewis, R. W. (1987). Theories, concepts, mapping and teaching. *University Bookman, 27*(4): 4–11.

Lewis, R. W. (1986). Teaching the theories of evolution. *American Biology Teacher, 48*(6): 344–347.

Lewis, R. W. (1980, Summer). Evolution: A system of theories. *Perspectives in Biology and Medicine,* pp. 551–572.

Lewis, R. W. (1977, August). *Biological theories: Organization and teaching.* Presentation to AIBS meeting, East Lansing, MI,

Lewis, R. W. (1975, December). Personal communication.

Linn, M. C., Pulos, S., and Gans, A. (1981). Correlates of formal reasoning: Content and problem effects. *Journal of Research in Science Teaching, 18*(5): 435–447.

Linn, M. C., and Thier, H. D. (1975). The effect of experimental science on development of logical thinking in children. *Journal of Research in Science Teaching, 12*(1): 49–62.

Locke, J. (1924). *Essay on the Human Understanding.* Oxford, England: Clarendon Press. Originally published 1690.

Lott, G. W. (1983). The effect of inquiry teaching and advance organizers upon student outcomes in science education. *Journal of Research in Science Teaching, 20*(5): 437.

Lovell, K. (1961). A follow-up study of Inhelder and Piaget's *The Growth of Logical Thinking. British Journal of Psychology, 52:* 143–153.

Lowery, L. F., Bowyer, J., and Padilla, M. J. (1980). The Science Curriculum Improvement Study and student attitudes. *Journal of Research in Science Teaching, 17*(4): 327–355.

Luria, A. R. (1961). *The Role of Speech in the Regulation of Normal and Abnormal Behavior.* Oxford, England: Pergamon.

MacGintie, G. E., and MacGintie, N. (1968). *Natural History of Marine Animals* (2nd ed.). New York: McGraw-Hill.

Mader, S. S. (1985). *Biology: Evolution, Diversity, and the Environment.* Dubuque, IA: Wm. C. Brown.

Malcolm, M. D. (1976). The effect of the Science Curriculum Improvement Study on a child's self-concept and attitude toward science. *Dissertation Abstracts, 36*(10): 6617A.

Mallon, E. J. (1976). Cognitive development and processes: Review of the philosophy of Jean Piaget. *American Biology Teacher, 38*(1): 28.

Marek, E. A., and Renner, J. W. (1979). Intellectual development, IQ, achievement, and teaching methodology. *American Biology Teacher, 41*(3): 145.

Markovits, H. (1985). Incorrect conditional reasoning among adults: Competence or performance? *British Journal of Psychology, 76:* 241–247.

Markovits, H. (1984). Awareness of the "possible" as a mediator of formal thinking in conditional reasoning problems. *British Journal of Psychology, 75:* 367–376.

Maxwell, D. E. (1974). The effect of selected science activities on the attainment of reading skills with kindergarten children. *Dissertation Abstracts, 35*(9): 6007A.

Mayer, R. E. (1983). *Thinking, Problem Solving, Cognition.* New York: W. H. Freeman.

Mayer, W. V., and Barufaldi, J. P. (1988). *The Textbook Chooser's Guide.* Berkeley, CA: National Center for Science Education.

McKinnon, J. W., and Renner, J. W. (1971). Are colleges concerned with intellectual development? *American Journal of Physics, 39:* 1047–1052.

Mead, M. (1949). *Coming of Age in Samoa.* New York: New American Library. Originally published 1928.

Meltzoff, A. N. (1990). Towards a developmental cognitive science. In A. Diamond (Ed.), *The Development and Neural Basis of Higher Cognitive Functions.* New York: Academy of Sciences.

Mendel, G. (1856). *Experiments in Plant Hybridization.* Cambridge, MA: Harvard University Press.

Miller, G. A. (1956). The magical number seven, plus or minus two: Some limits on our capacity for processing information. *Psychological Review, 63*(2): 81–97.

Minstrell, J. (1982). Conceptual development research in the natural setting of a secondary school science classroom. In M. R. Rowe (Ed.), *Education in the 80's: Science.* Washington, DC: National Education Association.

Minstrell, J. (1980). *Conceptual development of physics students and identification of influencing factors.* Unpublished research report, Mercer Island School District, WA.

Mishkin, M., and Appenzeller, T. (1987). The anatomy of memory. *Scientific American, 256*(6): 80–89.

Mokros, J. R., and Tinker, R. F. (1987). The impact of microcomputer-based labs on children's ability to interpret graphs. *Journal of Research in Science Teaching, 24*(4): 369–384.

Moon, T. C. (1969). A study of verbal behavior patterns in primary grade classrooms during science activities. *Dissertation Abstracts, 30*(12): 5325A.

Morgan, T. H. (1910). Sex-limited inheritance in *Drosophila. Science, 32:* 120–122.

Mussen, P. H., Conger, J. J., and Kegen, J. (1975). *Basic and Contemporary Issues in Developmental Psychology.* New York: Harper & Row.

Nachmias, R., and Linn, M. C. (1987). Evaluations of science laboratory data: The role of computer-presented information. *Journal of Research in Science Teaching, 24*(5): 491–506.

National Research Council. (1990). *Fulfilling the Promise: Biology Education in the Nation's Schools.* Washington, DC: National Academy Press.

Neimark, E. D. (1975). Intellectual development during adolescence. In F. D. Horowits (Ed.), *Review of Child Development Research.* Chicago: University of Chicago Press.

Neimark, E. D. (1970). A preliminary search for formal operations structure. *Journal of Genetic Psychology, 116:* 223–232.

Niaz, M. (1988). Manipulation of M-demand of chemistry problems and its effect on student performance: A neo-Piagetian study. *Journal of Research in Science Teaching, 25*(8): 643–658.

Nisbett, R. E., Fong, G. T., Lehman, D. R., and Cheng, P. W. (1987). Teaching reasoning. *Science, 238:* 625–631.

Nordland, F. H., Lawson, A. E., and Kahle, J. B. (1974). A study of concrete and formal reasoning ability in disadvantaged junior and senior high school science students. *Science Education, 58*(4): 569–575.

Northrop, F. S. (1947). *The Logic of the Sciences and the Humanities.* New York: Macmillan.

Novak, J. D., Gowin, D. W., and Johansen, G. T. (1983). The use of concept mapping and knowledge mapping with junior high school science students. *Science Education, 67*(5): 625–645.

Nussbaum, J. (1979). The effect of the SCIS's relativity unit on the child's conception of space. *Journal of Research in Science Teaching, 16*(1): 45–51.

Odum, E. P. (1971). *Fundamentals of Ecology* (3rd ed.). Philadelphia: W. B. Saunders Co.

Okebukola, P. A., and Jegede, O. J. (1988). Cognitive preference and learning mode as determinants of meaningful learning through concept mapping. *Science Education, 72*(4): 489–500.

Olsen, R. G. (1969). *Meaning and Argument: Elements of Logic.* New York: Harcourt, Brace, & Wold.

Overton, W. F., Ward, S. L., Black, J., Noveck, I. A., and O'Brien, D. P. (1987). Form and content in the development of deductive reasoning. *Developmental Psychology, 23*(1): 22–30.

Pascual-Leone, J. (1980). Constructive problems for constructive theories: the current relevance of Piaget's work and a critique of information processing simulation psychology. In R. H. Kluwe and H. Spada (Eds.), *Developmental Models of Thinking.* New York: Academic Press.

Pascual-Leone, J. (1977). *Cognitive Development and Cognitive Style.* Indianapolis, IN: Heath-Lexington Books.

Pascual-Leone, J. (1976). A view of cognition from a formalist's perspective. In K. F. Riegel and J. A. Meacham (Eds.), *The Developing Individual in a Changing World: Vol 1. Historical and Cultural Issues* (pp. 89–110). The Hague, Netherlands: Mouton.

Pasteur, M. L. (1862). Memoire sur les corpuscules organisés qui existent dans l'atmosphere, examen de la doctrine des generátions spontanés. *Annales de Chime et de Physique, 64.*

Piaget, J. (1978). *Behavior and Evolution.* New York: Random House.

Piaget, J. (1977a). *The Development of Thought: Equilibrium of Cognitive Structures.* New York: Viking Press.

Piaget, J. (1977b). *The Grasp of Consciousness.* London: Routledge & Kegan Paul.

Piaget, J. (1976a). Piaget's theory. In B. Inhelder and H. H. Chipman (Eds.), *Piaget and His School.* New York: Springer-Verlag.

Piaget, J. (1976b). *The Grasp of Consciousness.* Cambridge, MA: Harvard University Press.

Piaget, J. (1975). From noise to order: The psychological development of knowledge and phenocopy in biology. *Urban Review, 8*(3): 209.

Piaget, J. (1974). *Understanding Causality.* New York: W. W. Norton.

Piaget, J. (1973). *To Understand Is to Invent: The Future of Education.* New York: Grossman.

Piaget, J. (1972). Intellectual evolution from adolescence to adulthood. *Human Development, 15:* 1–12.

Piaget, J. (1971a). *Biology and Knowledge.* Chicago: University of Chicago Press.

Piaget, J. (1971b). Problems of equilibration. In C. F. Nodine, J. M. Gallagher, and R. H. Humphreys (Eds.), *Piaget and Inhelder: On Equilibration.* Proceedings of First Annual Symposium of the Jean Piaget Society.

Piaget, J. (1966). *Psychology of Intelligence.* Totowa, NJ: Littlefield Adams.

Piaget, J. (1965). *The Child's Conception of Number.* New York: W. W. Norton.

Piaget, J. (1964a). Cognitive development in children: Development and learning. *Journal of Research in Science Teaching, 2*(2): 176–186.

Piaget, J. (1964b). *Judgment and Reasoning in the Child.* Paterson, NJ. Originally published 1928.

Piaget, J. (1962). The stages of the intellectual development of the child. *Bulletin of the Menninger Clinic, 26*(3): 120–145.

Piaget, J. (1957). *Logic and Psychology.* New York: Basic Books.

Piaget, J. (1955). *The Language and Thought of the Child.* New York: World.

Piaget, J. (1954). *The Construction of Reality in the Child.* New York: Basic Books.

Piaget, J. (1952). *The Origins of Intelligence in Children.* New York: International Universities Press.

Piaget, J. (1929a). Les races lacustres de la *Limnaea stagnalis* and recherches sur la rapports de l'adaptation hereditaire avec la milieu. *Bulletin biologique de la France et de la Belgique, 62:* 424.

Piaget, J. (1929b). Adaptation de la *Limnaea stagnalis* aux milieux lacustres de la Suisse romande. *Revue Suisse de Zoologie, 36:* 263.

Piaget, J., and Inhelder, B. (1969). *The Psychology of the Child.* New York: Basic Books.

Piattelli-Palmerini, M. (Ed.) (1980). *Language and Learning: The Debate Between Jean Piaget and Noam Chomsky.* Cambridge, MA: Harvard University Press.

Piburn, M., Baker, D. R., and Treagust, D. (1988, April). *Misconceptions about gravity held by college students.* Presentation to annual conference of the National Association for Research in Science Teaching, St. Louis, MO.

Planck, M. (1949). *Scientific Autobiography* (E. Guynor, Trans.). New York: Philosophical Library.

Porterfield, D. R. (1969). Influence of preparation in the Science Curriculum Improvement Study on questioning behavior of selected second- and fourth-grade reading teachers. *Dissertation Abstracts, 30*(4): 1341A.

Posner, G. J., Strike, K. A., Hewson, P. W., and Gertzog, W. A. (1982). Accommodation of a scientific conception: Toward a theory of conceptual change. *Science Education, 66*(2): 211–227.

Prawit, R. S. (1991). Conversations with self and settings: A framework for thinking about teacher empowerment. *American Educational Research Journal, 28*(4): 737–757.

Preece, P. F. W. (1978). Exploration of semantic space: Review of research on the organization of scientific concepts in semantic meaning. *Science Education, 62*(4): 547–562.

Purser, R. K., and Renner, J. W. (1983). Results of two tenth-grade biology teaching procedures. *Science Education, 67*(1): 85–98.

Raghubir, K. P. (1979). The laboratory-investigative approach to science instruction. *Journal of Research in Science Teaching, 16*(1): 13–18.

Raven, J. C. (1958). *Standard Progressive Matrices.* London: H. K. Lewis & Co.

Raven, J. C. (1940). *Matrix Tests.* London: Mental Health.

Raven, R. J. (1974). Programming Piaget's logical operations for science inquiry and concept attainment. *Journal of Research in Science Teaching, 11*(3): 251–161.

Reif, F. (1987). Instructional design, cognition, and technology: Applications to the teaching of scientific concepts. *Journal of Research in Science Teaching, 24*(4): 309–324.

Rendel, J. M. (1967). *Canalization and Gene Control.* London: Logos Press.

Renner, J. W. (1982). The power of purpose. *Science Education, 66*(5): 709–716.

Renner, J. W. (1976). Significant physics content and intellectual development–cognitive development as a result of interacting with physics content. *American Journal of Physics, 44*(3): 218–222.

Renner, J. W., Abraham, M. R., and Birnie, H. H. (1988). The necessity of each phase of the learning cycle in teaching high-school physics. *Journal of Research in Science Teaching, 25*(1): 39–58.

Renner, J. W., Abraham, M. R., and Birnie, H. H. (1985). The importance of the form of student acquisition of data in physics learning cycles. *Journal of Research in Science Teaching, 22*(4): 303–325.

Renner, J. W., Abraham, M. R., and Birnie, H. H. (1983). *Sequencing Language and Activities in Teaching High School Physics—A Report to the National Science Foundation.* Norman: University of Oklahoma.

Renner, J. W., and Lawson, A. E. (1975). Intellectual development in pre-service elementary school teachers: An evaluation. *Journal of College Science Teaching, 5*(2): 89–92.

Renner, J. W., Stafford, D. G., Coffia, W. J., Kellogg, D. H., and Weber, M. C. (1973). An evaluation of the Science Curriculum Improvement Study. *School Science and Mathematics, 73*(4): 291–318.

Resnick, L. B. (1980). The role of invention in the development of mathematical competence. In R. H. Kluwe and H. Spada (Eds.), *Developmental Models of Thinking.* New York: Academic Press.

Rivers, R. H., and Vockell, E. (1987). Computer simulation to stimulate scientific problem solving. *Journal of Research in Science Teaching, 24*(5): 403–416.

Rogers, C. (1983). *Freedom to Learn for the '80s.* Columbus, OH: Charles E. Merrill.

Rogers, C. R. (1954). Toward a theory of creativity. *ETC: A Review of Semantics, 11:* 249–260.

Romer, A. S. (1959). *The Vertebrate Story* (4th ed.). Chicago: University of Chicago Press.

Roth, W. M. (1993). In the name of constructivism? Science education research and the construction of local knowledge. *Journal of Research in Science Teaching, 30*(7), 799–803.

Saunders, W. L., and Shepardson, D. (1987). A comparison of concrete and formal science instruction upon science achievement and reasoning ability of sixth-grade students. *Journal of Research in Science Teaching, 24*(1): 39–51.

Schneider, L. S., and Renner, J. W. (1980). Concrete and formal teaching. *Journal of Research in Science Teaching, 17*(6): 503–517.

Schwab, J. J. (1962). The concept of the structure of a discipline. *The Educational Record, 43:* 197.

Science Curriculum Improvement Study. (1974). *SCIS Teacher's Handbook.* Berkeley: University of California Press.

Science Curriculum Improvement Study. (1973). *SCIS Omnibus.* Berkeley, CA: Lawrence Hall of Science.

Science Curriculum Improvement Study. (1971a). *Communities: Teacher's Guide.* Chicago: Rand McNally.

Science Curriculum Improvement Study. (1971b). *Ecosystems: Teacher's Guide.* Chicago: Rand McNally.

Science Curriculum Improvement Study. (1970a). *Environments: Teacher's Guide.* Chicago: Rand McNally.

Science Curriculum Improvement Study. (1970b). *Subsystems and Variables: Teacher's Guide.* Chicago: Rand McNally.

Science Research Associates. (1970). *Iowa Tests of Educational Development,* Grades 9–12, Form X5.

Sharan, S. (1980). Cooperative learning in small groups: Recent methods and effects on achievement, attitudes and ethnic relations. *Review of Educational Research, 50*(2): 241–271.

Shayer, M., and Adey, P. (1981). *Towards a Science of Science Teaching.* London: Heinemann Educational Books.

Sherwood, R. D., Kinzer, C. K., Bransford, J. D., and Franks, J. J. (1987). Some benefits of creating macro-contexts for science instruction: Initial findings. *Journal of Research in Science Teaching, 24*(5): 417–435.

Shurter, R. L., and Pierce, J. R. (1966). *Critical Thinking: Its Expression in Argument.* New York: McGraw-Hill.

Shymansky, J. (1984). BSCS programs: Just how effective were they? *The American Biology Teacher, 46*(1), 54–57.

Siegler, R. S., Liebert, D. E., and Liebert, R. M. (1973). Inhelder and Piaget's pendulum problem: Teaching preadolescents to act as scientists. *Developmental Psychology, 9:* 97–101.

Simmons, H. N. (1974). An evaluation of attitudinal changes and changes in teaching behavior of elementary teachers enrolled in eleven SCIS workshops directed by leadership teams trained in a SCIS leader's workshop. *Dissertation Abstracts, 34*(7): 4068A.

Simon, H. A. (1974). How big is a chunk? *Science, 183:* 482–488.

Simpson, W. D., and Marek, E. A. (1988). Understandings and misconceptions of biology concepts held by students attending small high schools and students attending large high schools. *Journal of Research in Science Teaching, 25*(5): 359–372.

Slavin, R. E. (1980). Cooperative learning. *Review of Educational Research, 50*(2): 315–342.

Smith, C. L., and Millman, A. B. (1987). Understanding conceptual structures: A case study of Darwin's early thinking. In D. N. Perkins, J. Lochhead, and J. C. Bishop (Eds.), *Thinking: The Second International Conference.* Hillsdale, NJ: Lawrence Erlbaum.

Smith, E. L., and Anderson, C. W. (1987). Response to comments and criticism of "Plants as producers: A case study of elementary science teaching." *Journal of Research in Science Teaching, 24*(8): 771–772.

Snyder, L. H., and David, P. R. (1957). *The Principles of Heredity.* Boston: D. C. Heath.

Spearman, C. E. (1927). *The Abilities of Man.* London: Macmillan.

Spearman, C., and Wynn-Jones, L. (1951). *Human Ability.* London: Macmillan.

Sprick, R. S. (1985). *Discipline in the Secondary Classroom: A Problem-by-Problem Survival Guide.* West Nyack, NY: Center for Applied Research in Education.

Starr, C., and Taggart, R. (1978). *Biology: The Unity and Diversity of Life* (3rd ed.). Belmont, CA: Wadsworth.

Staver, J. R. (1986). The effects of problem format, number of independent variables, and their interaction on student performance on a control of variables reasoning problem. *Journal of Research in Science Teaching, 23*(6): 533–542.

Staver, J. R., and Walberg, H. J. (1986). An analysis of factors that affect public and private school science achievement. *Journal of Research in Science Teaching, 23*(2): 97–112.

Stebbins, R. C., and Allen, B. (1975). Simulating evolution. *American Biology Teacher, 37*(4): 206.

Sternberg, R. J. (1985). *Human Abilities: An Information-Processing Approach.* New York: W. H. Freeman.

Stewart, J. H. (1982). Difficulties experienced by high school students when learning basic Mendelian genetics. *American Biology Teacher, 44*(2): 80–84, 89.

Story, L. E., and Brown, I. D. (1979). Investigation of children's attitudes toward science fostered by a field-based science methods course. *Science Education, 63*(5): 649–654.

Suarez, A., and Rhonheimer, M. (1974). *Lineare function.* Zurich: Limmat Stiftung.

Suppes, P. (1968). The desirability of formalization in science. *Journal of Philosophy, 65:* 651.

Szent-Györgyi, A. (1964, December). Teaching and the expanding knowledge. *Science,* p. 1278.

TaFoya, M. E. (1976). Assessing inquiry potential in elementary science curriculum materials. *Dissertation Abstracts, 37*(6): 3401A.

Task Force on Laboratory Science (1985). *Final Report.* Phoenix: Arizona Board of Regents.

Terman, L., and Merrill, M. A. (1937). *Measuring Intelligence.* New York: Houghton Mifflin.

Thelen, J. N. (1979). Just because kids can't read doesn't mean they can't learn! *School Science and Mathematics, 79*(6): 457.

Thier, H. D. (1965). A look at a first-grader's understanding of matter. *Journal of Research in Science Teaching, 3*(1): 84–89.

Thomas, R., and Hooper, E. (1991). Simulations: An opportunity we are missing. *Journal of Research on Computing in Education, 23*(4): 497–513.

Tobin, K., and Gallagher, J. J. (1987). The role of target students in science classrooms. *Journal of Research in Science Teaching, 24*(1): 61–75.

Tomlinson-Keasey, C. (1972). Formal operations in females from eleven to fifty-four years of age. *Developmental Psychology, 6:* 364.

Tomlinson-Keasey, C., Williams, V., and Eisert, D. (1977a). Evaluation report of the first year of the ADAPT program. In *Multidisciplinary Piagetian-Based Programs for College Freshmen.* Lincoln: University of Nebraska.

Tomlinson-Keasey, C. and Eisert, D. (1977b). Second-year evaluation of the ADAPT program. In *Multidisciplinary Piagetian-Based Programs for College Freshmen.* Lincoln: University of Nebraska.

Torrence, E. P. (1967). Scientific views of creativity and factors affecting its growth. In J. Kagan (Ed.), *Creativity and Learning.* Boston: Beacon Press.

Towle, A. (1989). *Modern Biology.* New York: Holt, Rinehart & Winston.

Towler, J. A., and Wheatley, G. (1971). Conservation concepts in college students: A replication and critique. *Journal of Genetic Psychology, 118:* 265–270.

Ulerick, S. L., Bybee, R., and Ellis, J. (1988, April). *Research on computers in schools: From Plato to Logo and beyond.* Presentation to annual conference of the National Association for Research in Science Teaching, St. Louis, MO.

Van Deventer, W. C. (1958). A simplified approach to the problem of scientific methodology. *School Science and Mathematics, 58:* 99.

Vaughan, J. L. (1984). Concept structuring: The technique and empirical evidence. In C. D. Holly and D. F. Dansereau (Eds.), *Spatial Learning Strategies, Techniques, Applications, and Related Issues.* New York: Academic Press.

Vernon, P. E. (1947). The variations of intelligence with occupation, age and locality. *British Journal of Psychology, 1:* 52–63.

Victor, E. (1989). *Science for the Elementary School* (6th ed.). New York: Macmillan.

Vincent, D. V. (1952). The linear relationship between age and score of adults in intelligence tests. *Occupational Psychology, 26:* 243–249.

Von Foerster, H. (1984). In P. Watzlawick (Ed.), *The Invented Reality: How Do We Know What We Believe We Know?* New York: W. W. Norton.

Voss, J. F., Greene, T. R., Post, T. A., and Penner, D. C. (1983). Problem-solving in the social sciences. In G. H. Bowen (Ed.), *The Psychology of Learning and Motivation: Advances in Research Theory.* New York: Academic Press.

Vygotsky, L. S. (1962). *Thought and Language.* Cambridge, MA: MIT Press.

Waddington, C. H. (1975). *The Evolution of an Evolutionist.* Ithaca, NY: Cornell University Press.

Waddington, C. H. (1966). *Principles of Development and Differentiation.* New York: Macmillan.

Waddington, C. H. (1960). Evolutionary adaptation. In S. Tax (Ed.), *Evolution after Darwin: Volume I. The Evolution of Life.* Chicago: University of Chicago Press.

Waddington, C. H. (1959). Canalization of development and genetic assimilation of acquired characters. *Nature, 183*(4676): 1654.

Walker, R. A, Mertens, T. R., and Hendrix, J. R. (1979). Formal operational reasoning patterns and scholastic achievement in genetics. *Journal of College Science Teaching, 8*(3): 156–158.

Walker, R. A., Hendrix, J. R., and Mertens, T. R. (1980). Sequenced instruction in genetics and Piagetian cognitive development. *American Biology Teacher, 42*(2): 104.

Wallas, G. (1970). *The Art of Thought.* In P. E. Vernon (Ed.), *Creativity.* Middlesex, England: Penguin Education. Originally published 1926.

Wandersee, J. H. (1986). Can the history of science help science educators anticipate students' misconceptions? *Journal of Research in Science Teaching, 23*(7): 581–597.

Ward, C. R., and Herron, J. D. (1980). Helping students understand formal chemical concepts. *Journal of Research in Science Teaching, 17*(5): 387–400.

Washton, N. S. (1967). *Teaching Science Creatively in the Secondary Schools.* Philadelphia: W. B. Saunders.

Wason, P. C. (1966). Reasoning. In B. M. Foss (Ed.), *New Horizons in Psychology.* Harmondsworth, England: Penquin.

Wason, P. C., and Johnson-Laird, P. N. (1972). *Psychology of Reasoning: Structure and Content.* Cambridge, MA: Harvard University Press.

Werkmeister, W. H. (1948). *An Introduction to Critical Thinking: A Beginner's Text in Logic.* Lincoln, NE: Johnson.

Williams, R. J., Jr. (1959). *American Society: A Sociological Interpretation.* New York: Alfred A. Knopf.

Wilson, J. H. (1969). The "new" science teachers are asking more and better questions. *Journal of Research in Science Teaching, 6*(1): 49–53.

Wittrock, M. C. (1974). Learning as a generative process. *Educational Psychologist, 11:* 87–95.

Wollman, W. (1977). Controlling variables: Assessing levels of understanding. *Science Education, 61*(3): 371–383.

Wollman, W. T., and Lawson, A. E. (1978). The influence of instruction on proportional reasoning in seventh graders. *Journal of Research in Science Teaching, 15*(3): 227–232.

Wright, E. L. (1988, April). *Effect of intensive instruction in cue attendance on basic problem-solving skills of pre-service science methods students.* Presentation to the annual conference of the National Association for Research in Science Teaching, St. Louis, MO.

Yager, R. E. (1984). Defining the discipline of science education. *Science Education, 68*(1): 35–37.

Yager, R. E. (1983). The importance of terminology in teaching K–12 science. *Journal of Research in Science Teaching, 20*(6): 577.

Yap, K. C., and Yeany, R. H. (1988). Validation of hierarchical relationships among Piagetian cognitive modes and integrated process skills for different cognitive reasoning levels. *Journal of Research in Science Teaching, 25*(4): 247–282.

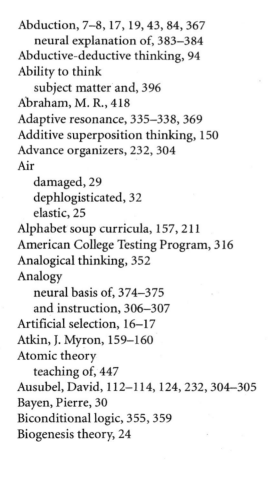

INDEX